Wissenschaftliche Untersuchungen
zum Neuen Testament

Begründet von Joachim Jeremias und Otto Michel
Herausgegeben von
Martin Hengel und Otfried Hofius

38

The Son of Man

Vision and Interpretation

by

Chrys C. Caragounis

J. C. B. Mohr (Paul Siebeck) Tübingen 1986

CIP-Kurztitelaufnahme der Deutschen Bibliothek
Caragounis, Chrys C.:
The son of man: vision and interpretation / by Chrys C. Caragounis.
– Tübingen: Mohr, 1986.
  (Wissenschaftliche Untersuchungen zum Neuen Testament; 38)
  ISBN 3-16-144963-0
  ISSN 0512-1604
NE: GT

Typeset by Sam Boyd Enterprise in Singapore; printed by Gulde-Druck GmbH in Tübingen; bound by Heinrich Koch KG in Tübingen.

Printed in Germany.

Dedicated to
Sophie
And our Daughters
Rosanna
Yvonne-Marie
Vivian
Eva-Corina

Preface

In the pages of this investigation parade the opinions of hundreds of scholars. I have agreed with practically each one of them on some point, though more often I have been in disagreement. This was unavoidable in an investigation of this kind which tries to engage one's fellow scholars in serious and honest but well-meaning discussion on a subject at once central and hotly debated. One thing needs to be put on record: I have learned from all the authors with whom I have been in *Auseinandersetzung*, often more from those with whom I have disagreed most.

This book does not claim to be the last word. It is hoped, however, that what it says may be a first word. Some of its statements may appear provocative or even audacious. But this may perhaps be because we are too conservative in our radical conclusions. The Son of Man has already in some circles become a "Phantom" and it would seem as if also Jesus' person and mission are about to vanish along with the "Phantom". What would remain then would be the Church, that paragon of ingenuity and inventiveness which was led by those obscure and unknown individuals, who self-effacingly left no traces of their names or activities, but who, nevertheless, formed and handed down to posterity this amazing synthesis of OT and Jewish apocalyptic traditions concretized in the person of their Master, who was totally innocent and unconscious of all this halo of Son of Man conceptualization attributed to him.

How seriously can one take this reconstruction? Maybe the time has come for a reappraisal of the evidence.

This book is a first step. Much work still remains to be done on the Gospels' SM. In this study I have tried to point out the directions or at least some of the directions which profitable and historically-based research ought to take. I have hardly done more than scrape the surface, but at least I hope to have scraped it. If this book stimulates interest and serious research in Jesus the Son of Man, the arduous toil of four years and more that has gone into it will have been well worthwhile.

Uppsala 14th Nov. 1984*   Chrys C. Caragounis

My thanks are due to Professors Martin Hengel and Otfried Hofius for their readiness to have this work published in the series of *WUNT* 1.

---

* The above date has been exceeded in one case, where I have cited the recently published (1985) Modern Greek Version of the New Testament.

VI   *PREFACE*

I would also like to express my sincere appreciation to Herrn Georg Siebeck for his fine co-operation.

Moreover, my appreciation is due to the typesetter in Singapore for his sound judgment, to Herrn Ulrich Gaebler of J.C.B. Mohr (Paul Siebeck), who co-ordinated the work, and to the printers and binders in Tübingen for the finished product.

Finally, I would like to thank Mr Douglas Jackson, Th. M., for help in checking the Manuscript. Words cannot pay off the debt I owe to my family for their understanding and patience.

Uppsala, July 1985   C. C. C.

Contents

Preface v

Contents vii

Introductory 1

I. A Survey of the Philological Investigation of the Expression 'Son of
Man' and a Critique of the Circumlocutional Theory 9
  A. Introductory 9
  B. In Past Research 11
  C. In Recent Research 19
  D. Conclusions. 33

II. The 'Son of Man' in the Old Testament in General and in Daniel
  in Particular 35
  A. Introductory 35
  B. Extra-Biblical Backgrounds 36
  C. Biblical Identifications 41
  D. The Old Testament Antecedents 48
  E. The Identification of the 'SM' in Daniel 61
    1. Philological Considerations 61
    2. The Character of the Beasts and a Comparison Between the
    Beasts' Ἄρχων and the 'SM'. 67
      a. The Nature of the Beasts. 68
        i. The Double Meaning of Ἀρχή / Ἐξουσία 68
        ii. The Referent of Ἀρχαί / Ἐξουσίαι. 68
        iii. The Component Parts of the Beasts 69
      b. A Comparison Between the Ἄρχων and the 'SM'. 70
        i. The Ἄρχων and the 'SM' are Spiritual Beings 71
        ii. The Ἄρχων and the 'SM' have each their Subordinates . . .71
        iii. The Power of the Ἄρχων and the 'SM' 71
    3. The Characteristics of the 'SM' 71
    4. The Identification of the 'SM'. 73
  F. Conclusions. 80

III. The 'Son of Man' in Some Strands of Jewish and Rabbinic
  Thought 83
  A. Introductory 83
  B. The *Parables* of I Enoch 84
    1. Excursus: The Date of the *Parables* 85

2. An Analytical Display of the Structure of I Enoch 46. 96

3. The Structure of I Enoch 46 98

4. A Comparison of I Enoch 46 with Daniel 7. 101

5. The Relation of the *Parables* as a Whole to Daniel. 104

6. The Interpretation of the Son of Man in the *Parables* 112

    a. Presentation 112

    b. Associations 113

    c. Origin 113

    d. Roles. 115

        i. Revealer 116

        ii. Judge. 116

        iii. Vindicator of the Righteous. 117

        iv. Universal Ruler. 118

        v. Object of Worship 119

C. IV Ezra 119

1. Date 119

2. A Jewish Composition with Christian Interpolations. 120

3. No Christian Influence on IV Ezra 13 121

4. The Messiah in IV Ezra 123

5. The 'One like a (Son of) Man' in IV Ezra 126

    a. The Text-critical Problem of the Expression 127

    b. Presented as Non-Human. 128

    c. Pre-existent 129

    d. Divine 129

    e. God's Son 130

    f. Messiah 130

    g. Judge. 131

D. Rabbinism. 131

E. The New Testament Evidence 136

1. A Jewish Convert to Jesus. 137

2. The Crowds. 138

3. The Jewish Authorities 139

    a. Jesus Before the Sanhedrin 139

    b. Stephen Before the Sanhedrin. .142

F. Conclusions. 143

IV. The New Testament Son of Man and the Danielic 'SM'. 145

A. The Organization of the Son of Man Sayings. 145

B. The Question of Authenticity and of Criteria 147

C. Defining the Task and the Procedure. 167

D. The Influence of Daniel's 'SM' upon the SM in the Teaching

of Jesus 168

1. The Fact of Influence 168

    a. The OT (apart from Dan) 'son of man' Cannot Explain

    the NT SM. 168

    b. A Comparison of the NT with Dan, I Enoch and IV Ezra . . .169

    c. The 'One like a son of man' Becomes the Son of Man. 173

    d. The Son of Man in Jesus' Teaching and the 'SM'
       in Daniel 174
       i. The Earthly Son of Man. 175
       ii. The Suffering Son of Man 190
       iii. The Exalted Son of Man. 201
    2. Some Areas of Influence 212
       a. The Nature and Extent of Influence 212
       b. A Son of Man Messianology 215
       c. The Nature of the Son of Man Messianology. 226
       d. The Son of Man and the Kingdom of God. 232
       i. The Kingdom of God 238
       ii. The Son of Man. 239
       iii. The Rebellious Powers 240
  E. Conclusions. 242

Vision and Interpretation (Epilogue and Conclusions) 245

Bibliography 251
  I. Abbreviations 251
  II. Texts and Translations 255
  III. Reference Works. 259
  IV. Secondary Literature. 260

Index of Passages. 279

Index of Authors. 296

Index of Names and Subjects 302

Introductory

The Son of Man (or in abbreviated form SM) problem has come well nigh to being regarded as insoluble[1]. Owing to its central place in the Gospel records of the life and teaching of Jesus, the expression Son of Man has at all times been looked upon as a possible key for unlocking some important secrets concerning Jesus' character and self-understanding[2]. But as this quest is in another, and perhaps just as real, sense tied up with the researcher's own understanding of Jesus' self-understanding, no consensus has thus far been possible. The disagreements were pronounced already in the last century, while the recent spate of Son of Man studies has, if anything, widened that gulf. Here it is not simply a question of two or three schools of interpretation. The views expressed are legion and no single book on the subject can hope to deal with or even mention all of them. This 'explosion' of scholarly opinion has of late been underscored through the production of resumé articles on the present state of the debate or of recent developments or of certain propositions emerging as a consensus among certain scholars[3].

The issue — or rather issues, since it is a question of one of the most complex areas in exegesis — is still hotly debated and there are at present no indications that the discussion will subside through arrival at a solution that will be acceptable to all. To be sure some studies have tried to assume the air of finality, but after perusing them it has become only too obvious that the last word has not yet been said. Indeed, such claims have only served to provoke more studies. So the 'summary-makers" work is definitely not ended!

---

1 Cf. the titles of two articles, one by Higgins, "Is the Son of Man Problem Insoluble?" (70–87 in *Neotestamentica et Semitica*) and the other by Hooker, "Is the Son of Man Problem really Insoluble?" (155–68 in *Text and Interpretation*).

2 Cf. M. Müller, "Über den Ausdruck 'Menschensohn' in den Evangelien", *ST* 31 (1977) 75 (= "Om udtrykket 'Menneskesønnen' i evangelien" *DTT* 40 (1977) 1–17).

3 See e.g. McCown, "Jesus, Son of Man: A Survey of Recent Discussion" *JR* 28 (1948) 1–12; Higgins, "The Son of Man Forschung since *The Teaching of Jesus*", in *NT Essays* 119–35; Black, "The Son of Man Problem in Recent Research and Debate" *BJRL* 45 (1962–3) 305–18; Marshall, "The Synoptic Son of Man Sayings in Recent Discussion" *NTS* 12 (1965–6) 327–51; *id.*, "The Son of Man in Contemporary Debate" *EQ* 42 (1970) 67–87; Marlow, " 'The Son of Man' in Recent Journal Literature" *CBQ* 28 (1966) 20–30; Kümmel, "Jesusforschung seit 1965; V. Der persönliche Anspruch Jesu" *TRu* 45 (1980) 40–84; Walker, "The Son of Man: Some Recent Developments" *CBQ* 45 (1983) 584–607. See also Haufe, "Das Menschensohn-Problem in der gegenwärtigen wissenschaftlichen Diskussion" *EvT* 26 (1966) 130–41.

However, amidst the multitude of ramifications of the Son of Man problem, it is possible to single out a few aspects that have been central to the discussion of the last few decades and which cannot be overlooked by any study seriously engaged in the quest for the Son of Man in the Gospel tradition. These problems can be summarized in the following way:

a) In recent years a strenuous effort has been made to explain the designation Son of Man in the Gospels as a circumlocution for 'I' etc. The thesis has been formulated that Son of Man is not a title, let alone messianic, but an ordinary Aramaic way of speaking of oneself in certain situations. The protagonist of this theory has been Vermes[4], who has found an energetic follower in Casey[5]. These claims have not passed unchallenged. For example, Borsch[6], Colpe[7], Jeremias[8] and especially Fitzmyer[9] have called Vermes' 'evidence' into question and in the ensuing debate have forced him to modify his original positions.

b) At the same time the connections previously thought to exist between the NT and 'apocalyptic' conceptions, current at the time of Jesus, have come under attack. In a characteristic fashion, Leivestad, for example, has called for the "Exit of the Apocalyptic Son of Man"[10] in what was a shorter form of an article with an equally provocative title in German, "Der apokalyptische Menschensohn ein theologisches Phantom"[11]. Leivestad denied the existence of the apocalyptic, transcendental Son of Man concept with judicial and kingly functions, as has often been found in the *Parables* of I Enoch, and consequently considered of importance for the use of the expression in the Gospels. Leivestad's call found an echo in Lindars[12], who in his most recent book[13] has come to speak of "The Myth of the Son of Man". For these writers there never existed any Son of Man concept prior to Jesus, or more correctly — since it is a question of a fully developed concept — prior to the Early Church. Leivestad and Lindars are, of course, by no means the only authors advocating this position, but may here suffice as representatives[14]. Even this position has been challenged and Higgins is able to write in his latest book[15], that "A majority of recent writers continue to support the view that there existed

---

4 I.e. cf. his programmatic essay "The Use of בר נש /בר נשא in Jewish Aramaic" (in M. Black, *An Aramaic Approach to the Gospels and Acts*, 3rd ed. 1967). See further Ch.I n.1.

5 E.g. *ZNW* 67 (1976) 147—54; id., *Son of Man*.

6 *The Son of Man in Myth and History.*

7 *TDNT* VIII, 400—77.

8 *ZNW* 58 (1967) 159—72.

9 In Review of M. Black's *An Aramaic Approach to the Gospels and Acts* in *CBQ* 30 (1968) 417—28; etc. see Ch.I n.1.

10 *NTS* 18 (1971—2) 243—67.

11 *ASTI* 6 (1967—8) 49—109.

12 "Re-enter the Apocalyptic Son of Man", *NTS* 22 (1975) 52—72.

13 *Jesus Son of Man* etc. 1983.

14 Another author that could be mentioned here is Dunn, *Christology in the Making*, 65—97.

15 *The Son of Man in the Teaching of Jesus*, 3.

in pre-Christian apocalyptic Judaism a concept of the eschatological Son of Man ...'' and cites as examples Tödt[16], Jüngel[17], Hahn[18], Nineham[19], Fuller[20], Barrett[21], Vielhauer[22], Conzelmann[23] and Teeple[24]. Lindars wrote, of course, after Higgins, but even so his book is not exempted from criticism. Quite recently it was subjected to an incisive critique by Black[25], who at the same time criticized Vermes' theory with which Lindars is aligned[26].

c) These tendencies in Son of Man research have received reinforcement from another quarter, which, in its own right, constitutes one more major problem confronting the student engaged in the Son of Man research. This relates to the date and character of the *Parables*. The old consensus that placed the *Parables* in the I century B.C. has recently been challenged by Milik[27] and others[28]. Milik's dating of the *Parables* in the third century A.D. has been rejected practically by all, even Black[29], but his declaration that no part of the *Parables* had been found among the Qumran fragments, despite the fact that all other parts of I Enoch are represented, has caused a great stir among scholars. The importance of this situation is easily deduced when it is recalled that the *Parables* has often been used as a link between what in Daniel has been thought to be a corporate figure, symbolical of the faithful Jews and the fully developed and individually conceived eschatological figure of the Son of Man in the Gospels. The absence of the *Parables* from Qumran has therefore been understood by some as decisive evidence that this work is post-Christian and consequently not an independent witness to a Jewish Son of Man concept prior to Jesus. Even this issue has been debated lively.

d) The corollary of these positions is that there was no Son of Man concept in Judaism prior to Jesus' time, and therefore Jesus could not have had any such apocalyptic figure in mind when — that is, if — he used the expression.

e) Though the apocalyptic content of the Son of Man has invariably

---

16 *The Son of Man in the Synoptic Tradition.*
17 In *Paulus und Jesus*, [4]1972, 215–62.
18 *The Titles of Jesus in Christology.*
19 *The Gospel of St. Mark.*
20 *The Foundations of New Testament Christology.*
21 *Jesus and the Gospel Tradition.*
22 In *Festschrift für Günther Dehn*, 51–79.
23 *ZTK* 54 (1957) 277ff.; "Jesus Christus" in *RGG* III 3rd ed. cols. 630f.; *An Outline of the Theology of the NT.*
24 *JBL* 84 (1965) 213–50.
25 "Aramaic Barnāshā and the 'Son of Man'" *ET* 95 (1984) 200–06. In this article Black expresses a number of views, which coincide with those held by the present author.
26 Cf. the change from his earlier study "Jesus and the Son of Man" *JSNT* 1 (1978) 4–18.
27 E.g. *The Books of Enoch.*
28 E.g. Hindley, *NTS* 14 (1967–8) 551–65.
29 Cf. the change of standpoint in Black, *ET* 95 (1984) 201 as compared with his article in *ET* 88 (1976) 5–8 and see Chapter Three 'Excursus on the Date of the *Parables*'.

been found in the *Parables*, all studies, with few exceptions[30], in one way
or another consider Dan 7 as the source of the expression. This might
sound as if Dan 7 is an exception in this complex of problems in enjoying
scholarly consensus. Actually nothing would be further from the truth. In
the course of my argument in Chapter Two, no less than a dozen interpretations of Dan 7:13f. are mentioned. Of these, the ones that have commanded the field are the older Israelite view[31] and the more recent angelic
view[32]. A major problem is posed here by the Danielic figure of 'One like
a son of man' (hence in abbreviated form always 'SM'[33]). The problem
this time relates more to its being neglected in Gospel SM research than
to questions intrinsic to any debate about it. Since, any relevance that has
been recognized in Daniel's 'SM' has normally been seen to come via the
developments in the *Parables*, NT scholars have generally contented themselves with merely referring *en passant* to Dan 7:13f. and citing the more
usual view of OT scholarship, viz. that this figure is a symbol for the pious
Jews. Now from the corporate symbol for the persecuted Jews in Dan 7 to
the exalted figure of the Gospel Son of Man, who comes as eschatological
Judge and King, is a very long way. The gap has been traditionally bridged
by postulating the *Parables* as an intermediary stage. It is therefore easy to
see how, in the view of some, the recent dismissal of the *Parables* is tantamount to a total collapse of the doctrine of a pre-Christian apocalyptic,
pre-existent Son of Man, who could have been a prototype for Jesus. But
are the current interpretations — or rather any one of the current interpretations of the Danielic 'SM' correct?

f) In view of the above problems which have been raised, it is not so
unusual to hear the claim that the messianic content in the Gospel sayings
was the work of the Early Church[34] in order to express her Easter faith in
Jesus, or as Dunn puts it, it was formed in the interests of Incarnation
Christology[35]. Again this conclusion is not free from difficulties and has
failed to convince other scholars.

g) Finally, the positions enumerated above have far-reaching consequences for the study of Jesus' person and especially his self-consciousness. If all roads lead to Rome, so too, all Son of Man studies are bound to
converge in Jesus. The ultimate question concerning the Son of Man is
the ultimate question about Jesus. Can or can we not know anything
about Jesus through our study of the Son of Man? Scholarly opinion goes

---

30 E.g. E.A. Abbott, *The Son of Man*, 82—102 and Harrison, *EvQ* 23 (1951) 46—50, derive it
    from Ezekiel.
31 Held by e.g. Montgomery, *Daniel*; Manson, *BJRL* 32 (1950); Hartman-DiLella, *Daniel*; Por-
    teous, *Daniel*; Russel, *Method and Message*; Dexinger, *Das Buch Daniel*.
32 E.g. Procksch, in *Christentum und Wissenschaft* 3; Noth, in *Gesammelte Studien*; Coppens,
    ETL 37 (1961) 5—19; *VT* 19 (1969) 171—82; Collins, *The Apocalyptic Vision*.
33 SM, or Son of Man is used in quoting or alluding to the term as a concept or expression (I En,
    IV Ez, NT) and son of man for the OT (apart from Dan) expression.
34 E.g. Perrin, *Rediscovering the Teaching of Jesus*, e.g. 198.
35 *Christology in the Making*, 82ff.

again its separate ways. For those who accept the positions outlined above, the Son of Man investigation is a blind alley: it cannot lead us to Jesus; it cannot tell us anything about Jesus. Others, some of whom have controverted (all or some of) the above positions consider it possible to reach some form of understanding concerning Jesus' view of himself.

To sum up, the problems that emerge from even a rudimentary ramification of the questions involved in the above positions are numerous and quite complex. The identity of the 'SM' in Dan 7, the date of the *Parables*, the nature of the 'Enochic' SM, the existence in Judaism of a SM concept, the existence of competing messianologies, the possibility of Jesus' acquaintance with such a concept, the content and significance of SM as a self-designation of Jesus and consequently his view of messianology and the question of his self-understanding, etc. etc. are issues with respect to which no consensus has been reached, nor is there one in sight for the near future.

The complexity of the subject as well as the number of studies already in existence, coupled with the phenomenal rate at which Son of Man studies are at present being turned out, would be enough to dissuade one from even entertaining thoughts of entering the arena[36]. That I do so despite the odds, is owing to *inter alia* the following circumstances:

First, the deeply contradictory picture which scholarship at present offers with respect to what according to the Gospels, was Jesus' favorite self-designation, makes a demand upon one who has not yet lost faith in the possibility of legitimate and profitable research in an area of the utmost significance for understanding the person of Jesus, to grapple with the task whatever the cost may be.

Second, for a number of years I have been interested in the possible Danielic antecedents to Jesus' concept of the Kingdom of God. This interest afforded me the opportunity of making a number of observations, which, I deem, are not altogether irrelevant to the study of the Son of Man problem.

Third, my preoccupation with Daniel has led me to the realization that previous studies on the Son of Man have often neglected or failed to notice certain features or data, which it would seem, have been germane to and formative for the Son of Man concept in subsequent works, and therefore also in the NT.

In the hope that my work shall not prove altogether superfluous in an already enormous body of literature on the subject, I take the step of offering my results for the consideration of my fellow scholars.

I propose to go about it in the following way: In Chapter One I address myself to the linguistic debate. This is a 'must' for anyone writing after Vermes. Inasmuch as this debate is not exclusively modern and 'Vermes-

---

36 It is reported by Hooker that when she announced her interest in working on the Son of Man problem to Prof. Black, he tried to dissuade her with a simple "Don't!", in *Text and Interpretation*, 155.

ean' or 'post-Vermesean', I begin with a survey of Son of Man research
from about the middle of the last century. Such a survey helps to set
Vermes' contribution in its historical setting and perspective by showing
that Vermes' theory is an old theory in new attire. I then concentrate on
Vermes and those who engaged in debate with him and end the Chapter
with a critique of the circumlocutional theory.

Next I address myself to the Book of Daniel (Chapter Two). First I deal
briefly with some of the *religionsgeschichtliche* backgrounds to the Danielic concept, paying special attention to the works of Mowinckel[37],
Emerton[38], Morgenstern[39] and Colpe[40]. Thereafter I proceed to a consideration of the biblical identifications, which admittedly are many and
varied but which show some healthy signs. As a prerequisite to the discussion of the Danielic expression I undertake an investigation of the OT expressions 'son of' and 'son(s) of man/men'. The object of the discussion of
Dan 7, to which I then turn, is to discover the clues which the author has
left for identifying correctly the 'One like a son of man'. This is of paramount importance for my entire investigation. The kind of 'SM' which
Daniel left as his legacy to his posterity is crucial for understanding the
material which later works, i.e. the *Parables*, IV Ezra, the NT, had at their
disposal and the modifications or embellishments which they carried out
in their respective presentations of the Son of Man.

Chapter Three is addressed to the question whether there developed in
post-Danielic times an interpretative tradition which took its cue from
Daniel's intended interpretation of his 'SM', or whether post-Danielic
works produced in their Son of Man conceptions something entirely different and new. To this intent the *Parables*, IV Ezra, rabbinic interpretations of Dan 7:13f. and certain NT passages — in so far as they may be
presumed to reflect ideas current at the time — are examined. Particular
attention is focused on the *Parables*, whose character as a literary work,
its relation to Daniel and the purpose of its composition are considered
important for the question posed. The discussion of IV Ez is more limited
and relates primarily to the *characteristica* of its Son of Man and their
relation to Daniel.

The Fourth Chapter is preoccupied exclusively with the NT. Following
some initial remarks about the grouping of SM logia, the question of authenticity and criteria is taken up. This question is of supreme importance
for the continued   investigation. The lack of any generally accepted criteria in the SM research leads to the formulation of certain methodological principles and criteria in dealing with the sources. The second (larger)
part of this chapter is addressed to primarily two questions, a) the establishment of literary relations between the Gospel (chiefly synoptic) SM

---

37 I.e. *He that Cometh*.
38 *JTS* 9 (1958) 225–42.
39 *JBL* 80 (1961) 65–77 and *VT* 10 (1960) 138–97.
40 Art. ὁ υἱὸς τοῦ ἀνθρώπου in *TDNT* VIII, 400–77.

and Daniel's 'SM', b) the areas in which Daniel's 'SM' has been influential in shaping the form and the content of the Gospel concept. The interest in this part turns partly on individual sayings and partly on larger patterns, i.e. the questions of messianology and of the Kingdom of God.

With regard to methodology the usual exegetical methods are brought to bear where applicable, but no slavish attitude towards them is shown. In addition I have utilized insights from Text linguistics, particularly semantics, especially in my investigation of the Danielic and Enochic material, and this needs a little explanation. In particular Dan 7 has been subjected to a rigorous linguistic/philological and logical/semantic analysis, though in the actual form of the present work (where this material is omitted) the argumentation has been simplified by taking a more 'classic' form. Nevertheless, the insights from the semantic analysis have been utilized. The reasons for excluding this material are a) for reasons of brevity (for Dan 7 that material would have claimed some 70 pages) and b) it is possible that in some future date I shall publish the rest of my findings in Daniel, where such an analysis might more appropriately appear. Nevertheless, any conclusions drawn from what has just been said, to the effect that I am imposing upon my readers results and conclusions from an analysis not given in public, and hence uncontrollable, would be unjustified, since the reasons for my identification, though simplified, are sufficiently argued in the present work.

In the case of the *Parables* too, I have analysed semantically-pragmatically all of the chapters containing the expression Son of Man. But of these, only the material pertinent from ch. 46 (the display and a short discussion of it without philological material) has been deemed advisable to include in the present work, because it brings to the fore its structural elements and underlines the *Parables'* relation to Daniel — a matter of paramount importance for the question addressed to these texts. The rest of the investigation is carried out in more 'classical' manner by means of statistics, compositional, motif, etc. considerations. IV Ezra 13 has not been analysed in this way, since its character and its relation to Daniel are different from those of the *Parables*, and it was judged that a semantic analysis would not contribute to the questions posed. Needless to say, this also applies to the rabbinic texts and to the NT.

With respect to the Fourth Chapter the situation is somewhat problematic. All the current methods have so far been used: *religionsgeschichte*, source- literary- tradition- form- and redaction-criticism, but the results have been largely unconvincing and contradictory. Hence, though the usefulness of these methods has been borne in mind, no inordinate optimism about their suitability to lead to authentic or assured results has apparently been entertained. This seems to explain why in addition to these methods certain criteria have occasionally been formulated as guidelines in Son of Man research, but even so, instead of a uniform picture, the most divergent interpretations of the SM have emerged. We cannot therefore speak of a scientific method or a set of criteria which are objective, valid and generally accepted in SM research. This state of affairs leads me to formulate certain principles and criteria in dealing with the Gospel SM logia. My method here, I am afraid, does not conform to Perrin's standard, who in reference to Tödt's methodology states, "it establishes the methodology . . . and by doing so immediately renders out of date any work not using this methodology"[41]. Perrin's methodology and findings involve him in considerable self-contradiction and his results have failed to convince the great majority of scholars. Perhaps his methodology is not *the methodology* for inquiring into the SM problem.

---

41 *Rediscovering*, 259.

Chapter I

A Survey of the Philological Investigation of the Expression 'Son of Man' and a Critique of the Circumlocutional Theory

A. Introductory

As indicated in the Introductory the last few decades have witnessed the appearance of an enormous amount of writing on the Son of Man question[1]. The rate of publication has been greatly accelerated in the years since 1960[2]. The majority of these studies are concerned with the

---

1 G. Vermes, "The Present State of the Son-of-Man Debate", *JJS* 29 (1978) 123ff. speaks of two waves of philological SM research prior to his 1965 lecture, printed under the title "The Use of בר נש / בר נשא in Jewish Aramaic" as Appendix E to the third edition of M. Black's *An Aramaic Approach to the Gospels and Acts*, in 1967. The first wave included the works of A. Meyer, *Jesu Muttersprache*, 1896; H. Lietzmann, *Der Menschensohn*, 1896; G. Dalman, *Die Worte Jesu*, 1898 and P. Fiebig, Der Menschensohn, 1901. The second wave comprised the works of J.Y. Campbell, "The Origin and Meaning of the Term 'Son of Man' ", *JTS* (1947) 145–55; J. Bowman, "The Background of the Term 'Son of Man' ", *ET* 59 (1947–8) 283–8; Black, "Unsolved Problems: The 'Son of Man' in the Old Biblical Literature", *ET* 60 (1948–9) 11–5; *id.*, "Unsolved Problems: 'The Son of Man' in the Teaching of Jesus," *ET* 60 (1948–9) 32–6. E. Sjöberg," בן אדם und בר אנש im Hebräischen und Aramäischen", *Ac Or*, 21 (1950–1) 57–65; 91–107 and Borsch "The Son of Man" *ATR* 45 (1963) 174–90. The third wave was initiated by Vermes' own 1967 publication, which has called forth the reaction of *inter alios* F.H. Borsch, *The Son of Man in Myth and History*, 1967; C. Colpe, Article Υἱὸς τοῦ Ἀνθρώπου, in *TDNT* VIII, 400–77, 1972 (German orig. 1969); J. Jeremias, "Die älteste Schicht der Menschensohn-Logien", *ZNW* 58 (1967) 159–72; J.A. Fitzmyer in his review of M. Black's book in *CBQ* 30 (1968) 417–28; "The Contribution of Qumran Aramaic to the Study of the NT", *NTS* 20 (1974) 382–407, and in "Methodology in the Study of Jesus' Sayings in the NT", in *Jésus aux origines de la christologie*, ed. J. Dupont, 1975, as well as the more congenial to Vermes' own viewpoint studies by Leivestad, "Der apokalyptische Menschensohn ein theologisches Phantom", *ASTI* 6 (1968) 49–105, shortened in "Exit the Apocalyptic Son of Man", *NTS* 18 (1972) 243–67; Lindars, "Re-enter the Apocalyptic Son of Man", *NTS* 22 (1975) 52–72; (for criticism of Leivestad and Lindars see M. Müller, *ST* 31 (1977) 65–82); M. Casey, "The Son of Man Problem", *ZNW*, 67 (1976) 147–54; and "The Use of the Term 'Son of Man' in the Similitudes of Enoch", *JSJ* 7 (1976) 11–29; J. Bowker, "The Son of Man", *JTS*, N.S. 28 (1977) 19–48; and R.E.C. Formesyn, "Was there a Pronominal Connection for the 'Bar nasha' Self-designation?", *NovT* 8 (1966) 1–35.

2 For this period the works are almost innumerable. A specimen is given in the footnotes of the

background and identification of the Son of Man. Nevertheless, a number of them have been addressed to the purely linguistic significance of the expression Son of Man. Though scholars have been interested in this question primarily for the bearing it may have on the meaning of the expression on Jesus' lips, such an investigation is also of some consequence for the use of the term in Daniel. Yet, on the other hand, for all its usefulness an investigation of this kind can under no circumstances predeter-

present study. Already in 1900 Baldensperger devoted about twenty-five pages (*TRu* 3 (1900) 200–10 and 243–55) on "die neueste Forschung über den Menschensohn", while by 1912 Charles (*The Book of Enoch*, 306) could speak of a "vast literature" for the "last eighteen years". The following is a specimen of works since the turn of the century: Rose, "Fils de l'homme et fils de Dieu" *RB* 9 (1900) 169–99; Drummond, "The Use and Meaning of the Phrase 'The Son of Man' in the Synoptic Gospels", *JTS* 11 (1901) 350–58; 539–71; Croskery,"Recent Discussions on the Meaning of the Title 'Son of Man'" *ET* 13 (1901–2) 351–55, Völter, "Der Menschensohn in Dan 7,13" *ZNW* 3 (1902) 173–74; Kristensen, "De term 'Zoon des Mensen' toegelicht uit de anthropologie der Ouden" *Theol. Tijdschr.* 45 (1911) 11–38; Badham, "The Title 'Son of Man'" *Theol. Tijdschr.* 45 (1911) 395–448; Gry, "La dénomination messianique 'Fils de l'homme' dans la Bible et les Apocalypses éthiopiens" in *Xenia. Hommage à l'université de Grèce*, 1912; Meloni, "Fillius Hominis" in *Saggi di Filologia Semitica* 315–9; Völter, *Die Menschensohnfrage neu undersucht, 1916*; Somervell, "The Son of Man", *ET* 29 (1917–8) 522–3; Dieckmann, "Ὁ υἱὸς τοῦ ἀνθρώπου" *Bib* 2 (1920) 69–71; Peake, "The Messiah and the Son of Man" in *Miscellaneous Essays on Theology*, 1–32 (= *BJRL* 8 (1924); Dupont, *Le Fils de l'homme*, 1924; James, "The Son of Man: Origin and Use of the Title", *ET* 36 (1924–5) 309ff.; Creed, "The Heavenly Man" *JTS* 26 (1925) 113–36; Schweitzer, *The Quest of the Historical Jesus*, [4]1926; von Gall, Βασιλεία τοῦ Θεοῦ, 1926; Huntress, " 'Son of God' in Jewish writings prior to the Christian Era" *JBL* 54 (1935) 117–23; Baeck, "Der Menschensohn" (*MGWJ* 81 (1937) 12–24; Bultmann, "Reich Gottes und Menschensohn" *TRu* N.S. 9 (1937) 1–35; Fridrichsen, "Människosonen och Israel" in *Festschrift G. Aulén* (1939) 100–16; Burkill, "The Son of Man", *ET* 56 (1944–5) 305–6; Torrey, "The Messiah Son of Ephraim" *JBL* 66 (1947) 253–77 Christensen, "Le fils de l'homme s'en va, ainsi qu' il est ecrit de lui" *ST* 10 (1956) 28–39; Schweitzer, *"Das Messianitäts-und Leidensgeheimnis"*, [3]1956; Otto, *Reich Gottes und Menschensohn*, [3]1954; Rost, "Zur Deutung des Menschensohnes in Daniel 7" in *Gott und die Götter*, ed. G. Delling, (1958) 41–3; Scott, "Behold, He Cometh with Clouds" *NTS* 5 (1958–9) 131; Guillet, "A Propos des Titres de Jésus Christ, Fils de l'homme, Fils de Dieu" in *A la rencontre de Dieu*, Memorial Albert Gelin, (1961) 309–17; Paul, *Son of Man*, 1961 Kruijf, *Der Sohn des lebendigen Gottes* (1962) 355–67; Newman, "Towards a Translation of 'The Son of Man' in the Gospels" *BT* 21 (1970) 141–46; Burkill, *New Light on the Earliest Gospels*, (1972) 1–38; Sabourin, "The Son of Man" *BTB* 2 (1972) 78–80; Hoffmann, *Studien zur Theologie der Logienquelle*, (1972) 82–233; Walker, "The Origin of the Son of Man Concept as Applied to Jesus" *JBL* 91 (1972) 482–90; Lebram, "Perspektiven der gegenwärtigen Danielforschung" (being a review of recent Literature) *JSJ* 5 (1974) 1–33; Kingsbury, "The Title 'Son of Man' in Matthew's Gospel", *CBQ* 37 (1975) 193–202; Wifall, "Son of Man – A pre-Davidic Social Class?" *CBQ* 37 (1975) 331–40; Brown, "The Son of Man: This Fellow", *Bib* 58 (1977) 361–87; Coppens, "Ou en est le problème de Jesus 'Fils de l'homme'", *ETL* 56 (1980) 282–302; Garnet, "The Baptism of Jesus and the Son of Man", *JSNT* 9 (1980) 49–65; Lindars, "The New Look on the Son of Man" *BJRL* 63 (1980–1) 437–62; Coppens, *Les Fils d'homme vétero- et intertestamentaire*, 1982; Duncan, "Daniel and Salvation-History" *Down Rev* no 338 (1982) 62–8; Bruce, "The Background to the 'Son of Man' Sayings" in *Christ the Lord*, ed. H.H. Rowdon, 1982, 50–70; Bietenhard, "Der Menschensohn – Hò huiòs toû anthrōpou" in *Principat 25.1. Religion* ed. W. Haase, 1982.

mine the significance and the content of this expression either in Daniel or in the NT. Thus, while the relevance of this pursuit is duly recognized, its pertinence must not be exaggerated.

B. In Past Research

In recent years a persistent attempt has been made to resolve the expression υἱός τοῦ ἀνθρώπου, by way of בר נשא, the Aramaic original thought to lie behind the Greek term, into an equivalent of the first person of the personal pronoun. As a matter of fact the attempt is not modern, but it has been intensified in modern times[3]. The equation of υἱός τοῦ ἀνθρώπου with 'I' had been made already by rationalists like H.E.G. Paulus[4] and C.F.A. Fritzsche[5] and was rejected as long ago as 1835 by D.F. Strauss[6].

However, no serious philological examination was applied to the expression until the last years of the XIXth century. Between the time of Strauss and the 1890's there appeared many studies indeed, which in one way or another, touched upon this question, but, with the chief interest lying with the Leben-Jesu-Forschung, and the question of Jesus' messianic self-consciousness or otherwise, these discussions inevitably suffered from the obsession of the times and the philological issue was drowned by other interests.

A. Neander[7] took an especially high view of the designation Son of Man, claiming that Jesus used it in reference to His humanity, His solidarity with mankind. Jesus being the embodiment of the idea of Man, He who realizes "das Urbild der Menschheit", is understood as the glorifier of human nature[8]. This spiritualized view of our term was shared by Ch.H.

---

3 Beside the studies by Vermes, Casey, Formesyn and others, cited above note 1, mention may be made of the recent monograph by Casey, *Son of Man*: The Interpretation and Influence of Dan 7, 1979.

4 *Exegetisches Handbuch*, I, B, 465.

5 *Quatuor N.T. Evangelia. Recensuit et cum Commentariis Perpetuis edidit. Tome I, Evangelium Matthaei*, 1829, 320: "Nam dubitare noli, quin Iesus se τὸν υἱὸν τοῦ ἀνθρώπου dixerit eo usu, quo suffecto in Pronominis 1. Nomine de nobis interdum loquimur, tanquam de altero ... h.s. *filius ille parentum humanorum* (ham τοῦ ἀνθρώπου sensu collectivo accipiendum), *qui nunc loquitur, homo ille, quem bene nosti* i.e. ego (sic h.l. infra 9,6. 11,19 Ioh 1,52 al.".

6 *Das Leben Jesu. Kritisch bearbeitet*, 4th ed. 1840, Vol.I, 489ff. (Eng. transl. *The Life of Jesus Critically Examined*, 1973, 281ff.).

7 *Das Leben Jesu Christi. In seinem geschichtlichen Zusammenhänge und seiner geschichtlichen Entwicklung*, 1837, 129ff. 5th ed. 1852, 152ff.

8 "Er nennt sich so in Beziehung auf seine menschliche Erscheinung als den der Menschheit Angehörenden, der in der menschlichen Natur für dieselbe so Grosses gewirkt hat, durch den dieselbe verherrlicht wird , welcher in dem vorzüglichsten , der Idee entsprechenden Sinne Mensch ist, der das Urbild der Menschheit verwirklicht". (*Leben Jesu Christi*, 153).

Weisse[9]. He considered the expression as an ascent of the human nature from its natural state to a spiritual one. In a similar vein P.de Lagarde[10], forty years later, declared that בר אנש means simply 'Man', but that through the use of this term Jesus ennobled mankind!

A diametrically opposite view was taken by F.C. Baur[11], who thought that Neander's view came into clash with the data of the synoptics. Jesus is nowhere portrayed as the one who glorifies human nature. Nor is the expression SM to be understood messianically. Such an understanding is expressed by υἱός τοῦ Θεοῦ. He therefore settled for a rather low view treating the expression as one which laid special emphasis on Jesus' being a mere man. A similar point was made by C.B.E. Uloth[12] who claimed that the Aramaic expression means simply "Man" and that it was used to underline Jesus' creatureliness, weakness and humiliation.

A third group of scholars worked along the lines laid down by Neander taking an exalted view of the SM concept. H. Holtzmann[13] considered that the term came into the NT from Daniel, where it signified humility. Jesus adopted this term and charged it with new meaning. The expression, accordingly, came to designate the bearer of all human values and rights. Jesus as SM is the Ideal Man. The concept of the Messiah is thus spiritualized into that of the Ideal Man. In Holtzmann and Baur we have the two extremes, the highest and lowest, of the interpretation of this expression. W. Beyschlag[14] followed suit in rejecting the rationalistic explanation that the expression was equivalent to 'I', claiming that Jesus in using the expression SM drew attention to His Messiahship. His motive in using this term, however, was to show how deeply conscious he was of His human nature. Nevertheless, a real distinction is found here: in differentiation from the rest of humanity, Jesus is the Man *par excellence*, the Ideal, Absolute, Heavenly Man, the embodiment of the whole of God's self-revelation. Against Holtzmann Beyschlag believed that the concept of the Ideal Man was already a part of Daniel's SM concept. To the same effect C. Wittichen[15], thought that the expression presented Jesus as the perfect description of the Idea of Man, or the Messiah, who was the instrument for the realization of this Idea in the world. The ideal interpretation is driven further by W. Brückner[16] who goes so far as to state that the

---

9 *Die evangelische Geschichte*, kritisch und philosophisch bearbeitet, 2 Vols., 1838. Vol.I, 319ff.

10 *Gesammelte Abhandlungen*, 25 n.1: " 'menschlich' ist bei den Indogermanen ein ehrendes, bei den Semiten ein tadelndes Beiwort ... erst Jesus adelte den בר נש = υἱὸς τοῦ ἀνθρώπου". Cf. *id.*, *Deutsche Schriften*, 1878, 230.

11 "Die Bedeutung des Ausdrucks ὁ υἱὸς τοῦ ἀνθρώπου", *ZwTh* 3 (1860) 274–92, esp. 278ff., and *Neutestamentliche Theologie*, 1864, 75–82.

12 *Godgeleerde Bijdragen*, 1862, 467ff.

13 "Über den neutestamentlichen Ausdruck 'Menschensohn' ", *ZwTh* 8 (1865) 212–37.

14 *Die Christologie des neuen Testaments*, 1866, 9–34.

15 *Die Idee des Menschen*, 1886, 60ff., 67ff., 97ff., 137ff.

16 W. Brückner, "Jesus 'des Menschen Sohn' "; *JpTh* 12 (1886) 244–78.

thought of the parousia relates not so much to Jesus' own "I", as to the Ideal Man, who as "Menschen Sohn" is carried in Jesus' breast.

The question whether the expression was influenced by the Danielic 'SM' or not as well as its messianic or non-messianic character found a divided scholarship. L.Th. Schultze[17], like Beyschlag, made Dan 7:13 his starting point and C. Holsten[18] thought that the term must, as the definite article before υἱός indicates its derivation from the well-known passage in Dan, have had messianic associations in Jesus' and his contemporaries' consciousness. For J. Weiss[19] the term is on Jesus' lips not so much a self-designation as a claim. Jesus hoped that people would soon see that he was the Danielic and Enochic SM[20]. On the other hand, J.M. Usteri[21], argued that the expression was a creation of Jesus. Like C.B.E. Uloth, he denied all influence from Ps 8:5 or Dan 7:13 even though the latter passage might have given the external impetus to its use. The term is to be understood as an expression of Jesus' peculiar vocation, which he decided upon through his incarnation.

The messianic significance of the term in the Gospels was upheld by A. Hilgenfeld[22], who derived the expression from Dan 7:13. Jesus had, however, put into the expression a significance which it lacked in the passage in Dan, i.e. that of the Messiah who was like a Son of Man. He thus encased the lowliness of the external appearance in the exaltedness of the Messiah[23]. For B. Weiss[24] the term is a messianic designation, whose connection with Dan 7 is especially apparent in the parousia utterances. C. Weizsäcker[25], on the other hand, prefers to see the address in Ez as the inspiring factor for what becomes a prophetic title on the lips of Jesus in the earlier occurrences of the term[26]. Only at a later stage in the life of Jesus did the Dan passage give rise to a messianic use of the term. The view of J. Weiss that the SM was on the lips of Jesus a claim rather than a self-designation, and that he hoped people would soon see in him the SM of Dan and I En, has been noted above. Differently from J. Weiss, W. Baldensperger[27] saw in the SM of Dan and I En only a picture, while in

---

17 *Vom Menschensohn und vom Logos.* Ein Beitrag zur biblischen Christologie, 1867, 67ff., 97ff., 137ff.

18 "Biblisch-theologische Studien III. Die Bedeutung des Ausdrucksform ὁ υἱὸς τοῦ ἀνϑρώπου in Bewusstsein Jesu", *ZwTh* 34 (1891) 1—79 (continued from 33, 1890).

19 *Die Predigt Jesu vom Reiche Gottes*, 1892, 51—9.

20 Weiss (*Die Predigt Jesu*, p. 56) was, however, willing to concede that in Mt 16:13; 11:19; Lk 7:34 the expression was the equivalent of 'I'.

21 *TZ*, a.d. Schweitz, 3 (1886) 1—23.

22 *ZwTh*, 6 (1863) 311—40, esp. 327—34.

23 For K.F. Nösgen, *Christus der Menschen- und Gottessohn*, 1869, 1—115, the expression is used to indicate Jesus' passible and human nature.

24 *Lehrbuch der biblischen Theologie des neuen Testaments*, 1868, 59—62, esp. 61.

25 C. Weizsäcker, *Untersuchungen über die evangelische Geschichte*, 1864, 426—31, 2nd ed. 1901, 274f.

26 He has a modern follower in Harrison, *EvQ* 23 (1951) 46—50.

27 *Das Selbstbewusstsein Jesu*, 2nd ed. 1892, 90ff., 171ff.

the *Parables* of I En the term was, according to him, used as a title of the Messiah. In the Synoptics the sayings relating to the parousia are to be differentiated from those relating to humiliation, the first group going back to Dan and I En. The term SM occurs everywhere as a clear, overt designation of the Messiah, which Jesus could not have espoused until after Caesarea Philippi[28]. Finally, G. Schnedermann[29] trying to avoid one-sidedness, understands Son of Man in Jesus' preaching as a picture by which, in line with Daniel's use, Jesus describes His peculiarity as a Messiah. However, since the Jews did not pay any particular attention to the Dan passage, the application of the expression SM ought so much the more to be ascribed to Jesus Himself. This does not necessarily mean that SM is =Messiah, but that Jesus with the help of Dan 7:13f. sought to create the impression that the SM is proclaimed as Messiah. In the minds of the people the expression could relate back to Dan, Ez, other prophetic passages, the people of Israel and even the "Ideal Man" — relations which should not be excluded from Jesus' own mind.

The diversity of scholarly opinion in the XIXth century was so great as to call forth H. Lietzmann's well justified remark: "Was hat nicht alles 'Menschensohn' bedeuten sollen! Idealmensch, der die Menschennatur verherrlicht; Messias, aber im Gegensatz zum Gottessohn der Juden, als armer, niedriger Mensch; Messias als Träger aller Menschenwürde und Menschenrechte; Messias als präexistenter himmlischer Mensch; Messias als Organ zur Verwirklichung des durch ihn zugleich dargestellten Menschenideales in der Welt; Messias ohne Nebenbedeutung; Bezeichnung des Berufes Jesu, wie sich derselbe durch seine Menschenwerdung bedingte; Messias im Sinne des 'Idealmenschen' als Gegensatz gegen den national beschränkten 'Davididen'; Messias als Erzeuger eines Menschen der Gattung Mensch angehörig; schliesslich soll es Messiasbezeichnung im Sinne eines in starkem Glauben erhobenen Anspruches sein"[30].

The last decade of the XIXth century saw two shifts in the investigation of the SM problem. The first was one of geography. Up to that time the debate had been confined primarily to Germany[31]. But in the early half of that decade the scene moved for a short time to Holland, to return again to Germany with the works of A. Meyer and H. Lietzmann. The

---

28 Half a century later Sjöberg, in reaction to Wrede, was to come to the opposite result of a hidden SM, dictated by the hidden character of the apocalyptic Messiah (See his *Der verborgene Menschensohn in den Evangelien*, utilizing his results from his earlier *Der Menschensohn im äthiopischen Henochbuch*).

29 *Jesu Verkündigung und Lehre vom Reiche Gottes*, II, 1895, 206–9.

30 H. Lietzmann, *Der Menschensohn*. Ein Beitrag zur neutestamentlichen Theologie, 1896, 23f.

31 Cf. the unproblematical remarks on the 'Son of Man' of British scholars writing before that date, in H. Alford, *The Greek New Testament*, 4 Vols., Vol. I, 6th ed. 1868, e.g. *ad* Mt 8:20; 16:13 and Jn 1:52, as well as the discussions in B.F. Westcott, *The Gospel of John*, 1881, 33–5; A. Edersheim, *Life and Times of Jesus the Messiah*, 3rd ed. 1886; here 29th impression used, no date, Vol. I, 351f. and F.W. Farrar, *The Life of Christ*, 31st ed. 1884, Vol. I, 158f. note.

other shift was that of approach. As early as 1862 the Dutch scholar Uloth had rejected Dan 7:13 as the antecedent to the NT expression, claiming that υἱός τοῦ ἀνϑρώπου must be understood in the light of the Aramaic בר נשא. This approach was seriously contemplated first in the works of Meyer and Lietzmann, both of which appeared in 1896. However, the renewed Dutch 'outburst' of the early 1890's could be regarded as a precursor to the new German approach.

In Holland the discussion was set off by H.L. Oort's dissertation[32], who for almost all synoptic occurrences of SM assumed a messianic sense. This conclusion was based on a detailed examination of the synoptic evidence. Then, noticing, as G. Volkmar[33] had done before him, that the expression is missing in Paul and that it does not have a titular sense in Rev 1:13, he considered that either the term was unknown to Paul or that Jesus actually had never used it. He renewed his investigation in an effort to establish the second alternative. His conclusion was that Jesus probably used the term as a picture, at all events not as a title. At a later time, under apocalyptic influence the Church put a messianic significance into it and ascribed its use to Jesus Himself.

This result was positively greeted by W.C.van Manen[34]. In reaction to Oort and V. Manen, B.D. Eerdmans[35] investigated the origin of the expression and its use by the evangelists. Among the many Gospel passages with messianic significance, he found three passages (Mt. 12:8 and par., 12:32 and par., and 16:13 and par.), where the expression referred simply to "man" in general. He went on to investigate four questions: a) The meaning of the Aramaic expression, b) Whether the expression was used as a title around Jesus' time, c) Which relation Jesus could have had to this expression, and d) Why the evangelists took the expression as a messianic title. After a brief examination of some Jewish-Aramaic texts, he concluded that *bar-nash* means simply "man". With regards to the second question he concluded that "Wij volstrekt geen recht hebben om aan te nemen, dat de uitdrukking omtrent Jezus' tijd als Messias-titel werd gebruikt"[36]. As for the third question he thought that Jesus did use the term in its everyday sense of "man", and that if any emphasis is to be found in it at all, it was that Jesus disclaimed being anything more than an ordinary man — to the disappointment of his would-be messianic partisans. The answer to the fourth question is that the Greek translators misunderstood the Aramaic expression and by relating it to Dan 7:13 interpreted it as a messianic designation and thought that Jesus had so used it[37].

---

32 *De Uitdrukking* Ο ΥΙΟΣ ΤΟΥ ΑΝΘΡΩΠΟΥ *in het Nieuwe Testament*, 1893.

33 *Die Evangelien: Oder Marcus und die Synopsis*, 1870, 199.

34 *Theol. Tijdschr.* 27 (1893) 517—72, on p. 543f.

35 *Theol. Tijdschr.* 28 (1894) 153—76.

36 *Theol. Tijdschr.* 28 (1894) 172.

37 Similarly Wellhausen, *Israelitische und jüdische Geschichte*, 312 note 1, considered the expression υἱὸς τοῦ ἀνϑρώπου a translation mistake of the evangelists.

Eerdmans' article was followed directly by a "Naschrift" by v. Manen[38], in which the latter criticized the former's exegesis of the texts, finding in them messianic significance, and concluding that Eerdmans' guess that υἱός τοῦ ἀνϑρώπου was a misunderstanding of the Aramaic term was superfluous.

Eerdmans, following up a line of thought concerning the messianic or otherwise character of the expression in I En, wrote a new study[39] in which he came to the same conclusion, viz. the non-messianic character of the expression. Even this article received a "Naschrift" from Prof. van Manen[40] and with this ended the Dutch *discussie*.

While the 'battle with words' was going on in the *Theologische Tijdschrift*, two German scholars, A. Meyer and H. Lietzmann, were forging their literary weaponry. These scholars were of the opinion that the problem should be attacked on Aramaic grounds, and in this they carried further Eerdmans' work. Meyer's book[41], which could be described as a precursor to G. Dalman's *Die Worte Jesu*, was of more general character and addressed itself only briefly to the question[42]. Meyer reviewed very briefly a few occurrences in the Gospels and concluded that in some instances the term referred merely to man generally, while in others it was equivalent to the personal pronoun "I", etc[43]. The latter conclusion was based on the supposition that in Galilean Aramaic the expression ההוא גברא and ההוא בר נשא occur on the lips of the speaker with reflexive meaning, i.e. "that man" = "I", or "someone", etc. The element of "son" in the expression is understood as "nur sprachliches Mittel zur Bezeichnung des Individuums in der Gattung"[44].

Lietzmann devoted to the subject a whole monograph of 95 pages. After briefly noticing the Targums of Onkelos and Jonathan, he discussed the material of five tractates of Talmud jeruschalmi: *Peâ, Demâi, Kelâim, Yoma* and *Taanîth*. He quoted about twenty passages from these tractates, where he translated חד בר נש with "jemand", בר נש/בר נשא with "dieser Mensch," "einen Mensch," "jener Mensch," with the negative particle לא = "niemand," the repetition בר נש ובר נש with "jedermann" and the

---

38 *Theol. Tijdschr.* 28 (1894) 177–87, dated eight days after Eerdmans article, i.e. 18th Oct. 1893.

39 *Theol. Tijdschr.* 29 (1895) 49–71, dated Aug. 1894.

40 *Theol. Tijdschr.* 29 (1895) 263–67.

41 *Jesu Muttersprache. Das galiläische Aramäisch in seiner Bedeutung für die Erklärung der Reden Jesu und die Evangelien überhaupt*, 1896.

42 It devoted a short discussion in pp. 91–101 and an excursus to the history of its interpretation, 140–49.

43 "Sind wir mit dem Gesagten auf dem rechten Wege, so handelt es sich in den genannten Stellen nicht um eine geheimnisvolle Selbstbezeichnung Jesu; vielmehr bietet die erste Gruppe nur allgemeine Reden, in der zweiten redet Jesus allerdings von sich selbst, aber unter Anwendung eines damals üblichen Sprachgebrauchs, der das 'ich' durch ein schärfer zugespitztes 'Mensch' umschreibt", *op.cit.*, 97f.

44 *Op.cit.*, 146.

plural בני נש with "Leute." He concluded that the singular is infrequent, but that the plural is more frequent with the sense of "Mensch" (p. 38), but found this use "die farbloseste und unbestimmteste Bezeichnung des menschlichen Individuums" (p. 38). The circumlocution בר נש for אנש was explained in the light of the semitic inability for abstract thought and its proneness to using picturesque language. The second word of the formula indicates the quality of the subject. בר indicates the particular individual, while נש indicates the genre, i.e. one of mankind. Lietzmann insisted that the term could not be used of a particular individual and refused to equate בר נש with ההוא גברא "this man", an Aramaic mannerism for "I" (p. 83f.). Lietzmann rejected the messianic interpretation of both Dan 7:13 and I En. Like others before him, he conceded that the rabbis interpreted the former passage messianically, but argued that the expression they used was not בר נשא but בר ענני = "Man of the Clouds"[45]. He closed his investigation by alleging that the expression was a technical term of hellenistic theology, which was possibly formed already in Jewish circles, and developed non-uniformly in different places (p. 95).

Lietzmann's extravagant positions were criticized two years later by G. Dalman[46]. Dalman considered that the Aramaic expression was a translation of the Hebrew בן אדם, where אדם was a term with collective significance, and that the expression signified a "Glied der Gattung Mensch" (p. 192). He found, moreover, that in earlier Aramaic[47], there was an analogous usage. First with the Jewish-Galilean and Christian-Palestinian do we meet with בר אנש as an equivalent for "Mensch" (p. 194f.). He continued: "Auf Grunde dieses ganzen Thatbestandes muss gesagt werden: das jüdisch-palästinische Aramäisch der älteren Zeit hatte אנש für "Mensch," verwandte zur Bezeichnung einer Mehrheit von Menschen gelegentlich בני אנשא . Das singularische בר אנש war ungebräuchlich und wurde nur in Nachahmung des hebräischen Bibeltextes angewandt, wo בן אדם der dichterischen Sprache angehört und übrigens auch nicht häufig gebraucht wird . . . Habe ich damit Recht, so ist auch Dan 7:13 בראנש blosse Übersetzung von hebräischem בן אדם " (p. 194). Dalman pointed out that though the Gospels speak often of "men", the designation is *never* υἱός τοῦ ἀνθρώπου , and the plural υἱοί τῶν ἀνθρώπων occurs only once, in Mk 3:28. This circumstance contradicts Holtzmann's contention[48] that Son of Man is the only possible expression for 'man' in Aramaic, of Wellhausen[49] that "Die Aramäer haben keinen anderen

---

45 See discussion below, in Ch. III: Rabbinism.
46 G. Dalman, *Die Worte Jesu*. Mit Berücksichtigung des nachkanonischen jüdischen Schrifttums und der aramäischen Sprache, 1898.
47 By which he means Mishnaic Hebrew, Onkelos Targum and the Samaritan Pentateuch Targum, as well as the inscriptions from Palestine, Palmyra, Nabatea and Tema.
48 *Lehrbuch der neutestamentliche Theologie*, 2 Vols., 1897, Vol. I, 256.
49 *Israelitische und jüdische Geschichte*, 381.

Ausdruck für den Begriff" and of Lietzmann[50] that "Jesus hat sich
selbst nie den Titel 'Menschensohn' beigelegt, weil derselbe im Aramäischen nicht existiert *und aus sprachlichen Gründen nicht existieren
kann"* (Dalman's italics) (p. 195). He is led to the conclusion that, contrary
to Lietzmann, בר אנשא is quite suited to designate a definite individual
(p. 197). Dalman gave a number of examples where one could say ההוא
גברא , "this Man", of himself, but insisted that ההוא אנשא or בר ההוא
אנשא was nowhere found in that sense (p. 205). He considered,
furthermore that ההוא גברא or its Hebrew equivalent האיש אותו
"this Man" had nothing to do with Son of Man and that although this
latter expression was unusual, there was nothing strange about it — if
Jesus preferred to speak of Himself in the third person. Though he did not
accept the messianic significance of the term, he criticized sharply Oort
and Lietzmann for denying its use by Jesus, attributing it, instead, to the
early Church (p. 207f.). Finally, he thought of the term as belonging to
the more exalted poetic or prophetic idiom and understood Dan 7:13 as
designating an individual, which, in combination with other OT passages,
had been taken by e.g. I En and IV Ezr messianically (pp. 199, 210f.).
Jesus' use of the term was not intended to set Him forth as the "Niedri-
gen", "wohl aber als *das seiner Natur nach schwache Menschenkind, wel-
ches Gott zum Herrn der Welt machen will* (Dalman's italics), und es ist
sehr warscheinlich, dass Jesus den Menschensohn von Dan 7 wiederfand
in dem Psalmwort (8:5f.)" (p. 218)[51].

Fiebig produced the most comprehensive investigation of the expression SM up to his time[52]. Lietzmann had leaned more heavily on the
Talmud jeruschalmi, Dalman on the Targum of Onkelos and Wellhausen
on the Syriac. Fiebig, striving for exhaustiveness, inquired into all these
groups of literature and into much else besides. His work is divided into
two parts: a) an investigation of the Aramaic usage, and b) the data of
the NT. He criticized sharply Lietzmann and Wellhausen and corrected
Dalman, but in the main his results corroborated Dalman's thesis (e.g. pp.
12, 15f., 28 and 47). Against Lietzmann he asserted that בר נש or בר
נשא was not the only Aramaic word for "man" in Jesus' time; אנש and
אנשא were just as frequent at all times (e.g. pp. 25, 44, 58). Nor was בר
נש the only word for "someone" in the Talmud jeruschalmi; the expression means also "the man" or "a man" (p. 28). Furthermore, he found
that neither the definite form nor the addition of בר to נש(א) is of any
significance: either may mean "the man" or "a man" (pp, 20, 44). He also
rejected outright Lietzmann's contention that בר נש was not suited as a
designation of a definite personality (p. 28). To Dalman's equation of

---

50 *Der Menschensohn*, p. 85.
51 Dalman's results were made available to English readers by Eaton, *ET* 10 (1898–9) 438–43,
   and opposed by N. Schmidt, *JBL* 45 (1926) 326–49.
52 *Der Menschensohn. Jesu Selbstbezeichnung mit besonderer Berücksichtigung des aramäischen
   Sprachgebrauchs für 'Mensch', 1901.*

בר אנשא with the Hebrew בן אדם as "das Menschenkind" or "Menschensohn", he posited that בר אנשא was equivalent with אנשא = "der
Mensch", claiming that in Biblical Aramaic the בר had lost its separate
meaning (pp. 9, 56). He closed this part of his study with a presentation
of the four expressions אנש, אנשא, בר (א)נש, and בר נשא, their different
meanings and the sources supporting each meaning (pp. 59f.).

a) אנש: a) jemand, b) ein Mensch, c) der Mensch, d) die Leute
   e) Menschen
b) אנשא: a) jemand, b) ein Mensch, c) der Mensch, d) die Menschen,
   e) Menschen
c) בר (א)נש : a) jemand, b) ein Mensch, c) der Mensch
d) בר נשא : a) ein Mensch, b) der Mensch, c) jemand

In the second part of his investigation Fiebig disproved the claim of
Wellhausen, Lietzmann and Meyer that Mt 12:32 par., Mk 2:10 par., Mt
8:20 par., Mt 11:19 par. and Mk 2:27f. par. involve a translation mistake
and regarded the expression as a self-designation of Jesus (p. 66). The expression, of course, means "man" but the peculiar form is retained in
Greek despite its ungrammatical character because it comes from Dan 7:
13. But though Dan 7:13 is the point of departure, it is transcended in
Jesus' use of this expression (p. 77ff.). Fiebig further claimed that Mt
9:8; IV Ez and Mk 2:27f. par. prove that the messianic title in contemporary literature was "der Mensch", not "das Menschenkind" and that IV Ez
and I En show that "der Mensch" was at the time of Jesus a current messianic title (p. 120).

C. In Recent Research

Following Fiebig there elapsed almost five decades before the next
philological study appeared, a study by J.Y. Campbell[53]. Meanwhile,
further progress in Aramaic language study brought about a modification
of approach. The priority which Dalman had assigned to the Targums of
Onkelos and Jonathan within the evolution of the Aramaic language was
reversed owing to the work of P.E. Kahle on the Cairo Geniza material[54].
The fragments of a targum from the Cairo Geniza exhibited an earlier
form of Palestinian Aramaic than that of Onkelos or Jonathan. The evidence of this Fragment Targum was vindicated ten years later by the dis-

---

53 *JTS* 48 (1947) 145–55. H.B. Sharman's, *Son of Man and Kingdom of God*, 1st ed. 1943, did
   not touch on the literary question.
54 See P.E. Kahle, *Masoreten des Westens*, Vols. I–II, 1927–30, esp. 1–15, and *The Cairo
   Geniza*, 1947, 2nd ed. 1959.

covery in 1957 in the Vatican Library of a complete Targum on the Pentateuch known as Neofiti I[55].

J.Y. Campbell[56] denied all connection with what in the words of H.L. Goudge he called "the stupid book of Enoch"[57], and was no less firm in rejecting the theory of a Danielic origin held *inter alios* by Dodd[58]. Furthermore, he took issue with Dalman for asserting that the indefinite sense 'someone', 'anyone', was a sign of lateness in the literature where it occurred — an argument possessing a circular character for Campbell, though he did not have recourse to the Geniza Targum. Instead, he suggested, using the analogy of II Cor 12:2f., that an indefinite phrase may at any time become definite, and that בר נש was used with reference to Jesus Himself. He made the further suggestion that the term was probably used with a demonstrative adjective, i.e. 'this (son of) man' and sought for parallels in the classical ὅδε (ὁ) ἀνήρ, whose Latin equivalent was *hic homo*. The phrase Jesus used would, on this theory, have been ההוא בר נשא or בר נשא ההוא. The demonstrative is unnecessary in Greek, the expression was misunderstood, and in translating it, it was thought to be a title, which accounts for the omission of the demonstrative from the Greek.

Campbell's article generated a fresh interest in the Son of Man debate. His publication was followed almost immediately by an article by Bowman[59]. Bowman was the first one to make use of the Geniza evidence, and countered Dalman's assertion that Targum Onkelos represented the earliest Aramaic, by citing the Geniza Palestinian Targum, which in Gen 4:14 and 9:5—6 evidences the use of *bar-nash(a)* with the sense of 'anyone' or 'a man'. However, the main concern of his study was to prove chiefly by means of I Enoch, IV Ezra and early rabbinic sayings that the term *bar-nash* was perhaps already in use in pre-New Testament times as a messianic title and that the Son of Man, though not so intended by Daniel, was, in conjunction with the *Ebed-Yahweh*, understood of the Messiah.

M. Black's two articles[60] have nothing in particular to offer on the philological level of the debate, other than that he stated categorically that there is no example of ההוא בר נשא in Aramaic. He also discountenanced the attempt to resolve the expression into "simply a synonym for the personal pronoun"[61].

---

55 Published by their discoverer A. Diez-Macho, *Neophyti I*, Vols. I—III, 1969—71.
56 "The Origin and Meaning of the Term Son of Man" *JTS* 48 (1947) 145—55.
57 In Campbell, *op.cit.*, 148. In a similar way Rowley, *The Relevance of Apocalyptic*, rev. ed. 1963, 83, considered I Enoch as an inferior immitator of Daniel.
58 *The Parables of the Kingdom* 1935, rev. ed. 1961, rp. Fount paperbacks, 1978, 67ff.
59 "The Background of the Term 'Son of Man' ", *ET* 59 (1947—8) 283—8.
60 *ET* 60 (1948—9) 11—5 and 32—6.
61 *ET* 60 (1948—9) 34. It may be noted that Vermes (in Black, *Aramaic Approach*, 314) trying to enlist Black's support to his circumlocutional theory, cites Black against Campbell, but

E. Sjöberg[62] made his starting point Dalman's work and therefrom proceeded to supplement and correct Dalman, as Fiebig had done before him. With regards to the Hebrew, Sjöberg maintained that excepting Dan 8:17 the singular בן אדם always occurs in poetic passages. As for the plural, it too, is mostly found in poetic or solemn style, a notable exception being Qoheleth, though its field is somewhat broader and the designation can be used in common, everyday contexts[63]. The situation with the Aramaic בר אנש is more complicated. In Daniel the plural does not appear to have any particular solemnity, while the singular is especially difficult to gauge because of the scarcity of comparative material[64]. Aramaic documents in general, such as Targum Onkelos, the Prophet Targum, the Elephantine Papyri, as well as inscriptions from Tema, Nabataea and Palmyra offer no example that is independent of the Hebrew. In contrast, the expression is very frequent in Galilean and Samaritan Aramaic, in the Palestinian targums of the Pentateuch, in Christian Palestinian Aramaic and in Syriac and Aramaic among Babylonian Jews. In this material the expression occurs in an individual and pronominal sense as 'a man' or 'someone' as well as in a generic sense, i.e. of a human being. Against Dalman, who based his findings on the Targum Onkelos, an artificial product of later times (p. 106f.), Sjöberg argued, in concurrence with Fiebig, that the expression בר (א)נש was probably common in Galilean Aramaic already by the time of Jesus. He closed his investigation by supposing that the use of the expression in Dan 7:13, which is closer to colloquial Aramaic than the language of official documents, was probably influenced by this association. At all events it was not a religious term[65].

The year 1967 saw the publication of the 3rd edition of M. Black's *An Aramaic Approach to the Gospels and Acts*, which contained an appendix by G. Vermes on "The Use of בר נש/בר נשא in Jewish Aramaic." This study, which was a lecture given in Oxford in 1965, awoke a new interest in the philological debate on the Son of Man — a debate which is still going strong.

In this, as well as in subsequent studies, Vermes has put forward the most powerful case for a circumlocutional sense of the expression Son of Man. Put in a nutshell, his thesis is that בר נש(א) was at the time of Jesus a common Aramaic circumlocution for different forms of the first

---

bypasses those other aspects of Black's thought which are against him and which are even more pronounced.

62 "בן אדם und בר אנש in hebräischen und aramäischen", *Act Or* 21 (1950–1) 57–65, 91–107.

63 Sjöberg, *Act Or*, (1950–1) 59.

64 Sjöberg, *Act Or*, (1950–1) 61, notes that the expression in the sing. is missing from the entire Aramaic literature (inscriptions and Papyri between VIII B.C. and III A.D.) discovered up to his time.

65 Thus, Thompson, in 1961 could write that the old circumlocutional theory is "discarded today"! *JTS* N.S. 12 (1961) 205.

person of the personal pronoun, e.g. 'I', 'me'[66]. Conscious of the limited material upon which Lietzmann had based his conclusions, some of which were unwarrantably extravagant and lacking in the diffidence which normally characterizes scholarly pronouncements, Vermes applied himself to the investigation of a much larger number of Aramaic writings, in which he included the new material from the Cairo Geniza. Vermes' evidence reinforced the conclusions of earlier scholars that (א)בר נש occurs in Aramaic literature in the generic sense of 'a human being' and in a sense which is equivalent to the indefinite pronoun 'someone', etc. In addition, and this is the crux of the matter, he presented nine passages where he claimed (א)בר נש had replaced the personal pronoun 'I', 'me'[67]. Vermes' thesis met with a mixed reception.

Already before Vermes made known his results in the above-mentioned publication, R.E.C. Formesyn[68] had taken a similar position, which was, however, not based on a, strictly speaking, philological investigation. Grappling with the question as to why the term Son of Man always occurs on Jesus' lips, Formesyn found the solution in the interchangeability of the expression with the personal pronoun. "In both the earthly and suffering Son of Man sayings this interchangeability gave rise to a messianic re-reading, or *messianization* of the pronoun[69]." In the case of the future Son of Man sayings the process worked in reverse. "This interchangeability, here in case the *potential pronominalization* of the Son of Man title gave perhaps the first push to the process of identification of Jesus with the future Son of Man whom he predicted"[70]. Without inquiring into Aramaic usage he considered *bar nash*, especially in the form ההוא בר נש, the equivalent of the personal pronoun[71]. The fact that no such example has turned up in Aramaic did not trouble him unduly because he thought that on the analogy of ההוא גברא this expression too must have existed. This, according to Kümmel[72], is "eine aus der Luft gegriffene Behauptung." The omission of the demonstrative in Greek is explained by the supposition that such "*slight* (italics mine) grammatical differences" are easily overlooked in oral transmission[73].

Among those who welcomed Vermes' study was Casey, who has written

---

66 For an earlier identification of בר נשא with 'I' see Appel, *Die Selbstbezeichnung Jesu: Der Menschensohn*, 5.

67 In Black, *Aramaic Approach*, 320–8. The passages are: Gen.R. VII. 2 (ed. Theodor, p. 51); *Y.Ber.* 5 c (lines 24ff. from bottom); *Y.Ber.* 5 c (lines 29ff.); *Fragment Targum*, (Geniza) on Gen 4:14; *Y.Ber.* 5 b (lines 5ff. from bottom); *Y.Ket.* 35 a (lines 9ff.); *Gen.R.* XXXIII 13 (ed. Theodor, pp. 363–4); *Y.Ber.* 3 b (lines 15ff.); *Y.Sheb.* 38 d (lines 24 ff.).

68 "Was there a pronominal Connection for the 'Bar Nasha' Self-designation?", *NovT* 8 (1966) 1–35.

69 *Ibid.*, 25.

70 *Ibid.*, 26.

71 *Ibid.*, 30ff. Though the expression was at the same time a messianic title.

72 *TRu* 45 (1980) 57.

73 *Ibid.*, p. 33.

repeatedly on the Son of Man question[74]. In his study on "The Son of Man Problem" he basically accepts Vermes' hypothesis that *bar nash* is a surrogate for 'I', but tries to put forward a mediating position between Vermes on the one hand and J. Jeremias and C. Colpe on the other, that *bar nash* can be interchangeable with 'I' in the case of general statements, which are true of all men and therefore of the speaker as well. This leads Casey to regard Jesus' utterances about his death and resurrection as expressions of belief that all men will eventually die and be resurrected[75]. Why such a roundabout expression is necessary to express the obvious, that is, that all men die, is never explained by Casey.

Vermes' thesis met with more criticism than approval. Among the first to react were F.H. Borsch[76], C. Colpe[77], J. Jeremias[78] and J.A. Fitzmyer[79]. Both Borsch and Colpe recognized that Vermes' evidence was far from persuasive since all his examples were generic statements, and therefore, could include the speaker as well[80]. Jeremias, in a similar manner, stated that the expression was of generic and indefinite character. According to him Vermes had missed the difference between בר נשא and ההוא גברא, the model on which the former was constructed. ההוא גברא means "Ich und kein anderer", it is, so to speak, limited to the speaker, while בר נשא means "Der (bzw. ein) Mensch, also auch Ich"[81].

Vermes reacted to this criticism by declaring that his critics had largely misunderstood the point he was making. They assumed, as J. Bowker also had done[82], that a circumlocution would function as an exact synonym, whereas he considered a circumlocution "roundabout and evasive speech[83]".

---

74 See "The Corporate Interpretation of 'One like a Son of Man' (Dan VII 13) at the time of Jesus", *NovT* 18 (1976) 167—80; "The Son of Man Problem" *ZAW* 67 (1976) 147—54; "The Use of the Term 'Son of Man' in the Similitudes of Enoch", *JSJ* 7 (1976) 11—29, as well as his recent book *Son of Man*.

75 *ZAW* 67 (1976) 149ff.

76 *The Son of Man*.

77 Art Υἱὸς τοῦ Ἀνθρώπου in *TDNT*, VIII, 400—77. See 403f. *id.*, *Kairos* N.F. 11 (1969) 241—63, esp. 245—50.

78 "Die älteste Schicht der Menschensohn-Logien", *ZNW* 58 (1967) 159—72.

79 Review of M. Black's *Aramaic Approach* 3rd ed. 1967, in *CBQ* 30 (1968) 417—28; "The Contribution of Qumran Aramaic to the Study of the NT", *NTS* 20 (1974) 382—407 "Methodology in the Study of the Aramaic Substratum of Jesus' Sayings in the NT" in J. Dupont (ed.), *Jésus aux origines de la christologie*, 1975. Both of the above (the last under the title "The Study of the Aramaic Background of the NT") together with other relevant studies, were reprinted in J.A. Fitzmyer, *A Wandering Aramean*, 85—113 and 1—27 respectively.

80 In Borsch's words: "The reference may still be just to *any man*. Though the speaker may occasionally include himself under this reference, this does not make it into a genuine circumlocution any more than would a comparable usage in English. E.g. 'A man can't work miracles. What do you expect of me?," *op.cit.* p. 23, n.4. Colpe, *TDNT* VIII, 403: "The Sfire example ... shows that in Aramaic both בר אנש and אנש were possible from the very first as indef. pronouns".

81 J. Jeremias, *ZNW* 58 (1967) 165, n.9.

82 "The Son of Man" *JTS*, N.S. 28 (1977) 19—48, esp. 30ff.

83 G. Vermes, "The Present State of the 'Son of Man' Debate" *JJS*, 29 (1978) 123—34, esp.

Fitzmyer's criticism is more damaging. In a number of lectures and articles appearing in various journals and lately printed in a volume of collected essays[84], he has raised the chronological and the morphological issues. All of Vermes' examples are late and this is confirmed by their morphology. They all lack the initial א, which is a sign of lateness[85]. In 1967 Fitzmyer had conceded[86] that some of Vermes' examples proved the circumlocutional use for the expression; however, in later publications this was withdrawn[87]. In a lecture given in Oxford in 1974[88] Fitzmyer finally admitted that the parallel targums, Neofiti I and Pseudo-Jonathan, on Gen 4:14, illustrate the circumlocutional use, but he is unwilling to date them in the first century A.D.[89]

Vermes pleaded that in the case of the Son of Man there is not sufficient evidence from the time of Jesus, so he did the best he could with the later evidence, some of which, at least, he hoped, possibly went back to a century or so after Jesus' time[90]. As for the criticism about the missing א, Vermes held fast to his position on the strength of Greek transliteration usage of semitic names such as *El'azar* into Lazar(os) (e.g. Jn 11:1; Jos., *BJ*, 5,567) and the verb אמר, which in Qumran occurs sometimes without the א[91].

So far it would seem that Vermes has succeeded in showing that the expression בר נש(א) occurs a sufficient number of times in Aramaic documents of post-Christian date in an indefinite sense, i.e. 'someone' etc., and in a generic sense, i.e. 'a man' etc. as well as once in Cairo Targum B on Gen 4:14 as a surrogate for 'I' (cf. Neofiti I: 'me'). Fitzmyer also has succeeded in eliminating the many vague examples of בר נש(א), which Vermes had marshalled to prove that the circumlocutional usage was ubiquitous in Aramaic literature. The net result of this debate has been enriching in that we now have become aware that an equivalent or near-equivalent of a peculiar NT Greek expression occurred occasionally in the Aramaic of later times with meanings not suspected from the NT texts. On at least one occasion the Aramaic expression has been proved to bear

125f. (The above article is printed also as "The 'Son of Man' Debate", in *JSNT* 1 (1978) 19–32 to which Fitzmyer's requested reply came in "Another view of the 'Son of Man' Debate" *JSNT* 1 (1978) 58–68.

84 *A Wandering Aramean:* Collected Essays, 1979.

85 See Fitzmyer's review of M. Black's *Aramaic Approach*, 3rd ed. 1967, 424–8. The same argument is more strongly reiterated following Vermes' *Jesus the Jew:* A Historian's Reading of the Gospels, 1973, 188ff., in "The NT Title 'Son of Man' Philologically Considered" in *A Wandering Aramean*, 143–60, esp. 149ff.

86 Fitzmyer, Review (of M. Blcak's *Aramaic Approach*) in *CBQ* 30 (1968) 427.

87 E.g. "The Contribution of Qumran Aramaic to the Study of the NT", *NTS* 20 (1974) 382–407, esp. p. 397, n.1.

88 Printed as ch. 6, "The NT Title 'Son of Man' Philologically Considered", in *A Wandering Aramean*, 143–60.

89 *Ibid.*, 152 and 154.

90 This point is argued afresh in *JJS* 33 (1982) 361–76.

91 G. Vermes, *JJS* 29 (1978) 123ff.

the sense of 'I'. Yet, on the other hand, the debate has not brought us any closer to the solution of the problem confronting the interpreter of the Greek expression in the NT. The reasons for this are many. In addition to the above arguments by e.g. Borsch, Jeremias and Fitzmyer, the following criticism may be made.

1. No convincing explanation has been forthcoming as to why if the term υἱός τοῦ ἀνϑρώπου was created by hellenistic theology[92] and was, in other words, 'significant' for Greek speaking Christianity, the term yielded to other titles so early in post-apostolic Christianity[93]. This would indicate that the term was not the product of the hellenistic Church, but came into it from earlier sources[94].

2. The advocates of the circumlocutional theory fail to appreciate that the term Son of Man by its exclusive occurrence on Jesus' lips (apart from sayings constituting quotations of his words and Acts 7:56) as a designation of his own person inevitably takes the place of the first person of the personal pronoun. Since Jesus is the speaker and the words refer to himself, it is obvious that this term as such can replace 'I' or 'me' (as it actually happens in Mt 16:13 as compared with Mk 8:27). However, to say that Son of Man is used in places where the personal pronoun *syntactically* might also have been used is a very different thing from saying that SM is used *semantically* as 'I', i.e., with the same meaning, content and connotations as 'I'. The interchangeability of SM with 'I' is a matter of verisimilitude only and relates to syntactics, not semantics. This point is illustrated well by Schmiedel's debate (in Protestant. Monatshefte, Berlin) against Wellhausen's theory (see above), as presented by Muirehead[95]: "Schmiedel's argument on this 'Machtspruch' (the polite German name for critical impudence) is worth quoting: 'Really! *Caesar commanded the attack*. Instead of this the words in the Gallic War might run: *The general commanded the attack*. But could it also be said: *The soldier commanded the attack*? or *Caesar exhorted the soldiers*. It might also be said: *The general exhorted the soldiers*: but what of: *The soldier exhorted the soldiers*? To show that the last example is not irrelevant, we need only quote (à la Wellhausen Mk 9:31: '*The Man will be delivered into the hands of men*'!" The latter example would, of course, not apply to Vermes, who unlike Wellhausen, would render SM with 'I', and not 'man'. But the former example exposes the bankruptcy of the circumlocutional theory.

---

92 This was the thesis of *inter alios* Eerdmans and Lietzmann.

93 Cf. Tödt, *The Son of Man in the Synoptic Tradition*, 117: "There is no proof whatsoever that this use of the name Son of Man originated in the Hellenistic sphere. Why should the Hellenistic community have been interested in transfering an Aramaic name to Jesus?".

94 Ciholas, "Son of Man in the Synoptic Gospels", *BThB* 11 (1981) 17–20 argues unconvincingly that "the Son of Man Christology may have belonged to one or several smaller groups which were sufficiently influential to create traditions which survived up to the time of the writing of the Gospels", and were thus incorporated into them. But there is no proof for such an assertion.

95 *ET* 11 (1899–1900) 62–5.

Even Leivestad is prepared to admit that the personal pronoun cannot replace every instance of the SM[96]. It is this distinction that SM and 'I' are
not coextensive in meaning that renders the production of ever so many
examples of the circumlocutional use of בר נשא in Aramaic literature a
wasted labour and their refutation a superfluous labour. For the point in
dispute is not whether the Aramaic expression can be used in a context
where 'I' could well have appeared, but whether Son of Man has no other
significance, no special overtones other than are carried by the personal
pronoun. This is patently not the case[97]. This even Vermes would be prepared to concede[98], and this decides the matter against his theory. For if
Son of Man does have a significance and overtones absent from 'I' — and
this is abundantly clear in the Gospels — it cannot be a 'surrogate' for
'I'![99] Strictly speaking the test ought to be: if the substitution of the one
term for the other introduces no change whatever in respect to the information conveyed, then the terms can be regarded as equivalent, but if

---

96 *NTS* 18 (1971–2) 256.
97 M. Müller, *ST* 31 (1977) 80: "Denn er (the term SM) wird nie an unbetonter Stelle verwen-
det, sondern kann überall — mit einer einzigen Ausnahme: Mt 16, 13 — durch die Bezeichnung 'Messias' ersetzt werden. Es ist also nicht zufällig, sondern in Gegenteil sehr wohl
beabsichtigt, dass durch den Ausdruck 'Menschensohn' ein ganz anderer Eindruck ensteht als
durch das blosse Personalpronomen".
98 Cf. his qualifications in Black, *Aramaic Approach*, 320, 327.
99 Vermes posits that ההוא גברא is used as circumlocution, a) "when a speaker wishes to
avoid undue or immodest emphasis on himself", b) "when he is prompted by fear or by dis-
like of asserting openly something disagreeable in relation to himself", c) "when he utters a
curse", and d) as "a protestation" (in Black, *Aramaic Approach*, 320). In a similar way he
thinks the replacement of 'I' by בר נשא(א) is owing to modesty or reserve (p. 327). It would
indeed be very interesting to see if the NT passages lend themselves to such an interpretation.
Since ὁ υἱὸς τοῦ ἀνθρώπου occurs in several places along with the personal pronoun, it ought
to be possible, on Vermes' theory, to distinguish the connotations of ὁ υἱὸς τοῦ ἀνθρώπου
from those of 'I' etc. A few examples may illustrate the point. In John 8:28 Jesus says: ὅταν
ὑψώσητε τὸν υἱὸν τοῦ ἀνθρώπου, τότε γνώσεσθε ὅτι ἐγώ εἰμί; Jn 6:26f. ἀμὴν ἀμὴν
λέγω ὑμῖν, ζητεῖτέ με οὐχ ὅτι εἴδετε σημεῖα, ἀλλ' ὅτι ἐφάγετε ἐκ τῶν ἄρτων καὶ
ἐχορτάσθητε· ἐργάζεσθε μὴ τὴν βρῶσιν τὴν ἀπολελυμένην ἀλλὰ τὴν βρῶσιν τὴν
μένουσαν εἰς ζωὴν αἰώνιον, ἣν ὁ υἱὸς τοῦ ἀνθρώπου ὑμῖν δώσει; Jn 6:62ff. τοῦτο
ὑμᾶς σκανδαλίζει; ἐὰν οὖν θεωρεῖτε τὸν υἱὸν τοῦ ἀνθρώπου ἀναβαίνοντα ὅπου ἦν τὸ
πρότερον; τὸ πνεῦμά ἐστιν τὸ ζῳοποιοῦν, ἡ σὰρξ οὐκ ὠφελεῖ οὐδέν· τὰ ῥήματα ἅ ἐγὼ
λελάληκα ὑμῖν πνεῦμά ἐστι καὶ ζωή ἐστιν; Jn 13:31ff. λέγει ὁ Ἰησοῦς· νῦν ἐδοξάσθη
ὁ υἱὸς τοῦ ἀνθρώπου καὶ ὁ Θεὸς ἐδοξάσθη ἐν αὐτῷ ... ἔτι μικρὸν μεθ' ὑμῶν εἰμί·
ζητήσετέ με.
    The synoptics present a similar situation. Cf. e.g. Mt 19:28 ἀμὴν λέγω ὑμῖν ὅτι ὑμεῖς
οἱ ἀκολουθήσαντές μοι ἐν τῇ παλιγγενεσίᾳ, ὅταν καθίσῃ ὁ υἱὸς τοῦ ἀνθρώπου ἐπὶ
θρόνου δόξης αὐτοῦ, καθήσεσθε καὶ ὑμεῖς ἐπὶ δώδεκα θρόνους ... Mt 26:23f. (cf. Mk 14:
20f.) ὁ ἐμβάψας μετ' ἐμοῦ τὴν χεῖρα ἐν τῷ τρυβλίῳ οὗτός με παραδώσει ... οὐαὶ δὲ τῷ
ἀνθρώπῳ ἐκείνῳ δι' οὗ ὁ υἱὸς τοῦ ἀνθρώπου παραδίδοται. Mk 8:38 (cf. Lk 9:26)
ὃς γὰρ ἐὰν ἐπαισχυνθῇ με καὶ τοὺς ἐμοὺς λόγους ... καὶ ὁ υἱὸς τοῦ ἀνθρώπου
ἐπαισχυνθήσεται αὐτόν. Mk 14:62 ὁ δὲ Ἰησοῦς εἶπεν· ἐγώ εἰμι, καὶ ὄψεσθε τὸν υἱὸν
τοῦ ἀνθρώπου ἐκ δεξιῶν καθήμενον τῆς δυνάμεως καὶ ἐρχόμενον μετὰ τῶν νεφελῶν
τοῦ οὐρανοῦ. Lk 12:8 πᾶς ὃς ἂν ὁμολογήσῃ ἐν ἐμοὶ ἔμπροσθεν τῶν ἀνθρώπων, καὶ ὁ

the semasiological information changes then the one term cannot be a surrogate for the other[100].

3. The circumlocutional theory fails to take account of the issue of communication. Thus, Vermes writes that what gave impetus to his study was the insight that "since 'the son of man' is not a Greek phrase, but Amaraic, if it is to make sense at all, it must be Aramaic sense"[101]. This is a surprising remark from the eminent scholar, since it implies that the communication line is broken. All communication between sender and receiver becomes impossible here. The author writes four Greek words whose message, however, can be decoded only if the reader knows that the Greek expression is the equivalent of an Aramaic expression meaning 'I'! This claim hardly squares with the very obvious concern of NT authors to communicate to their readers meaning (cf. e.g. their translation of semitic terms and expressions). Vermes' supposition is no doubt applicable to the magical papyri, but hardly to the NT, where every effort is made to render the message plain and understandable to all.

4. Despite every effort that has been made so far to dissociate the Son of Man sayings in the Gospels from Dan 7:13, the results have been largely unconvincing and in the end even those engaged in this pursuit have had to admit dependence on Dan 7:13 for at least certain sayings. Dan 7:13 is at present the only occurrence of the expression in Imperial Aramaic, being antedated by one example belonging to Old Aramaic i.e. the Sefire

---

υἱὸς τοῦ ἀνθρώπου ὁμολογήσει ἐν αὐτῷ ἔμπροσθεν τῶν ἀγγέλων τοῦ Θεοῦ. Lk 22:21f. πλὴν ἰδοὺ ἡ χείρ τοῦ παραδιδόντος με μετ' ἐμοῦ ἐπὶ τῆς τραπέζης. ὅτι ὁ υἱὸς μὲν τοῦ ἀνθρώπου κατὰ τὸ ὡρισμένον πορεύεται, πλὴν οὐαὶ τῷ ἀνθρώπῳ ἐκείνῳ δι' οὗ παραδίδοται. In all these texts it is difficult to see how ὁ υἱὸς τοῦ ἀνθρώπου occurs instead of 'I' with the mere distinction that it introduces 'reserve' or 'modesty' which are lacking in 'I' etc.! The point made here is that the present state of the SM sayings (Johannine and synoptic) does not support Vermes' theory. Neither can Vermes' theory be saved by questioning the authenticity of these sayings and by claiming that in the original sayings of Jesus SM was used according to Vermes' theory. Where are the Gospel traces of Jesus' original sayings in which SM on Jesus' lips was used to express 'modesty', 'reserve', 'fear', 'curse' or 'protestation', which are lacking in the personal pronoun? But if all those traces have been effectively obliterated by the evangelists, on what Gospel basis does Vermes base his theory? Vermes' theory is a mere *Vermutung* without basis. On the contrary a passage like Jn 5:26f. remains, on Vermes' hypothesis, unexplained: ὥσπερ γὰρ ὁ πατὴρ ἔχει ζωὴν ἐν ἑαυτῷ, οὕτως καὶ τῷ υἱῷ ἔδωκεν ζωὴν ἔχειν ἐν ἑαυτῷ. καὶ ἐξουσίαν ἔδωκεν αὐτῷ κρίσιν ποιεῖν, ὅτι υἱὸς ἀνθρώπου ἐστιν. Here the character of the Son of God as Son of Man gives him the right to hold judgment (the ὅτι is causal). (See also Moloney, *The Johannine Son of Man*, 84f.). In this place ὁ υἱὸς τοῦ ἀνθρώπου could not be replaced by 'I' without change of meaning. As for Jn 12:32, Sturch, *ET* 94 (1983) 333, argues that the replacement of the Son of Man by a pronoun is inapplicable, since the people's reaction in vs. 34 becomes, on Vermes' theory, meaningless. For a likely background for this text in Dan 7, see Martyn, *History and Theology in the Fourth Gospel*, 129ff.; Hamerton-Kelly, *Pre-existence, Wisdom and Son of Man*, 235ff., Moule, *The Phenomenon of the NT*, 92.

100 Cf. Pamment, *NTS* 29 (1983) 127.
101 *Jesus the Jew*, 177; *JJS* 29 (1978) 124.

inscription (Sf III, 16—17)[102] dated to the middle of the VIII B.C.[103] Now in Dan 7:13 it is entirely inappropriate to replace בר אנש with 'I'. If then, as is generally admitted, the expression in Dan 7:13 carries a particular significance, and the Gospels in some sayings quote that very passage, it is plain logic that ὁ υἱός τοῦ ἀνϑρώπου could not have the "farbloseste und unbestimmteste" significance of 'I', to borrow Lietz- mann's phrase. In Dan as well as in the Gospels, at least in the sayings that connect back to Dan, the sense must be other than 'I'[104].

Again, on the theory that in their present state the Gospel SM sayings reflect Church theology rather than Jesus' original usage of the expression, which in the absence of any other usage of the *bar nasha* expression, could have been only circumlocutional, it may be countered that the Danielic text alone witnesses to the existence of a different sense for this expres- sion than the circumlocutional one claimed by Vermes, and therefore also to the *prima-facie* possibility that Jesus both was acquainted with and made use of this other (older) import of the *bar (e)nash(a)* expression.

5. That Vermes' theory cannot be upheld becomes apparent not least from the fact that his own followers have been forced to modify it. The two full-scale studies acknowledging descent from Vermes' theory — Casey's[105] and Lindars'[106] — each goes its own way in interpreting the rabbinic 'evidence' on which Vermes had based his theory. Since Lindars' book is the later of the two, and since it is sufficiently critical of Casey's interpretation[107], I need only address myself to this study[108]. This re- presents a new mode of the circumlocutional theory.

After reviewing a few of Vermes' Aramaic texts, Lindars concludes: "There are thus three ways of referring to oneself by means of the third person. There is the general statement, in which the speaker includes him- self. It is the mistake of Casey to suppose that this is the clue to the mean- ing of the Son of Man sayings in the gospels[109]. Secondly there is the

---

102 In the indefinite sense of 'someone' cf. *ANET* p. 661 a and Beyerlin, *NERT*, 265, where it is rendered "a son of man" with a note "Here 'prince of the blood'. The Akkadian word 'man' can also mean 'king' ". Cf. Haag, בן אדם in *TDOT*, II, 161f. See further Fitzmyer, *The Ara- maic Inscriptions of Sefire*, (Bib Or 19) 1967, ad.loc.; Gibson, *Textbook of Syrian Semitic Inscriptions*, 3 Vols., Vol. II: *Aramaic Inscriptions from Zinjirli*, 1975, p. viif.; Whitehead, "Some Distinctive Features of the Language of the Aramaic Arsames Correspondence", *JNES* 37 (1978) 119f.

103 Cf. Fitzmyer, *The Aramaic Inscriptions of Sefire*, 115; Greenfield, "The Dialects of Early Aramaic", *JNES* 37 (1978) 94: "These (sc. Sefire etc.) are written in what may be called Early Standard Aramaic. This is clearly the literary dialect shared by the Arameans of Syria and the Arameans of other areas. It may have served as the base for later Official Aramaic". Fitzmyer, classes it as "Old Aramaic" (925—700 B.C.) in *A Wandering Aramean*, 60f., and "The Aramaic Language and the Study of the New Testament", *JBL* 99 (1980) 8.

104 Cf. Moule's remarks in *NT und Kirche*, 421.

105 E.g. *Son of Man*, 224ff.

106 E.g. *Jesus Son of Man*, 19.

107 Casey's position is discussed at several points in Lindars' study.

108 Casey's position is dealt with at many points of this study.

exclusive self-reference in which the speaker refers to himself alone. Vermes seems to be mistaken in thinking that this is the proper meaning of *bar nasha* in this type of speech. Thirdly there is the idiomatic use of the generic article, in which the speaker refers to a class of persons, with whom he identifies himself . . . It is this idiom, properly requiring *bar (e)nasha* rather than *bar (e)nash*, which provides the best guide to the use of the Son of Man in the sayings of Jesus"[110].

Lindars' thesis — a combination of Vermes' circumlocutional and Casey's generic views — involves the following positions:

a) The sporadic use of an Aramaic idiom of later times is supposed to have been current in Jesus' time, and this to such an extent as to occur fairly frequently on Jesus' lips[111].

b) At the time of Jesus no other usage of the SM expression was known or possible. Only what Lindars calls the generic idiom with self-reference could have been known to Jesus.

c) Only nine sayings have preserved the original sense which the expression bore when uttered by Jesus. All of these are found in Q and Mark[112].

d) All other SM sayings in the Gospels are inauthentic representing the evangelists' theologizing in the light of Dan 7:13 and their Easter faith.

e) In altering the import of the original *bar enasha* expression when translating the phrase into Greek, the evangelists misunderstood the way in which Jesus had used the expression and thus turned it into a title[113].

f) The characteristic feature of Jesus' usage of this expression is not "modesty", "reserve", etc., as Vermes thought, but irony.

On the basis of these postulates Lindars argues that in the nine authentic sayings Jesus says something which is true of a group of persons and, as a consequence of his identifying himself with that group, also of himself. Happily Lindars admits that his theory is highly speculative[114]. As a matter of fact it is based partly on precarious postulates and partly on demonstrably mistaken premises.

a) It is precarious to claim that Jesus could only have been acquainted with and have used so frequently an Aramaic idiom which is not extant in

---

109 I.e. Casey, *Son of Man*, 228–31.

110 *Jesus Son of Man.* 23f.

111 The nine 'authentic' occurrences, which Lindars finds, not taking into account other instances of that idiom in Jesus' sayings now 'lost' or altered (cf. p. 26), must be considered a very frequent use in such limited literature as the Gospels in comparison with the relatively few occurrences in the vast rabbinic literature.

112 I.e. Mt 8:20 = Lk 9:58; Mt 11:16–19 = Lk 7:31–35; Mt 12:32 = Lk 12:10; Lk 11:30; Mt 9:6 = Mk 2:10f. = Lk 5:24; Mt 10:32f. = Lk 12:8f.; Mk 8:31; 9:31; 10:33–4.

113 Thus Lk 17:24, 26, 30 and Mt 24:44 = Lk 12:40 which it was found possible to attribute to Q, "could not be considered authentic in their present form, because the titular Son of Man cannot correspond with the *bar enasha* idiom" (*Jesus Son of Man*, 165).

114 In *Jesus Son of Man*, 53 he calls it "a matter of guesswork" while on p. 73 he terms it a "necessarily speculative reconstruction".

contemporary literature, but is met only sporadically (Lindars presents one example and that "ambiguous" p. 23f.) several centuries later.

b) It is demonstrably mistaken to claim that Jesus could not have been acquainted with any other usage of *bar (e)nash(a)*, because such never existed, and that there was no SM concept prior to the Christian Church. Here the reader is referred to my discussion in Chs. Two and Three below. In his recent criticism of Lindars, Black upholds the titular use of SM in the *Parables*, while with respect to the Aramaic he says: "It is a capital error to assume that *Barnāshā/bar 'enāshā* in the Old Aramaic (or Hebrew *ben ha'ādām*), 'the Son of Man', cannot be used as a designation or with titular force for a particular individual ... The designation or title *Barnāshā* for the 'Son of Man' has the same force in the Old Aramaic as does Greek *ho uios tou anthrōpou*"[115]. Black therefore settles for the titular use of *bar nasha* prior to Jesus as well as the titular use of ὁ υἱός τοῦ ἀνθρώπου in Lindars' 'authentic' SM logia.

c) It is inconceivable that the Early Church, speaking the same language as Jesus, would have totally misunderstood Lindars' Aramaic irony, generic — self-reference, idiom on the lips of Jesus, and mistakenly have turned it into a title[116]. This is even more unthinkable when at the same time we are told (by Lindars) that this was the only usage in existence and that the idiom apparently was in widespread use!

d) There may be a subjective element in this, but surely the irony theory is hardly applicable on the so-called 'authentic' sayings of Jesus[117].

e) Finally, Lindars' exegesis is problematic. A few brief remarks may illustrate this.

In Mt 8:20 = Lk 9:58, "a man has nowhere to lay his head", since SM cannot be said to be identified with the class human beings (of whom it is not generally true that they are homeless) Lindars finds the "group" in the would-be-disciple. Note well the theory demands that what is said is applicable in a generic way first to a group and then in a particular application also to Jesus as a 'member' of that group. But one searches in vain for this here. Jesus' words refer exclusively to himself, to his own circumstances. It is, however, true that in the present context Jesus' words give an idea of what following him implies, but so far from identifying himself with this 'prospective disciple', I would suggest that Jesus actually turns him down by means of these words. This point can be better appreciated when we compare Jesus' attitude of *discouragement* to this scribe with his attitude of *encouragement* to the other man whom he actually urges to follow him and leave the dead to bury their own dead[117a]. Lindars' theory cannot be said to illuminate the passage. On the contrary, a Son of

---

115 *ET* 95 (1984) 202.
116 Cf. e.g. *Jesus Son of Man*, 31, 22, 43, 46, 57, 75.
117 Cf. e.g. *Jesus Son of Man*, 30, 31, 38, 57.
117a Similarly Dodd, *Parables*, 141: "This is the process of selection".

Man who has assumed the role of the Suffering Servant fits the conditions of the text quite satisfactorily[118].

Mt 11:16—19 = Lk 7:31—35 offers another interesting example. Lindars claims that Jesus here classes himself "with the Baptist as another of the same group"[119]. Black comments: "This is a strange exegesis, since the point of the saying is usually taken to be that this is exactly what Jesus is not doing"[120]. Neither can it be asserted that Jesus has his own disciples in mind. The point of the saying is the uncomprehending attitude of the Jews to two different servants of God who appear in diametrically different circumstances. The reference is surely exclusively personal.

With regards to Lk 11:30 Lindars says: "Just as Jonah was a sign to the Ninevites, i.e., bore witness to God through his preaching to them, so there is a man who will be a sign to the present generation"[121]. Again Black's objection is pertinent. He asks: "Jesus is referring to himself, but could a term 'a man' without any further qualification or meaning form a suitable parallel, in any language, to the prophet Jonah? And to what class of persons in the human family is *barnāshā* here referring?[122]. Lindars' theory has no satisfactory answer.

When it comes to Mt 12:41f. = Lk 11:31f. Lindars notes that the Greek uses $\pi\lambda\epsilon\tilde{\iota}o\nu$ rather than $\pi\lambda\epsilon\acute{\iota}\omega\nu$. "The reference is to the preaching (wisdom) of Jesus rather than to Jesus himself"[123]. In this way he hopes he can dispose of an otherwise bothersome exclusive self-reference, since in this context there is no group of persons with whom Jesus might be associated. However, the neuter form is no guarantee that $\pi\lambda\epsilon\tilde{\iota}o\nu$ cannot refer to Jesus. In Greek the neuter can be used to refer to persons[124]. In the actual text there is no mention of any $\kappa\acute{\eta}\rho\upsilon\gamma\mu a$ or $\sigma o\varphi\acute{\iota}a$ of Jesus that might be compared with Jonah's preaching or Solomon's wisdom. The comparison is actually on the level of persons[124a]. The neuter form is an idiomatic form of self-reference to divert undue attention to the speaker. The same idiom is used in Mt 12:6, $\tau o\tilde{\upsilon}\ \acute{\iota}\epsilon\rho o\tilde{\upsilon}\ \mu\epsilon\tilde{\iota}\zeta o\nu\ \acute{\epsilon}\sigma\tau\iota\ \tilde{\omega}\delta\epsilon$. Here Jesus, in whose presence and service the disciples broke the sabbath, declares himself to be greater than the temple, in which and in whose service the priests break the sabbath and yet are without guilt. The "here is something greater" in place of the direct "I am greater", is a Greek idiom to avoid an egotistic reference. At the same time the idiom often has a touch of irony. To the Greek copyists the idiomatic reference was so obvious that many of them did not hesitate to change $\mu\epsilon\tilde{\iota}\zeta o\nu$ to $\mu\epsilon\tilde{\iota}\zeta\omega\nu$ to make

118 So too Black, *ET* 95 (1984) 205.

119 *Jesus Son of Man*, 33.

120 *ET* 95 (1984) 205.

121 *Jesus Son of Man*, 41.

122 *ET* 95 (1984) 204.

123 *Jesus Son of Man*, 40. But see Hamerton-Kelly, *Pre-existence*, 34ff.

124 Cf. e.g. Jn 6:37, 39; 17:24; I Cor 1:17 (cf. Robertson, *Grammar*, 653).

124a Manson, *The Sayings of Jesus*, 90: "Jesus Himself is the sign".

it more explicit[125]. Black points out that the Aramaic *rab min* can be translated either way and that the Old Syriac has "a greater than Jonah/ Solomon is here" and concludes: "If the Greek should have rendered the original *meizōn Iōna*, then the words could only fittingly apply to the Son of Man Messiah"[126]. This is certainly the gist of the passage. The proposed theory is shown to be not merely unnecessary, but even a hindrance to a correct understanding of the text.

Mt 9:6 = Mk 2:10f. = Lk 5:24 is understood by Casey as a generic statement "a man has power to forgive sins on earth"[127]. Lindars modifies the generic statement so as to apply to a group of exorcists with whom Jesus identifies himself[128]. The theory is based on the supposed affinity of our text with 4QOrNab, according to which Nabonidus, the last Baby-lonian king, claims to have been forgiven, healed and urged by a Jew to give praise to God. The point of view here is clearly pagan, the text forms a parallel to Dan 4 and the agreement with the Gospel pericope is ex-tremely slender. Casey's and Lindars' theories presuppose the existence of Jewish exorcists who went about forgiving sins and healing people. There is, however, no evidence that such a practice ever existed[129]. All three evangelists testify unanimously that Jesus' declaration of forgiveness was regarded by the Jews as unambiguous blasphemy, Mark and Luke actually emphasizing the Jewish belief that only God has the right to forgive sins. This in itself is ample disproof of the existence of such a practice among the Jews. Moreover, if Jesus were to identify himself with a group of persons who had the right or were assumed to have the right to grant for-giveness of sins, the point of his being unique in this regard, so clearly emphasized in the pericope, would have been entirely lost. It is further-more to be noted that Jesus, as depicted in all three accounts, does not merely function as God's mouthpiece, thus comparable with the supposed Jewish exorcists, but acts as one who has that right in himself. The stand-point is similar to that in Jn 5:26f. Jesus does not controvert that forgive-ness is a divine prerogative, but claims that in his case, he, as Son of Man, has that right on earth. This is possible only for the kind of Son of Man we find in Dan 7 (see Ch. Two) and in the *Parables* (Ch. Three) as Thompson also has argued[130].

Finally, in Mt 10:32f. = Lk 12:8f. the theory is in grave difficulties.

---

125 E.g. C L Δ 0233 f[13] 1424.

126 *ET* 95 (1984) 204.

127 *Son of Man*, 228.

128 *Jesus Son of Man*, 44ff.

129 Casey and Lindars lean here on Vermes' discussion in *Jesus the Jew*, 58–82. In this chapter, however, all that Vermes has been able to produce is two individuals, Honi and Hanina ben Dosa, claimed by him to have lived in late first century A.D. and said to have performed a few miracles, chiefly to have called down rain. The description of these persons in the (late) Jew-ish sources are quite dissimilar from the description of Jesus, but quite apart from that, there is no hint of any forgiveness of sins recorded in those documents in connection with these individuals.

130 *JTS* 12 (1961) 203ff.

Lindars paraphrases "All those who confess me before men will have a man to speak for them (i.e., an advocate) before the judgment seat of God"[131]. Lindars refuses to understand the saying as exclusively self-referring because "The *bar enasha* idiom . . . forbids this simple interpretation"[132]. Note that the sense of the saying and of the context is subjected to the demands of the theory! But then the unanswerable question arises, with whom does Jesus here identify himself? On Lindars' theory there is no satisfactory answer to this compelling question. As Black remarks: "It is here an exclusive self-reference to Jesus as present Son of Man, but also as the One destined to take up the traditional role of the Son of Man Messiah, but as Advocate as well as Judge, on the day of Judgment"[133]. Black rightly concludes (with reference to Lietzmann's memorable expression). "For a term pregnant with messianic significance, Lindars would substitute what must surely be 'the most colourless and the vaguest' possible description of the human individual"[134].

D. Conclusions

To conclude, the philological debate of recent decades is essentially an old debate. What is often being put forward as new results has been said long ago.

Vermes' circumlocutional theory is of some interest for Aramaic syntax of later times, but has hardly any relevance for the NT Son of Man, whose antecedents are earlier and quite different.

Casey's generic reference version is too flat to make much sense of the Gospel logia and it is justly criticized by Lindars.

Lindars' generic — self-referring, irony theory is hardly applicable to the passages on which it has been based. The exegesis is not above serious criticism. The theory is based on unsubstantiated claims regarding a hypothetical Aramaic original which is beyond scientific scrutiny, on reconstructions which have no basis in any textual tradition, but which give the impression of being dictated by the theory.

The circumlocutional theory in all versions in which it has appeared has failed to provide the answer to the Son of Man problem in the Gospels. It has failed to produce Aramaic evidence that is both contemporary with Jesus and independent of the Gospels. Further, it has been unable to demonstrate that in his so-called 'authentic' SM sayings Jesus had actually used the expression as an Aramaic idiom and not in its older and well-established sense.

---

131 *Jesus Son of Man*, 54.
132 *Jesus Son of Man*, 54.
133 *ET* 95 (1984) 203.
134 *ET* 95 (1984) 203.

Chapter II

The 'Son of Man' in the Old Testament in General and in Daniel in Particular

A. Introductory

The expression son of man occurs five times in Daniel, as follows: in 2: 38 the בני אנשא along with "the beasts of the field and the birds of the air" have been given to Nebuchadnezzar's power. In 5:21 Daniel relates to Belshazzar that when Nebuchadnezzar became haughty, he was humiliated by being deposed from his kingly throne and "driven from among the בני אנשא". The two instances are identical and describe men in general. In 10:16 כדמות בני אדם ('one in the likeness of the sons of men') is used of an angelic figure, while in 8:17 בן אדם is employed by Gabriel as a term of address to Daniel. This last occurrence is quite similar to the use of the expression in Ez.

The fact that the expression in Dan has been found so far to have variable content — men in general, Daniel himself, the angel Gabriel — ought to be a warning to us that a fresh meaning for 7:13 cannot be ruled out. In fact in 7:13 the expression does carry a meaning different to the ones mentioned, as we shall presently see. We may thus say that the five instances of this term in Dan are applied in four different ways.

The study of the 'Son of Man' in Dan is inextricably tied up with two questions: the background and provenience of the term in Dan, and the Danielic use or application of it. These two questions are essentially separate matters and ought to be kept apart even though the former may be understood at times to influence the latter. Actually there are two kinds of backgrounds that are possible, an OT and an extra-biblical background, both of which have their advocates. The extra-biblical background again may be Iranian[1], Babylonian[2], or Canaanite[3]. The second question, namely, the identity of the one like a son of man in Dan, will be the chief con-

---

1 E.g. Mowinckel, *He that Cometh*, 346–50.

2 E.g. Jansen, *Die Henochgestalt: Eine religionsgeschichtliche Untersuchung*, 1939.

3 E.g. Morgenstern, "The King-god among the Western Semites and the Meaning of Epiphanes", *VT* 10 (1960) 138–97; " 'The Son of Man' of Dan 7:13f.: A New Interpretation", *JBL* 80 (1961) 65–77; Emerton, "The Origin of the Son of Man Imagery", *JTS* 9 (1958) 225–42.

cern of this chapter. However, before taking up that matter, it is considered pertinent to treat briefly the question of backgrounds.

B. Extra-Biblical Backgrounds

The postulation of a certain background need neither predetermine
nor predispose one to a particular interpretation of the figure termed
'SM' in Dan. An example of this principle is given in Mowinckel, who although deriving the concept ultimately from Iranian, or Indo-iranian
sources, considers that at a second stage, the stage of Daniel, the Son of
Man is a symbolic figure for Israel's people[4]. However, this is not the same
as saying that a correct identification and interpretation of the background cannot have some bearing upon the use of the term presently
under discussion. On the contrary, it is deemed that in this case, in particular, the background probably has some important dimension to add to
the discussion.

As hinted above the background of the Danielic Son of Man has been
sought in different directions. Each scholar has argued for his own view
and apparently with good reason has rejected alternative interpretations.
The reader, confronted with all the theories of possible backgrounds, is
thus at a loss when trying to decide which interpretation is to claim his
credence, since the one hypothesis seems to be as good as the other. It is
not feasible to undertake here an exhaustive examination of the various
backgrounds that have been proposed. Hence only a brief presentation
and discussion of the most representative ones will be attempted[5].

It is characteristic that Mowinckel, in his eagerness to forestall the rejection of his Iranian background hypothesis, brings in at the end of his
discussion even other possible backgrounds — Chaldean, Hellenistic,
Gnostic, etc. — and concludes that the ideas in question must have reached
the author of Daniel from many quarters and in many ways[6]. The one
thing that Mowinckel has not been able to show, however, is precisely
how these ideas would have reached the author of Dan, and how great

---

4 Mowinckel, *He that Cometh*, 350.
5 Cf. the exhaustive treatments by Borsch, *The Son of Man*; Colpe, *TDNT* VIII, 400—77, and
   Kraeling, *Anthropos and Son of Man*.
6 *He that Cometh*, 431. Similarly, Jeffery, *Daniel (The Interpreter's Bible*, VI, 451) and Russel,
   The Method and Message of Jewish Apocalyptic, 350, who, however, modifies, "It is safe to
   say that the Jewish apocalyptic writers would have no idea that the son of man was, or in origin had been, the Primal Man. Instead they identified him with the Messiah and so altered his
   whole appearance that only by the most careful scrutiny can we detect the influence of the
   Primal Man idea on the Jewish faith itself" (349). On the method of research of such messianic prototypes, see Colpe, *Kairos*, N.F. 11 (1969) 241—63; and 12 (1970) 81—112.

the possibility is for these ideas to have reached him. To postulate a variety of backgrounds as he does, the locus of which ranges from Phoenicia to Iran is, indeed, very diffuse argumentation. Certainly, if one kind of background is to be preferred to others, some very good reasons will have to be given as to why this particular background is to be preferred. In other words, it is not enough to produce a plausible combination of ideas, which through a particular interpretation can be related as antecedents to a biblical concept and then on the strength of such a plausible similarity to claim that one has found the actual background to that concept. Otherwise, the way is opened to many a flabby and whimsical interpretation, a good example of which is the Jewish scholar J. Morgenstern's hypothesizing[7]. More rigorous principles are necessary if loose thinking is to be eliminated.

Undoubtedly, the laying down of valid principles on the basis of which to decide the applicability or even relevance of a certain background is an intricate matter. It may be possible to construct a universal model for determining such matters. Nevertheless, in the absence of such a model at present, some conditions will have to be posited, whose satisfaction or otherwise may be taken as indicative of the relevance or non-relevance of a presumed background. These conditions are deemed necessary and sufficient as safeguards in the question of biblical backgrounds.

1. The first condition to be laid down is that the reconstruction of a presumed background should be made independently of the work whose background we are seeking to establish. Otherwise, we are running the risk of presenting the ideas of our text as the text's own background. This is particularly important in those cases where presumed background ideas are extremely fragmentary in the sources and where eager advocates of such 'backgrounds' fill in the details from the work which they wish to illuminate. This has happened notably with the so-called gnostic background of the NT, where Gnosticism takes its flesh and bones from the NT, and is then presented as the origin of NT ideas. Furthermore, the actual ideas and terminology in the background material must be used in the reconstruction and not simply biblical 'equivalents', which tend to brush aside real differences and often 'bridge' unbridgable gaps[8].

2. The second condition concerns the possibility of contact between the author of our text and the presumed background. This condition is multiple, entailing the components of geographical, temporal and possible acquaintance probability. This is obviously a difficult matter, since data on these three elements are often so hard to come by. Nevertheless, the principle must be adhered to rigorously if we are to be rid of a lot of nonsense offered as scientific findings.

---

7 Cf. Morgenstern, *JBL* 80 (1961) 65—77, who, to mention one point, suggests that Christians owe their doctrine of the Trinity to Antiochus Epiphanes!

8 Cf. Sarna, *Understanding Genesis*, XXVII, "To ignore subtle differences is to present an unbalanced and untrue perspective and to pervert the scientific method".

3. The third condition is that of congeniality in ideological standpoint between the presumed background and the author of our text. Again, this is a difficult question, since it can be supposed that an author may borrow a concept from a work whose general outlook he does not share. However, the value of the principle is that of several possible backgrounds, that background which ideologically and conceptually stands closest to the author of our text has the greatest claim to credence[9].

4. The fourth condition concerns other common denominators between the background material and the data supplied by our author outside of the particular concept under investigation.

When tests like these are applied upon such representative extra-biblical backgrounds as the following, Iranian or Indo-iranian, Babylonian, Ugaritic, Canaanite, these presumed backgrounds lose any persuasiveness that they may have been thought to possess at first sight[10]. Mowinckel tries to surmount the second test by positing a wide and diffuse geographical and ideological frame, but his reconstruction fails at least on the second, third and fourth grounds[11]. Nor is H.L. Jansen's interpretation of the SM

---

9 Cf. C. Westermann, *TLZ* 90 (1965) 490: "Ein dem Verstehen biblischer Texte dienender Vergleich muss von phänomenologisch fassbaren Ganzheiten herkommen auf sie zielen".

10 On the Ugaritic parallels in particular, see the sensible study by Ferch, *JBL* 99 (1980) 75–86, and *id.*, *The Apocalyptic 'Son of Man' in Dan 7*, 1979.

11 Mowinckel's thesis is that the concept of the Son of Man is not original to the Book of Daniel. Other sources of independent value are the Similitudes of I Enoch, IV Ezra and II Baruch. In all of these writings the Son of Man is an eschatological figure. With particular reference to I Enoch, the Son of Man is presented in Judaism as having divine rights, constituting God's greatest secret, and even having the right to raise the dead and to hold judgment. He is even associated with a kingdom although Jesus was the first one to connect the Son of Man with suffering. However, in certain Jewish quarters he came to be regarded as Messiah and is occasionally considered as divine Son of God (p. 369). Mowinckel accepts two stages of development for the concept. In Dan the figure of the Son of Man is a pictorial symbol of Israel (p. 350). However, this idea has no connection with the OT as e.g. Procksch thinks, "Der Menschensohn als Gottessohn" in *Christentum und Wissenschaft*, III, 1927, 425ff., who would derive it from Ez. Rather, the concept goes back to an earlier stage, to the idea of a primordial Man, the god-Anthropos, derived from Iranian myths (p. 422). He distinguishes between the Primordial Man, or the macrocosm and the First Man, or the microcosm. The Hellenistic "god-Anthropos" is of syncretistic Iranian and "Chaldean" origin (p. 426). Here motifs from all these quarters, Mandean, Hellenistic, Chaldean, Gnostic are blended together and "thus it is established that Judaism was familiar with many varying conceptions of the Primordial Man and the god-Anthropos" (p. 426). Therefore, since the Son of Man concept cannot be explained from the data of the OT, and since he must be understood as different from the Messiah, he must inevitably be interpreted with the help of all these backgrounds, or more correctly, kinds of background. But Mowinckel involves himself here in a circular argument, which is based upon a certain pre-understanding of the OT texts. At the end he makes a concession which is tantamount to admission that he has proved nothing in particular: "We certainly cannot point to any single one of the many variants of the anthropos myth as the only source and the direct source of the idea of the Son of Man. Everything suggests that the Jews acquired their knowledge of these myths and conceptions from many quarters, in many varying forms, and at different periods" (p. 431). Such a diffuse formulation not only shows desperation but also illustrates the habit of some scholars to reconstruct 'backgrounds' whose strength and appeal is their vague and intangible character.

in terms of Ea-Oannes, the Chaldean god of wisdom, more persuasive[12]. The theory of Emerton, that the imagery of Dan 7 presupposes certain Jebusite beliefs about enthronement, or the replacement of one deity by another, is interesting in some details, but is, as a whole, unsatisfactory[13] and quite uncongenial to the Book of Danial[14]. As Weimar puts it: "Der

---

12 *Die Henochgestalt*, etc. Jansen is concerned primarily with the Son of Man as found in I Enoch. Nevertheless, he too has a short section on Dan, where he declines identifying the 'SM' with the Jewish people, preferring to see in him a figure related to the Enochic Son of Man, whose background is Babylonian (e.g. 92ff.). See also P. Jensen, "Adapa" in *RLA* I, (1932) 33–5 and F.M.T. Böhl, "Die Mythen von weisen Adapa", *Welt des Orients*, 2, (1959) 416–31. F. Hommel, "The Apocalyptic Origin of the Expression 'Son of Man'," *ET*, 11 (1899–1900) 341–45, suggests the Babylonian hero Adapa and refers to A. Jeremias's article "Oannes-Ea" in *Roscher's ALGRM* III, p. 586, who calls attention to *Zir-amilûti* as an analogy to 'Son of Man' (345). But see Colpe's criticism, in *TDNT*, VIII, 409. Cf. also Shea, *AUSS* 15 (1977) 27–41.

13 According to Muilenburg, *JBL* 79 (1960) 207, the theory depends "upon assumptions ... quite precarious".

14 J.A. Emerton, *JTS* 9 (1958) 225–42, after criticizing T.F. Glasson's theory that Dan 7:13 is an adaptation of I En 14 (in *The Second Advent*, 2nd ed. 1947), uses as stepping stones A. Bentzen's hypothesis (*Daniel*, 1952, and *King and Messiah*, 1955), that the vision of the Ancient of Days and of the Son of Man goes back to an enthronement festival in ancient Israel, which, in line with Mowinckel's interpretation (*Psalmenstudien* II, 1922), shall have occurred in the autumn. It was via such a festival that the Canaanite mythological imagery reached Daniel. Emerton senses difficulties with the equation or correspondence of the SM with the Davidic king, thus enthroned. He therefore avails himself at this point of Prosksch's equation (*ZAW*, Beihefte 34, pp. 141ff.) of "one like unto a Son of Man" with Ez 1:26 "a likeness as the appearance of a man", as well as Feuillet's observation that the description of the Son of Man coming with the clouds is suggestive of a theophany, and puts forward the idea that the Son of Man is the apocalyptist's adaptation of the Ugaritic Baal, who is also said to fly with the clouds. Emerton is thus led to the conclusion that the Son of Man in the scene of Dan 7, whatever its precise use by Daniel, is a divine being. However, the passage introduces another divine being, the Ancient of Days! "How is the presence of two divine figures to be explained?" he asks. His solution is via the other three passages he discusses, I En 37–71; II Esdr 13 and Sib Or 5, 414–33, in which he thinks that the functions of the Son of Man overlap with the functions of the deity. This underlines the divine character of the SM but involves the problem of two divine beings. Emerton rejects N. Schmidt's interpretation (*JBL* 19 (1900)), who seems to think that Yahweh is dually conceived as Yahweh proper pictured as Ancient of Days, and Yahweh the dragon-slayer represented here by the SM. Emerton thinks instead, that the description of the Ancient of Days fits the Ugaritic El while that of the SM Baal, who in the Ugaritic pantheon is inferior to El. Then by an extremely dubious manner of hypothesizing, whereof no palpable evidence is forthcoming, Emerton suggests that Israel's Yahweh, originally inferior to El or El Elyon, was in the time of Dan identified with him. Emerton concludes his highly conjectural study by saying that "the main thesis of this paper is independent of the particular conjectures offered in the latter part. There are good grounds for believing that the enthronement of the Son of Man by an aged deity goes back to Canaanite myth and ritual, and that behind the figure of the Son of Man lies Yahweh, and ultimately Baal." The problem with Emerton's study is that his conjectures are not limited to its latter part. It is characteristic that a passage of twelve lines in the earlier part of his study contains no less than seven "probablies" and "likelies"! For a different criticism see Casey, *Son of Man*, 37. Glasson returned to the discussion in an article entitled "The Son of Man Imagery: Enoch XIV and Dan VII" *NTS* 23 (1976) 82–90. His chief argument against Emerton's antedating of Dan to I En 6–36, is that the similarities can neither be coincidental or derived

Menschensohn-Psalm (sc. Dan 7:13f.) steht so deutlich innerhalb einer israelitischen Traditionslinie"[15]. Besides, Emerton has not even attempted to reconstruct his background by drawing from extra-biblical sources. Disagreement is even more pronounced with respect to Morgenstern's vagaries[16].

To try to refute in detail theories of the kind referred to above and

---

from the OT; the one must have drawn upon the other. So Dan is on the borrowing side. This conclusion of Glasson's does not follow.

In discussions of interdependence, the more embellished account is usually said to be dependent upon the terser and less evolved one. Now a comparison between Dan and I En shows abundantly that Enoch has the embellishments and hence Enoch must be the borrower (so too H.H. Rowley, *Relevance of Apocalyptic*, 1944, etc., who calls I En "an inferior imitator of Daniel", and D.S. Russell, *The Method and Message of Jewish Apocalyptic*, 1964). For his thesis of the priority of Enoch Glasson leans heavily, if not primarily, upon an argument of dubious value. Since Daniel is to be dated after the commencement of the Jewish revolt but before the death of Judas Maccabaeus in 161 B.C., Enoch, which has borrowings from Greek sources in its descriptions of the underworld, etc., cannot have been written after Daniel, when the national Jewish fervour would hardly tolerate such borrowings from the culture of the hated regime. Glasson's chief problem is that he dates Daniel during the Maccabaean revolt. If the Book is dated earlier, this 'difficulty' is surmounted. Glasson concludes his study by referring to J.T. Milik's work (see "Problèmes de la littérature Hénochique à la lumière de fragments araméens de Qumrân", *HTR* 64 (1971) 333—78, and *The Books of Enoch*: Aramaic Fragments of Qumrân Cave 4, 1976), who supports a date for the Enochic fragments found in Qumrân in the 3rd century B.C. This, of course, does not necessarily make Enoch older than Daniel; it could just as well make Daniel still older.

15 In *Jesus und der Menschensohn*, 32.

16 In *VT* 10 (1960) 138—97, he develops the thesis that the background of Dan 7 is Tyrian religion as transformed by Hiram into a solar religion and updated by Antiochus Epiphanes. He bases his reconstruction chiefly on Josephus' account of Herodes' acclamation by the populace of Caesarea — presumably the event narrated in Acts 12:19—23 — and his sudden death, interpreted both in Acts and by Josephus as God's judgment. The festival involved the death of the older god, Baal-Haddad, and the birth of a younger deity, Tammuz-Adon, both of whom in time were transformed into Baal-Shamem or the Zeus Olympios of Josephus, and Melqart or the Heracles of Josephus. These were actually not two distinct deities, but essentially one deity which died as old Baal and rose as youthful Tammuz. Morgenstern thus identifies the Ancient of Days with Baal Shamem and the Son of Man with Melqart: "Plainly the entire scene in Dan vii, 9—14 has as its background the Tyrian festival ceremony of the coming of Melcarth and his replacement of Baal Shamem as lord of the world" (187). In a more recent study entitled "The 'Son of Man' of Dan 7:13f.: A New Interpretation," *JBL* 80 (1961) 65—77, Morgenstern reiterates his older thesis on the character of Tyrian religion and assumes that Solomon had introduced it into Israel. The scene of Dan 7:9—14 is to be understood against this background. The Ancient of Days, tired and weary of his administration, is ready to give up the government of the world to the younger deity, presented as the Son of Man. The difficulty that in Dan 7 the Ancient of Days and the Son of Man are contemporaneously on the scene, whereas in Tyrian religion the birth of Tammuz on the vernal equinox followed the death of Baal on the autumn equinox, is explained with reference to Antiochus Epiphanes, who is thought to have united the two feasts into one, when he acted himself the role of Melqart in 172 B.C., at which time he adopted the epithet 'Epiphanes' (*VT* 10 (1960) 164; *JBL* 80 (1961) 74). Morgenstern concludes that the schema of the two fused deities also applies to the way Jesus' relation to the Father is conceived, implying that Christians owe their concept of the Godhead as Trinity to Antiochus Epiphanes. Morgenstern is criticized by Colpe, *TDNT*, VIII, 416.

delineated briefly in the footnotes, is to attach to them far more significance than they actually possess[17]. It may suffice to observe that these hypotheses do not fulfill the conditions laid down above, and hence make
no serious claim to be the background of Dan 7:13[18].

There is, however, one ray of light in these interpretations, which is so
signally absent from those studies which merely deal with the identification of the 'SM' of Dan 7 with a biblical entity — be it Moses, Daniel, or
the people of Israel. This is the recognition that the 'SM' is of supernatural
character. Morgenstern is quite explicit on that point[19]. The others,
though supposing that the figure of the 'SM' in Dan is a symbol of Israel,
betray an uneasiness with this solution, which is symptomatic of their
search for a background presupposing either a Primal Man or a deity that
supplants another, older, one[20]. This dissatisfaction with the current symbolic interpretations, this search for a more exalted ancestry for the SM
concept, is the one positive contribution of the History of Religions approach. For the rest these interpretations are signally unconvincing.

C. Biblical Identifications

Most scholars have seen little, if any, value in religio-historical excur-

---

17 Colpe, *TDNT*, VIII, first criticises (esp. 408—15) hypotheses like the ones mentioned above,
    and then goes on (415—9) to present a particular form of the Canaanite hypothesis. Para-
    doxically enough he shows in some detail the untenableness of his hypothesis, but at the end
    having no other hypothesis to fall back to, he espouses it half-heartedly as the one coming
    "closest to the actual facts". The hypothesis involves the transfer of power from an older god
    to a younger one going back to Baal's wresting of power from El (419). The fact that Dan
    7:13f. betrays no such rivalry between the Ancient One and the 'SM' is tacitly bypassed.
    Colpe has actually demonstrated that all extra-biblical reconstructions of backgrounds, in-
    cluding his own, for the concept of Son of Man are extremely precarious. Cf. Maddox, *ABR*
    19 (1971) 40; Marshall, *EvQ* 42 (1970) 81. Besides, even those scholars who assume a *reli-
    gionsgeschichtlich* background, do not make the claim that Dan borrows directly or consciously
    from such backgrounds, which is tantamount to saying that the One like a Son of Man in Dan
    is not inspired by or conceived in those terms. All they are interested to show is patterns of
    thought common to the Ancient Near East. But when the matter is put like that, it becomes
    obvious that relevance to Daniel is lost. For other negative verdicts see Glasson, *The Second
    Advent*, ch. 3 and *NTS* 23 (1976) 83; E. Jacob, *Theology of the Old Testament*, 1958, 341,
    and Delcor, *VT*, 18 (1968) 290ff. Lindars, *NTS* 22 (1975) 60 says: "Theories which pre-
    suppose influence of Iranian ideas of the Primal Man on the New Testament and its Jewish
    background are scarcely tenable".
18 See criticism of Iranian and Gnostic 'Son of Man' (esp. directed against Schmithals, *Gnosticism
    in Corinth*) in Brandenburger, *Adam und Christus*, 131—5, and Schmithals' reply in third
    edition (in English) 74 n.
19 Cf. e.g. *JBL* 80 (1961) 72f.
20 Cf. Colpe, *TDNT*, VIII, 406 "Such traits could be transferred to an eschatological Son of Man
    only if he were a heavenly being ... being a representation of God's renewed dominion, might

sions in order to interpret the 'Son of Man' of Dan 7:13f[21]. Instead they have concentrated their efforts on the data of the Book itself. Nevertheless, the identifications proposed have been of quite diverse character: Judas Maccabaeus[22], Moses[23], Daniel[24], the people of Israel[25], the eschatological people of Israel[26], the saints of the kingdom[27], angels[28], Mic-

---

well have been a god before being demoted to angelic status in consequence of Jewish monotheism".

21 Engnell, *Critical Essays*, 241, for example, is of the opinion that "the origin of the idea of the Son of Man came from within Israel and was ancient".

22 H. Sahlin, *ST* (1969) 41–68 and G.W. Buchanan, *To the Hebrews* (Anch B), 1972, 42–8. This interpretation is ruled out by e.g. the following reasons: a) If Judas Maccabaeus occupied such a central place in the Book as the One like a Son of Man does in ch. 7, it is inexplicable that the Book should contain no explicit reference to him or to his movement. The only possible reference to Judas Maccabaeus in 11:34 (so understood by e.g. Montgomery, *Daniel*, p. 458; DiLella, *Daniel*, 300; G. Maier, *Daniel*, p. 399) is disparaging rather than adulatory (cf. G. von Rad, *The Message of the Prophets*, p. 281); b) to interpret the 'SM' of Judas Maccabaeus is to misunderstand the intention of the author and the nature of the Book; c) Neither the expression as such linguistically regarded nor the details pertaining to this figure lend themselves to such an interpretation.

23 M. Gaster, *The Search I*, 1931, 13–30 considers that the concept of the messiah – purely national – was first formed in Hellenistic times when the Jewish people underwent persecution. By translating Dt 33:2–4 in a novel way and transposing various verses in Dan 7 (i.e. 1–8, 13, 9–10, 14, 11, 12, 18, 16, 17 (p. 22)) he hopes that he proves that the One like a Son of Man is Moses *redivivus*, who comes to plead with God (for criticism see Casey, *Son of Man*, 33f.).

24 H. Schmid, *Jud* 27 (1971) 192–220. This interpretation is based on a misunderstanding of the similar address to Daniel in 8:17 (בן אדם but not כבר אבש!)

25 E.g. Driver, *Daniel*, 88; Montgomery, *Daniel*, 323; Heaton, *Daniel*, 184f.; Manson, *BJRL* 32 (1950) 175; Porteous, *Daniel*, 110f.; Hartman, *Daniel*, 218f.; DiLella, *CBQ* 39 (1977) 14; Russell, *Method and Message*, 325ff.; Poythress, *VT* 26 (1976) 213; Casey, *NovT* 18 (1976) 167 and *Son of Man*, 29; Hooker, *The Son of Man in Mark*, 25ff.; Zevit, *ZAW* 80 (1968) 385–96 Delcor, *VT* 18 (1968) 290–312.

The exact wording may differ. Thus Schubert in *Bibel und zeitgemässer Glaube*, 1965, I, 263ff. calls them "men of insight"; Dexinger, *Das Buch Daniel*, 54 "hasidim"; Brekelmans, *OTS* 14 (1965) 316ff. and Hanhart, "Die Heiligen des Höchsten" in *Hebräische Wortforschung* (VT Sup 16), 1967, 90ff. "pious or Frommen"; Delcor, *Daniel*, 38, "The persecuted of Israel" and Caquot, *Sem*. 17 (1967) 37ff. "elect people".

26 Weimar, in *Jesus und der Menschensohn*, 28f. Weimar understands both the "Menschensohn" and "die Heiligen des Höchstens", which in the Aramaic Book of Daniel (which he would date during Antiochus III's time i.e. 223–187 B.C. (34f.) referred to heavenly beings, with the Menschensohn being Gabriel, to refer in the Maccabaean reinterpretation, to the eschatological people of Israel, (35f.).

27 Beasley-Murray, *CBQ* 45 (1983) 58. Actually Beasley-Murray thinks that the SM represents also God in the exercise of the Kingdom and that the messianic interpretation is also probable for this figure.

28 O. Procksch, in *Christentum und Wissenschaft*, 3 (1927) 429, who was followed by Sellin, *Israelitische-jüdische Religionsgeschichte*, 1939, 129f. and *Theologie des Alten Testaments*, 1963, 85. Cf. also Gunkel, *Schöpfung und Chaos*, 328. Further M. Noth, in *Gesammelte Studien*, 274–90 (cf. Baumgartner, *TRu* 11 (1939) 201–28); Coppens, *ETL* 37 (1961) 5–19; *ETL* 39 (1963) 94–100; 485–500; *VT* 19 (1969) 171–82; Coppens-Dequeker, *Les Fils de l'homme et les Saints du Très-Haut en Dan VII, dans les Apocryphes et dans le Nouveau Testament*, 1961; and Dequeker, *ETL* 36 (1960) 353–92; and *OTS* 18 (1973) 108–87;

hael[29], Gabriel[30], an angel prince[31], the Kingdom of God[32], the divine glory[33], and the Messiah[34], etc. have been suggested as possible interpretations of the One like a Son of Man[35]. However, only three of these interpretations have competed for supremacy: the Israelite, the angelic and the messianic interpretations[36]. The rest are more or less curiosity cases.

Kruse, *VD* 37 (1959) 147–61; 193–211; Horst, *Hiob*, 1960, 79; Hahn, *Christologische Hoheitstitel*, 4th ed. 1974; Lindars, *NTS* 22 (1975) 55f.. Collins, *JBL* 93 (1974) 50–66, esp. 66; and Kearns, *Vorfragen zur Christologie*, II, 151ff.

29 Schmidt, *JBL* 19 (1900) 22–8, who was followed by several scholars (see Rowley, *Darius the Mede*, 63; U.B. Müller, *Messias und Menschensohn*, 19–60; Porter, *The Message of the Apocalyptic writers*, 131–4; Collins, *The Apocalyptic Vision of the Book of Daniel*, 144; Wedderburn, *Adam and Christ: An Investigation into the Background of I Corinthians XV and Romans V: 12–21* (Unpublished Cambridge diss. 1970. Typewritten copy at Tyndale Library, Cambridge), 100, thinks of 'SM' as performing a function similar to that of Michael, though he is "nearer to humanity than to divinity".

30 Zevit, *ZAW* 80 (1968) 395f.

31 Kruse, *VD* 37 (1959) 193–211 understands the One like a Son of Man as an angelic prince like the ones spoken of as being over Persia and Greece, but of higher status than those. Cf. also Barr, *Daniel* in *Peake's Commentary on the Bible*, 597f. K. Müller too identifies the 'SM' with "ein bestimmter Engel ... den der Hochbetagte dazu bevollmächtigt, authentischer Verkündiger und Vermittler seiner eschatologischen Strafgerichtsbarkeit zu sein" (in *Jesus und der Menschensohn*, 50; Colpe, *Kairos* N.F. 11 (1969) 244, with "ein himlisches Wesen".

32 Rowley, *Darius the Mede*, 62, n.2; Baumgartner, *TRu* 11 (1939) 214ff.; M. Müller, *Messias og Menneskesøn*, ch. 3; Plöger, *Daniel*, 112; Dequeker, *OTS* 18 (1973) 182ff., Delcor, *VT* 18 (1968) 290–312 fluctuates between the view that it is a picture for the Kingdom of God and the people of Israel and its King.

33 Feuillet, *RB* 60 (1953) 170–202; 321–46. For criticism see Coppens, in *Wisdom in Israel and the Ancient Near East*, 33–41. Feuillet is followed by B. Willaert, *ColBG*, 5 (1959) 515–36.

34 This is the oldest interpretation being held by Hellenistic Judaism (e.g. I En 37–71; IV Ez 13, Sib. Or 3), rabbinism (for references see Edersheim, *The Life and Times of Jesus the Messiah*, II, 733f. Str-B, I, 956–9; Bowman, *ET*, 59 (1947–8) 285) and the Christian Church (e.g. the Gospels; Rev; Justin Martyr, *Trypho*, 31f.; Hippolytus, *Danielem*, 11f.). Further, Hävernick, *Daniel*; Pusey, *Daniel*, 83–7; Behrmann, *Daniel*; Ewald, *Daniel*, 252, Rosenmüller, *Danielem*, 231; Kranichfeld, *Daniel*, 277–9; Hilgenfeld, *Jüdische Apokalyptik*, 45f.; Keil, *Daniel*, 234ff.; 269ff.; Riem, *Messianic Prophecy*, 193ff.; Bleek, *Jahrbuch für deutsch. Theol.* 5 (1860) 58 n.; Schultz, *Old Testament Theology*, II, 439; Oesterly, *The Jews and Judaism during the Greek Period*, 152ff.; Welch, *Visions of the End*, 129; Aalders, *Daniel*, 133f.; Eichrodt, *Theologie*, I 331 n. 96; Young, *Daniel*, 155f.; id., *The Son of Man*; Leupold, *Daniel*, 308ff.; Maier, *Daniel*, 279ff.; Guilding, *EvQ* 23 (1951) 210–2; Dhanis, *Greg*, 64 (1964) 5–59; France, *Jesus and the Old Testament*, 135f.; Marshall, *EvQ* 42 (1970) 81. Cf. further the remarks of Dexinger, *Das Buch Daniel*, 55–67; Goettsberger, *Daniel*, 56; Bowman, *ET* 59 (1947–8) 283–8; Cruvellier, *Etudes evangeliques*, 1955, 31–50; R. Longenecker, *JETS* 12 (1969) 158.

35 Grotius apparently understood the Son of Man and the fifth Kingdom of the Roman Imperium. Cf. e.g. *ad. Danielem*, p. 468: *"Quasi filius hominis veniebat. Populus Romanus nullum habens intra se Regum, ut dicitur* I Maccab. VIII. 14 ... *"* On 7:27 he writes: *"Regnum autem et potestas, et magnitudo regni, quae est subter omne coelum, detur populo sanctorum Altissimi. Imperium Romanorum latissime patens ... tandem perveniat ad Christianos Iudaïsmi perfectores."*

36 Rhodes, *Int* 15 (1961) 411–30, recognises as the principle interpretations, the Messianic,

In the past two to three decades scholarly interest has concentrated mainly on the Israelite and angelic interpretations. Up to that time the Israelite interpretation had been dominant in critical scholarship. But in the year 1955 M. Noth, following O. Procksch's lead, put forward the hypothesis that קדישי in Dan 7 referred to angelic rather than to human beings. This thesis found a number of adherents, among which Coppens[37] and Dequeker[38] have been quite active in augmenting and reinforcing it. As was natural, the advocates of the Israelite interpretation considered their interpretation threatened and reacted energetically. This resulted in the production of more studies from both sides.

In the line of argumentation that has been put forward by the Israelite and angelic interpretations, the identification of the One like a Son of Man in Dan 7:13, as a matter of fact, involves two stages of interpretation. At a first stage the One like a Son of Man is identified with the 'holy ones', and at a second stage the 'holy ones' are identified with the people of Israel or with angels. But notwithstanding this and apart from a few exceptions, which limit their pronouncements to the second one of these questions[39], the studies written in this debate, whether addressed explicitly to the question of the identity of the 'SM'[40] or to that of the holy ones[41], treat primarily, if not wholly, the problem at the second stage — the identity of the holy ones — though at the end they pronounce on the identity of the 'SM'[42]. The reason for this apparent incongruity, is that almost all authors of both interpretations take the identity of the 'SM' with the 'holy ones' for granted. Therefore, for them the real issue is the identification of the 'holy ones' either with the Jews or with angels. This is partly the reason why these studies have rather little to contribute by

---

the collective (i.e. the Israelite), the combined (Welch's view), and the mythological (e.g. Mowinckel, Emerton, Morgenstern). The angelic interpretation had not yet made itself sufficiently felt.

37 *ETL* 39 (1961) 5–19; *ibid.*, 100–4; *ETL* 39 (1963) 94–100; 485–500; *ETL* 44 (1968) 497–502; *VT* 19 (1969) 171–82; Coppens-Dequeker, *Les Fils de l'homme et les Saints du Très-Haut en Dan VII, dans les Apocryphes et dans le Nouveau Testament*, 1961. Albright, *From Stone Age to Christianity*, 378f.; W. Manson, *Jesus the Messiah*, 98–101, 173f.; Davies, *Paul and Rabbinic Judaism*, 279; Gese, *Zur biblische Theologie: alttestamentliche Vorträge*, 140–45.

38 *ETL* 36 (1960) 353–92; *OTS* 18 (1973) 108–87.

39 E.g. Hasel, *Bib.*, 56 (1977) 173–92 and Poythress, *VT* 26 (1976) 208–13.

40 E.g. Casey, *NovT* 18 (1976) 167–80; and the many studies by Coppens, as e.g. *ETL* 37 (1961) 5–51; *VT* 19 (1969) 171–82; *ETL* 40 (1964) 78–80; DiLella in Hartman DiLella, *Daniel*, 85 –102 being the paper published under a different title in *CBQ* 39 (1977) 1–19.

41 E.g. Noth, in *Gesammelte Studien*, 274–90; Dequeker, *ETL* 36 (1960) 353–92; Coppens, *ETL* 39 (1963) 94–100; Brekelmans, *OTS* 14 (1965) 305–29; Hanhart, in *Hebräische Wortforschung*, 90–101; Dequeker, *OTS* 18 (1973) 108–87.

42 A few studies include both elements in their title, as e.g. Coppens-Dequeker, *Le Fils de l'homme et les Saints du Très-Haut en Dan VII, dans les apocryphes et dans le Nouveau Testament*, 1961; Collins, "The Son of Man and the Saints of the Most High in the Book of Daniel", *JBL* 93 (1974) 50–66; DiLella, "The One in Human Likeness and the Holy Ones of the Most High in Dan 7", *CBQ* 39 (1977) 1–19.

way of positive arguments for the identification of the 'SM', but relatively much on the identification of the 'holy ones', especially by way of refuting the alternative interpretation. With the emphasis thus placed upon demolishing the rival interpretation, the impression is gained that in the opinion of at least some of these scholars such demolishing is in and of itself tantamount to having proved the correctness of their own interpretation of the 'SM'![43]

It will serve no purpose to enter the debate at this second stage — the identification of the 'holy ones' — and to reiterate the usual arguments against the angelic interpretation of the 'holy ones'. The studies by Brekelmans[44], Hanhart[45], and Hasel[46] have brought out the OT[47], the apocryphal-pseudepigraphic[48], and the Qumran[49] evidence fairly well and have

---

43 Cf. Montgomery, *Daniel*, 317–24, whose discussion is devoted almost wholly to proving his opponents wrong, and argues for his own identification only in the last short paragraph. Similarly, Rowley, *Darius the Mede*, 62f.; DiLella, *CBQ* 39 (1977) 1–19 and Hasel, *Bib.*, 56 (1975) 173–92.

44 *OTS* 14 (1965) 305–29.

45 In *Hebräische Wortforschung*, 90–101.

46 *Bib* , 56 (1975) 173–92.

47 Hasel, *Bib* 56 (1975) 176 n. 7 cites Job 15:15 wrongly as 15:10, while his reference to Ex 15:11, taken over from Brekelmans (op.cit. 307), uses the substantive קוֹדֶשׁ not קְדוֹשִׁים as in all other places. This passage is accepted on the basis of the LXX reading. Of the twelve instances of קְדוֹשִׁים in the OT, six refer to angelic beings (Dt 33:2; Ps 89:6, 8; Job 5:1; 15:15; Zech 14:5), one (Ps 34:10) refers to humans, and five (Dt 33:3; Ps 16:3; Prov 9:10; 30:3; and Hos 12:1) are disputed. The great likelihood is, however, that Dt 33:3 and Ps 16:3 refer to people, Prov 9:10 and 30:3 to God (cf. *G-K,* § 124 h, but see Brekelmans, *OTS*, 14 (1965) 308), while for Hos 12:1 the likelihood of pointing עִם as עַם supports the view that the reference is to men: "But Judah still roams/walks with God, and the people of the saints (i.e. the holy people) are faithful," The LXX, interestingly, understands עַם as = λαός! This means that eight instances refer to heavenly beings and four instances to human beings.

48 Of 47 passages found by Brekelmans (*OTS*, 14 (1965) 310ff.) in the Apocrypha-Pseudepigrapha, 17 instances refer to angels, 5 are doubtful, and 25 refer to men. Noth and Dequeker had failed to examine satisfactorily this material.

49 In his discussion (*OTS*, 15 (1965) 321–5) Brekelmans ascribed 13 passages to angels (1QM I, 16; X, 11f.; XII, 1, 4, 7; XV, 14; 1Q22 IV, 1; 1Q28b I, 5; 1Q36 I, 3; 1QH III, 21f.; X, 35; 1Q GenAp II, 1; 1QS XI, 7f.), 7 passages to men (1QM III, 4f.; VI, 6; X, 10; XVI, 1; 1Q 28b III, 25f.; IV, 23; 4QS1 I, 1 23–25), and 6 passages he considered uncertain (1QH IV, 24f.; XI, 11f.; 1QM XII, 8f.; XVIII, 2; CD XX, 8 and 4QFlor I, 4). In his ensuing discussion he presented some arguments for the possibility that some of the uncertain instances should refer to men, but Hasel, (*Bib*, 56 (1975) 183) reads too much in Brekelmans' words when he claims that Brekelmans assigns 13 passages to angels, 11 to men and 2 as doubtful. Brekelmans' figures have been somewhat modified by more recent studies. Thus, H.W. Kuhn, *Enderwartung und gegewärtiges Heil*, 93, considers 1QH XI, 11f. as applied to men rather than to angels, and Mertens, *Das Buch Daniel*, 54f., argues for CD XX, 8 to be included with those instances that refer to humans, while Hanhart, *Hebräische Wortforschung*, 95f. is of the opinion that 1QS XI, 7f. and 1QH III, 21f. (ascribed by Brekelmans to angels) ought to be considered as doubtful. If these observations are correct, the statistical situation is as follows : 11 instances for angels, 9 instances for men and 6 instances uncertain.

Against this Dequeker has reacted energetically (cf. his study in *OTS*, 18 (1973) 108–87), but his refusal (apparently) to allow any Qumran instances of קְדוֹשִׁים to refer to human

shown that קדישי is used of heavenly as well as of earthly beings[50], with a general preponderance for reference to humans[51]. Noth's problematic argumentation that יבלא (Dan 7:25) ought to be understood by way of the Arabic *balā* as "kränken"[52] has been answered well by Hasel, who has shown that Noth has not been sufficiently careful[53]. The plea that עם in Dan 7:27 should be referred to angels on the strength of 1QH III, 21 f., where עם has been wrongly pointed as עַם,[54] has also been shown to be unfounded[55]. The word עַם is never used of angels in the OT nor is there such an instance clearly attested in Qumran. However, the most serious objections to the angelic interpretation are: a) that it makes no sense to think of angels as being subjected to the persecutions of Antiochus Epiphanes, b) if by 'holy ones' angels are meant, the Book loses its relevance for the people of God, and c) the angelic interpretation annuls the contrasting parallelism between the people of God and the nations, each of which is placed under a suzerain power[56] — a matter of paramount importance for the understanding of Dan 7.

It is therefore not possible on any counts to interpret the 'holy ones' of angelic beings. The reference is clearly to human beings[57]. However, to reject the angelic interpretation of the 'holy ones' of Dan 7 and to identify them instead with human beings, does not necessarily imply the espousal of the Israelite interpretation at the first stage of the problem, which without positive argument, assumes the identity of the 'SM' with the 'holy

---

beings, points more to fanaticism rather than to candid scholarship. In addition, to extricate himself out of the hopeless position in which he placed himself, he had to devise an incredible hypothesis of Danielic redaction in order to rescue his theory of identification of the 'holy ones'.

Sometimes it seems as if it is not realized that the identification of the 'holy ones' in Dan 7 is to be made on the basis of a careful analysis of the context, and not by whether 'holy ones' in the sense of human beings occurs a sufficient number of times outside Daniel! For the purpose of establishing a precedent, or even the possibility for the expression to be taken in a certain way, it is enough to produce one single certain example. That there is at least one such example is not in doubt. From here on the meaning of קדישי in Dan 7 will have to be ascertained solely on internal grounds.

50 For one epigraphical instance of 'holy ones' in reference to humans, see N. Avigad, *IEJ*, 7 (1957) 241.

51 See also Hasel's presentation of the Ugaritic data, which evidences the use of the term for human beings (*Bib* 56 (1975) 180ff.

52 Noth, *Gesammelte Studien*, 286.

53 *Bib* 56 (1975) 185f. Collins, *The Apocalyptic Vision*, 142, concedes it tacitly.

54 Noth, *Gesammelte Studien*, 284, based his argument in Bardtke's translation, *Die Handschriftenfunde am Toten Meer*, I, 153. (Cf. *id., TLZ* 80 (1955) 415). Bardtke however, later (*Handschriftenfunde*, II, 1958, 237) changed his translation in line with other translations, e.g. Lohse, *Die Texte aus Qumran*, 40 and 122f., and Vermes, *The Dead Sea Scrolls in English*, 93 and 158.

55 See the criticism of Hasel, *Bib* 56 (1975) 186ff. and Poythress *VT* 26 (1976) 210ff.

56 On this point see my discussion, below, under The Identification of the One like a Son of Man in Daniel.

57 Dumbrell, *RTR* 34 (1975) 21ff.

ones'. These two questions are different matters and must be solved separately each on its own grounds.

The advocates of the Israelite interpretation have exhibited a conspicuous lack of sensivity in interpreting the delicate interplay of symbol
and reality in Dan 7. Often they have failed to grasp the real depth of
Daniel's symbols, the level at which he 'sees' and interprets, with the result that their interpretation becomes very prosaic. In other words, these
interpreters often make matters too easy for themselves[58]. Thus Casey,
for example, makes the imperceptive statement: "What the manlike figure
gets in vs. 14, the people of the saints of the Most High get in vs. 27; they
get nothing which was not granted to him"[59]. This is patently not true.
However, what such a statement reveals is how effortlessly the identification of the 'SM' with the 'holy ones' often is 'established'![60]

The adherents of the angelic interpretation — and this goes for all
varieties — have shown greater sensivity in the matter. It is actually their
insight into the nature of the chapter and the characteristics of the 'SM'
that has caused their dissatisfaction with the Israelite interpretation and
prompted them to espouse an interpretation which, as we saw, is untenable[61]. Yet, in one important respect they were correct: they saw clearly
that the 'SM' cannot be a symbol for Israel. Their failure to produce
convincing results is owing to their unfortunate assumption that the 'SM'
is identical with the 'holy ones' — an assumption that dictated interpreting the 'holy ones' at all events as superhuman beings. The various identifications of the 'SM' with Michael, Gabriel or an angel-prince are really
nothing but makeshifts. These scholars have clutched at whatever clues
the Book seemed to provide in order to pinpoint the entity symbolized by
the 'SM'. Collins, for example, is acutely conscious of this problem[62] —

---

58 So e.g. Casey, *NovT* 18 (1976) 167, 172f. and DiLella, *CBQ* 39 (1977) 3.

59 Casey, *Son of Man*, 24. To the same effect DiLella, *CBQ* 39 (1977) 11. Hasel, more judicious-
ly, is non-commital. He interprets the saints of the Jewish people (*Bib* 56 (1975) 190), but
leaves the 'One like a Son of Man' uninterpreted: "Then they shall receive the Kingdom
(7:18−22), apparently through the Son of Man to whom God has given it (7:14)" (191).

60 In criticism of the Israelite interpretation, Engnell, who espoused the Messianic interpretation
of Dan 7:13, remarks: "Of course, there are those who want to assert that, on the whole, this
passage does not pertain to an individual messianic figure, but is simply a personification of or
a symbol for the people of Israel, and they support this view by v. 27. But it is clear that this
interpretation is incredible or, to put it more exactly, impossible, because the 'Son of Man'
is described in very personal terms in vv. 13f.; it is an ancient, individual messianic term associated with the savior-king or Messiah, as pointed out above; and in Jewish apocalypticism in
the period after Daniel, the 'Son of Man' appears as an individual messianic figure, the savior
and judge of the last time. That the kingdom of the Messiah-Son of Man also signifies the
empire of the messianic people, Israel (as the interpretation given in v. 27 indicates), is wholly
natural. To play this collective aspect off against the individual is to misunderstand completely
the Old Testament way of thinking, in general, and the way of thinking in messianic circles, in
particular" (*Critical Essays*, 239).

61 Hanhart, *Hebräische Wortforschung*, 99, seems to show some appreciation for this dilemma.

62 Similary, R.H. Charles, *Daniel*, 187.

the existence in Dan 7 both of the heavenly or supernatural and of the human elements — and his interpretation whereby the 'SM' is at once Michael, the angelic host and the people of Israel[63], is a desperate attempt to come to terms with this problem. He is thus forced to assume that the 'SM' functions as a multireferential symbol — thus introducing confusing hermeneutical principles — and his method has been criticized not unjustly by DiLella[64]. At the same time it should be said that Collins, notwithstanding his unacceptable formulation, has seen more clearly than DiLella[65] the impossibility of reducing the figure of the 'SM' to a mere symbol for the pious Jews, and his work can be understood as underscoring just that insight.

Despite what has been said above against the angelic interpretation — in its different forms — its advent has made a positive contribution to the debate on the identification of the 'SM'. The very fact of its ever having been propounded is an eloquent commentary on the unsatisfactory character of the Israelite view. The angelic interpretation has underscored dimensions that had been missed by the rival view. The inroads it has made into scholarly circles have underlined the weakness of the Israelite interpretation and questioned its supremacy. Peradventure the time has come for a more radical break with the 'old' tradition.

But before addressing the question of the identity of the 'SM' in Dan 7, it is deemed necessary to examine the OT background briefly for whatever clues it may provide for a right understanding of the problem.

D. The Old Testament Antecedents

The expression son of man and its variants in the OT text is represented by several Hebrew expressions, and these, in turn, are translated in the LXX with analogous expressions in the singular and plural. In order to be better able to survey the distribution of the OT occurrences with their Hebrew and Greek forms, the following table is appended[66].

---

63 *JBL* 93 (1974) 66 "In summary, then, we have argued that the 'one like a son of man' in Daniel 7 symbolizes primarily the angelic host and its leader but also the faithful Jews ... " There is a little shifting in his *The Apocalyptic Vision*, 144, where he expresses the matter thus: "It seems most likely that the figure of the 'one like a son of man' represents the archangel Michael, who receives the Kingdom on behalf of his host of holy ones, but also on behalf of his people Israel".

64 DiLella, *Daniel*, 91f. On the question of the multireferential versus the unireferential in hermeneutical theory see Perrin, *JBL* 93 (1974) 3–14. Cf. also Davies, *JSOT* 17 (1980) 47.

65 Cf. e.g. DiLella's unproblematic assumption that the 'SM' is a symbol for the faithful Jews: "Hence, there seems to be no mystery at all as to the meaning and background of the 'one in human likeness' " (*CBQ* 39 (1977) 3).

66 These figures are based on Lisowski, *Konkordanz zum hebräischen Alten Testament*, 2nd ed.

REF.	בֶן אִישׁ	בֶן אֱנוֹשׁ	בֶן אָדָם בְּנֵי (הָ)אָדָם בֶן (הָ)אָדָם		בַר אֱנָשׁ	
			MT	LXX		
Gn	–	–	1 Pl.d. =	υἱοὶ τ. ἀνθρώπων	–	1
Nu	–	–	1 Sg. =	υἱὸς ἀνθρώπου	–	1
Dt	–	–	1 Pl. =	υἱοὶ Ἀδάμ	–	1
I S	–	–	1 Pl. d. =	υἱοὶ ἀνθρώπων	–	1
II S	–	–	1 Pl. =	υἱοὶ ἀνθρώπων	–	1
I K	–	–	1 Pl. d. =	υἱοὶ ἀνθρώπων	–	1
II Ch	–	–	1 Pl. d. =	υἱοὶ ἀνθρώπων	–	1
Jb	–	–	2 Sg. =	υἱὸς ἀνθρώπου	–	2
Ps	3 Pl. = 1X υἱοὶ ἀν- θρώπων 2X υἱοὶ τ. ἀν- θρώπων	1 Sg. = υἱός ἀν- θρώπου	26 ⌈Sg. 3X = ⌈Sg. 2X ⌊Pl. 1X (Sg. 1X omitted in MT) Pl. 21X = ⌈Pl. 18X Pl. 2X ⌊Pl. 1X ⌊Pl. d. 2X= Pl. 2X	υἱὸς ἀνθρώπου υἱοὶ ἀνθρώπων υἱοὶ τ. ἀνθρώπων υἱοὶ ἀνθρώπων γηγενεῖς υἱοὶ τ. ἀνθρώπων	–	30
Pr	–	–	3 Pl. = ⌈Pl. 2X ⌊Pl. 1X	υἱοὶ ἀνθρώπων ἄνθρωποι	–	3
Ec	–	–	10 Pl. d. = ⌈Pl. 8X Pl. 1X ⌊Pl. 1X	υἱοὶ τ. ἀνθρώπων υἱοὶ ἀνθρώπων υἱοὶ τ. ἀνθρώπου	–	10
Isa	–	–	3 ⌈Sg. 2X = ⌈Sg. 1X ⌊Sg. 1X ⌊Pl. 1X = Pl. 1X	υἱὸς ἀνθρώπου ἄνθρωπος ἄνθρωποι	–	3
Jer	–	–	5 ⌈Sg. 4X = Sg. 4X ⌊Pl. 1X = Pl. 1X	υἱὸς ἀνθρώπου υἱοὶ τ.ἀνθρώπων	–	5
Ez	–	–	94 ⌈Sg. 93X = Sg. 93X ⌊Pl. 1X = Pl. 1X	υἱὸς ἀνθρώπου υἱοὶ ἀνθρώπων	–	94
Dan	–	–	2 ⌈Sg. 1X = Sg. 1X (LXX,Θ) υἱὸς ἀνθρώπου ⌊Pl. 1X = Sg. 1X (LXX) χειρὸς ἀνθρώπου (Θ) υἱὸς ἀνθρώπου		3 Sg. 1X = LXX, Θ: υἱός ἀν- θρώπου Pl. 2X = LXX: 1X ἀνθρώπων Θ: 1X υἱοὶ ἀν- θρώπων LXX: 1X omit Θ: 1X ἀν- θρώπων	5
Jl	–	–	1 Pl. = Pl.	υἱοὶ ἀνθρώπων	–	1
Mi	–	–	1 Pl. = Pl.	υἱοὶ ἀνθρώπων	–	1
Total	3X	1X	154X		3X	161

1958; H. Hatch-H.A. Redpath, *A Concordance to the Septuagint*, 1897. R. Young, *Analytical Concordance to the Holy Bible*, no date (The Psalms section is curiously defective – no doubt owing to some circumstantial error – in this, otherwise, complete concordance, listing only 10 of its 30 occurrences). The references have been verified with the MT edition of N. Snaith, תורה נביאים וכתובים (BFBS), 1962 and the LXX ed. by A. Rahlfs, *Septuaginta*, 9th ed. 1971, as well as the RSV of 1952.

Of the four expressions totaling 161 occurrences, by far the most pre-
valent one is בן אדם, occurring no less than 154 times. Of these the singular occurs 106 times (of which 93 times in Ez) and the plural 48 times.
This expression for son of man occurs in the indeterminate singular form
בן אדם 106 times, in the indeterminate plural form בני אדם 32 times
and in the determinate plural form בני האדם 16 times. The LXX translates all of the MT forms with υἱὸς (τοῦ) ἀνϑρώπου , υἱοὶ τοῦ ἀνϑρώπου,
υἱοὶ (τῶν) ἀνϑρώπων, ἄνϑρωπος, ἄνϑρωποι, once χειρός ἀνϑρώπου,
once γηγενεῖς and once υἱοὺς Ἀδάμ.

Of the OT books containing the expression son of man all have the
form בן אדם or בני (ה)אדם. The Psalms, however, have, in addition,
the Hebr. forms בן איש and בן אנוש, and Daniel the Aramaic בר אנש.
What is the relevance of all this for Daniel? In Daniel the Hebr. expression
occurs twice, once in the singular and once in the plural. The Aram. form
occurs 3 times, once in the singular and twice in the plural. There are thus
two questions to be decided: a) the relation of the Aramaic to the Hebrew
form, and b) the relation of the singular to the plural.

With regards to the first question, it may be remarked that the fact
that the Hebrew and Aramaic forms occur both in the singular and in the
plural in the respective sections of Daniel, must indicate that the two
forms of the expression are equivalent[67]. No other distinction in sense
can be perceived and hence no other explanation is possible or necessary.

The second question is more complicated. Here there are actually two
related questions: a) the distinction between the singular and the plural,
and b) the distinction between the determinate and the indeterminate
forms of the expression.

Since the time of Dalman[68] it has been usual to regard בן אדם etc. as a
poetic expression[69]. In order to account for such instances of son of man
as do not occur in poetic passages, Sjöberg widened the category so as to
include also what he called 'solemn' passages[70]. Furthermore, since even
so not every instance of son of man occurs within the 'poetic or solemn'
passages, Sjöberg separated the occurrences in the singular form from
those in the plural in order to obtain for the singular greater uniformity.
Moreover, he distinguished between the determinate and the indeterminate

---

67 So, too, Dalman, *Die Worte Jesu,* 194ff. The discovery of the Sefire inscription (dated c. 750
   B.C.) after Dalman would not alter this judgment since at least some of the OT occurrences of
   בן אדם (esp. those in the first Book of the Psalms) are generally accepted to be older than
   that, see e.g. O. Eissfeldt, *Introduction,* 449f.; Harrison, *Introduction,* 986; A. Weiser, *Introduction,* 285. The occurrence in Num 23:19 is considered by Sjöberg, *AcOr,* 21 (1950–51)
   57, to be the earliest instance. Harrison, *Introduction,* 620, would date it to the XIIth century
   B.C.
68 Dalman, *Die Worte Jesu,* 194.
69 E.g. Sjöberg, *Der Menschensohn im äthiopischen Henochbuch,* 1946, 40; *AcOr* 21 (1950
   –51) 57.
70 E.g. Sjöberg, *AcOr* 21 (1950–51) 57: "Es wird nur im poetischen und feierlichen Stil
   gebraucht."

forms of the expression, but despite all these accommodations the results he obtained were unsatisfactory, and in the end he was obliged tacitly to admit that his conclusions were not compelling[71], albeit he held fast to his views.

Sjöberg's claims can be summarized into three:

a) The singular בן אדם "wird nur im poetischen und feierlichen Stil gebraucht".

b) "Auch der Plural steht meistens im poetischen oder feierlichen Stil . . ."

c) "Nur die indeterminierte Form belegt ist. Determiniert müsste בן האדם heissen, aber diese Form ist nirgends zu finden".

I will start with the last point. What Sjöberg claims applies only to the singular. The plural form of בן אדם occurs 32 X in the indeterminate form בני אדם [72], and 16 X in the determinate form בני האדם![73] Quite tendentiously Sjöberg tries to minimize the determinate form when he says, "Etwas gewöhnlicher als der Singular ist der Plural בני אדם. Er kommt im AT 47 mal vor — in Qoh. immer determiniert בני האדם, sonst gewöhnlich indeterminiert" and in a note, "ausserhalb Qoh. determiniert nur an 6 Stellen." In order to be fair Sjöberg ought to have also said that the indeterminate form occurs 'ausserhalb Ps nur an 11 Stellen'! And so when the 6 occurrences of the determinate form are set over against the 11 of the indeterminate form one can no longer speak of the plural as occurring *'gewöhnlich'* in the indeterminate form! This is not the case even when the 10 times of Qoh. are compared with the 21 times of the Ps. Sjöberg's conclusion here is, therefore, forced.

The point Sjöberg raises under (a) is concerned with the use of the

---

71 Cf. Sjöberg's ambivalent remarks in *AcOr* 21 (1950—51) 57ff. With regards to the 14 instances in the singular בן אדם he says: "Es wird nur im peotischen und feierlichen Stil gebraucht" (57), then a few lines further down he says: "Alle diese Belege ausser der Dan.-Stelle finden sich in poetischen Abschnitte". And with regards to the 4 X in the plural form he writes: "Auch der Plural steht meistens im poetischen oder feierlichen Stil, aber einige Beispiele zeigen, dass ihre Anwendung nicht auf solche Zusammenhänge begrenzt war" (58). Further down the writes: "Obgleich Qoh nicht poetische Form hat, handelt es sich auch hier um einen feierlichen Stil" (59), and a little below he says again: "I Sam 26:19 zeigt aber, dass der Ausdruck auch in ganz schlichtem Zusammenhang benutzt werden kann und auch Gen 11:5 steht in einer Erzählung ohne besonderen, feierlichen Klang" (59).

Dalman had spoken of 'poetic passages. Sjöberg widened the category in order to include e.g. the 93 instances of Ez in the sing. and the 10 instances of Ec in the plural, but at the end he was obliged to admit exceptions belonging to everyday contexts. Sjöberg cannot eat the cake and have it! In view of the dubiousness of his method and the untenability of his claims, it is best to dispense with the category of "poetisch oder feierlich" as characterizing the use of the expression 'son of man'.

72 Dt 32:8; 2 Sam 7:14; Ps 11:4; 12:1, 8; 14:2; 21:11; 31:20; 36:8; 45:3; 49:3; 53:2; 57:5; 58:2; 62:10; 66:5; 89:48; 90:3; 107:8, 15, 21, 31; 115:16; Prov 8:4, 31; 15:11; Isa 52:14; Jer 32:19; Ez 31:14; Dan 10:16; Joel 1:12; Mich 5:6.

73 Gen 11:5; 1 Sam 26:19; 1 Kin 8:39; 2 Chr 6:30; Ps 33:13; 145:12; Ec 1:13; 2:3, 8; 3:10, 18, 19, 21; 8:11; 9:3, 12.

singular, which is "immer in poetischem oder feierlichem Zusammenhang zu finden" (p. 57). This form, outside the 93 times in Ez, where it functions as an appelation of the prophet, occurs only 13 times in the OT[74]. But the Ez occurrences cannot be added to the 13 instances found in the rest of the OT. The 93 instances of Ez count only as 'one' occurrence, since they represent the repetition of the one and the same usage. There are thus only '14' occurrences of בן אדם in the OT and they occur always in the indeterminate form! All of the 12 times apart from Dan 8:17 and Ez, occur in poetic passages. Sjöberg regards Ez and Dan as 'solemn' passages and so his category is sustained in tact. One may ask, however, what distinguishes a solemn passage from a non-solemn passage? The problem is not defined by Sjöberg. There are several other passages in Dan where Daniel is addressed but the expression is never used[75]. This would tend to weaken Sjöberg's assertion that בן אדם belongs to poetic or solemn style. The most one could say here would seem to be that בן אדם occurs 12 times in poetic and twice in non-poetic passages. Whether any significance is to be attached to this circumstance and any conclusions drawn as to whether the expression belongs to poetry or not is pending upon an examination of the relation of the singular to the plural.

Sjöberg's third assertion is that the plural too occurs mostly in poetic or solemn style. Here Sjöberg is embarrassed by Gen 11:5 and I Sam 26: 19 which show that "der Ausdruck auch in ganz schlichtem Zusammenhang benutzt werden kann" (p. 59). The question is, however, whether these are the only passages that deviate. Dan 10:16 is certainly not poetry, and it is difficult to see why the expression here is due to solemn style. The same would hold true of the 10 instances in Ec. as well as other passages. The expression 'feierlich' is used by Sjöberg as an umbrella to include just about every instance of 'son(s) of (the) man' in the OT, but we are never told what the style would have looked like if it were not 'solemn', and what the equivalence of the expression would have been in that case. Furthermore, one wonders where the specially close connections lie between poetry — with all its freedom in expression — and solemn style — which is usually stiff and stale, and why just this particular expression should be so supremely appropriate for just these two types of literary genre! The difficulties hinted at here are enormous and tell against the distinctions assumed by Sjöberg. Moreover, the fact that the expression occurs as בן אדם, בני אדם, בני האדם, not to mention בן אנוש and בני איש, or the Aram. בר אנש and בני אנשא would indicate that we do not have to do with a stereotypical phrase created *ad hoc* for poetic purposes, etc., but with expressions of equivalent significance adapted to the particular context in the singular or plural form.

---

74 Num 23:19; Jb 25:6; 35:8; Ps 8:4; 80:18; 146:3; Isa 51:12; 56:2; 49:18, 33; 50:40; 51:43; Dan 8:17.
75 E.g. Dan 9:22; 10:11, 12; 12:4, 9.

Support for the view that the expression is poetic is often found in the
circumstance that בן אדם etc., on a number of occasions, occurs in parallelism along with another term for 'man'. This is the case in 21 instances[76].
It is supposed here that son of man is identical in meaning with 'man'
except for the poetic connotations of the longer expression. The use of
son of man as poetic equivalent for 'man' does not, however, explain the
many other occurrences of בן אדם, etc., without any parallel term for
'man', or even the few occurrences where בן אדם is used in parallelism
along with some other term[77].

If then the theory that the expression בן אדם owes its origin to the
need for a poetic and solemn expression for 'man' is found to be untenable[78], what is that which distinguishes it from the usual expression for
'man'?[79] To answer this question, namely the *raison d' être* of the term
son of man, is a very difficult undertaking, firstly, because of the scarcity
of material and secondly because the present state of OT studies in areas
relevant to this question is unsatisfactory. In point of order of occurrence
in the OT son of man is instanced in Gen, Num, Dt, I Sam, II Sam, I Kin,
II Chr, Jb, Ps, etc. But in point of date, there is no consensus in scholarly
opinion. Some of the Psalms are considered to be very early[80], in fact,
sometimes, earlier than the occurrence in Gen 11:5, while the most primitive instance of son of man is considered by some to be Num 23:19[81].

On the other hand, P.J. Wiseman[82] has tried to show that the first 36
chs. of Gen contain a number of tablets analogous to those found in
Mesopotamia, whose contents present a roughly chronological sequence
and whose standpoint is primeval, partriarchal and Mesopotamian. This
lead is developed further by R.K. Harrison[83], who presents an alternative
theory of Pentateuchal origins to the four document theory. Harrison
would, therefore, antedate Gen 11:5 to all other son of man occurrences
in the OT.

---

76 I.e. with איש Num 23:19; 2 Sam 7:14; 1 Kin 8:39 (= 2 Chr 6:30); Ps 31:20; 49:3; 62:10;
   80:18; Prov 8:4, Isa 52:14; Jer 49:18, 33; 50:40; 51:43; Mich 5:6. With אנוש Jb 25:6;
   Ps 8:4; 144:3; Isa 51:12; 56:2. With גבר Ps 89:48.
77 I.e. with נבל ('fool') Ps 14:2; with חסיד ('saints') Ps 145:12; with נדיב ('prince') Ps 146:3,
   and with יהוה ('Lord') 1 Sam 26:19.
78 Furthermore, a principally poetic use of 'son of man' in the OT stands in sharp contrast to the
   use of the equivalent expression in the NT, the Mishnah and other Jewish writings.
79 On אדם occurrences in the OT see Maas, in *TDOT*, I 75−87, esp. 79−87.
80 Oesterly-Robinson, *Introduction to the Books of the Old Testament*, 1934, 190 and O.
   Eissfeldt, *Introduction*, 448−51, consider a number of Psalms to be pre-exilic, some "perhaps
   very old indeed" (Eissfeldt, *Introduction*, 448). Similarly Weiser, *Introduction to the Old
   Testament*, 285.
81 E.g. Sjöberg, *AcOr* 21 (1950−51) 57. Oesterley, *The Jews and Judaism*, 152.
82 First published under the title *New Discoveries in Babylonia about Genesis*, 1936, and *Creation Revealed in Six Days*, 1946, they have been recently republished together by D.J. Wiseman, as *Clues to Creation in Genesis*, 1977, with the title of the first study changed to *Ancient
   Records and the Structure of Genesis*. The relevant pages are 34−74 and 143−68.
83 Harrison, *Introduction*, 548ff.

But however one may look upon the date of that passage, it is clear that Gen 11:5 along with Gen 6:1ff. afford us the most primitive account of the son of man terminology, a kind of explanation — at any rate on the theological level — of the creation, or at least the existence of the expression. Even if one accepts that the Gen texts in their present form are later than Num 23:19 or some of the Psalms occurrences of son of man, one ought none the less to concede that the two Gen passages afford a kind of key to the understanding of the expression. But more on this below.

The expression 'son of . . .' occurs a number of times in the OT. Quite often the term is a specification of a people. The plural word 'sons' stands for the individual members of the group, while another personal, or national, etc. name stands for their progenitor or their national denominator. Here belongs the oft-appearing phrase 'sons of Israel'[84]. The phrase is used also to specify age: thus a "son of thirty-two years"[85] is a man thirty-two years old. Occasionally the expression has attributive significance: thus "sons of exile"[86] means exiles. The attributive significance is even more pronounced in the characteristic phrase "son(s) of Belial"[87], meaning 'base or worthless man/men', as well as in a typically semitic construction "son of wickedness"[88]. Similar to this use is 2 Kin 14:14, where בני תערבות (= "sons of pledges") means 'hostages', but has been mistranslated by the LXX with υἱοὺς τῶν συμμίξεων. In Jud 16:12 υἱοὶ κορασίων designates Israelite soldiers, while 2 Kin 2:3 בני נביאים means 'prophets', or possibly disciples of prophets[89].

The expression son of man is different to all other constructions of 'son of . . .'. In each of the other expressions the individual spoken of as 'son of . . .' is existentially different from that which is denoted by the word in the genitive, whether that is a personal name (e.g. 'sons of Israel') or a characterizing abstract noun (e.g. 'son of wickedness'). Cf. Dan 12:1, בני עמך, "children of thy people". In the case of the expression son of man the term 'man' is coextensive in ontological and semantic significance with 'son'. Both 'son' and 'man' refer to the same ontological phenomenon, to the same entity, and hence 'son of man' is virtually nothing other than 'man', or 'human being'. This is owing to the absence of the definite article from 'man'. In English this result is obtained by the om-

84 E.g. Gen 50:25; Ex 1:1 and *passim*. Similar are Ez 23:9 *bene Asshur*; 23:15 *bene Babel*; 25:4 *bene Kedem*; 27:11 *bene Arwad*; 27:15 *bene Dedan*, etc., all translated by the LXX with υἱοί ... .
85 2 Kin 8:17. See further 15:2; 18:2. See also 1QM VI, 14; VII, 1ff.
86 Ezra 6:16. Also 8:35 and 10:7 (the LXX has υἱοὶ ἀποικεσίας, παροικίας and ἀποικίας respectively, while in 1 Esdr 7:12, 13, it has υἱοὶ τῆς αἰχμαλωσίας).
87 E.g. Dt 13:14; Judg 19:22; 20:13; 1 Sam 2:12; 10:27; 25:17; 1 Kin 21:10, 13; 2 Chr 13:7. 1 Sam 1:16 has "daughter of Belial". The alternative phrase "man of Belial" also occurs, e.g. 1 Sam 25:25; 30:22; 2 Sam 16:7; 20:1; 1 Kin 21:13.
88 Ps 89:23 (LXX 88:23: υἱὸς ἀνομίας). On the construct state see *G-K*, § 128.
89 For the call and conditions of discipleship, see Riesner, *Jesus als Lehrer*, 276ff., esp. 281. See further, Haag's treatment of the scope of the expression with 'son of ... ' *TDOT*, II, 150–3.

ission of the definite article from 'man', i.e. '(the) son of man'. Greek usually expresses category by the use of the definite article, i.e. (ὁ) υἱὸς τοῦ ἀνϑρώπου, where ἀνϑρώπου designates category. In Hebrew the expression is sometimes found without the definite article (אדם בן) and sometimes with it (האדם בן)[90]. In the latter case the article defines the word 'son' rather than 'man', so the categorical character of 'man' is retained. It is this circumstance — the effect of the absence of the definite article — that renders the collocation of these two words, 'son' and 'man', such a strange expression[91].

When we turn to the OT passages containing the term son of man, we find that the utterances fall into three contextual categories: positive, negative and neutral . There are two passages in which son of man occurs in positive light[92] — if in weakness — and two more possibly positive, or more probably, neutral passages[93]. Of the remaining instances outside of Ez and Dan the passages are about evenly divided between the negative and neutral categories.

It is not feasible to discuss fully every occurrence of the expression. The thrust of the evidence will become apparent by taking up a few representative cases. In a number of instances son of man occurs in parallelism with a word for 'man'[94]. This circumstance has led scholars to explain the phrase son of man as a mere poetic variation for 'man'. However, closer scrutiny reveals that in the majority of cases son of man either has intensified or rendered more poignant the statement made about 'man' in the previous line (an 'ascending' parallelism) or what is predicated of or said in relation to the son of man is more derogatory or negative than the statement about 'man' (a climactic predication)[95]. In no case, where 'man' and son of man occur in parallelsim, is the statement about the son of man clearly or with certainty milder or less negative than that about 'man'[96].

In one of the earliest instances, Num 23:19, lies are predicated of 'man' but fickleness of the son of man. Which of the two characteristics is stronger

90 Engnell's statement of "constant absence of the definite article" is clearly an overstatement (see his *Critical Essays*, 237).

91 In the NT the definite article is present in the Greek expression ὁ υἱὸς τοῦ ἀνϑρώπου, but the effect is retained because of the peculiarity of the Greek in using the article to express generic or categorical sense.

92 Ps 80:17 (on which see Hill, *NovT* 15 (1973) 261–9) and Isa 56:2.

93 Ps 45:2; Prov 8:31.

94 Smith, *CBQ* 45 (1983) 59f. cites a Ugaritic text first published in Craibl 1979, 289 and translated by A. Caquot in *Annuaire du Collège de France* 79 (1978–9) 488–90, where 'son of man' in the sense of a 'human being' occurs side by side with 'man'.

95 Interestingly Thorion, *RevQ* 10 (1980) 307, finds the same characteristic use of the terms אדם and אדם בן in Qumran: "Wenn es sich nicht um den sündhaften, nichtigen Menschen, sondern um den Menschen, oder die Menschheit, im neutralen Sinn handelt, so wird *'DM* verwandt".

96 Jb 35:8 is uncertain. In Mich 5:7 'sons of man' is equivalent to 'men'.

may be a matter of opinion. A similar uncertainty exists about Job 25:6: "man, who is a maggot, and the son of man, who is a worm"[97]. In 2 Sam 7:14 "stripes of the sons of men" is an amplification of "rod of men"[98]. Ps 8:4, a passage often figuring in Son of man discussions, and one of the admittedly earliest occurrences of the expression, affords an interesting comparison between 'man' (אנוש) and son of man. The Psalmist, after surveying the infiniteness and grandeur of the universe, is astonished to find that its Creator stoops down to *take thought* of אנוש and to *care* for בן אדם. Incontestably the verb פקד (= visit, care for) is stronger than זכר (= remember, take thought of) and though son of man here is in reality a synonym for 'man', the climactic parallelism whereby Yahweh's acts are contrasted to what 'man' or the son of man are respectively, underlines the 'lower status' of son of man in relation to 'man'[99]. In Ps 31: 19 f. "sons of men" has as apposition "plots of men" and "strife of tongues" — a definitely negative evaluation. It is interesting that Ps 49:2 גם בני-אדם גם בני-איש is rendered by the LXX (48:3) as οἵ τε γηγενεῖς καὶ οἱ υἱοὶ τῶν ἀνθρώπων. Here γηγενεῖς possesses a lower status than υἱοὶ τῶν ἀνθρώπων. The *RSV* translates accordingly, "both low and high"! Similar to this is Ps 62:9, where the *RSV* renders בני אדם with "men of low estate" and בני איש with "men of high estate". Another group of instances definitely sets son of man in a context of negative predication[100]. In I Sam 26:19 David remonstrates with Saul that his persecution by the king is not inspired by Yahweh, but by "the sons of man" (בני האדם), i.e. by base persons who deserve his cursing. Ps 145:10 contrasts "sons of men" with Yahweh's saints and in Ps 14:1 ff. and 53: 1 f. the "sons of men" are epitomized by the fool (נבל)[101]. In Ps 12: 1 f. the "sons of men" are ungodly, liars, and deceitful, and in vs. 8 there is given an appalling description of lawlessness: "on every side the wicked prowl, as vileness is exalted among the sons of men"!

But there are also passages where the content is more neutral, though these too are concerned with weakness, frailty, insignificance, etc. These characteristics which are not directly evil in an active sense, are nevertheless associated with a 'fall', i.e. an alienation from God. The son of man is insignificant (Job 25:6), transient (Ps 89:47; 90:3), weak and frail (Ps

---

97 Brown-Driver-Briggs, *A Hebrew and English Lexicon of the OT, sub* רמה and תולעה regard the first as a sign of decay while the second as a symbol of insignificance.

98 Cf also Ps 90:3.

99 Cf. also L. Köhler, *TZ*, 1 (1945), 77f. Differently Haag, *TDOT*, II, 151, who tries to understand Ps 8:5 by means of Ps 144:3. However, Ps 144:3 is similar only in form. The Hebrew terms for 'man' and 'son of man' are reversed and the verbs are entirely different. On Ps 8 see the recent article by F.J. Moloney, "The Reinterpretation of Psalm VIII and the Son of Man Debate" *NTS* 27 (1981) 656–72.

100 Cf. LXX Ps 30:20f.

101 Similarly Prov 8:4f.

102 Cf. Hengel, *Judaism and Hellenism*, I, 115ff.

103 Even the standing phrase "no man shall dwell there, no son of man shall sojourn in her" in

146:3), evanescent (Isa 51:12), fully searched out and known by God (e.g. I Kin 8:39; 2 Chr 6:30; Ps 33:13).

Finally, in the Wisdom Literature the son(s) of man(men) emerge(s) in a definitely negative light. In Prov 15:11 the "sons of men" will not be able to hide their evil from him before whom Sheol and Abaddon lie open. Ecclesiastes muses on the theme of vanity, transience and wickedness associated with the "sons of men" (e.g. Ec 1:13; 2:3; 3:10). Indeed, pessimism and resignation here reach extraordinary proportions for a biblical author[102] and the "sons of men" are compared to beasts: "God is testing them to show them that they are but beasts . . . as one dies, so dies the other . . . man has no advantage over the beasts" (3:18 ff.). Nay, more, "the heart of the sons of men is fully set to do evil" (8:11), in fact "the hearts of the sons of men are full of evil, and madness is in their hearts while they live, and after that they go to the dead" (9:3); Therefore, "like birds which are caught in a snare, so the sons of men are snared at an evil time" (9:12)[103].

This rapid survey has indicated that the expression 'son(s) of man (men)'bears in the OT a predominantly negative significance. In a number of occurrences it is a question of man's frailty, creatureliness and transience, yet even these so termed neutral characteristics, inasmuch as they are negating qualities, exhibiting a lack of relation or a broken relation to him who is Life, Power, Action, set forth man in his alienation from God. The two or so instances here termed positive significance son of man instances are too negligible a factor[104].

The astounding thing, therefore, is that the above examination has brought to light or at least underscored[105] the fact that the pedigree of the most beloved self-designation of Jesus is, to say the least, humble indeed.

Essentially, the neutral instances are not different from the negative ones. Both categories portray man as a weak, helpless, transient creature, sometimes (the neutral instances) in its helplessness, hopelessness and frailty struggling on with its finite power, but never coming far enough, at other times (the negative instances) as straying from its Creator in a more active sense, indeed, not infrequently its selfish and wayward attitude hardening into active resistance, lawlessness and evil. The various qualities by which the son of man is known epitomize his 'fall', his alienation from God. The intriguing question, therefore, is, How has man come to be a son of man?

Jer 49:18, 33; 50:40; and 51:43, occurs in contexts of judgment.

104 But even these instances do not indicate that 'son of man' possesses any intrinsically positive qualities; they merely show the absence of incriminating circumstances. Ps 80:17 could, for instance, be classed with the neutral instances, since the 'son of man' is said to be strengthened by God, i.e. the statement assumes the weakness of the 'son of man'.

105 It is not impossible, but I do not recall coming upon this in my fairly extensive reading on the 'Son of Man'.

It would seem that the key to understanding this transition of man's status is to be found in the earlier chapters of Genesis. Ch. 11 relates an ambitious scheme which mankind conceived to commemorate its power and technology. The biblical author construes the project as nothing short of a defiance against God, who at the right moment intervenes to thwart men's design: "And the Lord came down to see the city and the tower, which the sons of men had built" (11:5). This is the first use of the expression in biblical literature, though in point of date there is, as mentioned earlier, controversy. The matter of date is of little importance for my purpose, since I am not interested in presenting a strictly historical development of the expression — an impossible task in the present state of research anyway — but in inquiring into certain patterns of thought in OT literature, which account for a strange expression. It is the theological significance of the expression that is of any interest for the NT use of it.

Throughout biblical literature Babylon stands for an evil power which opposes God. In the Book of Revelation it is the symbol of opposition to God. The story in Genesis may remind us of other extra-biblical traditions about men, heroes, or demigods on earth banding together to fight the god of heaven[106]. Such traditions are essentially expressions of a common underlying sentiment in human societies, namely a striving upward, an attempt to liberate themselves from the traditional Supreme Power. It is man's age-long search for emancipation, for upgrading himself, for doing away with every form of superior power that might have a claim on him — aspirations, which to the biblical author are nothing short of a revolt against God. It is in such a context of alienation and rebellion against God that the expression is — shall I say? — born!, at least theologically. 'Son(s) of man (men)' is therefore, unlike 'man', a concept loaded with definite negative connotations. In itself 'man' is a sociological term, and as such it is thoroughly neutral; son of man, on the other hand, is a *theological* term, implying a God-ward relation that is disturbed. Both terms refer, of course, to the same entity, but whereas 'man' is man as created by God, son of man is man in his estrangement from God, he is man subjected to frailty and decay, man in his wayward shortcomings and vices, lastly, man whom finally and absolutely only God can restore.

But though Gen 11:1—9 offers the earliest biblical instance of this term, we are probably taken a step further back by Gen 6:1—7. The expression 'son of . . .' is used here in collocation with 'God', when it is said that "the sons of God saw that the daughters of men were fair." There has been much speculation about who these 'sons of God' were[107].

---

106 Cf. e.g. the Greek myths of the overthrow of Ouranos and Cronos by their sons and subordinates, Hesiod, *Theogony*, 176ff. and 71ff.; Apollodorus, *Bibliotheca*, I, i, 1— ii, 1, and the attempt of Otus and Ephialtes against Zeus, Homer, *Odyssey*, XI, 307—17.

107 Jewish inventiveness considered them often to be fallen angels, e.g. I En 6:1ff.; Philo, *Gig*, 6; Jub, 4:15; 5:1f. Test Rub, 5:6f.; Josephus, *Ant*, I, 73 (I, iii, 1). The LXX MS A rescriptor

If by the expression angels are meant[108], we are given an adequate explanation as to why the unions are considered unnatural, the offspring gigantic[109] and the ensuing judgment receives an adequate motivation. The biological issue is, however, unexplained, but this probably did not trouble Jewish interpreters. If, on the other hand, the author meant simply men it is difficult to account for the expression 'sons of God' in contradistinction to 'daughters of men', as well as for all those other points explained by the alternative hypothesis, though the biological question is duly accounted for. We may perhaps be better off if we concentrate on their status as 'sons of God', instead of looking for their essence. What is interesting from our point of view is that the outcome of the union of the 'sons of God' with the 'daughters of men' is not more sons of God, but a species possessing a new status, a new category! Logically, vs. 4 belongs directly after vs. 2, and vs. 3 should head vv. 5—9. The present form of the text — perhaps purposely — sets forth God's judgment in two stages. First, God shortens human life to 120 years by withdrawing His life-giving spirit. Humanity is characterized as mere "flesh". The second stage, or measure, called for by the proliferation of evil, is judgment by a flood. From this point on until the close of Ch. 10 the narrative is concerned with the flood, Noah and his descendants. As soon as the narrator resumes his description of human affairs, men, busy with the Babel project, are characterized as "sons of men"! Humanity has assumed a new status, a new role. Theologically, man is the product of God's hands; son of man is the product of man. Man was created in God's image and likeness, the son of man is born in the image and likeness of a fallen man (cf. Gen 5:3), i.e. in the son of man man's fall and all that is associated with it have become crystalized.

---

has ἄγγελοι Θεοῦ, which is presupposed in the above texts. Cf. also Bowker, *The Targums and Rabbinic Literature*, corrected ed. 1979, 153f.; Rowley, *Relevance of Apocalyptic*, 57f. and Morgenstern, in *HUCA*, 14 (1939), 29—126. For a full discussion of the evidence on this line of interpretation see F. Dexinger, *Sturz der Göttersöhne* 70—124.

108 Haag, *TDOT*, II, 157f. understands the 'sons of God' as divine beings in line with supposed Ugaritic parallels, of which he cites *CTA*, 32 (*UT*, 2), 16f. Cf. also Scharbert, *BZ*, N.F. 11 (1967) 66—78. Dexinger, *Sturz der Göttersöhne*, 37 likewise understands the expression of heroes, by invoking parallels in Ugaritic literature (cf. e.g. 130ff.).

109 The *waw* in וגם (vs. 4) is *waw-explicativum*. The fact has escaped the notice of D. Baker, *VT* 30 (1980) 129—39. The verse should be translated: "The Nephilim were on the earth in those days, *that is*, after the sons of God had gone into the daughters of men." Dexinger, *Sturz der Göttersöhne*, 132 n. 480, gratuitously excises the words וגם אחרי-כן as a late gloss, in order to identify the 'sons of God' with their children, the Nephilim: "Besagte Heroen lebten auf Erde in jenen Zeiten, die Helden, welche zu den Mädchen hingingen, so dass diese ihnen gebaren. Sie waren die Männer, die seit der Vorzeit weitberühmte Leute waren". This interpretation is forced and unnatural. Cf. Scharbert's remark *BZ* N.F. 11 (1967) 72, n. 21: "Diese Deutung scheint mir an der Syntax von 6, 4 zu scheitern, nach der zwar die 'Riesen' mit den 'Helden' und den 'Männern mit Namen' identisch sind, diese aber deutlich genug als Nachkommen der 'Menschentöchter' und 'Gottessöhne' gekennzeichnet sind. Die 'Gottessöhne' kommen also wohl nur als die 'Väter' der Heroen in Frage".

This way of looking at the OT son of man expression, as a concept possessing theological significance *vis a vis* 'man', rather than it being a mere poetic equivalent for 'man', it is deemed does more justice to the tenor of the various contexts where it occurs. But such a statement immediately raises the question, If the term son of man really has acquired such negative connotations as has been claimed here, how does one account for its use as a title of address in Ez? The answer is quite simple. My proposed interpretation of son of man actually gives the requisite depth of meaning to this expression in Ez, the point of which is missed by the usual interpretations.

The Book of Ezekiel opens with a grand vision of God's chariot-throne, at the sight of which the prophet is dismayed. The first word of God's reassuring voice is "Son of man"[110]! This "son of man" is commissioned with a message to "the people of Israel, to a nation of rebels" (2:3). On their account he is ordered to swallow a book, the like of which proved to be bitter when eaten by John (Rev 10:9f.). He is made their watchman (3:17) by being charged to warn the wicked whose blood, otherwise, God is to require from him (3:18). He is bound (3:25) and lays on a bed, now on one side and then on the other in a symbolic siege of Israel and Judah respectively, eating and drinking by ratio while bearing the punishment of his people (4:1–17). In all these passages he is constantly addressed as "son of man"[111]. But there is no need to multiply such instances. The cases cited amply show that the role which the prophet has assumed among his people is one of representative, intercessor and substitute. The appellation "son of man" is, therefore, not a characterization of him as a rebellious person, but is indicative of his identification with the wicked nation which he serves. Thus, the status of son of man is transferred from those to whom it properly belongs to one who has identified himself with them and becomes their substitute. This transferred use of son of man in Ez is therefore a development of the concept as used in the passages discussed heretofore. The appellation is no longer a descriptive designation, but a term denoting role or function. It introduces a new concept in Yahwism, whereby Yahweh's prophet-servant becomes identified with those to whom he channels God's message. He becomes a son of man in order to address the sons of men[112].

With this brief explication of the use of son of man in Ez I now turn to Daniel.

---

110 Bowman, *ET* 59 (1947–8) 284, considers it possible that Ez has been influenced by Ps 80.

111 See Houk, *JBL* 88 (1969) 184–90 for the bearing of the threefold Son of Man address on the question of the composition of Ezekiel, a matter of no interest in the present investigation.

112 Borsch's view that 'son of man' as used of Ezekiel bespeaks a very high status of the prophets is unconvincing (cf. his *Son of Man*, 137ff.).

E. The Identification of the 'SM' in Daniel

The first thing to note here is that what the seer sees is a figure that was *similar* to a son of man. It is, therefore, strictly speaking, incorrect to speak of the Danielic Son of Man as if he were on a par with e.g. Ezekiel's son of man, or the son of man idea as found in the Psalms. In all of the OT occurrences, with the exception of Dan 7:13 and 10:16, the son of man is a human being. Here the son of man is no actual human being, but a figure in human form symbolizing a non-human reality. This is underscored by the preposition כ in 7:13 and the expression כדמות (= "in the likeness of") in 10:16. This observation has far reaching consequences. The current interpretation that the 'SM' of Dan 7:13 is a symbol for the faithful Israelites breaks down already at this point. If the symbol of the 'SM' stands for human beings then the obvious language to use is to speak of a son of man without the preposition כ. If, however, the symbol stands for something essentially different, it is readily understood why "like a human being" is used in order to approximate its character.

Furthermore, the descriptions of the four beasts are also symbolical. What the seer saw was not a lion, a bear, or a leopard, but a reality of far different nature, which however, had certain characteristics that recalled in the mind of the seer the idea of a lion, or a bear, or a leopard. Similarly, the figure of 7:13 is not a son of man, i.e. a human being, but someone who is being compared to a human being. The analogy between the two sets of comparison, the "beasts" representing human kingdoms and the 'SM', symbolizing another reality, must be maintained. Therefore, the preposition כ (= "*like* a human being") and the analogical character of the expression to the symbolic nature of the "beasts", which are no ordinary animals at all, but symbols of human kingdoms, rules out the identification of the 'SM' with the people of Israel[113]. One might even press the analogy further: since the figure of animals is used to represent a reality of a higher order than the symbol itself (sc. human kingdoms are symbolized by beasts) by the same token one might argue that the 'SM' is probably used of a reality higher than human beings.

The investigation into the identification of the 'SM' will be carried out under four headings.

1. Philological Considerations

Those who identify the 'SM' with the 'holy ones of the Most High', who, in turn, are identified with the faithful remnant of Israel, quite simply compare vs. 14 with vv. 18, 22 and 27. In vs. 14 'dominion' (MT:

---

113 So Dumbrell, *RTR* 34 (1975) 19ff. On the animal symbolism of the four Kingdoms, see Cumont, *Klio* 9 (1909) 263–73.

שלטן ;Θ: ἀρχή ; LXX: ἐξουσία), 'glory'/'honor' (MT: יקר ; Θ: ἡ τιμή; LXX: –) and 'kingly rule' (MT: מלכו , Θ: ἡ βασιλεία; LXX: –) are given to the 'SM', while in vv. 18 and 22 'the kingdom' (MT: מלכותא; Θ: τὴν βασιλείαν; LXX: τὴν βασιλείαν/ τὸ βασίλειον) and in vs. 27 'the kindgom and the dominion and the greatness' (MT: מלכותא ושלטנא ורבותא; Θ: ἡ βασιλεία, ἡ ἐξουσία, ἡ μεγαλωσύνη; LXX: τὴν βασιλείαν, τὴν ἐξουσίαν, μεγαλειότητα) of the kings under the whole heaven are said to be given to the 'holy ones' or saints. The syllogism, therefore, is that the 'SM' is none other than the saints[114]. Yet, this conclusion has overlooked a number of serious textual and linguistic difficulties, let alone the further question of the identity of the saints. The problem is thus quite complex[115].

The first difficulty is met already at vs. 13. The LXX represents the earliest refusal to identify the 'SM' with the saints. Whereas the MT and Θ agree in speaking of 'One like a son of man' coming with the clouds of heaven to the Aged One and being presented before Him, the LXX identifies the 'One like a son of man' with the Aged One: ὡς υἱὸς ἀνθρώπου ἤρχετο, καὶ ὡς παλαιὸς ἡμερῶν παρῆν, καὶ οἱ παρεστηκότες παρῆσαν αὐτῷ[116]. This identification cannot possibly be explained as an error[117]. For even if ἕως had been changed inadvertently to ὡς through the influence of ὡς υἱὸς ἀνθρώπου, the change from παλαιοῦ to παλαιός is no doubt deliberate[118]. Moreover, since this understanding is reflected in Rev 1:14, this particular interpretation must go back at least to the first century A.D.[119] J. Lust, in his interesting article argues, on the

---

114 So e.g. Colpe, *TDNT* VIII, 422 and Casey, *Son of Man*, 24: "What the man-like figure gets in vs. 14, the people of the saints of the Most High get in vs. 27; they get nothing which was not granted to him". In a similar manner, Deissler, in *Jesus und der Menschensohn*, 91, says: "Die Gleichung 'Menschensohn' = 'Heiligen des Höchstens' = 'Volk der Heiligen des Höchstens' = 'endzeitliches Israel' ist für Dan 7 nicht nur exegetisch gesichert, sie ist vielmehr das Hauptthema dieses berühmten Kapitels".

115 Attention is also called to the enormous – and therefore incredible – jumb that the writer of the *Parables* must have made in respect to his source by personifying and deifying what was only a symbol for ordinary people and at that only a few years after the appearing of the source, according to these scholars.

116 Ziegler, who otherwise follows MS 88, in his edition, in this instance dismisses the reading of that MS and the Syrohexaplaric, which, now finds support in MS 967, the earliest LXX MS, dated in the II A.D. (cf. A. Geissen, *Der Septuaginta-Text des Buches Daniel 5–12*, 18) and emends to ἕως παλαιοῦ ἡμερῶν παρῆν καὶ οἱ παρεστηκότες προσήγαγον αὐτόν on the basis of Justin, *Trypho*, 31, Tertullian, and Cyprian, as well as Montgomery's suggestion that the other reading is an error of pre-Christian date (*Daniel* 304).

117 So explained by Montgomery, *Daniel*, 304.

118 Similarly F.F. Bruce, *OTS* 20 (1977) 25; J. Lust, *ETL* 54 (1978) 62ff. and Moloney, *DownRev* 98 (1980) 280–90 in criticism of Casey's *Son of Man*.

119 F.F. Bruce, *OTS* 20 (1977) 26, suggests the probable existence of such an interpretative tradition known to John, and relates it to Mk 14:62ff. to account for the rage felt by the Jewish authorities at Jesus' applying this verse to himself. This thesis is developed in some length also by A. Guilding, *EvQ* 23 (1951) 210–12. Cf. also E. Lohse, in *Jesus und der Menschensohn*, 1975, 415–20

basis of the reading of the oldest LXX manuscript (MS 967), that the LXX reading is the correct one and that it probably preserves an original Hebrew reading[120]. This hypothesis seems to me unwarranted, albeit the upshot of the discussion points in one unmistakable direction: very early, perhaps in the misty days when the first copies of Dan were made, it was recognized that the author intended the 'SM' to be understood in close conjunction with the Aged One[121].

Another group of problems — this time relevant to the MT, Θ and the LXX — occurs at vs. 27. This verse is fraught with difficulties, but no one would suspect the problems from the smooth rendering of the RSV: "And the kingdom and the dominion and the greatness of the kingdoms under the whole heaven shall be given to the people of the saints of the Most High; their kingdom shall be an everlasting kingdom, and all dominions shall serve and obey them"[122]. This translation betrays the underlying assumption that the 'SM' is identical with the saints of the Most High mentioned in vv. 18, 22, 25 and 27. The pronouns 'their' and 'them' in the expression "their kingdom" and "serve and obey them" are unwarranted. The Aramaic text reads מלכותה (= 'his kingdom') and לה יפלחון (= 'him shall they serve and obey'). The third person singular pronoun has been understood, of course, as referring to לעם (= 'to the people' (of the saints of the Most High)) and been turned to the third person plural in English. But the propriety of this procedure is hereby called into question. The LXX renders the relevant part of this verse with ἔδωκε λαῷ ἁγίῳ ὑψίστου βασιλεῦσαι βασιλείαν αἰώνιον, καὶ πᾶσαι (αἱ) ἐξουσίαι αὐτῷ ὑποταγήσονται καὶ πειθαρχήσουσιν αὐτῷ ἕως καταστροφῆς τοῦ λόγου. This translation corresponds with the Aramaic in the expression לעם קדישי עליונין and possibly in that it understands αὐτῷ (לה), which it repeats, as in reference to λαῷ . But thereby the RSV most certainly, the LXX very probably and the MT possibly[123] commit the gross blunder of subjecting the higher powers, the

---

120 Lust concludes that "The Septuagint of Dan 7:13 is not to be considered as being erroneous. It may well be the only witness of an original Hebrew text. It presents a theology differing from the one found in the TM and in the Theodotionic version but corresponding to the one in Ezekiel's visions which may be considered as its source" (68). The occasional superiority of the LXX to the MT for the OT in general is upheld also by Π. Σιμώτας, Αἱ ἀμετάφραστοι λέξεις ἐν τῷ κειμένῳ τῶν Ο', Thessaloniki, 1968, esp. 155. Lust's statement concerning Θ's theology reveals the current misunderstanding of what Θ's text really says.

121 J. Lust, *ETL* 54 (1978) 63–9, esp. 66–9. Lust would prefer to look upon the present Aramaic of Daniel as a targum of an original Hebrew.

122 The same essential understanding is reflected in the NEB and the recently printed Swedish translation of Daniel (Gamla Testamentet 2: Daniel).

123 There is uncertainty as to whether מלכותה refers to לעם or to עליונין. The latter word though plural in form is semantically a singular concept like אלהים (cf. *G-K*, § 124h) and therefore can take a correlative in the singular. The former word (עם) being collective can be construed either with a singular as here, or with a plural, i.e. *constructio ad sensum* (cf. *G-K*, § 132g). The collation of a number of instances of עם in the OT has shown that the verb with עם as subject occurs both in the singular (e.g. Gen 41:55; Ex 4:31; I Sam 9:13; Ps

'dominions' (MT: שלטניא ‎; Θ: ἀρχαί ; LXX: ἐξουσίαι) to the saints of the Most High, who, in the opinion of most scholars, represent the pious Jews! The basic fault with this view is that it misunderstands the meaning of 'dominions' in vs. 27 b[124].

How are we then to understand the expressions מלכותה (= 'his king-dom') and לה יפלחון וישתמעון (= "him shall they serve and obey")? To whom do 'his' and 'him' refer? There are only two possibilities: their antecedent is either 'the people', or 'the Most High'. The expression 'the saints of the Most High' (= קדישי עליונין) occurs only four times in Dan, all in this chapter (vv. 18, 22, 25 and 27). The use of עם in connec-tion with this expression in vs. 27 is unique. The *Vorlage*[125] of the most reliable translation of Dan, namely, the so-called Theodotion (Θ), ob-viously omitted עם, which is why Θ has in all four places ἅγιοι (ἁγίοις (2 times), ἁγίους) ὑψίστου![126] The expression עם קדישי (= λαὸν (τῶν)

81:12; Isa 32:18 Jer 2:13; Dan 12:1; Zech 14:2) as well as in the plural (e.g. Gen 11:6; Num 11:8; II Sam 18:5; I Kin 18:21; Neh 8:1; (5:13 where the substantive is קהל); Jer 23:32; Isa 43:21; Hag 1:2). When a participle has עם as correlate it normally occurs in the plural (e.g. Num 11:1; II Sam 15:23; Dan 11:32). The same applies to a verb that relates back to עם as subject (e.g. Ex 7:16; Jer 5:23). More pertinent for our text, which has a noun with suffix, מלכותה, relating back to another word, are the following instances: Isa 6:10; 29:13; 51:7; and 58:1. The first instance reads in the RSV rendering: "Make the heart of this people fat, and their ears (singular suffix ואזניו) heavy, and shut their eyes (singular suffix ועיניו)". To the same effect is Isa 29:13. These two passages show that it is possible to refer מלכותה to the people of the saints of the Most High. This is, however, not the only alternative. The following two passages construe the noun with the correlative עם by way of *constructio ad sensum* in the plural: Isa 58:1 "Declare to my people their transgression (pl. פשעם), and the house of Jacob their sin (pl. חטאתם)" (RSV). Similarly Isa 51:7.

As Hebrew syntax leaves both possibilities open, the matter will have to be decided on internal or contextual grounds.

124 See *infra* under the next subheading.
125 Such a *Vorlage* for the OT in general was postulated by H.St.J. Thackeray, *The Septuagint and Jewish Worship*, 2nd ed. 1923. See further the more recent work by A. Schmitt *Stammt der Sogennante Θ Text bei Daniel wirklich von Theodotion?* 1966, e.g. 112.
126 It is nowadays generally recognized that Θ whether in its present or an earlier form, is older than the reviser Theodotion (II A.D.) going back to pre-Christian times, e.g. G. Salmon, *Historical Introduction to the Books of the NT*, 1885, (who gave to the already raised Theo-dotionic problem its definitive shape); J. Gwyn "Theodotion" in *Dictionary of Christian Biography* ed. W. Smith, Vol. IV, 1887, 970ff.; Charles, *Revelation*, I, lxviif. Montgomery, *Daniel*, 46ff.; Roberts, *The OT Texts and Versions*, 132ff.; Ziegler, (ed.) *Septuaginta XVI, 2 Susanna Daniel Bel et Draco*, 1954, 22. For a history of the discussion of the Theodotionic problem see S. Jellicoe, "Some Reflections on the ΚΑΙΓΕ Recension" *VT*, 23 (1973) 15–24, esp. 16ff., and *The Septuagint and Modern Study*, Oxford, 1968, esp. 83–94.

The discussion now seems to focus on the date and place of this Proto-Theodotion. Thus, Barthélemy *Les Devanciers d' Aquila* (Sup *VT* XI), Leiden, 1963, finds in the so-called ΚΑΙΓΕ recension the work of 'Theodotion' whom he identifies with Jonathan ben Uzziel, previously considered to be the author of an Aramaic targum. This Jonathan-Theodotion is dated to the mid-first Christian century and is a predecessor of Aquila. In the opinion of F.M. Cross, *HTR* 57 (1964) 283, Barthelemy's theory "must remain *sub judice*". A. Schmitt, *Stammt der sogennante Θ-Text bei Daniel wirklich von Theodotion?*, rejects categorically any connection between Θ and Theodotion. Jellicoe, *VT* 23 (1973) 15–24, concludes that

ἁγίων, 'people of the saints') is really awkward, hence the LXX turns the noun קדישי into an attributive adjective despite the fact that the same term everywhere else in Dan functions as a noun. Moreover, this construction cannot be parallel to the *status constructus*, to indicate an adjectival idea, since the abstract substantive קודש should then have been used (sc. קודש עם as in Dan 12:7), or the more usual construction with the adjective קדוש (= Aramaic קדיש, i.e. עם קדוש as in Dt 7:6)[127]. Thus, the presence of עם in the present Aramaic text and of λαῷ in the LXX might conceivably be a later insertion into the text to make reference to the Jewish people more palpable[128].

Recognizing the corruption of the passage in the MT and in the LXX, we turn to the Θ text, where we read: καὶ ἡ βασιλεία καὶ ἡ ἐξουσία ἐδόθη ἁγίοις ὑψίστου, καὶ ἡ βασιλεία αὐτοῦ βασιλεία αἰώνιος, καὶ πᾶσαι αἱ ἀρχαὶ αὐτῷ δουλεύσουσι καὶ ὑπακούσονται. This translation not only evinces inner consistency, it also properly distinguishes the abstract words βασιλεία, ἐξουσία and μεγαλωσύνη in vs. 27a from the concrete use of the term ἀρχαί in 27b — a distinction of paramount importance, an importance which the LXX and the Modern Versions have missed[129].

The upshot of this is that Θ understands ἡ βασιλεία αὐτοῦ and αὐτῷ δουλεύσουσι καὶ ὑπακούσονται of vs. 27b as referring to ὑψίστου and not to the saints. With respect to the MT we saw, above, that מלכותה and לה purely grammatically could be referred either to עם— if original — or to עליונין[130]. What weighs in favour of the second alternative is firstly the

---

the KAIΓE recension is none other than the Ur-Theodotion, an Ephesian translator of the I cent. B.C., whose work was revised in the II century A.D. by the traditional Theodotion. In a short note K. Koch, "Die Herkunft der Proto-Theodotion-Übersetzung des Danielbuches", *VT* 23 (1973) 362–4, accepts the pre-Christian date for Θ and locates its place of provenience in the Syrian-Mesopotamian region. He refers to K.A. George, *The Peshitto Version of Daniel* (unpublished Diss., Hamburg, 1972), who brings Θ in close connection with the Peshitto.

From the foregoing it has become obvious that though our Θ goes back to pre-Christian times, its relation to the LXX still awaits elucidation. The state of research is such that F.F. Bruce, *OTS* 20 (1977) 38ff. can contemplate two solutions opposed to each other: either the LXX text — admittedly paraphrastic or targumic in character (Cf. Segal, *Two Powers in Heaven*, 202) — paraphrased a text of Theodotionic character, or Θ — admittedly a straightforward translation — corrected targumic LXX on the basis of the Hebrew and Aramaic. When such widely divergent options are possible, it is readily perceived not only how little we can assume about the Θ text, but also how much. The door has not been barred to regarding this version as of equal antiquity or even greater antiquity to that of the LXX, and this may have significance for the very problem engaging our attention at present. In whichever case, the Θ text is, by general consensus, of pre-Christian date and its theology about the One like a Son of Man is Jewish, not Christian!

127 See *G-K*, § 128 p.

128 I.e. by those who understood the passage as referring to the Jewish people, or, were inspired by polemic against the Christians, or, a Christian use of it. This would support the priority of the Θ reading. That the Θ reading should be a correction of the MT and the LXX is less likely in view of the wide acceptance of this text in the first century A.D.

129 On this see *infra*, under the Comparison between the Ἄρχων of the Beasts and the 'SM'.

fact that עליונין is the closer antecedent, and secondly the great likelihood that the MT also understood שלטניא as referring to concrete beings
— an understanding that demands reference to עליונין[131]. Moreover, the
two verbs יפלחון (= 'serve') and ישתמעון (= 'obey') are quite inappropriate if the reference is to the people of Israel, but find their proper use
if they refer to the Most High. The verb פלח occurs 9 times in Dan (i.e.
3:12, 14, 17, 18, 28; 6:17, 21 and 7:14, 27). Everywhere else outside of
chapter 7 the verb is used of serving a deity. If the 'SM', who is thus to be
served (7:14) is a symbol for Israel, and if 'serve' in vs. 27 refers again to
Israel, these are the only exceptions. However, since all other examples
are clear instances of service rendered to a deity, it is highly precarious to
understand these 'less clear' instances as constituting an anomaly evidenced nowhere else. The verb שמע too, occurs regularly of obedience to
God, and sometimes it is combined with עבד, one of the Hebrew equivalents to the Aramaic פלח, to indicate service and obedience to Yahweh,
e.g. Josh 24:24; I Sam 12:14; Job 36:11.

In conclusion, it may be said that the Θ text has the 'powers' subjected
to the 'Most High', whereas the LXX text has them subjected to the Jewish people. The MT is somewhat ambiguous; however, an understanding
in line with the explicit statement of the Θ text is far the more likely[132].
Taking into consideration the targumic nature of the present LXX text
of Dan, with its multitude of faulty renderings, as well as the early[133] and
widespread acceptance of the Θ text at a time when comparison with very
early Hebrew-Aramaic witnesses was still possible, there ought to be little
doubt that the Θ text has better preserved the original reading. Vs. 27 is
thus understood as saying:

> "And the kingly rule and the dominion and the greatness of the kingdoms under the whole
> heaven shall be given to the saints of the Most High, whose kingly rule is an everlasting kingly
> rule, and all the dominions shall serve and obey him."

The Interpretation Part contains two more grammatical peculiarities:
the designations for 'Most High' and the expression 'saints of the Most
High'. With regards to the term 'Most High' two distinct forms are used:
עליא (Kethibh, vs. 25) and עליונין (vv. 18, 22, 25 and 27). The Hebrew
form is עליון. The same form is presupposed in Aramaic, though in Dan
only the form עלי in the emphatic form עליא (Kethibh, for Qere עלאה)

---

130 Driver, *Daniel*, 104f. admits the option, though on p. 93 he refers the pronouns to the saints.
131 Dequeker, *OTS* 18 (1973) 181f. also understands 7:27b as referring to the Most High. His
    reasons, however, are very different from mine. He thinks that vs. 27b is a doxological refrain,
    whose first part is reflected in Dan 3:33 and Ps 145:13 and its second in Dan 7:14. Seeing
    7:27b as parallel in genre with Dan 3:33 and Ps 145:13 is, in my opinion, unjustified.
132 Of Jewish sources, which similarly understand לה in 7:27 as referring to the Messiah rather
    than the "people of the saints", may be cited Midr. Haggadol Gen 49:10, Pseudo-Saadia and
    Samuel ben Nissim.
133 MS 967 is dated in the II A.D.

is found occurring in the Aramaic section 10 times[134]. The expression 'saints of the Most High' occurs four times (all in chapter 7) and strangely enough uses the peculiar double plural עֶלְיוֹנִין[135]— a form attested nowhere else. That the term עִלָּיָא occurs no less than ten times in the Aramaic sections, alone or in association with 'God', whereas the expression 'saints of the Most High' always has another form, is surely not to be explained as a coincidence. The significance of this pecularity will be discussed below. For the time being it may suffice to underline that the 'saints' and the 'Most High' are thus closely related by the construct state construction[136], and that in vs. 27 both are said to receive kingly rule; the saints receiving the rule of the kings under the whole heaven, while the 'Most High' having the 'powers' or 'principalities' brought in subjection to him.

2. The Character of the Beasts and a Comparison Between the Beasts' Ἄρχων and the 'SM'

One of the main reasons for misinterpreting the intention of the Book of Daniel is the failure to recognize the dynamic nature of the Book. The Book cannot simply be compared to the mythologies of the Near East and be interpreted in that light. Nor does an understanding of its statements, in vision or interpretation, on the purely human or historical level, do justice to the nature of the Book. Daniel tries to grasp both history and supra-history, and to give an adequate explanation of history by penetrating beyond history into 'ultimate' causes, to those elements hidden behind the veil of historical occurrences which shape, indeed, determine, history. To do justice to the character of the Book, therefore, it is imperative that the interpreter keeps this duality, this double dimension constantly in mind. This means that the entities symbolized often are to be understood on two levels, the referent being neither constant nor static.

One of the few students of Daniel who has shown some appreciation for this dimension is J.J. Collins[137]. Unfortunately, however, he used that insight only for the purpose of identifying the 'saints' with angels and the 'SM' with Michael — what was basically Procksch's and M. Noth's hypo-

---

134 In 3:26, 32; 5:18, 21 together with 'God'; in 4:14, 21, 22, 29, 31; 7:25 alone.
135 *G-K*, § 124h; Baumgartner, (*K-B, sub voc.*); H. Bauer-P. Leander, *Grammatik des Biblisch-Aramäischen*, § 305g; and F. Rosenthal, *A Grammar of Biblical Aramaic*, § 22 and 187 explain the form as an imitation of אֱלֹהִים. See also Driver, *Daniel*, 90; Bevan, *Daniel*, 125; Charles, *Daniel*, 191.
136 The term 'saints' or 'holy ones' occurs in Dan 7 six times, four of which are in the expression 'saints of the Most High'. The proximity of the other two instances to this expression involves no evidence against regarding them as identical with 'saints' in the longer expression.
137 See his "The Son of Man and the Saints of the Most High in the Book of Daniel" (*JBL*, 93 (1974) 50–66) reprinted with modifications in his *The Apocalyptic Vision*, 123–52.

thesis[138]. Had Collins, however, been consistent in the application of this criterion he would have been obliged to abandon his identification.

The inerpretation I am presenting here and the reasons that led me to it, go as far back as 1975. The present thesis was put in print in a nutshell in 1977 as an excursus of my dissertation[139]. Prof. J. Coppens, who has written voluminously on the Danielic 'SM' wrote in a review of the above-mentioned work: "Les observations de l' auteur sur la version de Dan VII, 27 par Theodotion meritent toute notre attention. Elles tendent à prouver que Théodotion distinguait entre le Fils d' homme et les Saints du Très-Haut, et qu' en toute hypothèse il se refusait à voir dans le Fils d' homme le symbole du peuple de Dieu[140]." In the present study I intend to spell out the implications of the 1977 publication.

Before entering into a discussion concerning the points of comparison between the essential component parts of the beasts on the one hand, and the 'SM' on the other, it is necessary to elucidate the nature of the concept of 'beasts', in other words, to define the concept of the beast as closely as possible.

a) The Nature of the Beasts

i. The Double Meaning of 'Αρχή /'Εξουσία. In the Aramaic of Dan 7 the term שׁלטן occurs 7 times. All these instances are rendered by the LXX with ἐξουσία, while Θ has 3 times ἐξουσία and 4 times ἀρχή. Besides, the LXX uses ἐξουσία once more in vs. 27a in a phrase not found in the MT or Θ. Moreover, the MT, the LXX and Θ all agree in using the sigular in all of the first 6 instances (i.e. 7:12, 14 (3X), 26, 27a), and the plural in the seventh instance (i.e. 7:27b). The question immediately arises whether the term carries the same meaning in the plural as in the singular. To this the answer is categorically, No![141] In the singular the term is always used in an abstract sense of the 'power', 'dominion' or 'authority' as exercised by the different beasts and then given to the 'SM'

---

138 O. Procksch, "Der Menschensohn als Gottessohn" in *Christentum und Wissenschaft*, 3 (1927) 429. M. Noth, "Die Heiligen des Höchsten", *NorTT*, 56 (1955) 146–61 (reprinted in M. Noth, *Gesammelte Studien*, 2nd ed. 1960, 274–90. Others who have espoused this interpretation include H. Kruse, "Compositio libri Danielis et idea Filii Hominis," *VD* 37 (1959) 147–61, 193–211; J. Barr, *Daniel* in A.S. Peake's *Commentary of the Bible*, London, 1962, 597; L. Dequeker, *ETL* 36 (1960) pp. 353–92. J. Coppens, *VT* 19 (1969) 171–82; Z. Zevit, "The Structure and Individual Elements of Daniel VII", *ZAW* 80 (1968) 385–96., *et al.*

139 *The Ephesian Mysterion*: Meaning and Content, 157–61.

140 In *ETL* 53 (1977) 507.

141 The fluctuation in meaning of these terms, whereby they have sometimes the abstract sense and sometimes a concrete sense of 'authorities' or 'rulers', as well as the double reference of the latter sense to human and spiritual powers, obtains also in the NT. Cf. e.g. Eph 1:21; 3:10; 6:12; Col 1:16; 2:10, 15; I Cor 15:24 (I Cor 2:8 ἄρχοντες) for the personified use, and for the abstract sense of 'power', 'authority' see for ἀρχή Lk 20:20; Jud 6; and for ἐξουσία Mt 7:29; 8:9; Jn 5:27 and Rev 2:26.

(7:14) and to the saints (7:27a). In 7: 27b, however, the plural is used in a personified way as a designation of those who wielded the 'power' or 'dominion' (7:12) spoken of in the singular above, and who, at length, become subjected to the Most High[142]. This very important distinction has, as far as I know, been invariably overlooked, and this circumstance has contributed to the mistaken identification of the 'SM'.

ii. The Referent of Ἀρχαί/ Ἐξουσίαι. The next question is, What entity does the plural ἀρχαί/ἐξουσίαι refer to? Two answers are possible here: the first one is that the reference is to the kings of each beast. Such an answer is *a priori* possible since both the šemitic term שלטן as well as the Greek terms ἀρχαί/ἐξουσίαι can manifestly be used to carry such a sense. However, in Jewish and biblical usage the terms ἀρχαί/ἐξουσίαι in plural are used often to designate a non-human order of beings, which usually exercise a malevolent influence upon humanity[143]. In accordance with this usage and in the light of Dan's conception of history, the ἀρχαί of Θ and the ἐξουσίαι of the LXX (MT: שלטניא) in 7:27b are understood to refer to spiritual powers operative behind their human agents. This claim will be corroborated by the discussion following immediately.

iii. The Component parts of the Beasts. The third question is what constitutes the Beasts. Here it is important to observe that the term 'beasts' does not stand for any particular king[144], but for the whole series of kings involved in each kingdom. Moreover — and this is of extreme importance — the beast is not quite identical with this totality of kings. The oscillation between king and kingdom observable in the text, obtains also between the king on the one hand and an entity that is conceived of as being the core in the concept of 'Beast' on the other. The recognition of the dynamic nature of the text is of crucial importance for understanding the nature of the concept of 'Beast'.

Our author is grappling with his problem on a two-dimensional basis. While cogitating on human affairs the author goes beyond what is observable in the empirical realm. He introduces his readers to another plane, the plane of vision, where earthly phenomena are seen to have their invisible counterparts to 'events' beyond the world of senses. More than this, there

---

142 For the Semitic term cf. the Arabic *sultan* = the Turkish ruler.
143 Cf. e.g. Ascension of Isaiah 1:4; Test. Lev. 3:8; I En 61:10; II En (A) 20:1; Apoc Soph (apud Clemens Alexandrinus, *Stromata*, V, 11); Test Sol 20:15; 8:2. For the NT use of these terms see e.g. Eph 1:21; 2:2; 6:2; Col 1:16; 2:10.
144 This is maintained despite the personal tone in the address to Nebuchadnezzar (Dan 2:38). Nebuchadnezzar, the 'head of gold', is so addressed no doubt because he, as the real 'builder' of Babylon, is the most important representative of the first kingdom/beast. There is therefore nothing strange in his being singled out in this way. Besides, he is the only king personally involved in the event of this message. Cf Jer 27:7f. where Nebuchadnezzar sums up in himself the kings of Babylon.

is a causal connection between the invisible and the visible worlds. Earthly events are not simply the result of the whim of earthly potentates; they are to be explained by reference to realities in the invisible world. It is this double dimension in the author's perspective which renders the concept of 'Beast' a complex concept of ambivalent nature. Therefore, in the author's way of thinking the 'Beast's' essential character is neither the state nor the king. What is perhaps only implicit as yet in chapter 7 becomes quite explicit in 10:13, 20, 21. Here, two of the beasts/kingdoms, Persia and Greece, are described as having a 'prince'[145] (Θ: ἄρχων), who tries to thwart God's purposes by opposing the angelic emissary. That these 'princes' cannot possibly refer e.g. to Cyrus or Alexander, that is to ordinary or for that matter extraordinary human kings[146], is placed beyond reasonable doubt in vs. 21, which in identical terms speaks of the angel Michael as the 'prince' of the Jews[147]. Accordingly, the ἄρχων of 10:21 and the ἀρχαί of 7:27b are to be considered as equivalent[148].

Thus, the concept of 'Beast' in Dan 7 is a complex concept consisting in the first place of a spiritual power, which inspires actions directed against God and his people, and in the second place of the kings of each kingdom, who carry out their invisible suzerain's intentions, and in the third place of the state, which through its machinery, institutions and members makes possible the realization in time and space of the celestial overlord's designs. Of these three components the primary one is the invisible ἄρχων, who ultimately is responsible for the actions of those under his control[148a].

b) A Comparison Between the Ἄρχων *and the* 'SM'

Having analyzed the concept of 'Beast' as consisting of an invisible

---

145 The MT has always שר. The LXX misunderstands (probably) the angelic character of this 'prince' and renders with στρατηγός, except when שר is a designation for Michael, where the LXX translates with ἄγγελος.

146 The singular "prince of the Kingdom of Persia", "prince of Greece" inapplicable for a series of kings is admirably suited to designating the invisible ἄρχων at work behind each kingdom.

147 For the Hebrew-Jewish view (outside Daniel) that each nation is placed under a guardian angel, whereas the Jews are put directly under God, see Dt 32:8f.; Jubilees 15:31f.; Targum of Pseudo-Jonathan on Gen 11:7; Sirach 17:17; Late Hebrew Test. of Naphtali 9:4f. According to I En 20:7 Israel is placed under Michael's command, who according to Test.Lev. 5:7; I En 89:76; Test Dan 6:2ff., has as his task to help and intercede for Israel. These passages are obviously dependent on our passage.
    A similar notion occurs in Greek sources, cf. Plato, *Leges*, 4, 713Cff.; 5, 738D, where the guardian spirits of cities are called δαιμόνια. For their duties, cf. Plato, *Symposium*, 202E. See further Mertens, *Daniel im Lichte der Texten vom Toten Meer*, pp. 100–2.

148 The fluidity of the expression occurs also in other Jewish sources (e.g. Test Sol 20:15 ἀρχαί), and in the NT, (e.g. ἄρχων Mt 9:34; 12:24; Jn 12:31; 16:11; I Cor 2:6, 8; Eph 2:2; and ἀρχαί Rm 8:28; Eph 3:10; 6:12; Col 1:16, 2:10 (πάσης ἀρχῆς); 2:15).

148a The discussion by Welch, *Visions of the End*, 108f., wherein all of the beasts are considered simply in relation to human greed for power and human cruelty, and where the invisible ἄρχων is totally absent, is most inadequate.

potentate + the king + the state, I will now proceed to compare and contrast the details between the ἄρχων and the 'SM'.

i. The ἄρχων and the 'SM' are conceived as spiritual beings. The ἄρχων, as has been shown above, is a spiritual power. As for the 'SM', the very designation כבר אנש precludes his identity as a human being. Both the manner of his transportation before the Aged One and his investment with absolute power are indicative of his non-human nature[149].

ii. Both the ἄρχων and the 'SM' have each their subordinates. The ἄρχων has his subordinates in the king and the state, while the 'SM' has them in the saints. The appearing of the 'SM' before the Ancient One is to be understood undoubtedly in connection with the saints he seeks to vindicate[150].

iii. The Power of the ΄Αρχων and the 'SM'. There is, moreover, a parallel between the ἄρχων and the 'SM' in the matter of the power which each exercises in relation to that which their subordinates exercise or are to exercise. Thus, as the power of the invisible ἄρχων is visibly exercised by his beast/kingdom, so too the power of the 'SM' finds its visible expression in the dominion of the saints. In other words, the power of the kings and the power of the saints is authority delegated by the ἄρχων and the 'SM' respectively[151]. This parallelism demands, in its own rights, the distinction between the 'SM' and the saints or 'holy ones', and the postulation that the 'SM' bears to the saints a similar relation as the ἄρχοντες do to their respective kingdoms.

3. The Characteristics of the 'SM'

The two chief characteristics of the 'SM' are the manner of his approach to the Ancient One and the powers he is given. The seer catches a glimpse of this mysterious figure as he is transported with the clouds of heaven. Several scholars have noticed the inappropriateness of the clouds if the figure transported by them is a mere symbol for Israel. Feuillet[152],

---

149 Passages like I En 14:8, where Enoch is carried up to heaven by winds, and II En 3:1, where angels carry up Enoch on their wings, are to be considered as imitations of Daniel, constituting no anomaly against the biblical idea, where the clouds uniformly are the means for transportation of the deity.

150 The contingency between the 'SM' and the saints, apart from the expression 'saints of the Most High', for which see below, is evident from the circumstances of his appearing, i.e. at the end of their persecutions, to bring them deliverance. His coming is causally related to the destruction of the fourth beast.

151 On this point see further under "The Identification of the One like a Son of Man", below.

152 Feuillet, "Le Fils de l'homme de Daniel et la tradition biblique", *RB* 60 (1953) 173ff. and 321ff. Emerton, *JTS* 11 (1958) 229, and Beasley-Murray, *CBQ* 45 (1983) 44ff., concur in this.

in particular, has observed that the clouds suggest a theophany of Yahweh himself. He argues that if Dan 7:13 does not refer to a theophany, this must be the only exception out of about seventy instances[153]. This very important consideration — the problem, which the theophany raises against the Israelite interpretation — is totally bypassed by DiLella[154], in its proper place of discussion, being taken up at the end of his study, and at that as a mere means for distinguishing "the Israel of faith" thus transported from the four empires representing chaos and disorder[155]. But this is no solution of the problem at all. It must be emphasized that if the 'SM' is understood of the saints on earth, the clouds are inappropriate as a means for transportation; and if he, on the other hand, be understood as representing the martyred saints, these could not conceivably be entrusted with an earthly dominion (vs. 27a)!

The second point to be urged is the kind of exaltation offered to the 'SM':

> "And to him was given dominion, glory and kingly rule and/that all peoples, nations and languages shall/should serve him. His dominion is an everlasting dominion, which shall not fade/pass away, and his kingly rule shall not be destroyed."

The identification of the 'SM' with the saints of the Most High is the result of an uncritical equation of vs. 14 with the whole of vs. 27. Vs. 14 is parallel only to vs. 27b, whereas the first part of vs. 27 corresponds with vv. 18 and 22. Vs. 14 sets forth the 'dominion', 'glory' and 'kingly rule' given to the 'SM' in absolute terms, while vs. 27a speaks of the 'kingly rule', the 'dominion' and the 'greatness' *of the kings under the whole heaven (!)* as given to the saints. The difference between the two statements is very material and raises a serious obstacle to the identification of the 'SM' with the saints. Besides, in vs. 27b we find that the invisible powers — the primary component in the concept of Beast — are subjected to the Most High, and not to the saints, which would be an absurd idea[156]. We thus conclude that at the destruction of the Beasts the 'SM' assumes the power of the invisible ἄρχοντες, and that in dependence of this event, the saints are given the power of the kings (= kingdoms) under the whole heaven. The power of the saints is thus subservient

---

153 Procksch, *ZAW*, Beihefte, 34 (1920) 141–9, draws attention to the similarity between the expression 'one like a son of man' and 'likeness as the appearance of a man' (Ez 1:26) and suggests the superhuman character of the One like a Son of Man.

154 DiLella, *CBQ*, 1977, 1–19. See also his "The Son of Man" in Daniel", in Hartman – DiLella, *The Book of Daniel*, 101f.

155 DiLella deplores the fact that such a simple and straightforward phrase should have received a multitude of interpretations. The answer he holds, is simply that the One like a Son of Man is no mysterious figure at all, it is a symbol of the faithful Israel. DiLella makes matters a little too simple for himself and fails to appreciate the serious difficulties attaching to his 'simple' solution.

156 I Cor 6:3 is no proof for the supposition that in biblical thought the angelic powers shall be subjected to humans on earth.

to that of the 'SM' and constitutes a tangible proof of the triumph of God over his enemies.

But if the 'SM' is not a symbol for the saints, in the sense of the Jewish remnant, who is he then? This question will engage us in the discussion following immediately.

4. The Identification of the 'SM'

Following the statement in vs. 17 that the four beasts represent four kingdoms, vs. 18 simply mentions the net result of the whole process by saying that "the saints of the Most High shall receive the kingdom, and shall possess the kingdom for ever, for ever and ever." Here no mention of judgment is made. On the other hand, vs. 22, which has been preceded by the report on the persecution of the saints, appropriately does take up the theme of judgment: "Until the Ancient of Days came, and judgment was given to the saints of the Most High, and the time came when the saints received the Kingdom" (RSV). The Aramaic for "judgment was given to the saints" is ודינא יהב לקדישי. The preposition ל here has the meaning not of 'to' but more of 'for'[157], still better 'in favour of', precisely as in Ezra 6:10. The NEB gives the correct rendering: "Then judgment was given in favour of the saints . . ." The word 'judgment' becomes, accordingly, equivalent to 'verdict'. The picture is one of the vindication by the Almighty of the oppressed. Moreover, it must not pass unnoticed that vs. 22 describes two stages: one, until the Ancient One came (אתה) followed by the scene of judgment, and the other, the time came (מטה) when the saints took possession of the kingdom. The expression וזמנא מטה (= 'and the time came') implies some waiting on the part of the saints distinct from that during the persecution.

Turning to the Vision Section it seems at first sight as if the 'SM' appears after the destruction of the fourth beast (and the reduction of the first three beasts), and this might be understood as implying that whereas the saints, as part in the suit, are presumably thought of as being present during the judgment, the 'SM' comes on the scene first after the judgment. This would be an effective way to prove the distinction of the 'SM' from the saints. Unfortunately, it is not possible to make much of the apparent sequence of events here (i.e. the judgment of the beasts, the appearance of the 'SM'), since this is, in all probability, to be explained by the linearity of Hebrew thought. Moreover, the arrangement of the text whereby the 'SM' is presented as the last item in the vision helps enhance the climactic significance attached to this Figure in the total context of the vision.

Two, more important, considerations for the 'SM's' being present

---

157 So e.g. Montgomery, *Daniel*, 309f.; Driver, *Daniel*, 91.

during the judgment are the significant details that more than one throne was placed (implying more than one Judge) and that the 'SM' actually was escorted to the very presence of God (i.e. presumably to take his seat), which could hardly be said of any one of the parties engaged in the conflict. As for the 'SM's' distinctness from the saints, his being transported with the clouds of heaven is a serious obstacle to identifying him with them. In such contexts the clouds are the bearers of the divine presence[158].

Who is he then?

The request of Daniel to the bystander had been to tell him the meaning "of all this" (vs. 16), i.e., the entire vision. Of the vision elements which are not interpreted by name, the most conspicuous are the Ancient One and the 'SM'. With regards to the first of these there should be no surprise, since he is described in the vision in such detail and in such clear categories that his attributes and characteristics could apply only to One Being, namely, God. But the Figure of the 'SM' is by no means self-evident. Why is he not interpreted? Or, is he perhaps interpreted, though without being named expressly, but implicitly, by way of the associations made in the text?

We have seen reason, above, to relate the 'SM' with the saints in the matter of their possession of kingly rule. The 'SM' receives kingly rule in the absolute sense, while the saints receive the limited power of the kings under heaven. The power of the saints is contingent upon the assumption of kingly power by the 'SM'. In the Interpretation Section the designation 'saints' or 'holy ones' occurs four times in the expression 'saints of the Most High'. The saints and the Most High are brought into close relation in connection with the vindication of the former and their sharing, in a subordinate sense, in the royal power of the Most High. The absolute power spoken of in the Vision Section (vs. 14) as given to the 'SM', is, in the Interpretation Section (vs. 27b), given to the Most High. The 'SM' figures only in the Vision Part while the Most High only in the Interpretation Part. This is because the 'One like a Son of Man' has been interpreted as the Most High![159]

This interpretation solves the problems which all other interpretations share in common. The nature of the beasts, the ἄρχων's primacy, the identification of the saints with human beings — the only tenable identification —, the limited power given to the saints, the subjugation of the cosmic powers (the ἀρχαί) to a non-human being, all these questions find here a satisfactory interpretation. However, my identification raises one

---

158 See e.g. Ps 18:10ff.; 97:2; 104:3; Isa 19:1; Nah 1:3 and the numerous appearances of Yahweh in the cloud, e.g. Ex 16:10; 19:9.

159 Oesterly, *The Jews and Judaism*, 153ff. rejects the identification of the 'SM' with the "saints", and thinks that Daniel has made use of two incompatible traditions which he holds together in tension, with the former (regarding the 'SM') stemming from Iran. Such hypothesizing is both incredible and unnecessary in view of the identification which ch. 7 itself points to.

problematic question: Is the 'SM' the Most High or the Ancient One, namely, God? To this the answer is, No! This might be taken to imply that there are two divine principles posited here, but the answer to this is more complex. In the first place there is no *a priori* reason why the concept of God as consisting of more than One has to be laid to the credit of the NT, or to the later dogma of the Christian Church. Both Emerton and (even more pronouncedly) Morgenstern are able to conceive of two divinities — an older and a younger — being involved in Dan 7[160]. Morgenstern would, in fact, credit Antiochus Epiphanes with the creation of the concept of the Trinity! There is, furthermore, evidence that the Jewish rabbis could conceive of two divine principles[161]. But the author of Dan has been careful in his choice of language. In the Aramaic sections, the Most High as referring to God is described as עליא, a term occuring once in 7:25, where the reference is manifestly to the Being he otherwise describes as the Ancient One. But in the expression 'saints of the Most High', he uses a double plural of the Hebrew word עליון i.e. עליונין. This shows that the author distinguishes the 'Most High' spoken of in connection with the saints from the Most High as referring to God. In the author's conception these two are different entities. That this is so is confirmed strikingly by vs. 22, where again the author distinguishes between the Ancient One and the 'Most High' spoken of in relation to the saints. It ought therefore to admit of no doubt that the 'SM' is interpreted as being none other than the 'Most High' of the expression 'saints of the Most High' (of vv. 18, 22, 25 and 27), and that this Being is distinguished from the Most High in reference to the Ancient One, or God[162].

The implications of this for the Danielic use of the expression 'SM'

---

160 Similarly Black, "The Throne-Theophany Prophetic Commission and the Son of Man: A Study in Tradition History" in *Jews, Greeks and Christians*, 57—73, on 60f. understands the Son of Man as a divinity along with the Aged One, following Feuillet's thesis in *RB* 60 (1953) 170—202: "This in effect means that Dan 7 knows of two divinities, the Head of Days and the Son of Man. So far as our form-critical analysis of this Throne-vision pericope is concerned, it entirely confirms such a conclusion: Daniel 7 is not only in the form-tradition of Isaiah 6 (cf. I En 14) and Ezekiel 1, which are all *Theophanies*, but represents a highly significant development of it into a theology which seems virtually ditheistic". Since Black is still not willing to give up the Israelite identification of the 'SM', in view of his findings, he has no other choice than to speak of Israel's apotheosis (cf. his Festschrift article "Die Apotheose Israels" in *Jesus und der Menschensohn*, 92—99, esp. 98). Nevertheless he conceeds, that from his above conclusion "It is only a step to the identification of the second 'divinity' with the supra-mundane Messiah ... " This step is "not yet taken in Daniel: but it is the next logical development of the traditions of a corporate apotheosis ... Doctrinaire theology discovers this Son of Man messianism in the famous *Parables* of I Enoch", which in Black's opinion is both Jewish and earlier than Milik claims.

161 See references to rabbinic literature to this effect in *Str-B* I, 956ff., Bowman, *ET* 59 (1947—8) 287f. and Segal, *Two Powers in Heaven, passim*. See also my discussion in Chapter Three: Rabbinism.

162 The ascription of a similar title ('Most High') to the Ancient One as well as to the 'SM' need cause no surprise. A striking parallel is the term κύριος, which though ideally belonging to God, is, in the NT, used most frequently of Jesus Christ in its most exalted sense.

are of interest. The figure of the 'SM' appears before the judgment-seat of God. That scene is spoken of again in vs. 22, where the author concentrates only upon the saints, who in vs. 13 are represented by the 'SM'. Vs. 22, as also vv. 19—21, is essentially a part of the Vision Section, placed here for effect to make the referents in the interpretation clearer. This means that the Vision speaks both of the 'SM', who is transported with the clouds, and of the saints, who are vindicated. The 'SM' is thus the leader or representative of the saints in their humiliation and suffering. The designation 'One like a Son of Man' is meant to draw attention to this particular aspect. It is also required by the symbolism of the chapter, which uses animal symbolism to depict human entities and therefore cannot use the same symbolism for this Exalted Figure. The examination of the OT use of the expression, above, has shown that its meaning is one of wickedness, weakness, creatureliness, and inadequacy. Ezekiel is called son of man on account of his identification or solidarity with the people of Israel. In Dan 7:13 this figure appears in solidarity with his persecuted people and is therefore fittingly described as 'One *like* a son of man'![163] — but *not* a 'son of man'.

In the Interpretation Section, however, he is spoken of in connection with his vindicated people[164] and his own assumption of universal power, and this explains why the lowly designation of 'One like a son of man' has to give place to the exalted designation of 'Most High'! The designation 'Most High' may have been inspired by the appearance of the 'One like a son of man' with the clouds of heaven, that is, the 'One on high', or, the 'Exalted One'[165].

The Danielic 'SM', however, is not simply inspired by Ezekiel's son of

---

163 On this see Dodd, *According to the Scriptures*, 117, who says: "To say, as is often said, that the OT knows nothing of a suffering Son of Man is inaccurate." He also thinks that Ps 8, Ps 80 and Dan 7:13 were used by NT authors as *testimonia*. Another scholar who argues for a suffering Son of Man in Dan is C.F.D. Moule, *The Phenomenon of the NT*, 82—99, esp. 87ff. The idea of a suffering Messiah identified with the Son of Man is held also by Davies, *Paul and Rabbinic Judaism*, 280, esp. n. 1. France, *TynBul* 19 (1968) 52, on the other hand, objects that "to suggest that He (sc. Jesus) derived not only the future glory but also the earthly sufferings from Daniel 7 is not only inconsistent with His actual use of that passage, but also robs His self-understanding of its most distinctive feature, the combination into a single programme of the contrasting fates of the Servant and the Son of Man." Without doubt France has here overemphasized the future aspects of the 'SM' in Dan 7 to the detriment of the 'SM's' present solidarity with his people. The motif of humiliation (suffering) and exaltation is as much part of Dan as it is of the NT! There is therefore no good reason to dissociate the one from the other.

164 That vs. 25 speaks of the persecution of the 'saints of the Most High' rather than of the 'saints of the 'SM',' is owing to the fact that this Vision section is embedded within the Interpretation Part, which has already made the identification of the One like a Son of Man with the 'Most High'.

165 The term עליון apart from its use as a name for God (e.g. Gen 14:18ff.; Ps 21:8; 46:5) occurs 22 times with the meaning 'upper', 'high', 'highest', 'exalted' referring for the most part to things, but sometimes also to persons (e.g. Dt 26:19; 28:1; Ps 89:27).

man. In Ez the son of man is the prophet himself, who sees a vision of the glory of the Lord. In Dan the 'SM' is part of that vision. He is closely associated with the עתיק יומין (= 'the Ancient One'), who is the equivalent of Ezekiel's circumlocutional דמות כמראה אדם (= 'A Likeness like the appearance of a Human Being') and the still more circumlocutional הוא מראה דמות כבוד-יהוה (= 'The Appearance of the Likeness of the Glory of the Lord'). Daniel has boldly simplified Ezekiel's descriptions, but has ascribed to his 'SM' a higher function than that which Ezekiel's son of man has, and hence carried over to him characteristics belonging properly to Yahweh himself[165a].

The question now is, How has this come about? Or, Is it possible to account for Daniel's use of the expression "One like a son of man" to designate the exalted Figure which plays such an important role in this chapter? It seems to me that it is possible to answer this question affirmatively and to make a *prima-facie* case along the following lines.

To start with, it may be readily conceded that Daniel had at his disposal the OT concept of son of man, but that concept could not account adequately for Daniel's 'SM'. Daniel's 'SM' is neither a human being nor is he charged with the predominantly negative traits of the OT expression. It would, therefore, appear that the best avenue is to go via the Book of Ezekiel, which seems to provide a precedent for Daniel's procedure. It is true that Ezekiel uses the expression son of man of himself frequently, but that usage, for obvious reasons, cannot be the only or essential prototype for Daniel's 'SM'. Daniel 7 has at its core a theophany whose closest OT parallel is Ez 1. In that highly symbolical chapter two symbolical descriptions appear conspicuous, the description of the "living creatures" and the description of Yahweh. The dominant feature in the description of the "living creatures" (חיות) is their animal symbolism: each of the four creatures has *one* human face and *three* animal faces. But Yahweh is described entirely in human imagery. The depiction of Yahweh in human form may have part of its explanation in the genius of Hebrew religion (imitated in Christian art), which, unlike Egyptian, Babylonian, Canaanite, etc. religion, generally discouraged the portrayal of Yahweh in animal form. In fact the depiction of Yahweh by any image, animal or human, was strictly prohibited. However, Hebrew thought made allowance for metaphorical or symbolical language in speaking about Yahweh and this usually took the form of anthropomorphism. This explains Daniel's choice of a 'human being' to symbolize the second Figure. If Yahweh is to be spoken of in terms of symbols at all, then the most fitting imagery to use is the human form, the crown of God's creation (cf. Ps 8). But another, and perhaps more important, reason is undoubtedly the Hebrew belief that God had created man in his own "image" and in his own "likeness"

165a That Ez's throne-vision lies behind Dan 7 and 1 En 46f. is recognized by Fabry, TWAT IV, 270.

(בצלמנו כדמותנו) (Gen 1:24). It could, therefore, be reasoned that if man had been created in the image and likeness of God, then the most natural and fitting way to depict God would be in human form. Ezekiel's description of Yahweh as "A Likeness like the Appearance of Man"(דמות כמראה אדם) would thus seem to be essentially the reverse of "(let us make) Man in our Image, like our Likeness" (נעשה) אדם בצלמנו כדמותנו) of Gen 1:26!

Ezekiel's symbolism may well have functioned as a prototype for Daniel. At any rate it explains how a Jew, any Jew, (and therefore also Daniel) could reason. However, Daniel's vision involves two Beings. The Supreme Being and his throne are depicted in a way strongly reminiscent of Ezekiel's theophany, the most conspicuous difference being that in Daniel the Transcendent One is described as "Ancient of Days" (עתיק יומין). Ezekiel's description of Yahweh as דמות כמראה אדם seems to be the imagery drawn upon in the description of Daniel's second Figure (sc. the 'SM'). Ezekiel's circumlocution, originally applied to Yahweh himself, could not be simply transferred by Daniel to this other Figure without any modification. The depiction of Yahweh as "an Old Man" (i.e. "Ancient of Days" or "Aged One") has undoubtedly influenced the depiction of the Second Being as "a son of man". Though Emerton's and Morgenstern's theses are unacceptable in the way in which they have been presented, it must be recognized that the descriptions of the "Ancient of Days" or "Aged One" and of the ". . . son of man" imply the seniority of the former Figure. That 'son of man' actually means a 'human being' rather than 'a son of a/the man' is beside the point. On the analogy of Ezekiel's "A Likeness like the Appearance of a Human Being" Daniel could construct his own "One like a Human Being" and ascribe to this Figure characteristics and attributes which strictly were Yahweh's prerogative. It would, therefore, appear that Ezekiel's depiction of God and his throne has served to supply the raw material for Daniel's depiction of his "Aged One" and his throne, while Ezekiel's description of Yahweh as "A Likeness like the Appearance of a Human Being" was the prototype for Daniel's description of his "One like a Human Being". At any rate Ezekiel's theophany explains the thought process by which Daniel as a Jew could have come to describe his Second exalted Being as "One like a Son of Man".

Here, the Davidic, or political, messiah has to give place to a totally different conception of 'messianism' — one that is in line with the outlook of the Book as a whole[166]. If we understand the Danielic 'SM' messianic-

166 Many authors have advocated a messianic interpretation for the 'SM' in Daniel. Of these may be mentioned: Hävernick, Hengstenberg, Keil, Pusey, Zöckler, Von Lengerke, Ewald, Behrmann, Kranichfeld, Daniel, 277ff.; Bleek, in JdTh 5 (1860) 58 n.; Hilgenfeld, Jüdische Apokalyptik 45f. Rosenmüller, In Danielem, 231; Riem, Messianic Prophecy, 193ff. Schultz, Old Testament Theology, II, 439; Str-B, I, 956; Welch, Visions of the End, 129f.; Oesterly, The Jews and Judaism, 152ff.; Albright, From Stone Age to Christianity, 290ff.

ally we need at least to define the way in which we do so. If by Messiah is meant the Davidic King who sets his people free, causes them to dwell in peace and prosperity, exalts them over their enemies, etc., etc., then the 'SM' does not conform to this pattern. The concept of 'SM' belongs to a new messianic conception brought about by the events of the exile[167].

The 'SM' is no Davidic Messiah in the Jewish royal succession, but a heavenly being without descent. He does not win his kingly power by means of battle with Israel's armies against Israel's enemies, but receives it from God at the judgment. Nor is his kingly rule confined to Israel, rather it is universal, and not temporal, but eternal. His enemies are not merely human, but in the first place celestial beings.

If the 'SM' is to be understood of the Messiah, then Daniel's conception of messianism runs counter to what is often thought of as the traditional Jewish conception of an earthly messiah. The 'SM', distinct from the Ancient One, but possessing divine status[168], is ascribed glory and power

---

Muilenburg, *JBL* 79 (1960) 200f.; Young, *The Son of Man*, 1958; Dhanis, *Greg* 45 (1964) 5—59; Longenecker, *JETS* 12 (1969) 151—8; Marshall, *EvQ* 42 (1970) 81; France, *Jesus and the OT* 1971, e.g. 135ff.

    The notion that the Danielic 'SM' is the Messiah, is open to question, or at least to correction. In the first place the understanding of Dan 7:13f. at a later period (e.g. I En) is no guarantee in itself that Daniel understood the term so. In the second place, there is no overt notion of Messiah in chapter 7, though the term occurs at 9:25.

167 In dealing with the messianic hope Schürer rightly demarcates the earlier from the later hope: "The hope of the pre-exilic prophets was that the community would be morally purified and cleansed of all its bad elements; that it would flourish unmolested and respected in the midst of the Gentile world, its enemies either destroyed or forced to acknowledge Israel and its God; that it would be ruled by a just, wise and powerful king of the house of David, so that internal justice, peace and joy would prevail; and even that all natural evils would be annihilated and a condition of unclouded bliss come into being" (*History of the Jewish People*, II, 493). This vision, which was never fullfilled, says Schürer, "was ... substantially modified in later ages, partly during the time of the later prophets, but particularly in the post-biblical period" (493) ... "After the downfall of the last Gentile kingdom, God himself would take the sceptre in his hand and found a kingdom in which he, the heavenly king, would rule through his people" (493). Why God should need a people as intermediaries in order to rule the world is never explained, but the notion is apparently based on the supposition that the 'SM' symbolizes the people of Israel. Developments in messianic expectation, such as the extension of the hope to embrace all mankind and the Messiah's character as universal Judge and Ruler, "combined with the failure of political messianism in A.D. 70 and 135, are associated with a further characteristic distinguishing the later expectation from that of earlier ages: it became more transcendental, more and more transposed into the supernatural, the ultramundane ... By a miraculous act of God, the one (sc. world) would be destroyed and the other called into existence" (495). This fair summary of the transformation of messianic expectation halts in one important respect: the historical context in which it is placed. It is the thesis of the present study that the transformation of the messianic expectation from the strictly earthly and national Davidic messiah into a supernatural, universalistic and transcendental Messiah and the "universal act of God", whereby an end was to be put to the old aeon and the new aeon was to be ushered in, were not first attained after A.D. 70 and 135, as Schürer would have us believe, but are already the concepts with which the author of Daniel is wrestling. The 'SM' is not the faithful Jews, as Schürer thinks (497f.) but this new conception of the Messiah, this new type of Messiah, who bears hardly any resemblance

that are regularly predicated of God. Whether the author thought of two divine principles, of an older and a younger deity, of a concrete manifestation of God's glory, or of a self-projection of God, is idle to speculate. We are on the same wavelength as Daniel when we understand the nature of his 'SM' in the kind of way Jesus, in interpreting Ps 110:1, showed the fallacy of the current Jewish understanding of the messiah: εἰ οὖν Δαυὶδ καλεῖ αὐτὸν κύριον, πῶς υἱὸς αὐτοῦ ἐστιν; (Mt 22:45)[169]. No human messiah will do for Daniel.

It is simply a truism that the author of Dan has given up on humanity (which he considers as having been reduced to bestiality) and has centered his hopes upon a direct divine intervention. This is set forth in chapter 2 by means of the "Stone cut without human hands" and in chapter 7 by the 'SM'. It is not to be wondered at if the more personal representation of these — that of the 'SM' — in time established itself in certain circles (e.g. IV Ezra, I Enoch, the NT) as a serviceable messianic title.

F. Conclusions

The attempts to interpret the Danielic 'SM' with the help of various Near Eastern reconstructions of possible backgrounds are shown to be unsuccessful and lacking in credibility.

The great majority of scholars have concentrated their efforts on identifying the Danielic 'SM' with a biblical entity especially within Daniel itself. An examination of the two most widely held interpretations, the Israelite and the angelic, shows their inadequacy; these theories are based on a faulty exegesis of Dan 7.

A careful exegesis of Dan 7 reveals that the 'SM' is portrayed as a

---

to the traditional messiah. And the catalyst for the transformation of the messianic hope, was surely not the fall of Jerusalem in A.D. 70 or 135, but the exile and its aftermath.

168 Cf. his coming with the clouds. Furthermore, the plural 'thrones' probably indicates one for the Ancient One and one for the 'SM'. This understanding probably underlies Jesus' words to the Jewish authorities ὄψεσθε τὸν υἱὸν τοῦ ἀνθρώπου καθήμενον ἐκ δεξιῶν τῆς δυνάμεως (Mt 26:64). See also Guilding, EvQ 23 (1951) 212. According to bT Sanh 38b R. Akiba thought Dan 7:9 spoke of two thrones, one for the Ancient One and one for David, i.e. the Messiah. The Jewish aversion to the title 'Son of Man', because of the Christian application on Jesus, is here obvious. Despite that, Akiba did not escape the rebuke, "How long will you profane the divine glory, Akiba?" Cf. France, Jesus and the OT, 186f. See further Jocz, The Jewish People and Jesus Christ, 186 (see further Ch. Three: Rabbinism).

169 Perhaps in no other OT text is the Messiah — if it is a question of the Messiah — more clearly ascribed supernatural status than in the Danielic presentation of the 'SM'. No doubt this text must have contributed to forging the variant understanding of the 'Son of Man' held by Jesus. For Jewish understandings see the survey in Schürer, History of the Jewish People, rev. ed. II, 1979, 497–547.

heavenly Being with honors and powers normally predicated of God, and is, in the Interpretation Part of the chapter, identified with the *ʿElyônîn*.
This Figure is distinguished from the Most High, which is another name for the Ancient of Days or God. The 'SM', as a Figure alongside the Ancient of Days, may have been suggested by the concept of the Messiah as God's vicegerent on earth, but is quite different from this latter concept and has probably been developed from the imagery of Ez 1. The positing of such a Transcendental Figure is dictated by Daniel's dynamic conception of history and of the human situation (so-called apocalyptic), in which the concept of the traditional messiah is deemed insufficient and must, therefore, be superseded by a new conception of the Agent of God's Kingdom and the Vindicator and Leader of God's people. The nationalistic horizons are unable to bound the new ideas, whose perspective is universal, indeed, cosmic.

Chapter III

The 'Son of Man' in Some Strands of Jewish
and Rabbinic Thought

A. Introductory

Two points need to be made clear here. One, the understanding of Dan 7:13 in Jewish thought need not coincide with how the Book of Daniel intended its 'SM'. Certain Jews could have put a new content in an expression borrowed from Dan. However, if it is found that Jewish literature understood the SM in a way that is in harmony with our findings in the case of the Danielic 'SM', this circumstance ought to strengthen belief in the existence of an interpretative tradition reflecting the substantially correct understanding of Dan 7:13 f.[1] The other point is that the NT understanding of the Danielic 'SM' need not have come from or been conditioned by the understanding found in other literature. It is conceivable that the NT could have developed its own interpretative tradition, which peradventure was a continuation of Daniel's intended sense, or a departure from it, or which just happened to coincide with a particular Jewish interpretation, or stood over against it. However, if it is found that the Christian understanding of the SM has important similarities to an interpretation found in Jewish sources, it ought to strengthen the case for the existence of an interpretative tradition among the Jews which was more than a mere backyard oddity. This would moreover imply that the NT, so far from presenting an arbitrary or tendentious interpretation of the SM concept, actually belonged to an important stream of Jewish 'messianic' interpretation, at any rate, important enough to have survived[2]. Furthermore, and what is even more relevant to the recent debate on the SM, the substantial convergence of the Book of Daniel, some of the Jewish literature and the NT in their understanding of the SM ought, a) to have a bearing on the discussion of Dan 7 as a possible background to the NT concept of the SM[3], and b) if the previous point is secured, it ought to

---

1 'Correct' in the sense that the interpretation coincides with the Author's intention.
2 This finding is in agreement with Stone's findings about the existence in Judaism of various streams of tradition (see his *Scriptures, Sects and Visions*, 1980, esp. chs. 5–8).
3 Abbott, *The Son of Man*, 1910, 82–102, thinks that the NT title Son of Man is influenced by

raise a number of questions, such as the relation of this SM type of messianology to the OT messianic concept, whether the OT concept of the Messiah underwent severe changes in inter-testamental and NT times, whether there were competing interpretations of messianism, and others.

The term son of man occurs very sparingly in Jewish literature. The Apocrypha contain it six times[4]. Apart from Tob 7:7, which is a special case[5], the expression occurs in the usual OT senses of 'frailty', 'badness', etc. None of these instances is of any importance for the continuing discussion of Daniel's 'SM'.

In the Pseudepigrapha the expression son of man is found only in I Enoch, while the concept occurs in IV Ezra. The messianic time is furthermore described in II Baruch[6], the Psalms of Solomon[7] and the Sibylline Oracles III, 785 ff.[8], while V.414 ff. speaks of "a blessed man" "from the plains of heaven", who receives universal dominion from God[9]. Dan 7:13 is referred to occasionally in rabbinic writings. The concept is absent from the Qumran material[10].

Of this literature, the texts that make the most of Dan 7, interpreting its 'SM' with various embellishments, are the *Parables* of I Enoch and IV Ezra. The Sibyllines and II Baruch have more distant echoes of Dan 7. I shall therefore concentrate on I Enoch and IV Ezra.

B. The *Parables* of I Enoch

The term son of man occurs in the *Parables* (i.e. I En 37–71) 16

Ezekiel. Similarly, P. Parker, *JBL* 60 (1941) 151–57; G.S. Duncan, *Jesus, Son of Man*, 1947; R.K. Harrison, *EvQ* 23 (1951) 46–50.

4 I Esdr 4:37; Tob 7:7; Judith 8:12, 16; Sap 9:6; Sir 17:30.
5 Raquel on hearing that Tobias is Tobit's son, exclaims: ὁ τοῦ καλοῦ καὶ ἀγαθοῦ ἀνθρώπου (υἱός)! A B omit υἱός.
6 Especially chs. 29, 30, 39 and 40. See Charles, *The Apocalypse of Baruch*, in Charles, *AP*, II, 1913, 470–526; Violet, *Die Apokalypsen des Esra und des Baruch in deutscher Gestalt*, 1924; Klijn, *Die Syrische Baruch-Apokalypse* (*JSHRZ*, Bd. V), 1976, 103–84; id., *2 (Syriac Apocalypse of) Baruch* in Charlesworth, *OTP*, 615–52.
7 Especially Ps Sol 17 and 18. See edition by Holm-Nielsen, *Die Psalmen Salomos* (*JSHRZ*, Bd. IV, 1977).
8 The passage is reproduced in Virgil, *Eclogae* IV, esp. lines 21f.
9 Bowman, *ET* 59 (1947–8) 286 thinks "heavenly man" would represent the Aramaic *bar-nash* and be influenced by Dan 7:13.
10 F.F. Bruce, *Biblical Exegesis in the Qumran Texts*, 63ff., sees an implicit existence of the Son of Man concept in Qumran, which in 1QpHab V, 3–6 speaks of judgment being committed to God's elect. Since he identifies the Danielic 'SM' with the saints, and moreover, since in I Enoch the Son of Man is identified with the Elect One, Bruce considers that the Qumran elect ones are the Danielic 'SM'. In view of our discussion, above, this identification is considered inappropriate. Moreover, the term 'son of man' is actually absent from these texts, and no amount of indirect identifications can compensate for this absence. 1QS XI, 20 בן אדם

times[11] but nowhere else in I En. Scholarly opinion has generally dated this work, which is extremely difficult to date, in the I B.C.[12], though some, nowadays, would incline to a first century A.D. date[13]. Milik[14], on the grounds of its absence from Qumran, would prefer to place it around A.D. 270, and to regard it as a Christian composition[15].

1. Excursus: The Date of the Parables

The question of the date of the *Parables* has become a lively subject of debate in recent years, especially since the publication of Milik's work[16]. The impetus has been given by the fact that the *Parables* is not represented in the Qumran MSS, though all other parts of I Enoch are[17]. This negative evidence from Qumran has been evaluated differently;

(where the definite art. is probably an afterthought being written above the א, see Moule, *The Origin of Christology*, 16) is a reflection of the thought of Ps 8:4.

11 As a seventeenth instance may be considered the initial introduction of this figure (46:1), which in Danielic fashion, and in view of the employment of the expression 'son of man' in the ensuing description once for all makes clear that the figure spoken of was not a man or human being, but one "whose countenance had the appearance of a man". Hereby the author underlines his continuity with and indebtedness to Daniel.

12 E.g. Charles. *The Book of Enoch or I Enoch*, 1912, p. liv, 94—79 or 70—64 B.C. (Similarly in his *APOT* II, 171); Schürer, *History of the Jewish People*, etc. 3rd ed., 1898, 192—209: under Herod the Great; Frey, *Suppl. Dict. Bible*, I, cols. 360—4: Maccabaean; Foakes-Jackson, — Lake, *Beginnings of Christianity*, I, 354: mid first century B.C.. Oesterley, *Jews and Judaism*, 80: Post-Maccabaean; Sjöberg, *Der Menschensohn im äthiopischen Henochbuch*, 38 : during the time of the early procurators, i.e. c. 40 B.C.; Rowley, *Relevance of Apocalyptic*, rev. ed. 1963, pp. 54ff.: sometime in the II century B.C.; Russel, *Method and Message*, 52: presumably in the pre-Christian era; Stone, *Scriptures, Sects, Visions*, 59: I century B.C.; Hammershaimb, *Første Enoksbog* in *De Gammeltestamentlige Pseudepigrafer*, 74: I B.C.; Borsch, *The Son of Man*, 146: before the birth of Christ ;Jeremias, *TDNT* V, 687, n. 245 and Stuhlmacher, *Werden und Wirken*, 425 n. 49 in the last third part of the I century B.C.

13 E.g. Schürer *The History of the Jewish People*, Vol. II, new ed. 1979, 505. Knibb, *NTS* 25 (1979) 345—9. See further under Excursus on the Date of the Parables.

14 *The Books of Enoch*, 96.

15 The absence of I En 37—71 from the Qumran Library is far from decisive evidence that the work is post-Christian. Other explanations are possible. (Cf. Borsch, *The Son of Man*, 146 and Thompson, *ET* 72 (1960—1)125). Furthermore, the identification of Enoch with the Son of Man — so offensive to the Old Master of apocalyptic that he did not hesitate to change the 'thou' to 'He' etc. (Charles, *The Book of Enoch*, 144f.) — if not inadvertently made on account of a lost section there, may have been a later (post-Christian) intentional change to deprive Christians from further Jewish support for their Son of Man Christology. (So most recently Black, *ET* 95 (1984) 201). On the other hand there would have been no motive for such an identification before Christianity, and in the light of its description of the Son of Man, it is difficult to conceive of the original Jewish composition having created such an identification. See note 121.

16 *The Books of Enoch*, 1976.

17 The value of such negative evidence is diminished further when it is remembered that 1 Enoch is a collection of various independent works, written by different authors and at different times! Why expect that the tastes of the Ethiopic translator — especially if he also was the collector — should coincide with those of the Qumran community?

some have been undisturbed by it, while others seem to have made more
of it than such evidence from silence could warrant scientifically: they
gave up the pre-Christian date of the *Parables* overnight. This eagerness to
keep pace with scientific progress in the case of the dating of the *Parables*
contrasts sharply with the pronounced reluctance in giving up an out-
moded Maccabaean date for Daniel, as for example the Qumran evidence
seems to demand[18].

The reason for this behaviour in relation to the *Parables* has its explanation in another historical circumstance. The silence of Qumran would
have proved an altogether insufficient factor had it not concurred with a
trend in certain quarters to give an alternative interpretation of the title
Son of Man. As we saw in Chapter One, the attempt has been made during
the past hundred years to resolve this title to an Aramaic equivalent for
'one', 'someone' or 'I', etc. and that this attempt has been intensified in
the last two decades by Vermes and others[19]. The direction of movement
has been away from Christology to 'anthropology'. The titular use of the
expression came therefore to be contested and its messianic character to
be questioned. Since much of the Son of Man content in the Gospels was
understood against the background of an assumed Son of Man concept
current in Judaism before Jesus, and evidenced chiefly in the *Parables*, a
late dating of this work would result not only in undermining belief in
the existence of the Son of Man concept in Judaism, but also in depriving
Jesus of all knowledge, and consequently use, of such a concept. Thus, the
silence of Qumran, in itself an innocent fact, by being juxtaposed to the
current burning issue of the Son of Man debate, has received exaggerated
emphasis.

Milik allowed himself to be overimpressed by the Qumran silence and
set the pattern for others[20]. He pointed further to the silence of ancient
versions and early Christian writers. These arguments have been met e.g.

---

18 Some of the Qumran MSS of Daniel are quite old, particularly 4Q Dan[c], which is written in
    a "semicursive script" and, is dated by Cross to 100–50 B.C. (*The Bible and the Ancient
    Near East*, 149). The Aramaic dialect in which the Qumran MSS of Daniel are written is the so-
    called Imperial Aramaic, in use from 700 to 200 B.C. (cf. Fitzmyer, *A Wandering Aramean*,
    61). It is therefore a scientific *non-sequitur* when Hartman- DiLella, *Daniel*, 74, fully aware
    that "It seems best to place Daniel here" (i.e. 700–200 B.C.), still date it during the Macca-
    baean period. A similar conclusion would seem to be in order with respect to the comparison
    of Daniel with the Genesis Apocryphon. The MS itself was dated by the editors, Avigad-
    Yadin in the I B.C. while the original composition "must have been contemporary with or
    previous to the date of the composition of Jubilees, the Book of Noah etc". Its Aramaic
    seems to be later than the Imperial Aramaic found in Daniel and Ezra (Winter, *TLZ* 4 (1957)
    260 and Kutscher, in *Aspects of the Dead Sea Scrolls*, 161). Kutscher places it in the period
    I B.C. – I A.D., (22). Fitzmyer agrees with this (*Genesis Apocryphon*, 17ff.). However
    Vermes, *Scripture and Tradition*, 96 n. 2, prefers a date in II B.C. After comparing its gram-
    mar, style and vocabulary with those of Daniel, Archer (in *New Perspectives on the OT*,
    160–9) concludes that the Maccabaean date of Daniel is impossible.
19 Vermes' first results as presented in his Oxford lecture, date to 1965.
20 Cf. Black, *ET* 88 (1976) 5–8, "negative arguments, in particular the silence of Qumran and

by Mearns[21] and Knibb[22]. But this silence in itself could not determine the date of the book, so it had to be sought in other circumstances. By way of positive argument Milik argued that the *Parables* was in form close to the Sib. Oracles[23], and that its angels have wings (I En 61:1), a feature first known in Christian iconography of the fourth century, though he admits that the Seraphim and Cherubim (i.e. Isa 6; Ez 1) are an exception[24]. His main positive argument for dating the *Parables* around A.D. 270 is that he interprets I En 56:5—7 of the events of A.D. 260—70. However, these events hardly correspond with the conditions of the Enoch text. First, Sapor I was king of Armenia, not strictly of Parthia or Media. Second, Sapor I invaded Syria, not Palestine. Milik tries to obviate the difficulties by understanding "the Parthians and Medes" of I En 56:5—7 as the Palmyreans[25] under Zenobia, who took Syria and Egypt but "spared the city of Jerusalem, for Zenobia was well known for her Jewish and Christian sympathies"[26]. However, — and this is a third objection — the Enoch text seems to demand either successful resistance or successful political out-manoeuvering[27] as the salvation of Jerusalem from an invading force, rather than Zenobia's pro-Judeo-Christian feelings. Milik has failed to prove his case.

Prior to Milik, Hindley[28] had tried to find in I En 56:5—7 a description of Trajan's campaign towards the Persian Gulf in A.D. 113—17 when his rear was attacked and a Roman army was defeated. Again the chief actors were Armenians not Parthians or Medes. Hindley thinks that it is not impossible that the Armenians and their allies turned toward Antioch, which is only 300 miles from Jerusalem, and that this might be the 'event' alluded to by I En 56:5—7! There is, of course, no historical basis for this. It is a reconstruction of what Hindley hopes may have happened. It is obvious that Hindley has left the domain of history and wanders in that of speculation. To corroborate his reconstruction he interprets I En 53:7 of the Antioch earthquake of A.D. 115. It requires strong imagination to see even a faint echo in I En 53:7 of the Antioch earthquake as described by Dio Cassius[29]. Surely the *Parables* text relates to the general theme of

---

of versional and patristic tradition, seem absolutely decisive for the mediaeval origins" of the *Parables*. In the Paris Seminar, however, he acknowledged the Jewish character of the work (perhaps in reaction to Christianity) and placed it around A.D. 100. Even more radically in *ET* 95 (1984) 200—6 (see end of this Excursus).

21 *ET* 87 (1978) 118—9; *id.*, *NTS* 25 (1979), 361ff.

22 *NTS* 25 (1979), 346ff.

23 *The Books of Enoch*, 92ff. This has been contested by Knibb, *NTS* 25 (1979) 348f.

24 *The Books of Enoch*, 97. See also Mearns' remarks, *NTS* 25 (1979) 362.

25 This identification is called "pure fiction" by Greenfield-Stone, *HTR* 70 (1977) 59. See also Knibb, *NTS* 25 (1979) 349f.

26 Milik, *The Books of Enoch*, 95f.

27 Cf. 1 En 56:7 "But the city ... shall be a hindrance to their horses". Isaac, *OTP* I, 39, has the variant translation "stumblingblock".

28 *NTS* 14 (1967—8) 551—65.

29 Dio Cassius 68:25, § 6.

the Return and is inspired by Isa 30:25; 40:4; 41:15—18; 44:3. Hindley's thesis is unconvincing[30].

Knibb offers a number of good arguments against Milik and Hindley, but his positive arguments for dating the *Parables* to the end of the first century A.D. are slender and circular. As in Milik's case, the silence of Qumran weighs heavily. His other argument is that the presentation of the Son of Man in the *Parables* fits best the end of the first Christian century, because the judicial functions of the Son of Man are analogous to those of the Messiah and the Son of Man in II Bar 40:1 f.; 72:2 ff. and IV Ezra 12—13[31]. This argument is circular since these similarities can and have been explained as conscious echoes of the *Parables* in these works[32]. This is not the way to date the *Parables*. It is further weakened by Knibb's own admission that the *Parables* is wholly Jewish[33] — and not at all Christian — not akin to the Sibyllines[34] — as Milik suggests[35] — its original language was semitic[36] and although rejecting Charles' list of NT citations and allusions to the *Parables*, he does not seem to get the better of the argument against Theisohn, who rigorously and convincingly works out Matthew's use of the *Parables*[37].

Mearns[38] considers the *Parables* a Jewish-Christian work, from around A.D. 40, whose eschatology was taken over by the NT and hence there was no need for its dissemination in ancient authors. Its Christian provenience explains its absence from Qumran[39]. The direction of dependence is "from a cruder prototype in the *Parables* to a more developed version in the New Testament"[40]. The decisive factor in dating the *Parables* is its being known by the author of the Testament of Abraham, who in its shorter recension[41], polemicizes against Enoch's status as eschatological Judge in I En 71. Since Mearns thinks the NT contains clear allusions to the Test Abr, having been written before Paul developed his own eschatology in his Thessalonian correspondence[42], the date arrived at for the *Parables* is around A.D. 40[43]. I En 56:5—7 could have been inspired by the events of 40—38 B.C.[44]

---

30 See also the criticism by Knibb, *NTS* 25 (1979) 354f.

31 *NTS* 25 (1979) 258f. Knibb has no confidence in the historical value of 1 En 56:5—7.

32 See below.

33 *NTS* 25 (1979) 349, 351.

34 *Ibid.*, 349.

35 *The Books of Enoch*, 92ff.

36 *NTS* 25 (1979) 350.

37 Cf. his evasiveness in *NTS* 25 (1979) 357.

38 *ET* 87 (1978) 118—19; and *NTS* 25 (1979) 360—69.

39 *ET* 87 (1978) 118; *NTS* 25 (1979) 362f.

40 *ET* 87 (1978) 118; cf. *NTS* 25 (1979) 365.

41 Test. Abr. Recension B, ch. 11. Cf. also Milik, *The Books of Enoch*, 363f.

42 *NTS* 25 (1979) 363f.

43 *Ibid.*, 368f.

44 *Ibid.*, 362.

If it could be proved that the Test Abr has influenced the NT and has itself been influenced by the *Parables*, it would be a further corroboration of the other evidence for the early date of the latter work. However, Mearns' view that the *Parables* is a Jewish-Christian work lacks solid basis.

Greenfield and Stone[45] rightly reject the silence of Qumran as a valid argument for dating a book. They counter that the Book of Esther also is missing from Qumran. Would this imply that it did not exist?[46] On the positive side, they consider the title Son of Man as unmistakable evidence for the Jewishness of the work and, with Sjöberg, exclude Christian influence[47]. The Parthian invasion is identified as that of 40-38 B.C.[48], when the Parthians actually held Jerusalem for a short period. Greenfield-Stone see another historical circumstance in I En 67:8—9, where they identify the "waters" "for the healing of the body" as those of Callirhoe, to which Herod had recourse according to Josephus[49]. They thus conclude:

> "These two references indicate that the final composition of the *Similitudes* took place at some time during the first century C.E. They may be part of the original composition, or they may very well have been added to an already extant composition to give the reader historical instances of God's judgment. They strengthen the view that the *Similitudes* is a contemporary of the Qumran texts"[50].

The above brief review of some representative studies advocating a late date for the *Parables* has shown the complete absence of any compelling arguments for dating this work during the Christian era. Milik has found no following[51]. Nor is there any consensus among those who tentatively place the *Parables* in the first century A.D.: the exact date, the character of the work, the silence of Qumran, the NT use of it, all are at present open questions. Thus Charlesworth, in summarising the two Seminars on the Books of Enoch, held at Tübingen (1977) and Paris (1978), closes with the admission:

> "Yet the real issue remains open. Are these Jewish Parables pre-Christian and a source for understanding either Jesus' *ipsissima verba* or the theologies of the evangelists? Or, are they post-Christian and a significant development of the canonical gospels, or a Jewish reaction to Christianity"[52].

The excursion into the history of Parthia has not produced any concrete results. The chief problem here is the meagre content in the refer-

---

45 *HTR* 70 (1977) 51—66.

46 *Ibid.*, 55.

47 *Ibid.*, 58.

48 *Ibid.*, 58ff.

49 *Ant* 17, 6, 5 (171—3); *Bell. Jud.* 1, 33, 5 (657—8).

50 *HTR* 70 (1977) 60. One may object here that a reader could hardly see in 1 En 67:8—9 an obvious instance of God's judgment on Herod.

51 Even Black has given up Milik's date. An exception is Sanders, *Paul and Palestinian Judaism*, 374.

52 *NTS* 25 (1979) 322f.

ence to "the Parthians and Medes" in I En 56:5–7. The text seems to demand:

1. A Partho-Median invasion.
2. The capture of Palestine.
3. Failure to take Jerusalem, owing either to military reversals, or to diplomatic outmanoeuvering.
4. Dissention among the allied invading forces, resulting in
5. The dissipation or self-annihilation of their armies.

Considered purely as a possible threat to Syria and Palestine, it may be said that the Parthians proved a potential menace from the time they secured their independence in 230 B.C.[53] However, the only occasion on which they in fact took Palestine was in 40–38 B.C.[54] On this occasion Orodes and his son Pacorus, with the assistance of Labienus – a Roman deserter –, seized Asia Minor, Syria and Palestine and placed Antigonus as king and high priest in Jerusalem[55]. They were driven out by Ventidius Bassus in 39 B.C. and crushed by him the following year. This juncture of Partho-Jewish history seems to be the one that suits best, if not entirely, the conditions of I En 56:5–7[56]. However, it may all the same be that I En 56:5–7 treats of the general theme of God's wrath against the enemies of his people, patterned on the Sennacherib incident (II Kings 19:32–35) and Ezekiel's prophecies against Gog (chs. 38–39). I conclude, therefore, that though historical considerations cannot with certainty settle the question of the date of the *Parables*, the fact of the Parthian threat alone

---

53 These Asiatic hordes, vassals of the Seleucids, formed themselves into an independent king-dom around 230 B.C. and thereafter proved a constant menace to the Seleucids and Romans. (*IEE* IV, 402, 406f.) Wars against the Parthians, either to ward off their attack or recapture lands lost to them, were fought by e.g. Seleucus II (230 B.C.); Antiochus III (230–09 B.C.); Antiochus IV (164 B.C.), Demetrius II (141–39 B.C., who was captured by them); Antiochus VII (lost his life 130 B.C.); Antiochus X (lost his life 92 B.C.), (*IEE*, V, 179, 194).

54 The Parthian menace was particularly real during Mithridates II's reign, when he annexed Mesopotamia and Armenia around 97 B.C. A little later Tigranes of Armenia (related to the Parthians) extended his territories into Asia Minor, Media, a great part of Syria and styled himself "Great King" (*IEE* V, 194). Around 92 B.C. the Armenians actually took Damascus and threatened Judea and Jerusalem. Salome Alexandra, the widow of Alexander Jannaeus, had to buy Jewish freedom quite expensively (Jos., *Ant.* XIII, 419–21; *Bel. Jud.* I, 116; *IEE*, V, 194; Schürer, *History of the Jewish People*, I 231. This event seems to fit condition (3) above, more than any other known event, but the enemies were now Armenians not Parthians. The Parthians posed a threat again around 63 B.C. following Pompey's treachery, and especially in 53 B.C. after crushing Crassus at Carrhae. Their planned invasion of Antioch was staved off by Cassius in 51 B.C. (cf. Jos., *Ant.* XIV, 119ff., *Bel. Jud.* I, 180–2). But again nothing in all this meets the conditions of 1 En 56:5–7.

55 Jos., *Ant.* XIII, 330–69; *Bel. Jud.* I, 248–73; Schürer, *History of the Jewish People*, I, 278 –80; Bruce, *Israel and the Nations*, 189.

56 The objection has sometimes been made that according to Josephus, *Ant.* XIV, 337; *Bel. Jud.* I, 250, 256, the Jews far from seeing a threatening enemy, actually welcomed the Parthians. But this temporary friendliness, which after a while was given up (Jos., *Ant.* XIV, 398; *Bel. Jud.* I, 268f.), need not have been the view of our author. See Greenfield – Stone, *HTR* 70 (1977) 58.

points to some juncture of that people's history when they were a threat to the Jews, and that the most plausible juncture is obtained by the events of 40—38 B.C.[57] Absolute certainty is impossible here.

The only avenue open is to go via the literary connections of the *Parables* with works of the I century A.D.

1. *The Testament of Abraham*. In this work there are some striking conceptual and verbal parallels to the NT[58], so a literary connection is inescapable. The question however is: Which way did the influence move? Mearns has no doubt that the NT has borrowed from the Test Abr and that the latter polemicizes against the *Parables*. That would indeed be a neat way of settling the question of the date of the *Parables* prior to the NT, but it is, alas, not free from difficulties.

a. It is far from certain that Test Abr Recension B XI polemicizes against the supposed exaltation of Enoch to judgeship in I En 71. Enoch is nowhere in the *Parables* called judge, or raised to that function. Mearns deduces this from Enoch's supposed identity with the Son of Man, who is a Judge. (But see below.)

b. The judge in Test Abr B XI is Abel not Enoch! It may, therefore, with equal, if not better, reason be claimed that the Test Abr is on the borrowing side in its relation to the NT, and that it polemicizes against the NT claim that the eschatological Judge is the Son of Man (= Jesus).

c. Among the verbal phenomena — a number of which clearly bespeak a quite late date — two expressions seem to be decisive for a post-Christian date, at least for the final redaction with the Christian interpolations. One of them is the term τόν τρισάγιον ὕμνον (Test Abr Rec. A XX) which occurs first in Chrysostom[59]. The other is the expression δευτέρα

---

57 So Olmstead, *JAOS* 56 (1936) 255. It is clear that except for their identification of I En 67: 8—9 with Herod's visit to Callirhoe just before his death, Greenfield and Stone would have dated the *Parables* in the I century B.C., on the basis of the events of 40—38 B.C., just as Stone does in a later work, *Scriptures, Sects and Visions*, 59.

58   1. Test Abr A IV: ἐν ῥιπῇ ὀφθαλμοῦ of Michael's ascent to heaven may be compared with I Cor 15:52 of the translation of believers.

    2. Test Abr A VII: ἐγώ εἰμι Μιχαήλ ὁ παρεστηκώς ἐνώπιον καὶ ἀπεστάλην πρός σε is paralleled in Lk 1:19 of Gabriel's mission to Zacharias.

    3. Test Abr A XI: δύο ὁδούς · ἡ μία ὁδὸς στενή καὶ τεθλιμμένη καὶ ἡ ἐτέρα πλατεῖα καὶ εὐρύχωρος ... δύο πύλας· μία πύλη πλατεῖα, ... καὶ μία πύλη στενή ... ψυχὰς ὀλίγας εἰσερχομένας διὰ τῆς στενῆς πύλης ... ἡ ἀπάγουσα εἰς τὴν ζωήν ... ψυχὰς ὀλίγας εἰσερχομένας διὰ τῆς πλατείας πύλης ... ἡ ἀπάγουσα εἰς τὴν ἀπώλειαν is very close to Mt 7:13f.

    4. Test Abr A XIII: εἴ τινος τὸ ἔργον κατακαύσει τὸ πῦρ ... εἴ τινος τὸ ἔργον ... μὴ ἅψηται ... οὗτος δικαιοῦται has a parallel in 1 Cor 3:13f.

    5. Test Abr A XIII: of the place to which Abraham comes after death: ἔνθα οὐκ ἔστιν πόνος, οὐ λύπη, οὐ στεναγμός, ἀλλ᾽ εἰρήνη καὶ ἀγαλλίασις καὶ ζωὴ ἀτελείωτος recalls Rev 7:15—17 (with citations from Isa 25:8; 49:10 etc.); 19:6—8 and 21:3—4.

59 *Homiliae* 1:1. The term τρισάγιος occurs, according to Lampe, *Patristic Greek Lexicon*, 1409, for the first time in Didymus Maximus (died 398 A.D.), *Trinitate*, 2 :7 διὰ τοῦ τρισαγίου αἴνου, while τρισάγιος ὕμνος was introduced into the liturgy in 438 by Proclus, *CP*. The term does not occur in the early Christian authors according to *BAG*.

παρουσία (Test Abr Rec. A XIII), which is clearly Christian (cannot be Jewish) and occurs first in Justin[60].

d. Test Abr Rec. A XIII teaches three judgments: by Abel[61], by the twelve tribes of·Israel in connection with which the expression δευτέρα παρουσία is used, and by God himself at his ἐνδόξου ... παρουσίας. The substitution of Abel in the first judgment as well as of Israel's twelve tribes in the δευτέρα παρουσία, is no doubt in conscious polemic against the NT tenet of the Son of Man (= Jesus) as the eschatological Judge at his second parousia. Since neither the first nor the second judgment involves a transcendental figure, the Test Abr has to have a final — third — judgment by God himself. The polemic against Christianity is rather clumsily executed.

e. According to the Test Abr salvation is attained by having one's good deeds outweigh one's sins. This is in itself opposed to the corresponding teaching in the NT. However, when the author of Test Abr has Abraham himself admit and espouse that doctrine it sounds as an imitation of Paul's method in Galatians whereby he tries to prove the superiority of faith over the law by making Abraham the first believer. Once again the Test Abr is proved to be in conscious polemic against Pauline Christianity by using Paul's method in reverse.

On these and other grounds I consider the Test Abr to be a Jewish composition, which uses NT terminology and ideas consciously[62] to polemicize against Christian tenets[63]. This work cannot therefore be used to date the *Parables*.

2. *IV. Ezra.* There can hardly be any doubt that the author of IV Ezra was acquainted with and made use of the *Parables*. Charles has long ago presented a list of passages from the *Parables* that were utilized by IV Ezra: IV Ez 6:49–52 (cf. I En 60:7–9); IV Ez 7:32 f. (cf. I En 51:1, 3); IV Ez 7:37 (cf. I En 61:1; 60:6); IV Ez 7:36 (cf. I En 48:9 f., 27:3); IV Ez 7:125 (cf. I En 62:10). These parallels have been endorsed by Box[64], Myers[65] and recently by Metzger[66]. To these parallels I may add IV Ez 13:26 relating to the hidden character of the Son of Man, which is taken

---

60 See *Apology* 52:3; *Dialogue* 14:8; 31:1; 32:2; 40:4; 49:2; 51:2; 53:1; 54:1; 110:2; 111:1; 121:3.

61 Cf. οὗτος ἐστιν υἱος Ἀδάμ (easily recalling בן אדם or בר אנש) ... αὐτῷ δέδωκεν κρίσιν, κρῖναι τὸν κόσμον ... διὰ τοῦτο ἐνταῦθα ... ἐκ τοῦ υἱοῦ αὐτοῦ κρίνονται with Jn 5:27 καὶ ἐξουσίαν ἔδωκεν αὐτῷ κρίσιν ποιεῖν, ὅτι υἱὸς ἀνθρώπου ἐστίν.

62 Cf. e.g. Test Abr Rec. A XIII which contradicts Jesus (Mt 18:16) and Moses (Dt 19:15) by claiming that two witnesses are not enough to establish a charge.

63 Among those who hold a post-Christian date are James, *The Testament of Abraham*, II cent. A.D. Schmidt, *Le Testament d'Abraham* I, 117ff.: Recension B: I cent. A.D.; Recension A: II cent. A.D.; Janssen, *Testament Abrahams*, 198: Roman post-Christian times; Sanders, *Testament of Abraham*, (OTP I, 875) around 100 A.D.

64 *The Ezra-Apocalypse*, lxxf.

65 *I and II Esdras*, 310.

66 *The Fourth Book of Ezra*, 522f.

over from the *Parables*[67]. Finally, IV Ezra's treatment of the Son of Man
is reminiscent of I Enoch 46. Just as the author of the *Parables* had introduced the central figure of his work in Danielic fashion, but thereafter
dropped the simile part and made a title of the expression — that Son of
Man — so too, IV Ezra 13 probably introduced this figure with "(someone
in the) form of a Son of Man" (see below under IV Ezra), but then
dropped both 'form' and 'son of' and kept to 'Man' — the Man from the
Sea.

3. *The NT.* That the *Parables* are presupposed by the NT has been a firm
conclusion of scholarship. Charles, for example, presented a long list of
passages which, he thought, had been at work in the formation of many
NT ideas[68]. Knibb thinks that "in the case of most of these passages, there
is little more that a general similarity of thought or language"[69], but
granting that all of Charles' passages are not valid, there are at least some
that are and have "more than a general similarity in thought or language"!
One such example is the sitting of the Son of Man upon the throne of his
glory (see Mt 19:28, 25:31) — an expression which, especially in its contextual collocation, is to be found nowhere else[70].

Were it not for the silence of Qumran — a negative argument of dubious
value[71], — there would hardly be any reason to deny the pre-Christian
date of the *Parables* and the thesis that this work reflects a part of Jewish
thought at the time of Jesus[72]. With respect to the negative evidence of
Qumran, Black, one of the former champions of a late date on that score,
has recently made a radical turn. In his latest article on the Son of Man
problem, he writes: "Too much seems to me to have been made of the
argument from silence: the *Parables*, it is true, are not represented in the
Qumran fragments, but this argument is less impressive when it is realized
that these fragments constitute only about 5 per cent of the total Book."
He continues: "My own view is that the *Parables* contain pre-Christian
Jewish traditions, Hebrew and/or Aramaic, including some, at any rate of
the Son of Man visions, but I would now make one concession to the lateness of at least one part of the work: chapters 70—71, where Enoch is
himself identified . . . as the Son of Man . . . represents, as Lietzmann con-
tended, a later addition . . . It is even open to the suspicion that Enoch as

67 See e.g. 48:2, 6; 62:6f.; 69:26ff. Similarly Box, *The Ezra-Apocalypse*, 284f., and Myers, *I and II Esdras*, 310.
68 See the list in his *The Book of Enoch*, pp. xcv—ciii.
69 *NTS* 25 (1979), 355.
70 See my discussion in Chapter Four. See further the detailed study by Theisohn, *Der auserwählte Richter* — a book that came to hand just at the close of my investigation here — who comes to conclusions similar to mine.
71 This argument is rejected e.g. by Thompson, *ET* 72 (1961), p. 125; Borsch, *The Son of Man* 146f.; Mearns, *ET* 87 (1978), 118; *id. NTS* 25 (1979) 362ff.; Greenfield-Stone, *HTR* 70 (1977), 55f. See also Theisohn, *Der auserwählte Richter*, 149ff., for the influence of the Son of Man tradition on the Gospels.
72 Stone, *Scriptures, Sects and Visions*, 59.

Son of Man was an invention of late esoteric cabbalistic Judaism, as a Jewish rival to the gospel figure"[73]. This view accords well with my findings.

***

Though interpolations by writers acquainted with Christianity for I Enoch as a whole cannot be ruled out, it appears that the SM concept in the *Parables* is so integral to that work's contents[74], and the descriptions of him so widespread in the text, that it is practically impossible to think of "Christian" influence here[75]. The SM concept in the *Parables* may, therefore, be taken as a sure guide to one stream of Jewish messianic interpretation[76].

The *Parables* uses several titles in speaking of the Messiah (48:10; 52:4), a term which, according to Charles[77], occurs in its technical sense here for the first time. A fairly frequent title is the 'Elect One', which is met no less than 15 times[78]. Another, though uncommon, title is the 'Righteous One', which is found explicitly only twice[79], but which, as a concept is found also in 39:6[80] and 46:3[81]. But the most characteristic and fre-

---

73 *ET* 95 (1984) 201.

74 Against e.g. Lagrange, *Le judaïsme avant Jésus-Christ*, 1931, 224ff., who thought of two sources, one speaking of the Elect One and the other (a Christian source) of the Son of Man, and N. Messel, *Der Menschensohn in der Bilderreden des Henoch* (BZAW 35), 1922, who assumes that the Son of Man passages are later insertions. But as Mowinckel puts it, "Sjöberg has decisively refuted all objections to the authenticity of the passages and the integrity of the text" (*He that Cometh*, 355). C.P. van Andel, *De Struktuur van de Henoch-Traditie en het Nieuwe Testament*, 1955 and Borsch, *The Son of Man*, 146, agree with this position. No serious attempt in recent years to shake this position is known to me.

75 Black, *BJRL*, 45 (1962/3) p. 312 agrees that "there is nothing distinctively Christian about the Son of Man in the Similitudes". Borsch, *The Son of Man*, 147, similarly rejects all such influence on the Son of Man concept. Hammershaimb, *Første Enoksbog*, 74 says, "Menneskesønen helt igennem er tegnet som en jødisk messias, og at en Kristen interpolator næppe vilde have undladt at hentyde til Jesu jordiske liv og at understrege hans lidelse, død og opstandelse ..."

76 The Jewish character of the Son of Man in I Enoch is upheld by the basic study of Sjöberg, *Der Menschensohn*, 1ff. Further by Mowinckel, *He that Cometh*, 354f.; Borsch, *The Son of Man*, pp. 146f., Casey, *Son of Man*, 99ff., who, however, wrongly identifies him with Enoch. See also Coppens, *ETL* 57 (1981) 58–82.

77 *The Book of Enoch*, 95; also *id.*, *Daniel*, 187.

78 I.e. 39:6a; 40:5; 45:3, 4; 49:2, 4; 51:5a, 3; 52:6; 53:6; 55:4 ;61:5, 8, 11; 62:1.

79 I.e. 38:2 and 53:6. The first instance, which reads "And when the Righteous One shall appear before the eyes of the righteous" has a better-attested *v. l.* 'righteousness'. Charles chooses 'Righteous One', while Hammershaimb, *Første Enoksbog*, 99, 'retfaerdigheden', though in his commentary he takes the word as 'retfaerdige'.

80 "Mine eyes saw the Elect One of righteousness and of faith". The genitive construction is qualitative and therefore equivalent to 'Righteous One'.

81 "This is the Son of Man who hath righteousness". Even here the abstract 'righteousness' is not an object that can be possessed, but a personal quality. Thus, "the Son of Man who hath righteousness" is essentially "The Son of Man", that is, "The Righteous One".

quent concept is that of Son of Man, which occurs altogether 17 times[82].

That all these titles refer to one and the same entity is evident from the identification of the Elect One with the Righteous One[83], of the Righteous One with the Son of Man[84], of the Son of Man with the Messiah[85], of the Messiah with the Elect One[86], and of the Elect One with the Son of Man[87]. This data need not be explained as reflecting different sources, strata of tradition, or interpolations. The variations are to some extent, accounted for by the desire to illustrate different aspects of the Messiah, and determined by contextual considerations[88]. But the main reason is given below.

Though I have made an analysis of all seven chapters of the *Parables* (i.e. 46, 48, 62, 63, 69, 70, 71) in which the term son of man occurs, it has not been considered advisable to include here all these analyses. Such a procedure would have made the presentation unduly long and tedious. The analysis of chapter 46, will, nevertheless, be taken up because of its central importance in the study of the SM in the *Parables*. The structural elements of this chapter bear an unmistakable similarity to their counterparts in Daniel, especially chapter 7. A comparison of the two texts, therefore, it is hoped, will reveal the components integral to both texts as well as the 'divergent' material[89]. The similarities, moreover, disclose the necessary components to the concept, while the new material shows the accidental embellishments. It is those components which can be judged to be basic to the concept that are the primary guide in determining the nature of the SM in the *Parables*. The embellishments, though not anchored in Danielic tradition, are also important in revealing the author's conception of the SM, since those would not have been possible unless they were in general agreement with his overall interpretation of the SM.

---

82 I.e. 46:1 (see note 11), 2, 3, 4; 48:2; 62:5, 7, 14; 63:11; 69:26, 27, 29 (*bis*); 70:1; 71:14, 17.

83 53:6 "the Righteous and Elect One". Cf. further 39:6 "the Elect One of righteousness" (see note 80), and 49:2 "he is mighty in all the secrets of righteousness ... because the Elect One standeth before the Lord of Spirits."

84 46:3 "this is the Son of Man who hath righteousness" (cf. note 81).

85 48:2—10.

86 52:4—6 "All these things ... shall serve the dominion of his Anointed that he may be potent and mighty on the earth ... All these shall be in the presence of the Elect One, as wax before fire ... and they shall become powerless before his feet".

87 E.g. 62:1—5.

88 Thus, in both places where 'Righteous One' occurs, the title has its correlate 'righteous ones' (e.g. 38:2, "when the Righteous One shall appear before the eyes of the righteous", see also 53:6). In the majority of instances 'Elect One' is also correlated with 'elect ones' (e.g. 40:6; 45:3, 4; 61:11f.) or a verbal noun idea implying 'choice' (i.e. 49:4; 51:5a). In 39:6f. the double title of 'Elect One' and (the implicit) 'Righteous One' are correlated with both 'righteous ones' and 'elect ones': "Mine eyes saw the Elect One of righteousness (i.e. the Righteous One, cf. note 80) ... And the righteous and elect shall be without number before Him for ever and ever". Further analysis might give more cases. The term 'Messiah', (only twice) identifies this 'Righteous One' or 'Elect One' with the expected Messiah, while 'Son of Man' is used to link back to Daniel and to underline the continuity of messianic conception in this new manner.

89 On this cf. Emerton's remarks in *JTS*, 9, 1958, pp. 229, 235—37.

Here is presented a display of I En 46, which is segmented so as to show the structure of the author's thought[90]. This is followed by a discussion of the structure of I En 46 based on the display.

2. An Analytical Display of the Structure of 1 Enoch 46

1	And there I SAW One[91] who had a head of days	
2	And His head was white like wool	Attrib. Comment on 'head', 1
3	And with Him was another being whose countenance had the appearance of a man	Comment on 'One', 1
4	And his face was full of graciousness	Attrib. comment on 3
5	Like one of the holy angels	Comparison with 4
6	And I ASKED the angel[92] who went with me and showed me all the hidden things concerning that Son of Man	Reaction to 'I saw', 1
7	Who he was	Content of 'I asked', 6
8	And whence he was	Addit. content of 6
9	(And) why he went with the Head of Days	Addit. content to 6
10	And He ANSWERED and SAID unto me	Response to 'I asked', 6
11	This is the Son of Man	Content of 'said', 10
12	Who hath righteousness[93]	Comment on SM, 11
13	And with whom righteousness dwells	Emphatic equivalence with 12
14	And who revealeth[94] all the treasures of that which is hidden	Addit. comment on SM, 11
15	Because the Lord of Spirits hath chosen him	Reason for 14 (also 11–12?)
16	And whose lot hath the pre-eminence[95] before the Lord of Spirits in uprightness for ever	Addit. comment on SM, 11

---

90 Since the object of this analysis is not theoretical, the analysis has been executed only on such levels as were conducive to the purpose of it. Further segmentation would have been of no real value; on the contrary it would have made the presentation unduly long and cumbersome on the reader. In this analysis and the ensuing discussion I have utilized insights from semantics. An effort has been made to keep to terms readily understandable so as not to presuppose on the readers' part such specialized knowledge. Should any of the terms here used prove unfamiliar, reference to any handbook on linguistics will do to explain them. For a more connected discussion of semantic relations, Beekman – Callow, *Translating the Word of God*, may be consulted.

91 ONE: so Charles, Hammershaimb, Knibb. Beer: definite, 'den'.

92 THE ANGEL: so Charles, Beer. Hammershaimb: 'en af englene'; Knibb: 'one of the holy angels'. The reading chosen here, though lacking support in the MSS, is in keeping with this section of I Enoch, in which Enoch is said (see 40:2 ;52:3; 61:3) to be accompanied by one particular angel who interpreted what Enoch saw. This same angel is on other occasions called "angel of peace" (i.e. 40:8; 52:5; 53:4; 54:4; 56:2) and sometimes simply "the angel" (61:2; 64:2). Enoch therefore was not accompanied by many angels but by one.

93 RIGHTEOUSNESS: so Charles, Hammershaimb, Knibb. Beer: definite, 'die Gerechtigkeit'.

94 WHO REVEALETH: so Charles, Beer, Hammershaimb. Knibb: 'he will reveal'. The difference is that the reading adopted here makes the unit a characteristic of the Son of Man along with Unit (hence U) 13, whereas Knibb's reading makes it an act of his. According to my analysis the Son of Man's acts begin first with U 17, with the underlining resumption of the Son of Man's name. "And this Son of Man whom you have seen" is a clear marker that a new series begins (relating his acts), as distinguished from the previous Units (which relate to his characteristics, and form an answer to the question 'Who he was', U 7).

95 THE PRE-EMINENCE : according to earlier MSS followed by Charles. Beer and Knibb follow

17	And this Son of Man whom thou hast seen	Resumes 11
18	Shall raise up[96] the kings . . . from their seats[97]	Comment on SM, 17
19	And [he shall raise up] the mighty [from their seats]	Addition to 18
20	And [he shall raise up] the strong from their thrones	Addition to 18–19
21	And he shall loosen the reins of the strong	Addition to 18–20
22	And [he shall] break the teeth of the sinners	Addition to 18–21
23	And he shall put down the kings from their thrones and kingdoms	Addition to 18–22
24	Because they do not extol . . . him	Reason fron for 18–23
25	And [because they do not] praise [him]	Addit. reason for 18–23
26	Nor humbly[98] acknowledge whence the kingdom was bestowed upon them	Addit. reason for 18–23
27	And he shall put down the countenance of the strong	Resumes 18–23
28	And shall fill them with shame[99]	Amplification of 27
29	And darkness shall be their dwelling	Specific of 28
30	And worms shall be their bed	Addition to 29
31	And they shall have no hope of rising from their beds	Addition to 29–30
32	Because they do not extol the name of the Lord of Spirits	Reason for 27–31?
33	And these are they	Resumes 'kings' etc. from 18–32
34	Who cast down[100] the stars of heaven	Comment on 'they', 33

---

another reading, found mostly in later MSS: "through uprightness his lot has surpassed all before the Lord of Spirits". Hammershaimb combines elements of Charles's and Beer's ren-' derings and uses the verb 'har sejret' (= has been victorious). The difference is that according to the reading chosen by Beer, Knibb and, to some extent, Hammershaimb, the second reason (after the one in U 15, where the Actor is the Lord of Spirits) given for the Son of Man's role in revealing secret things lies in his own achievement of uprightness. The two reasons are thus God's choice of him and his own righteousness. The reading adopted in the presentation, above, on the other hand, presents both reasons as proceeding from the Lord of Spirits. Such an understanding also highlights the connection between 'chosen' (U 15) and 'lot' (U 16).

96 RAISE UP: so Charles, Beer, Hammershaimb. Knibb: 'rouse'. Charles compares this with what here is U 23, and considers the text corrupt. He regards the present Unit as original but its verb 'raise up' as giving the wrong sense, whereas he thinks that U 23 is an intrusion, though the verb is the right one. But there is perhaps another way of looking at the problem. A look at my presentation makes it likely that 'raise up from the seats' is used in the sense of 'rouse' or in a sense that indicates divestment of royal dignity. The verb is understood of all three, the kings, the powerful and the strong. This is the first stage of judgment. In the following three units (21–23) comes the second stage: 'he will loosen', 'he will break', 'he will cast down', where each succeeding unit constitutes an intensification of judgment. Finally, U 18 (rousing or divesting the kings of their power) and 23 (casting the kings down from their thrones) is most likely an *inclusio*.

97 SEATS: so Charles. Beer: 'Lagern'; Hammershaimb: 'lejer'. Knibb: 'resting-places'. The expression is to be understood as an equivalent to 'thrones', as U 20 and U 23 show.

98 HUMBLY: so Charles, Knibb. Beer and Hammershaimb: 'thankfully'.

99 SHALL FILL THEM WITH SHAME : so Charles and Hammershaimb. Beer follows another variant, passively: 'Schamröte wird sie erfüllen'; similarly Knibb. If the unit be understood passively, it must go along with the following two units 'darkness' and 'worms' — a somewhat unnatural connection. On the other hand, if the Agent is understood to be the Son of Man, the unit stands in appositional relation to U 27 and clarifies 'put down the countenance'. Such a relation is deemed more likely.

100 CAST DOWN. Charles, Beer, Hammershaimb and Knibb have 'judge'. 'Cast down' is here preferred, firstly, because it is entirely possible that as Charles points out, an original יורידו

35	And raise their hands against the Most High[101]	Addit. comment on 'they', 33
36	And tread upon the earth[102]	Addit. comment on 'they', 33
37	And dwell upon it	Addit. comment on 'they', 33
38	And all their deeds manifest uprighteousness[103]	Conclusion from 34—37
39	And their power rests upon their riches	Addition to 38
40	And their faith is in the gods which they have made with their hands	Addition to 39
41	And they deny the name of the Lord of Spirits	Consequence of 40?
42	And they persecute[104] the houses of his congregations	Addition of 41
43	And [sc. that is] of the faithful who hang upon the name of the Lord of Spirits	Amplification of 42

3. The Structure of 1 Enoch 46

I En 46 is here divided into 43 units (= U)[105]. These units are organ-

---

(= cast down) or even יפילו (= throw down) was corrupted to ידינו (= judge), secondly, because the text is so obviously dependent on Dan 8:10, and thirdly, because 'stars of heaven' is a standing expression for the 'righteous' (cf. 43:1, 4) who, according to Dan 8:10, which our author elaborates upon and adapts, are cast down by the wicked king, not judged.

101 The whole unit. Charles thinks it is displaced or interpolated because the stanza should be a distich, not a tristich, and because 'Most High' does not occur again in the *Parables*. However it does in 60:1, 22 (Book of Noah) and 62:7. There is no compelling reason why a distich is required nor is the absence of the title 'Most High' in the *Parables* a valid argument for the line being an interpolation. 'Raise their hands against the Most High' can be regarded as an expressive equivalent for blaspheming or threatening God. Dan 7:25, occurring in a quite similar context, is the inspiration of the expression here.

102 On the basis of Dan 8:10 Charles argues for reading units 36—37 as one: "And tread to the earth those who dwell upon it" because he thinks that an original יושביה was corrupted to וישבו בה. This explains why he is eager to excise U 35. The text will thus consist of two units, one concerned with the casting down and the other with the trampling of the righteous by the wicked kings. This is in itself plausible. For admittedly U 35 interrupts the flow of thought between U 34 and U 36—37 if Charles's reconstruction of the last two units is correct. However, U 36 and U 37 can also make sense as they stand. U 36 probably reflects Dan 7:23 "it shall ... trample it (sc. the earth) down", rather than 8:10 "and trampled upon them" (sc. the host of the stars)". "And dwell upon it" would signal the unlawful settling by the kings, etc. on God's earth, which really belongs to the righteous. The excision of the unit on the Most High is also problematic. It overlooks the fact that both in Dan 8:11 ("it magnified itself even up to the Prince of the host") and 7:25 ("he shall speak words against the Most High") blasphemy or threat against the Most High is coupled with tyrannical behaviour towards the righteous, and is of decisive importance for the condemnation of the wicked king, as here.

103 So Charles, Hammershaimb, Knibb. Beer adds with some MSS what is probably a repetition "und alle deren Thaten Ungerechtigkeit ist".

104 PERSECUTE: so Charles, Hammershaimb. A number of MSS here read "shall be driven from". So Beer, Knibb. The last rendition implies firstly that the kings once were within the houses of His congregations — a rather absurd idea. Secondly, it implies that this 'driving out constitutes their punishment, which can hardly be correct in the light of the foregoing text. Thirdly, the variant here adopted better suits the context, both U 41 and U 43. Fourthly, that U 42, U 43 are concerned with persecution of the righteous is corroborated by the text immediately following, i.e. 47:1—2. I therefore choose without hesitation the reading 'persecute', and understand 'And' of U 43 as being the literal translation of what was intended as a *waw-explicativum*.

105 Adherence to a more rigid segmentization doctrine would have given more units (cf. e.g. U 6,

ized as three sections. The first section is introduced with "And there I saw" (U 1), the second with "And I asked" (U 6) and the third "And he answered and said to me" (U 10). With regards to the organization of the text these three units are semantically more prominent than those following them, and hence they are indented to the far left. The first section (U 1–5) with the main unit "And there I saw" contains the vision. The second section "And I asked (U 6–9) containing the seer's reaction to what he saw, is related semantically to the previous section as result to reason. In both sections the Agent is the seer. The third section (U 10–43) constitutes the angel's dialogical response to the seer's questions and forms the interpretation of the vision. Here the Agent is the interpreting angel, though his words are embedded in the seer's report, while in them are embedded several other Agents or Actants.

The text is structured as follows. In the vision U 1 is in focus, implying that the One who had a head of days is the dominant Figure, and the chief Object of "I saw". In close conjunction with but subordinate to the Head of Days is introduced another personage who resembled a human being. Though this Figure lacks the prominence of the Head of Days at the introductory scene, he is described in greater detail. Thereby the author hints that the text looks forward, and this is a step in preparing the ground.

The sight elicits the seer's reaction (U 6), which is preoccupied entirely with the less prominent being in the Vision part. The cumbersome expression (U 3) is dispensed with, and the more formal one, Son of Man[106], is adopted. The visionary asks three questions, all about the SM, since for him the Head of Days posed no identification problem: who he was, whence he was, and why he went with the Head of Days[107]. The rest of the text is an answer to the seer's inquiry. However, it must not pass unnoticed that the answer given really corresponds to the first question alone[108]. The questions concern the SM's identity, origin and association with the Head of Days. Both the fact that questions are asked only about him as well as the form the third question (U 9) takes, indicate the transfer of focus from the Head of Days onto the SM[109]. This transferred focus

---

which contains four ideas: 'I asked', 'he went', 'he showed', and 'something is hidden') but would have been pointless in this analysis — unconcerned with theoretical linguistics — and have impeded surveyability.

106 Certain difficulties are associated with this expression in the Ethiopic text. See note 115 below.

107 Also this being, introduced through a circumlocution in U 1, now receives its formal designation.

108 With considerable difficulty an implicit answer to the third question might be claimed for some of the following units (e.g. U 16), but it is best to consider even these units as answering the first question.

109 Cf. "with Him was another being" where the focus is on the Head of Days, while the Son of Man is in passivity, with "And why he went with the Head of Days", where the focus is centered on the Son of Man.

is sustained down to U 31, while the Head of Days, or Lord of Spirits, lingers in the background.

U 11—43 relate to U 10 as content and constitute what the angel told the visionary. Even this longest of three sections is carefully structured into smaller constituent parts. U 11 with the deictic pronoun (resuming U 6—9) introduces the SM emphatically, thus announcing the main theme of the interpretation. The interpretation falls into three main divisions dealing with a) the characteristics of the SM (U 11—16); b) his acts of judgment upon the kings, etc. (U 17—32) and c) a description of the deeds of the kings, etc. (U 33—43), which function as grounds for the SM's judgment on them.

In the first part (U 11—16) the angel, complying with the seer's request, identified the SM by attributing to him certain characteristics: he is righteous, he reveals secrets, and his lot has pre-eminence before the Lord of Spirits. U 14 is especially emphasized through the reason unit 15, indicating the characteristic brought most into prominence in the text — that of revealing secrets! The second step in the description of the SM is by means of a summary of his acts. Actions, too, reveal a person's character. Essentially U 14 also belongs to the acts, but here the acts relate to judgment, which explains why U 14 is placed in the previous series. The second series is more complex than the first one. There is first a sequence of six units (U 18—23) dealing with what the Son of Man will do to the kings, the mighty and the strong. These six units seem to have a chiastic structure. U 18—20: kings — mighty — strong; U 21—23: strong — sinners — kings. 'Sinners' most probably corresponds to 'mighty' in U 19. In U 18—20 the same event-word is presupposed: "raise up from their seats/ thrones". i.e. divest them of their authority. In U 21—23 three different event-words are used, one with each category. Note also the 'crescendo': 'loosen' — 'break' — 'put down'. U 23 probably forms an *inclusio* with U 18.

These six units relating to the Son of Man's acts are followed by three reasons (U 24—26); "they do not extol", "they do not praise", and "they do not humbly acknowledge".

U 27 resumes the objects of the Son of Man's wrath by using one term, 'strong', of wider semantic range than 'kings', as representative of all three categories against whom now the eschatological doom is to be uttered: "put down their countenance". This judgment is amplified by U 28 with "fill them with shame". 'Shame' is undoubtedly a corollary of eschatological and final judgment. The last two units are more specific statements about the nature of the judgment than U 18—23. Judgment becomes more specific still by U 29—31, constructed passively, so as to indicate the final and abiding result of the Son of Man's acts. Even here we can notice a gradual intensification: "darkness shall be their dwelling", "worms shall be their bed", and "they shall have no hope of rising from their beds".

This group of units too (and with it the Son of Man's acts) is concluded by one unit (U 32) giving the reason. This is a virtual summary of the reasons previously given: "because they do not extol the name of the Lord of Spirits".

The third and final part of the angel's interpretation (U 33—43) is concerned with the deeds of the kings, etc. In the total organization of the text this part functions as the reason for the Son of Man's acts, while at the same time it highlights and climaxes the impact of the text upon the addressees.

U 33 is in focus. In its intent and function it resembles U 11 and 17. At the same time it functions as a link between U 11—32 and U 34—43. It resumes 'kings', etc. from the foregoing text which speaks of their being condemned, and couples it with a description of their deeds, which call down that judgment.

In U 34—37 the 'kings', etc. are the Agents. Their actions have three targets: the righteous, here called stars of heaven, the Most High, and the earth as God's creation. A group of three units (U 38—40) follows, predicating of them not acts, but characteristics: unrighteousness, reliance on riches, and idolatry. These are the conclusions to be drawn from U 34—37.

The final group of units (41—43) reverts attention to the acts of the kings, etc. The arrangement is chiastic in relation to U 34—35. Though the units here are three in number, there are only two events, sc. acts of which the kings and mighty are guilty: they deny the name of the Lord of Spirits — a direct outcome of U 40 — and they persecute the righteous. U 43 is either an amplification, the 'and' (also in Ethiopic an one-letter prefix as in Hebrew) reflecting a *waw-explicativum*, or else, the direct object of 'persecute' of U 42 (ω = *we* = 'and' being a textual error).

4. A Comparison of I Enoch 46 with Daniel 7

Some of the basic constituents of a narrative text are undoubtedly the participants, the order in which they are introduced, the priority or focus attached to them, and their roles, that is, the events for which they are responsible.

A comparison between I En 46 and Dan 7 indicates clearly that I En 46 has in general taken his schema over from Dan 7.

1) Participants (in Vision)	I En 46: The Head of Days and the Son of Man Dan 7: The Ancient of Days and the 'SM'
2) Order of presentation	I En 46: First the Head of Days, then the Son of Man is presented Dan 7: First the Ancient of Days, then the 'SM' is presented
3) Priority (focus)	I En 46: At first focus is centered on the Head of Days, thereafter on the Son of Man Dan 7: First the Ancient of Days is in focus, then the 'SM'

<table>
<tr><td>4) Roles</td><td>I En 46: The Head of Days is generally in the background; The
Son of Man is active as judge
Dan 7: The Ancient of Days is more in the background; the 'SM'
receives dominion, kingship, etc.</td></tr>
<tr><td>(roles of new participants
in Interpretation)</td><td>I En 46: The kings, etc.: defy God, persecute the righteous,
are condemned
Dan 7: The kings (esp. little horn) defy God, persecute the
righteous, are judged
I En 46: The righteous: are persecuted, and are vindicated
Dan 7: The righteous: are persecuted, and are vindicated</td></tr>
</table>

All of these ideas are common to both texts, and show that the similarities are more than a coincidence.

I shall now proceed to discuss in more detail the points of agreement between the two passages, I En 46 and Dan (esp. ch. 7).

1) Both texts contain visions of things not perceived by physical organs.

2) In both texts the vision prompts the seer to request an interpretation.

3) In both texts there is an angelic interpreter near at hand.

4) In both texts the angelic answer makes up the interpretation.

5) In both texts the focus is on the interpretation.

These general considerations relate to the basic circumstances of the texts. Their contents reveal no less striking similarities.

6) I En 46 initiates the vision by presenting One who had a head of days. Dan 7 opens this part of the vision by presenting One that was ancient of days. There is no doubt that the two descriptions are similar in character and refer to God[110].

7) The other being presented by I En 46 is described as "One whose countenance had the appearance of a man"[111].

8) Both the Head of Days and the Son of Man are first introduced by circumlocutions in both I En 46 and Dan 7; thereafter the first is referred to as Head of Days and the second as Son of Man. In Dan 7 the initial expression "One like a Son of Man" is never again mentioned, because it is interpreted[112].

9) The Head of Days is described as having a head that was like wool. He is similarly described in Dan 7:9.

10) In neither Dan 7:9 nor I En 46:1 is the comparative 'like' used in connection with the Head of Days.

11) This last point is in sharp contrast with the way both authors describe the other being: Dan 7:13 "One like a son of man"; I En 46:1 "another being whose countenance had the appearance of a man". Thus,

---

110 The Ethiopic term r'ĕsa is similar to the Hebrew ר א ש (= head), while mawâ'ĕl means 'the years of one's life'. This being thus had a head that indicated the many years of his life. Obviously the expression implies a very great age, or eternity, and corresponds to the Aramaic of Dan 7:9 עתיק יומין = 'ancient in respect of days', i.e. Eternal.

111 Cf. also Dan 10:16, כדמות בני ־ אדם.

112 See Ch. Two: The Identification of the 'SM' in Daniel.

while Dan and I En 46 use 'Ancient of Days' and 'Head of Days' as a non-anthropomorphic kind of adjectival denomination of God, they use 'One like a son of man' and '(One who had) the appearance of a man' in order to underline the anthropo*morphic* description of a 'non-anthropic' being.

12) The shifting of interest from the Head of Days to the Son of Man is evidenced in both texts.

13) In I En 46 the seer asks for an explanation only of the Son of Man. The implication is that the Head of Days needs no explanation. Dan 7 revealed exactly the same situation.

14) In the rest of I En 46 the Son of Man is in the foreground, while the Head of Days, under a new name (Lord of Spirits), lingers in the background. In like manner in Dan 7, the One like a son of man, interpreted as the Most High, dominates the rest of the chapter.

15) The chief function of the Son of Man in I En 46 is that of Judge of the kings and the mighty. In Dan 7 the 'SM' appears on the stage at the judgment, and his assumption of universal dominion makes it easy to ascribe to him the role of Judge.

16) In I En 46 the kings and the mighty act arrogantly against God. The same is true of the kings symbolized by the little horn of Dan 7.

17) In I En 46 the kings and the mighty persecute the righteous. This is also the case in Dan 7.

18) This hybristic and arrogant behaviour explains the Son of Man's wrath and judgment upon the kings, etc. That holds true also of Dan 7.

19) The reason given for the condemnation of the kings, etc., viz. that "they do not extol nor praise him, nor humbly acknowledge whence the kingdom was bestowed upon them" has obviously been inspired from Daniel, where God's judgment comes upon Nebuchadnezzar (as representative of the beasts of ch. 7) on account of his haughtiness (4:30) and his refusal to take to heart that "the Most High rules the kingdoms of men and gives it to whom he will" — a motif recurring at 4:17, 25; 5:21.

20) In I En 46 the righteous, thought of as 'stars of heaven', are said to be cast down. The same is said of the righteous in Dan 8:10 (cf. also 7:7).

21) In I En 46 the kings lift up their hands against the Most High, no doubt as a gesture of defiance and threat. This has a good parallel in Dan 7:25 "he shall speak words against the Most High".

22) In I En 46 and Dan 7 the righteous are closely connected with the Most High (though in I En 'Most High' is probably applied only to God).

23) In I En 46 and Dan 7 the judgment meted out against the kings seems to be final.

24) In both I En 46 and Dan 7 the righteous are vindicated.

---

113 I.e. 40:5—45:3 (67 lines) with astronomical secrets; 55:4—61:5 (136 lines) with the return of the exiles, Lights and Thunders Noah, etc.; 63:11—69:26 (143 lines) with Noah and Deluge, Promise to Noah, fallen angels, etc.

25) In both I En 46 and Dan 7 the Son of Man emerges victorious and evil is finally swept away.

The similarities are so deep-going and integral to the texts that one can only speak of direct dependence of I En 46 on Dan 7. The author of I En 46 has taken not only the general theme, but also the structure of Dan 7 and the different elements in particular. The roles of the participants are preserved intact.

The main dissimilarities are:

1) I En 46 does not contain a vision of the throne (Dan 7:9). This is, however, taken up in the section immediately following, sc. 47:3.

2) I En 46 does not refer to the clouds carrying the Son of Man as Dan 7:13 does. Nevertheless, the detail in 46:2 that the Son of Man "went" with the Head of Days may be a faint echo of the idea of divine transportation. Still, his being "named before the Head of Days" (48:2) may be a reflection of the presentation of the 'SM' in Dan 7:13.

3) I En 46:3 makes reference to the Son of Man's function as revealer of secrets. This is missing from Dan 7. Its presence in I En is, of course, quite natural since this was a thought most dear in the bosom of every would-be apocalyptist. Indeed, this role of the Son of Man is what made his book most relevant.

4) Finally, there are a number of details in the descriptions of the Son of Man, of the kings, of the judgment, etc., which do not have exact verbal counterparts in Dan 7. But this, so far from impairing the thesis of Enochic dependence upon Daniel, actually enhances it, by showing the kind of embellishments made in this reinterpretation of Daniel. None of these dissimilarities is such as to cancel out the similarities discussed above, often they are quite incidental. But they all fall in well with the basic schema of I En 46 as taken over from Dan 7.

5. The Relation of the *Parables* as a Whole to Daniel

Having seen that I En 46 is dependent on Dan 7, not only for its main ideas, but also for its structural elements, the question now is, What relation does the *Parables* as a whole bear to the Book of Daniel?

The best way to deal with this question is probably via a discussion of the various titles used. As mentioned earlier the *Parables* uses four titles, 'Righteous One', 'Elect One', 'Son of Man', and 'Anointed One', all of which are applied to the same entity. These four titles are strewn in the entire text fairly uniformly and indicate in the clearest possible manner that the *Parables* deals with just this personage, who is set forth by means of these four titles. Here follows the list of occurrences in the consecutive text of the *Parables*. The figures between the lines with the references indicate the number of lines intervening for each mention of anyone of the titles.

Line

15	Righteous	(38.2)	20			4		
30			278	Elect	(51:5a)	551	SM	(62:7)
45	Elect	(39:6a)	3			7		
29			281	Elect	(51:3)	558	SM	(62:9)
74	Elect	(40:5)	15			15		
67			296	Anointed	(52:4)	573	SM	(62:14)
141	Elect	(45:3)	6			41		
5			302	Elect	(52:6)	614	SM	(63:11)
146	Elect	(45:4)	13			143		
11			315	Elect	(52:9)	757	SM	(69:26)
157	Appear. of a Man	(46:1)	13			2		
			328	Righteous	(53:6)	759	SM	(69:27)
3			0			7		
160	SM	(46:2)	328	Elect	(53:6)	766	SM	(69.29)
2			30			3		
162	SM	(46:3)	358	Elect	(55:4)	769	SM	(69:29)
5			136			3		
167	SM	(46:4)	494	Elect	(61:5)	772	SM	(70:1)
46			8			52		
213	SM	(48:2)	502	Elect	(61:8)	824	SM	(71:14)
29			10			10		
242	Anointed	(48:10)	512	Elect	(61:11)	834	SM	(71:17)
7			16			2		
249	Elect	(49:2)	528	Elect	(62:1)	836	End of *Parables* text	
9			19					
258	Elect	(49:4)	547	SM	(62:5)			

The above list shows that in a running text of 836 lines (Charles', *AP*, II, pp. 208—37), these four titles occur 37 times altogether, giving an average of one occurrence per 22.3 lines. If we were to exclude the three large blocks dealing with asides and comprising 346 lines[113], the average would then become one occurrence per 13.2 lines. This average of lines would become still smaller if we were to reckon in those instances where in place of the actual titles the personal or relative pronouns are used.

The above figures show that the contents of the *Parables* are densely interspersed with one or other of these titles, and they underscore the point, made above, that the chief burden of the *Parables* is to set forth this personage described by four different titles[114].

Of particular interest is the way in which the author went about achieving his purpose. Though the order of the contents of the *Parables* in detail is a moot question, and minor transpositions have probably taken place, there is no reason to assume that the original order was radically different from the one we now have. According to the existing text, the first title to occur, practically at the very beginning, is that of 'Righteous One' (38: 2). This is followed by the title 'Elect One', which is repeated four times (39:6; 40:5; 45:3, 4), and only thereafter does the title of Son of Man

---

114 Contra de Villiers, in *Studies in I Enoch and the NT*, 50—68, who sees wisdom as the overriding interest of the *Parables*.

make its appearance, at first very carefully in a circumlocution (46:1) recalling Daniel's expression, and then as a fixed title[115]. From that point onwards, the four titles appear in the text interchangeably. Nevertheless, even after the introduction of the title Son of Man in 46:1—4 and 48:2, the author goes on to speak of the 'Anointed One', the 'Elect One' and the 'Righteous One' before he definitely settles down into using Son of

---

115 The Ethiopic has four renderings of the English Son of Man: *walda sab'ĕ* = 'son of man' (i.e. mankind, a human being): 46:2, 3, 4 ; 48:2; *walda b'ĕsī* = 'son of man' (i.e. in contradistinction to woman) 62:5; 69:29 (bis); 71:14; *walda 'ĕguâla 'ĕmahĕjâw* = 'son (of) of the offspring of the mother of the living': 62:7, 9, 14; 63:11; 69:26, 27; 70:1; 71:17, and once *walda b'ĕsit* = 'son of woman': 62:5 (in two MSS). The last type has been shown to be a textual corruption, cf. Charles, *The Ethiopic Version of the Book of Enoch*, 112 and 127 and Sjöberg, *Der Menschensohn,* 9 and 42ff. Charles, *The Book of Enoch* 1912, 85ff. argues that the variations may be the result of nonrigorous translation since the Ethiopic translator could only have had before him ὁ υἱὸς τοῦ ἀνθρώπου, which translates אדם בן or אנוש בן. Charles' explanation that the Ethiopic expressions are only variations of the same original expression is supported by Dillmann, *Lexicon lingua aethiopicae*, 1865, col. 519, and confirmed by Fiebig, *Der Menschensohn*, 42f., though Messel, *Der Menschensohn in der Bilderreden Henochs* (*ZAW* Beih. 35), 1922, tried, unsuccessfully, to disprove Charles. The second type *walde b'ĕsi* and *sab'ĕ* are used interchangeably in I En as Charles has shown. The longer expression, where 'son of ... ' may be taken in apposition to 'offspring of ... ' may be a 'Christianization' of the expression in the light of the comparison, indeed, the virtual identification, of Mary with Eve (see Justin, *Dialogue*, 124 and Irenaeus, *Adv. Haereses*, III, 22.4; V, 19.1; IV, 33.11. See J. Quasten's remarks (*Patrology*, Vol. I, pp. 211f., 297ff.) and W. Staerk, (*ZNW* 33 (1934) 97—104). What is practically certain is that the Ethiopic translator could not have had before him any other Greek form than ὁ υἱὸς τοῦ ἀνθρώπου, or any other Hebrew form than אדם בן. See also Charles, *The Book of Enoch*, 1912, pp. 1xvf.

Some have tried to make the most of the various Ethiopic expressions as well as the use of the demonstrative and the 'identification' of the Son of Man with Enoch in 71:14, in order to disprove the messianic character of the Son of Man in the *Parables*. Casey is one such recent example. His whole discussion (*Son of Man*, 99—112) is so vitiated by the concern to prove the non-titular use of Son of Man in the *Parables* (as indeed in the entire Jewish literature and in Jesus' use) that it becomes extremely one-sided, most unsatisfactory and singularly unconvincing. It fails to come to terms with the depth of the Son of Man concept in En 37—71. Casey seems to hide his head in the sand ignoring all the evidence concerning the Son of Man in the *Parables*, shortly discussed in this study, and merely quibbles about some minor points regarding the Ethiopic demonstrative, — which in all probability renders the Greek definite article (cf. e.g. Schmidt, *JBL* 15 (1896) 36—53 and Charles' discussion (*The Book of Enoch*, 1912, 86ff.; see also pp. lxiii ff.), which is still valid and Sjöberg, *Der Menschensohn im äth. Henoch.*, 44—8) — as well as the three expressions for Son of Man, and lastly, but not least, he makes ch. 71 the pivot and hinge for the interpretation of the Son of Man in the *Parables*. The variant renderings for Son of Man are not in the least surprising. For one, the most peculiar rendering *walda 'ĕguâla 'emahĕjâw* = "son of the offspring of the mother of the living" in 62:7, 9, 14; 63:11; 69:26, 27; 71:17, is the normal Ethiopic rendering in the OT, in Dan 7:13 and everywhere in the NT (cf. Borsch, *The Son of Man*, 147 and Colpe, *Kairos* 11 (1969) 249). Years ago, I pointed out that the Ethiopic translator in rendering the Greek μυστήριον did not content himself with his indigenous *hebu'*, but on occasion used a transliteration of the Greek term, viz. *mesṭir* (*The Ephesian Mysterion*, 24f. note 43). That he could therefore have rendered ὁ υἱὸς τοῦ ἀνθρώπου in more than one way need not surprise us. Bowman, *ET* 59 (1947—8) 287 points to the analogy of the Curetonian and Sinaitic Syriac NT, which render υἱὸς τοῦ ἀνθρώπου variously. As for Casey's identification of the SM with Enoch, reference may be made to note 121.

Man from 62:5 to the end of his work. These circumstances surely reveal the author's tactics in trying to introduce an unknown and non-messianic designation in 'messianic' contexts by means of other more feasible and usable titles.

What has just been said is corroborated by the following considerations. The titles 'Righteous One' and 'Anointed One' occur very sparingly and have a minimal context. According to 38:2f. the Righteous One appears as Judge, while according to 53:6 and context, the Righteous One, here also called the Elect One, is associated with the judgment of the wicked and the vindication of the righteous[116]. With regards to the Anointed One, 48:10 speaks of his having been denied along with the Lord of Spirits by the kings and the mighty, and 52:4 speaks of his wielding of dominion on earth. No characteristics and no other description is given of the person referred to by these titles. But then it must be remembered that the immediate context goes on to speak of the Elect One or the Son of Man, so that the description of one title merges into that of the other.

On the other hand, the title 'Elect One' receives a very full presentation, almost comparable to that of the Son of Man. But it is worthy of note that the description of the Elect One's character and actions is in all essentials identical with or similar to that of the Son of Man! Here follows a comparison of the main characteristics, privileges and actions of the Elect One and the Son of Man respectively.

THE SON OF MAN
I. Characteristics

46:1 Countenance like appearance of a man
Full of graciousness
Like one of the holy angels
46:3 Righteousness
Revealer
48:6 Chosen } before creation
Hidden }
Revealed to holy and righteous
Revealed to elect
69:26 Name revealed
71:14 Born unto righteousness
Righteous abides over him
Righteousness of Head of Days never
   forsakes him
71:15 From him proceeds peace
71:71 Length of days

THE ELECT ONE
I. Characteristics

39:6a Righteousness
Faith
49:2 Everlasting glory
Perpetual might
Spirit of wisdom, insight, understanding, might
62:2 Spirit of righteousness

---

116 The term 'Righteouse One' (38:2 and 53:6) no doubt embedded in Hebrew messianic expectation (as e.g. II Sam 23:3; Isa 32:1), finds its most normative form in the OT in Isa 53:11 "the Righteous One, my Servant" (*RSV*). The term clearly occurs as a messianic title in Apocalyptic and rabbinic writings (e.g. Ps. Sol. 17:35; P^esiqta R. 34 (159^a); P^esiqta R. 37 (163^a). See *Str-B* II, 289f. Cf. also G. Schneider, Art. δίκαιος-δικαιοσύνη in *EWNT*, I, cols. 781–84;

II. Privileges, Position, Things Granted

46:3 Chosen by Lord of Spirits
His lot has pre-eminence

48:2f. Is named at that hour before Lord
of Spirits
His name is named before Head of
Days
His name is named before sun, signs,
and stars were created

48:5 Worshipped by all earth-inhabitants

62:6 Kings, mighty, etc. bless, glorify,
extol him

62:7 Preserved by Most High in his presence

62:8 Elect to stand before him

62:9 Kings, etc. to fall down before him
Kings, etc. to worship him
Kings, etc. to set their hope in him
Kings, etc. to petition and suppli-
cate him

69:27 Sum of judgment given to him

III. Actions

46:3 Reveals treasures of secrets

46:4 Raises up kings, mighty, etc.
Loosens reins of strong
Breaks teeth of sinners

46:5 Puts down kings from throne and
kingly rule

46:6 Puts down countenance of strong
Fills strong with shame
(causes) darkness to cover them
(causes) worms to be their bed
(causes) them to have no hope

48:4 Shall be a staff to righteous
Shall be a light to Gentiles
Shall be a hope to those troubled

62:5 Sits on throne of his glory

62:6 He rules over all

62:14 The righteous and elect shall feast
with him
The righteous and elect shall lie down
and rise up with him

63:11 (Kings, mighty, etc.) shall be ashamed
before him
(Kings, mighty, etc.) shall be driven
from his presence
Sword (= judgment) before his face
for ever

II. Privileges, Position, Things Granted

39:4 Is Elect according to Lord of Spirits'
good pleasure

39:6a Is under the wings of Lord of Spirits

40:5 Is blessed by presences

49:2 Stands before the Lord of Spirits

51:3 Is given secrets by Lord of Spirits
Is glorified by Lord of Spirits

52:6 Mountains of silver, etc. melt before
him

Mountains of silver, etc. are destroyed
at his appearance

61:8 Is placed by Lord of Spirits on throne
of glory

62:2f Is seated by Lord of Spirits on throne
of his glory
Kings shall see him on throne
Kings shall see him judge in righteousness
Kings shall see that no lying word
is spoken before him

III. Actions

45:3 He sits on throne of glory
He tries the sinners' works

45:4 He dwells among faithful

49:4 He shall judge secret things
He cannot be deceived

51:5a He shall arise, choose righteous
Sits on God's throne
He shall speak secrets of wisdom

53:6 He shall cause the house of congrega-
tion to appear

55:4 Sits on throne of glory and judges
Azâzêl, etc.

61:8 Shall judge works of holy ones in
heaven (= angels)
Shall judge their secret ways according
to word of Lord of Spirits

61:8 Shall judge their paths according to
righteous judgment of Lord of
Spirits

61:11 Together with archangels praises God

62:2 His word slays sinners
Unrighteous are destroyed before him

L. Ruppert, *Jesus als der leidende Gerechte?* (*SBS*, 59), H. Dechent, *Der 'Gerechte' — eine Bezeichnung für den Messias,* (*TSK* 100), 1928) 439–43. The NT can take it for granted that it is so understood, (i.e. Acts 3:14: ὑμεῖς δὲ τὸν ἅγιον καὶ δίκαιον ἠρνήσασθε, 7:52: (your fathers) ἀπέκτειναν τοὺς προκαταγγείλαντας περὶ τῆς ἐλεύσεως τοῦ δικαίου, 22: 14 ; I Jn 2:1; Jas 5:6 (probably); II Tim 4:8). Apart from Isa 53:11, I En 38:2 and 53:6 are probably the earliest instances of the term's messianic use.

69:27 Sits upon throne of glory
    Causes sinners to pass away
    Causes sinners to be destroyed
69:28 Causes sinners to be bound with chains
    Causes sinners to be imprisoned
    Causes all their works to vanish
69:29 He appeared
    He seated himself on throne of glory
    Evil passes away before his face
    His word goes forth
    His word is strong before the Lord
      of Spirits

71:15 Proclaims peace to you
    The elect will have dwelling-place
      with him
    The elect will have a heritage with
      him
    The elect will not be separated from
      him for ever

This comparison shows unmistakably that the Elect One and the Son of Man are portrayed almost identically, and that their most conspicuous functions are to be the judge of the wicked and the Vindicator of the righteous. But the question arising here is: If the Son of Man received these characteristics from his portrayal in Daniel, from where did the Elect One acquire them? For the picture of the Elect One in the *Parables* cannot stem from the OT, since the ideas associated with this title here do not occur in the OT passages dealing with the Elect One[117]. Nor can we at the present state of research interpose another document as source of these ideas, for the simple reason that we do not possess such a document, nor do we have good reasons for assuming the existence of such a document. But the origins of the ideas are fully accounted for by the sources available within our purview. It has hopefully been demonstrated that the ideas associated with the Son of Man in the *Parables* are inspired by Daniel, especially chapter 7[118]. It has been further shown that the Elect One

---

117 Though בחיר occurs some thirteen times in the OT, only two instances may be considered as having messianic overtones, Ps 89:3(4) and Isa 42:1 (cf. G. Schrenk, *TDNT*, IV, 184). Yet in the *Parables* the term is definitely a title of the Messiah and is frequently associated with the 'elect ones', i.e. God's righteous (39:6; 40:6; 45:3,4; 61:11f.). The messianic import in this title no doubt derives from the conception of David as the chosen king of the Lord. It is so understood occasionally in the NT and is applied to Jesus (e.g. Lk 9:35; 23:35, – the last instance indicating that it was a messianic designation current at Jesus' time), see *TDNT*, IV, 189 and Eckert, *EWNT*, I, col. 1016.

118 This does not mean that all the details in the *Parables* are borrowed from or inspired by Daniel; the framework and the main ideas stem from Daniel, though details have laid many biblical books under tribute. Hartman (*Prophecy Interpreted*, 113–26) for example, has given a very helpful and full presentation of background material of various degrees of parallelism to I En 46 from most parts of the OT including Daniel. Casey, *Son of Man*, 107ff. has directed his efforts especially against Hartman's Danielic background material and tried to eliminate this source. But the attempt is unsuccessful (cf. Hartman's discussion).

is depicted with characteristics belonging properly to the Son of Man. It
is this identical schema underlying the presentation of the Son of Man and
the Elect One that makes it so easy to blend the two, by letting the description pass from the Son of Man to the Elect One and vice versa. The
same applies to the other two titles, Righetous One and Anointed One.
For all four designations have one and the same Figure in view — the
Figure set forth in Dan 7 as 'SM'[119]. Hence, it may be claimed that what
lies at the heart of the *Parables* is its Son of Man messianology, conceived
not in classical Hebrew theological thinking, but in a new thinking developed from the Book of Daniel, a messianology, furthermore, not con-
ceived· in terms of a Davidic king, but in terms of the heavenly being
portrayed in Dan 7[120]. In his great objective the author of the *Parables*
is hampered by one serious difficulty: the term 'Son of Man' is not a
current messianic title, at any rate, not in widespread use. The dilemma
is solved: a) by adopting three other messianic titles and portraying them
with characteristics belonging to the Son of Man; b) by solemnly introducing the Son of Man title itself and describing the figure so set forth with
the same characteristics (actually his own from the start), c) by blending
the Son of Man with the other titles in the description, d) by identifying
the Son of Man with the Elect One, the Righteous One and the Messiah,
and e) by using all four titles interchangeably. The bold stroke of the author of the *Parables* thus consists in his portrayal of three messianic titles
with the characteristics and descriptions of features belonging to a non-
messianic designation — the Son of Man — and by blending that designation with the current messianic titles, so as to raise the designation Son
of Man to the level of a messianic title[121].

---

119 Cf. Hartman, *Prophecy Interpreted*, 120, 'The author (sc. of the *Parables*) has accordingly
applied to the Daniel Son of Man epithets which in the OT are applied to David, the Davidic
Messiah, the Righteous Branch and the Servant of Yahweh. From this we may reasonably
suppose that he started from a biblical interpretation which identified those figures with each
other".

120 Cf. Davies, *Paul and Rabbinic Judaism*, 159.

121 The Son of Man of the *Parables* has sometimes been identified with Enoch (e.g. by Sjöberg,
Manson, Black, Casey). Perrin makes the unsubstantiated hypothesis: "What has happened in
I Enoch is then, in my view, that, in the course of the development of the Enoch saga, the
translation of Enoch has been interpreted in terms of Ezek. 1 and Dan 7, and Dan 7 has then
been understood as referring to the giving of the role of eschatological judge to the one represented by the Son of Man figure (a quite different interpretation from that given to this scene
by the author of Daniel), which in this saga is Enoch", (*BR* 11 (1966) 23. The same article is
printed as Ch. 3 in *A Modern Pilgrimage in NT Christology*).
    This interpretation has overlooked a number of serious difficulties:
    a) Appel ("Die Komposition des äthiopischen Henochbuches", *B Fch Th* 10:3 pp. 43ff.)
is probaBly correct in pointing out that between 71:13 and 71:14 there is a gap which originally described the appearance of the Son of Man with the Head of Days, a vision that called
forth Enoch's question about the Son of Man (as in 46:2) and in response to which the angel
uttered the contents of vv. 14—17. Though we cannot know with certainty what stood in the
lost text, there is an abrupt transition from vs. 13 to vs. 14 which makes likely the assumption
of a text like the one Appel presupposes.

But the question is again, Why introduce a designation not classically associated with the Messiah? or, Why not content oneself with portraying one's Messiah in the usual Hebrew imagery? To answer these questions is a very involved matter; it would take us into digressions about the nature of apocalypticism, the working-habits of apocalyptists, and others. But three very valid reasons for doing so, are: a) that the author of the *Parables* like Daniel has lost faith in a traditional human messiah of David's line, b) That with Daniel he sees not only mankind, but also the world of spirits in commotion and rebellion against God, and c) that with Daniel again he looks for a superhuman being as alone fit to deal with human as well as spiritual lawlessness, to definitely sweep away unrighteousness and sin, to vindicate and exalt the righteous and to usher in the reign of righteousness and bliss. To achieve this purpose the apocalyptist considered the Danielic 'SM' as the most suitable imagery and source of inspiration. Accordingly, he took over not only the 'SM' and the ideas immediately associated with this designation, but also the whole nexus of ideas connected with the 'SM', indeed, most of the structural elements of the Danielic presentation, especially chapter 7.

---

b) In 71:13 the subject of 'came' is the Head of Days. But in vs. 14, despite what Sjöberg says (p. 156), the speaker is the interpreting angel, not the Head of Days, who is actually spoken of in the third person in that verse!

c) The MS translated by Knibb corroborates this view (under b)) by reading at the beginning of vs. 14 "And that angel came to me and greeted me with his voice and said to me" instead of simply "And he came to me and greeted me with his voice and said to me" − the text to which Sjöberg *et al.* attach the Head of Days as grammatical subject!

d) The second personal pronoun in vs. 14 destroys the natural flow of thought in the passage.

e) The 'Enochic interpretation' assumes too much by having God come up to Enoch (an idea offensive in itself, instead of Enoch being brought before God) and speak to him in person (something unprecedented in this work) and inform him that all he witnessed in the *Parables* so far had him, Enoch, as its most central figure! This is most incongruous.

f) 71:15 is quite incongruous after 71:14 if the Son of Man is Enoch and the speaker is the Head of Days. But vs. 15 is quite understandable if the speaker is the angel and the subject of 'proclaims' is the Son of Man of vs. 14.

g) If then it is not possible to consider God the speaker in 71:14−17, the situation becomes even more untenable to have the interpreting angel, who accompanies Enoch, charged with a message from the Head of Days to the Son of Man, − telling him who he is! (viz. in vs. 14).

h) Vs. 17 reverts back to the third person in speaking of the Son of Man, as is the case in the entire work. This indicates that a tampering (conscious or unconscious) has taken place in regard to vv. 14 and 16. Such tampering was probably facilitated by vs. 15, which addresses Enoch, but *not* as Son of Man.

i) Finally the strongest argument against the 'Enochic interpretation' is the whole portrayal of the Son of Man in the *Parables*, which is inapplicable to Enoch's person. Cavallin (*Life after Death*, pp. 206f.) gives some evidence for Jewish belief in the exaltation of great men of the past, e.g. Enoch, Abraham. The latter is, according to Philo, "a prototype of immortalized men of God (*Sacr.* 5,4.5.6)" (p. 206). This is most probably due to hellenistic influence on Philo, while purely Jewish views of the resurrection and exaltation of the Patriarchs are something quite different from the descriptions of the Son of Man in the *Parables*.

6. The interpretation of the Son of Man in the *Parables*

Having considered the relation of the *Parables* to the Book of Daniel and argued that the author planned his work so as to advance a novel Son of Man messianology, I shall now proceed to discuss the picture of the Son of Man he presents. Having already put forth the case that the author used the three titles of Elect One, Righteous One and Anointed One as means of identifying his Son of Man, it is not necessary to discuss these titles again. The evidence they afford is, nevertheless, to be kept in mind and to be added to what will now follow[122]. The discussion here will be carried out under four subheadings.

a) *Presentation*

The presentation of the Son of Man in 46:1 *vis à vis* that of the Head of Days is of paramount importance for evaluating the understanding of the Son of Man by the author of the *Parables*. First he is presented as "another being whose countenance had the appearance of a man" (46:1). To forestall any possible misunderstanding the author adds immediately "His face was full of graciousness like one of the holy angels". This shows clearly the author's concern to underline the Son of Man's otherworldly character[123]. He is neither a human being nor an angel. He only resembles

---

On the other hand Melchisedek seems to be presented as a heavenly being in 11Q Melch (see Horton, *The Melchisedek Tradition*, (64—84). On Philo's 'heavenly man' and its possible connection to the SM, see Wedderburn, *NovT* 15 (1973) 301—26.

j) And yet this is so in the present text. Many explanations are possible: (i) Mowinckel ("Henok og Menneskesønnen" *NorTT* 45 (1944), 57—69) thought that "Son of Man" in 71: 14 is not titular; (ii) The change may have taken place by inadvertency; (iii) We must reckon with the possibility of a conscious change in the interests of opposing Christian claims about Jesus being the Son of Man predicted, for example, in the *Parables*. (iv) It is furthermore possible that if the the text of 71:14ff. has never been altered, chs. 70 and 71 are an addition to the text of the *Parables*, which, as a matter of fact, ends with ch. 69. (v) How much an interpolator — if there is such — would have thought of the incongruity he was hereby introducing in order to achieve his more immediate goals, need not detain us. But it is much easier for a person trying to uphold a certain cause to introduce a change in a text, in the belief that it will help him out of his present difficulties without paying heed to the incongruity thus brought into the text, than for the original author, the architect of the work, to involve himself in such a hopeless muddle and contradiction of concepts as we have in the present text.

k) As a parallel to Enoch's being taken up to the SM in 1 En 70—71 from which it becomes a smaller step to his identification with the SM, may be cited IV Ez 14:9, where this time Ezra is taken up to the SM: "For you will be removed from (among) men and henceforth be with my Son and those like you until the times are determined".

This may, of course, have been written by another hand, but it shows how apocalyptic circles were eager to elevate their teachers to positions of special honour. It is difficult to be certain if IV Ezra contributed to the higher 'elevation' of Enoch in I En 71, but it is not improbable.

122 To the same effect Colpe, *TDNT*, VIII, 425.

123 Cf. Collins in *Ideal Figures in Ancient Judaism*, 111—33.

a human being in certain respects (i.e. countenance), as he does angels in others (i.e. graciousness). He is of another order. These points agree well with the data of Dan 7, indicating that the author of the *Parables* had understood his prototype as a kind of theophany and accordingly strove to carry over the implications of his notion more overtly to his own work.

b) Association

From the very start the Son of Man is introduced in the company of the Head of Days: "With him was another being . . ." (46:1). The seer asks in amazement "Why he went with the Head of Days" (46:2). We are told a) that the Son of Man is chosen by the Lord of Spirits (46:3), b) that his lot has the pre-eminence before the Lord of Spirits (46:3), c) that he judges the kings and the mighty because they do not praise the Lord of Spirits (46:4ff.), d) that he was named before the creation of the world in the presence of the Head of Days (48:2f.), e) that he is preserved by the Most High in his presence (62:7), f) that he is seated on the throne of his (? the Most High's) glory (62:5; 69:27), g) that the sum of judgment is committed to him by the Head of Days (62:5ff.; 69:27ff.), h) that he is worshipped together with the Lord of Spirits (48:5f.; 62:6 ff.), etc., etc.

All these ideas surely put it beyond doubt that the Son of Man is thought of as possessing a unique relation to the Head of Days, which is not comparable to the relation which the angels, described in this work, bear to him. Even in this important respect the *Parables* follows Daniel who, out of all the thousands and myriads of angels, standing before the throne of the Ancient One, singles out the Being compared to a son of man, and has him brought before the Eternal One with extraordinary pomp and even has (apparently) a throne reserved for him.

Like Daniel the *Parables* has its Son of Man associated neither with mankind nor with angels, but with God Himself. He sits on God's throne[124].

c) Origin

On seeing the Son of Man the visionary had asked three questions: Who he was, Whence he was, and Why he went with the Head of Days. The first question was answered immediately in chapter 46. The second question, which concerns us here, comprises the kind of question apocalyptists delighted in and forms independent material (from Daniel), though such speculation could have been encouraged by Daniel's terse

---

124 E.g. 51:3; 61:8; 62:2.

and enigmatic presentation of his 'SM'. There are two passages that deal with the origin of the Son of Man:

48:2   a "And at that hour that Son of Man was named
       b In the presence of the Lord of Spirits,
       c And his name before the Head of Days
    3 a Yea, before the sun and the signs were created,
       b Before the stars of heaven were made,
       c His name was named before the Lord of Spirits
    6 a And for this reason hath he been chosen and hidden before Him
       b Before the creation of the world and for evermore
62:7   a For from the beginning the Son of Man was hidden,
       b And the Most High preserved him in the presence of His might
       c And revealed him to the elect.

There can be no doubt that the author of the *Parables* is hereby portraying a pre-existent Son of Man[125], who was hidden by the Most High
or the Lord of Spirits, and who is now revealed according to God's design[126]. The use of verbs such as "revealed" or "appeared" (e.g. 48:7;

---

125 Similarly Schürer, *History of the Jewish People*, new ed. II, 519ff. and Bowman *ET* 59 (1947
    —8) 228, who finds "actual pre-existence with God in heaven" both in the *Parables* and in
    rabbinic literature.
126 In an article in *BJRL*, 32 (1950) 171—93, T.W. Manson argued vigorously against Sjöberg
    and others who upheld the pre-existence of the Son of Man in the *Parables*. Manson thinks
    that it is more proper to speak of the Son of Man's "non-existence" (186). The passages in
    the *Parables* which indicate pre-existence are explained as involving only "premundane elec-
    tion" not "premundane existence" (184). What Manson is interested in doing here is to rule
    out the objective existence of the Son of Man before his revelation. To him this is important
    because he later intends to identify the Son of Man with Enoch. But quite apart from the
    problematic nature of this identification (see note 121), Manson does not take sufficient ac-
    count of the fact that one cannot hide something which does not exist. The way he attempts
    to interpret the Son of Man's 'hiding' and his being under the wings of the Lord of Spirits
    (184f.) is wholly unsuited to these texts. For example with regard to the latter point he says:
    "To bring a person under the wings of the Shekinah is a regular way of describing conversion
    to Judaism" (185). Unless Manson is of the opinion that the *Parables* advocates the Son of
    Man's conversion to Judaism, I cannot see the relevance of this remark for the problem at
    hand.
        Manson puts his finger on the weakness of the identification of the Son of Man with
    Enoch, which Sjöberg and others advocate. Sjöberg says: "Henoch begegnet nur Gott selbst
    und wird von ihm als der Menschensohn begrüsst. Aber wenn dies geschieht, ist die Bezei-
    chnung Menschensohn mit dem inhalt geladen, den sie nach der vorherigen Darstellung der
    Bilderreden hat. Damit ist der präexistente himmlische Menschensohn gemeint. Als *dieser*
    wird der erhöhte Henoch begrüsst und in seine Stellung in der himmlischen Welt tritt er ein.
    Wie dies möglich ist, können wir uns nicht konkret vorstellen" (187). Manson comments:
    "So the essential problem is stated and declared insoluble" (188).
        Manson finds the insolubility of the problem in the Son of Man's pre-existence: "I venture
    to think that the problem is insoluble precisely because Sjöberg insists on retaining the con-
    ception of the Son of Man as a pre-existent heavenly being, a being something lower than God
    and something higher than angels" (188) (Casey, unreflectively is not aware of the difficulty,
    cf. his expression "Enoch was pre-existent"! *Son of Man*, 106). Manson's solution is that "the
    remedy is to recognize that the premundane Son of Man in Enoch is, if I may so describe it,
    an idea in the mind of God" (188); again, "Enoch incarnates, not a 'pre-existent heavenly
    being' but a divine idea" (189), and again, "Now an idea, a piece of God's purpose, which
    has been actualized in a famous man in the past, is actualized in the people of the saints of

62:7; 69:29) is thus quite symptomatic[127]. The author evidently interpreted the 'SM' of Dan 7:13 as a pre-existent being, hidden, but now revealed to assume the role of Judge. Thereby the author bids good-bye to the traditional Hebrew idea of the messianic king of the seed of David. Speculation on this puzzling, enigmatic being, appearing for the first time on the stage of Hebrew theological thinking in such a peculiar manner, without any genealogical connections or explanations as to his origin, filled the visionary's inventive imagination, which quite fruitfully brought forth the creation we have before us[128]. His source was quite silent on the Son of Man's origin. Nevertheless, from his appearing with the clouds of heaven, his unique relation to the Ancient of Days, his investment with universal dominion, — from all these things only one conclusion could be drawn: that Being must have been pre-existent. To the question: Why he was not known either to the prophets, in general, or to his source of inspiration, in particular, the answer is found in his hiddenness, a doctrine that proved only too convenient for the apocalyptist's purpose[129]. The Son of Man was chosen and reserved for the end-judgment. While, therefore, the author's view of the Son of Man's pre-existence is an inevitable conclusion from Dan 7:13f., that doctrine is not found explicitly in that source.

d) Roles

Of the roles ascribed to the Son of Man, the following ones are perhaps the most significant.

---

the Most High in the days of the Maccabees, and is destined to be more fully actualized in the expected Messiah, is something specially characteristic of the Hebrew way of looking at life and history" (190).

Manson's thesis is unconvincing. The insoluble problem which Sjöberg admitted did not hinge on the Son of Man's pre-existence, but on Sjöberg's insistence on identifying the Son of Man with Enoch. This is precisely the problem which leads Manson to play down the statements on pre-existence. Sjöberg started from the *Parables* as a whole and let the texts speak for themselves, but when he came to ch. 71, he unfortunately stumbled over that miserable blunder of Ethiopic transcription. Manson starts from an obviously impossible identification, and goes on to minimize the significance of the statements on pre-existence in order to bring the description of the Son of Man in line with Enoch's person. According to the present thesis both of them use a wrong approach. One problem is that insufficient attention has been paid to the nature of the 'SM' in Daniel. Second, the close dependence of the *Parables* on Daniel has not been adequately appreciated. Third, the description and portrayal of the Son of Man in the *Parables* — the whole picture, not alone pre-existence — is such as to rule out his identification with Enoch, even in the qualified way which Manson suggests.

127 Similar verbs are used of the Elect One, e.g. 52:9.

128 Similarly Sjöberg (*Der Menschensohn*, 146), "Der Menschensohn wird nicht als irdischer Messias, als endzeitlicher König des Geschlechts Davids geschildert. Er ist ein aus dem Himmel kommendes, dort vorher präexistentes Wesen, dessen Erscheinung den Abbruch der bisherigen Zeitalter und den Einbruch eines neuen Äons bedeutet".

129 The asking of three questions (46:3) about the Son of Man, when only one was to be at the

i. Revealer. Of the texts using the Son of Man designation, 46:3 is the only passage in which his role as Revealer is mentioned[130]. As the analytical display shows one of the characteristics of the Son of Man is that he "reveals all the treasures of that which is hidden." This statement, though here placed among the Son of Man's characteristics, denotes actually one of his acts. In the context, however, the attention is directed to his role as Revealer, which explains its inclusion among his characteristics. What is significant in this case is that of the four characteristics of the Son of Man enumerated (U 12–14 and 16), this characteristic of Revealer is the only one that is underscored in the text through the ascription of a reason for it: "Because the Lord of Spirits has chosen him" (U 15). The author hereby claims quite clearly that God has chosen the Son of Man to be the Revealer of his mysteries to the elect.

ii. Judge. This is the most conspicuous role of the Son of Man in the Parables. The main passages dealing with this role are: 46:4–6; 62:3ff., 11; 69:27, 29.

Chapter 46:4–6 takes up the Son of Man's judgment of the kings, the mighty and the strong on account of their unrighteous deeds, acts of defiance against God and of persecution of God's faithful.

Chapter 62 interestingly enough begins with the Elect One as Judge, but then continues with the Son of Man in that function.

62:1 c Open your eyes and lift up your horns if ye are able to recognize the Elect One
    2 a And the Lord of Spirits seated him on the throne of his glory
    3 a And there shall stand up in that day the kings and the mighty
       c And they shall see and recognize
       d How he (sc. the Elect One) sits on the throne of his glory
       e And righteousness is judged before him
       f And no lying word is spoken before him
    5 a And one portion of them shall look on the other,
       b And they shall be terrified
       e When they see that Son of Man
       f Sitting on the throne of his glory.

Staggered by what they see,

    9 a All the kings and the mighty and the exalted and those who rule the earth
       b Shall fall down before him on their faces
       c And worship and set their hope upon that Son of Man
       d And petition him and supplicate for mercy at his hands.

---

time answered, may have been among other things, for the purpose of enhancing that Figure's enigmatic nature.

130 Though we here adhere strictly to a discussion of passages expressly using the Son of Man designation, the picture given is incomplete inasmuch as titles like Elect One and Righteous One (especially the former) are used interchangeably with Son of Man, and these occur often with ideas of pre-existence, roles, etc. discussed here. An exhaustive study of those aspects ought to take what is said in connection with all titles into consideration.

However, the Lord of the Spirits will drive them away from his presence (62:10).

In 69:26ff. the Son of Man is again seated on his glorious throne and the sum of judgment is committed to him. The picture of judgment here is fuller and the verdict final:

69:26 c Because the name of that Son of Man had been revealed unto them
    27 a And he sat on the throne of his glory,
       b And the sum of judgment was given unto the Son of Man
    28 a With chains shall they be bound
       c And all their works shall vanish from the face of the earth
    29 a And from henceforth there shall be nothing corruptible;
       b For that Son of Man has appeared,
       c And has seated himself on the throne of his glory,
       d And all evil shall pass away before his face.

In chapters 53—56, where the titles of Righteous One and Elect One are used, the Figure so represented figures in the judgment of the angels, e.g. 55:4:

Ye mighty kings who dwell on earth, ye shall have to behold Mine Elect One, How he sits on the throne of glory and judges Azâzêl, and all his associates, and all his hosts in the name of of the Lord of Spirits.

Of considerable interest is the circumstance that the Son of Man is depicted as Judge, not by virtue of his being a Saviour, though saviourhood aspects are not altogether lacking in the *Parables*, nor because he is conceived of as a Suffering Servant[131], but wholly by virtue of God's election of him. He has been chosen and hidden from the beginning to be revealed at the end-time and enter his pre-determined office of Judge. The mentality of the author of the *Parables* is quite different from that found in the Gospels, and makes improbable the view that the Son of Man of the *Parables* is of Christian inspiration.

iii. Vindicator of the Righteous. Already at the Son of Man's initial presentation in chapter 46, the role of Vindicator of the righteous is implicit in the statements concerning the Son of Man's judgment of the kings and the mighty because, among other things, they persecute the faithful. Thus in 48:4 he is called "The staff of the righteous whereon to stay themselves and not fall". In 62:12f. through their being condemned the kings and the mighty are made

A spectacle for the righteous and for His elect:
They shall rejoice over them
Because the wrath of the Lord of Spirits resteth upon them,
And his sword is drunk with their blood.
And the righteous and the elect shall be saved on that day,
And they shall never thenceforward see the face of the sinners and unrighteous

---

131 Similarly Muilenburg, *JBL* 79 (1960) 206.

This is the note on which the *Parables* ends:

71:17   And so there shall be length of days with that Son of Man
         And the righteous shall have peace and an upright way,
         In the name of the Lord of Spirits for ever and ever.

Once again dependence on Daniel is quite apparent (Dan 7:22, 25ff.).

iv. Universal Ruler. The idea that the Son of Man receives universal rule is implicit in his function as Judge. Accordingly, in 48:8ff. the kings, etc., are powerless in his hands. The matter is put in a most clear manner in 62:6f.:

    And the kings and the mighty and all who possess the earth
    Shall bless and glorify and extol him *who rules over all*, who was hidden.
    For from the beginning the Son of Man was hidden.

The text goes on to speak of the kings' fruitless repentance and commiseration of their sorrowful state:

63:4   a We have now learnt that we should glorify
       b And bless the Lord of kings and him who is king over all kings,
    7 a For we have not believed before Him
       b Nor glorified the name of the Lord of Spirits,
       c But our hope was in the sceptre of our kingdom,
       d And in our glory
   11 a And after that their faces shall be filled with darkness
       b And shame before that Son of Man
       c And they shall be driven from his presence.

The universal reign of the Son of Man carries with it the banning of all evil:

    And from henceforth there shall be nothing corruptible
    And all evil shall pass away before his face (69:29)

Further, the reinstatement and bliss of the righteous:

62:12 b They (sc. the righteous) shall rejoice over them
   13 a And the righteous and elect shall be saved on that day,
       b They shall never thenceforward see the face of the sinners and unrighteous
   14 b And with the Son of Man shall they eat
       c And lie down and rise up for ever and ever
   15 c And they shall have been clothed with garments of glory
   16 c And your garments shall not grow old,
       c Nor your glory pass away before the Lord of Spirits,

and lastly the reign of peace and righteousness under the Son of Man, with which the book closes:

71:15 c From hence has proceeded peace since the creation of the world
       d And so shall it be unto the end for ever and for ever and ever.
   16 a And all shall walk in his ways since righteousness never forsakes him
   17 a And so there shall be length of days with that Son of Man
       b And the righteous shall have peace and an upright way.

Similarly in Dan 7 the 'SM' is portrayed as assuming universal power (7:14, 27).

v. Object of Worship. The roles discussed so far, and especially the last one, lead the author quite naturally to ascribe to his Son of Man what only God can receive — worship. The thought is expressed already in 48:5, where the Son of Man is worshipped together with the Lord of Spirits:

> All who dwell on earth shall fall down and worship before him
> And will praise and bless and celebrate with song the Lord of Spirits.

Similarly, in 62:6 the kings, etc. "bless and glorify and extol him *who rules over all*". This is an indication of honors usually offered to a deity. The detail *him who rules over all* is a most superlative way of describing the Son of Man's exalted status. In 62:9 the notion becomes quite explicit:

> 62:9 a And the kings and the mighty and the exalted and those who rule the earth
> b Shall fall down before him on their faces,
> c And worship and set their hope upon that Son of Man
> d And petition him and supplicate for mercy at his hands.

We have seen that the author of the *Parables* struck out on a bold line of interpretation, whereby he tried to portray his Son of Man in a manner unprecedented before his time (for all we know) as Revealer of heavenly secrets, as Universal Judge, as Vindicator of the righteous and as Universal Ruler. All these functions or offices by implication have prepared the ground for the explicit claims of the last role, whereby the Son of Man attains the final honor possible — that of worship[132].

Even this role of the Son of Man in the *Parables* is inspired by the source. In Dan 7:27 we are told that "all dominions shall serve and obey him" — the two terms "serve" and "obey" being used of service and obedience rendered to a deity (cf. Chapter II: Philological Considerations).

C. IV Ezra

1. Date

The first issue of importance here, as in the case of the *Parables*, is to prove that the concept under discussion is genuinely Jewish and not inspired by Christian exegesis. The simplest way to do that would be by showing that the work is pre-Christian. But, alas, this is not possible in the case of IV Ezra. Therefore, recourse will be had to the other alternative remaining, namely, the presence or absence of Christian influence on IV Ezra.

---

132 So too Muilenburg, *JBL* 79 (1960) 206.

The date of IV Ezra is conjectured to be the first century A.D. Box[133] dates the Eagle Vision (chs 11–12) to A.D. 81–96 or A.D. 69–79 and the rest of the material, including chapter 13, before A.D. 70. Violet[134] decides for the completion of the work in A.D. 100. Rowley[135] dates the whole book to the first century A.D.; Eissfeldt[136] in the reign of Domitian (81–96) or rather, soon after his death; Russell[137] between A.D. 90 and 100; Myers[138] to the last decade of the first Christian century, and Schreiner[139] about A.D. 100. An exception is Kaminka[140], who places chapter 13 in the time of Alexander the Great, and dates the bulk of the book earlier.

The dating of IV Ezra has its starting-point in 3:1: "In the thirtieth year after the overthrow of the city". This "overthrow"is understood by Kaminka to refer to the capture of Jerusalem in 587 B.C. – hence his dating at 556 B.C. – while by others it is taken to refer to the events of A.D. 70.

2. A Jewish Composition with Christian Interpolations

The tendency in recent times is to regard the book (viz. chs. 3–14) as a unity[141].

If we accept a date for the book in the last decades of the first century A.D. as well as the substantial unity of the book as a working hypothesis, we still have to reckon with the possibiliy of Christian interpolations[142]. There are indeed a number of passages that recall NT ideas and expressions. The difficulty in determining the degree of NT influence is, however,

133 *The Ezra-Apocalypse*, etc., xxviii ff., and 249; IV *Ezra* in Charles' *AP* II, 552.
134 *Die Apokalypsen des Esra und des Baruchs in deutscher Gestalt* xlix f.
135 *The Relevance of Apocalyptic*, 115.
136 *Introduction*, 626.
137 *The Method and Message*, 63.
138 *I and II Esdras*, 129. Similarly B.M. Metzger, *An Introduction to the Apocrypha*, 22.
139 *Das 4 Buch Esra (JSHRZ, V)*.
140 *MGWJ* 76 (1932) 121–38; 206–12; 494–511; 604–07; 77, (1933) 339–55.
141 M.R. James, *JTS* 19 (1918) 347ff.; Violet, *Die Apokalypsen des Esra und des Baruch*, p. xliii; J. Keulers, *Die eschatologische Lehre des vierten Esrabuches*, (*Biblische Studien* 20, 2–3, 1922), 47ff.; Gry, *Les dires prophétiques d' Esdras*, Vol. I, xciv ff.; A. Weiser, *Introduction* 436; B.M. Metzger, *Introduction to the Apocrypha*, 22; Russell, *Method and Message*, 63; Myers, *I–II Esdras*, 120f.; Brandenburger, *Die Verborgenheit Gottes im Weltgeschehen*, 23ff., 86ff.; Schreiner, *4 Ezra*, 298; Breech, *JBL* 92 (1973) 267ff.
     Among those who see IV Ezra as a composite work are the originator of the theory, Kabisch, *Das vierte Buch Esra und seine Quellen untersucht*, 1889, and Box, *The Ezra-Apocalypse*, 1912, xxi ff. and in Charles' *APOT* II, 551.
142 The Jewish character of the book is universally accepted, cf. e.g. Box, *The Ezra-Apocalypse*, p. lviii ff.; Violet, *Die Apokalypsen des Esra und des Baruch*, xl; Oesterley, *The Jews and Judaism*, 158; Colpe, *TDNT* VIII, 427ff.; Myers, *I–II Esdras*, 121ff.; Schürer, *History of the Jewish People*, II, 512; Stone, *Scriptures, Sects and Visions*, 99ff. id., "Ezra, Apocalypse of", *Enc. Jud.*, VI, 1108f.

that many of these ideas occur in other pseudepigraphical works as well. Further, it is not initially clear whether and to what extent Christian interpolations or influence has taken place, or if it is simply a case of coincidence, whereby ideas in current circulation have become the common stock in trade of groups of different religious standpoints. Now the great number of such commonly shared expressions between the NT and IV Ezra would seem to point to Christian influence at least in some cases[143]. The clearest indication of Christian tampering is found in 7: 28f.[144]: "For my son Jesus[145], together with those who are with him, will be revealed . . . Then after those years, my son Christ will die . . ." This passage is immediately followed by a description of a resurrection and judgment: "The world . . . will be aroused and what is corruptible will pass away . . ." (7:31f.).

Thus, there seem to be good grounds for assuming a Christian interference with the text of an otherwise very Jewish writing.

3. No Christian Influence on IV Ezra 13

Prejudicial though this may be initially, there seem to be equally good grounds for assuming the practically complete absence of Christian interference in the Fifth and Sixth Visions[146]. The contents of the Sixth Vision, in which our immediate interest lies, are genuinely Jewish not Christian, and its picture of the One like a Man coming out of the Sea ought consequently to be regarded as a purely Jewish conception. This judgment is grounded on the following considerations:

---

143 As samples of probable 'Christian' influence may be cited: 4:26 "because the age is speedily coming to an end." With this cf. I Cor 7:29ff.; 4:35: "have not the souls of the righteous in their storehouse inquired ... How long must we stay here?", cf. Rev 6:9—11; 5:9 "and all friends will assault each other" (the Armenian text (see Violet, *Die Esra Apokalypse*, 57) adds "filii cum patribus, et patres cum filiis, matres cum filiabus, adversariae inter se, fratres cum fratribus". With this cf. Mk 13:12; 7:31: "what is corruptible will pass away," cf. I Cor 15:53, though I En 68:28f. is just as possible: "and all their works (shall) vanish from the face of the earth. And from henceforth there shall be nothing corruptible"; 8:3: "Many have been created but few will be saved" recalls Mt 22:14; 9:3: "so when there will appear in the world tremors in places, disorders of peoples, intrigues of nations ..." reminds us of Mt 24: 6ff. Cf. further 6:23 with I Cor 15:52; I Th 4:16; 6:25 with Mk 13:13; 8:31f. with Rm 3: 20ff. and *passim*; 13:30 with Mt 24:6ff.

144 For this and other interpolations see Bloch, *HTR* 51 (1958) 89ff.

145 According to the Latin translation. The Syriac, the Ethiopic and the Arabic read "Messiah" (see Box, *The Ezra-Apocalypse*, 114). Gero, *ZNW* 66 (1975) 264—7, mainly on the basis of the Georgian Version, argues that the reading 'son' is probably a variant translation of an originally ambiguous Hebrew בר meaning both 'son' and 'elect', and that the translation here need not be explained as a Christian interpolation, as e.g. Lohse, *TDNT*, VIII, 361.

146 Similarly Borsch, *The Son of Man*, 156: "these (i.e. the interpolations) do not seem to have affected the crucial vision in ch. 13". Bloch, *HTR* 51 (1958) 87—94, dealing with christological interpolations, finds no such in ch. 13. Of the few references to the NT which Myers cites, only 13:31 with Mt 24:6f.; and 13:32 with Mt 24:30 = Mk 13:26 may be considered as parallels; 13:10 with Rev 11:5 is doubtful.

a) In chapter 13, the Man from the Sea Vision (and this applies to the Eagle Vision, chs. 11–12), there are hardly any similarities in thought or in diction with the NT. For their inspiration as well as descriptions these visions lean heavily on the OT and particularly on Daniel[147].

b) In 12:10ff. after identifying his eagle with the fourth beast of Dan 7, the author proceeds to flatly contradict Daniel with respect to the identification of the fourth beast. Neither the OT nor the NT present another case of outright contradiction of foregone biblical authors[148]. The expression ". . . Daniel, your brother" (11:11) is aimed at bolstering up the apocalyptist's status by setting him not merely on a par with Daniel, but above him, by means of the superior, or rather, more valid revelation he has received.

c) The search for credentials leads him to make many assertions of self-commendation and self-praise[149]. Conscious of his inferior standing, the author here dwells upon his moral and religious qualities in an effort to make up for the lack of a direct divine calling, which does not seek its legitimization in the prophet's own person, but in the fact of God's call. Such self-complacent and self-exalting language has no parallel either in the prophets[150] or in the NT[151], but it has a parallel in IV Ezra's forerunner, the author of the *Parables*[152].

---

147 Of the same opinion is Stone, "The vision (viz. IV Ez 13) is greatly influenced by Daniel as is evident not only from the explicit reference to that chapter in 12:11 but from many other elements in the structure of the vision" (in *Religions in Antiquity*, 301). Similarly Keulers, *Die eschatologische Lehre*, 124.

148 Dan 9:2, 24ff. is not a contradiction of "the world of the Lord to Jeremiah the prophet." The author simply makes Jeremiah's prophecy of seventy years of captivity his starting point for a new vision involving seventy weeks of years, a vision that spans a period not foreseen by Jeremiah, according to him.

149 Some typical examples are the following: "If I am accounted by you more just than the many" (12:7); "You (sc. God) have already regarded me (sc. Ezra) worthy ..." (12:9); "You (sc. Ezra) alone have been deemed worthy to know this secret of the Most High" (12:36); "You (sc. Ezra) alone of all the prophets are left to us, like a grape from vintage, like a lamp in a dark place, like a safe harbor for a ship in a tempest" (12:42); "From the beginning you (sc. God) ... have considered me (sc. Ezra) worthy" (13:14); "You (sc. Ezra) alone have been informed: because you have relinquished your [own interests], and devoted yourself to mine; you have explored my law, you have dedicated your life to wisdom, and you have called understanding your mother" (13:53f.). In 8:47ff. the author of IV Ezra is proud of his humility " ... inasmuch as you (sc. Ezra) have frequently reckoned yourself among the unjust ... But in this too you will be [regarded] as commendable before the Most High, because you have humbled yourself ... and did not reckon yourself among the just so as to have gloried over much". The point made in all these statements is not simply that God considers Ezra worthy of the Almighty's confidence, but that Ezra actually deserves it!

150 Perhaps one of the boldest statements in Daniel is 10:11: "O Daniel, man greatly beloved". but it does not come anywhere near IV Ezra's self-complacent statements.

151 Even those Pauline statements, which can be interpreted as giving vent to an arrogant spirit, rightly understood fall in well with Paul's golden rule: μή ὑπερφρονεῖν παρ' ὅ δεῖ φρονεῖν ἀλλὰ φρονεῖν εἰς τὸ σωφρονεῖν (Rm 12:3).

152 Cf. I En 37:4: "Till the present day such wisdom has never been given by the Lord of Spirits as I have received according to my insight ..." Stone remarks with regard to the *Parables*

The above three points bespeak the Jewish character of IV Ezra.

d) The description of the central Figure of Vision Six, the One like a Man coming out the Sea, is strongly reminiscent of Daniel's "One like a son of man". His emergence from the depths of the Sea, at first somewhat puzzling, is, in due time, interpreted as symbolizing nothing other than his hiddenness (13:52, cf. also 13:26). This, at once, connects back to the Son of Man in the *Parables*, where some of the aspects of the Son of Man dwelt upon are his pre-existence, hiddenness and righteousness. IV Ezra conceives of the Son of Man similarly, which indicates that he is rooted in Jewish not Christian pietism.

e) Finally Ezra's conception of the Son of Man exhibits no Christian traits. It is, therefore, difficult to conceive of a Christian interpolator introducing this concept into IV Ezra's text and portraying the Son of Man in a way no Jewish author would ever hesitate to do, while at the same time denying him every peculiarly Christian feature. Indeed, in more senses than one it might be claimed that the 'One like a (son of) Man' of IV Ezra stands in contrast to or is a rival of the Son of Man of the Gospels[153]. IV Ezra attempted to give an alternative interpretation of the Son of Man figure in current messianic discussion, but in the process he was obliged to depart from his Danielic prototype[154] which was adhered to more strictly by Christians.

But what is of significance for our immediate purpose is not so much IV Ezra's reactionary interpretation of the One like a (son of) Man, but the fact that he too, independent of Christian interpretation, indeed in spite of it, understood the Figure of the 'SM' in Daniel (and in I En 37—71) messianically[155], albeit he depicted him in his own way[156].

4. The Messiah in IV Ezra

In the Fifth Vision the eagle is stated to represent the fourth beast of Dan 7 and it is interpreted in a manner that leaves no doubt that the beast symbolizes the Roman Empire (12:12—31). Several allusions which can be interpreted of the Fall of Jerusalem in A.D. 70[157], explain the author's

---

"they are close enough to IV Ezra to serve as comparative material" (in *Religions of Antiquity*, 301).

153 Cf. Baldensperger, *Die messianisch-apokalyptische Hoffnung des Judentums*, 128 n.2, and Tillmann, *Der Menschensohn*, 105.

154 Cf. Keulers, *Die eschatologische Lehre des vierten Esrabuches*, 125: "Esra sich ... viel radikaler von Daniel abgekehrt hätte."

155 So Keulers, *Die eschatologische Lehre*, 140.

156 The description of the Man from the Sea, the mountain cut without hands, the war of the wicked against the Son of Man and their destruction, the new multitude following the Son of Man, etc., are easily developed from various parts of Daniel's book.

157 E.g. 11:39 may imply that "sway over my world so that through them (i.e. the beasts) the end of my times might come" is fulfilled in Jerusalem's fall. Clearer is 11:42: "You have

vituperations against the Roman Empire[158], and probably fix the writing of the book not too long after that tragic event.

Within the confines of Danielic imagery, but contrary to Danielic symbolism, a lion, in Danielic manner, utters words of judgment against the Eagle, during which event "the remaining head . . . vanished" (12:1).

In the interpretation of the vision, the lion is said to symbolize "the Anointed One whom the Most High has reserved till the end of days, who will arise from the seed of David" (12:32). This description underlines three ideas about the Messiah, a) that he is hidden[159], i.e. preserved by the Most High, b) that he is to be revealed at the end of days, and c) that he is of the seed of David.

While still clinging to classical messianic expectations, the author supplements them by introducing conceptions of more recent vintage[160]. The ideas of the Messiah's hiddenness and appearing at the end of time[161]

---

razed the walls of those who did you no harm"; and still clearer is 12:44f.: "consumed in the conflagration of Zion! For we are no better than those who perished there." See Breech, *JBL*, 92, (1973) 270.

158 Cf. 11:40–45 (Myer's translation):
Holding sway over the world with great terror,
And over the entire earth with the utmost oppression;
You lived for so long in the world with duplicity;
You have not judged the earth with truth.
You have oppressed the meek,
You have injured the peaceful,
You have hated those who speak the truth,
You have loved liars,
You have destroyed the homes of the thrifty,
You have razed the walls of those who did you no harm.
Your arrogance has reached the Most High,
And your haughtiness the Almighty.
The Most High has considered his times;
Now they come to an end;
His ages have attained completion.
Therefore, you Eagle, you will vanish,
With your horrible wings,
With your evil winglets,
With your malicious heads,
With your ghastly talons,
With your whole sinister body.

159 On the thought of pre-existence, hiddenness and revealedness see also 7:28.

160 E.g. from Daniel and I En 37–71. Similarly Stone, "The roots of most of these elements lie deep in apocalyptic tradition and especially in Daniel 7 ... IV Ezra 12:11 makes it evident that the author is dependent on a tradition of interpretation or rather re-interpretation of Dan 7 and may not have been the first so to be" (in *Religions in Antiquity*, 302). Bloch, *HTR*, 51 (1958) 93f. considers the reference to David's seed an interpolation, following Oesterly, *II Esdras*, 141, who says that "it is most improbable that the transcendental Messiah and the earthly messiah should be spoken of together in this way in a Jewish writing" — as if the 'transcendental Messiah' could be introduced into a vacuum!

161 For a study of the technical term 'End' in IV Erza and its associations with the messianic king, see Stone, *JBL* 102 (1983) 229–43.

are clearly ideas loaned from the Son of Man description in the *Parables*[162]. IV Ezra hereby indicates that he is dissatisfied with the traditional idea of a human messiah, — no one of the messianic pretenders of the past hundred years had succeeded in ousting the Romans — and casts his hopes on a Figure "reserved till the end of days"[163]. The statement that this Personage "will arise from the seed of David" is not emphatic at all in IV Ezra[164]. It is probably his way of stressing the continuity in messianic thought, though the content is thoroughly transformed, as is seen from the function of the Messiah delineated immediately thereafter: (The Messiah will) "upbraid them (sc. the kings represented by the Eagle) for their wickedness, condemn them for their injustices, and confront them directly with their insults. First he will present them alive for judgment, and then after upbraiding them he will destroy them"[165]. It is incontrovertible that the picture of the Messiah here[166] is strongly reminiscent of the Son of Man as presented in the *Parables*, — a heavenly being rather than an earthly messiah, whose ordering in of the kings for judgment, upbraiding them and final destruction of them bear no relation to the functions of the traditional messiah. Rather these are the chief characteristics of the Son of Man as developed by I En 37—71 from Dan 7.

Lastly, the Messiah in IV Ezra 11—12 also has a role in regard to God's people: "But the remnant of my people who are left in my land he will set free with compassion and grant them joy until the end, the day of judgment (12:34)[167]. The reference to "land" as well as the futurity of the day of judgment may indicate that IV Ezra still hopes for a restored existence of Jewery in Palestine before the Judgment[168]. In this case

---

162 Cf. e.g. I En 48:6f.; 62:6f.; 69:29.
163 In 7:29, nevertheless, IV Ezra speaks of the death of the Messiah after a reign of "400 years". So the Latin and the Arabic of Ewald. The Arabic of Gildemeister has 1000 years; the Ethiopic omits and the Armenian has a lacuna, while the Syriac reads "30 years" (see Violet, *Die Apokalypsen des Esra u.d. Baruch*, 74; Box, *Ezra-Apocalypse*, 115, and Schreiner, *Das 4 Buch Esra*, 345). If the reference to the Messiah's death is not a Christian interpolation (30 years could be an approximation to Jesus' life), — so understood by P. Grelot in *La venue du Messie*, 19—50 — it may be an explanation as to why and how IV Ezra is able to combine in 12:32 characteristics of a heavenly Son of Man with the Davidic messiah (cf. II Bar 30:1). On the absence of the Messiah's vicarious sufferings in Jewish thought see Schürer, *History of the Jewish People*, II, 547ff. On the problem of the Messiah's death cf. Wilcke, *Das Problem eines messianischen Zwischenreichs bei Paulus*, 45.
164 Similarly Stone (in *Religions in Antiquity*, 311): "The reference to the Davidic descent of the Messiah in 12:32 should probably be regarded as a traditional element and not at all central to the concept of the book", while Lagrange, *Revue Biblique*, N.S.2, 1905, pp. 499, considers it an interpolation. According to Bloch, *HTR* 51 (1958) 93 the passage tries to connect the transcendental with the earthly messiah.
165 12:32f. Cf. I En 38:1; 41:2; 45:2, 5f.; 48:8ff.; 50:2ff.; 53:3ff.; 60:5ff.; 62:11ff.; 69:27f.
166 Similarly Stone in *Religions in Antiquity*, 296.
167 Cf. I En 62:13, 15f.; 69:26.
168 There is therefore the problem of how far 12:32—34 is to be related to 7:29—33. In 7:29ff. the Messiah and all who have human breath die. The world returns to primordial silence for

motifs from two different ideas or models of messianism have been
blended together[169]. But this, at its very best, only means that while IV
Ezra still hopes for certain earthly effects of the messianic reign as becomes a Davidic messiah, this will be effected by such means as are
associated with a heavenly Messiah, a being described in Dan 7 and I En
37—71 as Son of Man, etc. On the other hand, IV Ezra may have been
under pressure, in the face of Jerusalem's desolation, to make the pros-
pects of messianic times more tangible by dwelling on some aspects associated with the earthly messiah. What is important is not the terms
themselves (e.g the Davidic messiah, etc.) but the ideas and concepts
with which these terms are charged[170].

The above brief examination has shown that IV Ezra in presenting his
Messiah has utilized Son of Man ideas from the *Parables* and ultimately
from Daniel. IV Ezra's Messiah conforms more to the Son of Man concept than to the traditional Davidic messiah[171].

Our interest will now be directed to the Sixth Vision, in which we actually find the term 'One like a (Son of) Man' used.

5. The 'One like a (Son of) Man' in IV Ezra

The Son of Man of IV Ezra evinces neither the conformity nor the

---

seven days. Thereafter comes the resurrection and finally the Most High is seated on his
throne in judgment. In 12:32—34 a period of happiness is vouched for the remnant of Israel
in Palestine (12:34) after the final judgment of the oppressors (12:33)! Harnisch (*Verhängnis
und Verheisung der Geschichte*, 256f.) has noticed the incongruity but solves the problem in
a questionable manner. He thinks that the appearance of the Messiah does not imply the end-
stage of final salvation. The times of the Messiah appear as a closing phase of the old aeon. It
is a transitional period which ends with the Messiah's death. After the silence of the seven
days a new aeon is born. The earth, the dust and the storehouse give up those in their keeping
and the judgment takes place. Thus, Harnisch seems to think that either 12:34 alone or 12:
32—34 occurs prior to the Messiah's death in 7:29. This reconstruction makes too many
assumptions: a) that the statement of the Messiah's death in 7:29 is genuine; b) that the
judgment of 12:32—33 is not final; c) that the picture of the Messiah in 12:32ff. and 7:28ff.
is coherent. Finally, d) it fails to take account of the influence of the Son of Man motif on
12:32ff., which is not the same as that of the traditional Messiah. For example, while according to 12:32 the Judge is the Messiah, who 'wears' the Son of Man characteristics, the Judge
in 7:33 is the Most High (presumably = God). It is, therefore, entirely possible that we ought
not to blend the presentation of the two texts (7:28ff. and 12:32ff.) into a coherent messianic synthesis. Stone, too, is aware of the different conceptions involved at chs. 11—12 and
7:28ff. (in *Religions in Antiquity*, 310).

169 Similarly Myers, *I—II Esdras*, 302. See also Klausner, *Messianic Idea*, 365.
170 It is not the purpose of this investigation to enter into a discussion of IV Ezra's theology in
general. For such discussions see e.g. Keulers, *Die eschatologische Lehre des vierten Esrabuches;* Harnisch, *Verhängnis und Verheissung;* Rössler, *Gesetz und Geschichte;* and Sanders,
Paul and Palestinian Judaism, 409—18.
171 On the inconsequent presentation of IV Ezra's Messiah now with Davidic and then with Son
of Man traits, see Keulers, *Die eschatologische Lehre des vierten Esrabuches*, 140f. The best

multiformity of the Son of Man of the *Parables*. Here, the situation is much simpler. Its dependence on Daniel is more general in character rather than in details as I En 37—71. Consequently, our investigation will dispense with semantic analyses and detailed comparisons. In a simpler and more direct manner an answer will be sought to the question of how IV Ezra interpreted Daniel's 'SM', and the interpretative tradition to which he bears witness.

a) The Text-critical Problem of the Expression

The first problem facing us is that of the precise form of the expression used for what is usually translated as 'One like a Man'.

Owing to *homoioteleuton*[172], occasioned by the repetition of *Et vidi et ecce*, the Latin omits the text containing the crucial term. The Arabic, Ethiopic and Armenian Versions read: "The wind caused to come up out of the heart of the Sea as it were the form of a Man"[173]. The Syriac Version has *'yk dmwt' dbrnš' '*(One) like the appearance of a Son of Man'. Inasmuch as the Syriac is the closest of the existing Versions to the original Hebrew or Aramaic, using precisely the same expression as the corresponding one in Hebrew and Aramaic, it ought to admit of no doubt that the Hebrew was בן אדם rather than אדם, and the Aramaic בר (א)נש(א) rather than (א)נש(א)[174]. It is further entirely possible that the Latin, too, read *filius hominis* representing an original בן אדם or בר (א)נש(א). Absolute certainty on the matter is impossible[175], but to judge from I En 46:1 (since Dan 7 does not repeat the expression), the longer expression 'One like a Son of Man' was very likely used in the introductory presentation (13:3a), but was afterwards dispensed with as was done also in the case of the *Parables*[175a]. But even if the original did read 'One like a Man' instead of 'One like a Son of Man', it is not detrimental to the present thesis, since the weight is not placed

---

hypothesis to explain the discrepant pictures of the Messiah in IV Ezra is probably to assume the blending of two different models of Messiah.

172 See Box, *The Ezra-Apocalypse*, 287.

173 Syriac: "wie die Gestalt eines Menschen"; Ethiopic: "gleichwie ein Mensch" ("oder 'wie das Bild eines Menschen' "); Arabic of Ewald: "gleich der Gestalt eines Menschen"; Arabic of Gildemeister: "das Bild eines Menschen"; and the Armenian: "similitudinem hominis" (Violet, *Die Esra-Apokalypse*, 367f.).

174 This position coincides with the view of N. Schmidt, art. "Son of Man" (*Encyclopedia Biblica*) and Keulers, *Die eschatologische Lehre des vierten Esrabuches*, 126.

175 Casey, *Son of Man*, 124f., makes a remarkable syllogism. He admits that the Syriac reads "One like the appearance of a Son of Man". However, on the basis of the Latin, which here has a lacuna, but which he thinks it must have read *homo* (because elsewhere in the vision it reads *homo*) he decides that the Greek was ἄνθρωπος and the Hebrew אדם! — a reading for which there is not a shred of evidence.

175a See Moule, *Origin of Christology*, 15f.

upon the actual form of the term, but upon the content conveyed thereby[176]. In the vision of chapter 13 enough of the imagery of Dan 7 has been preserved[177] so as to leave no doubt as to who the Personage referred to in vs. 3 is. So, even if Ezra did use 'One like a Man' in this context, the presentation and the associations made leave no doubt whatever that he thereby intended none other than the particular Figure set forth by Daniel as "One *like* a Son of Man" or by the *Parables* as "One whose countenance had the *appearance* of a Man" or simply "that Son of Man".

Thus, while there are good grounds for assuming that the expression IV Ezra used was 'One *like* a Son of Man' (as the Syriac!), even the present expression in the other translations (except the Latin!) indicates that the Figure IV Ezra described was thought of as non-human — precisely as in Dan 7!

But how is this 'non-human' being, or rather 'One *like* a human being' conceived in IV Ezra? This will be the concern of the following discussion.

b) Presented as Non-human

Leaving aside the question as to whether the original expression contained the phrase 'son of' or not, we concentrate on the preposition 'like' (= כ), or the prepositional phrase 'in the likeness of' (= דמות). As in Dan 7:13 and I En 46:1, this was the means which the author employed in order to make it clear that the entity he described was non-human. The Personage only *resembled* a human being. This point is underscored in the interpretation[178]. It is further underlined by another phrase borrowed from Daniel, namely that the Figure observed is transported with the clouds of heaven. The importance of the motif of the theophany for the nature of the being here presented has already been discussed in connection with Daniel. What has therefore been said there applies here also. Another motif of Danielic provenience is the Sea, though the symbolism here is different, being explained of the hiddenness of the Figure.

These details leave the impression that we are here concerned with the 'same' supernatural being with which Daniel and I En 37—71 had occupied themselves.

---

176 A similar situation was registered with regard to the original behind the Ethiopic of the *Parables*, but that could not dim the fact that the Figure so portrayed was inspired by Dan 7. The elasticity of the expression is owing to the fact, that the expression son of man as such really means 'man' or 'human being'. The messianic content does not lie in the expression as such, but in the Entity referred to by this expression. Thus, though the particular form itself does not mean 'Messiah', it helps to identify the Person so referred to as the Messiah. Cf. also the discussion under The OT Antecedents, in Ch. Two.

177 Note the elements: "dream in the night" (13:1); "wind, sea, stirred up" (13:2); "one resembling a (son of) man" (13:3); "flying with the clouds of heaven" (13:3).

178 I.e. 13:32: "My son, whom you saw *as a man* rising up will be revealed".

c) Pre-existent

The reference to the Son of Man's coming up from the heart of the Sea is puzzling, and at first sight probably leads our thoughts to the role played by the Sea in Dan 7. The interpretation, however, makes it quite plain that the Sea motif is entirely different from that found in Daniel. In vs. 26 we are told that "the man you saw rising from the depths of the Sea represents the One whom the Most High has kept for many ages"[179]. As if this explanation is not enough, the seer, in imitation of Daniel (cf. Dan 7:19 with 7:16!), asks for more precise information about the symbolism of the "depths of the Sea", and is told: "Just as no one can search out or perceive what may be in the depths of the sea, so no one on earth will be able to see my son or those who are with him except in the time of his day" (13:52). There can hardly be any doubt that these passages conceive of the Son of Man as pre-existent, and that 7:28 and 14:9 are to be understood likewise[180].

d) Divine

The mention of the clouds carrying the Son of Man with its theophanic significance, hints at the supernatural or divine character of the Figure so transported. Other features betraying the Son of Man's nature are his voice and his way of annihilating his enemies. In 13:4 we read that "wherever the voice of his mouth sounded all who heard it melted as wax melts when it comes in contact with fire". In the OT such language occurs in connection with theophanies[181], even as in I En 1:6. Similarly in the *Parables* the elements and mankind tremble, quake or melt before the Head of Days[182], the Elect One[183], and the Son of Man[184]. His way of managing the hostile throng that attacks him, has no parallel whatever to that which is typical of the Davidic messiah, but is in keeping with Yahweh's theophanic appearances Discarding all human implements of war, "he discharged from his mouth, as it were, a torrent of fire and from his lips a flaming blast; and from his tongue he poured forth a gust of sparks . . .

---

179 Myers, *I–II Esdras*, 310 says: "Reference is to the heavenly Messiah of I Enoch 37–70, not to the Davidic Messiah". Cf. also Box's remarks in *The Ezra-Apocalypse*, 293 (and in Charles, *APOT* II, 618).

180 So Myers, *I–II Esdras*, 127 and Stone, in *Religions in Antiquity*, 310: "The Messiah is pre-existent in all texts". With this position agrees also Keulers, *Die eschatologische Lehre des vierten Esrabuches*, 127, 141. Breech's remarks (to the contrary) are rather curious, esp. as Breech reckons with the unity of IV Ezra (*JBL*, 92 (1973) 273).

181 E.g. Ps 46:6; 68:2(3); 97:5; Isa 34:3; Mic 1:4; Judith 16:15.

182 60:1–3.

183 52:6: "All these (sc. the mountains) shall be in the presence of the Elect One as wax before the fire"; 62:2.

184 62:5.

the torrent of fire, the flaming blast, and the powerful gust . . . cremated all [of them]. Suddenly nothing . . . was apparent except powdery ashes" (13:10–11). This imagery of divine vengeance[185] though unsuitable for a Davidic messiah, is in keeping with the supernatural status attributed to the Son of Man[186]. In the Interpretation we are given to understand that the "torrent of fire", the "flaming blast" and the "gust of sparks" are nothing else than his divine word of condemnation, which the Jewish author identifies with the law! (13:38).

e) God's Son

In the Interpretation Part, the entreaties of the seer for an explanation are answered by the Most High, who interprets the symbolism of the Son of Man who annihilated the multitudes, thus: "Moreover, when this takes place, the signs to which I directed your attention earlier will come about and then my Son, whom you saw *as a man* (!) rising up, will be revealed" (13:32). The reference here is to the first appearance of the 'One like a Son of Man' in 13:3a. The Son of Man is here explicitly called the Son of God. This is repeated in 13:37 in connection with the judgment and annihilation he is to bring upon the evil-doers. Not without reason 7:28f. is called to mind. Even though "Jesus" there is an interpolation, and the death of the Messiah has been regarded by some as a Christian tampering, there is no reason to doubt that the Messiah is in 7:28f. called the Son of God.

f) Messiah

There is no doubt that 7:28ff., 12:32ff. and chapter 13 all deal with the Messiah[187]. In 7:28 the Messiah is accompanied by an entourage. So in 12:34 he is said to bring deliverance and re-instatement to God's people. In 13:12 the seer sees the Son of Man "summon to himself another peaceful host". This is interpreted in 13:39ff. as the ten tribes, whose return to the promised land is facilitated by the recurrence of Exodus motifs, thus bringing the Son of Man's activity in direct connection with Salvation History. In 13:26 it is said expressly that "the One whom the Most High has kept for many ages *through whom to deliver his creation*" (italics mine) is the "SM"[188]. The Messiah, accordingly, functions as Sav-

---

185 Cf. Isa 11:4; Ps 18:8, 13.
186 So, too, in I En 62:2.
187 Ferch, *AUSS*, 15 (1977) 135–51.
188 So Myers following the Latin, Armenian and the Arabic of Ewald. Violet and Schreiner translate "erlösen" with Syriac, Ethiopic and the Arabic of Gildemeister.

iour of the newly collected people and as destroyer of their enemies (13: 48f.).

g) Judge

Finally, the Son of Man figures also as Judge. The description given of him in the vision, where he annihilates his enemies with a blast from his mouth, has led some to speak of the 'Warrior' motif of the Son of Man, and search for Ugaritic parallels[189]. This is however unnessary. In the Interpretation, which is no doubt by the same author as the Vision[190], we are given to understand what "the torrent of fire", "the flaming blast" and "the powerful gust" are: "My Son himself will berate for their impiety the peoples who have come [against him] . . . confront them face to face with their evil designs and with the tortures they are to undergo — these are like the flames — and crush them effortlessly with the law — these are like the fire" (13:37f.). With this may be compared 12:32f.: "The Anointed One . . . will . . . speak with them, upbraid them for their wickedness, condemn them for their injustics, and confront them directly with their insults. First he will present them alive for judgment, and then, after upbraiding them, he will destroy them." The ideas in the two passages are in all essentials identical, and confirm most conclusively the Son of Man's identification with the Messiah as well as the Son of Man's function as Judge.

D. Rabbinism

As is well known the rabbinic writings are all post-NT. However, so far from evidencing NT influence, they are often written in conscious polemic against Christianity. Hence, the evidence they present may be considered as a witness to an unbroken chain of interpretative tradition with regard to the Danielic 'SM'.

Dan 7:13f. does not figure as often as one might have expected in such a vast collection as the rabbinic literature. Nevertheless, where is occurs, it does so for the most part in a clearly messianic sense.

According to *B. T. Sanhedrin* 98 a R. Jehoshua ben Levi (c.A.D. 250) in speaking of the Messiah's coming, juxtaposed Dan 7:13 with Zech 9:9: "If they (sc. the people of Israel) are worthy, (he will come) with the

---

189 E.g. Stone, in *Religions in Antiquity*, 308.

190 Contra Stone, *Religions in Antiquity*, 305f. See Casey, *Son of Man*, 126ff.; Breech, *JBL*, 92 (1973) 273, and Harnisch, *Verhängnis und Verheissung*, for the unity of the book.

clouds of heaven; if not, lowly and riding upon an ass"[191]. In *Midrash R. Numb.* 13:14 in answering the question, How do we know that the Messiah will rule over the earth? the author supports his contention by citing Ps 72:11 and Dan 7:13f. and 2:35: "Because it is written 'All kings shall prostrate themselves before him, all nations shall serve him' . . . and it also says, 'Behold, there came with the clouds of heaven one like unto a son of man . . . and there was given unto him dominion . . . that all the peoples . . . should serve him,' etc. ". . . And the stone that smote the image became a great mountain, and filled the whole earth"[192]. Here not only the Son of Man but also the Stone cut without hands is interpreted messianically. *Midr. Hag-gadol Gen* 49:10 interprets "the sceptre shall not depart from Judah" messianically by citing various passages from the prophets as Deut 33:21; Ps 72:17; Jer 16:13; Isa 53:4; Am 5:18, as well as Dan 7:14 and 7:27!: ‏ולו יקהה עמים · הוא בא ומק'הה שניהן‎ ‏שלאומות וכולו משתעבדין לו שנ' וליה יהב שלטן ויקר ומלכו‎ ‏(דניאל ז' י'ד) .ואומ' וכל שלטוניא ליה יפלחון ויתמעון (שם‎ ‏כ'ז)‎ [193]. Of particular interest here is that the author understands not only Dan 7:13f. messianically but also ‏ליה‎ in 7.27 as referring to the Messiah (in Daniel's text, the Most High) rather than to the people of Israel[194]!

Agadath Bereshith offers two examples[195]. In 14:3 while speaking of the Redeemer the author cites 7:13 in a straightforward case of identification of the Son of Man with the Messiah. In 23:1 the Messiah, identified with the Son of Man of Dan 7:13 which the author cites, is supposed to come from the gates of Rome: ‏ראין את המשיח גצמח ד) משערי‎ ‏רומי , והן שמחין ,שכך דניאל אומר וארו עם ענני שמיע כבר‎ ‏אנש אתי הוה(דניאל ז יג),אותה שעה וראיתם ושש לבכם‎ [196].

According to *P.T.: Tannith* 2:1 R. Abbahu (c. A.D. 300) with a clear allusion to Num 23:19 said (in Hebrew! rather than Aramaic): "If a man say 'I am God', he lies; 'I am the Son of Man' (‏בן אדם‎), he will finally regret it; 'I ascend to heaven', he will not be able to fulfill it." This utter-

191 *The Babylonian Talmud: Sanhedrin*, Tr. and ed. by J. Shachter, H. Freedman, in I. Epstein's edition. *Der Babylonische Talmud*, Ed. L. Goldsshmidt, 1931.
192 Midrash Rabbah: *Numbers*, Eds. H. Freedman and M. Simon, 1939.
193 "And to him shall be the obedience of the peoples. He shall come and make the peoples' teeth blunted, and all shall serve him, as it is said, 'And to him was given dominion and glory and kingly rule' (Dan 7:13). It is also said: 'And all dominions shall serve and obey him'.
194 Though my interpretation (above, under The Identification of the 'SM' in Daniel: Philological Considerations) was based on the exegesis of the chapter, this rabbinic interpretation is corroborative.
195 *Agadath Bereschit*, ed. S. Buber.
196 "You will see the Messiah, who will spring up from the gates of Rome; then you will rejoice, for thus says Daniel: 'Behold, with the clouds of heaven there came one like a son of man (Dan 7:13) and you shall see him and your heart shall rejoice' ". *Str-B* I, 485ff. and 956ff. with some hesitation cite also Ps 2:9 and 21:5 for which there is some evidence that they were interpreted in the light of Dan 7:13.

ance was probably made in polemic against the Christian identification of Jesus with the Son of Man[196a]; however, it shows that according to R. Abbahu the designation Son of Man *was* a messianic title — and to judge from the rest of the quotation — the Messiah *was* understood by him as heavenly and divine[197].

With R. Akiba we touch on the so-called "Two Powers in Heaven" heresy[198]. This, according to Segal's investigation involved the worship of two Powers in heaven and it was practised by certain Jewish groups and, of course, Christians[199]. From rabbinic polemic against these 'heretics' it becomes apparent that the main text on which this doctrine hinged was Dan 7:9–14[200]. The 'SM', or Metatron, or a chief angel was understood to be seated beside God and function as his vizir[201]. The earliest datable text of rabbinic polemic against this doctrine comes from the time of Ishmael and Akiba[202]. However, when extra-rabbinical texts are taken into account, these ideas seem to go back to predecessors in the first century and to have their roots in Philo and still further back in Daniel and — what Segal regards as a possibility — in pre-Danielic I Enoch[203]. What seems to have been at the heart of the controversy was the problem of reconciling strict monotheism with certain OT statements which apparently implied the existence of Two Powers. The 'orthodox' rabbis chose to interpret such statements as involving God's various attributes or manifestations[204]. For example the two thrones of Dan 7:9 were claimed to symbolize two aspects of God's providence, rather than imply Two Entitles seated on them. It is against such a background that R. Akiba's position is to be viewed.

R. Akiba (died A.D. 132) was of the opinion that the plural 'thrones' in Dan 7:9 was to be understood so as to mean that one throne was intended for the Ancient of Days and one for David[205]. That by 'David' Akiba did

---

196a Similarly Dalman, *Worte Jesu*, 202: Herford, *Christianity in Talmud and Midrash*, 62f.; Meyer, in *Handbuch zu den Neutestamentlichen Apokryphen,* 61f.

197 Casey's quibble that "The context ensures that 'Son of Man' is correctly understood as a Christian title, and that it therefore follows that this passage is no evidence of the existence of a Son of Man concept in Judaism" (*Son of Man*, 91) is really a short circuit. Abbahu's objection "he will finally regret it" has meaning against the Christian identification of the Son of Man with Jesus *only* if Abbahu himself identified the Son of Man with the Messiah!

198 See Segal, *Two Powers in Heaven*. This is the usual rabbinic terminology, though it was not established until the end of the tannaitic period (261).

199 Segal, *op.cit.,* 71 and 260.

200 Segal, *op.cit.,* 35, 40 and 47ff.

201 Segal, *op.cit.,* 65 and 71. The Metatron of III En "is clearly dependent on the ancient 'son of man' traditions ..." (65). Similarly Hengel, *The Son of God*, 46.

202 Segal, *op.cit.,* 260.

203 Segal, *op.cit.,* 20f.

204 Segal, *op.cit.,* 35: "The proof-text for these statements is Dan 7:9f. which describes a heavenly enthronement scene involving two divine manifestations, 'the son of man' and 'the Ancient of Days'."

205 B.T. Ḥagiga II, 1 (14a) (*Der Babylonische Talmud*, ed. L. Goldschmidt).

not mean the historical David — a David *redivivus*, as Casey claims![206] —
is obvious from the objection of R. Jose the Galilean: "How long will you
profane the Divine Glory, Akiba?" The reason why Jose considered Akiba's saying blasphemous was no doubt because he understood 'David' of
the earthly messiah. On the other hand, Akiba did not apprehend his
statement as blasphemous because he probably thought of a heavenly
Messiah[207]. At all events unless Akiba interpreted the Son of Man of Dan
7:13 messianically he would not have him seated as 'David' on a throne
beside God[208].

Of special interest are *B.T. Sanhedrin* 96 bf. and *Tanhuma Toledoth* 20
(70 b). In the former text R. Nahman (died A.D. 320) asks R. Isaac "Have
you heard when *Bar Nafle* will come?" — "Who is *Bar Nafle*?" asks the
latter. The former answers: "The Messiah!" R. Isaac then asks in astonishment: "Do you call Messiah *Bar Nafle*?" R. Nahman explains: "Certainly,
as it is written 'In that day I will raise up the tabernacle of David *ha-
nofeleth*" (= 'that is fallen') (Am 9:11). The term *Nafle* in the expression *Bar Nafle* is clearly an allusion to *ha-nofeleth* in the quotation from
Amos. However, the participle נפלת (from נפל) only means 'fallen' and
it is clearly unsuitable as a messianic title even though it is referred to
David's tabernacle. Besides, the word *Bar*, an integral part of the messianic designation here, is missing from Am 9:11. What R. Nahman has
in mind is the expression *Bar enash* in Dan 7:13. That expression, however, affords no 'catchword' to relate it to Am 9:11. Nahman is apparently aware that 'clouds' (ענני) of Dan 7:13 figures as a messianic designation. But again ענני affords no connecting link to the vocabulary in Am
9:11. The solution is found in the transliteration of the Greek word translating ענני in Dan 7:13 in Θ and the LXX: νεφέλη[209]. This term is
admirably suited because of its resemblance to the participle *nofeleth*. So,
the *Bar-enash* is turned to *Bar-Nafle* (= 'Son of the Cloud', or 'Cloud
Man', i.e. 'One who comes with clouds')[210], and a connection is established with *nofeleth* of Am 9:11[211].

206 *Son of Man*, 87. Here Casey is in serious difficulties. To save his theory of the non-messianic
interpretation of Dan 7:13 he gives an explanation that is really desperate: "The passage
makes excellent sense if it is supposed that 'David' actually means 'David'. R. Akiba is then
saying that the real historical David will rise from the dead and take part in the final judgment, sitting on one of the thrones ... vs. 13 actually symbolizes the arrival of the people of
Israel."
207 That Akiba supported the Bar Cochba revolt need not imply that he was incapable of interpreting Dan 7:13 as referring to a heavenly being.
208 Cf. the discussion by Segal, *Two Powers in Heaven*, 47ff., who thinks that Akiba's 'recanta-
tion', namely that the two thrones were for mercy and justice, which is found in a later text,
came from his students as "a later addition, ascribing the 'orthodox' interpretation to a great
rabbinic leader," while "the messianic controversy over Dan 7:13 is probably from R. Akiba's
time." See Hengel, *The Son of God*, 46f.
209 Rabbinic literature evinces many Greek terms in transliteration.
210 The Editor of the B.T. H. Freedman, explains it similarly: "Lit. 'son of the fallen', *Bar Nafle*

Tanhuma Toledoth 20 (70 b) is a parallel case[212]. In explicating Anani
(עֲנָנִי, in I Chr 3:24), the last in a list of David's descendants, the author
puts into operation the usual rabbinical method: "Who is Anani?" he asks.
"He is the King, Messiah!" he says. "See Dan 7:13: 'behold, there came
with the clouds of heaven (עֲנָנֵי שְׁמַיָּא) one like unto a son of man."
From this Casey jumps to the rash conclusion that the rabbi of *Tanhuma
Toledoth* 20 thought that עֲנָנֵי שְׁמַיָּא (= 'clouds of heaven') was the
actual messianic title and that כְּבַר אֱנָשׁ was for this rabbi — as for Casey
— a symbol for Israel!, thus: "With Anani of heaven one like a son of man
(sc. Israel) was coming"[213]. Though Casey's method of argumentation is
a good example of rabbinic reasoning, it will hardly do for the purpose of
establishing the meaning in *Tanhuma Toledoth* 20. The first thing to be
laid down here is that this author considered Dan 7:13 as having messianic
significance. In advocating the messianic character of David's last descendant, Anani (of I Chr 3:24), the author of *Tanhuma Toledoth*, like R.
Nahman sought for the "peg" — to use Bowman's expression[214] — with
which to relate two totally unrelated texts. Since בַּר אֱנָשׁ was for obvious
reasons unusable the "peg" was found in עֲנָנֵי (= 'clouds'). That 'clouds'
was no messianic term as such, had as little significance for our author as
nofeleth (= 'fallen' of Am 9:11) had for R. Nahman. The important
thing was that a bridge was established between I Chr 3:24 and Dan 7:13,
whereby the messianic content of the latter passage could be applied to
Anani of the former passage. Furthermore, there was the precedent of
R. Nahman, who had used that very word in a transliteration of the Greek
(νεφέλη) translation of עֲנָנֵי as dictated by *nofeleth* in Am 9:11. This
time Anani of I Chr 3:24 demanded the Aramaic term of Dan 7:13, rather
than a transliteration of the Greek equivalent, and so עֲנָנֵי was adopted
without further ado — except for a minor change of a vowel in the pro-
nunciation.

Thus, it may be concluded that both *B.T. Sanhedrin* 96 b and *Tanhuma*

is generally assumed to represent the Greek υἱὸς νεφελῶν, the 'son of the clouds'; cf. Dan 7:
13 there came with the clouds of heaven one like a son of man, which R. Nahman gave a Hebrew connotation" (*Sanhedrin* Vol. II, 654). Goldschmidt (*Der Babylonische Talmud: Synhe-
drin* Vol. 9, p. 63) associates *Nafle* not with בַּפֵל (= 'to fall') but with " נְפִיל Riese, der
Riesensohn, Göttersohn". But in view of the above argument, this is considered improbable.

211 This is a typical example of the whimsical method of rabbinic interpretation. "Midrashic
interpretation cares nothing for the original meaning, nor does it read statements in their
contexts; it seizes a word, a phrase, and utilizes it as a peg for extraneous ideas" (Bowman,
ExpT, 59, 1947/8 285).
212 *Str-B* I. 486 and Vermes, *Jesus the Jew*, 171f. understand it as 'Cloud Man' and associate it
with other evidence for a messianic interpretation of Dan 7:13. Hengel, *The Son of God*, 46,
remarks that "in the time of the rabbis, titles like Son of Man and Son of God could no longer
be used because of competition with Christianity. Instead, Enoch (i.e. in III En 2:2; 3:2;
4:1) is given by God the mysterious designation 'na'ar', young man". See Alexander in
OTP I, 226ff.
213 *Son of Man*, 82.
214 *ET* 59 (1947–8) 285.

Toledoth 20 (70 b) are clear instances of the messianic interpretation of Dan 7:13. The liberties taken with the wording of this text reveal the intention to make the text prove the messianic character of other texts. Such a Greco-Aramaic hybrid as *Bar-nafle* or the improper use of עָנָנֵי שְׁמַיָא to support the name Anani only reveals how firmly the messianic interpretation of Dan 7:13f. was rooted in rabbinic thought[215].

We need not pursue the matter further[216]. The examples discussed above amply support the thesis that Dan 7:13f. and its 'SM' were understood by many rabbis (Casey would admit, most rabbis[217]) messianically.

The evidence of the *Parables*, IV Ezra and the (later) Rabbis is really sufficient to prove the thesis that has been developed in this chapter, that is, that the Book of Daniel gave rise to a new conception of the Messiah in terms of the Son of Man, and that this conception was current among the Jews at the time of Jesus, as is witnessed by IV Ezra and especially the *Parables*. This chapter might, therefore, end here. There is, however, one more area where similar, though indirect, evidence might be found, namely the NT. The treatment of the subject in hand would, therefore, be incomplete without some reference to the NT data. However, inasmuch as the value of the NT data as genuine evidence for a pre-Christian Jewish Son of Man concept is often questioned, and in view of the principle enunciated in Chapter Two, viz. to prove or illustrate a point that has a bearing for a particular book independently of that book in order to avoid circularity in argumentation, the NT will *not* be used to *prove* but merely to *corroborate* what has been sufficiently demonstrated through the *Parables* and IV Ezra.

E. The New Testament Evidence

It has often been overlooked that the NT ought to be reckoned among the possible sources for the existence of a pre-Christian Son of Man con-

---

215 Among those who follow an essentially similar line of interpretation may be mentioned Levy, *Neuhebräisches und Chaldäisches Wörterbuch über die Talmudim und Midraschim*, 1876—9, Vol. I, p. 259a; Eerdmans, *Theol.Tijdschr.* 28 (1894) 166f.; Driver, *Daniel*, 108; Goettsberger, *Daniel*, 56; *Str-B* I, 66, 957; Vermes, *Jesus the Jew*, 171f. Dalman, *Worte Jesu*, 201 is uncertain, while Casey, *Son of Man*, 82ff. (and *NovT* 18 (1976), 175ff.) tries to prove the opposite, but the attempt is not crowned with success.

216 For more examples see *Str-B*, I, 485ff., 956ff.; and Bowman, *ET* 59 (1947/8) 283—8.

217 *Son of Man*, 83. Casey finds the corporate interpretation in what he calls "The Syrian Tradition" comprised of ten authors, the earliest of whom is the philosopher Porphyry (A.D. 270—320) but the rest are both late and obscure, mere sideshoots: Aphrahat (A.D. 337), Ephraem (A.D. 360—73), Polychronius (A.D. 430), Cosmas Indicopleustes (A.D. 550), Peshitta glosses (VII—VIII A.D.), Theodore bar Koni (A.D. 790), Ishodad of Merw (IX A.D.), an

cept in Judaism[218]. For the importance of the NT evidence, if its genuineness can be upheld, lies in its being contemporaneous with Jesus[219].

However, it has not altogether escaped the attention of scholars that the Gospels never explicate the term SM. There is no record of either the disciples, or the multitudes, or the Jewish leaders ever demanding an explanation of this expression[220]. From this circumstance the logical conclusion would seem to be that no explanation occurred because no explanation was necessary, since the term was well-known. Moreover, it is difficult to explain why the evangelists, who often emphasize the Jews' imperceptiveness or their erroneous tenets, would in this crucial case ascribe to them a messianic understanding in terms of the Son of Man, which coincided with their own ideas of messianship, if the Jews did not actually hold such opinions.

At any rate, the few NT texts treated here would seem to imply that the titular import of the expression was not unknown to Jews of Jesus' time.

1. A Jewish Convert to Jesus (Jn 9:35)

When Jesus found the once blind man, now driven out by the Jewish authorities, he put to him the question: σὺ πιστεύεις εἰς τὸν υἱὸν τοῦ ἀνθρώπου [221]; The man, who evidently had had no prior personal contact with or knowledge of Jesus, and who, moreover, being blind from birth, could never have acquired such knowledge through personal reading, appears none the less not to be surprised at all by the expression SM[222]. Far from asking for an explanation, he seems to be quite acquainted with

Anonymous Commentator on Daniel (no date), R. Hayyim ben Galipapa (A.D. 1310–80). These authors are the mainstay for Casey's thesis that the term Son of Man is not a messianic title, or a title at all in the literature up to the death of Jesus, nor a title as often as assumed after the death of Jesus. Casey's thesis needs hardly any refutation.

218 As examples may be cited the commentaries on the Gospels and Acts mentioned in this section, (if not otherwise stated) none of whom seems to think of the passages here discussed as witnessing to such a belief among the Jews. Other studies are Arndt, *Luke*, 455f.; Munck, *Acts*, Part II, 66f.; Bauerfeind, *Apostelgeschichte*, 120; Marshall, *Acts*, 148f. For exceptions see below.

219 With respect to the genuineness of individual logia, discussed in this section see e.g. Moore, *The Parousia in the NT*, 184ff.; Borsch, *NTS* 14 (1968) 565ff.; Pesch, *Markusevangelium*, II, 437, and Blinzler, *Der Prozess Jesu*, 123–6.

220 See e.g. Bernard, *John*, I, p. cxxi. The problem cannot be simply explained away on the theory that Son of Man was understood to be the equivalent for 'I'. We have seen that the circumlocutional explanation fits neither the NT data (see ch. I) nor Dan 7:13, I En 37–71, IV Ezra, or the Rabbinic writings.

221 The majority of witnesses read υἱὸν τοῦ Θεοῦ. The reading adopted here is supported by p66, 75 ℵ B D W, etc. and is generally regarded as original, e.g. Bernard, *John* II, 338; Brown, *John* I, 375; Morris, *John*, 494 n.47; Lindars, *John*, 350; Barrett, *John*, 364; Schnackenburg, *John* II, 253.

222 So Bultmann, *Johannesev.* 257.

its significance[223]. The implication is that he owed his knowledge of the
SM concept to others. All he wanted to know was who the Son of Man
was[224]. And on Jesus' identifying himself as the Son of Man, the man
showed no hesitation whatever in worshipping him. Such a spontaneous
reaction would seem to be inexplicable unless the term SM in Jewish
consciousness had had a definite messianic content similar to the one observed in e.g. the *Parables* and IV Ezra.

2. The Crowds (Jn 12:34; 8:28)

When Jesus was apprised of the coming of certain Greeks or Hellenists,
he said: "The hour has come for the Son of Man to be glorified" (12:23).
In the following verses Jesus speaks of his coming death (vv. 24—33). At
this point the multitude reacts in bewilderment: $\dot{\eta}\mu\epsilon\tilde{\iota}\varsigma$ $\dot{\eta}\kappa o\acute{\upsilon}\sigma\alpha\mu\epsilon\nu$ $\dot{\epsilon}\kappa$ $\tau o\tilde{\upsilon}$
$\nu\acute{o}\mu o\upsilon$ $\acute{o}\tau\iota$ $\dot{o}$ $X\rho\iota\sigma\tau\grave{o}\varsigma$ $\mu\acute{\epsilon}\nu\epsilon\iota$ $\epsilon\dot{\iota}\varsigma$ $\tau\grave{o}\nu$ $\alpha\dot{\iota}\tilde{\omega}\nu\alpha$, $\kappa\alpha\grave{\iota}$ $\pi\tilde{\omega}\varsigma$ $\lambda\acute{\epsilon}\gamma\epsilon\iota\varsigma$ $\sigma\grave{\upsilon}$ $\acute{o}\tau\iota$
$\delta\epsilon\tilde{\iota}$ $\dot{\upsilon}\psi\omega\vartheta\tilde{\eta}\nu\alpha\iota$ $\tau\grave{o}\nu$ $\upsilon\dot{\iota}\grave{o}\nu$ $\tau o\tilde{\upsilon}$ $\dot{\alpha}\nu\vartheta\rho\acute{\omega}\pi o\upsilon$; $\tau\acute{\iota}\varsigma$ $\dot{\epsilon}\sigma\tau\iota\nu$ $o\tilde{\upsilon}\tau o\varsigma$ $\dot{o}$ $\upsilon\dot{\iota}\grave{o}\varsigma$ $\tau o\tilde{\upsilon}$
$\dot{\alpha}\nu\vartheta\rho\acute{\omega}\pi o\upsilon$; It is to be observed that 'Messiah' has not been used by Jesus
anywhere in this context. When he spoke of his sufferings and death he
designated himself as Son of Man. But when the crowds object to him,
they use the term 'Messiah'! By this the evangelist would seem to imply
that in the opinion of the Jews the Son of Man was identical with the Messiah[225]. It is from this identification that the problem arises[226]. In their
view the Messiah (= the Son of Man) was to abide forever[227]. This belief
was in all likelihood based, as scholars have observed, mainly on Dan 7:
13f. Why was Jesus now saying that the Son of Man was to die? Could it
be that Jesus was speaking of a different Son of Man to the One they had
been taught to identify with the Messiah? The last question $\tau\acute{\iota}\varsigma$ $\dot{\epsilon}\sigma\tau\iota\nu$
$o\tilde{\upsilon}\tau o\varsigma$ $\dot{o}$ $\upsilon\dot{\iota}\grave{o}\varsigma$ $\tau o\tilde{\upsilon}$ $\dot{\alpha}\nu\vartheta\rho\acute{\omega}\pi o\upsilon$; surely does not mean 'Who is this Son of
Man?' i.e. in contradistinction to the Messiah — as it is sometimes con-
strued[228] — but 'Who is this particular (cf. $o\tilde{\upsilon}\tau o\varsigma$!) Son of Man of whom

---

223 Haenchen, *Johannesev.* 381: "Der versteht die Bezeichnung 'Menschensohn' sofort, und zwar
in Sinne von, 'Christus', 'Messias', und wünscht nur zu erfahren, wer er ist". To the same effect Hoskyns, *The Fourth Gospel*, 359. This is also admitted by Barrett, *John*, 364. Dodd,
Historical Tradition, 114 thinks vs. 35 is confessional (preferably in the v. l. $\upsilon\dot{\iota}\grave{o}\varsigma$ $\tau o\tilde{\upsilon}$ $\Theta\epsilon o\tilde{\upsilon}$)
but Smaley, *NTS* 15 (1968—9) 296 argues against a confessional understanding of this verse.
224 Brown, *John* I, 375.
225 So Hoskyns, *The Fourth Gospel*, 427: "In this passage the Jews rightly understood the
phrase Son of Man to be equivalent to the Messiah." Further Haenchen, *Johannesev.*, 443.
For a different exegesis see Schnackenburg, *John* II, 253.
226 See Sturch, *ET* 94 (1983) 333.
227 This is in agreement with the presentation of the Son of Man in Daniel and the *Parables*,
where there is no hint of the Son of Man's death. Cf. also Ps 89:36; 110:4; Isa 9:6f.; Ez 37:
25.
228 E.g. Barrett, *John*, 428; Schnackenburg, *John*, II, 395; Bernard, *John*, II, 443f.; Leivestad,
NTS 18 (1972) 250. Similarly NEB: "What Son of Man is this?"!

you are speaking, i.e. who does not conform with our view of the Son of Man"[229]? What the people are really saying is: "According to our opinion the Son of Man is the same as the Messiah, who is to abide forever; but apparently *not* according to you"![230]

Jn 8:28 is, no doubt, another witness to a certain Jewish acquaintance with the SM concept. Jesus' words: ὅταν ὑψώσητε τὸν υἱὸν τοῦ ἀνθρώπου, τότε γνώσεσθε ὅτι ἐγώ εἰμι (sc. ἐκεῖνος, i.e. the Son of Man) imply that the Jews' problem was not one of accepting a SM concept, but of accepting Jesus' claim to be that Son of Man. Further, it may be that what suggested the use of ὑψόω in reference to Jesus' exaltation (through death) was the use of the term SM. The Son of Man was traditionally thought of as an *exalted* being. If he was now found in circumstances of humility, that was not his definitive state. He needed to be *exalted*. This observation seems to be supported by the fact that of the four occurrences of ὑψόω in John, three have ὁ υἱὸς τοῦ ἀνθρώπου etc. as subject/object and the fourth ἐγώ (of Jesus)[231].

3. The Jewish Authorities

a) Jesus before the Sanhedrin (Mt 26:62ff. = Mk 14:60ff. = Lk 22:67ff.)

The historical, traditional and redactional questions raised by these accounts and the arguments pertaining thereto are well-known and need not, therefore, be reiterated here in any detail[232]. In general, however, the basic reliability of the trial accounts can be considered as having been

---

229 This was already the understanding of Charles, *The Book of Enoch*, 309: "In St. John 12:34 it is just the strangeness of this new conception of this current phrase of a Messiah who was to suffer death, that makes the people ask 'Who is this Son of Man? We have heard of the law that the Christ abideth for ever' ". Bernard, *John*, II, 443f. concedes the full possibility of this interpretation, though at the end, he keeps to the other alternatives. See Thompson, *JTS* 12 (1961) 207.

230 In his interesting study Thompson, whose approach is somewhat different to mine, comes nevertheless to a similar conclusion: "The Son of Man is taken as a well-known title; what is strange is that he has to be exalted from the earth. The implication is that the Son of Man, with whom the Jews were familiar, was not a figure connected with the earth nor one that needed to be exalted. In other words, the reply of the crowds presupposes that the heavenly Son of Man as found in the Similitudes of Enoch was a concept known to the Jews in the first century A.D."

231 Ὑψόω could not possibly be explained as a synonym for the Son of Man's return, or going up to heaven. That idea is expressed by ἀναβαίνω whose antonym is καταβαίνω (cf. Jn 3:13).

232 See e.g. the discussions by Sherwin-White, *Roman Society and Roman Law in the NT*, 24–47; Blinzler, *Der Prozess Jesu, passim*; Catchpole, *The Trial of Jesus, passim*; Taylor, *The Passion Narrative*, 80ff.; id., *Mark*, 563ff.; Schneider, *Verleugnung, passim*; Lane, *Mark*, 528ff.; Marshall, *Luke*, 846ff.; Ellis, *Luke*, 269ff.

demonstrated[233]. Of the three accounts the fullest are those of Mt and Mk, but the Lukan one also has its interesting points. Both Mt and Mk agree in having the high priest ask σὺ εἶ ὁ Χριστὸς ὁ υἱὸς τοῦ Θεοῦ (Mk τοῦ εὐλογητοῦ); Objections have been raised to the identification of the Messiah with Son of God, but there now appear to exist sufficiently good grounds for the equation[234]. Both Mt and Mk agree in having Jesus give an assenting answer to the high priest's question (Mk more straightforward than Mt) and then quote the combined Ps 110:1 and Dan 7:13. It is as a reaction to the claim Jesus makes through this citation that the high priest tears his clothes and utters: Blasphemy!

Some scholars consider Luke's account as being based on a non-Markan source[235], more primitive than Mark[236]. Catchpole actually holds that the source did not originally contain the Son of Man saying (vs. 69), which was added later by Luke, who took it over from Mark[237]. The evidence

---

233 Sherwin-White, *Roman Society*, 44ff.; Blinzler, *Der Prozess Jesu*, e.g. 95–174; Catchpole, *The Trial of Jesus*, 136ff.; Taylor, *Mark*, 563; Marshall, *Luke*, 846ff. The authenticity of the accounts is presupposed by e.g. Borsch, *NTS* 14 (1967–8), 565ff.; *id., The SM in Myth and History*, 391ff.; Bruce, *OTS* 20 (1977) 26; Guilding, *EvQ* 23 (1951) 210–12; Lohse, in *Jesus und der Menschensohn*, 415ff.; Black, *ET* 95 (1984) 204; Kümmel, *Promise and Fulfilment*, 50f.; Moule, *The Origin of Christology*, 27; Leivestad, *NTS* 18 (1971–2) 264 and Colpe, *TDNT* VIII, 435.

234 Lane, *Mark*, 537, says: "There is evidence that contemporary Judaism also conceived of a Messiah sitting at God's right hand and coming in the clouds of heaven". Lane cites Mid Ps 2:7, which combines Ps 110:1 with Dan 7:13f. in explicating 'Thou art my son' – though the explication is there applied to Israel. Lohse, *TDNT* VIII, 361, objects: "Thus far there is no clear instance to support the view that in pre-Christian times Judaism used the title 'Son of God' for the Messiah". With this agrees Cullman, *Christology*, 279ff., who however, proceeds on that count to attribute the title 'Son of God' to Jesus himself. Lövestam, (*SEÅ* 26 (1961) 93–107) despite his initial statement that "Einem direkten Beleg dafür, dass 'Sohn Gottes' im Judentum als Messias-Titel gebraucht wurde, gibt es bisher nicht" (95), goes on to cite 4Q Flor, 1Q Sa II, 11f. as well as Midrash on Ps 2:7. etc., as evidence that the Jews had brought together Ps 2:7; 110:1, and Dan 7:13 in a messianic interpretation. He says, we may reckon with "dass die Bezeichnung 'Sohn Gottes' im Judentum zur Zeit Jesu auf den Messias angewandt werden könnte" (96, see also 99) and that Ps 2 offers an OT grounds for the "Nebeneinanderstellung von 'der Messias' und 'der Sohn Gottes' in der entscheidenden Verhörsfrage vor dem Hohen Rat vor" (97). More recent years have brought more direct evidence from Qumran. Pesch, *Markusevangelium*, II, 437, is now able to write: "Gegen die Verbindung von 'Messias' und 'Sohn Gottes' im Munde des Hohenpriesters ist historisch also nichts mehr einzuwenden." Pesch cites as support Fitzmyer, *NTS* 20 (1973–4) 397ff. and Hahn, *Christologische Hoheitstitel*, 287. Fitzmyer argues for the following translation of what is a defective text: "[But your son] shall be great upon the earth, [O King! All (men) shall] make [peace], and all shall serve [him. He shall be called the son of] the [G]reat [God], and by his name shall he be named. He shall be hailed (as) the Son of God (ברה די אל), and they shall call him Son of the Most High" (בר עליון) (4QpsDan Aᵃ) and relates to Lk 1: 32ff. See also Fuller, *Foundations*, 31ff.; Betz, *NovT* 6 (1963) 20–48, and Hengel, *The Son of God*, 44ff.

235 E.g. Schneider, *Verleugnung*, 105ff.; Catchpole, *The Trial of Jesus*, 139f., 200; Ellis, *Luke*, 260; Marshall, *Luke*, 847.

236 Catchpole, *The Trial of Jesus*, 140; Marshall, *Luke*, 847.

237 *The Trial of Jesus*, 140, 142, 200.

is "evenly balanced" between this and the alternative view that vs. 69 is original to that source, according to Marshall[238]. Lk 22:69 is occasionally seen as interrupting the continuity of thought from vv. 67f. to vs. 70[239]. But the removal of vs. 69 does not leave sufficient grounds for the *conclusion*[240] which the Sanhedrin draws and expresses in the form of a question (i.e. vs. 70). The conclusion σὺ οὖν[241] εἶ ὁ υἱὸς τοῦ Θεοῦ; is clearly drawn from Jesus' citation of Ps 110:1 and Dan 7:13 in which Jesus, in answering the original question (in his own way, rather than in the way expected by the Sanhedrin) σὺ εἶ ὁ Χριστός; (vs. 67) answered it in terms of the Son of Man[241a]. The terms Son of God and Son of Man (the former used by the Sanhedrin, the latter by Jesus) were therefore for the Jewish authorities equivalent. This agrees with Mt and Mk who also make Jesus' use of the term SM the cause for the high priest's exasperation.

The comparison of these accounts furnishes perhaps a good example of the difficulties which the current views of synoptic interrelationships involve. The drastic solutions proposed no doubt weaken the credibility of the hypothesis as a whole. If, on the other hand, the synoptics are understood as independent works based on independent though parallel traditions, all these accommodations and qualifications become superfluous[242]. For the question at hand it may after all be that, as Hooker expressed it in connection with the Son of Man sayings[243], all accounts need to be taken into account in order for us to obtain a true picture of what actually happened.

There can be no doubt, however, that all three evangelists make Jesus' claim to be the Son of Man the basis for the high priest's/Sanhedrin's charge of blasphemy. But why was it blasphemy? Surely not because Jesus had said that the Son of Man was to sit on the Majesty's right hand, or to come with the clouds of heaven! These were the very words of Scripture. For the high priest/Sanhedrin it was blasphemy because in the words of Jesus he/they discerned Jesus' claim to be that Son of Man[244]. Again, unless the designation SM was a current messianic title, loaded with the Danielic content — not to speak of the content which I En 37–71 (and later IV Ez 13) had added to the concept — there would seem to have

---

238 *Luke*, 848.
239 See in Marshall, *Luke*, 850.
240 Marshall, *Luke*, 851, seems to imply that this is a pure question.
241 To ease the difficulties of his theory (with respect to the excision of vs. 69), Catchpole, *The Trial of Jesus*, 197, tries to understand the οὖν as a simple connective referring to vs. 68, but this is hopelessly incongruent.
241a See Cullmann, *Christology*, 120f.
242 See discussion in Chapter Four.
243 *The Son of Man in Mark*, 79.
244 Similarly Ford, *JBL* 87 (1968) 262: "The charge of blasphemy must be due to using a substitute for the divine name. This substitute appears to be 'Son of Man'."

been no reason for the high priest to be so upset or to condemn Jesus to death[245]. Moreover, the equation of Son of Man with Son of God made by the Sanhedrin (Lk 22:69f.) in drawing its conclusions from Jesus' words (vs. 69) shows that for the Jewish authorities Son of Man was actually equivalent to Son of God[246]. The full implications latent in Daniel's 'SM'[247], developed and set forth more explicitly by I En 37—71 and IV Ez 13, had apparently been drawn and accepted by the Jewish leaders. In the last analysis it seems that it was Jesus' claim to be the Son of Man that became the final cause for his condemnation[248], because in Jewish eyes the term was connected with divinity and thus constituted the ultimate blasphemy[249].

b) Stephen before the Sanhedrin (Acts 7:56)

This text will be treated more briefly. It is essentially similar in character to the previous trial account[250]. On hearing Stephen's words: ἰδοὺ θεωρῶ τοὺς οὐρανοὺς διηνοιγμένους καὶ τὸν υἱὸν τοῦ ἀνθρώπου ἐκ δεξιῶν ἑστῶτα τοῦ Θεοῦ, the august assembly of the Jewish nation stop their ears and rush with fury upon Stephen. Again, we ask, Why? It could not possibly be because Stephen had claimed to have seen a vision[251], nor because he had spoken of the Son of Man as standing in the presence of God — this was the Son of Man's proper place, according to tradition[252]. Could it then be because the Jews knew very well that by Son of Man Stephen meant no one else but Jesus[253]? In that case, the Jews were put

---

245 Mark's version ἐγὼ εἰμι, καὶ ὄψεσθε τὸν υἱὸν τοῦ ἀνθρώπου ἐκ δεξιῶν καθήμενον τῆς δυνάμεως καὶ ἐρχόμενον μετὰ τῶν νεφελῶν τοῦ οὐραονῦ might tempt advocates of the circumlocutional theory to see in υἱὸν τοῦ ἀνθρώπου the equivalent of 'I', i.e. "It is me, and you shall see me sitting ..." Such an understanding is, nevertheless, shattered on the quotations from Ps 110:1 and Dan 7:13, where 'one like a son of man' cannot mean 'I'.

246 See Ellis, *Luke*, 262.

247 Cf. his reticent identification of the 'SM' with the 'Most High'.

248 Lövestam, in his interesting study (*SEÅ* 26 (1961) 93—107 gives the impression that Jesus was condemned on account of his assent to the high priest's question whether he was the Messiah, the Son of God — an admission that implied a share in God's majesty, and was thus a blasphemy (106f.). On this point I am compelled to disagree. Lövestam has not taken sufficient account of the part played by the Son of Man concept with which Jesus identifies himself. This is especially clear in Luke's account, though both Mark and Matthew imply that what brought about the felling word was primarily Jesus' answer whereby he applied Ps 110:1 and Dan 7:13 to hiinself.

249 Obviously, if Vermes' theory were right, Jesus would not have been condemned, since "the charge of balsphemy ... would not apply to a messianic claim" (sc. of the popular type of messianism) (Ellis, *Luke*, 263).

250 On this text see Blinzler, *BZ* N.F. 3 (1959) 252—70; Mussner, in *Jesus und der Menschensohn*, 283—99 and Barrett in *Apophoreta*, 32—8.

251 During this period it was quite fashionable to see visions.

252 E.g. Dan 7:13 (cf. 7:9); I En 46:1f.; 48:2, 5; 62:5ff.; 69:27.

253 On the assumption of the Son of Man's function as Judge by Jesus, see Pesch, *Bibel und*

in a dilemma. To acquiesce to Jesus' claim to be the Son of Man would be tantamount to confessing themselves guilty of having put to death the Son of God[254]!

From this brief examination it can be concluded that all four evangelists described the reactions of various persons toward Jesus in a way that leaves no doubt that the concept of Son of Man was well known to the Jews, apart from Jesus' use of the title, and that it was presupposed in their dealings with him. Are there any compelling reasons for rejecting this evidence?

F. Conclusion

The conclusion from the above examination is that the Rabbis, the *Parables* and IV Ezra all bear witness to a new type of messianic consciousness and expectation, one that had been developed from the Book of Daniel and which differed from the traditional messianic hope (i.e. the earlier type of hope of which Schürer speaks). The later hope existed side by side with the earlier hope.

It has, in fact, emerged from the above investigation that the *Parables* was composed in order to put forward an alternative understanding of messianology to the current one. The messianology of the *Parables* was inspired by and constructed on the model provided by Daniel, though Daniel's terse and severe description received the inevitable apocalyptic embellishments. The heart of the *Parables* has thus been shown to lie in its Son of Man messianology.

IV Ezra, though later than Jesus and despite Christian interpolations, also presents a Son of Man doctrine which is thoroughly Jewish in character and is inspired by Dan 7 and the *Parables*. Through its presentation of a Messiah in Son of Man terms and its presentation of a Son of Man in messianic terms, IV Ezra, along with the *Parables* which it actually copied, witnesses to the existence of a fairly widespread phenomenon regarding the messianic mood of the times: the gradual giving up of the older hope structured around an earthly, Davidic messiah, and the acceptance of the newer hope, whose core was a supernatural Messiah of heavenly origin and universal dimensions. Though IV Ezra is dated after the fall of Jerusalem and though the actual handling of themes and the particular way in which those themes are handled bear the marks left by that tragic event,

Leben, 6 (1965) 92–107; 170–83. See also Haenchen, *Acts* 292; Schneider, Die *Apostelgeschichte*, I 474f.

254 Cf. IV Ez 13:32, 37. According to Pesch, *Bibel und Leben*, 6 (1965) 92–107, 170–83, the function of this vision is judgment on Israel. A similar understanding is envisaged by Berger, *Die Auferstehung des Propheten*, 221ff.

his conception of the Son of Man messianology lies deeper in his Jewish consciousness, and evidences a prior confrontation with ideas already in vogue. These ideas have survived mainly in the *Parables*, laid under tribute by IV Ezra, and dated in all likelihood to the first century B.C.

The Son of Man messianology, which is found in the *Parables* and IV Ezra, has its inspiration in Dan 7 and its historical justification in the national disappointments following the Maccabaean uprising.

It is therefore the firm conclusion of the above investigation that Judaism at the time of Jesus (or even already earlier for that matter) was not monolithic as has sometimes been assumed. There were different trends, different theologies, different anthropologies (in the broadest sense) and different messianologies in vogue[255] — and all competed for supremacy.

Returning to the initial lines of the present Chapter we are now in a position to answer the questions posed there, affirmatively: Jewish apocalypticism gave an interpretation of the Danielic 'SM' that was in all essentials in accord with Daniel's intention, as explicated in Chapter Two, though it was one that greatly embellished the laconic and austere presentation of the prototype[256]. Rabbinic evidence, though later than the NT certainly witnesses to an unbroken chain of analogous interpretation. Bruce even considers that it is warranted to "place the Book of Daniel and the Qumran texts within one stream of tradition"[257].

Though this conclusion, for methodological, etc. reasons, has not been based upon the NT evidence, a brief examination of the latter shows its corroborative character.

---

255 See e.g. Stone, *Scriptures, Sects and Visions*, esp. chs. 5–8.
256 With this conclusion agrees also the author of a detailed examination of IV Ezra: "Man kann es also kein Missverständnis der Danielstelle nennen, dass die Bilderrenden Henochs, die Rabbinen (man denke hier an den rabbinischen Messiasnamen: Anani, Wolkenmensch) und auch der Verfasser der Esra-Apokalypse das Symbol Daniels wieder aufgreifen und auf den Messias deuten. Besonders in den Kreisen, in denen die transzendenten Hoffnungen Eingang gefunden hatten, muss die Figur des Menschensohn, dessen Kommen auf oder mit den Wolken Präexistenz und himmlische Natur vermuten liess, beliebt gewesen sein" (Keulers, *Die eschatologische Lehre des vierten Esrabuches*, 128).
257 In *Neotestamentica et Semitica*, 221.

Chapter IV

The New Testament Son of Man
and the Danielic 'SM'

A. The Organization of the Son of Man Sayings

The term ὁ υἱὸς τοῦ ἀνθρώπου occurs 69 X[1] in the synoptics (Mt 30 X, Mk 14 X, Lk 25 X) and 13 X in John.

Bultmann has divided the synoptic occurrences into three groups. These are sayings that describe the Son of Man as "(1) coming, (2) as suffering death and rising again, and (3) as now at work"[2]. This grouping of the Son of Man sayings has been largely accepted[3], though occasionally different groupings are substituted[4]. Bultmann's grouping is not completely satisfactory. The last class, in particular, is too vague to account for the character of a number of sayings placed under this heading, while a saying like Lk 6:22 properly speaking can hardly come under this or any other of the proposed categories. Another difficulty is that the feature of resurrection, which is associated with sayings about sufferings and death, occurs only in one third of these sayings. Besides, resurrection is really a form of, or the act leading to, exaltation. A third difficulty is that the first class contains a number of sayings in which the Son of Man is not "coming", but he is exalted! On the other hand, neither are the schemas of locality (i.e. grouping the Son of Man sayings according to their *locus*, viz. whether the event occurs in heaven or on earth) or of tem-

---

1 Mt 18:11 and Lk 9:56 can hardly be authentic.
2 *Theology*, I, 30. Actually the first to do so were Foakes-Jackson-Lake. *The Beginnings of Christianity*, I, 368—84.
3 E.g. E. Schweizer, *ZNW* 50 (1959) 185—209 and English tr. in *JBL* 79 (1960) esp. 120f.; Borsch, *The Son of Man*, 320—64; Higgins, *Son of Man*, 2, 29; Colpe, *TDNT* VIII, 430ff.; Ladd, *Theology*, 149; Marshall, *EvQ* 42 (1970) 67—87; Kieffer, *Nytestamentlig teologi*, 50.
4 E.g. Knox, *The Death of Christ*, 88ff. divides the Son of Man sayings into a) such as are colored by apocalypticism, b) such as refer to Jesus' sufferings, and c) the remaining Son of Man sayings; Riesenfeld, in *En Bok om nya testamentet*, 402, calls them a) Present, b) Future, and c) Sayings about suffering and exaltation; Lindars, *NTS* 22 (1975) 66—70, seems to divide them into four classes: a) Glorification sayings, b) Passion sayings, c) Two controversy sayings (i.e. Mk 2:10, 28), and d) Two Q tratition sayings (i.e. Mt 8:20 = Lk 9:58 and Mt 11: 19 = Lk 7:34).

porality (viz. present or future sayings) really happy solutions, despite their valuable distinctions. Apart from the fact that these terms are too vague to communicate any really important content, it will be difficult to classify a number of sayings under the one or the other of these labels[5]. The best approach is, no doubt, that of different categories, whereby Son of Man sayings are classified according to their content and the *Gattung* of the passages in which they occur. However, the number of categories arrived at is too prohibitive[6] for the system to be of practical value. Hence, despite my dissatisfaction, I consider the three-class system as perhaps the most practical one. My labels are, however, somewhat different to Bultmann's. My classification is as follows:

	Earthly Life[7]	Sufferings[8]	Exaltation[9]	Total
Mt	7	10	13	30
Mk	2	9	3	14
Lk	7[10]	8	10	25
	16	27	26	69[11]

The 'Exaltation' group includes all those sayings, which speak of the Son of Man's glorification, power, Judge/King function, and of his coming with the clouds of heaven.

The 'Sufferings' group includes all sayings (direct or alluding) concerning the Son of Man's sufferings, death and resurrection.

Finally, the 'Earthly Life' group contains all other sayings, which are, admittedly, of quite diverse nature, cf. Lk 7:34 with 12:10.

The Johannine Son of Man is not as diversified as the synoptic one.

---

5 Thus e.g. Knox and Schweizer classify some sayings differently, see Hodgson, *JR* 41 (1961) 91f.

6 I have carried out such a classification which resulted in over a dozen classes, so the schema was abandoned.

7 Mt 8:20; 9:6; 11:19; 12:8, 32; 13:37; 16:13; Mk 2:10, 28; Lk 5:24; 6:5, 22; 7:34; 9:58; 12: 10; 17:22.

8 Mt 12:40; 17:9, 12, 22; 20:18, 28; 26:2, 24 (bis), 45; Mk 8:31; 9:9, 12, 31; 10:33, 45 ;14: 21 (bis), 41; Lk 9:21, 44; 11:30; 18:31; 19:10; 22:22, 48; 24:7.

9 Mt 10:23; 13:41; 16:27, 28; 19:28; 24:27, 30 (bis), 37, 39, 44; 25:31; 26:64; Mk 8:38; 13: 26; 14:62; Lk 9:26; 12:8, 40; 17:24, 26, 30; 18:8; 21 :27, 36; 22:69.

10 Lk 6:22 is difficult to classify. It involves neither sufferings nor exaltation. The persecutions against Jesus' followers may actually be inspired by what people presumably know of the earthly Jesus, and therefore it may be preferable to classify the saying among those dealing with Jesus' earthly life.

11 If the parallels are eliminated there are 39 different Son of Man sayings: Mt 9:6 = Mk 2:10 = Lk 5:24; Mt 12:8 = Mk 2:28 = Lk 6:5; Mt 16:27f. = Mk 8:38 = Lk 9:26; Mt 17:22f. = Mk 9: 31 = Lk 9:44; Mt 20:18f. = Mk 10:33f. = Lk 18:31ff.; Mt 24:30f. = Mk 13:26f. = Lk 21:27; Mt 26:24 = Mk 14:21 = Lk 22:22; Mt 26:64 = Mk 14:62 = Lk 22:69; Mt 17:9 = Mk 9:9; Mt 17:12 = Mk 9:12; Mt 20:28 = Mk 10:45; Mt 26:45 = Mk 14:41; Mt 8:20 = Lk 9:58; Mt 11: 19 = Lk 7:34; Mt 12:32 = Lk 12:10; Mt 12:40 = Lk 11:30; Mt 24:27 = Lk 17:24 ;Mt 24:37 = Lk 17:26; Mt 24:44 = Lk 12:40; Mt 10:23; 13:4, 37; 16:13, 28; 19:28; 24:39; 25:31; 26: 2; Mk 8:31 = Lk 9:22; Lk 6 :22; 12:8f.; 17:22, 24, 30; 18:8; 19:10; 21:36; 22:48; 24:7.

Two instances, Jn 6:27 and 6:53, speak of the Son of Man as giving men life through his death[12]. Jn 1:51 describes the Son of Man as in constant contact with God through angelic instrumentality[13]; 9:35 presents him as the object of saving faith and 5:27 depicts him as entrusted with power to hold judgment. The majority of the instances, however, in one way or another imply his sufferings and death, though remarkably enough, the verbs used predicate neither sufferings nor death, but exaltation. In three of these cases (3:14; 8:28 and 12:34) the Son of Man is thought of as lifted up ($\dot{v}\psi\omega\vartheta\tilde{\eta}\nu\alpha\iota$)[14]. In two other cases (12:23 and 13:31) the Son of Man is said to be glorified or exalted ($\delta o\xi\alpha\sigma\vartheta\tilde{\eta}\nu\alpha\iota$) and in the last two cases (3:13 and 6:62) he is depicted as going up ($\dot{\alpha}\nu\alpha\beta\alpha\iota\nu\epsilon\iota\nu$) to heaven. Thus, the most characteristic view of the Johannine Son of Man is that in which his sufferings and death are viewed not merely as his way to exaltation, but as that exaltation itself. Thus, too, although the synoptics' two classes of Son of Man sayings, viz. those that speak of the Son of Man's sufferings and those that speak of the Son of Man's exaltation, are in John merged into one and the same type — a new type, — the Johannine conception of the Son of Man is in important respects rather different from that of the synoptics[15].

B. The Question of Authenticity and of Criteria

The question of the authenticity[16] of the Son of Man sayings has

---

12 On this see Barrett in *Jesus und der Menschensohn*, 342—54.

13 See Smaley in *Jesus und der Menschensohn*, 300—13, esp. 308—13.

14 On 3:14 see Ruckstuhl in *Jesus und der Menschensohn*, 314—41, and on 8:28 Riedl in *Jesus und der Menschensohn*, 155—70.

15 Lindars rightly deplores the fact that John is normally dismissed in investigations of the Son of Man concept, where the synoptics are considered not only the primary but frequently also the only evidence. For the Son of Man in John, see, in addition to the above mentioned works, Guthrie, *Theology*, 282—90; Schnackenburg *NTS* 11 (1964—5) 123—37; id., "Die Ecce-homo-Szene und der Menschensohn" in *Jesus und der Menschensohn*, 371—86; Smaley, *NTS* 15 (1968—9) 278—301; Lindars, in *Christ and Spirit in the NT*, 43—60; Dodd, *The Interpretation of the Fourth Gospel*, 241—9; Freed, *JBL* 86 (1967) 402—9; Ruckstuhl, in *Theologische Berichte* I, ed. Pfammatter-Furger, 171—284; Moloney, *The Johannine Son of Man*; Kinniburg, *S E* 4 (1968) 64ff.; Sidebottom, *ET* 68 (1956—7) 231ff., 280ff.; Maddox, in *Reconciliation and Hope*, 186—204; Coppens, *ETL* 52 (1976) 28—81, with extensive bibliography in n.3; Braun, in *La venue du Messie*, 133—47; Coppens, *Le Fils de l'Homme Néo-testamentaire*, 45—103; Hamerton-Kelly, *Pre-existence*, 218—42. Schulz, *Untersuchungen zur Menschensohn-Christologie im Johannesevangelium*, 96ff. argues that the Johanninie SM sayings belong to a special stratum of the tradition.

16 The terms "authentic" and "authenticity" are used by me throughout this study as referring to what can be considered as actually going back to Jesus, not in existential fashion as e.g. Robinson, *The New Quest of the Historical Jesus*, 99.

found no scholarly consensus whatever. The situation at present is deeply contradictory. What is authentic for one scholar is inauthentic for another and vice versa.

In general, however, scholarly opinion may be subsumed under three main positions: a) the rejection of all three classes of Son of Man sayings, b) the acceptance of only one (occasionally two of the three classes of Son of Man sayings, and c) the acceptance of all three classes of Son of Man sayings.

The first position had, according to Hodgson[17], one single advocate, H. Lietzmann[18]. Since Hodgson wrote we may add a few more names like Vielhauer[19], Teeple[20], and Perrin[21], as well as a couple of scholars overlooked by Hodgson, viz. Käsemann[22], and Conzelmann[23].

The second position is represented by a good number of scholars, but here there is agreement neither as to the class of sayings to be accepted nor as to the particular sayings to be accepted as genuine within the class chosen. A few examples will illustrate the point. Albert Schweitzer[24] followed by J. Jeremias[25], accepted as authentic only eschatological Son of Man sayings, which indicated Jesus' belief that he would be the heavenly Son of Man at the end-time. Bultmann[26] followed by Bornkamm[27], Tödt[28], Hahn[29], and Higgins[30], accepts only certain apocalyptic sayings as genuine, but as referring to someone other than Jesus[31]. E. Schweizer[32] accepts for the most part sayings referring to Jesus' earthly life, as well as a few glorification (= my 'Exaltation') sayings. Knox[33] accepts all nineteen Son of Man sayings belonging to his Group A (= more or less my 'Exaltation' group) but not as a self-designation of Jesus, and in addition he accepts four of the 'Earthly Life' sayings, but only in a generic sense.

---

17 *JR* 41 (1961) 91.

18 *Der Menschensohn.*

19 in *Festschrift G. Dehn*, 51—79 and *ZTK* 60 (1963) 133—77, rp. in *Aufsätze zum NT*, 55—91 and 92—140. See esp. 133.

20 *JBL* 84 (1965) 213—50.

21 *Rediscovering the Teaching of Jesus*, 164—99.

22 *ZTK* 51 (1954) 125—53.

23 *ZTK* 54 (1957) 277—96; *ZTK* 56 (1959) Beih. 1, 2—13: *SEÅ* 28/9 (1963/4) 39—53.

24 *Geschichte der Leben-Jesu-Forschung*, [4]1926, e.g. 390ff.

25 *Neutestamentliche Theologie*, I, 1971, 254f. (Engl. tr. 266f.).

26 *Theology* I, 30. According to Hodgson, *JR* 41 (1961) 104—6 only Mk 8:38 par.; Mk 13:26 par.; Mt 24:44 par.; and Lk 12:8.

27 *Jesus of Nazareth*, 162f.

28 *Der Menschensohn in der synoptischen Überlieferung.* 1959.

29 *Christologische Hoheitstitel* [4]1974 (Engl. tr. *The Titles of Jesus in Christology*, 1969).

30 *Jesus and the Son of Man*, 185—92: *The Son of Man in the Teaching of Jesus*, 2.

31 For criticism of this position, see Lindeskog, *S T* 28 (1968) 149—75; Cullman, *The Christology*, 152—64.

32 *ZNW* 50 (1959) 185—209 (= *JBL* 79 (1960) 119—29) and *NTS* 9 (1962/3) 258.

33 *The Death of Christ*, 88ff.

Jüngel[34] admits only certain future sayings. There is, furthermore, no agreement on the individual sayings considered as authentic even when the same group is accepted.

The third position, that of accepting Son of Man sayings of all three groups, has, among others, the following advocates: Turner[35], Mowinckel[36], Taylor[37], Cullmann[38], Maddox[39], Cranfield[40], Leivestad[41], Goppelt[42]. Stauffer[43], Moule[44], Barrett[45], Bruce[46], Hunter[47], Marshall[48], Colpe[49], Borsch[50], Ladd[51], Hooker[52], Lindars[53] and Guthrie[54]. But even here the individual sayings accepted as genuine differ from one scholar to another.

The above few paragraphs have hopefully shown how deeply scholarship is divided on one of the most central issues of NT theology, viz. Jesus' self-consciousness with its important consequences for the nature of the earliest Christology[55]. But what is even more surprising in this really contradictory picture which biblical science offers at present is the conspicuous absence of objective, valid and universally acceped criteria. The decisions arrived at are usually based upon criteria of a subjective and circular character[56]. Borsch summarizes the situation poignantly when he says: "What makes a number of the sayings suspect to many scholars

34 In *Paulus und Jesus* 215-62.
35 *Jesus Master and Lord*, 196—212.
36 *He that Cometh*, 346—450.
37 *ET* 58 (1946—7) 12—5; *The Names of Jesus*, 25—35; *The Gospel according to St Mark*, 119f.
38 *Christology*, esp. 155—61.
39 *NTS* 15 (1968) 45—74 and *ABR* 19 (1971) 36—51 (= in Germ. tr. *EvT* 32 (1972) 143—60), esp. 44—8.
40 *Mark* 1959 272—7.
41 *ASTI* 6, 1968 (= *NTS* 18 (1971/2) 243—67) 49—105.
42 In *Mensch und Menschensohn*, ed. H. Sierig, 20—32.
43 *NT Theology*, 108ff.
44 *The NT Gospels*, 1965, 46—9; *The Phenomenon of the NT*, 34—6; in *NT und Kirche*, 422 and *The Origin of Christology*, 19.
45 *Jesus and the Gospel Tradition*,
46 *This is That*, 26—30, 97—9.
47 *The Work and Words of Jesus*, 107f.
48 *NTS* 12 (1965/6) 327—51.
49 *TDNT* VIII, esp. 430—64.
50 *The Son of Man*, 314—64.
51 *A Theology of the NT*, 153—8.
52 *The Son of Man in Mark.* Cf. also Maddox, *ABR* 19 (1971) 48.
53 *NTS* 22 (1975) 52—72; esp. 65—71.
54 *Theology*, 270—91.
55 Cf. Lindars, *NTS* 22 (1975) 64: Lindeskog, *S T* 22 (1968) 149—75; Higgins, *The Son of Man in the Teaching of Jesus*, 126.
56 For a discussion of recent Son of Man work and often criticism of principles used, reference may be made to Mc Cown, *JR* 28 (1948) 1—12; Marlow, *CBQ* 28 (1966) 20—39; Higgins in *NT Essays* 119—35; Michel, *TZ* 27 (1971) 81—104; Marshall, *NTS* 12 (1965—6) 327—51; *EvQ* 42 (1970) 67—87; Birdsall, *EvQ* 42 (1970) 7—17; Higgins, *The Son of Man*, esp. 29—53; Tuckett, *Scripture Bulletin* 12 (1981) 14ff.; Kümmel, *TRu* 45 (1980) 40—84.

frequently has little to do with intrinsic, exegetical difficulties, but is rather due to suspicions based on assumptions about the kind of Son of Man Jesus could have known and with regard to the character of his ministry. Once such assumptions are rigorously questioned, many of the other arguments often appear to be insubstantial. In this light it is interesting that even scholars who tend to agree on a general line of approach are frequently inclined to present reasons for the omission of a particular logion which are quite contradictory"[57]. Borsch's remark was anticipated by Hodgson, who wrote: "Invariably, the argument for unauthenticity of one group of sayings rests upon a prior judgment that another group, or groups, *are* authentic"[58]. These observations by Borsch and Hodgson find an echo in Maddox[59], who, by way of a critique of the results and methodology of Hooker[60], Borsch[61], Colpe[62], and especially Perrin[63] finds it necessary to search for *valid* criteria for the Son of Man research.

It is not possible within the limits of the present work to discuss in any detail the principles by which this contradictory picture of the Son of Man research outlined above, has come about. It is, however, incumbent upon me that I delineate very briefly the false premises upon which much of the Son of Man research has been conducted. This is given partly as a justification for my parting company with many of the results of the present debate.

Bousset made much of the criterion of formal consistency. He stated that "If the Son of Man can only mean the supraterrestrial transcendent Messiah . . . then we cannot explain how Jesus already in the present could claim for himself the predicate and rights of the Son of Man"[64]. But as Ladd points out, "That the ideas of an apocalyptic and earthly Son of Man are not necessarily mutually exclusive is proven by the fact that these two concepts are brought together in the Gospels"[65]. Knox is conscious of the dependence of historical exegesis on theological presuppositions which decide on which standpoint the onus of proof is to be laid. Knox himself thinks the burden of proof is upon those who accept the Son of Man sayings as a self-designation of Jesus. As far as Knox himself is concerned, since Jesus could not possibly have predicted his death, the 'Sufferings' sayings cannot be authentic and certainly not a self-designation[66]. As for the 'Exaltation' sayings, it is incredible that a "sane"

---

57 *The Son of Man*, 314. Similarly Guthrie, *Theology*, 271.
58 *JR* 41 (1961) 91.
59 *ABR* 19 (1971) 36—51.
60 *The Son of Man in Mark*.
61 *The Son of Man*.
62 *TDNT*, VIII, 400—77.
63 *Rediscovering the Teaching of Jesus*.
64 *Kyrios Christos*, 40.
65 *A Theology of the NT*, 153.
66 *The Death of Christ*, 74ff.

or a "good" man could think of himself as divine[67]. However, since the
tradition that Jesus used the expression is so widespread in the synoptics,
it can be presumed that he did use the phrase, but not in self-reference[68].
Hodgson's criticism here is quite apt: "On the basis of his presuppositions
Knox has no alternative: he must prove that Group A (= my 'Exaltation'
sayings) is authentic and that Groups B and C are secondary. Theology
not only defines the problem but also narrowly prescribes the limits of
historical investigation. Knox must *prove* exegetically what he has *presumed* theologically . . . if Knox is wrong about the authenticity of Group
A, then his whole argument collapses, since his rejection of B and C depends upon the authenticity of A"![69]

Other scholars too, like Bultmann[70], F.C. Grant[71] and Higgins rule
out the possibility of Jesus' claim to be the eschatological Son of Man
because, in Higgins' words, "How could a sane man have entertained such
thoughts of himself"[72]? It will be readily apparent that Higgins' objection
can hardly be valid as a *geschichtswissenschaftliches Argument*. It is
practically impossible for Higgins to know what thoughts a "sane man"
of Jesus' time, of Jesus' Jewish background and of Jesus' calibre and
self-consciousness could or could not have entertained[73].

Leivestad, who called for the "exit", i.e. the banishment of the apocalyptic Son of Man"[74] claims categorically that "the existence of such a
title is incompatible with the New Testament"[75]. This is reminiscent of
Lietzmann's 'authoritarian' statement in which he sought to debar the
existence of the title Son of Man from Aramaic on linguistic grounds —
an extravagant claim that came to grief. Leivestad could, of course, have
added to his dogmatic statement the qualification "as *I* understand it"!

Leivestad argues that there was no Son of Man title in Jewish thought
chiefly because a) "Colpe . . . denies it"![76] — i.e. the titular use of Son of
Man in the *Parables*, — and b) because the *Parables* is late since it is absent
from the Qumran material[77]. Such 'arguments' are simply not adequate
to banish the "apocalyptic Son of Man" from Judaism. If one broaches
the question, then one will have to argue properly for it. As for the ab-

---

67 *The Death of Christ*, 58, 65ff.
68 *The Death of Christ*, 86.
69 *JR* 41 (1961) 95f.
70 *The History of the Synoptic Tradition*, 137.
71 *The Gospel of the Kingdom*, 63.
72 *Jesus and the Son of Man*, 19, 199. An almost identical thought is expressed by Knox, *The Death of Christ*, 58ff.
73 Cf. the criticism by Marshall, *NTS* 12 (1965/6) 329 and Hooker, *The Son of Man in Mark*, 183ff.
74 The title of the original German published in *ASTI* 6, (1968) 40—105 was characteristically "Der apokalyptische Menschensohn ein theologisches Phantom"!
75 *NTS* 18 (1971/2) 245.
76 I.e. in his article in TDNT, VIII, 400—77.
77 *NTS* 18 (1971/2) 246.

sence of the *Parables* from Qumran — if absence it is — it is admitting of other explanations than simply its late date. (See Chapter Three, above). Leivestad goes on to pronounce a number of Son of May sayings in the synoptics as authentic, but there is usually a tag attached: the condition that the saying is understood in a particular way, cf. his remark: "Thus understood the saying may very well be authentic"[78]. Leivestad's rejection of the "apocalyptic Son of Man" is due to his inability to find a qualifying "thus understood" for it. Thus, for Leivestad, authenticity or inauthenticity depends obviously not so much on intrinsically exegetical problems but upon whether or not a saying can be understood in a way that is in harmony with certain presuppositions.

Even Lindars' article[79], which to a considerable extent is a refutation of Leivestad, treats the question of authenticity more in an *a priori* way than by means of judgments based on the detailed exegesis of each passage. Lindars accepts as authentic sayings of all three categories. Nevertheless, this result is based upon the observation that since the expression Son of Man "cannot be derived from other sources, it must be traced back to Jesus himself"[80]. From this premise the conclusion is drawn that at least some Son of Man sayings of each group "must be authentic in order to explain the existence of the rest"[81]. Lindars supplies no list of sayings which, according to him, are authentic. Though there is much to be said for Lindars' procedure, the fact remains that this, too, is an *a priori* judgment. And one could, for example, argue, if one so wished, that the sayings of a particular class were created by the Earthly Church on the analogy of other classes. Lindars' argument is useful, if combined with others, but is not of itself of compelling value.

A priori principles seem to be at work also in both E. Schweizer's and Hooker's solutions. With respect to these scholars Maddox remarks: "Schweizer's solution involves rejection of the eschatological sayings as inauthentic, and Hooker's involves retaining them, but in a 'demythologized' way"[82]. Once again, rejection or retention of certain SM sayings is made to depend upon a prior understanding of the nature and character of the Son of Man sayings.

Perrin is one of those scholars who have explicitly indicated the criteria controlling their research. Three criteria are presented: a) the *criterion of dissimilarity* according to which "The earliest form of a saying we can reach may be regarded as authentic if it can be shown to be dissimilar to characteristic emphases both of ancient Judaism and the early

---

78 *NTS* 18 (1971/2) 259. See also 258ff. on Mt 16:13; Mk 2:10; 260 on Lk 17:22–30; 262ff., 267.
79 *NTS* 22 (1975) 52–72.
80 *NTS* 22 (1975) 65.
81 *NTS* 22 (1975) 68.
82 *ABR* 19 (1971) 48.

Church"[83]; b) the *criterion of coherence* according to which "material from the earliest strata of the tradition may be accepted as authentic if it can be shown to cohere with the material established as authentic by means of the criterion of dissimilarity"[84]; and c) the *criterion of multiple attestation* defined as "A proposal to accept as authentic material which is attested in all, or most, of the sources which can be discerned behind the synoptic Gospels"[85]. With regard to the last criterion Perrin says: "We shall . . . have only limited occasion to use the criterion of multiple attestation, *preferring* (italics mine) to work upon the basis of the establishment of the history of the tradition and the criteria of dissimilarity and coherence"[86], and in the chapter dealing with the Son of Man this criterion is altogether dropped. It will be seen, further, that the second criterion depends for its application upon and is conditioned by the results obtained by the first criterion. It is therefore hardly an exaggeration to say that Perrin bases his sweeping results essentially upon a single criterion, and that of doubtful validity, or at any rate, an application of it in a clearly cavalier manner.

Perrin thus rejects all of the Son of Man sayings on two grounds: a) because there never was a Son of Man concept in Judaism[87], and b) because he considers that "the burden of proof will be upon the claim to authenticity"[88] of the Son of Man sayings. The "claim to authenticity" will have been proven only if Perrin's "fundamental criterion for authenticity", i.e. the "criterion of dissimilarity" is satisfied[89]. This criterion implies that the advocate of authenticity "must be able to show that the saying comes neither from the Church nor from ancient Judaism"[90]. Since Perrin thinks that he has reasons to question all of the Son of Man sayings, it is concluded that authenticity is unproven and that rejection of them is justified. Perrin's first argument, the absence of the Son of Man concept in Judaism as a ground for rejecting the authenticity of the Son of Man in the NT, is a *non sequitur* with regard to his criterion of dissimilarity. In this case Perrin's "fundamental criterion for authenticity" clearly supports the authenticity of the Son of Man sayings since the concept was, according to Perrin, absent in Judaism and not in use in the early Church either! As for Perrin's other argument, that of laying the burden of proof upon the claim to authenticity, this has rightly been rejected by Kümmel, who pointed out, "I have already argued against the

---

83 *Rediscovering*, 39. Fuller's definition is somewhat fuller though essentially similar (see his *The Foundations* 18). This criterion was first suggested by Bultmann, *History of the Synoptic Tradition*, 205 and was made into a criterion by Käsemann, *Exegetische Versuche*, I, 205.

84 *Rediscovering*, 43.

85 *Rediscovering*, 45.

86 *Rediscovering*, 47.

87 *Rediscovering*, 198.

88 *Rediscovering*, 39.

89 *Rediscovering*, 39.

90 *Rediscovering*, 39.

acceptance of this basic viewpoint (*Theologische Rundschau*, xxxi, (1965/ 66), 43), while with regard to the synoptic tradition, too, the demand can only be that not the authenticity of a saying attributed to Jesus but its secondary formulation can and must be proven"[91]. Kümmel goes on "One can see very readily where this false methodological principle leads by examining Perrin's first example"[92]. Such negative commerce with the *criterion of dissimilarity* is castigated also by Riesner: "Heute ist weithin anerkannt, dass eine negative Handhabung des "criterion of dissimilarity" pseudokritisch wäre"[93]. For further criticism, see Maddox[94] and Hooker[95].

Even an open-minded application of this otherwise questionable *criterion of dissimilarity* would, as Ladd[96] observes, result in the acceptance of the 'Sufferings' sayings, since such a Son of Man is neither known in Judaism nor is he current in the christology of the Early Church! Moreover, Perrin might also have brought to bear on his Son of Man discussion, as he does in other parts of his book, his third criterion, that of *multiple attestation*. But quite arbitrarily he is "preferring to work upon the basis of the . . . criteria of dissimilarity and coherence"![97] This last criterion would, as Maddox well observes, tend to establish the authenticity of the Son of Man sayings since, in Perrin's own words in an earlier book[98], now repudiated[99], the Son of Man as Judge "is far too widespread in the tradition to be dismissed as no part of the expectation of the historical Jesus"[100]. We thus see that a more objective use of the criteria employed by Perrin would have led to the pronouncement of the 'Sufferings' and 'Exaltation' Son of Man sayings as authentic. But this at once implies that these criteria are not proof against misapplication, a circumstance that detracts considerably from their usefulness.

The three criteria 'used' by Perrin have been treated by other scholars as well. For example, Catchpole[101] has discussed their limitations and

---

91 Review of Perrin's *Rediscovering*, in *JR* 49 (1969) 60f.

92 *JR* 49 (1969) 61.

93 *Jesus als Lehrer*, 90, where more scholars are cited.

94 *ABR* 19 (1971) 44f.

95 *The Son of Man in Mark*, 79; *Theology*, 75 (1972) 570–81. See also Hooker, *NTS* 17 (1970– 1) 480–7.

96 *Theology*, 153.

97 *Rediscovering*, 47.

98 *The Kingdom of God in the Teaching of Jesus*, 139.

99 *Rediscovering*, 48.

100 Cf. Walker, *NTS* 28 (1981–2) 374–88, esp. 377–9, who in comparing and contrasting the Two Source Hypothesis and the Griesbach Hypothesis with regard to their respective consequences for the Son of Man concept, concludes that according to both hypotheses the Son of Man tradition is "fairly widespread". The difference between them is that in the former hypothesis there is a tendency to move from "Sufferings" Son of Man sayings to "Eschatological" Son of Man sayings, while in the latter the opposite is the case. A similar conclusion to Walker's in respect to the "Sufferings" sayings is reached by Tuckett, *JSNT* 14 (1982) 70.

101 In *NT Interpretation*, 177.

proneness to misuse. McArthur[102] has postulated four criteria: a) "multiple attestation", b) "discounting tendencies of developing tradition", c) "attestation by multiple forms" and d) "the elimination of all material which may be derived either from Judaism or from primitive Christianity". The third criterion is really a special form of the first one, while the second partly coincides with the fourth one, which is that of dissimilarity. McArthur is well aware of the limited use of these criteria and considers the first as the most objective one — which Perrin, with regard to the Son of Man question, relegated to the limbo of oblivion. Kümmel[103], too, thinks that McArthur's criteria cannot apply to every text. Kümmel does admit the limited usefulness of the criteria discussed above in a prudent application where relevant, but makes no attempt to supply any criteria of his own.

In conclusion of the above discussion it may be stated that two results have been forthcoming in relation to the Son of Man question and that both of them are equally remarkable. The first result is that a wide divergence of scholarly opinion, or outright contradiction, with regards to the authenticity of the Son of Man sayings has emerged. The second result is often the signal lack of any criteria in deciding for authenticity or inauthenticity, or where criteria have been explicitly applied, the intrusion of inevitable subjectivity. At any rate, the discussion above has underlined the fact that no criteria have as yet been proposed, which in themselves are so valid, objective and universal, as to be unsusceptible to misuse. The application of these criteria has not brought us any nearer to the solution of the Son of Man question.

The *criterion of dissimilarity* is clearly incapable of solving the Son of Man problem on account of its inherent weaknesses. The criterion stipulates that authentic words of Jesus must not correspond to characteristic emphases in Judaism or the Early Church[104]. The criterion here simply presupposes that we are thoroughly acquainted with all the conceptions of Judaism, with Jesus' whole teaching and with the entire thought of the Early Church[105]. But this is by no means the case. In the case of Judaism alone the discovery of the Dead Sea Scrolls has added so much that was completely unknown a few decades ago. And who is to say that today's picture(s) of Judaism is(are) not going to be modified by future discoveries? We simply do not have an adequate basis for applying the *criterion of dissimilarity* in such a way that genuine results will be forthcoming. Another difficulty, the gravest of all, lies at the core of the *criterion of dissimilarity*, with its underlying assumption that Jesus' teaching must always be distinguishable or dissimilar from the teachings

---

102 *Interpretation* 18 (1964) 39—55.
103 *TRu* 30 (1965—6) 44f.
104 Perrin, *Rediscovering*, 39.
105 See Calvert, *NTS* 18 (1971—2) 211.

of Judaism and of the Early Church. This would seem to presuppose that no continuity between Judaism and Jesus is permissible, nor is even any lasting influence of Jesus on the Early Church recognized. Both of these assumptions would fly in the face of modern scholarly consensus. Positing a world in a vacuum for Jesus' thought is problematic enough; but to even deny Jesus' influence on the Early Church and hence the Church's use of motifs and ideas first initiated by Jesus, would seem to be going altogether too far for sensible scholarship. The advocates of this criterion would, of course, recognize common elements shared between Judaism and Jesus on the one hand, and between Jesus and the Church on the other. But, they insist, these elements cannot divulge Jesus. Only the things in which Jesus differs from his contemporaries are a safe guide for finding the authentic Jesus[106]. But here our difficulties turn about the relation between Jesus and the Early Church. The *criterion of dissimilarity* does not take seriously Jesus' influence on the Early Church. It sets aside as inauthentic all those things in which Jesus influenced the Early Church, and tries to reconstruct Jesus on the few things that apparently have not left their imprint upon the Church, to judge from the fragmentary evidence available about the Church. It might as well be demanded of us to reconstruct Socrates' teaching from Plato's dialogues with the stipulation that we discount all 'platonic' elements from those dialogues! The undertaking would clearly turn out to be a fiasco. It might possibly succeed if we could presuppose that none of Plato's teachings could have originated with Socrates, but then what would be left *for* Socrates? All we would be doing would be taking all those original traits in which Socrates influenced Plato so deeply and which Plato perfected in his dialogues, and deny the scent of them to Socrates! How authentic would be our Socrates? However, we do know that Plato was deeply influenced by Socrates, as we also know that Jesus' influence on the Early Church was indelible. Hence to declare authentic only such ideas of Jesus as are not found in Judaism or Christianity is surely to present an unhistorical and inauthentic picture of Jesus. McArthur is in agreement with this when he says with regard to the application of this "negative criterion" that "it is so ruthless that it is difficult to know what can survive the test"[107]. The result would be to cut off Jesus from all contact with past, present or future and make him into an island. The *criterion of dissimilarity* is clearly unsuitable for determining the authentic Jesus.

With regard to the Son of Man concept in Judaism and the Early Church the application of this criterion leads to two contradictory results. The existence of the Son of Man concept in Judaism would *a priori* deprive Jesus of the claim of having used the title, while the consistent abstention of the Early Church from using the title would tend to authen-

---

106 Perrin, *Rediscovering*, 39.
107 *ET* 82 (1970–1) 117.

ticate Jesus' use of it. The *criterion of dissimilarity* could, of course, be so formulated as to signify that authentic words of Jesus must not have counterparts *either* in Judaism *or* in Christianity, and on the ground of its existence in Judaism still be possible to deny the use of the title to Jesus. It is, however, more surprising when advocates of this criterion claim that the Son of Man concept does not occur in Judaism, and that the title is the creation of the Early Church[108]. But this only makes the problem bigger. What clear or convincing arguments are there to show that while the Church could create the concept of Son of Man, Jesus could not? Furthermore if the title owed its existence to the Church's creative genius in inventing christological concepts, would that Church have been so consistent in abstaining from using what she perceived to be Jesus' most beloved self-designation? And is it, moreover, credible that the Early Church would have neglected to use the title in countless christological contexts in the Gospels, while at the same time making use of it in such a saying as the one that speaks of the Son of Man as "gluttonous" (Mt 11:9; Lk 7:34)?

Many scholars have pointed out the abuses to which this criterion is susceptible[109]. More radically I have tried to show that the criterion as such is unsuitable for reaching decisions regarding authenticity. Its usefulness is rather limited; it may help, for example, to emphasize what is new and prominent in Jesus: however, it cannot be used to tell us which words of Jesus are authentic and which are not. So, it is not merely a question as to whether the *criterion of dissimilarity* is used positively or negatively; rather the criterion is so constructed as to be untrustworthy as a guide to authenticity[110]. Thus, while even a positive use of this criterion, such as Ladd[111] has suggested above, needs to reckon with the criterion's negative side, — which would greatly circumscribe its usefullness, — its inexorably consistent use without restraint or check by other criteria, could only lead finally to the 'de-Judaization' of Jesus as well as the 'de-Jesus-ing' of the Early Church![112] In either case the Jesus of the *criterion of dissimilarity* would no longer be the Jesus of history[113].

---

108 Perrin, *Rediscovering*, 198.

109 E.g. Maddox, *ABR* 19 (1971) 44f.; Hooker, *Theology* 75 (1972) 570—81; Riesner, *Jesus als Lehrer*, 90.

110 That it may occasionally point to correct results, as pointed out above, is more of the nature of coincidence. However, this does not affect the verdict on it as a general principle.

111 *A NT Theology*, 153.

112 Cf. France *Jesus and the OT*, 20f.: "It requires a Jesus who was utterly eccentric, in that he took nothing from his environment, never endorsed a proverb or maxim of Jewish wisdom, and most unlikely of all, seldom if ever simply endorsed the teaching of the Old Testament. And it requires a church which was utterly unfaithful to its master's teaching, in that it hardly ever simply preserved and endorsed anything that he said, but altered and adapted it to such an extent that its teaching stands in sharp contrast with the few remaining genuine sayings of Jesus".

113 See Calvert, *NTS* 18 (1971—2) 211f.

The *criterion of coherence* is not an independent criterion, but works on the basis of what has been pronounced authentic by the application of other criteria. In applying this criterion a scholar seeks to discover material that is in harmony with material that is assumed to be authentic. This implies that if a wrong criterion has been used in establishing the 'norm', i.e. the 'hard core', and the result is accordingly untrusthworthy, the *criterion of coherence*, if used consistently, will produce more untrustworthy results. It can readily be seen which results are to be expected when this criterion is used in combination with the *criterion of dissimilarity*. The *criterion of coherence* is useful as a general principle, but it may be used only in those cases where traditions have been established by more objective criteria. Above all the combination of the *criterion of dissimilarity* with its 'appendix', the *criterion of coherence*, is to be regarded as a concurrence of errors[114].

The *criterion of multiple attestation* is independent of the above two criteria and tends to be more objective. In principle it is similar to the one used in Textual Criticism concerning the widespread occurrence of a reading in text-forms or geographical *loci*. But as in Textual Criticism, so here, it is not always a safe guide, since it can always be supposed that a tradition is authentic in spite of its being attested in only one strand of the Gospel tradition and vice versa. In particular the use of this criterion is hampered by the question of sources. In the present state of Source Criticism in which not only varied but also contradictory solutions are put forward, and where a 'certain consensus' has imposed itself as a working hypothesis for the 'lack' of better theories, it is not possible to speak of the assured results of modern Source Criticism upon which the *criterion of multiple attestation* can be unproblematically applied. Take for instance Q. In some of the Son of Man studies Son of Man logia are listed according to the 'source' in which they occur, and this means also Q[115]. But despite its widespread acceptance Q has always been hypothetical and detractors have never been wanting[116]. Among adherents to Q there is fairly broad disagreement as to its form and sphere of influucnec. In particular in the *Colloquium Biblicum Lovaniense* in Aug. 1981 on The Sayings of Jesus in Early Christian Tradition, the traditional neat picture of the nature and influence of Q was practically shattered[117]. Q is now claimed to lie behind Mark also and to have existed in several forms or

---

114 These two criteria have been subjected to devastating criticism by Hooker (*Theology* 75 (1972) esp. 574–9.

115 E.g. Hodgson, *JR* 41 (1961) 105f.; Tödt, *Der Menschensohn*, pp. 322f.; Higgins, *The Son of Man in the Teaching of Jesus*, pp. 55f.; Casey, *Son of Man*, 236; Lindars, *Son of Man*, 85–100.

116 Cf. Calvert, "The growing feeling that the synoptic problem is still with us, and that the two-source theory is no longer adequate, makes it difficult to build up a criterion on this basis" (*NTS* 18 (1971–2) 218). See also Riesner, *ThB* 8 (1977) 49–73, and Walker, *NTS* 28 (1981–2) 374–88.

117 See e.g. the Papers in *Logia* by Neirynck, "Recent Developments in the Study of Q" 29–75;

stages, thus disturbing the traditional thesis of Matthew's and Luke's dependence on Mark and Q[118]. The inherent weaknesses of the hypothesis have begun to emerge in the midst of its supporters.

The *criterion of multiple attestation* would come to its right if it could be applied to objective and well-defined sources, rather than to hypothetical reconstructions. The reconstruction of Q is surely interesting and may even have elements of truth in it, but Can it really be used scientifically as an objectively verified source on a par with Matthew, Mark and Luke?

As for McArthur's second criterion, that of *discounting tendencies of developing tradition,* it is susceptible to subjectivity. With regard to his third criterion, *attestation by multiple forms,* it has, no doubt, some usefulness, though I would suspect a rather limited one as far as the Son of Man question is concerned[119].

Teeple[120] delineates five criteria, which are hardly any more successful than the ones discussed already. For criticism of these see Kümmel[121] and Higgins[122]. As for Carlston's "positive criterion of authenticity"[123] that "A saying is authentic if it is characteristic of the known teaching of Jesus" it really begs the question as far as the Son of Man problem is concerned. In her book on the Son of Man in Mark, Hooker has pointed out the weakness of this type of reasoning as for example when scholars assume that the Exaltation sayings are the authentic teaching of Jesus and then reject the Sufferings and Earthly Life sayings as incoherent with the Exaltation ones.

Does this imply that we have definitely entered a *cul-de-sac,* or are groping in thickest darkness in a labyrinth without exit? Higgins[124] and Hooker[125] have both asked the question 'Is the Son of Man Problem insoluble?" The very fact that the question has been asked at all would indicate how close to, if not actually in the "slough of dispondency", NT scholarship has sometimes felt itself to be. Catchpole expresses this sentiment well when he writes: "The problems which emerge during any

Vassiliadis, "The Original Order of Q. Some Residual Cases", 379–81; Jacobson, "The Literary Unity of Q. Lc 10, 12–16 and parallels as a Test Case", 419–23; Hickling, "The Plurality of 'Q' ", 425–9 and cf. Vassiliadis, "The Nature and Extent of the Q-Document" *NovT* 20 (1978) 49–73.

118 Cf. Lambrecht, "Q-Influence on Mark 8, 34–9, 1" in *Logia,* 277–304. See Roland, *RB* 90 (1983) 23–79, for the quite different view that "Matthew and Luke used two parallel Greek versions of a semitic Gospel, whereas Mark harmonized the two versions and adapted them for his Roman readers" (Harrington in *NTA* 27 (1984) 18.

119 For more criteria, discussed and found insufficient or rejected, see Kümmel, *TRu* 30 (1965–6) 42ff.

120 *JBL* 84 (1965) 219–23.

121 *TRu* 45 (1980) 70f.

122 *The Son of Man,* 37–9.

123 *BR* 7 (1962) 33ff.

124 in *Neotestamentica et Semitica,* 70–87.

125 in *Text and Interpretation,* 155–68.

critical examination of criteria might suggest that there is no future for the inquiry except in pessimism or even agnosticism"[126]. It might be pointed out here by the way that the "problems which emerge" are not so much due to the Son of Man texts *per se* as to the invalidity of the criteria used. However, both Catchpole and Kümmel[127] rightly refuse to acquiesce in this attitude of resignation and despair. Indeed, if our criteria have been "false" as Kümmel objected against Perrin, there is no reason why they should not be substituted by more valid principles. As for the question of the authenticity of the Son of Man logia, this I think, must be decided on rather different grounds. The following considerations are here regarded as of decisive importance.

a) The trustworthiness of the sources.

Without doubt the data of the synoptics have all too easily been brushed aside as formulations to meet Church needs[128]. *Formgeschichte* has undoubtedly used the form to make verdicts about the history of sayigs attributed to Jesus more readily than was warranted[129]. Palmer goes so far as to dub the title of Bultmann's *History of the Synoptic Tradition*, in view of the concerns of the book, "a misnomer for this type of research"[130]. Further, it may be admitted that it is an embarrassment to the biblical scholar that classical scholars attach the same credibility to the historical data of the Gospels and Acts as they do to their profane sources. Apropos of this Sherwin-White writes: "It is astonishing that while Graeco-Roman historians have been growing in confidence, the twentieth-century study of the Gospel narratives, starting from *no less promising material* (italics mine), has taken so gloomy a turn in the development of Form Criticism that the more advanced exponents of it apparently maintain . . . that the historical Christ is unknowable and the history of his mission cannot be written"[131]. With regard to Acts, he says: "Any attempt to reject its basic historicity even in matters of detail must now appear absurd. Roman historians have long taken it for granted"[132], and with regard to the Gospels: "It would be no harder for the Disciples and their immediate successors to uncover detailed narratives of the actions and sayings of Christ within their closed community, than it was for Herodotus and Thucydides to establish the story of the great events

---

126 in *NT Interpretation*, 177.
127 *TRu* 45 (1980) 84.
128 Cf. Palmer's biting remark: "Were the first Christians adept at thinking up stories-of-Jesus to suit a situation in their Church? Form critics do not show this, but take it for granted in all their reasonings. These reasonings do, however, show how adept form-critics are at thinking up early-Church-situations to suit stories of Jesus" (*The Logic of Gospel Criticism*, 185).
129 Cf. Hooker, *Theology* 75 (1972) 570ff. and Palmer's criticism of Form-criticism in his *Logic of Gospel Criticism*, 184ff.
130 *The Logic of Gospel Criticism*, 188.
131 *Roman Society*, 187.
132 *Roman Society*, 189.

of 520–480 B.C."[133] In an interesting study[134] Mosley shows that the low view of ancient historians (Greek, Roman and Jewish) usually held by NT scholars, in the light of which the NT is judged[135], is too sweeping to do justice to the facts. He concludes that our standard ancient historians were aware of the difference between fact and fiction and that they made every effort to write down history "as it happened"[136]. (Cf. the equivalent phrase τῶν γενομένων τό σαφές σκοπεῖν in Thucydides I, 22). Stuhlmacher, who agrees with these judgments poignantly says: "Hinzu kommt, dass in Gesprächen mit Althistorikern und Altphilologen unserer Exegese in zunehmendem Masse Esoterik, hypertropher Kritizismus und mangelndes historisches Urteilsvermögen bescheinigt werden. All dies zwingt zur Selbstbesinnung"[137]. The fact that the Gospels and Acts are written after Easter need not imply that they are devoid of all interest in history[138]. Perhaps Gadamer's view[139] with regard to the subjectivity involved in the perception of historical truth has been allowed too great a scope in dominating NT hermeneutics. A more modern and more thorough investigation has come to a different conclusion: "Historische Erkenntnis ist nicht notwendig perspektivisch und standortgebunden; es kann sinnvoll gefordet werden, alle subjektiven Inhalte aus empirischen historischen Aussagen auszuschalten. Empirische Aussagen können von dogmatischen getrennt werden, aber auch diese sind in konditionaler Wendung einer verbindlichen Prüfung zugänglich. Historische Erkenntnis ist allgemeingültig möglich; der Historiker kann sagen, 'wie es eigentlich gewesen' "[140].

It is significant to note in this connection that developments are taking place in recent Gospel research, whereby the synoptics have come to be

---

133 *Roman Society*, 191.

134 *NTS* 12 (1965–6) 10–26.

135 Cf. e.g. McArthur's statement that the Gospel writers used "a freedom totally foreign to modern historiographers. In a sense *this was true of all ancient historians* (italics mine), but it was particularly true of the Early Christian writers" (*ET* 82 (1970–1) 117).

136 Mosley also cites the concurring judgment of other classical scholars. For a similar judgment on Herodotus see Atsalos, in *IEE*, III, B, 438f. and on Thucydides, see Cacrides, in *IEE*, III, B, 441ff. Cf. also Turner, *Grammatical Insights into the NT*, 24, who, with regard to Luke's account of the census, heretofore not substantiated by other sources, makes bold to say: 'However, we have St Luke's own testimony to the census and he should be accounted an authority." In a similar note Sherwin-White writes: "Luke should mean what he wrote" (*Roman Society*, 171). Cf. also Riesner, *Jesus als Lehrer*, 32.

137 *ZNW* 63 (1972) 26.

138 See Turner, *Historicity and Gospels*. As for the possibility of reliably preserving oral tradition, see the painstaking investigation of Vansina, *Oral Tradition*, and for the characteristics of ancient school formations – which would seem to obtain also in the case of Jesus and his disciples – see Culpepper, The *Johannine School*.

139 *Wahrheit und Methode*, (Engl. tr. *Truth and Method*, 1975). For a presentation and criticism of Gadamer, see Hirsch, *Validity in Interpretation*, 245–64.

140 Hedinger, *Subjektivität und Geschichtswissenschaft*, 663, quoted by Riesner, *Jesus als Lehrer*, 80.

regarded as independent parallel sources[141] i.e. each one is treated in its own right[142], and as constituting trustworthy sources for Jesus' teaching[143]. At any rate, in the light of developments in the fields of classics and the OT[144], where confidence in the trustworthiness of sources is growing, it is hardly defensible to single out the Gospels and continue to treat their accounts with suspicions inherited from the nineteenth century.

b) The burden of proof. This principle somehow hangs together with the above point. The recognition that the Gospel statements ought to be taken seriously and be tested objectively by scientific research has as a corollary the laying of the burden of proof upon the claim to inauthenticity. The starting-point is the Gospel text. That text claims that Jesus sometimes spoke of himself as the Son of Man. It is an unsound methodology to *a priori* pronounce the Gospel data as unreliable and then demand that the authenticity of each saying be proved individually. The proper scientific procedure is, no doubt, to give authenticity the benefit of the doubt at least as a working hypothesis, as long as no definite grounds pointing to inauthenticity exist[145]. Open-mindedness must continue to the end of the investigation so that where sound evidence points definitely to the secondary character of a saying, that evidence should not be brushed aside. In disagreement with the above position a number of scholars like Käsemann and Perrin have considered it axiomatic that the burden of proof is upon the claim to authenticity. But this has not been equally obvious to other scholars, who have found good reasons to question the validity of this axiom. Thus, in argumentation against Käsemann's standpoint that "wir . . . die Echtheit des Einzelgutes zu prüfen und glaubhaft zu machen haben"[146] Kümmel states unequivocally: "auch wenn wir der Jesustradition ohne Zweifel primär nur in der kerygmatischen Formung der Gemeinde begegnen, die Beweislast für das höhere Alter eines Überlieferungsstückes liegt bei denen, die die 'Unechtheit' behaupten, weil wir ja in der synoptischen Tradition das Kerygma in Gestalt einer in das Leben Jesu zurückreichenden Überlieferung der Worte und Taten Jesu vor uns haben"[147]. And against Perrin, whose reasoning is similar to Käsemann's, Kümmel objects: "With regard to the synoptic tradition . . . the demand

---

141 Frey, *Analyse ordinale des évangiles synoptiques, passim*, see e.g. 303ff., 134ff. Frey rejects synoptic interdependence positing, instead, a partially common dependence on short pre-synoptic sources. Cf. also Gerhardsson-Hartman, *STK* 58 (1982) 113.

142 Riesner, *Jesus als Lehrer*, 88.

143 Riesner, *Jesus als Lehrer*, 88; see also 4ff.

144 Cf. Maddox, *ABR* 19 (1971) 47 n.16.

145 Cf. Riesner, *TZ* 38 (1982) 513: "Trifft das hier skizzierte Bild vom Ursprung der Jesus-Überlieferung zu, dann haben jene Forscher Recht, welche die Beweislast für Unechtheitsurteile beim Exegeten sehen. Er darf von einem grundsätzlichen Vertrauen in die substanzielle Zuverlässigkeit der synoptischen Wortüberlieferungen ausgehen. Das macht die kritische Prüfung der Einzellogien nicht unnötig, wohl aber zu einem hoffnungsvollen Unternehmen".

146 *Exegetische Versuche*, 203.

147 *TRu* 30 (1965–6) 43

can only be that not the authenticity of a saying attributed to Jesus but its secondary formulation can and must be proven"[148]. McArthur[149] has put forth the mediating position that Perrin's three criteria should be reversed in point of order, with the criterion of multiple attestation given priority, and that of dissimilarity the least prominence. He thinks furthermore that if a motif is supported by three or four sources the burden of proof should shift on the claim to inauthenticity, but if a motif is supported by only one source or even two, the burden of proof should be laid on the claim to authenticity. It is obvious that such a mechanical application of criteria is, for reasons pointed out above, inadmissible and unsound[150].

It is again remarkable and symptomatic of current trends that recent synoptic studies (of quite different theological stance) reveal the increasing conviction that the onus of proof is to be laid on the claim to inauthenticity[151]. Inauthenticity cannot be considered as proven merely because a plausible case for it has been made; nothing short of definite proof must be required. Droysen has summarized well the demand to be made upon the claim to inauthenticity: "Zum vollen Beweis der Unechtheit gehört, dass der wirkliche Ursprung des Gefälschten, die Zeit, der Zweck der Fälschung nachgewiesen wird"[152]. In the face of such demands made upon the claim to inauthenticity it is easy to see how fragile such claims often have been.

The above two points are general considerations regarding the nature of the Gospel tradition and the proper approach to it. In the following five points more specific reasons will be given in support of the thesis that Jesus could use the term Son of Man.

c) We have already seen (Chapter Two) that the LXX of Dan 7:13 witnesses to the existence of a view whereby the 'SM' of Dan 7:13 was identified with the Aged One. This kind of interpretation is supported by Θ in Dan 7:27, where it clearly distinguishes the 'SM' from the saints, by identifying him with ʿElyônîn. The theology reflected in LXX Dan 7:13 and in Θ Dan 7:27 is carried further, as we have seen, by the *Parables* and IV Ezra, which overtly and explicitly identify their Son of Man with a pre-existent, supernatural being, in fact, one who is called the son of God (IV Ez 13:37). Furthermore, Rev 1:13ff. (cf. 1:7) portrays Jesus as One like a son of man with characteristics taken over from the description of the Aged One in Dan 7:9f. These facts amount to a demostration that

---

148 *JR* 40 (1969) 60. See also Hooker's criticism of Perrin, in *Theology* 75 (1972) 574ff.

149 *ET* 82 (1970–1) 118.

150 For a more recent discussion of criteria, see Stein, in *Gospel Perspectives* I, 225–63.

151 Cf. e.g. Kümmel, *Theologie*, 23f.; Colpe, *TDNT* VIII, 434f.; Jeremias, *Theologie*, 45 (Eng. tr. 37); Hooker, *The Son of Man in Mark*, 4ff.; Marshall, *EvQ* 42 (1970) 79; *id.*, *Historical Jesus*, 199f.; Stuhlmacher, *ZNW* 63 (1972) 24, and Riesner, *Jesus als Lehrer*, 80–95 and literature cited on p. 85 n.30.

152 *Historik*, 100.

there existed in the time of Jesus an interpretative tradition in which the Danielic 'SM' was attributed supernatural or divine status. It is against this background that some of the Gospel sayings make sense (e.g. Mt 9: 2–8 = Mk 2:3–11 = Lk 5:18–25; Jn 5:25; 10:31–39) the clearest of which is Mt 26:64 = Mk 14:62 = Lk 22:69, where Jesus' claim to be the Son of Man of Dan 7:13f. is pronounced a blasphemy. It is obvious, therefore, that the concept of Son of Man was current at the time of Jesus and that its *characteristica* were those of a primarily exalted, transcendental being, seated beside the Almighty and with prerogatives and functions identical to his. There is, therefore, no *a priori* reason for denying to Jesus the possibility of acquaintance with the term and hence also the possibility of his applying it to himself. That he did so is testified by the Gospel narratives, whose witness there are no compelling grounds of any kind to doubt.

d) The earliest writings of the NT, i.e. the epistles, make no explicit use of the title Son of Man. This is not to be explained as owing to ignorance on the part of these authors[153]. Paul, for example, was clearly acquainted with the title but refrained from using it[154]. That the evangelists, writing after Paul, did not consider it incongruent to use a title which was not current in the Church at that time, is an unmistakable indication that the term was well anchored in the tradition of Jesus, and that no account of the Master's life and teaching was deemed authentic which lacked the title. It is to be observed that by doing so the evangelists were not trying to introduce into the Christian community a new title of Jesus, but were impelled to take account of it in their narratives by the fact that the title was part of the tradition of Jesus.

e) The virtually exclusive use of the expression by Jesus. For J. Jeremias this is "the most important consideration in the question of authenticity"[155]. The fact that the title, though known both to the Early Church and to Paul[156], occurs only (except for Acts 7:56) on the lips of Jesus points to one unmistakable conclusion: "The title was rooted in the tradition of the sayings of Jesus right from the beginning; as a result, it was sacrosanct, and no one dared to eliminate it"[157].

---

153 Contra Lindars, *Jesus Son of Man*, 97.
154 Cf. e.g. The Adam-Christ typology in Rm 5:15ff.; Paul's designating Christ as ἄνθρωπος in I Cor 15:21; Rm 5:15 and the use of the imagery of Ps 8:4(5) in I Cor 15:27; Phil 3:21; Eph 1:22 and Phil 2:9ff., on which see Black, *BJRL* 45 (1962–3) 315. See further the discussions by Vögtle, "Die Adam-Christus-Typologie und 'der Menschensohn' " *TTZ* 60 (1951) 309–28 and " 'Der Menschensohn' und die paulinische Christologie" in *Studiorum Paulinorum Congressus Internationalis Catholicus*, 1961 I, 199–218, in which he admits Paul's knowledge but not any christological use of *bar nasha*. See also Brandenburger, *Adam und Christus* and Wilckens, ' Christus, der 'letzte Adam', und der Menschensohn" in *Jesus und der Menschensohn*, 387–403.
155 *Theology*, I, 266.
156 Jeremias, *Theology*, I, 26.
157 Jeremias, *Theology*, I, 266. See also Bernard, *John* I, cxxii. Casey's explanation of why Son

f) The impossibility of deriving the title Son of Man from other sources. This criterion is used particularly by Lindars. Lindars' argument is that the phrase Son of Man "cannot be derived from other sources, it must be traced back to Jesus himself"[158]. The corollary of this postulate is that at least some of the Son of Man sayings in each of the three groups "must be authentic in order to explain the existence of the rest"[159].

g) Son of Man sayings have withstood successfully diverse criticism. Borsch points out that "many of these sayings have over the years tren-chantly withstood assaults from almost every direction and what should have been a withering barrage of criticism convinces us that their claim on authenticity must be taken much more seriously"[160]. This was under-scored in my discussion, above, which — in spite of the fact that no at-tempt was made to achieve completeness — indicated that the great majority — if not actually each one — of the Son of Man sayings (and therefore at least some of each group) have been pronounced authentic by one or more scholars.

The above considerations ought to put it beyond reasonable doubt that in the expression Son of Man we have Jesus' own self-designation[161]. While it would seem that authentic Son of Man sayings belong to each one of the three types of such sayings, this does not imply that on occasion an original Son of Man saying could not, in the Gospel tradition, have been resolved into the personal pronoun or even vice versa. Of this Mt 16: 13 as compared with Mk 8:27 = Lk 9:18, Lk 6:22 as compared with

---

of Man occurs exclusively on Jesus' lips is that "he (sc. Jesus) is the only person in the Gos-pels who talks about himself to any extent" (*Son of Man*, 234), the implication being that Son of Man is used in lieu of 'I' and that other people do not speak sufficiently extensively to use the idiom of themselves. This is in itself a possible explanation, but it is neither the only nor the best explanation, and therefore of no compelling value. A number of other con-ditions (such as those raised in Chapter One) will need to obtain first before Casey's explana-tion can assume plausibility, but as it was shown in the latter part of Chapter One, these conditions do not obtain. With at least equal reason it might be countered, for example, that Jesus' exclusive use of the title as self-referring is owing to his being the only person who was in a position to give expression to his self-consciousness in this way. Others could use the title (as in Jn 12:34 a text which Casey excises without argument!) only in referring to Jesus' words, but obviously and understandably *not* in self-reference. If there do not occur more examples of the Jn 12:34 type, it is surely owing to the fact that Jesus is the only person in the Gospels who speaks to any extent!

158 *NTS* 22 (1975) 65. For Lindars' more recent views (i.e. in his *Jesus Son of Man*) see my dis-cussion at the end of Chapter One.

159 *NTS* 22 (1975) 68. So too Colpe, *TDNT* VIII, e.g. 438. In this connection it is perhaps per-tinent to quote a few sobering remarks by Hooker: "It is comparatively easy to argue against the authenticity of any particular saying considered in isolation; the arguments look less con-vincing when they are weighed against the total evidence of all the Son of Man sayings ... It may well be in fact that ... all together are needed to contain the whole truth about the Son of Man" (*The Son of Man in Mark*, 79).

160 *The Son of Man*, 314f.

161 Zorn, *VoxRef.* 34 (1980) 1—21; Sabourin, *RSB* 3 (1983) 129—34; Longenecker, *JETS* 12 (1969) 151—8.

Mt 5:11 and Lk 12:8f. as compared with Mt 10:32f might be some of the cases in point[162]. This is simply because syntactically 'Son of Man' is an equivalent of 'I', 'me', etc. though theologically it has a wholly different content. It is therefore quite probable that in some cases where no particular theological emphasis was recognized to lie in the expression Son of Man, the equivalent pronoun was felt sufficient to mark the grammatical subject or object of the sentence. But to use such an occasional practice as an argument for resolving the title Son of Man everywhere into the personal pronoun, as Vermes, Casey and Lindars have tried to do, or to explain the title as a creation of the Early Church is, in view of the massive evidence available for the meaning of the term as a title as well as its authenticity, surely to hide one's head in the sand[163].

Strictly speaking it is impossible to *prove* that Jesus used the Son of Man title on certain occasions. And the demand for such a proof is equally illegitimate. It is as illegitimate and unreasonable as the demand that unless Herodotus' accounts of the battles of Thermopylae, Salamis or Plataea be verified in some positivistic way, his statements are to be rejected. Needless to say, no student of ancient history would waste his time with such squabbles. The burden of proof is on the detractor. As Kümmel put it "what can and must be proven" is not the authenticity, but the inauthenticity of a tradition. Thus, to attempt to *prove* the authenticity of the tradition is to become guilty of a gross violation of the principle of legitimacy in scientific research, i.e. of trying to prove what cannot and should not be proved!

The most that can be reasonably demanded of me here is that I give some indications which show that the tradition accepted as genuine is not at variance with conditions obtaining around the time when the tradition was in vogue or was propagated. This has to some extent been done already in a general way a) by showing that "inauthenticity" verdicts did not rest on any intrinsic difficulties within the texts themselves, but on *a priori* presuppositions, and b) by my discussion of the seven principles which supported the general reliability of the SM sayings. And it will be done in more specific fashion (below) in discussing certain representative texts taken from each one of the three classes of SM logia.

This is not to deny, however, that the exact wording of the contexts in which the SM term is embedded is often the wording of the evangelists. After all we need to recall the fact of translation. But this does not necessarily mean that the evangelists created the contexts and the sayings in which they merely inserted Jesus' phrase *bar-nāshā*. Such sayings as con-

---

162 Higgins in *Jesus und der Menschensohn*, 117–23 argues for the authenticity of 'Son of Man' in Lk 12:8f. and for the secondary character of Mt 10:23f. On Mk 8:27–30 see Pesch, *BZ* 17 (1973) 178–95; 18(1974) 20–31 who argues for its going back to Jesus (*BZ* 17 (1973) 194f.).

163 As e.g. Sandmel in *In the Time of Harvest*, 355–67, who regards the title as Mark's literary device in conscious polemic against the Jews.

tain this title were no doubt too specific, too poignant, too 'catchy' to be forgotten in the tradition and therefore, had a better chance than other things Jesus had said to survive intact. The view that is best supported by the facts is that the SM sayings have faithfully preserved the gist of what Jesus said. And this is sufficient for the purpose of the present investigation, viz. to indicate the fact and scope of the influence of the Danielic 'SM' upon the SM concept in the teaching of Jesus.

C. Defining the Task and the Procedure

At this point the heart of the present investigation has been reached. The task remaining is to apply the results obtained above upon the Son of Man concept as found in the NT. The questions that might be asked here are many indeed. Is the expression Son of Man in the NT more than a circumlocution for 'I' etc.? Is the term titular? Is the apocalyptic Son of Man definitely banished from the NT? Are there influences from the OT in general, from Daniel's 'SM' in particular, or from the *Parables*? In how far is the NT Son of Man a reflection of the Son of Man conception obtained above? In what respects is he different? What is Jesus' original contribution to the Son of Man concept? What does the total Son of Man conception in the NT reveal of Jesus' self-consciousness? How is the Son of Man related to the Kingdom of God? Why is the title Son of Man missing in Paul? Is it really missing, or is it transformed into, or interpreted by another title? These and other similar questions arise and press for an answer in an investigation of this kind. What I can do is to make a serious attempt to indicate some of the underlying influences from my background material which come into fruition in the NT, and which, though not necessarily determinative in their totality, are, nevertheless, real factors in shaping the theology of the Son of Man conception, in Jesus' preaching.

In the discussion of the NT Son of Man concept no semantic analysis will be undertaken. The reasons for this are two: a) the texts containing the Son of Man sayings are too many to render a semantic analysis feasible, and b) a semantic analysis of some texts that might be chosen is considered unnecessary since the logia are usually short and the meaning of the expression does not depend upon the structure of the text in such a way that it can only yield important results after such an analysis has been carried out. In the case of I En 46 the semantic analysis was conducive to bringing out the similarity in structure between that chapter and Dan 7, and the consequent influence of the latter upon the former. The relation between Dan 7 and the Gospels' Son of Man texts is quite different from that betwen Dan 7 and I En 46.

Neither will any attempt be made to discuss each one of the Son of

Man sayings in detail. Since the primary object of the investigation is to discover the background influence on the concept of Son of Man in the NT, it is enough if a 'bridge' is established between the background material and some of the Son of Man sayings. For this purpose a few representative sayings of each class will be discussed individually with a view to showing a) that no valid objections can be raised against their authenticity, and b) that these sayings prove beyond all doubt the influence of the Danielic 'SM' upon the corresponding concept as used by Jesus. Other SM sayings can be derived from those already established. In a further section the SM concept will be treated thematically in order to give some idea of the areas in which the Danielic 'SM' has made its impact upon the teaching of Jesus.

D. The Influence of Daniel's 'SM' upon the SM in the Teaching of Jesus

We have now reviewed all the literature that contains the term Son of Man, viz. the OT, Daniel in particular, the Book of the *Parables*, IV Ezra and rabbinic tradition. Of these writings only the first three, the OT generally, Daniel and the *Parables* are chronologically relevant for the present investigation regarding influence on the NT concept of the Son of Man. IV Ezra lies chronologically at the fringe.

1. The Fact of Influence

a) The OT (apart from Dan) 'son of man' Cannot Explain the NT SM

As shown in Chapter Two[164], the term son of man in the OT is used in many different contexts, but it always designates a particular person or a group of persons. Apart from two instances[165], where the sense is probably positive, the occurrences of this term are about equally divided between a category connoting creaturely weakness with its attendant circumstances, and a category connoting evil, lawlessness and vice. The OT knows nothing of a Son of Man with the divine, majestic and otherworldly characteristics with which the NT Son of Man is for the most part portrayed. Even Ps 8:4 does not depict any Primal or Ideal Man, but simply humanity as it actually is[166]. Therefore, the predominantly exalted Figure of the Son of Man in the NT cannot derive from the OT. However,

---

164 See OT Antecedents, under Ch. II. In this section 'OT' is used for the OT except Daniel.
165 I.e. Ps 80:17; Isa 56:2.

it is possible, indeed probable, that the OT term son of man has contributed to the assumption by a Son of Man concept which was initially
characterized by exalted traits and inspired from other texts, of traits
connoting ordinary human aspects. Not only does a text like Mt 11:9 =
Lk 7:34, about the Son of Man's eating and drinking, unexplained by the
Son of Man in Daniel, the *Parables* and IV Ezra, find an adequate explanation in the corresponding term as met with in the OT, but it may well be,
moreover, that the OT son of man has been the verbal or ideational link
for the paradox of the Son of Man, who in the NT is presented at once as
divine and human. Texts like Ps 8:4; 45:2; 80:17; Isa 52:14 may quite
conceivably have functioned as 'bridges' to account for the Son of Man's
earthly traits[167]. It would, therefore, appear that the NT concept of the
Son of Man is composite in inspiration, having received its purely human
characteristics from the OT use of the term, while its most prominent
characteristics, especially those that depict the Son of Man as an exalted
Being must stem from elsewhere.

b) A Comparison of the NT with Dan, I Enoch and IV Ezra

A representative group of Son of Man sayings illustrating the exaltation
traits of the Son of Man — i.e. those traits most easily extracted from the
background material — occurs in the eschatological discourse in Mt 24
par. We may therefore concentrate on these.

A careful comparison of the Son of Man in this discourse with such OT
and Jewish material as Daniel, the *Parables*, and IV Ezra reveals important
affinities with these writings, particularly the former two. The comparison
presented here is not exhaustive.

The international wars, rumors of wars and diverse pestilences of Mt
24:6f. = Mk 13:7f. = Lk 21:9f. preceeding the Son of Man's coming, have
an exact equivalent in IV Ezra 13:19, 27—32, where, too, such conflicts

---

166 Similarly Guthrie, *Theology*, 273. Moloney, *NTS* 27 (1981) 662f. argues for an individualized
     interpretation of this text in the Targum, but even if this be so, it is a long way from the au-
     thor's original meaning. Moreover, though this Psalm is cited in messianic contexts in the NT
     (i.e. Mt 26:16; I Cor 15:27; Eph 1:22) it is not the verse containing the expression 'son of
     man' that is cited. In Heb 2:6f. the actual verse is cited, but it is interesting to note that the
     meaning is still one of humanity in general, and that Jesus is brought in not because the text is
     thought to apply directly to him but because of his partaking of human nature. It is by way
     of the incarnation (βραχύ τι παρ' ἀγγέλους ἠλαττωμένον) that Ps 8:4 is applied on Jesus
     and not because it is considered to be a concealed messianic title. Grässer, in *Jesus und der
     Menschensohn*, 404—14, comes to a similar conclusion. After presenting Moule's diagram (in
     the latter's article in *NT und Kirche*, 413—28) which shows that Heb 2:6 has direct connec-
     tion with Gen 1—3, Ps 8, etc. but only indirect connection with Dan 7, comments in agree-
     ment: "Mit Heb 2,6 haben wir kein Indiz für eine Menschensohn-Vorstellung nach Art der
     Evangelien".
167 So already Nestle, *ET* 11 (1899-1900) 238.

characterize the time preceeding the Son of Man's coming[168]. These commotions are in Mt 24:6 = Mk 13:7 = Lk 21:9 described as divinely ordained ($\delta\epsilon\hat{\iota}$ $\gamma\grave{\alpha}\rho$ $\gamma\epsilon\nu\acute{\epsilon}\sigma\vartheta\alpha\iota$) with an expression taken over from Dan 2: 28 ($\check{\alpha}$ $\delta\epsilon\hat{\iota}$ $\gamma\epsilon\nu\acute{\epsilon}\sigma\vartheta\alpha\iota$). As in Dan 12:1 these times are said to be unique in human history (Mt 24:21 = Mk 13:19). Interesting also is the fact that in both Mt 24:3 and IV Ezra 13:32 these turmoils are described as the 'sign' for the Son of Man's coming[169]. The comparison of the Son of Man's coming to a lightning (Mt 24:27 = Lk 17:24) — undoubtedly emphasizing suddenness and speed — could easily have been suggested by Dan 7:13. It has, however, some even closer parallels in apocalyptic works. In the *Parables* (I En 59) lightnings are ordained by the Lord of Spirits to execute judgment on earth, while more closely, II Bar 53 speaks of a lightning riding upon a Cloud risen from the great Sea[170]. The Lightning of the Cloud, which brings relief to earth, is a symbol of the Messiah, and the whole imagery is obviously dependent upon Daniel 7[171]. Not only does the accompanying of the Son of Man by an entourage of angels (Mt 24: 31 = Mk 13:27) find an echo in Dan 7:13, but also his sending them out to gather the elect seems to be explained by the Son of Man texts in apoclyptic works. In the *Parables* angels play an important role as emissaries of the Lord of Spirits. For example, in I En 47:2 angels take active part in interceding for the salvation of the righteous[172]. A number of other texts speak of angels of punishment who are sent out to gather and punish the wicked[173]. The saying Mt 24:31 = Mk 13:27 may have been formed by analogy. The linking of Noah with the Son of Man's coming (Mt 24: 37ff. = Lk 17:26f.) is another item of common interest. In the *Parables* there are a number of texts (I En 60—69) which connect Noah with the punishment of the wicked angels, kings, and mighty ones[174], in an overall context dealing with the Son of Man and his equivalent, the Elect One, as the SM or the Elect One appears in glory and majesty, and assumes his functions of Judge[175]. There was, therefore, traditional basis for bringing Noah in connection with the Son of Man's coming in judgment. Such

---

168 Cf. also I En 56:5ff.; II Bar 25—27.

169 On the sign see below under The Exalted Son of Man.

170 So Klijn: "2 Baruch" in Charlesworth, *OTP*, I, 639. Charles, "I Enoch" in *AP*, II, 510 has "a very great sea", which obscures the reference to the Great Sea. Violet, *Die Apokalypsen des Esra und des Baruch in deutscher Gestalt*, 281, has simply "Meere". On this passage, see K. Müller, *BZ* 17 (1973) 52f.

171 See Charles, *APOT* II, 510.

172 See also 40:6; 104:1: "I swear unto you that in heaven the angels will remember you for good before the glory of the Great One" (Isaac, "I Enoch" in Charlesworth, *OTP*, I, 85 and note at 104:1). On the intercession of angels for men, see Charles, *APOT* II, 93 (note at 9: 10) and *id., The Book of Enoch*, 21, in both of which works more passages are cited.

173 Cf. I En 51:2; 53:3—7; 54:5; 55:3 (!); 56:1—8. See Charles' comments in *The Book of Enoch*, ad 40:7; 53:3.

174 I.e. what Charles considered to be Fragments of a *Book of Noah*.

175 E.g. 61:8, 62:1ff.; 5ff., 63:11; 69:26ff.

a connection could not have been found in the OT account of Noah, since this conception of the Son of Man was altogether absent there.

Finally, texts like Mt 19:28 and Mt 25:31, where the Son of Man is said to be seated ἐπὶ θρόνου δόξης αὐτοῦ, are quite likely direct quotations from the *Parables*[176], in which the identical expression — attested nowhere else either in Daniel or in the OT[177] — occurs several times![178] Borsch[179] would go so far as to even argue for some kind of connection between Mk 14:62(= Mt 26:66 = Lk 22:69) and I En 62:5.

Already these few points have indicated how many and complex are the links between the eschatological discourse of the Gospels and apoc-lyptic conceptions in works antedating Jesus or being antedated by him by a few decades, works, which, in turn, are clearly dependent for their main ideas upon Daniel, and thus testify to a fairly developed cycle of Son of Man theology current in certain Jewish circles of pre-NT times. The Son of Man presentation, at least in this Gospel discourse, has such close and manifest parallels to corresponding Son of Man concepts in these works, that only a commonly shared background could adequately account for them. At the same time this examination also shows that the connections between the Gospel discourse and the *Parables* and IV Ezra are chiefly secondary. That the *Parables* and IV Ezra are dependent upon Daniel has been shown above. That the NT, too, in its turn, has Daniel as its primary source for its Son of Man ideas, is the unavoidable conclusion. This will be made clear in the following sections.

Here, however, in support of my contention that the NT Son of Man has affinities with the corresponding figure in Daniel, the *Parables* and IV Ezra, the following table is appended.

---

176 Cf. Marshall, *NTS* 12 (1965–6) 336 and Borsch *NTS* 14 (1967–8) 567, and especially the detailed investigation of these passages by Theisohn, *Der auserwählte Richter*, 152–82.

177 I Sam 2:8 "inherit a throne of glory" lacks "his" and the context is entirely different. Nor are I Chr 29:23 "Solomon sat on the throne of the Lord" (LXX, θρόνου Δαυίδ) or Jer 14: 21 "do not disgrace the throne of thy glory" really parallels. Isa 22:23 "he (sc. Eliakim the son of Hilkiah) shall be for a throne of glory" is quite different. This holds true of the other LXX instances: Jer 17:12: θρόνος δόξης ὑψωμένος, ἁγίασμα ἡμῶν, Dan 3:54 (v. 1.): εὐλογητὸς εἶ ἐπὶ θρόνου δόξης σου, as well as Sap. 9:10: ἐξαπόστειλον αὐτὴν (sc. σοφίαν) ... ἀπὸ θρόνου δόξης σου, Sir 47:11: Κύριος ... ἔδωκεν αὐτῷ ... θρόνου δόξης ἐν τῷ Ἰσραήλ, and T Lev 5:1: καὶ ἐπὶ θρόνου δόξης τὸν ὕψιστον. The same is true of 4QpJsA 19 כבוד כסא(כ) . See Alegro, *DJD* V, 14 and Vermes, *Dead Sea Scrolls in English*, 227. In some of the above samples it is true, the throne of glory is referred to God, however, the conditions that here need to be fulfilled are a) The expression θρόνου δόξης αὐτοῦ, b) The idea of being seated upon the throne of glory and c) The Son of Man who is to be seated on it. In this concurs also Theisohn, *Der auserwählte Richter*, 152ff.

178 I En 45:3; 51:3; 55:4; 61:8; 62:2 (this last passage according to Charles, *The Book of Enoch*, 123, following Dillmann; Isaac in *OTP* I, 43, otherwise); 62:5; 69:27, 29. In I En 9:4 ὁ θρόνος τῆς δόξης σου occurs metonymically of God's everlasting rule, while the idea of 'sitting' on it as well as that of the 'Son of Man' are absent from the context. The idea of sitting occurs at I En 14:18–20, but the One who sits is God, not the Son of Man and the expression is θρόνον ὑψηλόν, a passage dependent on Dan 7:9f.

179 *NTS* 14 (1967–8) 565ff.

Daniel	I Enoch	IV Ezra	Gospels
Non-human	Non-human	Non-human	–
(Pre-existent)	Pre-existent	Pre-existent	Pre-existent (Jn 3:13; 6:62)
Divine	Divine	Divine	Divine
Coming w. Clouds	–	–	Coming with Clouds
Vindicator	Vindicator	–	Saviour (Lk 19:10)
(Messiah)	Messiah	Messiah	Messiah
Judge	Judge	Judge	Judge
Subjects evil powers	Condemns evil powers	–	Subjects evil powers (Mt 13:40; 25:41)
Universal King	Universal King	–	Universal King
Worshipped	Worshipped	–	Worshipped
–	Revealer	–	Revealer (Jn 3:12f.)
–	–	God's Son	God's Son (Lk 22:69f.)
–	–	–	Forgives sins (Mt 9:6; Mk 2:10; Lk 6:5)
			Lord of sabbath (Mt 12:8; Mk 2:28; Lk 6:5)
			Human (Mt 11:19; Lk 7:34)
			Servant (Mt 20:28; Mr 10:45)
			Poor and Despised (Mt 8:20; Lk 9:58)
			Suffering
			Dying
			Rising
			Coming again

This table shows that practically all of the characteristics of the Son of Man in Daniel and the *Parables* recur in the Gospels. The features common with IV Ezra are fewer, but nonetheless just as clear. In choosing between Daniel and the *Parables* as the background to the Gospel concept of the Son of Man preference is to be given to Daniel. The reasons for this are: a) Daniel is the source for the *Parables* b) Daniel is expressly mentioned and repeatedly cited, whereas the *Parables* is neither mentioned nor expressly cited, though in "the throne of his glory" we may actually have a direct quotation; c) the Son of Man's coming "with the clouds of heaven" is not only expressly said to be a quotation from Daniel, but also the corresponding expression does not occur in the *Parables*; and d) Daniel's influence on the NT is widespread, whereas the similarities with the *Parables* seem to presuppose a common background, sometimes perhaps only on the oral level[180]. Thus the influence from the circles of the *Parables* and IV Ezra — in as far as this is recognized — is mainly indirect,

---

180 Lindars, *ET* 92 (1981) 295–99 argues that the fact that Ps 110:1 does not play any part in the *Parables*, indicates that whatever similarities exist between it and the Christology of the NT were arrived at separately. But this does not rule out knowledge of the *Parables* by the NT authors.

whereas Daniel's influence is both direct and palpable. Can this influence or part of it actually be shown to go back to the teaching of Jesus? Before I address myself to this question it is necessary for me to clarify one important detail.

c) The 'One like a son of man' Becomes the Son of Man

Here we take up a detail that has occasionally been overlooked. As we saw in Chapter Two the Figure which Daniel saw in his vision and described was not 'the Son of Man' or even 'a son of man', i.e. a designation of the ordinary type which we meet in the OT generally. What Daniel saw was a Figure that was *"like* a son of man"". The Gospels, however, speak simply of 'the Son of Man'. Thus, what in Daniel's vision is only an unidentified entity spoken of in terms of a simile, in the Gospels, standing at the end of the process of concretization and identification, the "like" is dropped and the "son of man" is identified with Jesus and thus becomes *'the* Son of Man'! This process had begun already in Daniel with the equation of the 'One like a son of man' with the 'Most High'[181]. It continued in I Enoch 46 where, after an initial use of the Danielic expression, the simile part was dropped and the expression was elevated to the

status of a title of a supernatural Messiah variously spoken of as "Anointed One", "Elect One". and "Righteous One". But even here we have a description of the Son of Man and his activities, but no identification with a concrete person[182]. The end of this process is reached in the NT, according to which Jesus was unique in claiming to be the 'SM' of Daniel. The "like" of Dan 7:13 had both a concealing and a disclosing function. On the one hand it veiled the real character of the entity thus disclosed by *comparing* him to a human being, while on the other hand it unveiled the entity's otherwordly character by underlining his *mere similarity* (but no more) to a human being[183]. Jesus took over this as yet non-titular description in Daniel — already made titular in the *Parables*, IV Ezra and perhaps other Jewish writings lost to us — and applied it to himself not only with the content which it had in Daniel, but with a content which he added to it. He apparently looked upon himself as *that* Son of Man[184]. Hence, the "like" had played out its role and was definitely dropped.

The misplaced assumption that the Danielic 'SM' is a representation of the pious Jews has been a serious hindrance to a full appreciation of the

---

181 But observe that strictly speaking this was only an equation, not an identification, which would presuppose the identifying of an unknown with a known entity.

182 With regard to the alleged identification of the Son of Man with Enoch, see Ch. Three, above.

183 The 'like' is already dropped at the equation of the One like a son of man with the 'Most High'.

184 Moule, *The Origin of Christology*, 13ff. has come to a similar conclusion.

Son of Man as understood by Jesus. The NT evidence points to an understanding of the Son of Man which, not only suits the Danielic Figure as
discussed briefly in Chapter Two, but which, moreover, is inexplicable
apart from it! In support for this contention, it may be pointed out that
an understanding of the Danielic 'SM' as the one claimed for Jesus here,
was by no means unique for Jesus. As indicated in Chapter Three, the *Parables*, IV Ezra and the Jewish rabbis had an interpretation that was basically similar to Jesus' own. What was altogether new in Jesus over against
these Jewish authors was that according to the Gospels he also attached
to the concept some unheard of characteristics, like suffering and death.
Over and above that, Jesus was also unique in believing himself to be the
personification of the 'SM'.

d) The Son of Man in Jesus' Teaching and the 'SM' in Daniel

Criticism has been occasionally leveled by scholars against a sharp
division of the sayings into three classes[185], while my own dissatisfaction
with such a classification has been registered above[186]. The classification
is artificial. Sayings of different 'types' often blend together and the contexts in which they occur are not always 'pure'[187]. This is because the
evangelists did not distinguish the SM sayings into different types, and
that because in all probability there was no such distinction in the tradition of Jesus' SM sayings. At least none is apparent. The unifying principle
was understood to lie in the title Son of Man. Once Jesus had applied this
title to himself there was nothing to forbid his use of the title in speaking
of certain aspects of his mission, which *ex hypothesi* might not be covered
by the original background concept. There is certainly no compelling
critical ground for the thesis of some scholars[188] that Jesus could have
uttered sayings of only one or the other type, but not of all three types
into which modern scholarship has divided his SM sayings[189]. Hence, it
is strictly speaking unnecessary to provide evidence (as I have taken upon
myself to do) that Jesus actually did use the SM title in all three types
of SM sayings. That such evidence actually exists only confirms what I
have been saying, and my discussion of it in this section serves to underscore the fact that the seeds for Jesus' full-fledged development of the SM
concept in the Gospels were all present in the Danielic background.

---

185 O. Betz, *Wie verstehen wir das NT?*, 30ff.; Neugebauer, *Jesus der Menschensohn*, 21ff.;
    Hooker, *The Son of Man in Mark*, 80; *id.* in *Text and Interpretation*, 159f.
186 At the beginning of this chapter.
187 Cf. e.g. Mk 8:31–38 (where a Suffering saying is blended with an Exaltation saying) and Lk
    17:22–30 (where a Earthly Life saying occurs side by side with a Suffering saying and two
    Exaltation sayings).
188 E.g. Tödt, *Der Menschensohn*, 116.
189 Most scholars have accepted the authenticity of all three types.

i. The Earthly Son of Man. Mt 8:20 = Lk 9:58. The authenticity of this saying cannot be seriously doubted. The logion, setting forth the cost of discipleship, is in line with other similar sayings of Jesus, which are characteristic of his teaching[190]. The great stumbling block to authenticity for Tödt is the title SM:

> Man steht vor einer unüberwindlichen Schwierigkeit, wenn man behauptet,, dass Jesus in den Parusiesprüchen vom Menschensohn als einer transzendenten Gestalt gesprochen hat, während er daneben andere Worte formulierte, in denen der Menschensohn alle bisherigen Prädikate verlor und nach Jesu eigenem, irdischem Tun gedeutet wurde[191].

Tödt's problem relates to what already has been discussed above, namely, the assumption of some scholars that if a particular class of SM sayings is accepted as authentic, it automatically renders inauthentic the other classes. But it has never been satisfactorily explained why, for example, Jesus could not have used the designation SM in earthly at the same time as he used it in exaltation sayings. Why is the possibility excluded that Jesus might use a traditional motif to apply to his own person in more than one way? Unimpressed by Tödt's argument scholars such as Schweizer[192], Borsch[193], Goppelt[194], Colpe[195], Casey[196], Marshall[197], Lindars[198], and Black[199] have accepted the authenticity of this saying[200].

However, the above scholars are united neither as to their reasons for accepting the genuineness of this saying nor as to their interpretation of it. Lindars, for example, accepts it as genuine because he thinks that he can find in it what he considers to be the original Aramaic idiom of *bar nasha*, while Black thinks of the Isaianic Servant. In what follows I shall try to indicate what seems to me to be the correct understanding of this saying, which, at the same time, will provide an answer to Tödt's objection, by showing that this saying is not incompatible with what underlies the exaltation sayings. At the same time its relation (as an earthly saying!) to Dan 7 will hopefully become apparent.

Manson's suggestion that "foxes" and "birds" are symbols for the Ammonites and the gentiles respectively and that SM has collective signifi-

---

190 E.g. Mt 10:37ff. = Lk 14:26f. (cf. Lk 12:51ff.); 16:24ff. = Mk 8:34ff. = Lk 9:23ff.; 19:21 = Mk 10:21−25 = Lk 18:22−25; 19:27ff. = Mk 10:28ff. = Lk 18:28ff.

191 *Der Menschensohn*, 116.

192 *ZNW* 50 (1959) 199; *id., JBL* 79 (1960) 121; *NTS* 9 (1962−3) 258.

193 *The Son of Man in Myth and History*, 325.

194 *Mensch und Menschensohn*, 20ff.

195 *TDNT*, VIII, 432f.

196 *Son of Man*, 229.

197 *NTS* 12 (1965−6) 340f.

198 *Jesus Son of Man*, 29ff.

199 *ET* 95 (1984) 205.

200 Dibelius, *Jesus*, 88 and Hamerton-Kelly, *Pre-existence*, 43 and also inclined to regard this saying as authentic.

cance, i.e. "everybody is at home in Israel's land except the true Israel"[201] is far-fetched and is justly rejected by Tödt[202].

The first part of the saying consists of two statements: αἱ ἀλώπεκες φωλεοὺς ἔχουσιν and τὰ πετεινὰ τοῦ οὐρανοῦ κατασκηνώσεις. Though the first statement cannot be related to any OT saying, there are several passages in the OT which can be brought into relation with the second, and some of them are capable of explaining the first as well. Since the expression τὰ πετεινὰ τοῦ οὐρανοῦ occurs frequently in the OT it is, in itself, no pointer to any connection. When, however, the whole expression is taken into account, i.e. with κατασκηνώσεις, the candidate passages become six[203]. Of the two Ezekiel instances 17:23 has the peculiar כל צפור כל־כנף "every bird of every wing" i.e. NEB: "winged birds of every kind", rendered by the LXX with πᾶν πετεινόν, though the predicate is actually שכנו "dwell" (LXX ἀναπαύσεται). Neither the MT nor the LXX text can be considered a probable background to Mt 8:20 par. Ez 31:6 קננו כל־עוף השמים, which the LXX translated with ἐνόσσευον τὰ πετεινὰ τοῦ οὐρανοῦ, comes closer to Mt 8:20 par. קנן occurs five times in the OT and it is always rendered with νοσσεύω by the LXX, which also uses the same verb once for דור (Dan 4:9) and once for שכן (Dan 4:18). On the other hand, שכן is in the LXX normally rendered by κατασκηνόω. Thus, the only similarity between Ez 31:6 and our text is the phrase "birds of the air". There are no contextual similarities to connect the two texts. Ps 104:12 עוף־השמים ישכון (LXX: τὰ πετεινὰ τοῦ οὐρανοῦ κατασκηνώσει) comes very close to Mt 8:20 par. especially with its use of שכן which is understood to underlie σκηνόω of Jn 1:14. However, the context, once again, affords no more similarities. It must, therefore be concluded that no conscious allusion to any of these passages can be demonstrated. This leaves us with the three Deniel texts.

In Dan 2:38, in describing Nebuchadnezzar's greatness and dominion, the author says that God has given into his hand בני־אנשא חיות ברא ועוף־שמיא (LXX ἀπὸ ἀνθρώπων καὶ θηρίων ἀγρίων καὶ πετεινῶν οὐρανοῦ· Θ: οἱ υἱοὶ τῶν ἀνθρώπων, θηρία τε ἀγροῦ καὶ πετεινὰ οὐρανοῦ). In the context of chapter 2, however, in which Nebuchadnezzar represents the first of four kingdoms destined to be crushed and to be replaced by God's everlasting Kingdom, the sons of men, the beasts of the field and the birds of the air are associated first with the concept of kingdom as such (the theme of the book as a whole), and second they enjoy the benefits of one of the kingdoms doomed to destruction. This connection becomes more explicit at 4:9 (LXX, Θ 4:12), where Nebuchadnezzar relates another dream, and at 4:18 (LXX, Θ 4:21), where

---

201 Manson, The Sayings of Jesus, 72f.
202 Der Menschensohn, 113. There is equally no ground for Bultmann's suggestion (History of synoptic Tradition, 28) that the saying is an old proverb.
203 Ps 104:12 (LXX 103:12); Ez 17:23; 31:6; Dan 2:38, 4:9 (LXX, Θ:4:12); 4:18 (LXX, Θ: 4:21).

Daniel, in semitic fashion, repeats the dream before giving his interpretation of it. At 4:9 we are told תחתוהי תטלל חיות ברא ובענפוהי ידרוֹן צפרי שמיא . The LXX translates ὑποκάτω αὐτοῦ ἐσκίαζον πάντα τὰ θηρία τῆς γῆς, καὶ ἐν αὐτῷ τὰ πετεινὰ τοῦ οὐρανοῦ ἐνόσσευον, while Θ has ὑποκάτω αὐτοῦ κατεσκήνουν τὰ θηρία τὰ ἄγρια, καὶ ἐν τοῖς κλάδοις αὐτοῦ κατῴκουν τὰ ὄρνεα τοῦ οὐρανοῦ. At 4:18 the LXX text is either defective or follows another textual tradition. The Θ text agrees with the MT: תחתוהי תדור חיות ברא ובענפוהי ישכון צפרי שמיא is rendered by Θ: ὑποκάτω αὐτοῦ κατῴκουν τὰ θηρία τὰ ἄγρια καὶ ἐν τοῖς κλάδοις αὐτοῦ κατεσκήνουν τὰ ὄρνεα τοῦ οὐρανοῦ (LXX τὰ πετεινὰ τοῦ οὐρανοῦ). Here it may be pointed out in passing that for Θ τὰ ὄρνεα τοῦ οὐρανοῦ (4:12, 18) and πετεινὰ οὐρανοῦ (2:38) are interchangeable expressions. No doubt the "beasts" and the "birds" along with the "tree" are but symbols for human beings. But we may stay on the level of the symbol. The first thing which we note here is that these beasts and birds are said to dwell securely and pleasantly enjoying the shade, the protection and the nourishment which the tree provided for them! The second thing is that the "tree" which provides these benefits is the same as the golden part of the statue in chapter 2 and the lion of chapter 7, in other words, one of the beasts which is to lose its power and dominion to the 'SM'. The connection of the 'SM' with this imagery becomes therefore quite obvious[204].

But could this connection between the imagery of the tree with its beasts and birds and the Kingdom of God or the 'SM' who is its Agent, have been present in the mind of Jesus? Can it actually be shown that Jesus had noticed Dan 2 and 4 and employed them in his teaching? It seems to me that it is possible to answer these questions affirmatively. First, let us take Lk 20:17f. Though that logion begins with a quotation from Ps 118:22 (the stone which the builders rejected) setting forth the Messiah's rejection by men but his acceptance by God, it goes on to describe his function in judgment in terms of the 'Stone' of Dan 2:35, 45, which crushes to powder the disobedient and ungodly. We should note here that judgment is one of the functions of the 'SM' in Dan 7 as well as in the *Parables* and in the NT. Second, scholars have been struck by the imagery of the tree's immense growth in Dan 4:10ff., 20f. as a parallel to the parable of the mustard seed (Mt 13:31ff. = Mk 4:30ff. = Lk 13: 19)[205]. Actually, there is more than mere coincidence. The parable is chiefly an illustration of the astounding growth of the Kingdom of God, after a humble or insignificant beginning[206], coming to contain all kinds

---

204 The "Stone" of ch. 2 and the 'SM' of ch. 7 are symbols of the same entity, the Agent of God's Kingdom, who is to pound Nebuchadnezzar's kingdom to powder (see Θ 2:44 λικμήσει and cf. Lk 20:18 [= Mt 21:44]).

205 Plummer, *Luke*, 345; Lane, *Mark*, 171; Ellis, *Luke*, 187; Marshall, *Luke*, 561; Taylor, *Mark*, 270; Dodd, *Parables*, 142.

206 The attempt by some to eliminate this feature is shattered on the fact of μικρότερον (Mt 13:

of "birds", i.e. people of all nations, so the allusion to Dan 4 is quite obvious. With Dan 4 it has the following points in common: a) the original smallness of the tree, b) the tree's immense growth, c) the tree's functioning as a symbol for a kingdom, d) the nestling of the birds in the tree's branches[207], e) the birds' functioning as a symbol for human beings. With the exception of the probably different types of trees involved in the two texts, all other details in the parable can be derived from Dan 4.

But this really implies that Dan 4 was actually used as illustrative material in Jesus' teaching. But if Dan 4 could be used by Jesus to illustrate the tiny and humble beginning of the Kingdom of God, which eventually grows and fills the whole earth, why could it not also be used by him to illustrate the apparently insignificant and humble beginning of the Son of Man's work in proclaiming God's Kingdom, at a time when its future glory was still out of sight, but was nonetheless implicit in his message? What valid arguments can be brought against this?

We have already shown the probability of deriving τὰ πετεινὰ τοῦ οὐρανοῦ from Dan 2 and 4. It may, however, be objected that Dan 4 does not speak of foxes but of animals or beasts of the field. True, but that is not detrimental to my argument. Jesus is not quoting Dan 4 verbatim, but is merely alluding to it. The fox is nevertheless one of the animals intended by Dan 4! Moreover, in antiquity, as in modern times, the fox was the most common wild animal in the Middle East. Samson is said to have caught 300 of them! (Jd 15:4)[208]. No other animal gave more trouble to people than the fox, and no other animal had been more closely observed and known by man, or made the subject of countless stories or anecdotes (cf. Aesop's fables). The fox even figured in metaphorical speech in order to portray human craftiness (cf. Lk 13:32 of Herod)[209]. There is therefore nothing unnatural about Jesus' use of the fox as a representative of the animals of Dan 4. The two categories of Dan 4, "beasts of the field" and "birds of the air" are therefore certainly preserved intact in this dominical saying.

In addition to these two common elements, i.e., a) the beasts of the field represented in Mt 8:20 par. by the foxes, and b) the birds of the air, there are four more contact points between our passage and Dan 2 and 4. c) The sayings of both Mt 8:20ff.= Lk 9:58ff. and Dan 2 and 4 occur

---

32 = Mk 4:31), on the fact that the mustard seed was considered as proverbially the smallest seed (cf. Michel, *TDNT* III, 810f.), and on the feature of growth both in Dan 2:35 and 4: 11ff., 20ff., the latter of which is clearly the background of the parable.

207 Cf. the almost identical wording of Lk 13:19 τὰ πετεινὰ τοῦ οὐρανοῦ κατεσκήνωσεν ἐν τοῖς κλάδοις αὐτοῦ with Dan (Θ) 4:21 ἐν τοῖς κλάδοις αὐτοῦ κατεσκήνουν τὰ ὄρνεα (or πετεινά in 2:38) τοῦ οὐρανοῦ.

208 See also LXX 3 Kings 21:10 (not in MT); Neh 3:35; Ca 2:15; Lam 5:18; Ez 13:4. According to Jos, *Ant* XII, 146 a decree had to be issued to prohibit the sale of fox meat or its fur in Jerusalem.

209 See also Plutarch, *Solon*, 30, 2; *Sulla*, 28, 3.

in a kingdom context. As far as Mt 8:20ff. = Lk 9:58ff. is concerned, the passage deals (especially in its Lukan form) with the reactions of three men to the challenge of the Kingdom. Jesus advances the claims of the Kingdom and the consequent cost of discipleship. It is "the process of selection", as Dodd expressed it. Even in the Matthean form of the pericope, which, unlike Luke, lacks an express reference to 'kingdom', the idea of Kingdom is nevertheless present, since the scribe's proposal to follow Jesus has actually nothing but the Kingdom as its aim! This means that the saying about foxes, birds and the Son of Man is embedded in the concept of the Kingdom. Similarly in the case of Dan 2 and 4 the idea of kingdom is the matrix for the saying about beasts and birds.

d) Mt 8:20 par. implies a contrast between the present insecurity involved in accepting the claims of the Kingdom and following Jesus on the one hand, and the security of the "foxes" and "birds", which in Dan 4 enjoy the benefits of the tree/kingdom on the other.

e) The Son of Man's homelessness, or rather, present rejection by the societies of men, is both a contrast to the thriving circumstances of those under the protection of the tree/kingdom of Dan 4 (or the beast of Dan 7) as well as an apt summary of the rejection, indeed, persecution by the beasts (while in power) of God's people (Dan 7), whose leader and representative is the 'SM'.

f) Finally, there is an implicit promise for the final triumph of the Kingodm of God over the beasts/kingdoms. The Son of Man's rejection is only temporary. "Go and proclaim the Kingdom of God," far from being a defeatistic injunction, is a command that carries with it the idea of hope, of triumph and of future glory. By contrast the seeds of decay or destruction of the tree/kingdom in Dan 2 and 4 are there apparent. The contrast is unmistakable. The time will come when the "beasts of the field" and the "birds of the air" of Dan 4 at the destruction of the "tree" will lose their security, while the Son of Man and his followers will no longer be homeless or rejected.

The convergent lines of thought between our text and the Danielic material are so many and so deep-going that it is impossible to miss Jesus' allusion to that complex of ideas (the Danielic conception of God's Kingdom and the 'SM'), which exerted such a decisive influence upon his thinking as a whole.

The conclusion from the above discussion, therefore, is that Mt 8:20 par. is much more intricate than it appears at first sight. So far from being an 'innocent' saying about foxes and birds, it is deeply allusive, and is in conscious reference to Dan 2 and 4, describing the first phase of the Kingdom of God, i.e. its onset through its representative, the Son of Man, against the kingdoms of evil. The reward, the glory is not in sight yet, though it is implied in the call; here the emphasis is rather placed on the labour and the pains preceding it.

Mt 9:6 = Mk 2:10 = Lk 5:24. This saying is interwoven in the miracle

story of the healing of the paralytic. The connection of the SM saying
with this healing story is sometimes considered secondary[210]. Tödt, appealing to Bultmann for regarding the *Streitgespräche* as *Gemeindebildun-*
gen, considers the SM saying inauthentic[211]. This judgment is questioned
by Marshall, who warns against "a sweeping condemnation of their (sc.
the Streitgespräche) contents"[212]. Hooker[213] in fact champions the essential unity of Mk 2:1–12 and Lindars[214], opposing the separation of the
SM saying from its context, says. "the only reason why critics have sought
to remove it is the difficulty caused by the Son of Man in it"![215] This appears to be the case with *inter alios* Lane, who, however, like others, tries
to base his rejection of Mk 2:10 formally on syntactical grounds.

Lane speaks of the homogeneous character of vv. 5–9, 11–12 in which
"The fact of pardon is announced in verse 5, questioned in verses 6–9,
validated by the healing in verse 11, and recognized by the crowd in verse
12. The homogeneous development demonstrates the literary unity of
the pericope. It also puts in clear relief the 'commentary' character of
verse 10"[216].

For this proposal Lane appeals to Duplacy, who espousing Sharp's
hypothesis[217], argues that in Hellenistic and Byzantine Greek ἵνα cum
subjunctive "introduit une proposition indépendante exprimant une
décision ou, plus souvent, un ordre adouci, une prière, un souhait"[218].
Lane understands this as giving him the right to translate vs. 10 as: "Know
that the Son of Man has authority . . ." and to construe it as the evangelist's comments to his readers rather than as Jesus' words to the scribes.
That Lane's latter procedure does not follow from his translation – even
if that were correct – it quite obvious.

As for his translation, Lane, like Murphy O'Connor, appeals to Duplacy's above formulated rule, for what is variously explained as a post-
classical use of ἵνα, like ὅπως, with verbs of command and entreaty
(LSJ[219]), or with verbs of will, striving, command and entreaty (Δημητ-

210 E.g. Dibelius, *Formgeschichte des Evangeliums*, 63ff. is of the opinion that vv. 6–10 consti-
       tute an imaginary conversation on Jesus' right to forgive sins inserted into a paradigm. Bult-
       mann, *History of the Synoptic Tradition*, 14ff. regards it a controversy dialogue with vv. 5b–
       10 as a secondary interpolation. Tödt, *Der Menschensohn*, 121.
211 *Menschensohn*, 121.
212 *NTS* 12 (1965–6) 341.
213 *The Son of Man in Mark*, 83ff.
214 *Jesus Son of Man*, 44.
215 Cf. e.g. Ceroke, *CBQ* 22 (1960) 383; Murphy O'Connor, *RB* 2 (1967) 183: Lane, *Mark*, 98.
216 *Mark*, 97.
217 *ET* 38 (1926–7) 428f. Sharp, in his 22 line long note, did not produce any evidence for this,
       but merely availed himself of an enlightening article by H. Pernot (*ET* 38 (1926) 103–8), –
       in which the latter pointed out the significance of Modern Greek for a correct understanding
       of NT Greek, including its use of ἵνα, – but unlike Pernot, jumped to the conclusion that Mk
       2:10, too, should be understood imperatively.
218 In *Mélanges Bibliques A. Robert*, 424.
219 Sub ἵνα II, 1.

ῥάκος [220]), or as ἵνα cum subj. in commands in lieu of ὅπως cum fut. ind.
(Moulton[221] and Robertson[222]), or elliptically in commands introducing
a principle sentence (LSJ[223] and Δημητράκος[224]), or "with subjunctive as
a periphrasis for the imper." (BAG[225]). All these variations simply reflect
the fact that ἵνα, commencing its course in Hellenistic and completing it
in Modern Greek, underwent a dramatic development. It first rose around
NT times to being almost the sole final conjunction[226], thus provoking
the reaction which gradually reintroduced (in literary style) ὅπως and
ὥστε[227], and then "sank to a proclitic"[228] gradually losing its "classical
force"[229] and (in Modern Greek) being "reduced to νά"[230] — often
with imperative sense[231] and not infrequently in independent clauses[232].

However, the observation that ἵνα cum subjunctive can have a quasi-
imperative sense since post-classical times as well as a clearly imperative
sense in Modern Greek, does not necessarily mean that Mk 2:10, too,
must have imperative force. Duplacy's error, taken over by e.g. Murphy
O'Connor[233] and Lane, is that, without proof, he jumps from a semi-
imperative use of ἵνα cum subjunctive in Hellenistic, etc. Greek to such
a use in Mk 2:10. Duplacy has contented himself with merely referring
to a few standard works pointing out this use of ἵνα — which no one
contests — and with citing a few (mainly NT) texts[234], none of which is
really a parallel to Mk 2:10! It must, therefore, be concluded that Duplacy has not established the imperatival significance of Mk 2:10 par. Needless to say, Sharp did not even attempt to prove it, he just took it for granted.
Pernot was only interested in eliminating the parenthetical character of
λέγει τῷ παραλυτικῷ, an interest that led him to treat vs. 10 as a complete sentence. He tried to justify this by appealing to Modern Greek: "I
believe we see here another use of ἵνα , well known to all those who have
studied Modern Greek a little: 'well, you will realize (or see) that the Son
of Man has power on earth to forgive sins (since he is going to do the

---

220 Μέγα Λεξικόν sub ἵνα 3.
221 *Prolegomena*, 178.
222 *Grammar*, 994.
223 Sub ἵνα II, 3, b.
224 Μέγα Λεξικόν, sub ἵνα 4.
225 Sub ἵνα III, 2.
226 Jannaris, *Historical Grammar*, § 1761f.
227 Jannaris, *Historical Grammar*, § 1761f.
228 Jannaris, *Historical Grammar*, § 1766.
229 Jannaris, *Historical Grammar*, § 1767.
230 Jannaris, *Historical Grammar*, § 1769.
231 For examples see Δημητράκος, Μέγα Λεξικόν Vol. 6, p. 4836, sub νά 7.
232 For examples see Δημητράκος, Μέγα Λεξικόν, Vol. 6, p. 4836, sub νά 7.
233 *RB* 2 (1967) 183.
234 I.e. Tob (LXX) 8:12; 2 Mc 1:9; Dan (LXX) 6:6; 2 Cor 8:7; Eph 5:33; Gal 2:9; Mk 5:23; 6:
   25; 9:12; 10:51; 12:15, 19; 14:38, 49. Of these passages only Tob 8:12; 2 Mc 1:9; 2 Cor 8:
   7; Eph 5:33; Mk 6:25 and 12:19 could possibly be considered as 'imperative'. The rest have
   no imperative sense.

more difficult task of the two)'. The sentence stops there, it is complete. Mark then takes up the rest of his narrative: 'he saith to the sick of the palsy' "[235]. It seems to me that Pernot has overreached himself here. I would like to know what the Modern Greek rendering would look like which would support his English translation while at the same time representing a correct reflection of the original. It must be firmly asserted that Pernot's translation is not a natural rendering of Mk 2:10 into Modern Greek! (see below). Cadoux[236] speaks of "four unmistakable cases" in the NT[237] but then proceeds to briefly address some twenty more passages, to which he gives imperative sense[238] and finally quotes another twenty-seven texts which are "conceivably" imperatival[239]. He closes by suggesting that his inquiry may have some relevance also for Mk 2:10 par. and Mk 4:12 par. Cadoux's four unmistakable cases are among Moulton's examples (see below). With respect to the twenty examples which he discusses, Cadoux has always to use an auxiliary English verb, 'to have to', 'must', or 'need' — in other words, not one single case can be translated as a straightforward imperative — and the resultant translation implies that it has a very strange Greek as its original. Modern Greek, which is supposed to support such renderings, can surely in no single instance contain Cadoux's proposed translations[240].

Moulton says: "In the NT the clearest ex. is Eph 5:33"[241]. It should be noted, however, that the imperatival import of ἵνα φοβῆται is dependent on the imperative ἀγαπάτω![242] Neither the rest of Moulton's NT examples[243] nor LSJ, Moulton-Milligan[244], Sophocles[245] or Δημητράκος 's profane examples provide a parallel to Mk 2:10 par. Duplacy and Lane tacitly bypass the particle δέ — as if it was not there! — which

---

235 *ET* 38 (1926–7) 106.

236 *JTS* 42 (1941) 167.

237 I.e. Mk 5:23; 2 Cor 8:7; Eph 5:33 and Gal 2:9f.

238 *JTS* 42 (1941) 168-72.

239 *JTS* 42 (1941) 172. Of these only 1 Cor 14:1; 16:15f.; Col 4:16; Jn 13:34b may be considered as imperatival, and of these, again, only 1 Cor 16:15f. seems to be an independent sentence.

240 Meecham, *JTS* 43 (1942) 179f. rejected Gal 2:10 from Cadoux's unmistakable cases, and reduced Cadoux's twenty-seven instances to only two, Rm 16:1f. and Col 4:16f. But then he tried to add Mk 5:12; 10:51 par.; Hb 13:17; 1 Th 4:13 and Tit 3:13f. But none of these is imperatival.

241 Other passages cited by Moulton are: 1 Cor 7:29; 2 Cor 8:7; Mk 5:23 and Gal 2:10. An imperatival sense for 1 Cor 7:29 can be disputed. The imperatival sense, implying an exhortation to spiritual marriages, makes nonsense of Paul's words in vv. 2–5, 9, 12–13, and 27–28. The sense could jsut as well — if not actually better — be futuristic-eschatological (cf. vs. 31).

242 Mk 5:23 ἵνα ἐπιϑῇς is probably dependent on παρεκάλει (cf. *BDR* § 387 note 4). As for Gal 2:10 it is surely elliptical, presupposing a verb like 'they wished' or 'they asked us'. So the 1967 Modern Greek translation by four professors of Athens University (Η ΚΑΙΝΗ ΔΙΑΘΗΚΗ) : ἐξήτησαν μόνον νὰ ἐνθυμηθοῦμε ...

243 I.e. Mk 10:51 par.; 6:25; 10:35; Jn 17:24 — all follow ϑέλω!

244 *The Vocabulary of the Greek Testament*, 304f.

245 *Greek Lexicon of the Roman and Byzantine Periods*, 598–600.

joins vs. 10 to the foregoing, as well as leave out of account the context
(in which vs. 10 occurs) and the verse's structure. These considerations
are decisive against the proposed translation. Thus Lane's neat translation "Know that the Son of Man has authority . . .", which, when standing by itself appears plausible, becomes impossible when compared with
the Greek which it is supposed to represent. If we seek for translational
sense as our guide to the interpretation of the verse, then the test ought
to be *not* what a free English translation can make of the text, but
whether Modern Greek, exhibiting identical structural and syntactical
peculiarities, in short, the same idiom with historical continuity, supports the proposed translation or not. Here the answer is a categorical
'No'! Ἵνα δὲ εἰδῆτε ὅτι . . . can only be rendered by ἀλλὰ γιὰ νὰ
μάθετε ὅτι. . .[246]. The cluase is a subordinate final clause and *not* a command[247].

Moulton himself does not class Mk 2:10 par. as imperatival, while all
the other Grammarians are unequivocal in treating the passage as a final
clause[248].

Lane also speaks of "the awkward syntactical structure" in that. "Jesus
appears (Lane's italics) to be addressing the scribes . . . The text, however,
proceeds with the abrupt transition, 'he says to the paralytic' . . ." Lane
furthermore thinks that "the function of 10b ('he said to the paralytic') is
to indicate the end of Mark's "commentary and the return to the incident
itself"[249]. These are in themselves hair-raising remarks. Hahn, too, speaks
of "the exceedingly harsh transition from vs. 10 to vs. 11[250]. Similarly,
Ceroke speaks of "this literary awkwardness"[251] referring to Taylor's[252]
problem with vs. 10b: λέγει τῷ παραλυτικῷ. The 'awkwardness' here is
supposed to lie in the circumstance that vs. 10b "he said to the paralytic"
is a repetition of vs. 5b! Therefore, Taylor thinks that two original stories,
a "Miracle-story" and a "Pronouncement story", have been blended together here. Taylor was reacting against Bultmann's theory that Mk 2:
5b—10 was secondarily interpolated in a "Miracle-story", 2:3—5a, 11—
12[253], and Dibelius' theory, which considered vv. 6—10 the preacher's

246 Jannaris, *Historical Grammar*, § 1769. See also § 1523; Δημητράκος, Μέγα Λέξικον, Vol. 2,
   p. 1611 sub γιά 5; and Vol. 6, p. 4836 sub νά 1.
247 Cf. Prof. Vamvas' translation (ΤΑ ΙΕΡΑ ΓΡΑΜΜΑΤΑ) in literary Modern Greek *ad loc.*:
   ἀλλὰ διὰ νὰ γνωρίσητε ὅτι ... as well as the 1967 Modern Greek Version, in virtually colloquial Greek: at Mt 9:6 and Mk 2:10 ἀλλὰ διὰ νὰ μάθετε ὅτι ... and at Lk 5:24 the equivalent: διὰ νὰ μάθετε ὅμως ὅτι ... Similarly the most recent Modern Greek translation (Η
   ΚΑΙΝΗ ΔΙΑΘΗΚΗ, 1985) in all three places: γιὰ νὰ μάθετε λοιπόν ...
248 Robertson, *Grammar*, 999: "In Mk 2:10 ἵνα we have real purpose;" also 1203; Turner,
   Syntax, 344; *BDR* § 470 note 4 and § 483, 1.
249 *Mark*, 98.
250 *Titles of Jesus*, 50.
251 *CBQ* 22 (1969) 373.
252 *The Formation of the Gospel Tradition*, 66ff.
253 *History of Synoptic Tradition*, 14f.

announcement to his Christian audience of the reality of Jesus' forgiveness[254]. Dibelius' problem was that whereas in vs. 5 the paralytic's sins
were merely declared by Jesus as forgiven, in vs. 10 it is Jesus who is said
to forgive them. This is a theological rather than a literary problem. The
passive ἀφίενται is supposed to be a 'divine passive', and hence Jesus is
understood as being merely God's mouthpiece in declaring forgiveness.
This, accoring to the theory, clashes with vs. 10, where Jesus is the one
who actually forgives. The falsity of this reasoning is sufficiently proven
by the scribes' objections following Jesus' first statement (vs. 5), who
clearly understood ἀφίενται as Jesus' own forgiving![255]

Ceroke makes a remarkable syllogism. Since the words "he said to the
paralytic" in vs. 10 are inappropriate as part of a saying of Jesus, he thinks
that the whole of vs. 10 must be editorial. For this he finds support in
the Marcan climax which "takes cognizance of the miraculous cure only
in allusion to vs. 5b, 'Thy sins are forgiven,' while failing to allude to vs.
10"[256]. Where in the Marcan climax allusion is made to vs. 5b but not to
vs. 10, and why the fact that 10b is Marcan must necessitate. also the
redactional character of 10a is something that Ceroke does not explain,
but notwithstanding this he concludes that the whole of vs. 10 is the
evangelist's addition!

I must confess that I am totally confounded in the face of all these
allegations as to the awkwardness of the text which is supposed to betray
its composite character[257]. Whether this is owing to deep ignorance or
obtuseness, I, for one, am incapable of detecting all these subtle 'difficulties', 'problems' and 'awkwardnesses' in Mk 2:5–11 par., which lead
those who are capable of penetrating to the division of soul and spirit,
to sort out Jesus' words from the evangelist's comments. As a native
speaker of Greek I cannot see any awkwardness on the literary or syntactical level of the text. The text makes perfect sense as it is. Vs. 10 is a
dramatic continuation from vs. 9 where Jesus, challenged by the objections of the scribes about his right to forgive sins, undertakes to demonstrate his authority in deed, by turning to the paralytic and commanding
him to stand up. The words "he said to the paralytic" (vs. 10b) are, of
course, editorial. This repeated λέγει τῷ παραλυτικῷ is necessitated by
the intervening dialogue with the scribes (vv. 8–9). It is most necessary in
vs. 10 in order to make clear that Jesus, having addressed the scribes by
what amounts to an acceptance of the challenge to prove his authority
to forgive sins, now turns to the paralytic to address to him the words
σοί λέγω. . . The personal pronoun is emphatic, distinguishing Jesus'

---

254 Die Formgeschichte des Evangeliums, 63ff.
255 Similarly Marshall, Luke, 210f.
256 CBQ 22 (1960) 381f.
257 Farrer, A Study in Mark, 76, exclaims in astonishment: "What is there to complain of here?
The effect is magnificent, and could not be bettered. Such is my judgment, and I claim to
follow St. Matthew and St. Luke".

earlier words in vs. 10, addressed to the scribes, from the words now following, which are addressed to the paralytic. The sentence is elliptical,
lacking its main clause. The complete sentence would have been something like: "But in order that you may know that the Son of Man has
authority to forgive sins on earth, I will now heal this man". The sentence
really amounts to: "But in order that you may know that my words of
forgiveness are not an empty claim or boast, I will now demonstrate their
validity by actually healing this man." The main clause "I will heal the
man" is omitted, and we get instead its equivalent in the form of a command to the paralytic. This is more effective than a main clause would
have been and it must be further judged to be perfectly acceptable and
vivid Greek[258].

Appositely Farrer[259] draws attention to a similar construction in Ex 4:
4f.: εἶπεν Κύριος πρὸς τόν Μωϋσῆν, Ἔκτεινον τὴν χεῖρα σου καὶ
ἐπιλαβοῦ τῆς κέρκου, καὶ ἐγένετο ῥάβδος ἐν τῇ χειρὶ αὐτοῦ· ἵνα πιστε-
ύσωσίν σοι . . . Farrer comments:

> Both in Exodus iv and in Mark ii a 'that' (*hina*) clause concerned with belief in divinely
> given authority is made to have its grammatical dependence not upon a statement, but on an
> attesting action. Exodus does not say: 'I bid you take up the snake, and I will make it a staff
> in your hand, that they may believe ...' Nor does Mark say, 'That ye may know ... I command
> the paralytic to arise, and enable him to do so'. It is superfluous to talk, when action supplies
> the place of words."

The pertinence of this text for Mk 2:10 is obvious. Farrer, in fact, thinks
that Mk 2:10 is consciously constructed on the model of Ex 4:4f. The
only dissimilarity — of no consequence, whatsoever, — lies in that Ex 4:
4f. has both the ἵνα clause and the command addressed to the same person (Moses), whereas Mk 2:10, understandably, addresses the ἵνα clause
to the scribes and the command to the paralytic. What is of consequence,
however, is that the ἵνα clause and the command are related to one
another exactly as in Mk 2:10[260].

An even closer parallel is provided by Philostratus[261], a passage mentioned by Duplacy, but set aside by him on the ground that it is —
"unique"![262] In order to prove to Apollonius that they possessed equal
powers as the Indians, of whom Appolonius was inordinately fond, the
head of the Egyptian Nudist philosophers said to him: "ὅτι δ᾽ οὐκ ἀδυνατοῦμεν σοφίζεσθαι, τὸ δεῖνα" ἔφη, "δένδρον", πτελέα δὲ ἦν, τρίτον
ἀπ᾽ ἐκείνου, ὑφ, ᾧ διελέγοντο, "πρόσειπε τὸν σοφόν Ἀπολλώνιον",
καὶ προσεῖπε μὲν αὐτόν, ὡς ἐκελεύσθη τὸ δένδρον. F.C. Conybeare
translates: " 'But you shall see that we are not unable to work tricks if

258 Jannaris, *Historical Grammar,* § 2031 remarks that the change from indirect to direct discourse "which lends vivacity to speech has been popular through all times".
259 *A Study in Mark,* 76.
260 The difference in order is of no consequence.
261 *Life of Apollonius,* VI, 10.
262 *Mélanges Bibliques A. Robert,* 423.

we like. Heigh! you tree yonder,' he cried, pointing to an elm tree, the third in the row from that under which they were talking, 'just salute the wise Appolonius, will you?' And forthwith the tree saluted him"[263]. The similarity in structure between this text and Mk 2:10 is total. That Philostratus uses ὅτι δ᾽οὐκ ἀδυνατοῦμεν rather than ἵνα δὲ εἰδῆτε is of no consequence. The passage could easily have been e.g. ἵνα δὲ εἰδῆτε ὅτι οὐκ ἀδυνατοῦμεν . . . This kind of structure involving direct speech and action is natural not only in Greek, but as Farrer shows, also in English[264].

There are thus no syntactical grounds for considering Mk 2:10a par. as alien to the rest of Jesus' words in that pericope. This does not in itself rule out the theoretical possibility that the pericope might have been of composite origin in its pre-literary stage, but it means that when it was written down, it was composed as a unity, and that since no palpable difficulties can be discovered in its present form indicating the secondary nature of vs. 10a[265], that theoretical possibility is and shall remain a pure theoretical speculation which cannot be made the subject of scientific criticism. In fact the suspicions against the unity of the passage are inspired by theology rather than syntax and relate to the kind of Son of Man presented in this text (i.e. One who forgives sins)[266]. This fact, however, has often been obscured by the attempt to prove the 'syntactical awkwardness' of the text, that is if vs. 10a is understood as Jesus' words, but its perfect harmony, if the saying is understood as the evangelist's comment and thus the creation of the Early Church! But as we have seen all these allegations as to the 'awkwardness' of the structure of the text as well as the 'naturalness and harmony' of the proposed solutions are mere platitudes, with no basis in post-classical, Byzantine and Modern Greek syntax. They rather give the impression of being a "device to get rid of the unwanted Son of Man"[267].

Vs. 10 is dependent upon vv. 8—9 and together they are dependent upon vs. 5b. The syntax of vv. 5—12 evinces perfect harmony, unity and a natural flow of thought. Bultmann, who was too competent a Greek scholar to indulge in the vagaries I have discussed, recognized the unity of vv. 5b—10[268] though he considered them an interpolation into a miracle-story. That was, however, not based on syntactical problems which he discovered in vs. 10, but it was for reasons of his own peculiar

---

263 In the edition of Loeb Classical Library.

264 *A Study in Mark*, 76.

265 Cf. Marshall, *Luke*, 211, who, speaking of the Lucan parallel (5:17—26), says: "This section is unlikely ever to have circulated on its own".

266 Though forgiveness of sins is not of frequent occurrence in the Gospels, it is nevertheless present (see Lk 7:47 and cf. Jn 8:11). It is also implicit especially in Jesus' fellowship with prostitutes, publicans and sinners.

267 Marshall, *NTS* 12 (1965—6) 342.

268 *History of the Synoptic Tradition*, 15.

theological stance. There are, however, no evident 'seams' between the parts belonging to the 'miracle-story' and those belonging to the 'pronouncement-story' to warrant Bultmann's hypothesis. If such there were once, they must have been effectively obliterated when the pericope was written down. Besides, vv. 5—10 are not concerned purely with forgiveness, so as to make it possible just to excise these verses from the 'miracle-story'. In the midst of the pericope, vs. 9, reference is made to the contemplated healing. The healing material and the forgiveness material are inextricably interwoven. Which is the more probable: that Mark should have brought two unrelated traditions together, (especially if one was a creation of the Early Church), or that Jesus should have healed a paralytic while at the same time dealing with his greater problem of sin? Moreover, that it was Jesus' habit to avail himself of a healing occasion to teach something else of greater importance than the healing itself, is shown by e.g. Mt 12:9ff. = Mk 3:3ff. = Lk 6:6ff. In that text, as here, Jesus did not proceed directly to the act of healing, but first engaged his religious antagonists in conversation. As for Mk 2:5 par. Jesus surely knew that his words "Thy sins are forgiven thee" would raise a storm of protest, but as we know from his insistence in frequently choosing the sabbath-day to perform his miracles[269], he did it purposely to create occasions for debate with the scribes and pharisees in order to expose their inconsequence, unreasonableness and hypocrisy to the audience!

I conclude, therefore, that there are no literary grounds for separating the material dealing with the forgiveness of sins from that dealing with the miracle, or any other valid grounds for regarding it impossible or even improbable for Jesus to have uttered these words. This logion, therefore, is rightly regarded as authentic by e.g. Farrer[270], Taylor[271], Kümmel[272], Thompson[273], Hamerton-Kelly[274], Leivestad[275], Marshall[276], Casey[277], Lindars[278], Colpe[279], Hooker[280], Borsch[281], Hill[282], Goppelt[283].

Now I turn my attention to the question of possible Danielic influence. This logion of Jesus' contains four ideas: ἐξουσία, ὁ υἱὸς τοῦ ἀνθρώπου,

---

269 Cf. Mt 12:1ff. = Mk 2:23ff. = Lk 6:1ff.; Mk 3:1ff. = Lk 6:6ff. = Mt 12:9ff.; Mk 1:21ff. = Lk 4:31ff.; 13:10ff.; 14:1ff.; Jn 5:9, 16ff.; 7:23; 9:14, 16.
270 *A Study in Mark*, 267ff.
271 *The Names of Jesus*, 27; *The Formation of the Gospel Tradition*, 66ff.; *Mark*, 200.
272 *Heilsgeschehen und Geschichte*, 435f.
273 *JTS* 12 (1961) 203ff.
274 *Pre-existence*, 61ff.
275 *NTS* 18 (1971—2) 259.
276 *NTS* 12 (1965—6) 341f.; *Luke*, 211.
277 *Son of Man*, 159ff.
278 *Jesus Son of Man*, 44ff.
279 *TDNT*, VIII, 430f.
280 *The Son of Man in Mark*, 81ff.
281 *The Son of Man in Myth and History*, 321f.
282 *The Gospel of Matthew*, 170. Schweizer, *JBL* 79 (1960) 121, is uncertain.
283 In *Mensch und Menschensohn*, 20ff.

ἀφιέναι ἁμαρτίας and ἐπὶ τῆς γῆς. A comparison of this logion with the MT, the LXX and Θ of Dan 7:14 reveals that the first, second and fourth of these ideas obtain in the latter passage as well. What is more, the comparison shows that the three ideas are collocated in Mk 2:10 par. in exactly the same way as in Dan 7:14. In both texts it is said that a) *The Son of Man* b) *has power* c) *on earth* (to do certain things). The only difference is the absence in Dan 7:14 of the third item in the Gospel account: ἀφιέναι ἁμαρτίας. But as we shall see this absence is only apparent.

We have seen above[284] that Casey's generic interpretation "a man has power . . ." and Lindars' modified view according to which Jesus identifies himself with a group of persons to which the idiom properly refers, are impossible. These views are modern restatements of a view propounded by Wellhausen[285], which is nowadays rejected "on the excellent ground that it produces an untrue statement"[286]. The same may be said of Colpe's similar view according to which "Not only God may forgive, but man too in Me, Jesus"[287]. No contrast between God and man is here intended; in fact, the idea of man is totally absent! What we have here is the Son of Man; but this expression cannot be resolved into its constituent parts, it is one idea. Jesus has on his own authority pronounced the forgiveness of the paralytic's sins, and on being charged by the scribes with usurping God's prerogative, he proceeds to justify his action as something "legitimately belonging to him on the grounds of his claim to be the Son of Man"[288]. Jesus has the right to forgive, not because he is a member of the human race[289], — an absurd idea — but because he is the Son of Man!

Apart from his right to forgive sins, Jesus also claims the right to bestow healing (and elsewhere even life!), i.e. another expression of divine activity. There is no doubt, therefore, that Jesus' claims here are of the most superlative kind[290] and that they have their explanation in his claim to be the Son of Man!

The kind of Son of Man presented here, far from being adequately explained by a colourless Aramaic circumlocution which can apply to any person, is conceived as a definite Figure with well-defined powers and rights. In no other body of literature do we find another Figure which comes closer to the requirements of our text (Mk 2:10 par.) than Dan 7 and its 'extension', I En 37—71. My analysis of Dan 7 (in Chapter Two, above) has shown that the 'SM' is conceived not as a symbol for the pious

---

284 At the close of Ch. One in criticism of Lindars.
285 *Das Evangelium Marci*, 17f.
286 Marshall, *NTS* 12 (1965—6) 342. See also *id., Luke*, 215.
287 *TDNT*, VIII, 430. On Wellhausen's ambiguous views see Colpe, *TDNT*, VIII, 431 note 236.
288 Marshall, *Luke*, 210f.: "Hence the miracle of healing was meant not simply to prove the reality of the act of forgiveness, but also to corroborate Jesus' claim to be the Son of Man".
289 As McNeile, *Matthew*, 116f.
290 Cf. Higgins, *Jesus and the Son of Man*, 26f.

Jews, but as a pre-existent, heavenly Being, who appears as the leader of the saints. In that capacity the 'SM' is granted the powers of the beasts in an absolute sense, and he exercises henceforth his authority here on earth (LXX: τὰ ἔϑνη τῆς γῆς) upon all peoples (Θ: πάντες οἱ λαοί). To the Danielic 'SM' ἐξουσία (LXX), ἀρχή, τιμή and βασιλεία (Θ after MT) are given, and all peoples, tribes and languages do him homage (Θ: δου-λεύσουσιν, after MT) or offer to him their worship (LXX: λατρεύουσα). It would be idle to argue that the Danielic 'SM' does not have the right to forgive sins, because that right is not explicitly mentioned in Dan 7. If he has the absolute power over all peoples, that of forgiving sins may safely be considered as being included[291]. The continuator of the Danielic tradition, the author of the *Parables*, understood this right as being included in the Son of Man's exalted functions, and has therefore made repeated references to the petitions for forgiveness which the ungodly address to the Son of Man[292].

One more detail must not pass unnoticed. Jesus' healings are in all likelihood to be understood in connection with his claim to be the Son of Man. In Jewish eyes illness was not only a consequence of sin, but also the result of demonic activity upon humans. In Dan 7 we see that the emergence of the 'SM' is connected with the destruction of the beasts, from whose repressive rule humans are freed in order to be placed under the rule of the 'SM'. It is extremely probable that Jesus saw his bestowal of healing on those oppressed by the evil powers as part of his rights and task as Son of Man.

The expression ἐπὶ τῆς γῆς has not only its equivalent in Dan 7:14, but also by contrast with Mt 28:18, where Jesus following his resurrection claims to have received (cf. the Danielic ἐδόϑη!) πᾶσα ἐξουσία ἐν οὐρανῷ καὶ ἐπὶ γῆς, the present authority of the Son of Man is confined to earth. The absolute authority of Mt 28:18, corresponding to the full powers of the 'SM', is granted to Jesus after the resurrection. However, authority on earth is a prerogative exercised by him already in the present.

It must be therefore concluded that a comparison of Mk 2:10 par. with Dan 7 reveals not only the very similar wording between the two texts, but, what is more, a similarity of ideas, as well as their identical colloca-tion, which shows clearly that the activity of the Son of Man as envisioned by Jesus cannot but have been conceived in dependence upon Dan 7:14. By concentrating upon and developing the ideas of the 'SM's' royal au-thority and the exercise of that authority upon earth in the Danielic text,

---

291 Cf. Thompson, *JTS* 12 (1961) 206, and Hamerton-Kelly, *Pre-existence*, 62.

292 Cf. e.g. I En 62:9f.; 63:1—11; 69:26ff. It is interesting to note, that the Son of Man is never said to forgive sins in heaven. This circumstance compared with such Gospel statements as Mt 18:18 and Jn 20:23 would seem to imply that forgiveness is an activity of the Son of Man confined to earth, whereas his activity in heaven takes the form of judgment. Such a distinc-tion would seem to explain the data of the *Parables* and Jesus' claim to forgive sins on earth in Mk 2:10 par.

Jesus has been able to connect the heavenly Being of the prototype with his own earthly activity as Son of Man[293].

ii. The Suffering Son of Man. One of the suffering SM sayings[294] is Mt 20:28 = Mk 10:45:ὥσπερ (Mk: καὶ γὰρ) ὁ υἱὸς τοῦ ἀνθρώπου οὐκ ἦλθεν διακονηθῆναι ἀλλὰ διακονῆσαι καὶ δοῦναι τὴν ψυχὴν αὐτοῦ λύτρον ἀντὶ πολλῶν. In an interesting article[295] Stuhlmacher has made a *prima-facie* case for the authenticity of this logion against Pesch[296], who considers Mk 10:45 as "eine sekundäre Bildung, die wahrscheinlich erst in der griechischsprechenden judenchristlichen Gemeinde entstanden ist"[297].

For reasons of brevity I shall content myself with presenting only a brief summary of Stuhlmacher's arguments.

1. I Tm 2:5f., which is a hellenized form of Mk 10:45 (Mt 20:28)[298], shows that the Gospel logion "zu den Überlieferungen rechnet, die für die deuteropaulinische Christologie über Paulus hinaus massgeblich geworden sind"[299].

2. Since the important terms ὁ υἱὸς τοῦ ἀνθρώπου, διακονηθῆναι-διακονῆσαι and λύτρον ἀντὶ πολλῶν fail in the Last Supper, Mk 10:45 par. cannot have its origin "in der urchristlichen Abendmahlstheologie", as some have supposed[300]. The similarities between Mk 10:45 and Isa 53 are limited to (παρα) διδόναι, ψυχὴ αὐτοῦ and πολλοι. This, while sufficient to connect our text with Isa 53, is incapable of explaining its whole content.

3. Against Jeremias[301], who derives the entire logion from Isa 53 treating λύτρον as the equivalent of אשם, Stuhlmacher objects that the LXX never uses λύτρον for אשם but for כפר, but this term is missing in Isa

---

293 The attempt by some (e.g. Eerdmans, *Theol.Tijdschr.* 28 (1893) 153ff.; Vermes, *Jesus the Jew,* 180, Casey, *Son of Man,* 161, 228f.; Lindars, *Jesus Son of Man,* 46) to overcome the stumbling block of the Son of Man's authority to forgive sins, by reducing the title, via ἀνθρώποις of Mt 9:8, to a mere circumlocution for man, is inexcusably bad exegesis. First, it is unjustifiable to use a comment made by the astonished and unenlightened crowd as the key to the understanding of the title Son of Man. Second, from the point of view of the crowds, it seemed as if God actually had given such authority to men (since Jesus was a man). Third, and more importantly, the plural ἀνθρώποις does not refer to any other persons who *ex hypothesi* are here classed together with Jesus. The plural is a Greek idiom indicating the class, human beings, to which Jesus belongs. The reference is exclusively to Jesus.
294 See classification in note 8, above.
295 "Existenzstellvertretung für die Vielen: Mk 10, 45 (Mt 20, 28)" in *Werden und Wirken des Alten Testaments,* für C. Westermann, eds. R. Albertz – H.P. Müller – H.W. Wolff – W. Zimmerli, pp. 412–27.
296 *Das Markusevangelium,* II 2, 162ff.
297 In *Werden und Wirken,* 412.
298 As shown by Jeremias, *Jud* 3 (1947–8) 249ff.; id., *Abba* 216ff.; id., *Theologie,* I, 277ff.
299 *Werden und Wirken,* 415.
300 *Werden und Wirken,* 415.
301 *Theologie* I, 277f.

53. Thus, though affinities between Mk 10:45 and Isa 53 are recognized, these are not strong enough to warrant the theory that the logion is the creation of the Palestinian Church on the basis of Isa 53.

4. The fact that the title SM in the NT (outside of Jesus' sayings) occurs only in Acts 7:56 (apart from the quotations of Dan 7:13 in Rev 1:13 and 14:14 and of Ps 8:5 in Heb 2:6) indicates that the Church was mindful that Son of Man was Jesus' peculiar self-designation and therefore abstained from using it. What is remarkable, however, is that all of these sayings speak of the SM in his glory, whereas Mk 10:45 par. of the SM's service. An even more peculiar contrast is seen to exist between our text and Dan 7:9—14 and I Enoch. In these works the SM is presented as an exalted Ruler and Judge who is served by angels and worshipped by the peoples, whereas in Mk 10:45 par. the SM rejects such an exalted position and instead looks upon himself as a λύτρον for many[302]. Where does the idea of διακονεῖν come from? Certainly not from Isa 53. Stuhlmacher, following the Syriac translation thinks that διακονεῖν corresponds to the Aramaic שמש which in the OT occurs only at Dan 7:10, of the angels' service before God. He argues: "Der traditionsgeschichtliche Ort des *diakonein* von Mk 10,45 (Mt 20,28) . . . ist die hoheitliche Menschensohnüberlieferung von Dan 7 und der äthiopischen Henochapokalypse! Das Wortspiel: 'nicht um sich bedienen zu lassen-sondern um zu dienen' meint, dass der Menschensohn freiwillig den Dienst der stellvertretenden Selbstpreisgable der himmlischen Würdestellung des angebeteten Gerichtssherrn vorzieht". With reference to the *criterion of dissimilarity*, he concludes that since this logion cannot be derived from the theology of the Early Church, biblical-Jewish sources, or simply from Isa 53, "Bei Mk 10: 45 (Mt 20:28) handelt es sich aller Wahrscheinlichkeit nach um ein echtes Jesuslogion"[303].

5. In further support of the authenticity of this logion, he appeals to Grimm[304], who points to an even closer parallel in Isa 43:3f. (MT). "In Jes 43,3f. findet sich das sprachlich echte Äquivalent von *lytron*, nämlich kōfaer; dem *anti (pollōn)* entspricht das wiederholte *taḥat* genau, und die auffällige Wendung vom Menschensohn, der sein Leben dahingeben will, findet in dem *wᵉ 'aettēn 'adām* Jahwes eine interessante Entsprechung: Der Menschensohn von Mk 10,45 nimmt die Stelle der Menschen ein, die Jahwe als Lösegeld für Israels Leben (*taḥtaekā bzw. taḥat nafšaekā*) dahingeben will"[305]. Since this text did not figure as a testimonium, Mk 10: 45 par. cannot be attributed to the Early Church. "Den messianischen Menschensohn als leidenden Gerechten und Gottesknecht zu interpretieren, ist sein (sc. Jesus') persönliches Werk"[306]. Stuhlmacher concludes:

---

302 *Werden und Wirken*, 419.
303 *Werden und Wirken*, 422.
304 *Weil ich dich liebe. Die Verkündigung Jesu und Deuterojesaja.*
305 *Werden und Wirken*, 422.
306 *Werden und Wirken*, 425.

"Die Jesus von Dan 7, 9—14 und dem äthiopischen Henoch her vorgegebene Menschensohntradition ist ein komplexes Phänomen . . . Wenn Jesus die ihm als dem messianischen Menschensohn eigentlich zukommende Bedienung durch die Engelheere und die Proskynese der Völker ausschlägt und es statt dessen als seinen Sendungsauftrag bezeizhnet, sein Leben dem (in der stellvertretenden Selbstpreisgabe gipfelnden) Dienst an den Vielen zu weihen, dann prägt er das ihm überkommene Bild vom Menschensohnweltenrichter entscheidend um"[307].

Stuhlmacher's double thesis, that Mk 10:45 par. is a genuine saying of Jesus and that the saying bears a conscious relation to Dan 7 must be deemed not only interesting but also persuasive[307a].

Among the passion sayings the most significant are Jesus' three predictions of his suffering, death and resurrection (Mt 16:21 = Mk 8:31 = Lk 9:22; Mt 17:22f. = Mk 9:31 = Lk 9:44; Mt 20:18f. = Mk 10.33f. = Lk 18:31ff.) as well as the saying during the last Supper (Mt 26:21ff. = Mk 14:18ff. = Lk 22:21f.) which has a parallel in Jn 13:21, 31.

This class of SM sayings has been treated with greater suspicion than the other two classes, while its wholesale rejection has by no means been an infrequent phenomenon[308]. Despite this, there are signs of a change in attitude towards these sayings, because it seems that there actually exist some good grounds for taking these sayings more seriously.

Borsch has set forth the essential arguments against the authenticity of this class of SM sayings and has devoted over twenty pages to refuting them[309]. These arguments will not be reproduced here. Borsch's position is that "once certain *possible* (Borsch's italics) accretions are removed, the residue of these sayings presents a hard core, the authenticity of which cannot easily be dismissed"[310] Borsch is also of the opinion that the Markan evidence is supported by John who represents an independent tradition[311].

We have already seen that Stuhlmacher has recently made a good case

---

307 *Werden und Wirken*, 425f.

307a This saying is treated in even greater detail by Kim, in his fine study *The 'Son of Man' as the Son of God, 38—73*. Kim's findings corroborate Stuhlmacher's conclusions, e.g. "He (sc. Jesus) understood himself to be 'the "Son of Man" ', i.e. the heavenly figure seen by Daniel כבר אנש in a vision ... He understood that he was to fulfill this mission as 'the "Son of Man" ' by carrying out the functions of the Ebed Yahweh." (72f.). Unfortunately this study came to hand after the completion of the present investigation, and could not therefore be taken into account in the present investigation.

308 See discussion with Knox, above.

309 *The Son of Man in Myth and History*, 329—53.

310 *The Son of Man*, 333.

311 Cf. *The Son of Man*, 349: "One may try to explain this in various ways, but still the fact is there. The sayings are so different that they can hardly be the result of later cross-influences. They must come from an earlier stratum. We find them well explained by the supposition that they stem from levels in authentic tradition. And actually, once one ceases to assume that Jesus could not have said these things in this way, we see no reason why this theme should not have been authentic and much to indicate that it probably was."

not only for the authenticity of Mk 10:45 par. but also for the independence of this logion from the Last Supper tradition[312]. As it happens Mk
10:45 (Mt 20:28) is one of the suffering sayings and the significance of
Stuhlmacher's demonstration is that Jesus did in fact understand himself,
in the light of Dan 7:9—14, Isa 43:3f. and 53:10—12, as a messianic Son
of Man who was to give his life as a ransom for his people[313].

A further corroboration of the general authenticity of the suffering
sayings comes from the study of the language of these sayings which
shows that they are of pre-Marcan provenience[314]. Tödt has shown that
terms like "ausgeliefert werden in die Hände", "verworden werden",
"verachtet werden", etc. etc. go back to pre-Marcan Palestinian and probably Aramaic tradition[315].

In addition to the above considerations, four arguments will be presented here for the essential trustworthiness of the passion sayings.

1. It is remarkable that of the fifteen SM sayings found in Mark, no
fewer than nine are suffering sayings. Of those remaining, two are Earthly
Life and three Exaltation sayings. This surely indicates that the suffering
SM belonged to a very broad stream of pre-Markan tradition.

2. The suffering SM sayings are very widespread in the synoptic tradition being the only type that receives about an equal amount of attention
in all three Gospels. Thus the three suffering predictions together with the
Last Supper prediction, which is independently corroborated by John,
testify to a solid tradition behind the Gospels. This evidence, according
to the *criterion of multiple attestation*, ought to imply that the tradition
of a suffering Son of Man is authentic.

3. The suffering Son of Man is not a part of the Jewish tradition.
Neither Daniel, nor the *Parables*, nor IV Ezra give the least hint of a suffering Son of Man. Nor is a suffering Son of Man part of the Church's
tradition. According to the *criterion of dissimilarity*, this state of affairs
would seem to speak in favour of the genuineness of the suffering sayings.

4. The main grounds for rejecting this class of sayings is that acceptance
of these sayings would somehow necessitate the assumption of the possibility of prediction[316]. This objection has of late lost most of its force
owing to the growing consensus among scholars that the circumstances in
which Jesus found himself could easily have led him to conclude that he
too, like others before him, might suffer a violent death at the hands of
the Jewish authorities[317]. Not only had he come into serious conflict

---

312 *Werden und Wirken,* 413f.
313 See also Hengel, *The Atonement,* 34ff., 42, 49ff., 71ff.
314 Borsch, *The Son of Man,* 341; Marshall, *Luke,* 368.
315 *Der Menschensohn,* e.g. 144—67. Marshall, NTS 12 (1965—6) 349 would go further back to
Jesus.
316 Cf. Marshall, NTS 12 (1965—6) 329.
317 Cf. Riesner, *Jesus als Lehrer,* 478. See also Jeremias, *The Servant of God,* 100, "that Jesus
reckoned with the possibility of a violent death has the strongest historical probability behind

with the Jewish leaders by the time of the first prediction (Mt 16:21 par.)[318], but his life had also been threatened repeatedly[319]. These circumstances, in conjunction with his knowledge of the violent end which many prophets had met in Jerusalem[320] could hardly have failed to evoke in him premonitions of his own approaching fate[321]. The conviction is indeed growing among scholars that Jesus' death did not come upon him unawares. As Riesner expresses it: "Selbst von einem kritisch gesicherten Minimum an Überlieferung her wird eine Geisteshaltung Jesu sichtbar, die es ausschliesst, dass er diese Gefahr als blindes Schicksal auf sich zukommen liess"[322]. And Lindars observes: "The three Son of Man sayings (i.e. Mk 8:31; 9:31; 10:33–4) . . . testify to the resolution and deliberation with which he faced the inevitable march of events. This is no Stoic indifference, but a deep sense of responsibility and commitment to the mission which he had undertaken in the name of God . . . It thus seems likely that Jesus did see the necessity of death in terms of sacrifice . . . Jesus' sacrificial approach to his death does not need to be dependent on Isa 53, but it is certainly consistent with it"[323]. It is also highly probable that Jesus' sharp rebuke to Peter as "Satan" at Caesarea Philippi, which can hardly be the creation of the Early Church[324], is to be explained in the light of Jesus' resolution to go to his death, a death from which Peter was trying to dissuade him[325].

There appear thus to exist *prima-facie* grounds for accepting an essential core in the passion predictions as Jesus' authentic teaching about himself. With this result agree such scholars as Marshall[326], Taylor[327], Borsch[328], Farrer[329], Riesner[330], Lindars[331], Schweizer[332], Goppelt[333], and Leivestad[334].

---

it." See further, Hengel, *The Atonement*, 71ff.; Schürmann, *Jesu ureigene Tod*, 33 and literature cited in note 68 and Kümmel, *Promise and Fulfilment*, 99.

318 Cf. e.g. Mt 15:1–14; 16:4–12; Mk 7:5–13; 8:11–15; Lk 6:6–11.

319 Cf. e.g. Mt 12:14 = Mk 3:6 = Lk 6:11. Cf. also Jn 7:1; 30, 32; 8:20, 37, 59; 10:31.

320 Cf. Mt 5:12; 13:57 = Mk 6:4 = Lk 4:24; Mt 23:29–35 = Lk 11:47–51.

321 As later in Mt 23:37–39 = Lk 13:33–35.

322 *Jesus als Lehrer*, 478.

323 *Jesus Son of Man*, 84.

324 Cf. Schweizer, *JBL* 79 (1960) 121: "For this statement only or a very similar one could have caused the protest of Peter and the harsh rebuke of Jesus calling him 'Satan' which cannot have been invented by the church."

325 See Riesner, *Jesus als Lehrer*, 479.

326 *NTS* 12 (1965–6) 348f. and *Luke*, 367ff.

327 *Mark*, 377f., 402.

328 *The Son of Man*, 330–53.

329 *A Study in Mark*, 286f.

330 *Jesus als Lehrer*, 478ff.

331 *Jesus Son of Man*, 60, 84.

332 *JBL* 79 (1960) 120f.

333 In *Mensch und Menschensohn*, 20ff.

334 *NTS* 18 (1971–2) 263f.

A more difficult task is to isolate the hard core with any certainty. The following table shows the significant words in each prediction.

Mt 16:21	Mk 8:31	Lk 9:22
δεῖ αὐτὸν (sc. υἱὸν τ. ἀν.) πολλὰ παθεῖν	δεῖ τὸν υἱὸν τ. ἀνθρώπου πολλὰ παθεῖν καὶ ἀποδοκιμασθῆναι	δεῖ τὸν υἱὸν τ. ἀνθρώπου πολλὰ παθεῖν καὶ ἀποδοκιμασθῆναι
ἀπὸ πρεσβυτ. ἀρχ. γραμμ. ἀποκτανθῆναι τῇ τρίτῃ ἡμέρᾳ ἐγερθῆναι	ὑπὸ πρεσβυτ. ἀρχ. γραμμ. ἀποκτανθῆναι μετὰ τρεῖς ἡμ. ἐγερθῆναι	ἀπὸ πρεσβυτ. ἀρχ. γραμμ. ἀποκτανθῆναι τῇ τρίτῃ ἡμέρᾳ ἐγερθῆναι

Mt 17:22f.	Mk 9:31	Lk 9:44
μέλλει ὁ υἱὸς τ. ἀνθρ. παραδίδοσθαι εἰς χεῖρας ἀνθρώπων ἀποκτενοῦσαν αὐτὸν τῇ τρίτῃ ἡμέρᾳ ἐγερθήσ.	ὁ υἱὸς τοῦ ἀνθρώπου παραδίδοται εἰς χεῖρας ἀνθρώπων ἀποκτενοῦσιν αὐτόν μετὰ τρεῖς ἡμερ. ἐγερθήσ.	ὁ γὰρ υἱὸς τ. ἀνθρ. μέλλει παραδίδοσθαι εἰς χεῖρας ἀνθρώπων

Mt 20:18	Mk 10:33f.	Lk 18:31–34
ἰδοὺ ἀναβαίν. εἰς Ἱερ. ὁ υ. τ. ἀνθρ. παραδοθήσεται τοῖς ἀρχιερ. κ. γραμματ. κατακρινοῦσιν θανάτῳ	ἰδοὺ ἀναβαίν. εἰς Ἱεροσ. ὁ υ. τ. ἀνθ. παραδοθήσεται τοῖς ἀρχιερ. κ. γραμματ. κατακρινοῦσιν θανάτῳ	ἰδοὺ ἀναβ. εἰς Ἱερουσαλήμ
		τελεσθ. τὰ γεγρ. διὰ προφητῶν
ταραδώσουσιν τ. ἔθνεσιν εἰς τὸ ἐμπαῖξαι	παραδώσουσιν τ. ἔθνεσιν καὶ ἐμπαίξουσιν αὐτῷ	παραδοθήσεται τ. ἔθνεσιν καὶ ἐμπαιχθήσεται καὶ ὑβρισθήσεται
	καὶ ἐμπτύσουσιν	καὶ ἐμπτυσθήσεται
καὶ μαστιγῶσαι σταυρῶσαι τῇ τρίτῃ ἡμ. ἐγερθήσεται	καὶ μαστιγώσουσιν καὶ ἀποκτενοῦσιν μετὰ τρεῖς ἡμ. ἀναστήσεται	καὶ μαστιγώσαντες ἀποκτενοῦσιν τῇ ἡμέρᾳ τῇ τρίτῃ ἀναστήσεται

This table shows:

a) that there is a substantial correspondence between the three evangelists for each one of the three predictions.

b) that the first prediction makes the Jewish leaders the agents of the SM's sufferings, while according to the second prediction the SM meets his fate at "the hands of men".

c) that the third prediction speaks of a double delivering of the SM (to the Jewish authorities and by them to the Gentiles), and as well contains a number of details on the SM's humiliation failing in the first two predictions.

d) that all three predictions speak of the SM's rising after three days or on the third day.

If we discount the details of the third prediction (mainly), there do not appear to be any compelling grounds for rejecting the substantial authenticity of the first and second predictions, as well as of the main items of the third prediction. We have already seen that Jesus in all probability had concluded that he would meet a violent death in the hands of the Jewish leaders. Words like πολλὰ   παθεῖν, ὑπὸ (ἀπὸ) τῶν πρεσβυτέρων καὶ ἀρχιερέων καὶ γραμματέων and ἀποκτανθῆναι in the first prediction are just the kind of words that would have been used to express such a conviction. The same is surely true of παραδίδοται εἰς χεῖρας ἀνθρώπων (ἁμαρτωλῶν) and of ἀποκτενοῦσιν in the second prediction, as well as of παραδοθήσεται τοῖς ἀρχιερεῦσιν καὶ γραμματεῦσιν and κατακρινοῦσιν θανάτῳ in the third prediction. The idea of necessity expressed by δεῖ (in the first prediction) is hardly a problem in view of the use of this term in the Gospels (see below).

There are two outstanding items in the third prediction: the SM's being delivered to the Gentiles and his resurrection after three days (Mk) or on the third day (Mt, Lk), (also in the first and second saying)[335]. The problem which the mention of resurrection raises is essentially a pseudo-problem. It is highly improbable that Jesus could have regarded his eventual death as an abrupt or tragic end of his mission. Such an assumption is contradicted by his teaching, his claims about himself and his actions, and in addition it is unsupported by his spiritual heritage. The OT spoke unequivocally of the final triumph of the Righteous One or the Servant of Yahweh beyond death (cf. e.g. Isa 53:10ff.). As for Jesus himself, he had spoken for example of the part he was to play both as witness[336] and as Judge at the final judgment[337]. Besides, the critical question arises: How could he promise his followers a life after death[338] if he could not himself look beyond his own death to vindication and triumph?[339] In view of the fact that the resurrection of the dead was an established tenet in certain sectors of Judaism, there does not seem to exist any reason for supposing that Jesus could not have spoken of his own resurrection[340]. As for the detail of the third day, this could have been concluded from Hos 6:2[341]. That Jesus had actually used an expression with such import becomes extremely probable from the fact that it is cited as Jesus' own words (though they are misconstrued) by the false witness at the trial (Mt 26:61 = Mk 14:58)[342].

To conclude this part of the discussion, we may note that the elements that have the greatest claim to authenticity are: δεῖ τὸν υἱὸν τοῦ ἀνθρώπου, which regards the SM as suffering, and at that by divine necessity,

---

335 The two expressions μετὰ τρεῖς ἡμέρας and τῇ τρίτῃ ἡμέρᾳ are equivalent in Greek. See also Taylor, *Mark*, 378.
336 Mt 10:32 = Lk 12:8.
337 Mt 16:27; Mk 8:28 = Lk 9:26.
338 Mt 10:37–38; 16:24–26 = Mk 8:34–37 = Lk 9:24–25.
339 Cf. Marshall, *Luke*, 368f.
340 Marshall, *Luke*, 371.
341 According to 1 Cor 15:4 this was a pre-Marcan tradition.
342 Lindars, *Jesus Son of Man*, 71: "it is very widely held that the saying is authentic. The witness is false in that the saying is misused to suggest a criminal intention on Jesus' part." Cf. also Borsch, *The Son of Man*, 353, 392f.; Marshall, *NTS* 12 (1965–6) 350.

and is thus unparalleled in Jewish tradition[343]; the frequent[344] and variously-used[345] παραδοθῆναι (16 times!) with the related εἰς χεῖρας ἀνθρώπων (ἀμαρτωλῶν) (6 times) and perhaps also τοῖς ἔθνεσιν (3 times, see below)[346]; and the widespread idea of resurrection (11 times!) without which the announced death is unthinkable (9 times with the specification on the third day, etc.)[347]. The expression πρεσβυτέρων, ἀρχιερέων, γραμματέων is, in view of Jesus' clash with them, also to be regarded as original[348]. This does not however imply that expressions like πολλὰ παθεῖν, ἀποκτανθῆναι, κατακρινοῦσιν θανάτῳ are automatically to be excluded as secondary. The probability is that these terms too go back to Jesus as they were necessary to the theme.

Can we relate the passion sayings to any relevant OT texts? It is not impossible that details like ἐμπαίξουσιν, ἐμπτύσουσιν, μαστιγώσουσιν and ὑβρισθήσεται are inspired by Isa 53:3: ἠτιμάσθη, καὶ οὐκ ἐλογίσθη, or still better Ps 22:7f. ὄνειδος ἀνθρώπων καὶ ἐξουδένημα λαοῦ ... ἐξεμυκτήρισάν με. There are however no verbal parallels which can demonstrate the connection. The closest parallel which the suffering sayings have with this Servant Song, is betwen παραδοθήσεται (in various forms) and κατακρινοῦσιν αὐτὸν θανάτῳ on the one hand and Isa 53: 12: ἀνθ' ὧν παρεδόθη εἰς θάνατον ἡ ψυχὴ αὐτοῦ ... διὰ τας ἁμαρτίας αὐτῶν παρεδόθη on the other. These two central words, παρεδόθη and θάνατον, are sufficient to connect the suffering sayings with Isa 53 and to bring the concept of the Servant into relation with that of the Son of Man. But at the same time it should be recognized that this text fails to account for the other important elements in the passion sayings. We are thus forced to conclude that though Isa 53 can explain some elements in the suffering sayings, it cannot account adequately for the phraseology of these sayings.

The connections with Daniel are both more copious and closer. To start with, the word δεῖ (102 times in the NT, of which 42 times in the Gospels) though impersonally construed and at times aligned with Greek and Hellenistic usage which expresses logical necessity or fate[349], has

---

343 The idea that Jesus' suffering is part of God's overall purpose is very widespread in παραδοθήσεται sayings of different types and points to its authenticity. See Mt 17:12 = Mk 9:12; Mt 16:21 = Mk 8:31 = Lk 9:22; Mt 26:24 = Mk 14:21 = Lk 22:22; Mt 20:28 = Mk 10:45.

344 E.g. Schweizer, *JBL* 79 (1960) 120.

345 Lindars, *Jesus Son of Man*, 68.

346 Though here we stand on less certain ground, τοῖς ἔθνεσιν cannot be rejected offhand. If it is true that the Sanhedrin did not have the right to inflict capital punishment, (cf. Blinzler, *Der Prozess Jesu*, 163–74) this expression would explain why the eventual death was expected to be carried out by the Gentiles. This circumstance might also explain the meagerly attested σταυρῶσαι.

347 Schweizer, *JBL* 79 (1960) 120f: "Thus it is probable that Jesus spoke of himself as the Son of Man who was to be humiliated and rejected by men, yet exalted by God".

348 Cf. Marshall, *NTS* 12 (1965–6) 349.

349 Cf. Grundmann, *TDNT*, II, 21f. For classical examples see Δημητράκος, *Μέγα Λεξικόν*, II, 1772f. and for the Hellenistic and the NT use see *BAG*, *sub* δεῖ.

in the NT its most characteristic usage in the idea of the personal will of God, or in the necessity which God's will implies[350]. Thus, the appearance of Elijah before that of the SM (Mt 17:10), Jesus' being about his Father's business (Lk 2:49), the fulfillment of Scripture with respect to Jesus' death (Lk 24:44), the eschatological events preceding the SM's coming (Mt 24:6 = Mk 13:7), the SM's sufferings and death (Mt 16:21 = Mk 8:31 = Lk 9:22, 24:7), the SM's being lifted up on the cross/exaltation (Jn 3:14; 12:34) and his resurrection from the dead (Jn 20:9) are all demanded by the $\delta\epsilon\hat{\iota}$ of God's will.

It is remarkable that in the LXX (apart from Daniel), in which the word occurs about 45 times, it is never used directly of God's will[351], let alone of what God's will has in store for the future or of what is decreed and must take place. The four examples of Daniel (LXX, Θ:2:28, 29 (bis); Θ: 2:45) are thus unique in the LXX in expressing the sovereign will of God to the performance of which all history is bent[352]. All these instances of $\delta\epsilon\hat{\iota}$ are in reference to Nebuchadnezzar's dream, which like the vision of chapter 7 is preoccupied with the course of events leading to the downfall of the four kingdoms and to the establishment of God's everlasting Kingdom through God's Agent, the Stone of chapter 2 or the 'SM' of chapter 7[353]. Here the expression $\ddot{\alpha}$ $\delta\epsilon\hat{\iota}$ $\gamma\epsilon\nu\acute{\epsilon}\sigma\vartheta\alpha\iota$ covers the remainder of human history, that is, the events which lead up to the 'SM's appearance and his investment with absolute power. The expression is taken over by Mt 24:6 = Mk 13:7 = Lk 21:9 in a similar context and is used to describe the events preceding the Son of Man's appearance with the clouds of heaven, as he who comes to put an end to human history and to initiate the new order of the Kingdom of God. In the first passion saying Jesus applies this Danielic $\delta\epsilon\hat{\iota}$ more narrowly to his own personal history and in particular to his destiny in his capacity as Son of Man. The Danielic $\delta\epsilon\hat{\iota}$, originally denoting the necessity of God's will with regard to the occurrence of historical events demanded for the accomplishment of his purpose, becomes for Jesus the inexorable *must* of divine necessity in reference to his own role and place as Son of Man in that divine purpose[354]. Here we reach bedrock. By means of this innovation, the traditional nature and function of the SM is widened to include that which according to Jesus' conviction is God's call to humiliation and suffering as the necessary preliminary to exaltation and glory[355]. In this Danielic $\delta\epsilon\hat{\iota}$, we have the key

---

350 Cf. Grundmann, *TDNT*, II, 23.

351 In Lev (LXX) 5:17 $\delta\epsilon\hat{\iota}$ is used in connection with prohibitive commandments. Prov (LXX) 22:14 is even more indirect.

352 The Aramaic expression מה די להוא (reflected in the LXX of 2:45:τὰ ἐσόμενα) denoting more futurity than necessity, may lie behind the passion variants μέλλει ὁ υἱὸς τοῦ ἀνθρώπου ... (Mt 17:22 = Mk 9:31 = Lk 9:44) and the future form which παραδίδοσθαι often takes. See Grundmann, *TDNT* II, 23.

353 Cf. Driver, *Daniel*, 26.

354 Cf. Mt 26:24 = Mk 14:21 = Lk 22:22.

355 Cf. e.g. Lk 17:22—25 which connects suffering with exaltation. See further Lk 24:26; Mt 26: 54.

to Jesus' view of his mission expressed by the phrase δεῖ γὰρ τὸν υἰὸν
τοῦ ἀνθρώπου . . .

We saw above that παραδοθήσεται etc. might be derived from Isa 53:
12. But that text cannot explain the important phrases . . . εἰς χεῖρας
ἀνθρώπων (ἀμαρτωλῶν) and . . . τοῖς ἔθνεσιν. These expressions can
however be explained in light of Dan 7. In describing the extraordinary
ascendancy to absolute rule and hybristic exercise of power of the little
horn, the author says: καὶ ῥήματα εἰς τὸν ὕψιστον λαλήσει καὶ τοὺς
ἁγίους τοῦ ὑψίστου κατατρίψει (Θ; παλαιώσει, MT: יבלא‎) . . . καὶ
παραδοθήσεται πάντα εἰς χεῖρας αὐτοῦ ἕως καιροῦ καὶ καιρῶν καὶ ἕως
ἡμίσους καιροῦ (LXX 7:25). Here we meet with an idea of παραδοθήσεται
which is much closer than that in Isa 53:12 to the παραδοθήσεται of the
suffering sayings. In Isa 53:12 παρεδόθη is used of the Servant's being
delivered up to death, whereas the suffering sayings demanded a being
delivered up to the power of authorities[356]. This is precisely what we find
in Dan 7:25. The saints are delivered to the power of the beast: they are
defeated (7:21) and decimated (7:25, BDB: "harass continually") by the
little horn.

Thus Dan 7:25 not only supplies a perfect parallel to the usage of
παραδοθήσεται in the suffering sayings, which is absent from Isa 53, it
also explains the phrases . . . εἰς χεῖρας ἀνθρώπων (ἀμαρτωλῶν) and
. . . τοῖς ἔθνεσιν. The first of these phrases has its equivalent in . . . εἰς
τὰς χεῖρας αὐτοῦ (Dan 7:25) said of the little horn to whose power
the saints are delivered. The expression ἀνθρώπων ἀμαρτωλῶν has a
dynamic correspondence to αὐτοῦ in Dan 7:25 used of the little horn. In
Jewish tradition the Gentile Antiochus Epiphanes (i.e. the little horn) is
known as ἀμαρτωλός [357]. This understanding is reflected in 2 Th 2:3ff.
which, in reference to the little horn of Dan 7:25 (and 11:36), speaks
of ὁ ἄνθρωπος τῆς ἀνομίας (or ἀμαρτίας according to the Majority reading).

The expression μετὰ τρεῖς ἡμέρας is probably derived from Hos 6:2.
Nevertheless the idea of the temporary abandonment of the Son of Man
in the hands of his enemies is actually found in the Danielic expression
ἕως καιροῦ καὶ καιρῶν καὶ ἡμίσους καιροῦ (7:25) said of the temporary abandonment of the saints in the hands of the little horn. Another
similarity between the passion sayings and Dan 7:25 is that vindication
and exaltation are held out to the Son of Man, as in the case of the
saints, following the time of their abandonment.

---

356 Thus, παραδοθήσεται εἰς θάνατον never occurs in the Suffering sayings. Mt 26:2 παραδίδοται εἰς τὸ σταυρωθῆναι implies a being delivered to such as have the right/power to
crucify him.

357 Cf. 1 Mc 1:10 which describes Antiochus as ῥίζα ἀμαρτωλός and 2:48 which designates
him as ἀμαρτωλός absolutely. Also the contingent in whose charge Antiochus placed the
captured Jerusalem is spoken of as ἔθνος ἀμαρτωλόν (1 Mc 1:34). With this cf. Sib Or, III,
388—400. Cf. also Hengel, Judaism and Hellenism, 225, 267—309 passim, for the impression
of Antiochus on the Jews; Goldstein, I Maccabees, 219f. and Rowley, Darius the Mede, 115—
22.

Finally, there is a correspondence of another kind between the suffering sayings and Dan 7:25. Jesus' betrayal and sufferings are characterized as his hour[358]. It is the hour in which the Son of Man is to all appearances placed at the disposal of the Jewish leaders, or of sinful men, or of the Gentiles. Yet Luke lets us see another dimension when he has Jesus address his captors: αὕτη ἐστὶν ὑμῶν ἡ ὥρα καὶ ἡ ἐξουσία τοῦ σκότους [359]. It is a well established conclusion of scholarship that NT terms like ἀρχαί and ἐξουσίαι often fluctuate in meaning between cosmic powers and earthly potentates, and that sometimes a double reference is intended[360]. This is often said to be the case for example in 1 Cor 2:6ff., where the reference to the ἄρχοντες τοῦ αἰῶνος τούτου who crucified Jesus is supposed to go beyond Caiaphas and Pilate, to the powers of darkness at work. Now this is exactly what we find in the Book of Daniel. We have analyzed the Danielic concept of the Beast as consisting of an evil spiritual power acting behind the king of a given state. To such a power the saints are said to be delivered up and such is the power in control behind those to whose disposal Jesus is abandoned. Jewish tradition, which represents the Son of Man in royal dignity and as Judge of the world (Dan, 1 En) has these powers subjected to him and offering to him their service (Dan 7:27b). But in assuming the role of a suffering Son of Man Jesus accepts his abandonment to these powers!

We thus see that not only the specific phraseology of certain expressions like δεῖ τὸν υἱὸν τοῦ ἀνθρώπου, παραδοθήσεται, εἰς χεῖρας ἀνθρώπων (ἁμαρτωλῶν), τοῖς ἔθνεσιν, (even πολλὰ παθεῖν by deduction) is derived from Dan 7 (esp. vs. 25), but what is even more impressive other important ideas underlying the suffering sayings, like his being delivered up to the powers of darkness operating behind earthly authorities, the temporary character of abandonment and the ensuing vindication and exaltation, are derived directly from Daniel.

One final matter calls for attention. In Dan 7:25 it is the saints not the 'SM' who is said to suffer at the hands of the little horn. With what justification then have I derived the Gospel SM's sufferings from this text, especially in view of my refusal to identify the 'SM' with the saints[361]? It is indeed true that the Danielic 'SM' is conceived of as a heavenly being, is distinct from the saints, and is equated only with ʾElyônîn. There is thus no question of the 'SM' personally suffering at the hands of Antiochus. The only connection of the 'SM' with suffering in Dan 7 is on account of his solidarity as leader of the saints who suffer. The situation with Jesus is however different. As Stuhlmacher has pointed out, Jesus assumes the role of substitute for his people. It is a question of Jesus'

---

358 Mt 26:45; Mk 14:35, 41; Cf. also Jn 7:30; 8:20; 12:23, 27; 13:1; 17:1.

359 Lk 22:53.

360 See discussion in Chapter Two, and Caragounis *The Ephesian Mysterion*, pp. 157–61 for discussion and references.

361 See Chapter Two. See also the discussion under 'The nature of the SM Messianology' below.

Existenzstellvertretung für die Vielen![362] Since Jesus assumed this role it was natural for him to apply all those ideas, which in Dan 7 relate to the suffering of the saints, to himself and to see his role as the suffering Son of Man along the lines described in Dan 7 of the saints. A suffering Son of Man is unknown in Daniel, 1 Enoch and IV Ezra. In the Gospels such a figure is a development by Jesus himself, who understanding his mission to be to give his life as a ransom for many, combined in his new conception of the Son of Man, the exalted traits of the Danielic 'SM' with the humiliation and suffering of the saints, and thus gave a new meaning to the idea of exaltation and royal rule — one that goes via suffering.

iii. The Exalted Son of Man. Of the three classes of SM sayings this is the one which has been traditionally considered the most authentic one[363]. Hence, the case for the authenticity of an exalted SM is more straightforward. Three sayings (actually one of them being a group) will be considered: Lk 12:8f. par.; Mt 26:64 = Mk 14:62 = Lk 22:69 and the SM saying in the eschatological discourse, Mt 24 = Mk 13 = Lk 21.

Before entering the discussion of the individual sayings it may be pointed out that the inquiry into the Suffering sayings showed that there are no valid grounds for rejecting the authenticity of the tradition that Jesus had looked beyond his death to vindication and exaltation[364], and that he had promised his followers a reward after death. This implies that the Exaltation sayings not only are in line with the Suffering sayings, but are even presupposed[365]. Jesus' event does not end in defeat and death, there is also the sequel of exaltation. That humility goes before honour is a well-known OT tenet[366], while the schema of Suffering-Exaltation in the NT[367] appears to have been influenced by Jesus' own teaching about himself[368]. Moreover, the connections of the Suffering sayings with the Danielic antecedents as well as the implicit promise of vindication in the latter, were also established. Finally, in the case of the Earthly Life sayings we were able to show that Jesus exercised an authority on

---

362 *Werden und Wirken,* 426.

363 Schweizer, *Geschichte der Leben-Jesu-Forschung,* 390ff.; Jeremias, *Theologie* I, 254f.; Bultmann, *Theology* I, 30; Bornkamm, *Jesus of Narazeth,* 162f.; Tödt, *Der Menschensohn,* 29; Hahn, *Titles of Jesus,* 28ff.; Higgins, *Jesus and the Son of Man,* 185ff.; *id., The Son of Man in the Teaching of Jesus* 2. Even Vielhauer, *Aufsätze,* 133, who rejects all SM sayings, thinks this type is oldest.

364 Cf. Bowker's interesting thesis of how suffering is combined with vindication, in *JTS* 28 (1977) 44−8. See further Farrer, *A Study in Mark,* 285−89.

365 Cullmann, *Christology,* 164.

366 Cf. e.g. the story of Joseph's exaltation after his degradation. See further Job 5:11; Prov 15:33; 18:12; 22:4; Isa 53:12.

367 E.g. Rm 8:17; Phil 2:5−11; 2 Tim 2:12; Heb 2:9f.; 5:8f.; Ja 4:10; 1 Pt 3:18−22; 4:13f.; 5:6; Rev 5:9−13.

368 E.g. Mt 16:29ff. = Mk 8:34ff. = Lk 9:23ff.; Mt 18:4; Mt 20:26ff. = Mk 9:35; 10:43ff.; Mt 23: 12; Lk 14:11; 18:14; 22:27.

earth which had its justification in his identification of himself with the Danielic 'SM'. These general considerations indicate that there is really nothing surprising or unnatural about it if Jesus sometimes spoke more directly of the SM's more typically Danielic characteristics (i.e. the exalted traits of the 'SM') with respect to his future vindication.

1. Lk 12:8f. par. In discussions of Exaltation sayings a not infrequent procedure is to begin with the above text. Especially those scholars who are of the opinion that Jesus differentiated between the SM and himself[369] usually make this saying their starting point[370] and then proceed to look for a differentiation in other sayings as well. The majority of scholars, however, with good reason have rejected what might perhaps be described as a scholarly aberration[371]. In favour of the authenticity of Lk 12: 8f. may be urged that there is nothing in this saying which might not have been said by Jesus. On the contrary a confessional *Sitz im Leben* for this saying in the post-Easter Christian kerygma is shattered on the fact that the term SM does not figure in the kerygma of the Early Church. In addition, the superficial possibility afforded by the wording of the saying for distinguishing the SM from Jesus tells against the saying's being a creation of the Church, which clearly believed in only one Son of Man, namely Jesus[372]. Further, that by SM Jesus could not possibly have referred to another person than himself is proved beyond all reasonable doubt by the finality which he assigned to his own person and teaching, leaving no room for another figure after him[373]. The saying is accepted as authentic without the condition of differentiating between the SM and Jesus by

---

369 E.g. Bultmann, *History,* 112; Tödt, *Der Menschensohn,* 53ff.; Higgins, *Jesus and the Son of Man,* 58ff.; Hahn, *Titles of Jesus,* 28ff.; Bornkamm, *Jesus of Narazeth,* 175ff., 228. See also Maddox, *ABR* 19 (1971) 44.

370 Cf. Jeremias, *Theology* I, 275; Vögtle, in *Logia,* 77.

371 See e.g. the refutations by Marshall, *NTS* 12 (1965–6) 338f.; Leivestad, *NTS* 18 (1971–2) 249, 261f., and Jeremias, *Theology,* I, 275f. Further see Lindars, *Jesus Son of Man,* 48–59, who is totally unconcerned with the theory of differentiation; Cullmann, *Christology,* 156; Schweizer, *JBL* 79 (1960) 120ff.; Stauffer, *NovT* 1(1956) 81ff.; Fuller, *The Mission and Achievement of Jesus,* 95ff.; T.W. Manson, *The Teaching of Jesus, passim;* Casey, *Son of Man,* 167.

372 The parallel in Mt 10:32f. has replaced the title with the personal pronoun. Jeremias, *Theology* I, 262f., cannot be said to have proved that whenever a SM saying has an alternative ἐγώ form, the latter is to be regarded as the original form. Cf. Mt 16:21 (αὐτός) with Mk 8:31 (υἱὸν τοῦ ἀνθρώπου). The fact that this saying is so widespread in the titular form speaks for the originality of the SM title in it. See also Lindars, *Jesus Son of Man,* 48ff.

373 Cf. e.g. his claim to be the coming one whose forerunner is John (Mt 3:3–15; Mk 1:2–11; Lk 3:3–17; Jn 1:19–34 with which cf. Mt 11:10; Lk 7:24); his implicitly affirmative answer to the question whether he was the Messiah (Mt 11:2–10; Lk 7:18–27); his authoritative declaration of God's final revelation and will (e.g. Mt 5:21–48); his claim to forgive sins (Mt 9:6 par.), and his claim that men's future destiny would be decided in accordance with their acceptance or rejection of his message (e.g. Mt 7:24–29).

most scholars, a specimen of whom includes Goppelt[374], Higgins[375], Marshall[376], Borsch[377], Lindars[378], Leivestad[379], Maddox[380] and Riesner[380a].

This saying is undoubtedly related to Mk 8.38 = Lk 9:26 (= Mt 16: 27)[381]. Both sayings have one and the same theme: the confession of Jesus on earth as a condition for the SM's confession of his confessors before God and his angels[382] at his exaltation. The connections with Dan 7:13f. are so obvious that it is unnecessary to belabour the point: the Son of Man, the Father (i.e. the Aged One[383]), the presence of angels, the theme of judgment and of acknowledgment or rejection make these texts a clear and conscious echo of the contents of Dan 7:9–14, 27[384]. In addition, our texts sustain good parallels with the thought of the *Parables*[385], which also develops the Danielic theme.

2. Mt 26:64 = Mk 14:62 = Lk 22:69. For the problems associated with the trial accounts as well as for the demonstration of their substantial reliability reference may be made above[386]. The key place which the SM saying holds in the trial scene and its being the decisive factor for Jesus' condemnation is widely recognized[387]. In the Matthean and Marcan versions Jesus answers the high priest's question with a quotation of Dan 7: 13 and Ps 110:1. Ps 110:1 is embedded within the quotation from Daniel. The reason for this appears to be that the 'lord' of Ps 110:1 was too indefinite a term, and hence was substituted by SM of Dan 7:13. On the other hand, $\kappa\alpha\vartheta\dot{\eta}\mu\epsilon\nu o\nu$ $\dot{\epsilon}\kappa$ $\delta\epsilon\xi\iota\tilde{\omega}\nu$ adds the dimension of final exaltation, on God's right hand which is only implicit in Dan 7 9–14 and was thus necessary. That Dan 7:13 is not quoted in full before the allusion to

---

374 In *Mensch und Menschensohn*, 20ff.
375 *The Son of Man in the Teaching of Jesus*, 81 (apparently). Higgins has changed his position *vis à vis* his earlier work.
376 *NTS* 12 (1965–6) 343ff.; *id., Luke*, 515.
377 *The Son of Man in Myth and History*, 358.
378 *Jesus Son of Man*, 48ff., 87.
379. *NTS* 18 (1971–2) 261 (apparently).
380 *ABR* 19 (1971) 44 note 10.
380a *Jesus als Lehrer*, 346f.
381 Lindars, *Jesus Son of Man*, 48. See also Lindeskog, *ST* 22 (1968) 150–60.
382 I cannot share Higgins' view (*Jesus and the Son of Man*, 58) that "angels of God" is "a circumlocution for God". Rather, "angels" is a conscious echo of Dan 7:10ff.
383 Cf. Moule, *The Origin of Christoloty*, 26.
384 On Lindars' view of Lk 12:8f. and my objections to it see Chapter One, In Recent Research.
385 See e.g. I En 62:5 and 69:27, 29 said of "that Son of Man" and 45:3; 49:2; 55:4 and 62:2 said of the Elect One.
386 Chapter Three: The NT Evidence.
387 E.g. Taylor, *Mark*, 564; Beyer, *TDNT* I, 623; Guilding, *EvQ* 23 (1951) 210–2; Borsch, *NTS* 14 (1967–8) 567; Bruce, *OTS* 20 (1977) 26; Derrett, *The Trial of Jesus*, 31: Catchpole, *The Trial of Jesus*, 141ff.; Linton, *NTS* 7 (1960–1) 260f.; Marshall, *Luke*, 851. Ford, *JBL* 87 (1968) 262; Farrer, *A Study in St. Mark*, 286.

Ps 110:1 is made, is most probably owing to the desire to portray the Son of Man first in his exalted state on God's right hand and then depict him as coming to hold judgment, by citing the well-known words of Dan 7: 13. Ὄψεσθε is in all probability not derived from Zech 12:10 (ἐπιβλέψ-ονται), but from ἐθεώρουν . . . ὡς υἱὸς ἀνθρώπου . . . of Dan 7:13. The divergences in Lk 22:69 are so many that he appears to be following another tradition[388]. However, even though the quotation from Dan 7: 13 fails, the presence of the title and its interpretation by the Jewish authorities in terms of Dan 7:13f. is sufficient to bring also Lk 22:69 into connection with Dan 7. In all three accounts it becomes thus obvious that by applying to himself the designation and functions of the exalted Figure of Dan 7, who is there equated with the exalted Being styled ʾElyônîn, Jesus had committed, in the eyes of the Sanhedrin, the final blasphemy.

3. Mt 24 = Mk 13 = Lk 21. The group of SM logia found in Lk 17:22–30 = Mt 24:27, 37 have been defended as authentic sayings of Jesus by e.g. Colpe[389] and Jeremias[390]. Jeremias expresses the matter thus:

> In the sayings of Jesus, as in Jewish apocalyptic, Son of man is a term of glory. If we keep to what was recognized on p. 263 as the earliest stratum of Son of man *logia*, something like the following picture emerges. When the persecution of the community has reached its climax (§22), the vision of Daniel 7.13, understood as a prophecy, will be realized. It will come suddenly, like a flash of lightning from a clear sky (Matt. 24.27 par. Luke 17.24), when no one expects it (Matt. 24.37, 39 par. Luke 17.26; also without parallel, 17.30). Veiled in clouds, surrounded by hosts of angels, in divine glory, the Son of man will appear (Matt. 13.26; cf. John 1:51). He will sit down on the throne at God's right hand (Luke 22.69) and send out his angels to gather together his elect from the four winds (Mark 13.27). He will hold judgment (Luke 21.36; Luke 22.69 is also a threat of judgment) with the twelve representatives of the people of the twelve tribes as assessors (Matt. 19.28 par. Luke 22.30, cf. Dan 7.9f.; I Cor 6. 2f.)[391].

Jeremias refuses to distinguish between Jesus and the Son of Man. "The third person", he says "expresses the 'mysterious relationship' which exists between Jesus and the Son of Man: he is not yet the Son of man, but he will be exalted to be the Son of man" i.e. the "term of glory derived from Dan 7.13"[392]. Jeremias therefore has no doubt that Jesus spoke of himself as the coming Son of Man exalted and empowered to hold judgment and that in doing so he derived the whole imagery of the Son of Man, his exaltation and his Judge-function from Dan 7:13f.

Jeremias actually holds eight synoptic SM sayings to be authentic: Mt 24:27 = Lk 17:24 ; Mt 24:37 = 39 = Lk 17:26; Mt 10:23; 25:31; Lk 17:

---

388 Similarly Catchpole, *The Trial of Jesus*, 183ff.; Marshall, *Luke*, 847f. and authors cited there.
389 *TDNT* VIII, 433–37. Colpe does not seem to include Lk 17:22. This saying is accepted by Cullmann, *Christology*, 156.
390 *Theology* I, 263, 272.
391 *Theology* I, 272.
392 *Theology* I, 276.

22, 30; 18:8; 21:36 (as well as Jn 1:51)[393] all (with the exception of Lk 17:22) Exaltation sayings. This list is significant because apart from Mt 25:31 and Lk 17:22 it coincides with the sayings which Colpe accepts as authentic, he however adds Lk 22:69 = Mt 26:63ff. = Mk 14:62 and Mt 24:30a[394].

Colpe's arguments for accepting the authenticity of these sayings are as follows: Mt 24:27 par. is considered authentic because it "plainly sets aside the idea of a political Messiah in favour of a heavenly bringer of salvation"[395]. Mt 24:37 par. "goes back in substance to Jesus Himself" because it sustains a comparison between the Son of Man's sudden coming and the coming of the Flood of Noah (and the destruction of Sodom Lk 17: 30)[396]. Lk 21:36 is accepted as genuine on the "principle that inauthenticity has to be proven rather than authenticity"[397]. With regard to Lk 18:8 Colpe says that "the point made here in a question is made again in Lk 17:24, 26, 30, as an intimation and in Lk 21:36 as a demand". The grounds for authenticity here is: "If one cannot understand Lk 18:8b more precisely, it must be regarded basically as part of Jesus' own preaching"[398]. Lk 22:69. which is to be assessed independently of Mk 14:62, and in which the phrase μετὰ τῶν νεφελῶν τοῦ οὐρανοῦ has not yet been added, is accepted as genuine because the Son of Man's activity as Judge is in line with Mt 24:27 = Lk 17:24 and 24:37 = Lk 17:26[399]. Mt 10:23 is accepted as authentic partly on the ground of it being unfulfilled prophecy and partly because only as such could it have "survived the tendency, which is particularly clear in Mt., to ascribe to Jesus a work among the Gentiles"[400]. Lastly, "the sign of the Son of Man" (Mt 24:30) is probably older "than Mk 13:26, and par. which is plainly modelled on Dan 7:13". It is authentic because "It is hardly possible that there could be any other source for it than Jesus' own preaching"[401].

If Colpe and Jeremias are right, we have here a sufficiently broad basis of Exaltation sayings which can actually, in one way or another, be related to the Danielic 'SM'. The question, however, is whether the four sayings of Mt 24:27, 30a, 37 and 39 accepted by Colpe and Jeremias, are the only SM sayings in the eschatological discourse that can make a reasonable claim to authenticity[402]. To be more specific, the question needs

---

393 *Theology* I, 263.
394 *TDNT* VIII, 433–37.
395 *TDNT* VIII, 433.
396 *TDNT* VIII, 434.
397 *TDNT* VIII, 434.
398 *TDNT* VIII, 435.
399 *TDNT* VIII, 435. Cf. also 436: "The authenticity of Lk 22:69 can be contested only if the historicity of the whole judgment scene is called in question".
400 *TDNT* VIII, 437.
401 *TDNT* VIII, 437.
402 Cf. Colpe, *TDNT* VIII, 438: "at least this basic core of sayings is authentic". See also Kümmel, *Promise and Fulfilment,* 95–104.

to be put, What constitutes an adequate basis for rejecting e.g. Mt 24:30b = Mk 13:26 = Lk 21:27? To apply Colpe's own criteria for his acceptance of certain SM sayings, Doesn't this saying "plainly set aside the idea of a political Messiah in favour of a heavenly bringer of salvation" just as Mt 24:27 par.? And can't it sustain a comparison with the suddenness of judgment at the flood and the destruction of Sodom as Mt 24:37 par.? And doesn't it imply the Son of Man's activity as Judge, and is this not in line with Mt 24:27 par.? And if Mt 24:30a is accepted as authentic because there could hardly be any other source for it, could not the same be said of 24:30b, in view of Jesus' application of Dan 7 to himself? And why is "the principle that inauthenticity has to be proved rather than authenticity", which was invoked as the sole and adequate argument for accepting Lk 21:36, not applied in the case of Mt 24:30b? If therefore five of Colpe's arguments for the authenticity of five different logia demonstrably give Mt 24:30b their combined support, is it not, on Colpe's principles, unjustifiable to refuse this saying authentic status?

Colpe's grounds for rejecting this saying are twofold: one, because the saying occurs in a "sequence of eschatological events", and two, because it makes "direct reference to Dan 7:13"![403] These are rather strange grounds for rejecting a SM saying. With respect to the first objection it may be pointed out that Mt 24:27 and 24:30a too, occur in a "sequence of eschatological events" but are nonetheless accepted by Colpe! As for the sayings' "direct reference to Dan 7:13" it may be asked: What is strange about it? Why could not Jesus have cited Dan 7:13?[404] In this study abundant proof is forthcoming[405] that Dan 7 lies at the basis of Jesus' proclamation and forms one of the main presuppositions for his message. That Jesus actually could cite Daniel 7:13f. is proved for example from Mt 25:31 accepted by Jeremias and especially from Mt 26:64 = Mk 14:62 = Lk 22:69 accepted by most scholars[406] and — Colpe himself![407] Jeremias, so far from attaching any weight to Colpe's objections, actually makes the presence of Dan 7 motifs in Jesus' SM sayings one of his criteria for accepting certain SM sayings as genuine![408]

It must therefore be concluded that Colpe has not produced compelling arguments for rejecting Mt 24:30b. In favour of the authenticity of Mt 24:30b two additional arguments may be urged: a) Given Jesus' use of Dan 7 motifs in speaking of himself as the Son of Man, there is hardly any reason why he might not have utilized the most conspicious character-

---

403 *TDNT* VIII, 450.
404 Cf. Hartman, *Prophecy Interpreted,* 246, "He (sc. Jesus) used the teaching methods of his time ... sometimes at least He based His teaching on the Scriptures".
405 See also discussion below.
406 See above (note 387) and Chapter Three: The NT Evidence.
407 *TDNT* VIII, 435. Cf. Colpe's own words: "The direct reference to Dan 7:13 in Mk 13:26, for which there is a parallel in the older tradition only at Mk 14:62 ..." How does the fact that "there is a parallel ... only at Mt 14:62" make Mt 24:30 inauthentic?
408 *Theology* I, 265.

istics of the Danielic 'SM', such as his glorious coming, his exaltation, his kingly and Judge functions, in other words, just those traits that were the most relevant in describing his future and exalted state as Son of Man. b) A subject so special as the eschatological discourse and hypothetically so different from Jesus' characteristic teaching could hardly be the invention of the Early Church.

Another argument urged against the authenticity of 24:30b is the alleged problem of the structure of vs. 30, as a whole, which is supposed to indicate the secondary nature of 24:30b. This is somehow connected with the interpretation of 24:30a "the sign of the SM". The options here are that the genitive τοῦ υἱοῦ τοῦ ἀνθρώπου is either subjective-possessive or appositional-explanative. Higgins[409] opts for the former alternative and interprets the sign as the cross. This interpretation is based on three grounds:

a) In Lk 11:30 the sign is the SM himself (just as in Jonah's case), but in Mt 12:40 the sign cannot be equated with the SM because the text speaks of Jonah's "submarine adventures"[410]. Higgins concludes: "This renders unlikely the equation of the sign of the Son of man with the Son of man in Matt. xxiv. 30"[411]. This is a false reasoning. In Isa (LXX) 8: 18 Ἰδοὺ ἐγὼ καὶ τὰ παιδία ἅ μοι ἔδωκεν ὁ Θεός, καὶ ἔσται εἰς σημεῖα καὶ τέρατα τῷ οἴκῳ Ἰσραήλ shows that Isaiah and his children are no signs in themselves, but become signs to Israel by performing or undergoing certain actions (e.g. walking "naked and barefoot" 20:2ff.) demanded by the prophetic calling[412]. Similarly, the sign of Jonah is not Jonah as such, nor his preaching[413], but is to be found in his "submarine adventure" which functioned as God's seal upon his mission and brought the Ninevites to repentance[414]. Thus, Mt 12:40 does not rule out the equation of the sign with the SM in 24:30, as Higgins claims.

b) Higgins' second argument is that the tribes of the earth mourn at the sight of the sign, that is, before they have seen the SM[415]. This interpretation is difficult to justify. Higgins presumes what he is supposed to prove (i.e. the difference of the sign from the SM). To assume the result and then use it as a basis to prove its correctness is surely circular argumentation. Mt 24:30 surely does not differentiate between the sign and the SM. The verb φανήσεται is punctiliar[416]. Here it is used ingressively of the inbreaking of the SM's appearance. It corresponds to the ἐξέρχεται ἀπὸ ἀνατολῶν (said of the lightning in 24:27) with which the SM's com-

409 *NTS* 9 (1962–3) 380–2 and more fully in *Jesus and the SM,* 108–14 and 133–40.
410 Manson, *The Sayings of Jesus,* 89.
411 *NTS* 9 (1962–3) 381.
412 See Helfmeyer, *TDOT,* I, 186.
413 See Jeremias, *TDNT* III, 409.
414 Lk 11:30 does not specify, but Mt 12:40 does so. See also Jeremias, *TDNT* III, 409.
415 *Jesus and the SM,* 111f.
416 Cf. Jannaris, *Historical Grammar,* § 1882; Moulton, *Prolegomena,* 150; Robertson, *Grammar,* 356f., 871.

ing is compared. The future ὄψονται as such can be linear (as in Mt 5:8, Jn 1:50; 19:37: ὄψονται εἰς ὃν ἐξεκέντησαν!; Rev 22:4) or punctiliar (as in Jn 1:39; Heb 12:4)[417]. Here, as in the similar saying at Jn 19:37 the sense is linear and corresponds to the linear φαίναται ἕως δυσμῶν of 24:27. The duration of linearity is, of course, a relative matter and often depends on the nature of the verb, but the ὄψονται here surely envisions the descent in glory, the entourage, the mission of the angels and the ingathering of the elect, i.e. a clearly linear aspect. The mourning begins at the first glimpse of the SM. That the third clause καὶ ὄψονται... is not intended as a third scene, as Higgins thinks, is shown by the omission of τότε. This word occurs twice: once in connection with the appearance of the sign, i.e. the Son of Man, and once in connection with the reaction of the tribes. The ὄψονται clause is intended as a direct continuation of the τότε φανήσεται clause. The mourning is placed in between because only in this way can Matthew, free from the negative effects of the SM's coming, concentrate upon the positive ones, which actually form the climax.

c) Higgins' third argument is that Mt 24:30 answers the disciples' question in 24:3 "What will be the sign of your parousia"[418]. Therefore 24:30a must supply the sign, which Higgins, without a shred of evidence in the NT, supposes to be the cross. He admits, however, that "the explanation of the sign here supported is incapable of proof"[419]. The most decisive objection to this interpretation is that Mt 24:30 does not describe any sign. In the absence of any other explanation the explanation of "the sign" ought to be found in the explanative-genitive "the Son of Man".

In support of my reasoning are the following considerations: Mt 24:3 contains three questions[420], concerning the destruction of the temple, the sign of his coming and the end of the world. The absence of the second question in Mark and Luke as well as their omission of the text of Mt 24:30a might appear to support Higgins' thesis that vs. 30a gives the sign demanded in vs. 3. However, it should not be overlooked that Mk 13:4f. and Lk 21:8 presuppose a question like the one in Mt 24:3: "What will be the sign of your parousia?" Since therefore Mk 13:4f. and Lk 21:8 are unthinkable without some such question, we should suspect one of those not too infrequent lapses of authors, whereby they write down less than they actually have in mind. The sign for which the disciples were asking was the sign of the times (Mt 16:3) which would help them determine the time of his return. In 24:4—29 we have an attempt to supply chiefly

---

417 Robertson, *Grammar*, 871. To the above linear examples may be added Acts 26:16.
418 *Jesus and the SM*, 109f.
419 *Jesus and the SM*, 114. Higgins' view is rejected by e.g. Rengstorf, *TDNT* VII, 237 note 264 and Colpe, *TDNT* VIII, 437.
420 It is not one question, as Higgins construes it and then finds it answered in 24:30 a (*NTS* 9 (1962–3) 381). In *Jesus and the SM*, 109f. he modifies a little, although in the end it comes to the same thing.

by means of Danielic imagery, an answer — but only an answer — to these questions, especially the first and third, by describing in general terms the upheavals, pestilences, natural catastrophes and the rise of false messiahs who will precede the end[421]. Any more definite sign is not given. This is thoroughly coherent with Jesus' consistent refusal to furnish signs[422], and with the idea of watchfulness. The day and the hour are known to the Father alone[423]. The SM is to come suddenly as a thief in the night[424]. Mt 24:30a is certainly an allusion to 24:3[425], but not as supplying 'the sign', but as refusing to supply it! The text says in effect that no sign can be given outside of the SM himself[426], let alone the monstrous idea of some that the sign will afford a last chance for repentance. The ultimate and most authentic sign is the presence of the Son of Man himself[427]. No sign preceding him will be given; he will be his own announcer or herald![428]

The conclusion from the above investigation is that there are no compelling grounds, either structural or contextual, for separating Mt 24:30a from 24:30b, nor any other decisive grounds for rejecting the authenticity of 24:30b[429]. This verse is accepted as genuine by e.g. Torrey[430], Borsch[431], Kümmel[432], Hooker[433], Marshall[434], and France[435].

---

421 Ellis, *Luke*, 242.

422 Cf. e.g. Mt 12:39; 16:4; Mk 8:12; Lk 11:19; Acts 1:7.

423 Mt 24:36 = Mk 13:32.

424 Mt 24:42–44 = Mk 13:35–36.

425 This probably explains why it fails in Mk and Lk.

426 Similarly Gundry, *Matthew*, 488; Schniewind, *Matthäus*, 244f.; Allen, *Matthew*, 258f. and Lindars, *Jesus SM*, 128f. There may actually be an allusion to the personal character of the sign as in Mt 12:39f. par.

427 Glasson, *JTS* 15 (1964) 299–300, has put forward the thesis that the occurrence of σημεῖον and σάλπιγξ in Mt 24:30f. points to the influence of certain texts in Isa, Jer, the Eighteen Benedictions, etc., which speak of the gathering of Israel. The meaning of σημεῖον is "ensign" or "standard". Glasson's thesis is impressive, and might have been accepted were it not for the fact that it too, like Higgins' thesis, is subject to the decisive criticism made above, which applies to any theory of differentiation between the sign and the SM.

428 Cf. Herodotus' apt description (I, 79) of how Cyrus with unprecedented speed pursues Croesus to Sardeis and becomes himself the herald of his own coming: ἐλάσας γὰρ τὸν στρατόν ἐς τὴν Λυδίαν αὐτὸς (sc. Cyrus) ἄγγελος Κροίσῳ ἐληλύθεε!

429 Casey's argument against the authenticity of Mt 24:30 (*Son of Man*, 165–78) is unfortunately vitiated by erroneous assumptions (e.g. regarding the interpretation of the 'SM', see my criticism, *passim* and cf. Farrer, *A Study in Mark*, 269), incorrect reasoning (see my frequent criticism) and an almost fanatic argumentation for the Aramaic idiom being the key to the NT Son of Man. Casey's claim that the Church by combining the Aramaic idiom with Dan 7 turned Jesus' innocent, reticent 'I' into a full fledged messianic title and made of Jesus something he had never dreamed of hardly squares with the NT data.

430 *Documents of the Primitive Church*, 12ff.

431 *The SM in Myth and History*, 361ff.

432 *Promise and Fulfilment*, 103, note 50 (in principle).

433 *The SM in Mark*, 148ff.

434 *Luke*, 777.

435 *Jesus and the OT*, 90, 106f.

The eschatological discourse is considered to be the finished product of the Early Church. It is widely held, however, that this finished product has grown around an authentic nucleus which goes back to Jesus[436]. Hartman speaks of an "original 'midrash' " given by Jesus in private[437]. Busch considered the isolation of Jesus' sayings from the accretions an impossible undertaking[438], and Hartman abstained from the attempt to isolate the hard core, though he saw it in Mk 13:5b–8, 12–16, 19–22 and 24–27[439] and was of the opinion that it contained the main Danielic elements including the Son of Man. Since a minimum of it is presupposed by 1 and 2 Th, that is, only "about 15 years after the death of Jesus"[440], Hartman considered it highly probable that the original midrash went back to Jesus.

Though the following presents a comparison of the eschatological discourse *as it stands now*, it can still give a valid impression of Danielic connections, especially as several SM sayings — even if Mt 24:30b were to be rejected — are now widely accepted as authentic sayings of Jesus. This discourse not only makes several allusions to Daniel but also in its structure it owes much to the thoughts expressed in that Book[441]. Hartman has given an almost exhaustive list of elements in the eschatological discourse which he considers have their main source of inspiration in Daniel[442]. More importantly Mt 24:15 (= Mk 13:14) claims to be actually citing "Daniel the prophet" (sc. 9:27; 12:11), while Dan 7:13 is expressly cited in Mt 24:30 (= Mk 13:26 = Lk 21:27): ὄψονται τὸν υἱὸν τοῦ ἀνθρώπου ἐρχόμενον ἐπὶ τῶν νεφελῶν τοῦ οὐρανοῦ (Mk 13:26:ἐν νεφέλαις; Lk 21:27.ἐν νεφέλῃ). The Matthean version is the closest one to the Danielic text: Θ: μετὰ τῶν νεφελῶν τοῦ οὐρανοῦ ὡς υἱὸς ἀνθρώπου ἐρχόμενος ; LXX: ἐπὶ τῶν νεφελῶν τοῦ οὐρανοῦ ὡς υἱὸς

436　E.g. Kümmel, ˉPromise and Fulfilment, 99; Lane, Mark, 449; Borsch, The SM in Myth and History, 355f.; Marshall, Luke: 758; Hartman, Prophecy Interpreted, 245ff.; Ellis, Luke, 241f.

437　Hartman, Prophecy Interpreted, 246. See also 235.

438　Zum Verständnis der synoptischen Eschatologie: Mark 13 neu untersucht, 30ff. Also Kümmel, Promise and Fulfilment, 99.

439　Prophecy Interpreted, 235f.

440　Prophecy Interpreted, 246.

441　The most obvious echoes from Daniel are: Mt 24:6 δεῖ γὰρ γενέσθαι (cf. Dan 2:28); 24:10 τότε σκανδαλισθήσονται (Dan LXX 11:41 v.l.); 24:15 τὸ βδέλυγμα τῆς ἐρημώσεως (Dan 9:27; 11:31; 12:11); 24:21 θλίψις μεγάλη (Dan 12:1); 24:30 τὸ σημεῖον τοῦ υἱοῦ τοῦ ἀνθρώπου (Dan 7:13); Mk 13:7 δεῖ γενέσθαι (Dan 2:28, 45); 13:13 ὁ δὲ ὑπομείνας (Dan Θ 12:12); 13:14 βδέλυγμα τῆς ἐρημώσεως (Dan 11:31; 12:11; 9:27); 13:19 θλίψις οἵα οὐ γέγονεν τοιαύτη ἀπ'ἀρχῆς κτίσεως (Dan 12:1); 13:26 ὄψονται τὸν υἱὸν τοῦ ἀνθρώπου ἐρχόμενον ἐν νεφέλαις (Dan 7:13f.); Lk 21:8 ὁ καιρὸς ἤγγικεν (Dan 7:22); 21: 9 δεῖ γὰρ ταῦτα γενέσθαι (Dan 2:28); 21:22 πλησθῆναι πάντα τὰ γεγραμμένα (Dan LXX 12:7); 21:24 Ἱερουσαλὴμ ἔσται πατουμένη ὑπὸ ἐθν˙ " (Dan 8:13; 9:26); 21:24 ἄχρι οὗ πληρωθῶσιν καιροὶ ἐθνων (Dan 12:7); 21:27 ὄψονται τὸν υἱὸν τοῦ ἀνθρώπου ἐρχόμενον ἐν νεφέλῃ (Dan 7:13f.).

442　Prophecy Interpreted, 145–77.

ἀνθρώπου ἤρχετο. The MT agrees with Θ: שמיא כבר אנש עם עֵנָנֵי
אָתֵה הוֹה. Matthew may have used the Θ text (cf. ἐρχόμενος) and
changed μετά to ἐπι'. But he may also have used the LXX text (cf. ἐπί)
and changed ἤρχετο to ἐρχόμενος to fit the quotation in his sentence[443].
Such syntactical modifications are called for in Greek by the demand of
case-agreement.

    The contexts of Mt 24 par. and Dan 7 are quite similar in character.
In both texts there is a cosmic struggle going on. In Dan 7 four evil kingdoms dominate the world scene with the last kingdom being both the
most evil and the most thorough in its destructive work. In Mt 24 nations
and kingdoms are drawn in a life-or-death struggle and these upheavals
are accompanied by natural catastrophes and pestilences. In Dan 7 the
fourth kingdom's wrath is vented in particular upon the saints, while in
Mt 24 (cf. also 10:17—21) the followers of Jesus are singled out as special
targets. Thus in both texts the extermination of God's people as well as
the replacement of God's rule by the reign of evil seem to be the ultimate
end in view. In Dan 7 at the peak of the saints' sufferings the Ancient
One takes his seat at court in the presence of myiads of his servants, and
a Heavenly Being, styled as 'One like a son of man', is transported by the
clouds of heaven and with divine pomp and honours is led to the Ancient
One to take his seat beside him and collaborate in the work of judgment.
The one like a son of man is the supernatural vindicator of the saints. He
assumes the power and the kingly rule of the four beasts and thus delivers
the saints from the beasts' power. As we have already seen the main agents
in the concept of 'beast' are not human, but invisible powers, who are
conceived of as being at work behind their human instruments. It is these
spiritual potentates which are disarmed by the 'SM'[444]. In Mt.24 at the
peak of the saints' persecution there occur certain phenomena in the sky
whereby the sky is darkened and the heavenly powers are shaken. These
powers (δυνάμεις) may be the equivalent of what in Dan 7:27 is called
ἀρχαί / ἐξουσίαι and refer to the powers in control of the heathen kingdoms. Against the background of this cosmic confusion or perplexity Mt
24:30 sets the appearance of the sign of the Son of Man. As in Dan 7:13
the Son of Man is coming on the clouds of heaven. He appears in power
and glory and as in Dan 7 he is accompanied by an angelic court. In Dan
7 the theophany appearance of the One like a son of man marks the end
of the old aeon, the reign of terror, and the beginning of the new aeon,
the reign of righteousness. In Mt 24 par. the Son of Man's coming similarly puts an end to troubles and commotions of an unprecedented nature,
and ushers in the eschatological reign of the Son of Man. Angels are sent
out to gather the elect. The motif of judgment in Dan 7 has its counter-

---

443 Charles, *Daniel*, 186, argues for the originality of the LXX (followed by Mt), against the MT
    and Θ which he considers corrupt.

444 Cf. the similar Pauline understanding in Col 2:15 ἀπεκδυσάμενος τὰς ἀρχὰς καὶ τὰς ἐξου
    σίας.

part in several texts in the Gospels, but especially in Mt 25:31 — a text very much akin to Mt 24[445].

These important elements shared in common by Mt 24 par. and Daniel make the eschatological discourse the Son of Man text of the Gospel tradition most obviously dependent upon Daniel[446]. Despite the existing disagreement as to its composition and interpretation[447], this dependence is well recognized[448].

The conclusion to be drawn from the discussion in this section is that there are authentic sayings in each one of the three classes. Jesus' thought was deeply influenced by Daniel from which he drew the underlying elements in his portrayal of himself as the Son of Man in his earthly activity, in his suffering and in his exaltation. At the same time the discussion has underlined Jesus' creativity in exceeding the germinal scope of his raw-material and in his synthesis of the ideas found in it with ideas from other sources.

Nothing more is to be gained by a further discussion of individual SM sayings. It will be more meaningful if I concentrate, instead, on some areas of Jesus' teaching upon which the Danielic 'SM' has left its imprint.

2. Some Areas of Influence

a) The Nature and Extent of Influence

When it is here claimed that Daniel's 'SM' has been influential in shaping the SM concept in the NT, that influence may conceivably be understood in connection with such NT statements as present a *prima facie* parallel to Dan 7:13f. Particularly, in light of the above discussion on the relation which the Gospel SM sayings bear to Daniel's concept, it may be assumed that the continued discussion will be concerned solely with the most ob- vious parallels. Although those verbal parallels are actually the backbone for the claim made in this study regarding Danielic influence, nothing would be further from the intention of this investigation than to content oneself merely with the most obvious literary connections. The purpose

---

445 Manek's thesis (in *Christ and Spirit in the NT*, 15—25) that the Son of Man of Mt 25:31 is distinct from the "king" of vv. 34ff., being a community term expressing Jesus (= the King) and the "brethren" is impossible. The King in vs. 34 is none other than the SM of vs. 31.

446 Dunn, *Christology in the Making*, 67.

447 See Beasley-Murray, *NTS* 29 (1983) 414—20.

448 Cf. even Casey, *Son of Man*, 165—78, who however, argues in circles in order to prove the inauthenticity of the sayings. Kümmel, *Promise and Fulfilment*, 95ff. is of the opinion that Mk 13:26 (= Mt 24:30 = Lk 21:27) is not incompatible with authentic sayings of Jesus. Cf. also Busch, *Zum Verständnis der synoptischen Eschatologie: Mark 13 neu untersucht*, 30ff.; 60—120; Bowman *The Intention of Jesus*, 55ff.; Hartman, *Prophecy Interpreted*, 145—77; Lane, *Mark*, 449—77; Grayston, *BJRL*, 56 (1974) 371—87; Marshall, *Luke*, 774ff.; Borsch, *The Son of Man*, 362f.; Hooker, *The Son of Man in Mark*, 148ff.

of this study is *inter alia* to give a specimen of the total impact of the Danielic 'SM' concept on the corresponding concept in the NT.

The total impact of Daniel's 'SM' upon the NT concept will be appreciated in its full extent only by taking the concept of 'SM' along with the cluster of ideas in which this concept is embedded. Setting the 'SM' of Daniel in its proper matrix and recognizing that the role which the *concept* — not necessarily the term itself! — plays extends beyond Dan 7:13f., is of paramount importance in accurately gauging the breadth and depth of the 'SM's' influence upon the NT SM. Thus, although the expression 'SM' occurs just once in Dan, the concept it represents underlies much more than Dan 7:13–14, while the ideas with which it is intertwined constitute the central theme of that book[449]. The wealth of content and associations belonging to the concept 'SM' in Dan is easily perceived from the following list of descriptions and statements made of or in connection with the 'SM' in Dan 7[450]. The 'SM' is:

1. associated with none other than the Aged One
2. portrayed as a heavenly being
3. transported on God's 'chariot', sc. the clouds of heaven
4. escorted by a heavenly retinue
5. seated upon a throne beside the Aged One
6. manifested in connection with the judgment of the beasts, which ultimately represent the rule of malevolent spiritual forces
7. vindicator of the suffering saints
8. given the kingly rule previously exercised by the evil spiritual powers, while by virtue of his assumption of universal power, the saints are granted the dominion of the kings under the whole heaven
9. the eschatological Agent of God's everlasting Kingdom
10. equated, in the interpretation, with the *'Elyônîn*, to whom the rebellious powers are subjected.

This list makes it abundantly clear that among the features of the Danielic 'SM', is to be reckoned his connection with the Kingdom of God. Indeed, the concept of the Kingdom of God is more than a mere feature[451]. It forms the matrix within which the concept of 'SM' "lives, moves and has its being"! — to use Luke's expression (Acts 17:28). The 'SM' is the indispensable Agent of God's eschatological Kingdom!

It is nevertheless proper to remind ourselves that the expression 'SM' in Dan is not a constant, i.e. it is not a fixed title of the Agent of God's Kingdom, but a metaphor appropriate to other metaphors used in the context[452]. What is constant is the Entity spoken of in Dan 7 in terms

---

449 I.e. the Kingdom of God. Cf. Charles, *Daniel* cxii ff.
450 Cf. the discussion in Chapter Two.
451 It constitutes the scarlet thread throughout the Book. Cf. the motif of God's sovereignty over the kingdoms of men, that permeates the whole book e.g. 2:21, 39f., 44; 4:3, 17, 25, 32, 34ff.; 5:18–21, 30; 6:26; 7:12, 18, 22, 26f.; 8:21–25; 10:13, 20; 11:36; 12:7. See also Dequeker, *Wereldrijk en Godsrijk in Daniel*.
452 For the application on Dan 7 and 8 of the Interaction theory of metaphor as developed by

of the 'SM' symbolism. Therefore, the constant, the Agent of God's Kingdom, may, in a different context, which employs different symbolism, be depicted in a radically different manner. Accordingly, in Dan 2, in a context of metals and clay, the Agent of God's Kingdom is appositely described as a 'Stone'. The 'Stone' of Dan 2 and the 'SM' of Dan 7 typify the same Entity, the Agent for the destruction of the heathen kingdoms, representing the reign of evil, and for the establishment of God's everlasting rule[453].

Now when it comes to the NT use of the concept of the Agent of God's Kingdom as presented in Dan 2 and 7, it is obvious that the imagery of Dan 7, which described that Agent in human-like characteristics, i.e. as "One *like* a son of man", had a better chance than the imagery of the 'Stone' of Dan 2 to assert itself as a title or designation of the eschatological Agent of God's Kingdom. Hence, the SM and not the 'Stone' became the standing self-designation of Jesus. Nevertheless — and this is both significant and corroborative of my reasoning, above — the 'Stone' of Dan 2, in combination with Ps 118:22[454], is also treated messianically in Mt 21:44 = Lk 20:18, i.e. as applying to the Agent for the destruction of the kingdom of evil and for the establishment of God's Kingdom, moreover, the Agent who in the context, is identified with Jesus[455].

The understanding of Dan 2 by Jesus in a way that is consonant with the original intention of its author, corroborates the present thesis that Daniel's 'SM' was originally intended as a heavenly being mediating God's Kingdom, and that the understanding of the Figure in messianic categories by the *Parables*, IV Ezra, certain rabbis and Jesus is not a departure from the author's original meaning, but a logical development of it along the lines he had indicated[456]. This implies that we are even entitled to speak of the existence of an interpretative tradition faithful to the sense intended by the author. What has just been said has far-reaching consequences for the question of Jesus' self-consciousness[457].

Max Black (*Models and Metaphors*, and *Metaphor and Thought* 19—43) see Porter, *Metaphors and Monsters* esp. 3—12 and 34ff.

453 That Dan 2 and 7 are parallel treatments of the same major theme is universally accepted, see e.g. Eissfeldt, *Introduction*, pp. 524, 526; Rowley, *Darius the Mede*, 67ff.; Lenglet, *Bibl* 53 (1972), pp. 169—90. Beasley-Murray, *CBQ* 45 (1983) 53f. Montgomery, *Daniel*, 61 says: "In cc. 2 and 7 we find a parallelism of a system of four kingdoms, which parallelism is admitted by all."

454 The λίθος of Ps 118:22 cited in Mt 21:42, passes on to the λίθος of Dan 2:34, 45 in Mt 21: 44. Mt 21:44 is missing in D 33 etc., but has overwhelming support in Alexandrian, Byzantine and other independent witnesses. Even if vs. 44 were not original in Mt, it is found in the parallel text in Lk 20:18. Besides, Mt 21:43 is an all too overt allusion to the Danielic theme according to which God puts down one kingdom and sets up another.

455 The Jews are presented as having understood it so, cf. Mt 21:45 = Lk 20:19. Cf. Marshall, *NTS* 12 (1965—6) 349.

456 On the question of the Son of Man and the Messiah, see Rowe in *Christ the Lord*, 71—96; McNeil, *NTS* 26 (1979-80) 419—21 and K.Müller, *BZ* 16 (1972) 159—87; 17 (1973) 52—66.

457 On this see Mussner, *BZ* N.F. 12 (1968) 161—72.

In view of the above observations with regard to the conceptual context of the Danielic 'SM', particularly its relation to God's Kingdom, it is most significant to find that in the NT the majority of the SM logia, whether they set forth the SM as Judge, King, Son of God, as casting out demons, or as suffering, are, in the last analysis, also concerned with the Kingdom of God[458]. It may, therefore, be laid down that the idea of the Kingdom of God constitutes the matrix within which the concept of SM is developed in its various forms and expressions both in Daniel and in the teaching of Jesus!

SM is really a many-sided concept. A brief look at the SM sayings reveals how broad the concept is, encompassing a wide variety of messianic titles and functions. The SM is depicted as Saviour, Messiah, King, Judge, Divine, Son of God, Suffering Servant, Lord of the sabbath and as One who has authority to forgive sins. He is, moreover, an ordinary man eating and drinking, as well as the most lowly and despised of men, and the one destined to die and rise again. The variety of attributes and functions subsumed under this title is so great as to make the title the broadest of all titles used by Jesus, as well as the one best-suited to contain such diverse and seemingly mutually-exclusive properties. In a word, the title SM is a unique term with a unique scope of functions admitting both of divine and human aspects. The term thus functions as an umbrella that gathers under it most of the aspects relating to Jesus' person and mission. But the 'umbrella' feature of the SM is peculiar to the NT. The background material is less variegated, at least as far as explicit statements go. Nevertheless, that material, as has been argued, contains the seeds to most of the concepts associated with the SM conception in the NT.

b) A Son of Man Messianology

One of the most important impressions gained from a perusal of the Gospels with regard to the question of messianology[459], is the substantial difference between the most widespread and popular Jewish understanding of it on the one hand and Jesus' conception of it on the other. All of the Gospels lay considerable emphasis upon this distinction. The rank and

---

458 It is therefore all the more surprising to find that a number of scholars actually claim that the Son of Man is never brought into connection with the Kingdom of God except secondarily, e.g. Sharman, *Son of Man and Kingdom of God,* 89; Vielhauer, *Aufsätze,* 58ff. Riesner, *Jesus als Lehrer,* 480, sees secondary connections in Mt 16:27f. par.; Mt 10:7, 23; 13:37—43; Lk 17:21f.; 21:27—31. Further Schweizer, *JBL* 79 (1960) 124; *id., NTS* 9 (1962—3) 257. On Mt 10:23 see Chamberlain, *Interpr.* 7 (1953) 3—13. Jüngel (in *Paulus und Jesus,* 261f.) is one of the exceptions.

459 As defined by Neugebauer, *NTS* 21 (1974—5), pp. 81f., that is, in its relation to the character of the Messiah as distinguished from Christology, which deals with the identification of the Messiah.

file looked for a scion of David's lineage, who would heal their illnesses[460], restores speech to the dumb and sight to the blind[461] and advance towards Jerusalem as its rightful king and liberator[462]. Such expectations were evidently fostered by scribal teaching on the Davidic descent of the Messiah[463], which apparently found an echo in many OT utterances[464]. According to John 6:14f. the feeding of the five thousand became a catalyst for the crowds' decision to use force, if necessary, to install Jesus as king. Here nationalistic fervour ran high, though Jesus as depicted by John, disappointed their hopes by his flight. The same basic attitude is revealed by John 7:41f., where a more sceptical part of the crowd found in Jesus' assumed Galilean origin an insurmountable stumbling block to his suitability as a messianic candidate, since according to their convictions, the Messiah would be ἐκ σπέρματος Δαυὶδ καὶ ἀπὸ Βηθλεέμ. To be sure the historicity of John's data is often questioned. However, in this case, John seems to be in substantial agreement with the synoptists. The acclamation of Jesus on his entering Jerusalem surely was conceived by the majority of the crowds in terms of a nationalistic Davidic messianism[465]. But once again Jesus is presented as having 'failed' to satisfy popular sentiment.

Was Jesus' 'recalcitrant' conduct owing to diffidence in the face of the 'exacting tasks' of the Messiah, or was it owing to his holding a radically different view of the messianic office than the one his contemporaries envisaged?[466] No doubt the second alternative seems to commend itself as the correct one[467]. Jesus' repudiation of the popular Jewish view of

---

460 Cf. the oft-repeated plea for help υἱὲ Δαυὶδ ἐλέησόν με, etc. in Mt 9:27; 15:22; 20:30f.; Mk 10:47f.; Lk 18:38f.

461 E.g. Mt 12:22f.

462 Mt 21:9 = Mk 11:9f. = Lk 19:38 = Jn 12:13f.

463 Cf. Mk 12:35. See Lohse, TDNT VIII, 480ff.

464 E.g. II Sam 7:16; Ps 89:20ff.; Isa 9:2–7; 11:1–9; Jer 23:5f.; 33:14ff.; Ez 34:23f.; 37:24; Hos 3:5; Am 9:11.

465 Cf. the nationalistic tone in the 'slogans' ὡσαννὰ τῷ υἱῷ Δαυὶδ (Mt 21:9); εὐλογημένη ἡ ἐρχομένη βασιλεία τοῦ πατρὸς ἡμῶν Δαυὶδ (Mk 11:10); εὐλογημένος ὁ ἐρχόμενος ὁ βασιλεύς (Lk 19:38); εὐλογημένος ... ὁ βασιλεὺς τοῦ Ἰσραήλ (Jn 12:13). All of these renditions of the acclamations of the crowds express the strong Jewish yearning and expectations for the ousting of Roman domination and the restoration of the Davidic sceptre.

466 Jewish messianic expectation was, as argued in ch. III, not uniform. An impression of the confused or even conflicting views in circulation is gained from Jn 6:14f., where the crowds are represented as thinking of the coming prophet (probably the one of Dt 18:15) in terms of a Messianic king. Cf. Dodd, Historical Traditions, 215: "The passage in Josephus (sc. Ant xx, 97, 167f., 168–70; Bel Jud ii, 261f.) show (as Strack-Billerbeck observe ad loc.) 'how closely in the thought of the populace in the decades before the destruction of Jerusalem the conceptions of the coming Prophet and of the Deliverer-Messiah belonged together; and the same thing comes out in John vi. 14 sq.' " Side by side with this we find that in Jn 7:40ff. (some of ?) the crowds seem to distinguish between the Prophet and the Messiah.

467 What finally issued into the overt declaration ἡ βασιλεία ἡ ἐμὴ οὐκ ἐστιν ἐκ τοῦ κόσμου τούτου ... (Jn 18:36f., cf. Mt 26:53 and see Dodd, Historical Traditions, 121f.) must be understood to imply a long-held implicit conviction of otherworldly destiny on the part of Jesus. See Sabourin R S B 3 (1983) 129–34.

messianology finds its most poignant expression in Mt 22:41—46 = Mk 12:35—37 = Lk 20:41—44. Countering the scribal claim that the Messiah is David's son, Jesus is reported as citing Ps 110:1 LXX: εἶπεν κύριος τῷ κυρίῳ μου . . . and then asking the question: εἰ οὖν Δαυίδ καλεῖ αὐτὸν κύριον, πῶς υἱὸς αὐτοῦ ἐστιν? This *logion* has sometimes been thought to have had its *Sitz im Leben* in the Early Church[468]. It could then be interpreted as a defence against Jewish allegations of Jesus' non-Davidic descent[469], or as a Christian concern to prove the divine character of the Messiah[470]. However, the apophthegmatic nature of the saying seems to be typical of Jesus. Taylor[471] argues against Bultmann for the authenticity of the saying chiefly on the grounds of its allusive character in half concealing and half revealing the 'Messianic Secret', and that it is difficult to conceive that the Church, whose conviction that Jesus is the Son of God exalted to his right hand, rings out in no uncertain terms, would have expressed its doctrinal belief in this obscure manner. Taylor's arguments have been accepted by France who says: "A saying which must have been at least puzzling, perhaps embarrassing, for those who proclaimed Jesus as Son of David is hardly likely to have been created and circulated by the Christian Church"[472], and Lövestam who adds that this rabbinic type of question fits Jesus' milieu well, and that its interpretation of Ps 110:1 in a messianic sense agrees with the use of this text in Jesus' self-defence before the Sanhedrin, a saying whose genuineness can hardly be controverted[473]. The saying is also accepted as authentic by e.g. Lane[474], and Marshall[475].

How is Jesus' question to be understood? It has been usual since Daube's work [476], to view Jesus' question as an instance of the Haggada-question type of reasoning, whereby two seemingly contradictory OT texts can be reconciled by being viewed in their special contexts, a procedure that betrays the inner harmony of the texts. Thus, Lane says: "It is the failure to recognize that Jesus was posing a Haggada-question which has led a number of commentators to affirm that Jesus denied the Davidic

---

468 E.g. by Bultmann, *Geschichte*, 145ff. (Eng. tr. 136f.); Bousset, *Kyrios Christos*, 43; Hahn, *Christologische Hoheitstitel*, 113ff. (Eng. tr. 104ff.).

469 Cf. the Jewish charge according to Celsius *apud* Origen, *Contra Celsum* i, 31, that Jesus was the son of a Roman soldier named Panthera. But see the explanation by Bruce, *Jesus and Christian Origins*, 54ff. See further Burger, *Jesus als Davidssohn*, pp. 52ff. Bultmann, *History*, 136, too, discountenances this explanation.

470 Hahn's arguments (*Titles of Jesus in Christology*, 104ff.) to this effect are not decisive. See Marshall, *Luke*, 746ff.

471 *Mark*, 493.

472 *Jesus and the OT*, 101.

473 *SEÅ* 27 (1962) 81f.

474 *Mark*, 435ff.

475 *Luke*, 743—49.

476 *The NT and Rabbinic Judaism*, 158—63; *id.*, *ZNW* 48 (1957) 119—26; *id.*, *NTS* 5 (1959) 174—87.

descent of the Messiah"[477]. In this view Jesus' question was not so much meant to question the Davidic descent of the Messiah, as "to invite thought and decision"[478]. "It is thus a matter of bringing the different statements into a correct relation to each other" writes Lohse[479]. But the question is: In which way is that harmony to be effected? Lane contents himself with paraphrasing the Marcan interrogative particles $\pi\tilde{\omega}\varsigma$ (vs. 35) and $\pi\acute{o}\vartheta\epsilon\nu$ (vs. 37) as "*What do* the scribes *mean* when they say . . ." and "*In what sense* then is he his lord?" respectively[480]. Apart from the inherent linguistic difficulties in taking $\pi\tilde{\omega}\varsigma$ and $\pi\acute{o}\vartheta\epsilon\nu$ in the proposed senses, Lane's 'explanation' still leaves the texts unexplained and in tension. Lane does not explain satisfactorily *how* the 'contradiction' was solved[481]. Daube himself suggests two possible solutions: "Say, the Messiah is David's son up to a certain moment in history, but his lord from then; or — this would mean that we have before us an adumbration of Paul's teaching in Romans — he is David's son according to the flesh, but his lord according to the spirit"[482]. Similar is Hahn's position that Jesus was David's son during his earthly life, but became David's lord after his resurrection[483] — a solution that presupposes that the saying is the creation of the Early Church[484]. If, however, as there is reason to believe[485], the saying is original, the resurrection factor cannot in itself be the answer to how the Messiah can be David's lord[486].

Daube's suggestion that Mt 22:41—46 par. is to be understood in light of the rabbinic Haggada-question exegesis may well be a correct observation. But that in itself does not solve the enigma. We need to indicate the solution explicitly. Lane's interpretation of $\pi\tilde{\omega}\varsigma$ and $\pi\acute{o}\vartheta\epsilon\nu$ as "What do . . . mean . . . " and "In what sense . . . " is, for obvious reasons, unacceptable. Besides, it is open to an interpretation whereby Jesus can be presumed to concede that the scribes 'mean it' in a way not understood by

---

477 Lane, *Mark*, 436. Similarly Lövestam, *SEÅ* 27 (1962) 74—80.

478 Lane, *Mark*, 437.

479 *TDNT*, VIII, 485.

480 Cf. Hahn, *The Titles of Jesus in Christology*, 253.

481 See his remarks in 437f. His proposed solution, which is based on Acts 2:29—34 etc. along exaltation lines involves the further difficulty of looking for the harmony of the 'contradictory' texts in David's mind.

482 *The NT and Rabbinic Judaism*, 163.

483 Perrin, *BR* 13 (1968) 17—28 develops the thesis that the apocalyptic Son of Man owes its origin and development to the Christian reflection upon the resurrection in the light of Ps 110:1, whence came the christological concept of Jesus as man. Zech 12:10f. and Dan 7:13 were introduced later to account for Jesus' standing at God's right hand, and the expectation of his return as SM.

484 *Christologische Hoheitstitel*, 259ff. (Eng. tr. 246ff.). To the same effect Lohse, *TDNT*, VIII, 485.

485 See Marshall, *Luke*, 746ff.

486 The fact the Ps 110:1 occurs in Acts 2:34f. in an argument on the resurrection, does not prove that it has to be understood of the resurrection also in connection with Mt 22:41—46 par.

the crowds, but which was, however, in essential agreement with Jesus' own solution. There is, of course, nothing of the sort here. The $\pi\tilde{\omega}\varsigma$ and $\pi\acute{o}\vartheta\epsilon\nu$ underline the untenability of the scribes' claim that the Messiah is David's son: $\epsilon\grave{\iota}$ $o\grave{\upsilon}\nu$ $\Delta\alpha\upsilon\grave{\iota}\delta$ $\kappa\alpha\lambda\epsilon\tilde{\iota}$ $\alpha\grave{\upsilon}\tau\grave{o}\nu$ $\kappa\acute{\upsilon}\rho\iota o\nu,$ $\pi\tilde{\omega}\varsigma$ $\upsilon\grave{\iota}\grave{o}\varsigma$ $\alpha\grave{\upsilon}\tau o\tilde{\upsilon}$ $\grave{\epsilon}\sigma\tau\iota\nu$[487] = "if therefore — as it is established — David calls him lord, how then *can he be* his son?" The apodosis of this first class condition[488] is in the form of a rhetorical question, which implies the answer 'He cannot be'[489]. Jesus appears here to be concerned not with the scribes' dialectical way of handling two "contradictory" texts of scripture, but with questioning the validity of the scribes' tenet that the Messiah is to be a literal descendant of Daivd, i.e. an earthly and political messiah.

This last statement raises the question: Does Jesus repudiate the OT texts that speak of a messiah of David's lineage? A number of scholars would answer this question affirmatively[490]. Taylor objects: "It is ... improbable that Jesus ever contested the Davidic descent of the Messiah. But if so, the case for supposing that he knew that he was not of David's line disappears; for the only reason for this assumption is his alleged attack upon this doctrine. Had he known that he was not of David's lineage, He would have been compelled, in claiming to be the Messiah, to denounce scribal teaching and to reject the testimony of the OT"[491]. Taylor's objections are too sweeping. Furthermore, Taylor's making the question of Jesus' eventual knowledge of the story of his birth depend upon whether he repudiated or not the OT messianic texts speaking of Davidic descent is unsound. It involves an illegitimate linking together of two distinct questions as if they were logically in indisoluble union with each other.

It would seem that the correct solution to the complex of problems at hand lies in finding a correct answer to the two issues which Taylor raised: Jesus' view of the OT texts and of himself. The fact that Jesus questioned the scribal view concerning the Davidic sonship of the Messiah does not mean that Jesus necessarily also repudiated the OT teaching on the Davidic descent of the Messiah. Nor does his non-repudiation of the OT, for that matter, necessarily imply that Jesus was not aware "that he was not of David's lineage". Here we need to recall the 'dynamic' or 'transformed' rather than literal way in which many of the OT prophecies are understood as being fulfilled in the NT. Such an example is Mt 17:10—13 = Mk 9:11—13, where the promise of Elijah's coming (Mal 4:5f.), taught and ex-

---

487 Mt 22:45. The Marcan $\pi\acute{o}\vartheta\epsilon\nu$ has identical function here.
488 Robertson, *A Grammar of the Greek NT*, 1004—22 calls this type of conditional sentence "Determined as fulfilled"; *BDR* § § 371 terms it "Realis"; Turner, *Syntax*, 113ff.
489 Schenk, *EWNT*, III, cols. 491f., renders similarly with "unmöglich" and "völlig ausgeschlossen".
490 E.g. Bultmann, *History*, 136f.; Lohmeyer, *Markus*, 262; van Iersel in *La venue du Messie*, 121ff.
491 *Mark*, 491.

pected by the scribes in a literal sense[492], is said by Jesus to have already been fulfilled in the coming of John the Baptist: John 'is' Elijah! In a similar way the Messiah's 'Davidic descent' can be fulfilled by other means than through a literal (i.e. biological) descent. Rejection of the scribes' literalistic interpretation of the OT, need not also imply the repudiation of the OT.

The other question is more complicated. It relates to the question of the evangelists' idea of Davidic descent and to Jesus' possible acquaintance with what the evangelists later came to record. To start with it may be conceded that the evangelists (only Matthew and Luke come into question here) never explicitly repudiate the Davidic descent of the Messiah[493]. They make a serious attempt to indicate that Jesus stands in a relation of continuity to David's lineage[494], and in this they seem to agree with the Jewish view. But at the same time it must be underscored that the relation of continuity, as they envisage it, is more sophisticated than the ordinary Jewish one. Thus, in contrast to the Jewish belief in a literally Davidic scion of political character, the Gospel tradition presents the alternative of a Messiah who has *theological* rather than biological continuity to David's lineage. Hence Joseph, through whom the Davidic descent is reckoned on Jesus[495], is, according to Matthew and Luke, Jesus' 'father' only by virtue of his being married to Jesus' mother![496] In other words, Jesus is 'adopted' into the Davidic line of descent. Thus, both Matthew and Luke present as much — if not actually more — evidence for Jesus' *not* being a descendant of David (understood biologically) as they do for Jesus' belonging to David's lineage (theologically). Now the evidence for Jesus' *not* being a literal descendant of David is the more special evidence of the two and is intended as a corrective on their more general statements that Jesus does belong to David's lineage. Are the evangelists here caught between a Scylla and a Charybdis! Is it their conception of the messianic role that is responsible for their conceiving of Davidic continuity — as they indeed must, according to the OT — in non-naturalistic terms?[497] Is this presentation of Jesus dictated by christolog-

---

492 And similarly understood by the disciples.

493 See Jeremias, *Jerusalem*, 276ff.; 290ff.; Cullman, *Christology*, 131; Lane, *Mark*, 435ff.; Marshall, *Luke*, 744ff.

494 See Mt 1:16f., 20; 2:1, 6; Lk 1:27, 32, 69; 2:4, 11.

495 Sometimes the attempt is made, indeed, to derive Jesus' Davidic descent through Mary (e.g. Stewart, *ZPEB*, IV, 106–12). The evidence that Mary was of Davidic descent is practically non-existent, see Jeremias, *Jerusalem*, 290, n. 69. If anything Mary would seem to be of Levitical descent, being a συγγενίς of Elisabeth (Lk 1:36). See Jeremias, *Jerusalem*, 290 n. 69.; Cullmann, *Christology*, 128. Matthew and Luke are unequivocal in deriving Jesus' Davidic descent through Joseph, so Lohse, *TDNT*, VIII, 486; Ellis, *Luke*, 84; Marshall, *Luke*, 62ff., 71; Cranfield, *Romans* I, 59.

496 Cf. Mt 1:16. Luke bases Jesus' Davidic descent on Jesus' being the 'adopted' son of Joseph (Lk 1:27, 32, 69; 2:4) as well as on Jesus' being born in Bethlehem (Lk 2:4ff., 11, 15). At the same time Luke stresses Jesus' supernatural origin (Lk 1:32, 35, 76; 2:49; 3:22f.).

497 I.e. Mt 1:18–25. Cf. Lk 3:23: ὢν υἱός, ὡς ἐνομίζετο, Ἰωσήφ! Cf. also the references to

ical considerations accute in the hellenistic Church, or do we have to do here with very old traditions?[498] Issues like these have been argued for and against times without number, but from our viewpoint they are still peripheral to the central question here, viz.: Is it possible that Jesus was acquainted with such stories about his birth as were later crystalized in the first and third Gospels?[499] or, – to put it more impertinently, – What constitutes the sure basis for denying to Jesus such knowledge? Purely apriorically there is nothing decisive against such a supposition. For if Alexander the Great could have been told that he was Olympias' son by Ammon rather than Philip[500] and he had apparently accepted it, or, at least, taken it sufficiently seriously as to make use of the 'joke'[501], it is not at all obvious why Jesus could not have been the recipient of analogical information, or have been influenced by such a belief. Indeed, it is taunting that many details in the Gospel narratives seem to make sense only on the basis of some such supposition[502]. For example, Riesner shows that Jesus is unique in 'binding' his disciples directly to his own person rather than to his teaching (as was the case with the rabbis who 'bound' their disciples to the Torah), and especially in demanding no less than that the disciple should be prepared to follow him to death![503] Such conduct on Jesus' part is inexplicable unless Jesus rightly or wrongly had come to look upon himself in a way not true of other men. The air

---

Mary's cogitations over unusual events or statements in connection with Jesus, Lk 2:19, 51, 33.

498 To postulate conflicting traditions reaching the evangelists and being preserved by them is no solution, since the problem is on the redactional level.

499 Many scholars would reject the possibility outright, especially as the 'accretions' are absent from Mark. The silence of Mark, for whatever it is worth, is of some force only on the presupposition of its priority. But as this ninetheenth-century dogma has come under so much fire of late, Mark can hardly be allowed an arbiter's role.

500 See Arrian, *Anabasis*, III, 3; IV, 9f.; Plutarch, *Alexander*, 28f. (680f.); 50 (694); Curtius X, 1–2; Strabo XVII, 1, 43. Cf. also Lucian, *Dialogi Mortuorum*, 395.

501 On the question of προσκύνησις and the drinking-bout at Bactra, see in addition to the texts of the previous note, Arrian, *Anabasis*, IV, 11,12 and Plutarch, *Alexander*, 51 as well as the discussions of Tarn, *Alexander the Great*, 123–66; id., *Hellenistic Civilization*; Robinson, *AJPh* 64 (1943), pp. 286–301; Brown, *AJPh* 70 (1949), 225–48; Dascalakis, *St Cl* 9 (1967) 93–105; Κανελλόπουλος, in *IEE* IV, 224–30.

502 Cf. his otherwise 'overbearing' attitude in e.g. his setting himself above Moses' law (Mt 5:22, 28, 33, 34, 39, 44); his claiming to be greater than the temple (the neuter μεῖζον referring to himself, according to Greek usage) and the sabbath (Mt 12:6ff. = Mk 2:27f.); his 'audacity' in forgiving people's sins (Mt 9:2–6 = Mk 2:5–10 = Lk 5:20–24). On this last point see Thompson, *JTS* 12 (1961) 203–6, who sees evidence for the existence of a Son of Man concept in Judaism. In my judgment this is not compelling, since ἐν τοῖς οὐρανοῖς (of God's right to forvgive sins) can always be assumed as the corresponding opposite to ἐπὶ τῆς γῆς (of the SM's right). See further Hay, *JBL* 89 (1970) 69–75; Kertelge in *Orientierung an Jesus*, 205–13 and Feuillet, *RSR* 42 (1954) 161–92, who claims that texts like Mk 2:5–10 par. and Mk 2:27f. par. exemplify Jesus' own consciousness, and are no statements of the disciples' post-resurrection interpretation of Jesus.

503 *Jesus als Lehrer*, 417f. referring to Schlatter, *Theologie des NT* I, 123f.; Rengstorf, *TDNT* IV, 444ff. and Schnackenburg in *Christliche Existenz* I, 91.

of authority, of high destiny, of special relation to God[504] etc. so permeate the Gospel narratives of his actions and teachings that he becomes a riddle apart from some such theory that he had somehow come to be imbued with thoughts stemming from a self-consciousness which probably had its basis in the kind of rumours which later took form in Mt and Lk as birth stories[505]. It should be clear that I am not here concerned with the historicity of the birth narratives — since this lies outside the domain of historical research — but with the possibility of Jesus' acquaintance with such stories[506]. However vague, scant,or false some such knowledge would seem to form the basis of Jesus' psychology and self-consciousness[507].

To return to Jesus' question to the crowds, "If David calls the Messiah his lord, how then can he be his son?", it is a question that cannot be answered meaningfully on the scribes' presuppositions. Indeed, the text does not indicate whether the scribes were at all bothered by this thought. Hence, it is not clear that this was a Haggada-question for them. The impression rather is that Jesus was original in using Ps 110:1 to counter the scribes' unacceptable view of a messiah in terms of a political liberator of David's lineage[508]. Alternatively, Jesus was using an already effected synthesis of Ps 110:1 with a current SM messianology. The question now is: How was Jesus led to apply to himself Ps 110:1 messianically and to ex-

---

504 Cf. his use of "Abba". See the standard discussion by Jeremias, *Abba,* 33—67, and Marshall's utilization of Jeremias' results for the Son of Man question in *Int* 21 (1967) 88ff.: "The fundamental point in Jesus' self-understanding was his filial relationship to God and that it was from this basic conviction that he undertook the tasks variously assigned to the Messiah, Son of Man and Servant of Yahweh" (93). Also Higgins, in *Promise and Fulfilment,* 135f.

505 Riesner, *Th B* 12 (1981) 177—87, in argumentation against Raatschen, shows that Jewish-Christian authors of the first century A.D. drawing on analogous tenets in Jewish tradition respecting Wisdom, would relate Jesus' pre-existence to his virgin birth.

506 The different forms in Mt and Lk indicate the existence of different traditions prior to the evangelists. The frequent claim that Paul was unacquainted with the tradition of the virgin birth cannot be maintained categorically. Through its use of γενόμενον Gal 4:4 seems to imply that Paul purposely avoided the use of τίκτω or γεννάω. This would seem to imply that Paul was acquainted with this tradition at the latest some 15—18 years (if not earlier!) after Jesus' death (see also Cranfield, *Romans* I, 59, who shares my understanding here, and who also draws attention to Phil 2:7). Perhaps Jn 8:40 takes us further back to Jesus (so Brown, *John* I, 357; Morris, *John,* 462, and esp. Cranfield, *Romans* I, 59 with literature in notes 3 and 4).

507 Cf. Kurichianil, *Biblebhashyam* 9 (1983) 114—25, who claims that a large number of synoptic sayings indicate that Jesus had accepted from the start the role of suffering in the light of the Servant concept.

508 Cf. Cullmann, *Christology,* 131f.: "He refutes this false conception by indicating that David would not have called the Messiah his 'lord' if the Messiah were his own physical descendant", and Stauffer, *NovT* 1 (1956) 102: "Die Messiashoffnung war vor allem die Hoffnung der jüdischen Widerstandsbewegung, die Zukunftshoffnung der politischen Religion. Jesus will mit dieser Messiashoffnung nichts zu schaffen haben ... Darum hat Jesus sich nicht als den Messias bezeichnet, sondern als den Menschensohn."

press a view of messianology that was so obviously different from the one most current among his contemporaries?[509]

Two circumstances seem to converge here pointing to the solution of this question. The first of these is that Jesus was acquainted with an interpretation of Dan 7:13f. which considered the 'SM' as a heavenly, preexistent being of transcendental character[510], which was chosen to be the Mediator of God's eschatological Kingdom on earth[511]. We have already seen in this chapter that the modern interpretation of the 'SM' in terms of the people of Israel, or even the angelic interpretation, for that matter, is foreign to the Gospel tradition[512]. The only interpretative tradition known — a tradition bequeathed, according to the present investigation, by Daniel himself — and which was treasured among certain circles of pre-Christian Judaism[513], had invested this Figure more and more with messianic characteristics, until the concept of messianology was, in the said circles[514], thoroughly transformed, and the old, official messianism, based on other texts, was superceded. The traditional, official view of a Davidic messiah with worldly functions, was, of course, very much alive in the time of Jesus, and often found expression both in the revolt tendencies of the Jewish people as well as in the rising up of various impostors[515]. But side by side with this attitude there had developed since the time of Daniel another attitude — usually called 'apocalyptic' — which spiritualized the idea of deliverance as well as that from which deliverance was sought, and consequently saw God himself, or a heavenly representative of his, as the solely adequate deliverer[516]. For these circles, whose beliefs were evidently shared by Jesus[517], a messiah of the type expound-

---

509 It seems that Ps 110:1 had not attained wide current use as a messianic prophecy. Cf. Marshall, *Luke,* 748. Dodd, *According to the Scriptures,* 101f. and Seitz, *SE* 6 (1973) 478–94, have independently argued for Ps 80:17 rather than Dan 7:13f. having led to the juxtaposition of the Son of Man with God's right hand. For sympathetic criticism of this position see Moule, *Origin of Christology,* 25f.

510 *Contra* Moule in *NT und Kirche,* 414.

511 See Hamerton-Kelly, *Pre-existence,* 39.

512 Equally foreign to the NT is e.g. Manson's interpretation of Mk 2:27f. that "He (sc. Jesus) and they (sc. the disciples) together, so long as they adhere to him, constitute the 'Son of Man' " (*In honorem A. Fridrichsen,* 146).

513 Cf. Davies, *Paul and Rabbinic Judaism,* 159, who, in reference to I En 48:1–7 and 49:2, says: "We need not cavil at the fact that these words are written of the Son of Man and not of the Messiah. The figure of the latter was highly complex and in Judaism as in the thought of Jesus and of the early Church the lineaments of the Son of Man and of the Messiah had become inextricably merged". Davies cites Robinson, *The NT Doctrine of the Christ* and Bonsirven, *Le Judaïsme Palestinien,* I, 360, who "regards the term 'Son of Man', etc. as a name for the Messiah"; similarly Moore, *Judaism,* II, 323f. (*ibid.* 159 n. 2).

514 Reflected in extant literature in the *Parables,* IV Ezra, certain rabbis, the NT and Justin, *Dial.* 32, 2.

515 See e.g. Josephus, *Bel Jud* II, 261–2; *Ant* XX, 97; 167–70.

516 Jeremias, *Theology,* I, 271.

517 So already Charles, *ET* 4 (1892–3) 504, who argued for an explicit messianic claim on Jesus' part, based on the *Parables* (similarly in *The Book of Enoch* 306–9), against whom Bartlet,

ed by the scribes was otiose and superfluous. This circumstance is reflected in the *Parables* — and in a smaller degree in IV Ezra — where
the title Messiah is, in comparison with that of the Son of Man, in re-
treat. Indeed, if the thesis put forward in this investigation is correct,
that work was composed for the purpose of setting forth a new type
of messianology, viz. in terms of Daniel's 'SM'. Similarly in the Gospels the title Χριστός is seldom on Jesus' lips, being consistently substituted[518] by that of the SM[519]. This substitution is not dictated merely
by Jesus' seeking to avoid e.g. Roman suspicion, on account of the political overtones of that term, but also — and perhaps more so — by his new
conception of messianology: οἶνον νέον εἰς ἀσκοὺς καινοὺς βλητέον![520]
The term Messiah, subject to popular misuse and charged with compromis-
ing or even incriminating implications, was felt inadequate and unsuitable
for conveying the new content of Jesus' teaching. The very passage under
discussion[521] is a witness to Jesus' attempt to free the term Χριστός from
the political and earthly connotations it had acquired by raising the Figure
of the Messiah — not the term! — to the level of a heavenly, transcendental being conceived of in terms of the 'SM' of Dan 7:13f.[522] "If David
calls him lord, then he cannot be his son" is Jesus' way of showing that
the Jewish conception of messianology fell far short of his own understanding of it, which he, moreover, in effect claimed was in accordance
with scripture, i.e. Ps 110:1; Dan 7:13f.[523] The combination of Ps 110:1
with Dan 7:13f. has been claimed to be the creation of the Early
Church[524], but Borsch, for example, with good reason, holds it to be pre-
Christian[525], and it may be said in Lindars' recent words: "There can be
no doubt that he (sc. Jesus) did use it (sc. the title SM) from time to time
in order to refer to himself . . . In fact some, at least, of the Son of Man
sayings imply that Jesus identified himself with the visionary figure of
'one like a son of man' in Dan 7:13"[526].

This interpretation is strikingly confirmed by Mt 26:64 = Mk 14:62 =
Lk 22:69[527]. In answer to the high priest's question whether he was the

who held an implicit messianic claim, tried to controvert, *ET* 4 (1892–3) 403 and *ET* 5
(1893–4) 41–2.

518 The expression is legitimate since the Son of Man in the Gospels, *contra* Stauffer, *NovT* 1
(1956) 81–108, has the functions of the Messiah, see above.
519 In the Epistles Χριστός has a wholly different content from that current in Jewish parlance.
520 Lk 5:38.
521 I.e. Mt 22:41ff. = Mk 12:35ff. = Lk 20:41ff.
522 See Zorn, *VoxRef.* 34 (1980) 1–21.
523 Cf. Sabourin, *R S B* 3 (1983) 129ff.
524 E.g. Perrin, *NTS* 12 (1965–6) 150ff.; *id., Rediscovering*, 173ff.
525 *NTS* 14 (1967–8) 566f.
526 *BJRL* 63 (1980–1) 437.
527 For the authenticity of this text, see Borsch, *Son of Man*, 391ff.; *id., NTS* 14 (1967–8) 565
ff.; Catchpole, *The Trial of Jesus*, 141ff.; *id., NTS* 17 (1970–1) 213–26; Riesner, *Jesus als
Lehrer*, 302.

Messiah, the Son of God[528], Jesus answers with a qualified 'Yes'[529], and then proceeds to correct the high priest's understanding of the nature of the Messiah by interpreting the Messiah in terms the 'SM' of Dan 7:13f. and of David's lord of Ps 110:1[530]. This implies that in Jesus' view the Messiah is David's lord, not so much on account of his resurrection or exaltation[531], but because he was conceived from the outset in Danielic fashion as a heavenly, pre-existent Agent of God's Kingdom[532]. With regard to the authenticity of Mt 22:41ff. par. and Mt 26:64 par. Black[533] has recently remarked "he (sc. Jesus) employs Ps 110:1 as a messianic *testimonium*. If he can do so here, he can also be the author of the conflated texts of Ps 110:1 and Dan 7:13 at Mk 14:26 par." Pesch seems to hold a similar view[534].

However, the application to himself of a view of messianology in terms of Ps 110:1 and Dan 7:13f. is inadequately explained if it cannot be combined with awareness of such stories as we find in Mt and Lk concerning Jesus' nativity. The other alternative, that of attributing this type of messianology to the christological creativeness of the Early Church (advocated by e.g. Dunn[535]), is first unnecessary (since the combination of Ps 110 with Dan 7 is probably older than Jesus), and secondly, it still leaves unexplained Jesus' peculiar psychology, unless one is prepared to deny all possibility of knowing anything at all about Jesus.

It would therefore seem that unless Jesus somehow had come to believe that his relation to Joseph was only formal or legal, there is no satisfactory explanation as to how he could be led to identify himself with the transcendental 'SM' of Dan 7:13f. and look upon himself as a Messiah, who is David's lord rather than son. It appears therefore probable that according to Mt and Lk it was the combination of acquaintance with the rumours regarding his birth and with the current interpretation of the 'SM' of Dan 7:13f. in terms of a supernatural being, that best explains how Jesus could come to question the scribal view of the Messiah's literal, descent from David[536].

---

528 Mk 14:61 has the semitic periphrasis υἱὸς τοῦ εὐλογητοῦ. Lk 22:67 has simply εἰ σὺ εἶ ὁ Χριστός.

529 Mt 26:64: σὺ εἶπας; Mk 14:62 the unequivocal ἐγώ εἰμι; Lk 22:70: ὑμεῖς λέγετε ὅτι ἐγώ εἰμι (though this is placed a little later in the dialogue). Matthew's and Luke's expressions are circumlocutional, though the import is virtually affirmative. See Taylor, *Mark*, 568; Lane, *Mark*, 536f.; Marshall, *Luke*, 851. It is often regarded as an evasive answer, see Flender, *Luke*, 45; Colpe, *TDNT*, VIII, 436; Vermes, *Jesus the Jew*, 148f.; Stauffer, *NovT*, 1 (1956), 89.

530 This answer of Jesus was, according to Catchpole, *The Trial of Jesus*, 141ff., made the ground for condemning him to death.

531 *Contra* Hahn, *The Titles of Jesus in Christology*, 253.

532 The theory of Smith, *ET* 18 (1906–7) 553–5, that 'Son of Man' was "in the first instance an oprobrious epithet, in fact a nickname" which Jesus having overheard, decided to use, is too frivolous to merit attention.

533 *ET* 95 (1984) 205.

534 *BZ* 18 (1974) 30.

535 *Christology in the Making*, esp. 65–97.

536 See Farrer, *A Study in Mark*, 287.

c) The Nature of the Son of Man Messianology

If Jesus' view of messianology was not identical with that of the scribes' and of the ordinary people's, what were its chief characteristics? We are here faced with the type of question which prompted Hahn's solution, referred to above, namely that the Messiah had two roles to play and hence bore two relations to David[537]. This is the schema of *Erniedrigung und Erhöhung*[538]. But the question again may be: Were these two motifs present in the tradition inhertied by Jesus, was he responsible for bringing them together[539], or is this combination the work of the Early Church? As far as the third question goes, we have seen reason, above, to accept the basic authenticity of all three types of Son of Man logia despite the inevitable colouring in matters of detail from the post-Easter situation. With regard to the first two questions the answer is more complex and will engage the following discussion.

The two main features of the Son of Man messianology are that he is depicted on the one hand as an exalted, heavenly and transcendental[540] being, as King[541] and Judge of the last days[542], and on the other hand as one who came to seek and to save what is lost[543], by serving and giving his life as a ransom for many[544]. In short, this class of sayings presents a Son of Man who is rejected and betrayed, who suffers and is put to death[545], but whom God finally exalts by raising him from the dead[546]. The two classes of sayings are connected by various means in the context of the various sayings, but the most overt connection is perhaps made in Lk 17:23—25 ὥσπερ γὰρ ἡ ἀστραπὴ . . . οὕτως ἔσται ὁ υἱὸς τοῦ ἀνθρώπου (ἐν τῇ ἡμερᾳ αὐτοῦ). πρῶτον δὲ δεῖ αὐτὸν πολλὰ παθεῖν καὶ ἀποδοκιμασθῆναι ἀπὸ τῆς γενεᾶς ταύτης. The exaltation of the Son of Man is thought to be indissolubly connected with that of his sufferings. The one is the condition for the other. The schema of Humiliation–Exaltation is, of course, rather well-known in Judaism[547] and the Early Church[548], but the question is: What basis was there in the tradition for

---

537 Cf. *The Titles of Jesus in Christology*, 253.
538 Schweizer, *JBL* 79 (1960) 124.
539 Riesenfeld, *En Bok om Nya Testamentet*, 403.
540 Mt 19:28; 25:31; 16:27 = Mk 8:38 = Lk 9:26; Mt 24:30 = Mk 13:26 = Lk 21:27; Mt 24:39 = Lk 17:30; Mt 26:64 = Mk 14:62 = Lk 22:69.
541 Mt 13:41; 16:28 (cf. also Mk 9:1 and Lk 9:27); See also references to the Son of Man's sitting on a throne, which implies kingship, Mt 19:28; 25:31.
542 Mt 19:28; 16:27 = Mk 8:38 = Lk 9:26; Mt 25:31ff.; 13:40ff.
543 Lk 19:10.
544 Mt 20:28 = Mk 10:45.
545 E.g. Mt 17:12 = Mk 9:12; Mt 17:22 = Mk 9:31 = Lk 9:44; Mt 20:28 = Mk 10:33f. = Lk 18:31f.; Mt 26:2; 26:45 = Mk 14:41; Lk 24:7; Mk 8:31 = Lk 9:21f. See Michel in *Tradition und Glaube*, 310—6.
546 Mt 17:22 = Mk 9:31 = Lk 9:44; Mt 20:18 = Mk 10:33f. = Lk 18:31ff.; Mt 19:9 = Mk 9:9; Mk 8:31 = Lk 9:22; Lk 24:7.
547 E.g. Prov 15:33; 18:12 and the classical instance in Isa 52:13—53:12.
548 Cf. e.g. Rm 8:17; I Cor 4:10ff.; Ph 2:6—11; II Tm 2:12.

bringing in the Son of Man in connection with this schema?

As we have already seen neither IV Ezra nor the *Parables* give the least indication of a suffering Son of Man[549]. In both of these works the Son of Man is a heavenly, transcendental being, chosen and hidden by God and reserved for the last days, in which he is to function as Judge of both men[550] and angels[551]. In the case of Daniel the situation is more complicated. For many of those who identify the 'SM' with the suffering saints Dan 7 clearly is evidence for a suffering Son of Man[552]. In this study, however, it has been argued that the 'SM' is to be equated with *'Elyônîn*, not with the saints, and this complicates matters.

We have seen in Chapter Three that the *Parables* has taken over and developed the main ideas connected with the 'SM' in Daniel, and made them more explicit. If suffering were such a pronounced component in the concept of 'SM' in Dan 7, as the Israelite view would imply, it is inexplicable that the author of the *Parables* altogether missed or wholly neglected that feature. The interpretative tradition of the 'SM' of Dan 7 seems to rule out such a feature.

In Dan 7 the relation of the 'SM' to suffering is somewhat intricate. There are two verses that speak of the saints' sufferings, both found in the Interpretation Part related to 7:7f. Verse 21 summarily mentions that the horn prevailed against the saints, while vs. 25 consists of two alternating parallel statements:

A
- a. "He shall speak words against the Most High (עליא)
- b. And shall wear out the saints of the 'Most High'* (עליונין)
- c. And shall think to change the times and the law;
B
- d. And they shall be given into his hand for a time, two times, and half a time" (RSV)

(* The quotation marks around 'Most High' are mine).

The attack is directed against the Most High (i.e. The Aged One) and against the saints of *'Elyônîn*. The attempt to make the times and the law 'different' (להשניה!) (c) are an affront to God's decrees and rule, and parallels the first line (a), of which it is an explication. Similarly, the wearing out of the saints (b) has its parallel in their being given into the horn's hand for a specified period of time (d). The *'Elyônîn*, with whom the 'SM' is here equated is not at all molested or subjected to suffering. As for

---

549 *Contra* Engnell, *Critical Essays*, 240; and Davies, *Paul and Rabbinic Judaism*, 278f., who follows W. Manson, *Jesus the Messiah*, 173f. in considering the Son of Man of the *Parables* merged with the Suffering Servant. Manson's passages, which Davies compares with Isaiah (I En 46:3 with Isa 42:1; 42:6; 53:11; I En 46:4 with Isa 49:7; 52:15; I En 48:4 with Isa 42: 6; 49:3; 50:4–5; 52:13; 53:11) appear to me rather far-fetched.

550 The *Parables* and IV Ezra.

551 Only the *Parables*.

552 Cf. Taylor, *Mark*, 542; Moule, *The Phenomenon of the NT*, 89; Davies, *Paul and Rabbinic Judaism*, 280; Barrett in *NT Essays*, 1–18. Against the presence of the idea of suffering argues France, *Jesus and the OT*, 128ff. Cf. Dodd, *According to the Scriptures*, 117: "To say, as is often said, that the OT knows nothing of a suffering Son of Man is inaccurate". Porteous, *Daniel*, 111, is in agreement with this.

the Vision Part, in which the 'SM' is presented before the Aged One
during the judgment of the four beasts, there is a verisimilitude of sufferings in the context, in as much as it is the outrageous conduct of the
beasts, especially the fourth one, that calls for the assembling of the divine
assize. However, no explicit statement to the effect that the 'SM' suffers
is to be found there.

   This seems to leave Jesus' ascription of suffering and death to the Figure of the Son of Man without real parallel in the sources, and without
adequate basis in the interpretative tradition regarding the Son of Man. A
confirmation of this standpoint is probably to be found in Jn 12[553]. In
vv. 23f. Jesus is presented as speaking of the Son of Man's death in terms
of exaltation or glorification ($\delta o \xi a \sigma \vartheta \tilde{\eta}$). In vs. 32 he substitutes Son of
Man by the personal pronoun: $\kappa \grave{a} \gamma \grave{\omega} \; \grave{e} \grave{a} \nu \; \dot{v} \psi \omega \vartheta \tilde{\omega} \; \grave{e} \kappa \; \tau \tilde{\eta} \varsigma \; \gamma \tilde{\eta} \varsigma \; \ldots$ The
crowds, which, on account of their Jewish legacy, are already acquainted
with the messianic significance of the concept of Son of Man, as presented
in Dan 7 and the *Parables*, ask in bewilderment: $\dot{\eta} \mu \epsilon \tilde{\iota} \varsigma \; \dot{\eta} \kappa o \dot{v} \sigma a \mu \epsilon \nu \; \grave{e} \kappa$
$\tau o \tilde{v} \; \nu \acute{o} \mu o \upsilon \; \ddot{o} \tau \iota \; \dot{o} \; X \rho \iota \sigma \tau \grave{o} \varsigma \; \mu \acute{e} \nu \epsilon \iota \; \epsilon \grave{\iota} \varsigma \; \tau \grave{o} \nu \; a \grave{\iota} \tilde{\omega} \nu a \; , \kappa a \grave{\iota} \; \pi \tilde{\omega} \varsigma \; \lambda \acute{e} \gamma \epsilon \iota \varsigma \; \sigma \grave{v} \; \ddot{o} \tau \iota$
$\delta \epsilon \tilde{\iota} \; \dot{v} \psi \omega \vartheta \tilde{\eta} \nu a \iota \; \tau \grave{o} \nu \; \upsilon \grave{\iota} \grave{o} \nu \; \tau o \tilde{v} \; \grave{a} \nu \vartheta \rho \acute{\omega} \pi o \upsilon \; ; \tau \grave{\iota} \varsigma \; \grave{e} \sigma \tau \iota \nu \; o \grave{\upsilon} \tau o \varsigma \; \dot{o} \; \upsilon \grave{\iota} \grave{o} \varsigma \; \tau o \tilde{v}$
$\grave{a} \nu \vartheta \rho \acute{\omega} \pi o \upsilon$; Several observations are in order. First, Jesus had not spoken
of the Son of Man's $\dot{v} \psi \omega \vartheta \tilde{\eta} \nu a \iota$ but of his own, (vs. 32). The crowds,
however, understood that Jesus was identifying himself with a figure they
knew of as Son of Man. Second, Jesus had not mentioned any Messiah,
but only the Son of Man (vs. 23). The crowds, however, which thought of
the Messiah's exaltation under the Figure of the Son of Man — who, moreover, was to abide forever — found in Jesus' words, which implied a suffering and dying Son of Man, an insurmountable stumbling block. Third,
$T \grave{\iota} \varsigma \; \grave{e} \sigma \tau \iota \nu \; o \grave{\upsilon} \tau o \varsigma \; \dot{o} \; \upsilon \grave{\iota} \grave{o} \varsigma \; \tau o \tilde{v} \; \grave{a} \nu \vartheta \rho \acute{\omega} \pi o \upsilon$ means "Who is this Son of Man of
whom *you* are speaking?" The idea of a suffering Son of Man was incom-
prehensible to them, and thoroughly foreign to the kind of Son of Man
they had been taught to identify with the Messiah[554].

   We must therefore concude that the idea of 'suffering', which is such a
pronounced feature of the Son of Man of the Gospels, especially the
Synoptics, is, to judge from the sources available, not an explicit part of
the Son of Man tradition, which Jesus might have inherited. Nor is there
any basis for presupposing any other tradition, which might now be lost.

   Does this mean that our sources fail to supply any indications which
might explain how the Figure of the SM could come to be connected with
suffering? There are two important considerations in Dan 7 which need
to be taken into account. The one relates to the tension which is involved
in the juxtaposition of 'SM' with *'Elyônîn*. As was noted in Chapter
Two, the lowly designation of 'One like a son of man' in the Vision Part

---

553 The relation of the Johannine Son of Man to that of the synoptic is recognised e.g. by Schnackenburg, *NTS* 11 (1964–5) 129.
554 For a closely similar position see Thompson, *JTS* 12 (1961) 206ff.

gave place to the exalted designation 'Most High' (= *'Elyônîn*) in the Interpretation Part. To be sure the figure presented as 'One like a son of
man' is as such neither human nor in overt humiliation, and his being
compared to a human being is, in this context, where human kingdoms
are symbolized by beasts, carrying the idea of human dignity over against
the beasts. Nevertheless, in comparison with who the 'SM' actually is,
this presentation as a human-like being carries assuredly the idea of *Erniedrigung*. Therefore, it may be said that Dan 7 involves an upgrading
of this Figure from Vision to Interpretation, and in this sense the schema
of *Erniedrigung und Erhöhung* is at least vaguely recalled[555]. Moreover,
the presentation of this Figure as one like a *human* being inevitably carries
the connotations so characteristic of human beings, especially those connected with the expression 'son(s) of man/men' in the OT[556] and hence
makes it feasible to attribute to the concept characteristics of lowliness,
creatureliness, weakness and humiliation.

This consideration alone is not sufficient to explain the NT Suffering
Son of Man, but makes it in principle possible for the concept to assume
characteristics of suffering. The other consideration is that, given the ancient idea of the leader's or king's becoming the representative and substitute for his people, there would be nothing strange if the 'SM' of Dan
7 were seen as involved in the suffering of his saints. Thus, if Jesus had
come to understand himself as a substitute for his people there would
be nothing unnatural in his application to himself of the role of the 'SM'
as well as the suffering of the saints. That in the original vision of the 'SM'
suffering could not be directly connected with him was a matter of no
consequence. The saints suffered. That was all that mattered. Since he,
Jesus, understood himself as their substitute, their suffering was carried
over to him. Thereby Jesus modified the original concept of the 'SM', and
in true semitic fashion carried over to it the characteristics of suffering
which at best were only implicit as far as the heavenly Being thus portrayed was concerned, but explicit as far as his saints were concerned. As we saw
above[557], Jesus used much of the terminology and imagery of Dan 7 in
his descriptions of the SM's sufferings. In doing so he conflated the Son
of Man concept with that of the Suffering Servant[558], and thus opened
the way for him to draw upon Isaianic and other material as well. Thereby

555 See Lohmeyer, *Kyrios Jesus*, who traced the idea of Erniedrigung (and exaltation) in Phil 2:
5–11, i.e. σχήματι εὑρεθεὶς ὡς ἄνθρωπος to Dan 7:13. Black, *BJRL* 45 (1962–3) 315
says that ἐν ὁμοιώματι ἀνθρώπου "is the Danielic *Kᵉbarnash*". On the Jewish concept of
Erniedrigung und Erhöhung see Schweizer, *Erniedrigung und Erhöhung*.
556 See Chapter Two.
557 See above under "The Suffering SM".
558 Ross, *EvQ* 6 (1934) 36–49; Black, *SJT* 6 (1953) 1–11; Bowman, *ET* (1947–8) 283–8;
Cruvellier, *Etudes evangeliques* 15 (1955) 31–50; Riesenfeld in *En Bok om Nya Testamentet*,
359ff.; France, *Jesus and the OT*, e.g. 121ff.; esp. 148; *id., TynBul* 19 (1968) 26–52, esp.
49–52. See also Coppens *ETL* 39 (1963) 104–13, and *id., De Menschenzoon-logia in het Markus evangelie*.

he created a conception of the Son of Man, which went a long way beyond the traditional one in Dan, the *Parables*, or IV Ezra.

In a number of Gospel Suffering sayings the *characteristica* of the Son
of Man are taken from various quarters and blended together. Dan 7 is
combined with e.g. Isa 53, Ps 22 and Ez 34 in order to express adequately
the content of the new concept. Thus, the theme of the Son of Man's
παραδοθήσεται τοῖς ἀρχιερεύσιν καὶ γραμματεύσιν (Mt 20:18 = Mk 10:
33f. = Lk 18:31ff.; Mk 8:31 = Lk 9:21f. (or of his παραδίδοσθαι εἰς
χεῖρας ἀνθρώπων (ἁμαρτωλῶν) (Mt 17:22 = Mk 9:31 = Lk 9:44; Mt 24:
45 = Mk 14:41; Lk 24:7), or of his παραδοθήσεται . . . τοῖς ἔθνεσιν (Lk
18:31), not only recalls Dan (LXX) 7:25: καὶ παραδοθήσεται πάντα εἰς
τὰς χεῖρας αὐτοῦ (sc. the little horn) ἕως καιροῦ καὶ καιρῶν καὶ ἕως
ἡμίσους καιροῦ, spoken of the suffering saints of 'Elyônîn, but also (more
distantly) of Isa 53:12: παρεδόθη εἰς θάνατον ἡ ψυχή αὐτοῦ . . . καὶ
διὰ τὰς ἁμαρτίας αὐτῶν παρεδόθη and Ps 22:16 (LXX 21:17): ὅτι
ἐκύκλωσάν με κύνες πολλοί, συναγωγὴ πονηρευομένων περιέσχον με.
Similarly, the SM's sufferings and the contemptuous treatment which he
is to receive (Mk 9:12: πολλὰ πάθῃ καὶ ἐξουδενηθῇ) can have been inspired by Ps (LXX) 22:7f.: ἐγὼ εἰμι . . . ὄνειδος ἀνθρώπων καὶ ἐξουδένημα λαοῦ , πάντες οἱ θεωροῦντές με ἐξεμυκτήρισάν με and Isa 53:4—
8: ἠτιμάσθη καὶ οὐκ ἐλογίσθη . . . ἡμεῖς ἐλογισάμεθα αὐτὸν εἶναι ἐν
πόνῳ καὶ ἐν πληγῇ καὶ ἐν κακώσει. The idea that the Son of Man οὐκ
ἦλθεν διακονηθῆναι ἀλλὰ διακονῆσαι καὶ δοῦναι τὴν ψυχὴν αὐτοῦ
λύτρον ἀντὶ πολλῶν (Mt 20:28 = Mk 10:45) is a clear reflection of Isa
43:3f., 53:10ff. and Dan 7:9—14 as Stuhlmacher has shown[559]. Finally
his coming in order to ζητῆσαι καὶ σῶσαι τὸ ἀπολωλός (Lk 19:10) has
in all probability Ez 34:16 as its source: τὸ ἀπολωλὸς ζητήσω καὶ τὸ
πλανώμενον ἐπιστρέψω .

These few indications are offered only by way of illustrating how the
SM, as conceived in the Gospels, is of composite background, and that the
basic source, Dan 7, has been supplemented with material from other
sources. It is, however, not my intention to pursue the discussion further
in this direction. I only wished to indicate that all the crucial components
that go to the making of the Gospel Son of Man concept what it is, were
to be found in the background material — given the condition of bringing
that disparate material together, a matter of no particular difficulty for
Jews, — and that hence it is gratuitous to look with e.g. Dunn[560] to the
Early Church as the matrix in which the SM concept was formed in the
interests of Incarnation Christology.

In this section I have dwelt primarily upon the *Erniedrigung* aspects of
the SM and their relation to Dan 7. The exaltation aspects have not been

---

559 See under "The Suffering SM" above.

560 *Christology in the Making*, 82—97. Dunn's conclusions are based on a number of presup-
    positions with respect to Daniel, the *Parables*, etc. which are not supported by this study.

particularly treated because hardly anyone would challenge the role of
tradition here. Exaltation is clearly the most dominant feature of the Son
of Man in Daniel, the *Parables* and IV Ezra, so there was no particular
reasons to expatiate on this.

However, a word or two ought to be said about the character of deliverance whose Agent the Son of Man is. It was noted, above, that Jesus rejected the role of a nationalistic Messiah which, according to John, was
offered to him by the populace. At the same time it may be observed
that Jesus spoke frequently about deliverance or salvation[561]. The verb
σώζω is used often of the healing which the people received at Jesus'
hands[562]. Sometimes it is used of deliverance from an untoward situation[563]. But at quite a number of places the verb carries the sense of eschatological salvation relative to the future destiny of believers[564]. Not
only is the promised Child to be called symbolically *Jeshua* , but he is,
moreover, explicitly assigned the task of saving his people from their
sins (Mt 1:21). In the teaching of Jesus salvation is conceived of primarily
as a metaphysical and eschatological occurrence[565], whose Agent is none
other than the Son of Man: ἦλθεν γὰρ ὁ υἱὸς τοῦ ἀνθρώπου ζητῆσαι
καὶ σῶσαι τὸ ἀπολωλός [566].

The ascription of Saviourhood aspects to the Son of Man is all the more
interesting and significant, especially when we recall that Danielic hints
of this kind were not developed in the *Parables* or IV Ezra. At the same
time we ought not to distinguish too sharply between σώζω in the sense
of delivering the body (from physical illness) and σώζω in the sense of
delivering the soul (from Gehenna). Physical deliverance from illness
and decay, often attributed to the activity of demonic powers, and spiritual deliverance through conversion to the Kingdom of God, are two
aspects of the Son of Man's activity oriented towards the whole man. A
saying like ὁ υἱὸς τοῦ ἀνθρώπου οὐκ ἦλθεν διακονηθῆναι ἀλλὰ διακονῆσαι καὶ δοῦναι τὴν ψυχὴν αὐτοῦ λύτρον ἀντὶ πολλῶν [567] combines
these two aspects of the Son of Man's mission. Thus, the healings of Jesus
are part and parcel of his preaching of the Kingdom of God, whose Agent
the Son of Man is. Through these the powers of the Kingdom become operative by means of the victory of the Son of Man over the forces of evil.
The connection with Dan 7 becomes particularly obvious when we recall
the double nature of the deliverance of the saints. On the one hand they

---

561 Ἐλεύθερος-ἐλευθερία occurs only a handful of times in the Gospels, but σώζω is found
   51 X according to Moulton-Geden's *Concordance* and 54 X according to the *Computer-
   Konkordanz zum Novum Testamentum Graece*.
562 E.g. Mt 9:21f.; Mk 6:56; Lk 7:50; 8:48; 17:19.
563 E.g. Mt 8:25; 14:30; Mk 13:13; Lk 23:35ff.
564 E.g. Mt 10:22: 16:25; 19:25; 24:13; Mk 8:35; Lk 9:24; 13:23.
565 Negatively, e.g. Mt 10:28; positively e.g. Mt 24:13 = Mk 13:13;
566 Lk 19:10. Mt 18:11 and Lk 9:56 are to the same effect, but their genuineness is in question
   on account of their weak MS support.
567 Mt 20:28 = Mk 10:45.

experience an earthly deliverance from the little horn's power, which symbolizes the rule of demonic powers (ἀρχαί, ἐξουσίαι), and on the other, a more metaphysical deliverance implied in their coming under the everlasting protection and care of 'Elyônîn (= 'SM'). These embryonic ideas of Dan 7 etc., are, in the NT, developed quite explicitly, especially when they are expressed in Servant language (e.g. Lk 4:18 quoting Isa 61:1f.).

The idea of messianology is transformed by being understood in terms of the Son of Man, who is divested of all earthly functions, characteristic of the Davidic messiah, except that the object of his mission is the whole man, soul and body. Whereas the Davidic messiah was thought of primarily as a political figure, in the new type of messianology, in the role of Servant and Saviour, the Son of Man affects the sons of men both in what relates to their present situation and in what relates to their future destiny. Politics are set aside. Only man, as created by God, becomes the object of the Son of Man's activity. Deliverance or salvation becomes spiritualized by juxtaposing a host of evil spiritual powers — rather than human enemies (i e. the Romans) — as the tyrants from which the Son of Man comes to deliver his people and lead them safe into the Kindom of God.

d) The Son of Man and the Kingdom of God

H.B. Sharman prefaces the second part of his study[568] with the words:

> "The Son of Man is not represented as functioning for the realization of the Kingdom of God, either in the Present or in the Future; the Kingdom of God is not made dependent upon any form of activity by the Son of Man, whether on earth or from the heavens. Both Son of Man and Kingdom of God are represented as belonging both to the Present and to the Future, but not by virtue of any bond of actual relationship between them. Each moves independent of the other throughout the course of the synoptic record. The Son of Man has no Kingdom and the Kingdom of God has no Son of Man" [569].

It is the thesis of the present study that this summary is not a fair statement of the Gospel situation. Firstly, this viewpoint undoubtedly has its presuppositional basis in the faulty identification of the 'SM' in Dan 7 with the pious Jews, instead of with the pre-existent, transcendental being, who, as we saw, is the chosen Agent in God's eschatological Kingdom. But even quite apart from the question as to who the 'SM' actually is, he is in Dan 7:14 in fact presented as being invested with dominion and kingship! Secondly, both the *Parables* and IV Ezra clearly present their Son of Man in kingly dignity. There was therefore good traditional

---

Sharman, *Son of Man and Kingdom of God*, 89f.

569 Similarly Käsemann, *NTS* 1 (1945–5) 248–60; Conzelmann, *ZThK* 54 (1957) 277–96; and Vielhauer, in *Festschrift für G. Dehn*, 51-79 (= *Aufsätze zum NT*, 55–91). For criticism of these three works see Colpe, *Kairos* N, F. 14 (1972) 244ff.

basis for the linking of the Son of Man with the Kingdom of God[570]. Thirdly, as far as the Gospels are concerned, Sharman admits the existence of some texts in which the Son of Man is actually brought into connection with the Kingdom of God, though he reduces their number to four sayings[571], whose significance he then tries to minimize[572]. Furthermore, he admits that in two more texts[573] a kingdom is ascribed to Jesus, which "may or may not be associated with the concept of the Son of Man"[574]. The idea that Jesus as Son of Man should have a kingdom that is distinct from the Kingdom of God, whose Messenger and Agent he is, is indeed a curiosity[575]. These six texts in themselves disqualify Sharman's statement that "The Son of Man has no Kingdom and the Kingdom of God has no Son of Man". Hence, his proposed methodology to discard the concept Son of Man altogether in the study of the Kingdom of God[576] is to be rejected. Fourthly, there are more Gospel texts which connect the Son of Man with the Kingdom of God than Sharman has allowed.

In Mt 12:28–32 the point of departure is the Pharisees' attribution of Jesus' miracles to satanic activity. Jesus retorts that his works are performed with the cooperation of God's Spirit and that they attest the coming of the Kingdom of God. Were the Pharisees' blasphemy merely directed against the Son of Man as such, (i.e. Jesus' person) it would be forgivable. But now it is directed against the Spirit's manifestation through the Son of Man's works which reveal the Son of Man's real character and mission, and is therefore unforgivable[577]. Here the Son of Man is clearly presented as the Agent for the coming of God's Kingdom through whom the Spirit of God is operative![578] In Lk 17:20–30, in the Lukan redaction, the Pharisees' question about the time of the coming of the Kingdom, is answered for the disciples by a description of the signs preceding the Son of Man's coming. Though this collocation is probably not original, it strengthens the view that for the evangelists as they knew the tradition of Jesus' sayings there was nothing incongruent in juxtaposing the Son of Man with the Kingdom of God. Mt 25:31–40 is a most interesting

570 Jüngel, too, thinks that the Kingdom of God and the Son of Man belong together (in *Paulus und Jesus*, 261ff.). Similarly Ashby, *ET* 72 (1960–1) 362.
571 I.e. Mt 16:28; Lk 21:31; Mt 13:41; Lk 22:30.
572 *Son of Man and Kingdom of God,* 89–90.
573 I.e. Mt 20:21; Lk 23:42.
574 *Son of Man and Kingdom of God,* 90.
575 *Son of Man and Kingdom of God,* 90. On the identity of the Kingdom of the Father with the Kingdom of the Son of Man, see Walker, *CBQ* 30 (1968) 573–79, esp. 579.
576 Cf. e.g. Lk 23:42; "thy kingdom" addressed by the thief to Jesus, with Mt 6:10 "thy kingdom" addressed to God, and Lk 22:16ff., "the kingdom of God" in the institution of the Lord's Supper. In Lk 22:29f. Jesus evidently receives God's Kingdom.
577 See Ladd, *Theology,* 154f.
578 The Lukan parallel has δακτύλῳ Θεοῦ. Hamerton-Kelly, *NTS* 11 (1964–5) 167–9, argues that " 'finger of God' is a variation of 'hand of God' " and that "in view of the OT background, χείρ may be interchanged with δάκτυλος" (168). He contends, furthermore, that "the two phrases πνεῦμα Θεοῦ and δάκτυλος Θεοῦ are interchangeable" (169).

piece of evidence. Verse 31 begins by speaking of the coming of the Son of Man in glory together with his angels, of his being seated upon a throne of glory and engaging in the work of judgment. Here we have a picture of the typically Danielic and Enochic Son of Man. Having presented the Son of Man in this glorious manner, the speaker continues his story by referring to him as "King"! It is unthinkable that the Son of Man would be referred to as King unless he had a Kingdom, and it is again unthinkable that there would exist more than one Kingdom, the Kingdom of God[579]. There are, in fact, many more texts that present the Son of Man as coming in majesty and glory[580], as being escorted by a heavenly retinue[581], as sitting on a throne of glory[582], in fact, on the right hand of God[583], viz. *characteristica* which are exclusively predicated of kings[584].

Sharman's standpoint has been adopted by e.g..Vielhauer[585]. Vielhauer's thesis that the SM is not connected with the concept of the Kingdom is tied up with his rejection of the authenticity of every SM saying. Vielhauer's procedure in order to prove the lack of connection between the SM and the Kingdom of God is by way of proving that none of the SM sayings which connect the two concepts is authentic. His arguments, however, cannot be said to carry conviction. A few examples will illustrate the point[586]. Vielhauer argues that in Mk 8:38—9:1 the two themes of SM and Kingdom of God did not belong together originally as is shown by 9:1a "And he said to them"[587]. But even if we should disregard 9:1, which actually is a fitting sequel to 8:34—38 (and the introductory phrase could be understood as a redactional marker to emphasize the saying on the Kingdom), the description of the SM's coming in the glory of his father and with his retinue of angels is an unmistakable reference to his kingly status and alludes to the similar status of the 'SM' in Dan 7: 13f.[588] It cannot therefore be justifiably conceded that Mk 8:38 does

---

579 So e.g. Walker, *CBQ* 30 (1968) 579. The connection of the Kingdom of God with the Son of Man is recongized by e.g. Doeve, *Jewish Hermeneutics*, 119—67; Borsch, *The Son of Man*, 381; France, *Jesus and the OT*, 136; Schweizer, *JBL* 79 (1960) 124; Marshall, *NTS* 12 (1965— 6) 336f.; Michel, *TZ* 27 (1971) 87ff.; Engnell, *Critical Essays*, 239, and Colpe, *Kairos*, N.F. 14 (1972) 247ff., who expresses himself thus: "In der Gottesreichpredigt parallelen Prophezeiung des Menschensohns kann nun das Verhältnis der Person des Menschensohns zur Person Jesu nur in Analogie zum Verhältnis der Gottesherrschaft zu Jesu Wirken verstanden werden. So wie in Jesus das Gottesreich anbricht, so muss in ihm auch der künftige Menschensohn in Funktion treten, und zwar bereits nach seinem eigenen Selbstverständnis" (248).

580 Mt 16:27 = Mk 8:38 = Lk 9:26.

581 Mt 25:31; 24:31 = Mk 13:27.

582 Mt 19:28; 25:31.

583 Mt 26:64 = Mk 14:62 = Lk 22:69.

584 For a passion saying connecting the Son of Man with the Kingdom of God — if genuine — see Mt 26:21—24 = Mk 14:18—21 = Lk 22:15—22, and the discussion by Pesch in *Jesus und der Menschensohn*, 165—95, esp. 181—95.

585 E.g. *Aufsätze*, 55—91.

586 See also the criticism by Colpe, *Kairos*, N.F. 14 (1972) 244f.

587 *Aufsätze*, 58.

588 See also *Aufsätze*, 77ff.

not bring together the concept of the SM with that of the Kingdom of God. With regard to Mk 13:28ff. Vielhauer reasons that the parable of the fig tree is connected with the SM's coming, while in the parallel text in Lk 21:29ff. it is "möglicherweise" related to the Kingdom of God. In that case the parable originally would have nothing to do with the SM, as in the Marcan context it has nothing to do with the Kingdom of God. Vielhauer continues: "Ist die Vermutung über den ursprünglichen Sinn des Gleichnisses richtig, dann hätte Markus oder schon die ihm vorliegende Tradition ein ursprüngliches Reich-Gottes-Wort in ein Menschensohn-Wort verwandelt; aber dieser Schluss bleibt unsicher". Though Vielhauer admits that he builds upon a "Vermutung" and that his result is "unsicher", he nevertheless tacitly assumes it as sufficiently proven and continues to discuss Matthew's "ähnliches Bild wie Markus" with respect to the non-connection of the SM with the Kingdom of God! This is a peculiar way of building up one's accumulated argument. Finally, with reference to Mt 25:31—46 Vielhauer differentiates the SM (vs. 31) from the King (vv. 34, 40), and thus assails the authenticity of the SM logia, on the basis of the following arguments: a) SM and King are not interchangeable concepts, b) the SM is only occasionally presented as King, but never designated as such, and c) that King is a favourite Jewish metaphor for God[589]. These arguments (actually the first and the third — since the second one really is against Vielhauer's thesis!) are not decisive. The SM is the Agent of God's Kingdom in Daniel and I Enoch where he is invested with kingly rule. The same holds true of many NT texts[590]. As for the third question, God's being presented as King in pre-Danielic, pre-Enochic literature as well as in post-Danielic Jewish thought can in no way constitute a valid objection to the SM's assumption of a similar role, as indeed he does in, for example, Dan, I Enoch and — in the NT!

In conclusion, Vielhauer admits that "Die Grunde waren nicht überall gleich stringent. Einmal blieb es bei einem Wahrscheinlichkeitsbeweis (Mt 10:23), und einmal (Mt 24:37—39 par.) blieb die Frage offen; sie konnte von diesem Einzelspruch aus nicht mit Sicherheit oder Wahrscheinlichkeit entschieden werden"[591]. However, this does not deter Vielhauer from using also these "offene" cases as 'verdicts' against authenticity!

How deeply entrenched the idea that the SM and the Kingdom of God were unassociated in the teaching of Jesus is in some circles, is exemplified by the peculiar position suggested by Bammel[592], who unconvinced by Vielhauer's arguments, resorted to the other extreme, claiming the centrality of the SM idea in the teaching of Jesus and minimizing that of the Kingdom of God. This looks desperate.

---

589 *Aufsätze*, 63.
590 See above.
591 *Aufsätze*, 79f.
592 *SE* 3 (1964) 3—32.

The evidence produced in this study is deemed sufficient to base the claim that there is every presupposition for speaking of a fundamental connection between the two chief concepts in Jesus' preaching, viz. the Kingdom of God and its Agent, the Son of Man[593].

This question shall not be pursued any further, in as much as the interest of this section turns on the way in which the related themes of God's Kingdom and the 'SM' of Dan 7 can have contributed to shaping the corresponding ideas in the NT.

The idea of God's Kingdom or God's Rule has its inception in the election of Israel to be Yahweh's people[594]. The anarchy prevailing at the time of the Judges[595], which culminated in the impious conduct of Samuel's sons, issued into the popular demand for a king[596]. This demand, initially looked upon as a rejection of Yahweh's rule in a theocratic regime[597], was finally acceded to and a monarchy was established[598]. But the disappointment caused by the first king[599], coupled with the satisfaction experienced in respect to the second king, David[600], led to the promise: "I have made a covenant with my chosen one, I have sworn to David my servant: 'I will establish your descendants for ever and build your throne to all generations' "[601]. The monarchy was looked upon as operating under the suzerainty of Yahweh and as being a concrete manifestation of his Rule. Solomon's apostasy led to his rejection, though a semblance of a kingdom was ensured to his posterity, and was understood to preserve the Davidic dynasty[602]. Attention was now focussed on a future messiah, who would rule over the original kingdom of David in peace, righteousness and prosperity. The Davidic kingdom was thus somehow conflated with Yahweh's Rule. However, when even this semblance of Davidic kingdom was swept away by the Babylonian invasion, the

---

593 The probability that Jesus' teaching on the Kingdom was public while his teaching on the SM was private can hardly be used as an argument for dissociating the two sets of sayings. Firstly, this would still leave the two sets of logia connnected in Jesus' mind and teaching, and secondly, the question may be raised, Why would it have been more dangerous for Jesus to claim publicly that he was the SM than to claim that he was the Agent of God's Kingdom?

594 See Eichrodt, *Theology of the OT*, I, 39–41; von Rad, *OT Theology*, I, 39ff. Bright, *History of Israel*, 149, says: "The covenant was Israel's acceptance of the overlordship of Yahweh. And it is just here that that notion of the rule of God over his people, the Kingdom of God, so central to the thought of both Testaments, had its start." So, too, Bultmann, see Perrin, *The Kingdom of God*, 113.

595 Cf. the pessimistic way in which the era of the Judges is summarized by a supporter of royalty: "In those days there was no king in Israel; every man did what was right in his own eyes" Judg 21:25.

596 I Sam 8:4f.

597 Cf. I Sam 8:6–8.

598 Cf. I Sam 8:9ff.

599 Cf. I Sam 15:10; 16:1.

600 Cf. II Sam 7:15f.

601 Ps 89:3f. reflecting II Sam 7:15f.; Ps 132:11f.

602 I Kin 11:11–14.

promise made to David underwent in some circles a radical reinterpretation.

The post-exilic Book of Daniel has as its central theme the Kingdom or Rule of God. But the Kingdom of God of the Book of Daniel is conceived of on a wholly different plane than the mundane, this worldly, kingdom of David. Of decisive importance for the understanding of the Danielic conception of the Kingdom of God is Daniel's presentation of human kingdoms as wild beasts and the criteria used in evaluating the degree of evil in each beast. The various nations are weighed and evaluated on the balances of Yahwistic religion and ethics. From that standpoint no other culture or religion is more hybristic or repugnant than the culture and religion of Greece. Hence, the fourth beast is described as "different" from all others[603].

But in evaluating the various human dominions with such special criteria and in such dynamic terms, the author of Daniel was concerned to show that the kingdoms of men are in a strict sense more than the manifestation of purely human rule. The various kings/kingdoms are represented as being under the control of invisible malignant powers. These powers are in open warfare against the God of heaven and vent their wrath upon his people on earth. The author of Daniel saw how futile and naive the expectation and hope for the restoration of Davidic rule would be. Behind the Babylonian, Persian, or 'Greek domination he sighted the reign of invisible evil powers, which he called שלטניא (LXX: Θ: ἀρχαί, ἐξουσίαι), an idea that was to exert a deep influence on Paul[604]. He anticipated Paul in recognizing that the fight was essentially not "against flesh and blood, but against the principalities, against the powers, against the world rulers[605] of this present darkness, against the spiritual hosts of wickedness in the heavenly places"[606]. A messiah of Davidic character is here deemed to be a pure incongruity.

Whether this new element was or was not influenced by Iranian dualism, the fact remains that the author of Daniel postulated the existence of another world and another plane than the empirical one, a world that is constantly seeking to assert itself by intruding into the world of men and trying to determine their actions. The various beasts are nothing less than the manifestation of the reign of evil. Daniel's dualism surpasses all

---

603 Dan 7:19. I have dealt with these questions in a number of studies, which I hope to publish one day.

604 Cf. e.g. I Cor 2:6ff.; Gal 4:3–9; Eph 1:21; 2:2; 3:10; 6:12; Col 1:16; 2:8–10, 15, and see Caragounis, *The Ephesian Mysterion,* 157–61 and literature cited there.

605 The term κοσμοκράτωρ, for example, occurs in rabbinic literatur in the transliterated form קוזמוקרטור (see *Str.-B*, II, 552) often of kings of worldwide rule (e.g. *Ber. Rabba* 57:1; *Shir Rab.* 3:4), though in the Test. Sol. 8:2 (cf. 18:2) it is used of the demons: ἡμεῖς ἐσμεν τὰ λεγόμενα στοιχεῖα, οἱ κοσμοκράτορες τοῦ κόσμου τούτου. and see Dulling, *Test Sol* in Charlesworth, *OTP* I, 969f.

606 Eph 6:12.

previous conceptions of dualism in Yahwism. Moreover, in the last days, it is said, evil shall reach unprecedented proportions and nothing but a direct intervention of God or of his representative will be able to stay it. Here the Davidic messiah is thrown overboard. A new understanding of the human situation and consequently a new understanding of the nature of God's Kingdom or Rule has as its corollary a new conception of the Agent of God's Kingdom. In Daniel the old type of Davidic, earthly messianism dies, and a new 'messianic' type is born. In these two *foci* of the Book of Daniel — the Kingdom of God and the 'SM' — is to be found an influence on the teaching of Jesus, without a peer in the rest of the OT. The two Danielic *foci* become also the two central *foci* in the teaching of Jesus; but not as two unrelated *foci* as Sharman alleged, but as two *foci* in the closest connection with one another. The Danielic legacy to the NT is its conception of the Kingdom of God in abstract, dynamic terms and its conception of a heavenly, transcendental Agent for God's Kingdom, presented variously as 'Stone' and especially as 'SM'. Consequently too, in the Gospels the Agent for God's Kingdom is not the Davidic messiah, but the Son of Man. In this complex of ideas we have the main stream of Danielic influence on the Gospels, which surpasses all other areas of influence mentioned so far in this Chapter[607].

This may now be summarized in the following three points.

i. The Kingdom of God. The character of the Kingdom of God is abstract and dynamic. The subject of the Kingdom of God in the teaching of Jesus is extremely intricate and many questions regarding its precise character, its relation to Jesus' teaching and works, its relation to the present or future, etc. have been hotly debated[608]. It is neither possible nor necessary at this juncture to go into any of these questions. Suffice it to register the general agreement that by Kingdom of God Jesus did not refer to any messianic kingdom of the Davidic type, but to some form of God's total Rule over those who accepted Jesus' claims, whether it was conceived of as already begun through his ministry, or as about to begin at some future point in history, or as being atemporal and existential[609]. Many indeed are the texts that could be cited to support this claim — the dynamic nature of the Kingdom of God — but no discussion of these is possible within the limits of this study[610]. Bultmann's words are, however, worth quoting:

---

607 Bultmann, *Theology*, I, 4f. has a similar understanding in most of the points taken up, above.

608 Cf. e.g. Ladd, *Jesus and the Kingdom, passim;* Schnackenburg, *Gottes Herrschaft und Reich, passim,* Kümmel, *Promise and Fulfilment, passim;* Lundström, *The Kingdom of God in the Teaching, of Jesus,* e.g. 3f.; Perrin, *The Kingdom of God in the Teaching of Jesus, passim;* Bultmann, *Theology,* I, 4f.

609 This last is the position of Bultmann and his school, see Perrin, *The Kingdom of God in the Teaching of Jesus,* 113—29.

610 See e.g. Mt 6:10, 33; 12:28; 13:11 etc. 16:28; Mk 9:1; Lk 9:27; 10:9, 11:20; 12:31; 17:20f.

"It is clear that his (sc. Jesus') thought is not determined by the *national* hope then still alive in certain circles of the Jewish people, in which the time of salvation to be brought in by God was thought of as the restitution of the idealized ancient kingdom of David. No saying of Jesus mentions the Messiah-king who is to crush the enemies of the People, nor the lordship of Israel over the earth, nor the gathering of the twelve tribes, nor the joy that will be in the bounteous peace-blessed land. Rather, Jesus' message is connected with the hope of other circles which is primarily documented by the *apocalyptic* literature, a hope which awaits salvation not from a miraculous change in historical (i.e. political and social) conditions, but from a cosmic catastrophe which will do away with all conditions of the present world as it is. The presupposition of this hope is the pessimistic-dualistic view of the Satanic corruption of the total world complex . . . when the day he (sc. God) has determined is here, the judgment of the world will be held by Him or by His representative, the Son of Man, who will come in the clouds of heaven"[611].

Since such a view of the Kingdom of God was contrary to the current expectations of the Jews[612], Jesus' new doctrine must either have some other source as its origin, or have been his original contribution to the subject. Without wishing to deny the originality of Jesus — an undertaking that is bound to fail, anyway — the coincidence of his conception of the Kingdom of God with the Danielic presentation of it, especially in the light of his use of other Danielic concepts related to the theme of the Kingdom, is admitting of only one explanation : Jesus adhered to the Danielic tradition of an otherworldly, dynamic Kingdom of God.

This concept he took and reshaped and filled it with a content all of his own. Thus, the call to enter the Kingdom, the conditions and means for getting into it, the Kingdom's implications and ethics, etc. are matters in which Jesus exhibited his originality. But even so, it is still permissible to say that the kind of Kingdom which Jesus proclaimed was essentially a development of the Danielic conception rather than of the old national hope. Therefore, as far as the question of God's Kingdom is concerned, Jesus stands firmly rooted in the Danielic tradition.

ii. The Son of Man. It is significant, as Bultmann pointed out, above, that in the teaching of Jesus no "Messiah-king" is presented to act as the Agent or King in the Kingdom of God. On the contrary, that Agent or King is the Son of Man. In no other background than that of Daniel and the *Parables* does the Son of Man figure as the Agent and King in God's Kingdom. In Daniel the 'SM's' role in the condemnation and destruction of the beasts is implicit. In the *Parables* he is explicitly presented as Judge[613]. As for the Gospels, there too, that function is quite explicit[614]. But with regard to the Son of Man's role as Agent for and King in God's

---

611 *Theology*, I, 4f.
612 Contra Sharman, *Son of Man*, 107.
613 See Chapter Three, above.
614 Cf. Mt 12:28f. = Mk 3:27 = Lk 11:20ff.; Mt 13:41; 16:27 = Mk 8:38 = Lk 9:26; Mt 25:31ff. Cf. also Jn 5:27.

Kingdom, there is complete agreement between Daniel and the Gospels. Cf. e.g. the Θ text with a few parallels from Mt par.

7:13f. ἰδοὺ μετὰ (LXX: ἐπὶ) τῶν νεφελῶν τοῦ οὐρανοῦ ὡς υἱὸς ἀνθρώπου ἐρχόμενος (LXX: ἤρχετο) καὶ ἕως τοῦ παλαιοῦ τῶν ἡμερῶν ἔφθασε (LXX v. 1.: ὡς παλαιὸς ἡμερῶν παρῆν) καὶ προσήχθη αὐτῷ (LXX: καὶ οἱ παρεστηκότες προσήγαγον αὐτόν). καὶ αὐτῷ ἐδόθη ἡ ἀρχή (LXX: ἐξουσία) καὶ ἡ τιμὴ καὶ ἡ βασιλεία, καὶ πάντες οἱ λαοί, φυλαί, γλῶσσαι (LXX: πάντα τὰ ἔθνη τῆς γῆς) δουλεύσουσιν αὐτῷ (LXX: πᾶσα δόξα λατρεύουσα αὐτῷ) ἡ ἐξουσία αὐτοῦ αἰώνιος, ἥτις οὐ παρελεύσεται (LXX: οὐ μὴ ἀρθῇ) καὶ ἡ βασιλεία αὐτοῦ οὐ διαφθαρήσεται.

7:27. καὶ ἡ βασιλεία αὐτοῦ βασιλεία αἰώνιος (LXX: βασιλεῦσαι βασιλείαν αἰ-ώνιον), καὶ πᾶσαι αἱ ἀρχαὶ (LXX: πᾶσαι αἱ ἐξουσίαι) αὐτῷ δουλεύσουσιν καὶ ὑπα-κούσονται (LXX: ὑποταγήσονται καὶ πει-θαρχήσουσιν αὐτῷ ἕως καταστροφῆς τοῦ λόγου).

13:41. ἀποστελεῖ ὁ ΥΑ ... ἐκ τῆς βασιλείας αὐτοῦ.

16:27. μέλλει γὰρ ὁ ΥΑ ἔρχεσθαι ἐν τῇ δόξῃ τοῦ Πατρὸς αὐτοῦ.

16:28. ἕως ἄν ἴδωσιν τὸν ΥΑ ἐρχόμενον ἐν τῇ βασιλείᾳ αὐτοῦ.

19:28. ὅταν καθίσῃ ὁ ΥΑ ἐπὶ θρόνου δόξης αυτοῦ ...

24:30. ὄψονται τὸν ΥΑ ἐρχόμενον ἐπὶ τῶν νεφελῶν τοῦ οὐρανοῦ μετὰ δυνάμεως καὶ δόξης πολλῆς ...

25:31ff. ὅταν δὲ ἔλθῃ ὁ ΥΑ ἐν τῇ δόξῃ αὐτοῦ καὶ πάντες οἱ ἄγγελοι μετ' αὐτοῦ, τότε καθίσει ἐπὶ θρόνου δόξης αὐτοῦ ... τότε ἐρεῖ ὁ βασιλεύς ...

26:64. ἀπ' ἄρτι ὄψεσθε τὸν ΥΑ καθήμε-νον ἐκ δεξιῶν τῆς δυνάμεως καὶ ἐρχόμε-νον ἐπὶ τῶν νεφελῶν τοῦ οὐρανοῦ.

28:18. ἐδόθη μοι πᾶσα ἐξουσία ἐν οὐ-ρανῷ καὶ ἐπί γῆς ... καὶ ἰδοῦ ἐγὼ μεθ' ὑμῶν εἰμι πάσας τὰς ἡμέρας ἕως συντε-λείας τοῦ αἰῶνος.

It goes without saying that in all these cases the connections back to Daniel cannot be explained as mere coincidence. As for Mt 28:18 it is a clear allusion to the Son of Man's assumption of absolute authority in heaven and on earth as depicted in Dan 7:14, 27b.

iii. The rebellious powers. Both in the teaching of Jesus and in Daniel 7 these powers play a central role and are directly connected with the Kingdom of God and with the Son of Man. It was shown in my discussion in Chapter Two that these powers are thought of as evil celestial poten-tates who have taken control of the world and through their subordinates, the empires, direct all their efforts against the Aged One and the saints of 'Elyônîn. Their one goal is to thwart the establishment of God's Rule[615]. Whether the 'SM' is thought of as causally related to their overthrow is not made explicit. Presumably he is co-Judge when the beasts are judged[616].

---

615 Cf. Dan 7:25.

616 That in Dan 7:13 he seems to be presented after the judgment on the beasts has taken place, need not cause any difficulty. This is in line with the semitic mentality in thinking linearly and relating sequentially rather than presenting the events in their intricate interrelationship and overlapping as they actually take place.

617 Cf. Mt 4:17–24.

What is, however, crystal clear is that he receives the dominion and rule which these powers once exercised. He thus displaces and replaces them in the government of the world. The 'SM' receives the dominion of the celestial overlords, while his saints are awarded the earthly dominion of the kings/kingdoms under the whole heaven. These circumstances find striking affinities in the Gospels. From the very start of his mission[617] Jesus was aware that the proclamation of the Kingdom of God implied a declaration of war against the demonic powers who held the 'children' of the Kingdom captive through various physical scourges, direct posses-sion, or blindness to the truth. He proclaimed the Kingdom of God in word and deed. His miracles were so integral to the message of the King-dom that he did not deem it right to entrust his disciples with its pro-clamation without first equipping them with the power to heal and to drive out demons[618]. The miracles of Jesus are thus not something extra, something additional, to the proclamation of the Kingdom of God, but an essential part of the Kingdom. The healing of the sick, the opening of the eyes of the blind, etc. are, of course, part of the mission of the Servant[619]. but in Jesus' mission these works receive new significance by being col-oured by the Danielic conception of reality, thus receiving the character of Son of Man attacks on the kingdom of evil[620]. His miracles, especially his driving out of demons, are construed as proof that Satan's power is broken[621] and that the Kingdom of God is breaking in: εἰ δὲ ἐν πνεύματι Θεοῦ ἐγὼ ἐκβάλλω τὰ δαιμόνια, ἄρα ἔφθασεν ἐφ' ὑμᾶς ἡ βασιλεία τοῦ Θεοῦ[622].

To conclude, the collocation of Son of Man, Kingdom of God and the evil powers shown by such striking parallels to be the common concern of both Daniel and the Gospels, so far from being a question of coincid-ence, is the most solid evidence for the vital significance of the Danielic concepts of 'SM' and Kingdom of God for the teaching of Jesus. This rare collocation of these three concepts is to be found only in Daniel, the *Parables* and the teaching of Jesus according to the Gospel tradition. Our discussion has shown that Daniel must be regarded as the source.

Any serious attempt to explicate either or both of the two central *foci* of Jesus' teaching will have to take account of these facts. The Son of Man can be made the subject of profitable study, not à la Vermes, à la Casey, or à la Lindars, but by being viewed within its natural matrix, viz. the Kingdom of God. Conversely, the Kingdom of God will remain 'Kingless' and inexplicable unless the Son of Man is allotted his rightful place within it. Finally, the two can become meaningful only by being juxtaposed with and viewed against the context of the evil spiritual

---

618 Cf. Mt 10:5ff.; Lk 10:17.
619 Cf. Isa 61:1f.
620 Cf. Mt 12:22–29.
621 Cf. Lk 10:18: ἐθεώρουν τὸν σατανᾶν ὡς ἀστραπήν ἐκ τοῦ οὐρανοῦ πεσόντα.
622 Mt 12:28.

powers, from whose grip the Son of Man delivers his people and leads them into the Kingdom of God[623].

E. Conclusions

The discussion in the Fourth Chapter showed that the SM research is in deep crisis. Many scholars have entered the discussion without indicating for their readers the criteria controlling the evaluation of the evidence in their research. Their results often contradict one another, while not too seldom they are self-contradictory. A few scholars have been particularly careful to indicate their criteria, but even here there has been no agreement either as to the criteria to be used, or as to the results obtained. The basic fault here is the unwarrantably negative view that has by and large been taken with regard to the sources. This suspicion has been largely determinative in the reconstruction of a Son of Man concept that is at such variance with the data of the sources.

The contradictory picture which emerged from a brief consideration of the criteria used and the results obtained, showed that the exclusion of some, or most, or all of the SM logia by various scholars was not the result of intrinsic problems associated with these sayings, but of *a priori* decisions as to what a particular scholar thought should be regarded as genuine or otherwise. It is obvious that SM research cannot be carried out in this way. This led me to the formulation of certain interpretative principles and criteria reflecting the general nature of the sources, especially in the light of very recent research about them. The discussion showed that the title Son of Man goes back to Jesus himself, and that though in the Gospel tradition some SM sayings may have been resolved into the personal pronoun or vice versa, the evangelists have given us what Jesus' disciples (in a wider sense) preserved in the tradition on account of the importance which they attached to Jesus' teaching, viz. an authentic picture of his teaching about himself as Son of Man.

A further result is that the NT Son of Man who has affinities with the Son of Man of the *Parables* and of IV Ezra as well as Daniel, is nevertheless directly dependent upon the last-named work, but may even occasionally have cited the *Parables*. The influence of Daniel is seen in particular sayings belonging to each one of the three classes of SM sayings. In gauging the breadth of Danielic influence upon Jesus' concept of the Son of Man it was found that it is not merely a question of some verbal parallels — which undoubtedly exist and are presented — but more than that a question of the total conception which Jesus evinces of himself, his mission and of the Kingdom of God. This means that I am led to the con-

---

623 These ideas play an important part also in the (esp. later) theology of Paul.

clusion that the Son of Man and the Kingdom of God are in Jesus' teaching indissolubly connected with each other, as they were in Daniel, and that in conjunction with Jesus' fight against the powers of darkness — another Danielic ingredient!, — the nexus between Jesus' teaching about the Son of Man in earthly work, in death and in exaltation, his defeat of the evil powers and the coming of the Kingdom of God constitutes the most interesting and the most important area of Danielic 'SM' legacy to the teaching of Jesus.

Vision and Interpretation
(Epilogue and Conclusions)

The subtitle of the present investigation is "Vision and Interpretation".
I have chosen to use this subtitle as the title of my epilogue and conclusions. The reader may interpret the first element in it, "Vision", in light
of the use of the term in Daniel, and the second element, "Interpretation", in light of the Gospels' Son of Man. That would certainly be a
valid way of interpreting my subtitle. It would be justified in as much as
the Danielic 'SM' is a κατ᾽ ἐξοχήν 'visionary' term with all the elements
of the obscure, the mysterious, the strongly allusive and at the same time
the elusive so characteristic of the apocalyptic genre. And yet that would
not be the whole truth. It would lead to the false impression that in the
Gospels we have *the Interpretation*, and by doing so invalidate the central
element in the Gospels' Son of Man, who is still the great enigma — if no
longer as to *who*, at least as to *how*! We may change the metaphor since
what is characteristic of the Gospels is not the visionary but the parabolic.
The parabolic teaching of the Gospels finds its most outstanding example
in the 'parable' of *Jesus the Son of Man*. In this 'Parable', all that in Jesus'
parables is obscure, incomprehensible, and offensive finds its consumma-
tion, in as much as it concerns his own person. The 'Parable' is — obscure.
The Aramaic *bar nasha* might have been understood by some of Jesus'
contemporaries as a usable, though by no means frequent, form of self-
reference, and thus the real import of the title could have eluded them[1].
Jesus could put into this title his own content without arousing the multitude's or anyone else's suspicions. It is — incomprehensible. The content
which Jesus seemed to put into it appears to have defeated the audience's
ability to assimilate the new information with the old content associated
with the term. 'Who is this Son of Man?' — was the reaction. It is — offensive (i.e. a *skandalon*). In the final analysis, it was Jesus' claim to be the
Son of Man — in the full sense of the Danielic 'SM' — that brought about
his condemnation by the Sanhedrin.

Nor would it appear that the disciples — on the theory that Son of Man
belonged to Jesus' private teaching, an attractive theory, but one which
is not entirely free from difficulties — were more successful in decoding

---

1 Cf. the similar character of the closing remarks by Lindars, *BJRL* 63 (1980–1) 462: "There
is an elusive quality about Jesus, which I believe is not merely a matter of intractable historical problems, but is part of his authentic personality and is one facet of his genius."

the full significance and implications of the claim. A parable without interpretation is merely dark, unmeaning words. The 'Parable' found its interpretation at the resurrection. The vision of Jesus the Son of Man in the Gospels, itself constituting an interpretation of the original vision of the 'SM' and hence an advance on it, is now finally and definitely interpreted following the Easter events. Every piece of the puzzle now falls into place. Now we know not only who the Son of Man is, but also *why* and *how* Jesus is the Son of Man.

In the present state of the Gospels, Jesus the Son of Man is both parable (or vision) and interpretation. The two parts of a parable, the *Bild*-part and the *Sach*-part, do not always stand in the Gospels separate from one another as in the analysis of the modern interpreter, but are often blended together, with elements of the *Sach*-part being anticipated in the *Bild*-part[2]. So it would seem is the case with the 'Parable' of the Son of Man. In the Gospels we have the interpreted 'Parable' of Jesus the Son of Man. But to say this is not the same as saying that the 'Parable' is created by the Interpretation. Rather it was the 'Parable' that necessitated the Interpretation. And that 'Parable' in its unexplained state was sufficiently perceived by those it confronted. Even if they did not understand all its details, they grasped its gist: ἔγνωσαν γὰρ ὅτι πρὸς αὐτοὺς τὴν παραβολὴν εἶπεν![3] The modern interpreter, however, who is concerned to separate the vision from its interpretation, the historical from the theological, is indeed confronted with a difficult, if not insoluble problem. On the other hand, it may be asked: How valid is history without explanation? Is it just a case of statistics or of meaningful communication?

The interpretation of Jesus the Son of Man impresses itself in another way. It does so by its eloquent absence in most of the NT writings, which at the same time happen to be, for the most part, the earlier ones. Could this mean that Son of Man is a late creation, which is why it fails in e.g. Paul? Not at all! The term Son of Man fails in all of the books of the NT which do not purport to deal with the historical Jesus. Its mention in Acts 7:56 is placed in the context of Jerusalem Christianity only a short time after Jesus' death, and has, moreover, in that context, the added significance of bringing home to the Jewish authorities Jesus' words in "the first book" (Lk 22:69), even though the Son of Man is, in the latter book, not "sitting". The only other occurrence outside the Gospels, Rev 1:13, is clearly necessitated by the description of the risen Christ in terms of the Aged One of Dan 7:9 and 7:13 (Cf. Rev 1:7)[4]. Why then does it not occur in Paul? Simply, because it is interpreted! Daniel himself had set the pat-

---

2 Cf. e.g. The words ἀγαθός, πονηρός in Mt 7:17f. used improperly of trees (by anticipation), which actually symbolize good and bad people respectively. Cf. also Mt 13:19ff., where words strictly applying to the interpretation are introduced in sentences dealing with the *Bild*-part of the parable.

3 Mk 12:12 = Mt 21:45 = Lk 20:19.

4 Heb 2:5 is not a case in point. Its character has been discussed above.

tern for this. While in the Vision Part he had spoken of the 'One like a son of man', in the Interpretation Part he kept consistently to the exalted term 'Elyônîn. Paul was certainly acquainted with the title Son of Man, as Jeremias has shown[5], but in the light of Christ's exaltation following his resurrection, Paul preferred to refer to him with the title Κύριος (cf. e.g. Phil 2:5–11)[6], which is a good dynamic equivalent of 'Elyônîn[7], rather than with a title whose human associations in the Greek form were as obvious as the term was incomprehensible. Thus Paul could say: εἰ καὶ ἐγνώκαμεν κατὰ σάρκα Χριστόν, ἀλλὰ νῦν οὐκέτι γινώσκομεν (II Cor 5:16). Thus the title Son of Man never won any currency in the Early Church, which chose to keep to Χριστός and Κύριος[8], a circumstance that receives corroboration from the fact that the evangelists attribute its use exclusively to Jesus[9], and also corroborates the trustworthiness of the evangelists' tradition.

That the evangelists, writing after Paul, make use of a non-current title, is evidence of their interest in history, and an indication of the historicity of the use of the term by Jesus. Unlike Paul and the other authors of letters, who are concerned with Interpretation, the evangelists are primarily interested in History. Even though their history-writing does not meet modern standards of historiography, it is in fact quite comparable to the kind of biography-writing generally practiced in the ancient world[10]. The title Son of Man had been used by Jesus and it was the concern of the evangelists to present the traditions which had reached them. In doing so it was inevitable that Interpretation would come to interact with Vision and leave its marks on It. But this recognition does not warrant the thesis that in the title Son of Man we meet Interpretation and nothing else. Though the phraseology of the contexts in which the term is embedded has taken its final shape in the hands of the evangelists, the traditions behind it evidence a stable core of Son of Man conceptualization attributable to Jesus and involving sayings of all three classes as discussed in Chapter Four.

The main conclusions of the above study will now be summarized briefly. But first the following remarks are in order. The first chapter though introducing the problem and therefore a necessary part of the in-

---

5 *Theology*, 265ff. (*Theologie*, 252ff.).

6 Cf. Hofius, *Der Christushymnus Phillipper 2, 6–11*, pp. 27f.

7 Semantically rather than etymologically considered. Tödt, *Der Menschensohn*, 86ff. concedes the parallelsim of *Kyrios* and Son of Man, from which Massingberd-Ford, *JBL* 87 (1968) 266, draws the conclusion that " 'Son of Man' was a substitute for 'the Name',"

8 To the popularization of Χριστός in the Early Church may have contributed the very early nickname Χριστιανός given to Jesus' followers apparently by Romans, a circumstance that would, of course, presuppose the prior use of Χριστός by his followers.

9 Except when his words are being quoted (Jn 12:34).

10 Cf. the biographies written by e.g. Plutarch (*Parallel Lives*), Diogenes Laertius (*Lives of Philosophers*), Suetonius (*Lives of Caesars*), not to mention Philostratus' *Life of Apollonius of Tyana*.

vestigation is, as far as the positive theses of this work are concerned, somewhat in isolation from the other three chapters which belong more closely together. As far as this last point goes, the thesis or theses of each chapter is argued for on its own grounds. This means that if the theses of one chapter were to fall, that would not automatically involve the invalidation of the theses of the other chapters. On the other hand, this may not be understood as implying that the present work is a string of unrelated theses brought together merely by the general similarity of theme. The accumulated *Thesis* from Chapter Two to Chapter Three to Chapter Four, indeed, in important respects, already from Chapter One, would lose its thrust and effectiveness if the theses of each chapter were considered in isolation. The work is a unity, and with the qualification made, must be considered as a unity.

The first chapter showed that the interest in the linguistic or philological aspects of the term Son of Man is at least a century old. Its resuscitation by Vermes' research has been of some interest as far as Aramaic texts go, but is unsuccessful as far as the Gospel Son of Man is concerned. This does not mean that the Gospel Son of Man expression cannot on occasion be substituted by 'I'. It can. That is, however, owing to the fact that the term is used in the third person and as self-reference, and not to any intrinsic significance relative to the term itself. In Aramaic texts it actually occurs indefinitely with the sense of 'one', 'someone' and once instead of 'I'. Besides, Vermes' theory is unnacceptable because it does not make even grammatical sense when applied to many of the NT passages, and because Son of Man is not co-existensive in semantic content with 'I' and therefore not a true substitute. Nor would Vermes' theory apply to Dan 7:13, which after all is the text that has inspired the NT term. Casey's and Lindars' work can hardly be said to have led to any more convincing results.

In the second chapter all of the current interpretations of Daniel's 'SM' are 'weighed' and found 'wanting' and are therefore rejected. The most widespread view that the 'SM' represents the pious Jews has been undermined from two quarters, by the History of Religions approach as well as by an interpretation that has been in vogue for some time, i.e. the so-called 'angelic' interpretation (e.g. Procksch, Noth, Coppens). But these interpretations too are shown to be untenable. A detailed examination of Dan 7 based on a historical, philological and Text-linguistic analysis reveals that Daniel did not intend its 'SM' as a symbol of the persecuted Jews, but as a symbol — consciously contrasting with the symbols of the beasts — of the figure with which he associates the saints in the Interpretation Part, namely *'Elyônîn* — the Exalted One. The *'Elyônîn* is not the traditional messiah, since Daniel's concept of history and reality are far different from the traditional Jewish conception and messianic expectations. Daniel sees salvation as coming from a divine intervention, and thus presents the Agent for God's eschatological Kingdom as a heavenly being in Ezekielian imagery.

The Danielic 'SM' is then found to be an important factor in the Jewish conception of messianic expectations. There are good grounds for the view that in post-Danielic thought the conception of the messiah was not monolithic, but different views of messianology competed with one another in Jewish religious circles. Side by side with the 'classical' expectation of a Davidic messiah of earthly origin and character, there developed in certain circles, a 'messianism' which took its cue from Daniel. The *Parables* of I Enoch is at present the most important witness to this development. Its author consciously constructed his composition in such a way as to put across an alternative view of messianism, one which he considered he had found in Dan 7. In doing so he went a long way beyond Daniel, and what was for the most part only implicit in the former book, became quite explicit in the latter. In the *Parables* the new insights regarding God's Rule as set forth in Daniel are merged with the messianic hope of Israel, though the Messiah, or the Righteous One, or the Elect One, or the Son of Man as this figure is called in this work, is closer to the Danielic 'SM' than to the traditional messiah. It is thus a question of a Messiah, but a Messiah of heavenly origin and character. This view was in important respects shared by IV Ezra. Together these works witness to an interpretative tradition of Daniel's 'SM' which, in essentials, was in agreement with Daniel's own conception of the corresponding figure. This finding is further confirmed by the identical interpretation of Dan 7 by the rabbis, and the currency of such an understanding among the Jews of Jesus' time seems to be presupposed by certain NT texts.

As far as the NT is concerned, the conclusions may be summarized in the following way. My discussion of the criteria often used in SM research has shown their unreliable character and highlighted the need for the formulation of more stringent criteria. This result is in line with a growing scholarly dissatisfaction with the criteria currently in use. At the same time the discussion showed that there are no incontrovertible grounds for rejecting wholesale the sayings of any one of the three classes into which modern scholarship has divided the SM sayings. This division is problematic. Neither Jesus nor the evangelists differentiated between the various sets of functions of the SM. It is therefore strictly speaking improper to play the one class of sayings against the other. The present investigation showed that at least some of the sayings of each class are authentic.

No connection could be established between the NT Son of Man concept and the Aramaic idiom of *bar (e)nash(a)*. This goes also for the latest version of this theory, which is based on one single Aramaic example and at that of confessedly "ambiguous" character. The titular character of the expression is shown not least by the 'hard core' of the ideas with which it occurs on the lips of Jesus. Jesus' use of the SM title looks backward to his spiritual heritage, and underscores his conscious continuity with the SM tradition.

The associations of the NT concept with the OT (apart from Dan) are extremely meagre, being limited for the most part to some general characteristics of lowliness, etc., primarily applicable to a few sayings of the Earthly Life group. The main guidelines for the development of the concept in Jesus' thought stem incontestably from Daniel.

Jesus' bold identification of himself with the Danielic 'SM' was not a reinterpretation or an individualization of a 'corporate' figure (i.e. the unfortunate identification of the 'SM' with the saints). Jesus spoke of himself as ὁ υἱὸς τοῦ ἀνθρώπου. In the definite article he put not only a definite sense (which the term lacked in Daniel) but practically a demonstrative sense (which the article could carry since Homeric times), alluding to the Danielic 'SM'. Jesus believed that he was *that Son of Man*, i.e. the One of whom Daniel had spoken.

A detailed examination of a few sayings taken from each one of the three classes of SM logia, shows that no cogent arguments can be brought against their authenticity and that the Danielic influence on each one of them is palpable. Though the Danielic 'SM' is primarily an exalted being, the concurrence of Jesus' understanding of his mission with the semitic view of the representative function of the leader led him to combine in himself as the Son of Man the traits of the Danielic 'SM' with those of the saints whom the latter represented, and thus achieve the synthesis of a Suffering and an Exalted Son of Man.

Jesus' view of himself as the Son of Man coloured his whole conception of himself, his work and his teaching. His idea of messianology differed from that of his contemporaries because he followed another interpretative tradition. This tradition had begun with Daniel and was carried on by I Enoch, IV Ezra and certain rabbis. The tradition entailed a dynamic interpretation of the messianic texts whereby the Messiah was understood to be David's lord rather than son, by being identified with the transscendental SM of Daniel and the apocalyptists. Jesus understood himself as the Son of Man Messiah, whose role was to give his life for his people, but thereafter also to appear in glory and to function as the eschatological Judge.

Contrary to the opinion of some the SM and the Kingdom of God cannot be proved to be mutually exclusive concepts. On the contrary, the SM idea is associated with God's Rule from the very beginning (in Daniel). As an earthly SM Jesus understood his task to be to announce the Kingdom of God. Daniel's influence had led him to think of God's Kingdom as opposed by invisible evil powers, powers which corresponded to those celestial rulers who in Dan 7 were the primary and moving agents in the concept of the beasts. Jesus' miracles were not merely acts of mercy towards the oppressed, but had the deeper significance of attacks on those malignant powers who opposed the establishment of God's Kingdom. His miracles were therefore an integral part of his proclamation of the Kingdom. It is primarily in this triad of Gospel concepts: Jesus as the Son of Man, his warfare against the rebellious celestial powers and his proclamation of the Kingdom of God in time as well as his future function as Judge and King, that Daniel's legacy to Jesus can be best appreciated and the person of Jesus can be best understood.

Bibliography

I. Abbreviations

AB	The Anchor Bible
ABR	Australian Biblical Review
AcOr (H)	Acta Orientalia (Havniae)
AJPh	American Journal of Philology
ALGRM	Ausführliches Lexikon der griechischen und römischen Mythologie
AnBib	Analecta Biblica
ANET	Ancient Near Eastern Texts Relating to the OT ed. J.B. Pritchard
APOT	The Apocrypha and Pseudepigrapha of the OT ed. R.H. Charles
ASTI	Annual of the Swedish Theological Institute
ATANT	Abhandlungen zur Theologie des Alten und Neuen Testaments
ATR	Anglical Theological Review
AUSS	Andrews University Seminary Studies
BAG	Bauer, W − Arndt, W.F. − Gingrich, F.W., A Greek-English Lexicon of the NT and Other Early Christian Literature
BC	Bible Commentary, St. Louis
BDB	Brown F. − Driver, S.R. − Briggs, C.A., A Hebrew and English Lexicon of the OT
BDR	Blass, F. − Debrunner, A. − Rehkopf, F., Grammatik des neutestamentlichen Griechisch
ΒΕΠΕΣ	Βιβλιοθήκη Ἑλλήνων Πατέρων καὶ Ἐκκλησιαστικῶν Συγγραφέων
BFBS	British and Foreign Bible Society
BFChTh	Beiträge zur Forderung christlicher Theolgie
Bib	Biblica
BibLeb	Bibel und Leben
Biblebhashyam	Biblebhashyam
BibOr	Biblica et Orientalia
BibS (F)	Biblische Studien (Freiburg)
BJRL	Bullentin of the John Rýlands Library
BKAT	Biblischer Kommentar: Altes Testament
BR	Biblical Research
BT	Bibliotheca Teubneriana
BT	The Bible Translator
BTB	Biblical Theology Bulletin
BZ	Biblische Zeitschrift
BZAW	Beihefte zur ZAW
CBQ	The Catholic Biblical Quarterly
CGTC	Cambridge Greek Testament Commentary
ConNT	Coniectanea Neotestamentica
CTA	Corpus de tablettes en cunéiformes alphabétiques découvertes à Ras-Shamra − Ugarit de 1929 à 1939
DJD	Discoveries in the Judaean Desert

Down Rev	The Downside Review
DTT	Dansk Teologisk Tidsskrift
EBib	Études Bibliques
EncBib	Encyclopedia Biblica
EncJud	Encyclopaedia Judaica
ET	The Expository Times
ETL	Ephemerides Theologicae Lovenienses
EvQ	Evangelical Quarterly
EvT	Evangelische Theologie
EWNT	Exegetisches Wörterbuch zum Neuen Testament
FRLANT	Forschungen zur Religion und Literatur des Alten und Neuen Testaments
GCS	Die griechischen christlichen Schriftsteller
G-K	Gesenius, W., Hebrew Grammar, ed. by E. Kautzsch. Engl. tr. by A.E. Cowley
Greg	Gregorianum
HAT	Handbuch zum Alten Testament
HSM	Harvard Semitic Monographs
HTCNT	Herder's Theological Commentary on the NT
HTKNT	Herders Theologischer Kommentar zum Neuen Testament
HTR	Harvard Theological Review
HUCA	Hebrew Union College Annual
HUT	Hermeneutische Untersuchungen zur Theologie
IB	The Interpreter's Bible
ICC	The International Critical Commentary
IDB	The Interpreter's Dictionary of the Bible
IEE	Ἱστορία τοῦ Ἑλληνικοῦ Ἔθνους
IEJ	Israel Exploration Journal
Int	Interpretation
JAOS	Journal of the American Oriental Society
JBL	Journal of Biblical Literature
JdTh	Jahrbuch für protestantische Theologie
JETS	Journal of the Evangelical Theological Society
JJS	Journal of Jewish Studies
JNES	Journal of Near Eastern Studies
JpTh	Jahrbuch für protestantische Theologie
JR	The Journal of Religion
JSHRZ	Jüdische Schriften aus hellenistisch- römischer Zeit
JSJ	Journal for the Study of Judaism in the Persian, Hellenistic and Roman Period
JSNT	Journal for the Study of the NT
JSOT	Journal for the Study of the OT
JTS	The Journal of Theological Studies
Jud	Judaica
Kairos	Kairos
K-B	Koehler, L. – Baumgartner W., Lexicon in Veteris Testamenti Libros
KEKNT	Kritisch- Exegetischer Kommentar über das Neue Testament
Klio	Klio
LCL	Loeb Classical Library
LSJ	Liddell, H G. – Scott, R. – Jones, H.S., A Greek-English Lexicon

MGWJ	Monatsschrift für Geschichte und Wissenschaft des Judentums
NAb	Neutestamentliche Abhandlungen
NCB	New Clarendon Bible
NCBC	New Century Bible Commentary
NEB	The New English Bible
NERT	Near Eastern Religious Texts Relating to the OT
NICNT	The New International Commentary on the New Testament
NIGTC	New International Greek Testament Commentary
NorTT	Norsk Teologisk Tidsskrift
NovT	Novum Testamentum
NTA	New Testament Abstracts
NTA	New Testament Apocrypha, ed. E. Hennecke — W. Schneemelcher
NTS	New Testament Studies
OCT	Oxford Classical Texts
OTP	Old Testament Pseudepigrapha
OTL	Old Testament Library
OTS	Oudtestamentische Studiën
PTA	Papyrologische Texte und Abhandlungen
PVTG	Pseudepigrapha Veteris Testamenti Graece
RB	Reveu Biblique
RechBib	Recherches Bibliques
RevQ	Revue de Qumran
RGG	Die Religion in Geschichte und Gegenwart
RLA	Reallexicon der Assyriologie
RSB	Religious Studies Bulletin
RSR	Recherches de Science Religieuse
RSV	The Revised Standard Version of the Bible
RTR	The Reformed Theological Review
SB	Sources Bibliques
SBLMS	Society of Biblical Literature Monograph Series
SBM	Stuttgarter Biblische Monographien
SBS	Stuttgarter Bibel-Studien
SBT	Studies in Biblical Theology
SBU	Svenskt Bibliskt Uppslagsverk
ScrB	Scripture Bulletin
ScrH	Scripta Hierosolymitana
SE	Studia Evangelica
SEÅ	Svensk Exegetisk Årsbok
Search	The Search
Sém	Sémetica
SJLA	Studies in Judaism in Late Antiquity
SJT	Scottish Journal of Theology
SNT	Studien zum Neuen Testament
SNTSMS	Society for NT Studies Monograph Series
ST	Studia Theologica
StCl	Studii Clasice (Bucharest)
STK	Svensk Teologisk Kvartalskrift
Str-B	Strack, H. — Billerbeck, P., Kommentar zum Neuen Testament aus Talmud und Midrasch
SUNT	Studien zur Umwelt des Neuen Testaments

TDNT	Theological Dictionary of the New Testament
TDOT	Theological Dictionary of the Old Testament
ThB	Theologische Beiträge
THBW	Theol. -homiletisches Bibelwerk
Theology	Theology
TheolTijdschr	Theologische Tijdschrift
TLZ	Theologische Literatur-Zeitung
TNTC	Tyndale New Testament Commentary
TRu	Theologische Rundschau
TSK	Theologische Studien und Kritiken
TTKi	Tidsskrift for Teologi og Kirke
TTZ	Trierer Theologische Zeitschrift
TWAT	Theologisches Wörterbuch zum Alten Testament
TynBul	Tyndale Bulletin
TynMon	Tyndale Monograph
TZ	Theologische Zeitschrift
UBS	United Bible Societies
UT	Ugaritic Textbook, by C.H. Gordon
VD	Verbum Domini
VoxRef	Vox Reformata
VT	Vetus Testamentum
VTSup	Vetus Testamentum Supplements
WBKM	Wissenschaftliche Beiträge zur Kunde des Morgenlandes
WMANT	Wissenschaftliche Monographien zum Alten und Neuen Testament
WUNT	Wissenschaftliche Untersuchungen zum Neuen Testament
ZAW	Zeitschrift für die alttestamentliche Wissenschaft
ZKT	Zeitschrift für katholische Theologie
ZNW	Zeitschrift für die neutestamentliche Wissenschaft und die Kunde der älteren Kirche
ZPEB	The Zondervan Pictorial Encyclopedia of the Bible
ZTK	Zeitschrift für Theologie und Kirche
ZwTh	Zeitschrift für wissenschaftliche Theologie

II. Texts and Translations

1. The Bible

Biblia Hebraica, ed. R. Kittel, 16th ed. by P. Kahle, A. Alt, O. Eissfeldt Stuttgart 1971.

תורה נביאים וכתובים ed. N. Snaith (BFBS), London 1962

Das Fragmententhargum: Thargum Jeruschalmi zum Pentateuch, Hrsg. von M. Ginsberger Berlin 1899, rp. Jerusalem 1966

The Targum of Onkelos and Jonathan Ben Uzziel on the Pentateuch with Fragments of the Jerusalem Targum, Trans. J.W. Etheridge, 2 Vols., London 1862–65, rp. N.Y. 1968.

Neophyti 1. Targum Palestinense, MS de la Bibliotheca Vaticana, ed. A. Diez-Macho, 6 Vols., Madrid, Barcelona 1968–79.

Septuaginta, ed. A. Rahlfs, 2 Vols., 9th ed. Stuttgart 1935, rp. 1971.

––. Vetus Testamentum Graecum auctoritate societatis litterarum Göttigensis editum. Vol. XVI. 2 Susanna, Daniel, Bel et Draco, ed. J. Ziegler, Göttingen 1954.

Der Septuaginta-Text des Buches Daniel. Bd. I: Kap. 1–2 nach dem Kölner Teil des Papyrus 967. Bd. II: Kap. 3–4 nach dem Kölner Teil des Papyrus 967 (PTA). Hrsg. von W. Hamm, Bonn 1977.

––. Kap. 5–12, zusammen mit Susanna Bel et Draco, sowie Esther Kap 1, 1a–2, 15 nach dem Kölner Teil des Papyrus 967 (PTA). Hrsg. von A. Geissen, Bonn 1968.

Novum Testamentum Graece, ed. Eb. Nestle, Er. Nestle, K. Aland, M. Black, C.M. Martini, B.M. Metzger, A. Wikgren, 26th ed. Stuttgart 1979.

Η ΚΑΙΝΗ ΔΙΑΘΗΚΗ, ed. E. Nestle, G.D. Kilpatrick, 2nd ed. London 1958.

The Greek New Testament, ed. K. Aland, M. Black, C.M. Martini, B.M. Metzger, A. Wikgren (UBS), 3rd ed., Stuttgart 1966.

ΤΑ ΙΕΡΑ ΓΡΑΜΜΑΤΑ, ἤτοι ἡ Παλαιὰ καὶ ἡ Νέα Διαθήκη, (Trans. into Literary Modern Greek by N. Vamvas), rp. London, 1955.

Η ΚΑΙΝΗ ΔΙΑΘΗΚΗ, (Trans. into Colloquial Modern Greek), Ἀθῆναι, 1967.

––. Τὸ πρωτότυπο κείμενο μὲ νεοελληνικὴ δημοτικὴ μετάφραση (Modern Colloquial Greek), Athens, 1985.

The Revised Standard Version, London etc. 1952.

The New English Bible, Oxford 1970.

Gamla Testamentet 2: ... Daniel ... Översatt av Bibelkommissionen, Stockholm 1984.

2. Apocrypha and Pseudepigrapha

Die Apokryphen und Pseudepigraphen des Alten Testaments, hrsg. E. Kautzsch, 2 Vols., Tübingen 1900.

The Apocrypha and Pseudepigrapha of the Old Testament With Introductions and Critical and Explanatory Notes to the several Books, Edited in conjunction with many Scholars by R.H. Charles, 2 Vols., Oxford 1913, rp. 1969.

De Gammeltestamentlige Pseudepigrafer I–IV. Ed. E. Hammershaimb, J. Munck, B. Noack, P. Seidelin, Kφbenhavn etc. 1953–63.

The Old Testament Pseudepigrapha. Vol. I: Apocalyptic Literature and Testaments. Ed. J.H. Charlesworth, London 1983.

Jüdische Schriften aus hellenistisch-römischer Zeit. Hrsg. von W.G. Kümmel in Zusammenarbeit mit Chr. Habicht, O. Kaiser, O. Plöger und J. Schreiner, Gütersloh 1973–

Fragmenta Pseudepigraphorum quae supersunt Graeca. Una cum Historicum et Auctorum Judaeorum Hellenistarum Fragmentis (PTVG III) A.-M. Denis, Leiden 1970.

The Testament of Abraham. The Greek Text now first edited with Introduction and Notes, etc. M.R. James, Cambridge 1892.

Le Testament d'Abraham. Introduction, édition de la recension courte, traduction et notes. 2 Vols. (Typewritten diss.) F. Schmidt, Strasbourg 1971.

The Testament of Abraham. The Greek Recensions. (Texts and Translations 2. Pseudepigrapha Series 2. SBL). M. Stone. Missoula 1972.

Testament Abrahams, (pp. 193—256 in Jüdische Schriften aus hellenistisch- römischer Zeit, Vol. III), E. Janssen, Gütersloh 1975.

Testament of Abraham. A New Translation and Introduction (in Old Testament Pseudepigrapha, Vol. I pp. 871—902 ed. J.H. Charlesworth) by E.P. Sanders.

II Baruch. The Syriac Apocalypse of Baruch, Tr. R.H. Charles, in R.H. Charles, *APOT* II, 470—526.

——. Die Syrische Baruch-Apokalypse Tr. A.F.J. Klijn (in *JSHRZ* V, Gütersloh 1976).

2 (Syriac Apocalypse of) Baruch, Tr. A.F.J. Klijn (in J.H. Charlesworth, *OTP* I, 615—52, London 1983).

The Ethiopic Version of the Book of Enoch, ed. R.H. Charles, Oxford 1906.

Apocalypsis Henochi Graece (PVTG III), ed. M. Black, Leiden 1970.

The Books of Enoch. Aramaic Fragments of Qumrân Cave 4, ed. J.T. Milik with the Collaboration of M. Black, Oxford 1976.

The Ethiopic Book of Enoch, ed. M.A. Knibb, 2 Vols., Oxford 1978.

Das Buch Henoch, Tr. G. Beer (in E. Kautzsch, Die Apokryphen und Pseudepigraphen des AT, 217—310).

Book of Enoch, Tr. R.H. Charles (in R.H. Charles, *APOT* II, 163—281).

The Book of Enoch or 1 Enoch. Translated from the Editor's Ethiopic Text etc. R.H. Charles, Oxford 1912.

Første Enoksbog, Tr. E. Hammershaimb (in *De Gammeltestamentlige Pseudepigrafer* II, 69—174, København 1956).

1 (Ethiopic Apocalypse of) Enoch, Tr. E. Isaac (in J.H. Charlesworth, *OTP* I, 5—89, London 1983).

2 Enoch, or The Book of the Secrets of Enoch, Tr. N. Forbes — R.H. Charles (in R.H. Charles, *APOT* II, 425—69).

2 (Slavonic Apocalypse of) Enoch, Tr. F.I. Andersen (in J.H. Charlesworth, *OTP* I, 91—213).

3 Enoch or The Hebrew Book of Enoch, Edited and translated for the first time with Introduction, Commentary and Critical Notes by H. Odeberg, Cambridge 1928.

3 (Hebrew Apocalypse of) Enoch, Tr. by P. Alexander (in J.H. Charlesworth, *OTP* I, 22—315).

Das vierte Esrabuch nach seinem Zeitalter, seinen arabischen Übersetzungen und einer neuen Wiederherstellung. Hrsg. von H. Ewald, Göttingen 1863.

Esdrae Liber Quartus Arabice, Hrsg. von J. Gildemeister, Bonnae 1877.

The Ezra-Apocalypse. Being Chs. 3—14 of the Book Commonly Known as 4 Ezra (or II Esdras), Tr. and Commentary by G.H. Box, London 1912.

IV Ezra, Tr. G.H. Box (in R.H. Charles, *APOT* II, 542—624).

Die Esra-Apokalypse (IV Esra). Erster Teil: Die Überlieferung. Herausgegeben von B. Violet (GCS), Leipzig 1910.

Die Apokalypsen des Esra und des Baruch in deutscher Gestalt. Hrsg. von B. Violet (GCS), Leipzig 1924.

II Esdras (The Ezra Apocalypse). With Introduction and Notes, by W.O.E. Oesterley, London 1933.

I and II Esdras. Introduction, Translation and Commentary, by J.M. Myers, (AB), N.Y. 1974.

4 Esra-Buch, Hrgs. J. Schreiner (in *JSHRZ* V).

The Fourth Book of Ezra, Tr. B.M. Metzger (in J.H. Charlesworth, *OTP* I, 517—59).

Die Oracula Sibyllina, Ed. J. Geffcken (GCS), Leipzig 1902.

Sibylline Oracles, Tr. J.J. Collins (in J.H. Charlesworth, *OTP* I, 317—472).

The Sibylline Oracles, Tr. H.C.O. Lanchester (in R.H. Charles, *APOT* II, 368—406).

Die Psalmen Salomos, Tr. S. Holm-Nielsen (in *JSHRZ* IV).

The Psalms of Solomon, Tr. G.B. Gray (in R.H. Charles, *APOT* II, 625-·52).

Testament of Solomon, Tr. D.C. Duling (in J.H. Charlesworth, *OTP* I, 934—87).

Apocalypse of Sophonias. For Greek fragments, see Clemens Alexandrinus, *Stromata* V. 11 (in Βιβλιοθήκη Ἑλλήνων Πατέρων καὶ Ἐκκλησιαστικῶν Συγγραφέων, Vols. 7—8, Ἀθῆναι 1956).

Apocalypse of Zephaniah, Tr. O.S. Wintermute (in J.H. Charlesworth, *OTP* I, 497—515).

Testamenta XII Patriarcharum. Edited according to Cambridge University Library MS Ff. 1.24, M. de Jonge (*PVTG* 1), 2nd ed. Leiden 1970.

A Late Hebrew Testament of Naphtali, Tr. R.H. Charles (in R.H. Charles, *APOT* II, 361—3).

New Testament Apocrypha, Ed. E. Hennecke — W. Schneemelcher. Engl. tr. R. McL Wilson, 2 Vols., London 1965.

The Ascension of Isaiah, Tr. J. Flemming — H. Duensing (in W. Hennecke — W. Schneemelcher, *NTA*, II, 642–63).

3. Qumran

Discoveries in the Judaean Desert. I: Qumran Cave 1. Ed. D. Barthélemy, J.T. Milik, Oxford 1955.

Discoveries in the Judaean Desert. V: Qumran Cave 4. Ed. J.M. Allegro, Oxford 1968.

Die Texte aus Qumran. Hebräisch and deutsch. E. Lohse, Darmstadt 1964.

The Dead Sea Scrolls in English, Tr. G. Vermes, Penguin, rev. ed. 1968.

The Genesis Apocryphon: A Scroll from the Wilderness of Judaea. Description and Contents of the Scroll, Facsimiles, Transcription and Translation of Columns II, XIX–XXII. Eds. N. Avigad, Y. Yadin, Jerusalem 1956.

The Genesis Apocryphon of Qumran Cave I: A Commentary (BibOr) J.A. Fitzmyer, 2nd rev. ed. Rome 1971.

4. Rabbinic Texts

The Mishnah. Translated from the Hebrew with Introductory and Brief Explanatory Notes, H. Danby, Corrected ed. Oxford 1938, rp. 1977.

Mishnayoth, ed. Ph. Blackman, 7 Vols. N.Y. 1963–64.

Der Babylonische Talmud. Neu übertragen durch L. Goldschmidt, 12 Vols., Berlin 1930–6.

The Babylonian Talmud. Translated into English with Notes, Glossary and Indices, Vols. I–XXXVI, Ed. I. Epstein, London 1935–52.

מדרש הגדול. על המשה הומשי תורה. ספר בראשית. הוציא לאור על פי מארץ
תימן. עם הערות והקדמה. שניאור זלמן שעכטער. במצות סוכני בית
הדפוס אשר לבית מדרש החכמות. בעיר קנטאבריגיא שנת תרֹסֹב לפ״יק
(Midrash Hag-gadol. Forming a Collection of Ancient Rabbinic Homilies to the Pentateuch. Edited for the first Time from various Yemen manuscripts and provided with Notes and Preface by S. Schechter: Genesis, Cambridge 1902).

Midrash Rabbah. Translated under the editorship of Rabbi Dr. H. Freedman and M. Simon. *Numbers.* Translated by Judah J. Slotki, 2 Vols. London 1939.

Midrash Hag-gadol on the Pentateuch: Numbers. Ed. S. Fish, Manchester 1940.

The Midrash on the Psalms. Translated from the Hebrew and Aramaic by W.G. Braude, 2 Vols. New Haven 1959.

אגדת בראשית. תכיל מדרש אגדת על ספר בראשית. בתהלה פרשת תורה
ואח״כ פרשת נביאים ואח״כ פרשת כתובים. יצא עתה לאור ... ערוך
ומסוד ... ממני שלמה באבער מלבוב קראקא תרס״ג. — (*Agadath Bereschit.*
Midraschische Auslegungen zum ersten Buch Mosis. Nach den ältesten Druckwerken, in Vergleichung mit einer Oxforder Handschrift cod. 2340 herausgegeben. Mit Erklärungen und einer Einleitung versehen von Salomon Buber, Krakau 1902).

Pĕsikṭa Dĕ-Raḇ Kahǎna. R. Kahana's Compilation of Discourses for Sabbaths and Festal Days. Translated from Hebrew and Aramaic by W.G. Braude and I.J. Kapstein, London 1975.

Pesikta Rabbati. Discourses for Feasts, Fasts, and Special Sabbaths. W.G. Braude, 2 Vols., New Heaven 1968.

5. Near Eastern Texts

Beyrlin, W. (Ed.) *Near Eastern Religious Texts Relating to the OT*, Philadelphia 1978.

Gibson, J.C.L. *Textbook of Syrian Semitic Inscriptions* 3 Vols. (Vol. III: *Aramaic Inscriptions including Inscriptions from Zinjirli*, 1975) Oxford 1971–82.
Gordon, C.H. *Ugaritic Manual.* Newly Revised Grammar; Texts in Translation; Cuneiform Selections; Paradigms – Glossary – Indices, Roma 1955.
–– *Ugaritic Textbook*, Rome 1965.
Herdner, A. *Corpus des Tablettes en Cunéiformes alphabétiques.* Découvertes à Ras-Shamra – Ugarit de 1929 à 1939, Paris 1963.
Pritchard, J.B. (Ed.) *Ancient Near Eastern Texts Relating to the OT* 3rd ed. Princeton 1969.

6. Christian Authors

The Apostolic Fathers, ed. K. Lake 2 Vols. (LCL), London rp. 1970.
Βιβλιοθήκη ῾Ελλήνων Πατέρων καὶ ᾿Εκκλησιαστικῶν Συγγραφέων, ᾿Αθῆναι 1955.
Chrysostom, *Homiliae* 1–6 in J.P. Migne (ed.) *Patrologia Graeca* Vol. 56.
Clemens Alexandrinus, *Stromata* in ΒΕΠΕΣ Vol. 7 pp. 234–361 and Vol. 8 pp. 11–316.
Didymus Maximus, *Trinitate* in J.P. Migne (ed.) *Patrologia Graeca*, Vol. 39.
Hippolytus, *On Daniel* in ΒΕΠΕΣ Vol. 6 (Text after ed. of G. Nath. Bonwetsch, *Hippolyt's Kommentar zum Buche Daniel*, Leipzig 1897 (completed by parts edited by C. Diobouniotis from Meteora MS, Leipzig 1911).
Irenaeus, *Adv. Haereses* in J.P. Migne (ed.) *Patrologia Graeca*, Vol. 7.
Justin Martyr: *Apology, Dialogue with Trypho the Jew.* in ΒΕΠΕΣ Vols. 3–4 (Text after ed. of E. Goodspeed, *Die Apologeten*, Göttingen 1914).
Proclus CP, in J.P. Migne (ed.) *Patrologia Graeca* Vol. 65.

7. Ancient Authors

Apollodorus. Ed. J.G. Frazer, 2 Vols. (LCL), London etc. 1921.
Arrian, *Anabasis Alexandri et Indica.* Ed. P.A. Brunt – E.I. Robson, 2 Vols. (LCL), London 1976.
Curtius, *History of Alexander*, Ed. J.C. Rolfe, 2 Vols. (LCL), London etc.
Dio Cassius, *Roman History*, Ed. E. Cary, 9 Vols. (LCL), Lodnon etc. 1914–27, rp. 1961.
Diogenes Laertius, Ed. H.S. Long, 2 Vols. (LCL), London etc. 1963.
Herodotus, Ed. H.R. Dietsch 2 Vols. (BT), Lipsiae 1887.
Hesiod, *Theogony. Hesiodi Theogonia Opera et Dies Scutum*, edidit F. Solmsen; Fragmenta Selecta ediderunt R. Melkelbach et M.L. West (OCT), Oxford 1970.
––, The Homeric Hymns and Homerica. With an English tr. by H.G. Evelyn-White (LCL), London etc. 1970.
Homer, Ed. D.B. Munro – T.W. Allen 5 Vols. (OCT), Oxford 1911–20.
Homer, Ed. A.T. Murray 4 Vols. (LCL) London etc. 1919–25 rp. 1975–78.
Josephus, Eds. H. St. John Thackeray, R. Marcus, A. Wikgren, L.H. Feldman, 9 Vols. (LCL) London etc. 1926–65, rp. 1966–77.
Lucian, Eds. A.M. Harmon – K. Kilburn – M.D. Macleod, 8 Vols. (LCL) London 1913–61 rp. 1959–79.
Philo, Eds. F.H. Colson – G.H. Whitaker – J.H. Earp 10 Vols. (LCL), London etc. 1929–53.
Philostratus, *Life of Apollonius of Tyana*, Ed. F.C. Conybeare, 2 Vols. (LCL), London etc. 1912, rp. 1969.
Plato, *Opera*, Ed. I. Burnet, 5 Vols. (OCT), Oxford 2nd ed. 1905–15, rp. 1958–62.
Plutarch. *Lives*, Ed. B. Perrin, 11 Vols. (LCL) London etc. 1914–26.
Strabo, Ed. H.L. Jones, 8 Vols. (LCL), London etc. 1917–32, rp. 1959–60.
Suetonius, Ed. J.C. Rolfe, 2 Vols. (LCL), London etc. 1914, rp. 1965.
Thucydides, *Historiae*, Ed. H.S. Jones, 2 Vols. (OCT), Oxford 2nd ed. 1942, rp. 1966.
Virgil, Ed. H.R. Fairclough, 2 Vols. (LCL), London etc. 1978.

III. Reference Works

Bauer, W.—Arndt, W.F.— Gingrich, F.W., *A Greek-English Lexicon of the New Testament and Other Early Christian Literature*, Chicago 1957, rp. 1974.

Bauer, H.—Leander, P., *Grammatik des Biblisch-aramäischen*, Halle 1927.

Baumgartner, W. *Wörterbuch zum aramäischen Teil des Alten Testaments in deutscher und englischer Sprache*, in L. Koehler — W. Baumgartner, *Lexicon in Veteris Testamenti Libros*, Leiden 1958.

Blass, F.—Debrunner, A.—Rehkopf, F., *Grammatik des neutestamentlichen Griechisch*, 14 völlig neubearbeitet, erweit. Auflage, Göttingen 1976.

Brown, F.—Driver, S.R.,—Briggs, C.A. *A Hebrew and English Lexicon of the Old Testament*. Based on the Lexicon of W. Gesenius. Tr. by E. Robinson, Oxford 1907, corr. rp. 1953, rp. 1978.

Computer-Konkordanz zum Novum Testamentum Graece. Herausgegeben vom Institut für neutestamentliche Textforschung und vom Rechenzentrum der Universität Münster, unter besonderer Mitwirkung von H. Bachmann und W.A. Slaby, Berlin—N.Y. 1980.

Δημητράκος, Δ., (Ed.), Μέγα Λεξικὸν ὅλης τῆς Ἑλληνικῆς Γλώσσης, 9 Vols. Ἀθῆναι 1933—53, rp. 1964.

Dillmann, A. *Lexicon Linguae Aethiopicae cum Indice Latino*, Leipzig 1865.

Encyclopaedia Judaica, 16 Vols., Jerusalem 1971—9.

Exegetisches Wörterbuch zum Neuen Testament, Hrsg.H.R.Balz—G. Schneider, 3 Vols., Stuttgart 1978—83.

Gesenius, W., *Hebrew Grammar*. As edited and enlarged by the Late E. Kautzsch. Tr. by A.E. Cowley, Oxford 1910, rp. 1963.

Hatch, H.,—Redpath, H.A., *A Concordance to the Septuagint*, etc. Oxford 1897.

Huck, A.—Lietzmann, H., *Synopsis of the First Three Gospels*. Eng. ed. by F.L. Cross, Oxford 1968.

Huck, A.—Greven. H., *Synopse der drei ersten Evangelien* mit Beigabe der johanneischen Parallelstellen, 13 Auflage, völlig neu bearbeitet von H. Greven (rubrics in German and English), Tübingen 1981.

The Interpreter's Dictionary of the Bible. An Illustrated Encyclopaedia, 4 Vols. and Supplement (1976), N.Y. 1962.

Jannaris, A.N., *An Historical Greek Grammar*. Chiefly of the Attic Dialect, London 1897.

Koehler, L.—Baumgartner, W. *Lexicon in Veteris Testamenti Libros* etc., Leiden 1958.

Kuhn K.G. *Konkordanz zu den Qumrantexten*, Göttingen 1960.

Lampe, G.W.H. (Ed.) *A Patristic Greek Lexicon*, Oxford 1961—68.

Levy, J. *Neuhebräisches und Chaldäisches Wörterbuch über die Talmudim und Midraschim*, Leipzig 1876—79.

Liddell, H.G.—Scott, R.—Jones, H.S. *A Greek-English Lexicon*, Oxford 1953.

Lisowski, G. *Konkordanz zum Hebräischen Alten Testament*, Stuttgart, 2nd ed. 1958.

Moulton, J.H. *A Grammar of New Testament Greek*, Vol. I. *Prolegomena*, 3rd ed. Edinburgh 1908.

Moulton, J.H.—Milligan, G., *The Vocabulary of the Greek Testament*. Illustrated from the Papyri and Other Non-Literary Sources, London 1930, rp. 1972.

Moulton, W.F.—Geden, A.S., *A Concordance to the Greek Testament*, Edinburgh 15th ed. 1978.

Redpath, H.A. See Hatch, H.—Redpath, H.A.

Die Religion in Geschichte und Gegenwart. Handwörterbuch für Theologie and Religionswissenschaft. Herausgegeben von K. Galling, 6 Vols. and Register, 3rd ed. Tübingen 1957—65.

Rengstorf, K.H. *A Complete Concordance to Josephus*, Vols. I—IV, Leiden 1973—83.

Robertson, A.T., *A Grammar of the Greek New Testament in the Light of Historical Research*, rp. Nashville 1934.

Rosenthal, F., *A Grammar of Biblical Aramaic*, Wiesbaden 1961. rp. 1974.

Smith, W. (Ed.), *Dictionary of Christian Biography*, London 1887.

Sophocles, E.A., *Greek Lexicon of the Roman and Byzantine Periods* etc. N.Y., Leipzig 1893.

Strack, H., *Einleitung in Talmud und Midrasch*, 6. Aufl., München 1976.

Strack, H.—Billerbeck, P., *Kommentar zum Neuen Testament aus Talmud and Midrasch*, Vols. I—VI, München 1922—61.

Tenney, M.C. (Ed.), *The Zondervan Pictorial Encyclopedia of the Bible*, Grand Rapids 1975—6.
Theological Dictionary of the New Testament, Eds. G. Kittel — G. Friedrich, Transl. by G.W. Brom-
iley, 10 Vols., Grand Rapids 1964—76.
Theological Dictionary of the Old Testament, Eds. G.J. Botterweck—H. Ringgren. Transl. J.T.
Willis, Grand Rapids 1974—.
Theologisches Wörterbuch zum Alten Testament, Hrsg. G.J. Botterweck—H. Ringgren, Stuttgart
1970ff.
Turner, N., *A Grammar of New Testament Greek*. Vol. III: *Syntax*, Edinburgh 1963.
——, *Grammatical Insights into the New Testament*, Edinburgh 1965, rp. 1977.
Young, R., *Analytical Concordance to the Holy Bible*, London, no date.
The Zondervan Pictorial Encyclopedia of the Bible, Ed. M.C. Tenney, Grand Rapids 1977.

IV. Secondary Literature

Aalders, G. Ch., "The Book of Daniel. Its Historical Trustworthiness and Prophetic Character",
EvQ 2 (1930) 242—54.
Abbott, E.A. *The Son of Man*, or Contributions to the Study of the Thought of Jesus (Diatessarica
Part VIII). Cambridge 1910.
Albright, W.F., *From Stone Age to Christianity*. Monotheism and the Historical Process, New York
1946, ^{2}1957.
Alford, H., *The Greek Testament*. With a Critically Revised Text: A Digest of Various Readings:
Marginal References to Verbal and Idiomatic Usage: Prolegomena: And A Critical and Exege-
tical Commentary, London, etc., Vol. I ^{6}1868; II ^{5}1965; III ^{4}1965; IV ^{3}1866.
Allen, W.C., *A Critical and Exegetical Commentary on the Gospel of St. Matthew* (ICC) Edinburgh
^{3}1922.
Appel H., *Die Komposition des äthiopischen Henochbuches*, (BFChTh 10:3), Gütersloh, 1906.
——, *Die Selbstbezeichnung Jesu: Der Menschensohn*, 1896.
Archer, G.L., "The Aramaic of the 'Genesis Apocryphon' compared with the Aramaic of Daniel",
New Perspectives on the OT, ed. J.B. Payne, pp. 160—69, Waco, Texas—London, 1970.
Arndt, W.F., *The Gospel According to St. Luke* (BC), St. Louis 1956.
Ashby, E., "The Coming of the Son of Man" *ET* 72 (1960—61) 360—3.
Άτσαλος, Β.Α., "'Ιστοριογραφία", IEE Vol. III, B, 430—40, 447—51.
Avigad, N., "Excavations at Beth She'arim, 1955". Preliminary Report" *IEJ* 7(1957) 73—92,
239—55.
Badham, F.P., "The Title 'Son of Man'" *Theol. Tijdschr.* 45 (1911) 395—448.
Baeck, L., "Der Menschensohn", *MGWJ* 81 (1937) 12—24.
Baker, D.W., "Further Examples of the Waw-Explicativum", *VT* 30 (1980) 129—36.
Baldensperger, W., *Die messianisch-apokalyptische Hoffnung des Judentums*, Strassburg 1903.
——, *Das Selbstbewusstsein Jesu im Lichte der messianischen Hoffnungen seiner Zeit*, Strassburg
1888, ^{2}1892.
——, "Die neueste Forschung über den Menschensohn", *TRu* 3 (1900) 200—10; 243—55.
Bammel, E. "Erwägungen zur Eschatologie Jesu" *SE* 3 (1964; *TU* 88) 3—32.
Banks, R.J. (Ed.), *Reconciliation and Hope*. New Testament Essays on Atonement and Eschato-
logy, L. Morris Festschrift, Exeter 1974.
Bardtke, H., *Die Handschriftenfunde am Toten Meer*, Vol. I Berlin, 1953: Mit einer kurzen Ein-
führung in die Text-und Kanongeschichte des Alten Testaments. Vol. II Berlin, 1958: Die
Sekte von Qumran.
——, "Der gegenwärtige Stand der Erforschung der im Palästina neu gefundenen Hebräischen
Handschriften, 29. Die Kriegsrolle von Qumran übersetzt", *TLZ*, 80 (1955) 401—24.
Barr, J., *Daniel*, in A.S. Peake's *Commentary on Bible*, London 1962.
Barrett, C.K., "Das Fleisch des Menschensohnes (Joh 6, 53)" in *Jesus und der Menschensohn*
für A. Vögtle, ed. R. Pesch—R. Schnackenburg, pp. 342—54, Freiburg etc. 1975.

——, *Jesus and the Gospel Tradition*, London 1967.

——, "Stephen and the Son of Man" pp. 32–8 in *Apophoreta*: Festschr. für E. Haenchen, Berlin 1964.

——, "The Background of Mark 10:45" in *New Testament Essays*, Studies in memory of T.W. Manson, ed. A.J.B. Higgins, pp. 1–18, Manchester 1959.

——, *The Gospel According to St. John*, An Introduction with Commentary and Notes on the Greek Text, 2nd ed. London 1978.

Barthélemy, D., *Les Devanciers D'Aquila* (Suppl. *VT* 10), Leiden 1963.

Bartlet, V. "Christ's Use of 'The Son of Man' ", *ET* 4 (1892–3) 403.

——, "The Son of Man: A Rejoinder", *ET* 5 (1893–4) 41–2.

Bauernfeind, O., *Kommentar und Studien zur Apostelgeschichte* (WUNT 1:22), Tübingen 1980.

Baumgartner, W., "Ein Vierteljahrhundert Danielforschung", *TRu* 11 (1939) 59–83; 125–44; 201–28.

Baur, F.C., *Neutestamentliche Theologie*, Tübingen 1864.

——,"Die Bedeutung des Ausdrucks: ὁ υἱὸς τοῦ ἀνθρώπου" *ZwTh* 3, (1860) 274–92.

Beasley-Murray, G.R., "The Interpretation of Daniel 7" *CBQ* 45 (1983) 44–58.

——, "Second Thoughts on the Composition of Mark 13" *NTS* 29 (1983) 414–20.

Beekman, J.–Callow, J., *Translating the Word of God*, Grand Rapids 1974.

Behrmann, G., *Das Buch Daniel,* übersetzt und erklärt, (*Nowack's Handkommentar* ... III. 3.2.), Göttingen 1894.

Bentzen, A., *King and Messiah*, Lutherworth 1955.

——, *Daniel* (HAT), Tübingen ²1952.

Berger, K., *Die Auferstehung des Propheten und die Erhöhung des Menschensohnes.* Traditionsgeschichtliche Untersuchungen zur Deutung des Geschickes Jesu in frühchristlichen Texten. (SUNT 13), Göttingen 1976.

Bernard, J.H., *A Critical and Exegetical Commentary on the Gospel According to St. John*, 2 Vols., Edinburgh 1928, rp. 1963.

Best, E.–McL Wilson. R. (Eds.), *Text and Interpretation*, Festschrift for M. Black, Cambridge 1979.

Betz, H–D., "Jesus as Divine Man" pp. 114–33 in *Jesus and the Historian*, in honour of E.C. Colwell, ed. F.I. Trotter, Philadelphia 1968.

Betz, O., "Die Frage nach dem messianischen Bewusstsein Jesu", *NovT* 6 (1963) 20–48.

Bevan, A.A., *A short Commentary on the Book of Daniel*, for the Use of Students, Cambridge 1892.

Beyer, H.W., Art. βλασφημέω etc. *TDNT* I, 621–5.

Beyschlag, W., *Die Christologie des Neuen Testaments, ein biblisch-theologischer Versuch*, Berlin 1866.

Bietenhard, H., " 'Der Menschensohn' – Ho huios toû anthrōpou. Sprachliche und religionsgeschichtliche Untersuchungen zu einem Begriff der synoptischen Evangelien, I. Sprachlicher und religionsgeschichtlicher Teil, in W. Haase (Hrsg) *Principat* 25.1. *Religion.* (Vorkonstantinisches Christentum: Leben und Umwelt Jesu; Neues Testament [kanonische Schriften und Apokryphen]) 265–350, Berlin 1982.

Birdsall, J.N., "Who is this Son of Man?" *EvQ* 42 (1970) 7–17.

Black, M., "Unsolved NT Problems: The 'Son of Man' in the Old Biblical Literature", *ET* 60 (1948 –9) 11–15.

——, "Unsolved NT Problems: 'The Son of Man' in the Teaching of Jesus", *ET* 60 (1948–9) 32–6.

——, "The Throne-Theophany Prophetic Commission and the Son of Man: A Study in Tradition History" pp. 57–73 in *Jews, Greeks and Christians.* Religious cultures in Late Antiquity. Essays in Honour of W.D. Davies, ed. R. Hamerton–Kelly & R. Scroggs, Leiden 1976.

——, "Jesus and the Son of Man", *JSNT* 1 (1978) 4–18.

——, "Die Apotheose Israels: Eine neue Intrepretation des danielischen 'Menschensohns' " in *Jesus und der Menschensohn*, ed. R. Pesch–R. Schnackenburg, Freiburg 1975.

——, "Servant of the Lord and Son of Man", *SJT* 6 (1953) 1–11.

——, "The Son of Man Problem in Recent Research and Debate", *BJRL* 45 (1962–3) 305–18.

——, "The 'Parables' of Enoch (1 En 37–71) and the 'Son of Man' ", *ET* 88 (1976) 5–8.

——, *An Aramaic Approach to the Gospels and Acts*, Oxford ³1967.

——, "Aramaic Barnāshā and the Son of Man", *ET* 95 (1984) 200–206.

Black, Max, *Models and Metaphors*, Studies in Language and Philosophy, London 1962.

——, "More about Metaphor" in *Metaphor and Thought*, ed. by A. Ortony, Cambridge 1979.

Bleek, F., "Die messianische Weissagungen im Buche Daniel" *JdTh* 5 (1860) 45–101.

Blinzler, J., *Der Prozess Jesu*. Das jüdische und das römische Gerichtsverfahren gegen Jesus Christus auf Grund der ältesten Zeugnisse dargestellt und beurteilt von Jos. Blinzler, Regensburg ³1960.

——, 'Der Stephanusbericht (Apg 6, 8–15 und 7, 54–8, 2)", *BZ* N.F. 3 (1959) 252–70.

Bloch, J., "Some Christological Interpolations in the Ezra-Apocalypse", *HTR* 51 (1958) 87–94.

Böhl, F.M.T., "Die Mythe von Weisen Adapa", *Die Welt des Orients*, (WBKM) 2, 1954–9, pp. 416–31, Göttingen.

Bonsirven, J., *Le Judaïsme Palestinien au Temps de Jésus-Christ*, 2 Vols., Paris 1934–5.

Bornkamm, G., *Jesus von Nazareth*, Stuttgart ²1957.

——, *Jesus of Nazareth*, N.Y. 1960.

Borsch, F.H., "Mark XIV. 62 and 1 Enoch LXII. 5", *NTS* 14 (1967–8) 565–7.

——, "The Son of Man", *ATR* 45 (1963) 174–90.

——, *The Son of Man in Myth and History*, London 1967.

——, *The Christian and Gnostic Son of Man*, Naperville, Illin. 1970.

Bousset, W., *Kyrios Christos*. Geschichte des Christusglaubens von den Anfängen des Christentums bis Irenaeus, Göttingen ²1921 (Engl. transl. by J.E. Steely, N.Y., 1970).

Bowker, J., *The Targums and Rabbinic Literature*. An Introduction to Jewish Interpretations of Scripture, Corrected ed. Cambridge 1979.

——, "The Son of Man" *JTS*, N.S. 28 (1977) 19–48.

Bowman, J., *The Intention of Jesus*, London 1945.

——, "The Background of the Term 'Son of Man' ", *ET* 59 (1947–8) 283–8.

Brandenburger, E., *Adam und Christus*. Exegetisch-religionsgeschichtliche Untersuchung zu Röm. 5:12–21 (1. Kor. 15) (WMANT 17) Neukirchen 1962.

——, *Die Verborgenheit Gottes im Weltgeschehen*. Das literarische und theologische Problem des 4. Esrabuches (*ATANT* Bd. 68) Zürich 1981.

Braun, F–M., "Messie, Logos et Fils de l' Homme" pp. 133–47 in *La Venue du Messie*, Recherches Bibliques ... VI, Bruges 1962.

Breech, E., "These Fragments I have stored against My Ruins: The Form and Function of 4 Ezra", *JBL* 92 (1973) 267–74.

Brekelmans, Ch. W., "The Saints of the Most High and Their Kingdom", *OTS* 14 (1965) 305–29.

Bright, J., *A History of Israel*, rev. ed. London 1972.

Brown J.B., "The Son of Man: 'This Fellow' ", *Bib* 58 (1977) 361–87.

Brown, R.E., *The Gospel According to John* (AB), 2 Vols. London, 1966 rp. 1971.

Brown, T.S., "Callisthenes and Alexander", *AJPh* 70 (1949) 225–48.

Bruce, F.F., "The Oldest Greek Versions of Daniel", *OTS* 20 (1977) 22–40.

——, *Biblical Exegesis in the Qumran Texts*, London 1960.

——, "The Background to the 'Son of Man' Sayings", pp. 50–70 in *Christ the Lord*, ed. H.H. Rowdon, Leicester, etc. 1982.

——, "The Book of Daniel and the Qumran Community" pp. 221–35 in *Neotestamentica et Semitica*, ed. E.E. Ellis–M. Wilcox, Edinburgh 1969.

——, *Jesus and Christian Origins Outside the New Testament*, Grand Rapids 1974.

——, *This is That*, Exeter 1968.

——, (Ed.) *Promise and Fulfilment*. Essays Presented to Prof. S.H. Hook in Celebration of his Ninetieth Birthday 21 January 1964., Edinburgh 1963.

Brückner, W., "Jesus 'des Menschen Sohn' ", *JpTh* 12 (1886) 254–78.

Buchanan, G.W., *To the Hebrews (AB)*, Garden City, N.Y. 1972.

Bultmann, R., *The History of the Synoptic Tradition*, Oxford 1968 trans. fr. Germ. ²1931.

——, *Das Evangelium des Johannes* (KEKNT), 11th ed. Göttingen 1950.

——, "Reich Gottes und Menschensohn", *TRu* N.S. 9 (1937) 1–35.

——, *Theology of the NT*, 2 Vols., London 1952, rp. 1968.

Burger, C., *Jesus als Davidssohn*, Göttingen 1970.

Burkill, T.A., "The Hidden Son of Man in St. Mark's Gospel" pp. 1–38 in T.A. Burkill: *New Light on the Earliest Gospel*, Ithaca, London 1972.

——, "The Son of Man", *ET* 56 (1944–5) 305–6.

Busch, F., *Zum Verständnis der synoptischen Eschatologie.* Mark 13 neu untersucht, Gütersloh 1938.

Cadoux, C.J., "The Imperatival Use of ἵνα in the New Testament" *JTS* 42 (1941) 165–73.

Callow, J., See Beekman, J.–Callow, J.

Calvert, D.G.A., "An Examination of the Criteria for Distinguishing the Authentic Words of Jesus", *NTS* 18 (1971/2) 209–19.

Campbell, J.Y., "The Origin and Meaning of the Term Son of Man", *JTS* 48 (1947) 145–55.

Caquot, A., "Les quatre bêtes et le 'fils d' homme' (Daniel 7)", *Sém* XVII (1967) 31–71.

Caragounis, C.C., *The Ephesian Mysterion — Meaning and Content,* Lund 1977.

Carlston, C.E., "A *Positive* Criterion of Authenticity?", *BR* 7 (1962) 33–44.

Casey, M., "The Corporate Interpretation of 'One Like a Son of Man' (Dan VII 13) at the Time of Jesus", *NovT* 18 (1976) 167–80.

——, "The Son of Man Problem", *ZNW* 67 (1976) 147–54.

——, "The Use of the Term 'Son of Man' in the Similitudes of Enoch", *JSJ* 7 (1976) 11–29.

——, *The Son of Man:* The Interpretation and Influence of Dan 7, London 1980.

Catchpole, D.R., "The Answer of Jesus to Caiaphas (Matt XXVI 64)", *NTS* 17 (1970/71) 213–26.

——, *The Trial of Jesus.* A study on the Gospels and Jewish Historiography from 1770 to the Present Day (Studia Post-Biblica). Leiden 1971.

——, "Tradition History" pp. 165–80, *NT Interpretation,* H.I. Marshall (ed.). Exeter 1977.

Cavallin, H.C.C., *Life after Death,* Lund 1974.

Ceroke, C.P., "Is Mk 2, 10 a Saying of Jesus?", *CBQ* 22 (1960) 369–90.

Chamberlain, W.D., "Till the Son of Man Be Come", *Int* 7 (1953) 3–13.

Charles, R.H., *A Critical and Exegetical Commentary on the Book of Daniel,* Oxford 1929.

——, *A Critical and Exegetical Commentary on the Revelation of St. John* (ICC), 2 Vols., Edinburgh 1920.

——, *The Book of Daniel,* London 1913.

——, "The Son of Man", *ET* 4 (1892–3) 504.

Charlesworth, J., "Seminar Report. The SNTS Pseudepigrapha Seminars at Tübingen and Paris on the Books of Enoch", *NTS* 25 (1978–9) 315–23.

Christensen, J., "Le fils de l' homme s'en va, ainsi qu'il est ecrit de lui", *ST* 10 (1956) 28–39.

Ciholas, P., "Son of Man in the Synoptic Gospels", *BTB* 11 (1981) 17–20.

Collins, J.J., *The Apocalyptic Vision of the Book of Daniel (HSM),* Missoula 1977.

——, "The Heavenly Representative: The 'Son of Man' in the Similitudes of Enoch" (in *Ideal Figures in Ancient Judaism.* Profiles and Paradigms, pp. 111–33, eds. J.J. Collins & G.W.E. Nickelsburg, Scholars Press, Chico 1980.

——, "The Son of Man and the Saints of the Most High in the Book of Daniel", *JBL* 93 (1974) 50–66.

Colpe, C., Art. ὁ υἱὸς τοῦ ἀνθρώπου, *TDNT* VIII (1972) 400–77.

——, "Der Begriff 'Menschensohn' und die Methode der Erforschung messianischer Prototypen", *Kairos* N.F. XI (1969) 241–63;

            XII (1970) 81–112;

           XIV (1972) 241–57.

Conzelmann, H., *An Outline of the Theology of the New Testament,* London 1969.

——, "Jesu självmedvetande", *SEÅ* 28–29 (1963–4) 39–53.

——, "Jesus Christus", in *RGG* III, 3rd ed. cols. 619–53.

——, "Gegenwart und Zukunft in der synoptischen Tradition", *ZTK* 54 (1957) 277–96.

——, "Zur Methode der Leben–Jesu–Forschung", *ZTK* 56 (1959) Beih. I, pp. 2–13.

Coppens, J., "Le Messianisme sapiental et les origines littéraires du Fils de l' Homme danielique" pp. 33–41 in *Wisdom in Israel and in the Ancient Near East* (Festschrift H.H. Rowley), Sup. *VT* 31, Leiden 1955.

——, *Le Fils de l' Homme néotestamentaire* (La Relève apocalyptique du messianisme royal, III) (Bibliotheca Ephemeridum Theologicarum Lovaniensium, LV), Leuven 1981.

——, *Le Fils d' Homme Vétero-et Intertestamentaire* (La Relève apocalyptique du messianisme royal, II) (Bibliotheca Ephemeridum Theologicarum Lovaniensium) (ed. posthumously by J. Lust), Leuven 1983.

——, "Les Origines du symbole du Fils de l' Homme en Dan VII", *ETL* 44 (1968) 497—502.

——, "Le Fils d' Homme daniélique et les relectures de Dan VII, 13 dans les apocryphes et les écrits du Nouveau Testament", *ETL* 37 (1961) 5—51.

——, "Le Serviteur de Yahvé et le Fils d' Homme Daniélique sont-ils des Figures Messianiques?" (in *Miscellannés Bibliques*), *ETL* 39 (1963) 104—113.

——, "*L' origine du symbole 'Fils d' Homme'*, *ETL* 39 (1963) 100—4.

——, *De mensenzoon-logia i het Markus-evangelie* (Mededelingen van het Koninklijke Akademie voor Wetenschappen, Letteren en schone Kunsten von Belgié, Kl. der Letteren, 35/3 Brussels —Paleis der Academién), 1973.

——, "Ou en est le problème de Jesus 'Fils de l' Homme' ", *ETL* 56 (1980) 282—302.

——, "Le fils d' Homme dans les Traditions juives post bibliques hormis les livre des Páraboles de l' Hénoch Ethiopien", *ETL* 57 (1981) 58—82.

——, "Les Saints du Très-Haut sont-ils à identifier avec les Milices célestes?", *ETL* 39 (1963) 94—100.

——, "Le Fils d' Homme daniélique, vizir céleste?", *ETL* 40 (1964) 72—80.

——, Review of C.C. Caragounis *The Ephesian Mysterion: Meaning and Content*, in *ETL* 53 (1977) 507.

——, "La Vision Daniélique du Fils d' Homme", *VT* 19 (1969) 171—82.

——, "Le Fils de l' Homme dans l' évangile Johannique", *ETL* 52 (1976) 28—81.

Coppens, J.—Dequeker, L., *Le Fils de l' homme et les Saints du Très-Haut en Dan VII, dans les apocryphes et dans le Nouveau Testament*, Louvain 1961.

Cortes, J.B.—Gatti, F.M., "The Son of Man or the Son of Adam", *Bib* 49 (1968) 457—502.

Cranfield C.E.B., *A Critical and Exegetical Commentary on the Epistle to the Romans*, 2 Vols. (ICC) Edinburgh 1975—79.

——, *The Gospel according to Saint Mark. Introduction and Commentary* (CGTC), Cambridge 1959.

Creed, J.M., "The Heavenly Man", *JTS* 26 (1925) 113—36.

Croskery, J., "Recent Discussions on the Meaning of the Title 'Son of Man' ", *ET* 13 (1901—2) 351—55.

Cross, F.M., "The Development of the Jewish Scripts" in *The Bible and the Ancient Near East*, ed. G.E. Wright, N.Y. 1961.

——, "The History of the Biblical Text in the Light of Discoveries in the Judaean Desert", *HTR* 57 (1964) 281—99.

Cruvellier, J., "La notion de 'Fils de l' homme' dans les Evangiles", *Études Évangéliques* 15 (1955) 31—50.

Cullmann, O., *Christology of the NT*, London 2nd ed. 1963.

Culpepper, R.A., *The Johannine School*, Missoula 1975.

Cumont, F., "La plus ancienne géographie astrologique", *Klio* 9 (1909) 263—73.

Dalman, G., *Die Worte Jesu. Mit Berücksichtigung des nachkanonischen jüdischen Schrifttums und der aramäischen Sprache*, Leipzig 1898.

Dascalakis, A.B., "La déification d' Alexandre le Grand en Egypte et la réaction en Grèce", *StCl* (Buchurest) 9 (1967) 93—105.

Daube, D., "Evangelisten und Rabbinen", *ZNW* 48 (1957) 119—26.

——, *The New Testament and Rabbinic Judaism*, London 1956.

——, "The Earliest Structure of the Gospels", *NTS* 5 (1959) 174—87.

Davies, Ph. R., 'Eschatology in the Book of Daniel", *JSOT* 17 (1980) 33—53.

Davies, W.D., *Paul and Rabbinic Judaism. Some Rabbinic Elements in Pauline Theology*, London 1962.

Dechent, H., "Der 'Gerechte' — eine Bezeichnung für den Messias", *TSK* 100 (1927—8) 439—43.

Deissler, A., "Der 'Menschensohn' und das Volk der Heiligen des Höchsten in Dan 7" in *Jesus und der Menschensohn*, ed. Pesch — Schnackenburg, 81—91.

Delcor, M., *Le Livre de Daniel* (SB), Paris 1971.

——, "Les sources du Chapitre VII de Daniel", *VT* 18 (1968) 290—312.

Delobel, J. (ed.), *Logia. Les Paroles de Jésus — The Sayings of Jesus*. (Mémorial Joseph Coppens. Bibliotheca Ephemeridum Theologicarum Lovaniensium LIX), Leuven 1982.

Dequeker, L., "Dan VII et les Saints du Tres-Haut", *ETL* 36 (1960) 353—92. .

——, "The 'Saints of the Most High' in Qumran and Daniel", *OTS* 18 (1973) 108—87.

——, *Wereldrijk en Godsrijk in Daniel II en VII*. Status quaestionis en exegetisch onderzoek, Leuven 1959.

Derrett, J.M.D., *An Oriental Lawyer Looks at the Trial of Jesus and the Doctrine of Redemption*, London 1966.

De Villiers, P.G.R., "Revealing the Secrets. Wisdom and the World in the Similitudes of Enoch" in *Studies in I Enoch and the New Testament* (Neotestamentica 17; Annual Publication of the NT Society of South Africa), 50—68, Stellenbosch 1983.

Dexinger, F., *Sturz der Göttersöhne oder Engel vor der Sintflut?*, Wien 1966.

——, *Das Buch Daniel und seine Probleme* (SBS 36), Stuttgart 1969.

Dhanis, E., "De filio hominis in Vetere Testamento et in iudaismo", *Greg* 45 (1964), 5—59.

Dibelius, M., *Die Formgeschichte des Evangeliums*, 2nd ed. Tübingen 1933.

Dieckmann, H., " Ὁ υἱὸς τοῦ ἀνθρώπου", *Bib* 2 (1920), 69—71.

Di Lella A., " 'The Son of Man' in Dan 7" in L. Hartman—A. Di Lella: *The Book of Daniel* (AB) pp. 85—102.

——, "The One in Human Likeness and the Holy Ones of the Most Hight in Daniel 7", *CBQ* 39 (1977) 1—19.

Dodd, C.H., *The Parables of the Kingdom*, rp. of 1961 ed. Found paperbacks, Glasgow 1978.

——, *According to the Scriptures*, London 1952.

——, *The Interpretation of the Fourth Gospel*, Cambridge 1953, rp. 1980.

——, *Historical Tradition in the Fourth Gospel*, Cambridge 1965.

Doeve, J.W., *Jewish hermeneutics in the Synoptic Gospels and Acts*, Assen 1954.

Driver, S.R., *The Book of Daniel*, Cambridge 1905.

Droysen, J.G., *Historik*. Vorlesungen über Enzyklopädie und Methodologie der Geschichte, herausg. R. Hübner, München-Berlin [5]1965 rp. 1937.

Drummond, J., "The Use and Meaning of the Phrase 'The Son of Man' in the Synoptic Gospels, Parts I and II", *JTS*, 11 (1901) 350—58; 539—71.

Dumbrell, W.J., "Daniel 7 and the Function of OT Apocalyptic", *RTR* 34 (1975) 16—23.

Duncan, G.S., *Jesus, Son of Man*, London 1947.

Duncan, J.—Derrett, M., "Daniel and Salvation-History", *Down Rev*, No. 338 (Jan. 1982), 62—8.

Dunn, J.D.G., *Christology in the Making*: An inquiry into the Origins of the Doctrine of the Incarnation, London 1980.

Duplacy, J., "Marc, 2, 10 Note de syntax" in *Mélanges Bibliques* Rédigés en l' Honneur de Andre Robert, (TICP), Paris 1955, 420—27.

Dupont, G., *Le Fils de l' Homme*, Paris 1924.

Dupont, J., (Ed.), *Jésus aux Origines de la Christologie*, Gembloux 1975.

Eaton, D., "Prof. Dalman on 'The Son of Man' ", *ET* 10 (1898—9) 438—43.

Eckert, J., Art. Ἐκλεκτός, *EWNT* I, col. 1014—20.

Edersheim, A., *The Life and Times of Jesus the Messiah*, 2 Vols. Grand Rapids [2]1886.

Eerdmans, B.D., "De Uitdrukking 'Zoon des Menschen' en het Boek Henoch", *Theol. Tijdschr.* 29 (1895) 49—71.

——, "De Oorsprong van de uitdrukking 'Zoon des Menschen' als evangelische Messiastitel", *Theol. Tijdschr.* 28 (1894) 153—76.

Eichrodt, W., *Theology of the Old Testament*, 2 Vols., London 1961—7.

Eissfeldt, O., *The OT: An Introduction*, Oxford 1965.

Ellis, E.E., *The Gospel of Luke*, (NCBC), Grand Rapids 1981.

Ellis, E.E.—Wilcox, M., *Neotestamentica et Semitica*. Studies in Honour of M. Black., Edinburgh 1969.

Emerton, J.A., "The Origin of the Son of Man Imagery", *JTS* 9 (1958) 225—42.

Engnell, I., "The Son of Man" pp. 237—41, in *Critical Essays on the Old Testament* by I. Engnell. Ed. by J.I. Willis with Collaboration of H. Ringgren (earlier printed in *SBU* 2nd ed. Vol. II, cols 229—32: "Människosonen"), London 1970.

Ewald, H., *Commentary on the Prophets of the OT*. Transl. by J.F. Smith, Vols. 1—5 (Theological Translation Fund Library), London 1875—1881.

Fabry, H.J., Art. כּׁס, *TWAT* IV, 247—72.

Farrar, F.W., *The Life of Christ*, London etc. Vol. I, ^{3l}1884, Vol. II 23 ed. no date.

Farrer, A.M., *A Study in St. Mark*, London 1951.

Ferch, A.J., "Daniel 7 and Ugarit: A Reconsideration", *JBL* 99, (1980) 75–86.

——, "The Two Aeons and the Messiah in Pseudo-Philo, 4 Ezra and 2 Baruch", *AUSS* 15 (1977) 135–51.

——, *The Apocalyptic 'Son of Man' in Dan 7* (Unpublished Dissert. for G. Hasel, Andrews University: Seventh-Day Adventist Theol. Seminary) 1979.

Feuillet, A., "Le fils d' Homme de Daniel et la tradition biblique", *RB* 60 (1953) 170–202; 321–46.

——, "L' exousia du Fils de l' Homme", *RSR* 42 (1954) 161–92.

Fiebig, P.W.J., *Der Menschensohn*. Jesu Selbstbezeichnung mit besonderer Berücksichtigung des aramäischen Sprachgebrauchs für 'Mensch', Tübingen, Leipzig 1901.

Fitzmyer, J.A., "The Languages of Palestine in the First Century A.D.", *CBQ* 32 (1970) 501–31.

——, "The Phases of the Aramaic Language", pp. 57–84 of *A Wandering Aramean* 1979.

——, "The NT Title 'Son of Man' Philologically Considered" in *A Wandering Aramean*, ch. 6, pp. 143–160.

——, *A Wandering Aramean*: Collected Aramaic Essays, (SBLMS 25), Missoula, 1979.

——, "The Study of the Aramaic Background of the NT" pp. 29Cff., in *A Wandering Aramean*: (= "Methodology in the Study of Jesus' Sayings in the NT").

——, *The Aramaic Inscriptions of Sefire* (*Bib Or* 19), Rome 1967.

——, "Review: M. Black: *An Aramaic Approach to the Gospels and Acts, Oxford* ³1967. With G. Vermes: Appendix on Son of Man", *CBQ* 30 (1968) 417–28.

——, "The Aramaic Language and the Study of the NT", *JBL* 99 (1980) 5–21.

——, "The Contribution of Qumran Aramaic to the Study of the NT", *NTS* 20 (1973–4) 382–407.

——, "Methodology in the Study of Jesus' sayings in the NT" pp. 73–102 of *Jésus Aux Origines de la Christologie*, ed. J. Dupont, Gembloux 1975.

——, *Essays on the Semitic Background of the New Testament*, Missoula 1974.

——, "Another View of the 'Son of Man' Debate", *JSNT* (1979) 58–68.

Flender, H., *St. Luke Theologian of Redemptive History*, London 1967.

Foakes–Jackson, F.J.,–Lake, K., *The Beginnings of Christianity*, 5 Vols, London 1920–33.

Ford, J.M., " 'The Son of Man' — A Euphemism?", *JBL* 87 (1968) 257–66.

Formesyn, R.E.C., "Was there a Pronominal Connection for the 'Bar Nasha' Selfdesignation?", *NovT* 8 (1966) 1–35.

France, R.T., "The Servant of the Lord in the Teaching of Jesus", *TynBul* 19 (1968) 26–52.

——, *Jesus and the OT*, London 1971.

Freed, E.D., "The Son of Man in the Fourth Gospel", *JBL* 86 (1967) 402–9.

Frey, J–B., "Apocalyptique", Vol. I, cols. 326–54 in *L. Pirot's Supplément au Dictionaire de la Bible*, Paris 1928.

——, "Apocryphes de l' Ancient Testament. I. Le Livre d' Hénoch" in *Supplém. Dict. Bible*, I, cols. 357–71.

Frey, L., *Analyse Ordinale des Évangiles Synoptiques*, (Mathématiques et Sciences de l' Homme XI), Paris 1972.

Friedrichsen, A., "Människosonen och Israel" in *Festschrift G' Aulén*, pp. 100–16.

Fritzsche, C.F.A., *Evangelium Matthaei*. Recensuit et cum Commentariis Perpetuis edidit, Lipsiae 1829.

Fuller, R.H., *The Foundations of the New Testament Christology*, London 1965.

——, *The Mission and Achievement of Jesus* (SBT 12), London 1954.

Gadamer, H–G., *Wahrheit und Methode*, Tübingen 1960.

——, *Truth and Method*, London 1975.

Garnet, P., "The Baptism of Jesus and the Son of Man", *JSNT* 9 (1980) 49–65.

Gaster, M., "The Son of Man and The Theophany in Daniel, Ch. VII: A New Interpretation", *Search 1* (1931) pp. 15–30.

George, K.A., *The Peshitto Version of Daniel*, (Unpublished Diss.), Hamburg 1972.

Gerhardson, B.–Hartman, L., "Situationen inom den nytestamentliga exegetiken", *STK* 58 (1982) 109–16.

Gero, S., " 'My Son the Messiah'. A Note on 4 Ezra 7: 28–29", *ZNW* 66 (1975) 264–7.

Gese, H., "Der Messias", *Zur Biblische Theologie: Alttestamentliche Vorträge*, pp. 140–45, München 1977.

Glasson, T.F., "The Son of Man Imagery: Enoch XIV and Daniel VII", *NTS* 23 (1976) 82–90.

——, "The Ensign of the Son of Man (Matt XXIV 30)", *JTS*, NS XV, (1964) 299–300.

——, *The Second Advent: The Origin of the NT Doctrine*, London ³1963.

Goettsberger, J., *Das Buch Daniel*, Übersetzt und erklärt, Bonn 1928.

Goldstein J.A., *I Maccabees*. A New Translation with Introduction and Commentary (AB), N.Y. 1977.

Goppelt, L., "Zum Problem des Menschensohns: das Verhältnis von Leidens- und Parusieankündigung" pp. 20–32, in *Mensch und Menschensohn*, ed. H. Sierig, Hamburg 1963.

Grant, F.C., *The Gospel of the Kingdom*, N.Y. 1940.

Grässer, E., "Beobachtungen zum Menschensohn in Hebr 2, 6", in *Jesus und der Menschensohn*, Hrsg. Pesch–Schnackenburg, pp. 404–14.

Grayston, K., "The Study of Mark XIII", *BJRL* 56 (1974) 371–87.

Greenfield, J.C., "The Dialects of Early Aramaic", *JNES* 37 (1978) 93–99.

Greenfield, J.C.,–Stone M.E., "*The Enochic Pentateuch and the Date of the Similitudes*", *HTR* 70 (1977) 51–66.

Grelot, P., "Les Messie dans les Apocryphes de l' Ancient Testament". État de la Question, pp. 51 –63, in *La Venue du Messie*. Messianisme et Eschatologie (*RechBib VI*), Bruges 1962.

Grotius, H., *Ad Danielem*, in *Opera Omnia Theologica in Quatuor Tomos Divisa*, Basileae 1732.

Grundmann, W., Art. δεῖ, *TDNT* II, 21–5.

Gry, L., "La dénomination messianique 'Fils de l' Homme' dans la Bible et les Apocalypses éthiopiens" in *Xenia. Hommage à l' Université de Grèce*, Athenes 1912.

——, *Les Dires Prophétiques d' Esdras* (IV. Esdras), Vol. I–II, Paris 1938.

Guilding, A., "The Son of Man and the Ancient of Days (Daniel 7:13)", *EvQ* 23 (1951) 210–12.

Guillet, J., "A Propos des Titres de Jésus Christ, Fils de l' Homme, Fils de Dieu", in *A la Rencontre de Dieu*, Mémorial Albert Gelin, Le Puy 1961, 309–17.

Gundry, R.H., *Matthew*. A Commentary on His Literary and Theological Art, Grand Rapids 1982.

Gunkel, H., *Schöpfung und Chaos in Urzeit und Endzeit*. Eine religionsgeschichtliche Untersuchung über Gen 1 und Ap Joh 12, Göttingen 1895.

Guthrie D., *New Testament Theology*, Leicester 1981.

Gwyn, I., Art. "Theodotion" in *Dictionary of Christian Biography*, ed. W. Smith Vol. IV, London 1887.

Haag, H., Art אָדָם בֶּן, *TDOT* II, pp. 159–65.

Haenchen, E., *Das Johannesevangelium*. Ein Kommentar herausgegeben von Ulrich Busse, Tübingen 1980.

——, *The Acts of the Apostles*, Oxford 1971.

Hahn, F., *The Titles of Jesus in Christology*. Their History in Early Christianity, London 1969.

——, *Christologische Hoheitstitel*. Ihre Geschichte im frühen Christentum (FRLANT 85), Göttingen ⁴1974.

Hammerton–Kelly, R.G., "A Note on Matthew XII. 28 Par. Luke XI. 20", *NTS* 11 (1964–5) 167–9.

——, *Pre-existence, Wisdom, and the Son of Man*. A Study of the Idea of Pre-existence in the NT, (SNTS Mon. ser. 21), Cambridge 1973.

Hamerton–Kelly, R.–Scroggs, R., (eds.), *Jews, Greeks and Christians*. Religious Cultures in late Antiquity. Essays in Honour of W.D. Davies, Leiden 1976.

Hanhart, R., "Die Heiligen des Höchsten" in *Hebräische Wortforschung* Festschrift für W. Baumgartner, VT Sup 16, Leiden 1967, pp. 90–101.

Harnisch, W., *Verhängnis und Verheissung der Geschichte*. Untersuchungen zum Zeit-und Geschichtverständnis im 4. Buch Esra und in der syr. Baruchapokalypse (FRLANT 97), Göttingen 1969.

Harrington, D.J., Entry: Roland, *RB* 90 (1983) 23–79 in *NTA* 28 (1984) 18.

Harrison, R.K., "The Son of Man", *EvQ* 23 (1951) 46–50.

——, *Introduction to the OT*, Grand Rapids 1969.

Hartman, L., *Prophecy Interpreted*. The Formation of Some Jewish Apocalyptic Texts and of the Eschatological Discource Mk 13 Par., Lund 1966.

Hartman, L.F.–Di Lella, A.A., *The Book of Daniel* (AB), N.Y. 1978.

Hasel, G.F., "The Identity of 'The Saints of the Most High' in Daniel 7", *Bib* 56 (1975) 173–92.

Haufe, G., "Das Menschensohn-Problem in der gegenwärtigen wissenschaftlichen Diskussion", *EvT* 26 (1966) 130–41.

Hävernick, H.A. Ch., *Kommentar über das Buch Daniel*, Hamburg 1832.

Hay, L.S., "The Son of Man in Mark 2:10 and 2:28", *JBL* 89 (1970) 69–75.

Heaton, E.W., *The Book of Daniel*, London, 1956.

Hedinger H.W., *Subjektivität und Geschichtswissenschaft*. Grundzüge einer Historik, Berlin 1969.

Helfmeyer, Art. אות, *TDOT* I, 167–88.

Hengel, M., *The Son of God*. The Origin of Christology and the History of Jewish-Hellenistic Religion, London 1976.

——, *Judaism and Hellenism*. Studies in their Encounter in Palestine during the Early Hellenistic Period, London 1974.

——, *The Atonement*. The Origin of the Doctrine in the New Testament, London 1981.

Hengstenberg, E.W., *Dissertations on the Genuineness of Daniel and the Integrity of Zechariah*, (Transl. B.P. Pratten), Edinburgh 1848.

Herford, R.T., *Christianity in Talmud and Midrash*, London 1903.

Hickling, C.J.A., "The Plurality of 'Q' " in *Logia* ed. J. Delobel, Leuven 1982.

Higgins, A.J.B., *The Son of Man in the Teaching of Jesus*, Cambridge 1980.

——, "Is the Son of Man Problem Insoluble?" pp. 70–87 in *Neotestamentica et Semitica* Studies in honour of M. Black, eds. E.E. Ellis, M. Wilcox, Edinburgh 1969.

——, *Jesus and the Son of Man*, Philadelphia 1964.

——, "Son of Man – *Forschung* since *The Teaching of Jesus*" in *New Testament Essays*: Studies in Memory of T.W. Manson (ed. A.J.B. Higgins), Manchester, 1959 pp. 119–35.

——, "The Sign of the Son of Man (Matt 24:30)", *NTS* 9 (1962–3) 380–2.

——, " 'Menschensohn' oder 'ich' in Q: Lk 12, 8–9 / Mt 10, 32–33?" in *Jesus und der Menschensohn*, Hrsg. Pesch–Schnackenburg, pp. 117–23, Freiburg, etc. 1975.

——, "The OT and some Aspects of the NT Christology" in *Promise and Fulfilment*. Essays presented to S.H. Hooke, Ed. F.F. Bruce, Edinburgh 1963.

Hilgenfeld, A., *Die Jüdische Apokalyptik in ihrer geschichtlichen Entwicklung*, Jena 1857.

——, "Die Evangelien und die geschichtliche Gestalt Jesu", *ZwTh* 6 (1863) 311–40.

Hill, D., " 'Son of Man' in Psalm 80 v. 17", *NovT* 15 (1973) 261–69.

——, *The Gospel of Matthew* (NCB), London 1972, rp. 1977.

Hindley, J.C., "Towards a Date for the Similtudes of Enoch. An historical Approach", *NTS* 14 (1967–8) 551–65.

Hirsch, E.D., *Validity in Interpretation*, New Haven 1967.

Hitzig, F., *Das Buch Daniel erklärt*. (Kurzgefastes exegetisches Handbuch zum Alten Testament), Leipzig 1850.

Hodgson, P.C., "The Son of Man and the Problem of Historical Knowledge", *JR* 41 (1961) 91–108.

Hoffmann, P. "Jesus, der Menschensohn", (Part II of *Studien zur Theologie der Logienquelle*, (N Alc, N.F. 8), Münster 1972.

Hofius, O. *Der Christushymnus Philipper 2, 6–11*. Untersuchungen zu Gestalt und Aussage eines urchristlichen Psalms (WUNT 2:17), Tübingen 1976.

Holsten, C., "Biblisch-theologische Studien: III. Die Bedeutung der Ausdrucksform ὁ υἱὸς τοῦ ἀνθρώπου im Bewusstsein Jesu", *ZwTh* 34 (1891) 1–79.

Holtzmann, H.J., *Lehrbuch der neutestamentlichen Theologie*, 2 Vols., Freiburg, Leipzig 1897.

——, "Ueber den nt: lichen Ausdruck 'Menschensohn' ", *ZwTh* 8 (1865) 212–37.

Hommel, F., "The Apocalyptic Origin of the Expression 'Son of Man' ", *ET* 11 (1899–1900) 341–45.

Hooker, M.D., *The Son of Man in Mark*, A Study of the Background of the Term 'Son of Man' and its Use in St. Mark's Gospel, London 1967.

——, "Is the Son of Man problem really insoluble?" pp. 155–68 in *Text and Interpretation*, Studies in the New Testament Presented to M. Black, Eds. E. Best and R. McL. Wilson, Cambridge 1979.

—, "On Using the Wrong Tool", *Theology* 75 (1972) 570—81.

—, "Christology and Methodology", *NTS* 17 (1970—1) 480—7.

Horst, F., *Hiob* (BKAT 16.1), Neukirchen 1960—68.

Horton, F.L., *The Melchisedek Tradition* (SNTSMS 30), Cambridge 1976.

Hoskyns, E.C., *The Fourth Gospel*. Ed. F.N. Davey, London 1947.

Houk, C.B., *"Ben 'Adam*. Patterns as Literary Criteria in Ezekiel", *JBL* 88 (1969) 184—90.

Hunter, A.M., *The Work and Words of Jesus*, London ²1973.

Huntress, E., "'Son of God' in Jewish Writings prior to the Christian Era", *JBL* 54 (1935) 117—23.

Ἱστορία τοῦ Ἑλληνικοῦ Ἔθνους, 15 Vols., Ἀθῆναι 1970—78.

Jacob, E., *Theology of the OT*, London 1958.

Jacobson, A.D., "The Literary Unity of Q. Lc 10, 2—16 and Parallels as a Test Case" in *Logia*, ed. J. Delobel, Leuven 1982.

James, J.C., "The Son of Man: Origin and Use of the Title", *ET* 36 (1924—5) 309—14.

James, M.R., "Salathiel qui et Esdras", *JTS* 19 (1918) 347—9.

Jansen, H.L., *Die Henochgestalt*: Eine Vergleichende Religions-Geschichtliche Untersuchung. (Skrifter utgitt av Det Norske Videnskaps-Akademi i Oslo), Oslo 1939.

Jeffery, A., "The Book of Daniel", *IB* VI, 339—549, Nashville 1956.

Jellicoe, S., *The Septuagint and Modern Study*, Oxford 1968.

—, "Some Relfections on the KAIGE Recension", *VT* 23 (1973) 15—24.

Jensen, P., Art. "Adapa" in *RLA*, I Ed. E. Ebeling, Berlin 1928, pp. 33—35.

Jeremias, A., Art. "Oannes" in W.H. Roscher's *Ausführliches Lexikon der griechischen und römischen Mythologie*, Vol. III, cols, 577—93, Leipzig 1897—1909.

Jeremias, J., "Das Lösegeld für die Vielen (Mk 10, 45)", *Jud* 3 (1947—7) 249—64.

—, *Abba*, Studien zur neutestamentlichen Theologie und Zeitgeschichte, Göttingen 1966.

—, Art. Ἰωνᾶς, *TDNT* III, 406—10.

—, "Die älteste Schicht der Menschensohn-Logien", *ZNW* 58 (1967) 159—72.

—, Art. παῖς Θεοῦ, *TDNT* V, 677—717.

—, *New Testament Theology*, Vol. 1: The Proclamation of Jesus, London 1971.

—, *Neutestamentliche Theologie*, Erster Teil: Die Verkündigung Jesu, Gütersloh 1971.

Jocz, J., *The Jewish People and Jesus Christ*. A Study in the relationship between the Jewish People and Jesus Christ, London 1949.

Jüngel, E., *Paulus und Jesus*: eine Untersuchung zur Präzisierung der Frage nach dem Ursprung der Christologie (HUT 2), 4th ed. Tübingen 1972.

Kabisch, R., *Das Vierte Buch Esra und Seine Quellen Untersucht*, Göttingen 1889.

Kahle, P.E., *Massoreten des Westens*, Stuttgart 1927—30.

—, *The Cairo Geniza*, London ²1959.

Κακριδής, Ι., "Ἱστοριογραφία: Θουκυδίδης", *IEE*, III, B 440—47.

Kaminka, A., "Beiträge zur Erklärung der Esra-Apokalypse und zur Rekonstruktion ihres hebräischen Urtextes", *MGWJ* 76, 1932, 121—38; 206—12; 494—511; 604—7; 77, 1933, 339—55.

Κανελόπουλος, Π., "Τὸ κράτος τοῦ Μεγάλου Ἀλεξάνδρου", *IEE* IV 1973, 218—35.

Käsemann, E., "Sätze heiligen Rechts in NT", *NTS* 1 (1954—5) 248—60.

—, "Das Problem des historischen Jesus" pp. 187—214 in *Exegetische Versuche und Besinnungen I*.

—, "Das Problem des Historischen Jesus", *ZTK*, 51 (1954), 125—53.

—, *Exegetische Versuche und Besinnungen I*, Göttingen 1960.

Kearns, R., *Vorfragen zur Christologie I—II*, Tübingen 1978—80.

Keil, C.F., *The Book of Daniel* (*Commentary on the OT*, ed. C.F. Keil — F. Delitzsch), rp. Grand Rapids 1978.

Kertelge, K., "Die Vollmacht des Menschensohnes zur Sündenvergebung (Mk 2, 20)" pp. 205—12 in *Orientierung an Jesus*. Für J. Schmid, ed. P. Hoffmann, Freiburg, etc. 1973.

Keulers, J., *Die Eschatologische Lehre des Vierten Esrabuches*. (BibS(F) XX, nos. 2—3), Freiburg 1922.

Kieffer, R., *Nytestamentlig Teologi*, Lund 1977.

Kingsburry, J.D., "The Title 'Son of Man' in Matthew's Gospel" *CBQ* 37 (1975) 193—202.

Kinniburgh, E., 'The Johannine Son of Man", *SE* 4 (1968) 64ff.

Klausner, J., *The Messianic Idea in Israel*, N.Y. 1955.

Knibb, M.A., "The Date of the Parables of Enoch: A Critical Review", *NTS* 25 (1979) 345–59.

Knox, J., *The Death of Christ*, The Cross in New Testament History and Faith, London 1959, rp. 1967.

Koch K., "Die Herkunft der Proto–Theodotion–Uebersetzung des Danielbuches", *VT* 23 (1973) 362–65.

Köhler, L., 'Alttestamentliche Wortforschung. Ps 8, 5", *TZ* 1 (1945) 77–8.

Kraeling, C.H., *Anthropos and Son of Man*: A Study in the Religious Syncretism of the Hellenistic Orient (Columbia Univ. Oriental Studies 25), N.Y. 1927.

Kranichfeld, R., *Das Buch Daniel*. Erklärt, Berlin 1868.

Kristensen, W.B., "De term 'Zoon des Mensen' toegelicht uit de anthropologie der Ouden" *Theol. Tijdschr.* 45 (1911) 11–38.

Kruijf. Th. de, *Der Sohn des Lebendigen Gottes*, Ein Beitrag zur Christologie des Matthäusevangeliums, (An Bib 16), Roma 1962.

Kruse, H., "Compositio Libri Danielis et Idea Filii Hominis", *VD* 37 (1959) 147–61; 193–211.

Kuhn, H.W., *Enderwartung und gegenwärtiges Heil*. Untersuchungen zu den Gemeindelieder von Qumran mit einem Anhang über Eschatologie und Gegenwart in der Verkündigung Jesu (SUNT 4), Göttingen 1966.

Kümmel, W.G., *Promise and Fulfilment*. The Eschatological Message of Jesus, 2nd ed. London 1961.

——, *Die Theologie des Neuen Testaments* nach seinen Hauptzeugen Jesus·Paulus·Johannes, Göttingen 1969.

——, "Jesusforschung seit 1950", *TRu* 30 (1965–66) 13–46.

——, *Heilsgeschehen und Geschichte*. Gesammelte Aufsätze 1933–1964, Hrsg. E. Grässer, O. Merk, A. Fritz, Marburg 1965.

——, "Jesusforschung seit 1965", *TRu* N.F. 45 (1980) 40–84.

——, "*Review* of N. Perrin's *Rediscovering the Teaching of Jesus*", *JR* 49 (1969) 59–66.

Kurichianil, J., "Jesus' Consciousness of His Passion and Death According to the Synoptic Gospels", *Biblebhashyam* 9 (1983) 114–25.

Kutscher, E.Y., "The Language of the Genesis Apocryphon: A Preliminary Study" in *Aspects of the Dead Sea Scrolls* (ScrH 4), Jerusalem 1958.

Ladd, G.E., *A Theology of the NT*, Grand Rapids 1974.

——, *Jesus and the Kingdom*. The Eschatology of Biblical Realism, London 1966.

Lagarde, P.A. de, *Deutsche Schriften*, Göttingen 1878.

——, *Gesammelte Abhandlungen*, Leipzig 1866.

Lagrange, M.J., *Le Judaïsme avant Jésus-Christ*, (EBib), Paris ³1931.

——, "Notes sur le Messianisme au Temps de Jésus", *RB*, NS.2 (1905) 481–514.

Lake, K.– Foakes-Jackson, F.J., See Foakes-Jackson–K. Lake.

Lambrecht, J., "Q – influence on Mark 8:34–9:1" pp. 277–304 in *Logia*, ed. J. Delobel, Leuven 1982.

Landmann, L., (Ed.), *Messianism in the Talmudic Era*, N.Y. 1979.

Lane, W., *The Gospel According to Mark* (NICNT), Grand Rapids 1974.

Lebram, J.C.H., "Perspektiven der gegenwärtigen Danielforschung", *JSJ* 5 (1974) 1–33.

Leivestad, R., "Der apokalyptische Menschensohn ein theologisches Phantom", *ASTI* 6 (1967–8) 49–109.

——, "Exit the Apocalyptic Son of Man", *NTS* 18 (1971–2) 243–67.

Lenglet, A., "La structure littéraire de Daniel 2–7", *Bib* 53 (1972) 169–90.

Leupold, H.C., *Exposition of Daniel*, Grand Rapids 1949, rp. 1978.

Leitzmann, H., *Der Menschensohn*. (Ein Beitrag zur neutestamentlichen Theologie), Freiburg 1896.

Lindars, B., "The Son of Man in the Johannine Christology" pp. 43–60 in *Christ and Spirit in the New Testament*: in honour of C.F.D. Moule, ed. B. Lindars–S.S. Smaley, Cambridge 1973.

——, *The Gospel of John* (NCB), London 1972.

——, "Enoch and Christology", *ET* 92 (1981) 295–99.

——, *Jesus, Son of Man*. A Fresh Examination of the Son of Man Sayings in the Gospels in the Light of Recent Research, London 1983.

——, "Re-Enter the Apocalyptic Son of Man", *NTS* 22 (1975) 52–72.

—, "The New Look on the Son of Man", *BJRL* 63 (1980—1) 437—62.

Lindars, B.—Smaley, S.S. (Eds.), *Christ and Spirit in the NT*, in honour of C.F.D. Moule, Cambridge 1973.

Lindeskog, G., "Das Rätsel des Menschensohnes", *ST* 22 (1968) 149—76.

Linton, O., "The Trial of Jesus and the Interpretation of Ps CX", *NTS* 7 (1960—1) 260.

Lohmeyer, E., *Kyrios Jesus*. Eine Untersuchung zu Phil. 2, 5—11, Heidelberg 1928.

—, *Das Evangelium des Markus*, Göttingen 1963.

Lohse, E., "Der Menschensohn in der Johannesapokalypse" in *Jesus und der Menschensohn*, Hrsg. R. Pesch — R. Schnackenburg, Freiburg 1975.

—, Art. Υἱός: II Palestinian Judaism, *TDNT* VIII, pp. 357—62.

—, Art. Υἱός Δαυίδ, *TDNT* VIII, pp. 478—88.

Longenecker, R.N., " 'Son of Man' Imagery: Some Implications for Theology and Discipleship", *JETS* 18 (1975) 3—16.

—, " 'Son of Man' as a Self-Designation of Jesus", *JETS* 12 (1969) 151—8.

Lövestam, E., "Die Davidssohnfrage", *SEÅ* 27 (1962) 74—80.

—, "Die Frage des Hohenpriesters (Mk 14:61; par. Mt 26:63)", *SEÅ* 26 (1961) 93—107.

Lundström, G., *The Kingdom of God in the Teaching of Jesus*, Edinburgh, London 1963.

Lust, J., "Daniel 7:13 and the Septuagint", *ETL* 54 (1978) 62—9.

Maas, F., Art. אדם, *TDOT* I, 75—87.

Maddox, R., "The Quest for Valid Methods in 'Son of Man' Research", *ABR* 19 (1971) 36—51.

—, "Methodenfragen in der Menschensohnforschung", *EvT* 32 (1972) 143—60.

—, "The Function of the Son of Man According to the Synoptic Gospels", *NTS* 15 (1968—69) 45—74.

—, "The Function of the Son of Man in the Gospel of John" pp. 186—204 in *Reconciliation and Hope*. NT Essays on Atonement and Eschatology. For L. Morris, Ed. R. Banks, Exeter 1974.

Maier, G., *Matthäus-Evangelium*, 2 Vols., Neuhausen, Stuttgart 1979—80.

—, *Der Prophet Daniel*, Brockhaus, Wuppertal 1982.

Manek, J., "Mit wem identifiziert sich Jesus (Matt. 25:31—46)?" pp. 15—25 in *Christ and Spirit in The New Testament*, Eds. B. Lindars, S.S. Smaley in Honour of C.F.D. Moule, Cambridge 1973.

Manson, T.W., "The Son of Man in Daniel, Enoch and the Gospels", *BJRL* 32 (1950) 171—93.

—, *The Sayings of Jesus*. As Recorded in the Gospels According to St. Matthew and St. Luke with Indrod. and Comm., London 1949.

—, "Mark ii. 27f.", *In honorem Antionii Fridrichsen (Con N, XI)*, Lund, Köpenhamn 1947.

—, *The Teaching of Jesus*. Studies in its Form and Content, 2nd ed., Cambridge 1935.

Manson, W., *Jesus the Messiah: The Synoptic Tradition of the Revelation of God in Christ — with special Reference to Form Criticism*, London 1943.

Marlow, R., " 'The Son of Man' in Recent Journal Literature", *CBQ* 28 (1966) 20—30.

Marshall, I.H., "The Divine Sonship of Jesus", *Int* 21 (1967) 87—103.

—, *I Believe in the Historical Jesus*, London 1977.

—, *The Gospel of Luke*, A Commentary on the Greek Text (NIGTC), Exeter 1978.

—, "The Son of Man in Contemporary Debate", *EvQ* 42 (1970) 67—87.

—, (Ed.) *New Testament Interpretation*, Exeter 1977.

—, "The Synoptic Son of Man Sayings in Recent Discussion", *NTS* 12 (1965—6) 327—51.

—, *The Acts of the Apostles*. An Introduction and Commentary (TNTC), London 1980.

Martyn, J.L., *History and Theology in the Fourth Gospel*, N.Y. 1968.

McArthur, H.K., "Basic Issues, A Survey of Recent Gospel Research", *Int* 18 (1964) 39—55.

—, "The Burden of Proof in Historical Jesus Research", *ET* 82 (1970—1) 116—9.

McCown, C.C., "Jesus, Son of Man: a Survey of Recent discussion", *JR* 28 (1948) 1—12.

McL Wilson, R., See Best, E.—McL Wilson, R.

McNeile, A.H., *The Gospel According to St. Matthew*, London 1915.

McNeil, B., "The Son of Man and the Messiah. A Footnote", *NTS* 26 (1979—80) 419—21.

Mearns, Ch. L., "Dating the Similitudes of Enoch", *NTS* 25 (1979) 360—69.

—, "The Parables of Enoch — Origin and Date", *ET* 89 (1978) 118f.

Meecham, H.G., "The Imperative Use of ἵνα in the New Testament", *JTS* 43 (1942) 179—80.

Meloni, G., "Filius Hominis" in *Saggi di Filologia Semitica*, 315—9, Rome 1913.

Mertens, A., *Das Buch Daniel im Lichte den Texte vom Toten Meer* (SBM 12), Würzburg 1971.

Messel, N., *Der Menschensohn in den Bilderreden des Henoch* (BZAW 35), Giessen 1922.

Metzger, B.M., *An Introduction to the Apocrypha,* Oxford 1957.

Meyer, A., "Jesus, Jesu Jünger und das Evangelium im Talmud und verwandten jüdischen Schriften" in E. Hennecke (hrsg.) *Handbuch zu den Neutestamentlichen Apokryphen,* Tübingen 1904.

——, *Jesu Muttersprache.* (Das Galiläische Aramäisch in seiner Bedeutung für die Erklärung der Reden Jesu und der Evangelien überhaupt, Freiburg, Leipzig 1896.

Michel, O., Art. κόκκος, *TDNT* III, 810–12.

——, "Der Menschensohn. Die eschatologische Hinweise. Die apokalyptische Aussage. Bemerkungen zum Menschensohn – Verständnis des NT", *TZ* 27 (1971) 81–104.

——, "Der Umbruch: Messianität = Menschensohn: Fragen zu Markus 8:31", pp. 310–16 in *Tradition und Glaube,* Festschrift K.G. Kuhn, eds. G. Jeremias, H–W. Kuhn, H. Stegemann, Göttingen 1971.

Μικρογιαννάκης, E., (with Cooperation of) "Ἡ κατάλυση τῶν ἑλληνιστικῶν κρατῶν τῆς Ἀνατολῆς (145–30 π.Χ.) in *IEE* V, 179–194.

Milik, J.T., "Problèmes de la littérature Hénochique à la lumière de fragments araméens de Qumrân", *HTR* 64 (1971) 333–78.

Moe, O., "Der Menschensohn und der Urmensch", *ST* 14 (1960) 119–29.

——, "Menneskesønnen og Urmennesket", *TTKi* 32 (1961) 65–73.

Moloney, F.J., "The End of the Son of Man?". *Review* (of M. Casey, *Son of Man*: The Interpretation and Influence of Dan 7, *DownRev* 98 (1980) 280–90.

——, *The Johannine Son of Man* (Biblioteca de Scienze Religiose, 14), Rome 1976.

——, "The Re-Interpetation of Ps VIII and The Son of Man Debate", *NTS* 27 (1981) 656–72.

Montgomery, J.A., *A Critical and Exegetical Commentary on the Book of Daniel* (ICC), Edinburgh 1927.

Moore, A.L., *The Parousia in the New Testament,* Leiden 1966.

Moore, G.F., *Judaism in the First Centuries of the Christian Era: The Age of the Tannaim,* 3 Vols., Cambridge Mass. 1927–30.

Morgenstern, J., "The Mythological Background of Ps 82", *HUCA* 14 (1939) 29–126.

——, "The Son of Man of Dan 7:13f.: A New Interpretation", *JBL* 80 (1961) 65–77.

——, "The King-god among the Western Semites and the Meaning of Epiphanes", *VT* 10 (1960) 138–97.

Morris, L., *The Gospel According to John.* The English text with Introduction, Exposition and Notes, Grand Rapids 1971.

Mosley, A.W., "Historical Reporting in the Ancient World", *NTS* 12 (1965–6) 10–26.

Moule, C.F.D., *The Origin of Christology,* Cambridge 1977.

——, *The New Testament Gospels,* London 1965.

——, "Neglected Features in the Problem of 'The Son of Man'" pp. 413–28 in *Neues Testament und Kirche,* für R. Schnackenburg ed. J. Gnilka, Freiburg i Br. 1974.

——, *The Phenomenon of the NT* (SBT), London, 1967.

Mowinckel, S., "Henok og Menneskesønnen", *NorTT* 45 (1944) 57–69.

——, *Psalmenstudien* II, Kristiania, 1922.

——, *He that cometh,* Oxford, 1956, rp. 1959.

Muilenburg, J., "The Son of Man in Daniel and the Ethiopic Apocalypse of Enoch", *JBL* 79 (1960) 197–209.

Muirhead, L.A., "The Name 'Son of Man' and the Messianic Consciousness of Jesus", *ET* 11 (1899 –1900) 62–5.

Müller, K., "Menschensohn und Messias: Religionsgeschichtliche Vorüberlegungen zum Menschensohnproblem in den synoptischen Evangelien", *BZ* 16 (1972) 159–187; 17 (1973) 52–66.

——, "Der Menschensohn im Danielzyklus" in *Jesus und der Menschensohn,* ed. Pesch–Schnackenburg, pp. 37–80, Freiburg etc. 1975.

Müller, M., *Messias og 'Menneskesøn' i Daniels Bog, første Enoksbog og fjerde Ezrabog,* København 1972.

——, "Ueber den Ausdruck 'Menschensohn' in den Evangelien", *ST* 31 (1977) 65–82.

——, "Om udtrykket 'Menneskesønnen' i evangelien", *DTT* 40 (1977) 1–17.

Müller, U.B., *Messias und Menschensohn in Jüdischen Apokalypsen und in der Offenbarung des Johannes* (SNT 6), Gütersloh 1972.

Munck, J., *The Acts of the Apostles*. Introduction. Translation and Notes, (AB), N.Y. 1967.

Murphy O' Connor, J., "Péché et Communauté dans le Nouveau Testament", *RB* 74 (1967) 161– 93.

Mussner, F., "Wege zum Selbstbewusstsein Jesu. Ein Versuch", *BZ* N.F. 12, (1968) 161–72.

— —, "Wohnung Gottes und Menschensohn nach der Stephanusperikope (Apg 6, 8 – 8, 2)" in *Jesus und der Menschensohn* Hrsg. R. Pesch – R. Schnackenburg, pp. 283–99, Freiburg etc. 1975.

Neander, A., *Das Leben Jesu Christi*. In seinem geschichtlichen Zusammenhange und seiner geschichtlichen Entwicklung. Hamburg 1837, 5th ed. 1852.

Neirynck, F., "Recent Developments in the Study of Q" pp. 29–75 in *Logia*, ed. J. Delobel.

Nestle, E., "The 'Son of Man' in the OT", *ET* 11 (1899–1900) 238.

Neugebauer, F., "Die Davidssohnfrage (Mark XII, 35–37 par.) und der Menschensohn", *NTS* 21 (1974–5) 81–108.

Newman, B.M., "Towards a Translation of 'The Son of Man' in the Gospels", *BT* 21 (1970) 141– 46.

Nineham, D.E., *The Gospel of Saint Mark*, Harmondsworth 1963.

Nösgen, K.F., *Christus der Menschen-und Gottessohn*. Eine Erörterung der Selbstbezeichnungen Jesu Christi in ihrer Grundlegenden Bedeutung für die Christologie, Gotha 1869.

Noth, M., "The Holy Ones of the Most High" in *The Laws in the Pentateuch and other Essays*, London 1966.

— —, "Die Heiligen des Höchsten", *NorTT* 56 (1955) (reprinted in *Gesammelte Studien*, pp. 274– 90).

— —, "Zur Komposition des Buches Daniel", pp. 11–28 in *Gesammelte Studien*.

— —, *Gesammelte Studien zum Alten Testament* II, München 1969.

Oesterley, W.O.E., *The Jews and Judaism during the Greek Period*. The Background of Christianity, London 1941.

Oesterley, W.O.E.–Robinson, Th.H., *Introduction to the Books of the OT*, London 1934.

Olmstead, A.T., "Intertestamental Studies", *JAOS* 56 (1936) 242–57.

Oort, H.L., *De uitdrukking O ΥΙΟΣ ΤΟΥ ΑΝΘΡΩΠΟΥ in het Neiuwe Testament*, Leiden 1893.

Otto, R., *Reich Gottes und Menschensohn*, München ³1954.

Palmer, H., *The Logic of Gospel Criticism*, London etc. 1968.

Pamment, M., "The Son of Man in the First Gospel", *NTS* 29 (1983) 116–29.

Parker, P., "The Meaning of 'Son of Man' ", *JBL*, 60–61, (1941) 151–57.

Paul, L., *Son of Man*, London 1961.

Paulus, H.E.G., *Exegetisches Handbuch* über die drei ersten Evangelien, 3 Vols., Heidelberg 1830 –42.

Peake, A.S., "The Messiah and the Son of Man" (in *Miscellaneous Essays on Theology*, pp. 1–32), rp. *BJRL* 8 (1924).

— —, *Commentary on the Bible*, London 1962.

Perrin, N., *The Kingdom of God in the Teaching of Jesus*, Philadelphia 1963.

— —, "Eschatology and Hermeneutics: Reflections on Method in the Interpretation of the New Testament", *JBL* 93 (1974) 3–14.

— —, *Rediscovering the Teaching of Jesus*, London 1967.

— —, "Mark XIV. 62: The End Product of a Christian Pesher Tradition?", *NTS* 12 (1965–6), 150– 5.

— —, *A modern Pilgrimage in NT Christology*. Philadelphia 1974.

— —, "The Son of Man in Ancient Judaism and Primitive Christianity: A Suggestion", *BR* 11 (1966) 17–28.

— —, "The Son of Man in the Synoptic Tradition", *BR* 13 (1968) 3–25.

Pesch, R., "Das Messiasbekenntnis des Petrus (Mk 8:27–30). Neuverhandlung einer alten Frage", *BZ* 17 (1973) 178–95; 18 (1974) 20–31.

— —, "Die Vision des Stefanus. Apg. 7, 55f. im Rahmen der Apostelgeschichte", *BibLeb* 6 (1965) 92–107, 170–183.

— —, *Das Markusevangelium*, (HTKNT) 2 Vols., Freiburg 1976–77.

— —, "Die Passion des Menschensohnes. Eine Studie zu den Menschensohnworten der vormarkinischen Passionsgeschichte" pp. 166—95 in *Jesus und der Menschensohn*, Hrsg. R. Pesch, R. Schnackenburg, Freiburg etc. 1975.

Pesch, R.—Schnackenburg, R., (eds.) *Jesus und der Menschensohn*. (Festschrift Anton Vögtle), Freiburg 1975.

Pfammatter, J.—Furger, F., (eds.) *Theologische Berichte* I, Zürich 1972.

Plöger, O., *Das Buch Daniel*, Gütersloh 1965.

Porteous, N., *Daniel*. A Commentary (OTL), Philadelphia 1976.

Porter, F.C., *The Messages of the Apocalyptical Writers*, New York 1905.

Porter, P.A., *Metaphors and Monsters*: A Literary-Critical Study of Daniel 7 and 8, Lund 1983.

Poythress, V.S. "The Holy Ones of the Most High in Dan VII", *VT* 26 (1976) 208—13.

Procksch, O., "Der Menschensohn als Gottessohn" in *Christentum und Wissenschaft* 3 (1927) 429.

——, "Die Berufungsvision Hesekiels", *ZAW* (Beihefte 34) 1920, 141—9.

Pusey, E.B., *Daniel the Prophet*. Nine Lectures Delivered in the Divinity School of the University of Oxford, Oxford 1869.

Quasten J., *Patrology*. The Beginnings of Patristic Literature, Utrecht-Antwerp 1966.

Rawlinson A.E.J., *The New Testament Doctrine of the Christ*, London 1926.

Rengstorf, K.H., Art. μανθάνω etc., *TDNT* IV, 390—461.

——, Art. σημεῖον, *TDNT* VII, 200—69.

Rhodes, A.B., "The Kingdoms of Men and the Kingdom of God. A Study of Daniel 7:1—14", *Int* 15 (1961) 411—30.

Riedl, J., "Wenn ihr den Menschensohn erhöht habt, werdet ihr erkennen (Joh 8, 28)", in *Jesus und der Menschensohn*, Hrsg. R. Pesch, R. Schnackenburg, pp. 355—70, Freiburg etc. 1975.

Riehm, E.K.A., *Messianic Prophecy*: Its Origin, Historical Growth and Relation to NT Fulfilment, (tr. L.A. Muirhead), Edinburgh 1891.

Riesenfeld, H., "Nytestamentlig Teologi" in *En bok om Nya Testamentet* ed. B. Gerhardsson, pp. 359—459, Lund 1971.

Riesner, R., "Wie sicher ist die Zwei—Quellen—Theorie?", *ThB* 8 (1977) 49—73.

——, *Jesus als Lehrer*. Untersuchung zum Ursprung der Evangelien-Ueberlieferung (WUNT 2:7), Tübingen, 1981.

——, "Präexistenz und Jungfraugeburt", *ThB* 12 (1981) 177—87.

——, "Der Ursprung der Jesus-Ueberlieferung", *TZ* 38 (1982) 493—513.

Roberts, B.J., *The OT Texts and Versions*, The Hebrew Text in Transmission and the History of the Ancient Versions, Cardiff 1951.

Robinson, C.A., "Alexander's Deification", *AJPh* 64 (1943) 86—301.

Robinson, J.M., *A New Quest of the Historical Jesus* (SBT), London 1959, rp. 1971.

Rolland, P., "Marc, première harmonie évangélique?", *RB* 90 (1983) 23—79.

Rose, V., "Fils de l' homme et fils de Dieu", *RB* 9 (1900) 169—99.

Rosenmüller, E.F.C., *Scholia in Vetus Testamentum Pars Decima. In Danielem*, Lipsiae 1832.

Ross, A., "The Title 'Son of Man' ", *EvQ* 6 (1934) 36—49.

Rössler, D., *Gesetz und Geschichte*. Untersuchungen zur Theologie der jüdischen Apokalyptik und der pharisäischen Orthodoxie. (WMANT 3), Neukirchen 1960.

Rost, L., "Zur Deutung des Menschensohnes in Daniel 7", pp. 41—3 in *Gott und die Götter*, Hrsg. G. Delling, Berlin 1958.

Rowdon, H.H. (Ed.), *Christ the Lord*. Studies in Christology Presented to Donald Guthrie, Leicester, Downers Grove Il. 1982.

Rowe, R.D., "Is Daniel's 'Son of Man' Messianic?", in *Christ the Lord*, pp. 71—96, ed. H.H. Rowdon, Leicester, etc. 1982.

Rowley, H.H., *Darius the Mede and the Four World Empires*. A Historical Study of Contemporary Theories, Cardiff 1935, rp. 1964.

——, *The Relevance of Apocalyptic*, London ²1947.

Ruckstuhl, E., "Abstieg und Erhöhung des johanneischen Menschensohns" pp. 314—41 in *Jesus und der Menschensohn*, Hrsg. R. Pesch, R. Schnackenburg, Freiburg 1975.

——, "Die johanneische Menschensohn-Forschung 1957—1969" pp. 171—284 in *Theologische Berichte I*, Hrsg. J. Pfammatter—F. Furger, Zürich 1972.

Ruppert, L., *Jesus als der leidende Gerechte?* (*SBS* 59), Stuttgart 1972.

Russel, D.S., *The Method and Message of Jewish Apocalyptic*, London 1964.

Sabourin, L., "About Jesus' Self-understanding", *RSB* 3 (1983) 129–34.

——, "The Son of Man", *BTB* 2 (1972) 78–80.

Sahlin, H., "Antiochus IV. Epiphanes und Judas Mackabäus: Einige Gesichtspunkte zum Verständnis des Danielsbuches", *ST* 23 (1969) 41–68.

Salmon, G., *A Historical Introduction to the Books of the New Testament*, London [7]1894.

Sanders, E.P., *Paul and Palestinian Judaism*, London 1977.

Sandmel, S., "Son of Man" pp. 355–67 in *In the Time of Harvest*, Essays in honour of Abba Hillel Silver's 70 Birthday, ed. D.J. Silver, N.Y. 1963.

Sarna, N., *Understanding Genesis*, N.Y. 1966.

Scharbert, J., "Traditions-und Redaktionsgeschichte von Gen 6, 1–4", *BZ* N.F. 11 (1967) 66–78.

Schenk, W., Art. Πῶς, *EWNT* III, cols. 489–92, Hrsg. A. Balz – G. Schneider.

Schlatter, A., *Die Theologie des Neuen Testaments* I: Das Wort Jesu, Calw – Stuttgart 1909.

Schmidt, H., "Daniel, der Menschensohn", *Jud* 27 (1971) 192–220.

Schmidt, N., Art. "Son of Man" in *EncBib*, Eds. T.K. Cheyne – J. Sutherland Black, London 1899 –1903.

——, "Recent Study on the Term 'Son of Man' ", *JBL* 45 (1926) 326–49.

——, "Was בר נשא a Messianic Title?", *JBL* 15 (1896) 36–53.

——, "The 'Son of Man' in the Book of Daniel", *JBL* 19 (1900) 22–8.

Schmithals, W., *Gnosticism in Corinth*. An Investigation of the Letters to the Corinthians, N.Y. [3]1971.

Schmitt, A., *Stammt der Sogenannte "Θ"-text bei Daniel wirklich von Theodotion?* (Mitteilungen des Septuaginta-Unternehmens 9), Göttingen 1966.

Schnackenburg, R., *Gottes Herrschaft und Reich*. Eine bibeltheologische Studie, Freiburg 1959.

——, "Die Ecce-homo-Szene und der Menschensohn" pp. 371–86 in *Jesus und der Menschensohn*, Hrsg. R. Pesch, R. Schnackenburg.

——, "Der Menschensohn in Johannesevangelium", *NTS* 11 (1964–65) 123–37.

——, *The Gospel According to St. John* (HTCNT), Vol. I–II, London, 1980.

——, "Nachfolge Christi" pp. 87–108 in *Christliche Existenz nach dem Neuen Testament I*, München, 1967.

Schnedermann, G., *Jesu Verkündigung und Lehre vom Reiche Gottes* in ihrer geschichtlichen Bedeutung, 2 Vols., Leipzig 1893–95.

Schneemelcher, W. (Ed.), *Festschrift Günther Dehn*, Neukirchen 1957.

Schneider, G., Art. Δίκαιος – Δικαιοσύνη, *EWNT* I, cols. 781–4.

——, *Die Apostelgeschichte*, I. Teil. Einleitung. Kommentar zu Kap. 1, 1 – 8, 40 (HTKNT), Freiburg, Basel, Wien 1980.

——, "Die Davidssohnfrage (Mk 12: 36–37)", *Bib* 53 (1972) 65–90.

——, *Verleugnung, Verspottung und Verhör Jesu* nach Lukas 22:54–71, München, 1969.

Schniewind, J., *Das Evangelium nach Matthäus*, Göttingen 1956.

Schrenk, G., Art. Λέγω etc., *TDNT* IV, 168–92.

Schubert, K. (Ed.), *Bibel und zeitgemässer Glaube*, I, Klosterneunburg, 1965.

——, "Das Zeitalter der Apokalyptik" pp. 263–85 in *Bibel und zeitgemässer Glaube*, I, Hrsg. K. Schubert.

Schulz, H., *Old Testament Theology*, 2 Vols., Edinburgh 1892.

Schulz, S., *Untersuchungen zur Menschensohn-Christologie im Johannesevangelium*, Göttingen 1957.

Schulze, L. Th., *Vom Menschensohn und vom Logos*. Ein Beitrag zur biblischen Christologie, Gotha 1867.

Schürer, E., *Geschichte des jüdischen Volkes im Zeitalter Jesu Christi*, 3 Bd., 3rd ed., Leipzig 1898–1901.

——, *The History of the Jewish People in the Age of Jesus Christ*, Tr. S. Taylor – P. Christi, 3rd ed. Edinburgh 1898.

——, *The History of the Jewish People in the Age of Jesus Christ* (175 B.C. – A.D. 135), revised by G. Vermes – F. Millar, Edinburgh Vol. I 1973, Vol. II 1979.

Schürmann, H., *Jesu ureigener Tod*. Exegetische Besinnungen und Ausblick, Freiburg etc. 1975.

Schweitzer, A., *The Quest of the Historical Jesus*: A Critical Study of Its Progress from Reimarus to Wrede, Eng. tr. W. Montgomery, 3rd ed., London 1954.

——, *Geschichte der Leben-Jesu-Forschung*, 4th ed., Tübingen 1926.

——, *Das Messianitäts-und Leidensgeheimnis*, Eine Skizze des Lebens Jesu, Tübingen [3]1956.

Schweizer, E., *Erniedrigung und Erhöhung bei Jesus und seinen Nachfolgern* (ATANT, 28), Zürich 1955

——, "The Son of Man", *JBL* 79 (1960) 119–29.

——, "The Son of Man Again", *NTS* 9 (1962–3) 256–61.

——, "Der Menschensohn (Zur eschatologischen Erwartung Jesu)", *ZNW* 50 (1959) 185–209.

Scott, R.B.Y., "Behold, He Cometh with Clouds", *NTS* 5 (1958–9) 131.

Segal, A.F., *Two Powers in Heaven*. Early Rabbinic Reports about Christianity and Gnosticism (SJLA 29), Leiden 1977.

Seitz, O.J.F., "The Future Coming of the Son of Man: Three Midrashic Formulations in the Gospel of Mark", *SE* 6 (= TU 112), (1973) 478–94.

Sellin, E., *Theologie des Alten Testaments*, Leipzig 1936.

——, *Israelitisch-jüdische Religionsgeschichte*, Leipzig 1933.

Sharman, H.B., *Son of Man and Kingdom of God*, N.Y. 1943.

Shea, W.H., "Adam in Ancient Mesopotamian Traditions", *AUSS* 15 (1977) 27–41.

Sherwin-White, A.N., *Roman Society and Roman Law in the New Testament* (The Sarum Lectures 1960–1), Oxford 1963.

Shippers, R., "The Son of Man in Matt XII, 32 = Lk XII, 10, Compared with Mk III, 28", *SE* 4 (1968) 231–5.

Shorp, D.S. "Mark ii, 10", *ET* 38 (1926–7) 428–29.

Sidebottom, E.M., "The Son of Man in the Fourth Gospel", *ET* 68 (1956–7) 231ff., 280ff.

Sierig, H. (Ed.), *Mensch und Menschensohn*, Hamburg 1963.

Σμιώτας, Π.Ν.,'Αἱ ἀμετάφραστοι λέξεις ἐν τῷ κειμένῳ τῶν Ο ', Θεσσαλονίκη 1968.

Sjöberg, E., *Der verborgene Menschensohn in den Evangelien* (Skrifter utgivna av Kungl. Humanistiska Vetenskapssamfundet i Lund), Lund 1955.

——, *Der Menschensohn im äthiopischen Henochbuch*, Lund 1946.

——, " אדם בו und בר אנש im Hebräischen und Aramäischen", *AcOr* (H) 21 (1950–1) 57–65, 91–107.

Smaley, S.S., "Johannes 1, 51 und die Einleitung zum vierten Evangelium" pp. 300–13 in *Jesus und der Menschensohn*, Hrsg. R. Pesch – R. Schnackenburg.

——, "The Johannine Son of Man Sayings", *NTS* 15 (1968–9) 278–301.

Smith, D., "The Nickname 'Son of Man' ", *ET* 18 (1906–7) 553–5.

Smith, M.S., "The 'Son of Man' in Ugaritic"; *CBQ* 45 (1983) 59–60.

Somervell, R., "The Son of Man", *ET* 29 (1917–8) 522–3.

Staerk, W., "Eva-Maria. Ein Beitrag zur Denk-und Sprechweise der altkirchlichen Christologie", *ZNW* 33 (1934) 97–104.

Stauffer, E., "Messias oder Menschensohn'" *NovT* 1 (1956) 81–102.

——, *New Testament Theology*, London 1955.

Stein, R.H., "The 'Criteria' for Authenticity" pp. 225–63 in *Gospel Perspectives* I, eds. R.T. France, D. Wenham, Sheffield 1980.

Stephenson, T., "The Title 'Son of Man' ", *ET* 29 (1917–8) 377–8.

Steward, D.G., Art. "Mary", *ZPEB* IV, (ed. M.C. Tenney), pp. 106–12.

St. John Thackeray, H., *The Septuagint and Jewish Worship*, London [2]1923.

Stone, M., "The concept of the Messiah in IV Ezra" pp. 295–312, in *Religions in Antiquity*. E.R. Goodenough Memorial Volume, ed. J. Neusner, Leiden 1968.

——, "Coherence and Inconsistency in the Apocalypses: The Case of 'the End' in IV Ezra", *JBL* 102 (1938) 229–43.

——, *Scriptures, Sects and Visions*, Philadelphia 1980.

——, "Ezra, Apocalypse of", *EncJud* VI, 1971, 1108f.

Stone, M.–Greenfield, J.C., See Greenfield, J.C.–Stone, M.

Strauss, D.F., *Das Leben Jesu, kritisch bearbeitet*, 4th ed., Tübingen 1840.

——, *The Life of Jesus: Critically Examined*, London rp. 1973.

Stuhlmacher, P., "Thesen zur Methodologie gegenwärtiger Exegese", *ZNW* 63 (1972) 18–26.

——, "Existenzstellvertretung für die Vielen: Mk 10, 45 (Mt 20:28)" in *Werden und Wirken des*

Alten Testaments. Festschrift C. Westermann zum 70. Geburtstag. Hrsg. R. Albertz, H. − P. Müller, H.W. Wolff, W. Zimmerli, pp. 412−27, Göttingen 1980.

Sturch, R.L., "The Replacement of 'Son of Man' by a Pronoun", *ET* 94 (1983) 333.

Tarn, W.W., "Alexander the Great and the Unity of Mankind" (British Academy Proceedings 19), 1933, 123−6.

−−, *Hellenistic Civilization*, London, ³1961.

Taylor, V., *The Formation of the Gospel Tradition*, London 1935.

−−, *The Names of Jesus*, London 1953.

−−, "The 'Son of Man' Sayings Relating to the Parousia", (in V. Taylor, *NT Essays*, London 1970 (= *ET* 58 (1946−7) 12−15).

−−, *The Gospel According to St. Mark*, London 1966.

−−, *The Passion Narrative of St. Luke*, Cambridge 1972.

Teeple, H.M., "The Origin of the Son of Man Christology", *JBL* 84 (1965) 213−50.

Theisohn, J., *Der auserwählte Richter. Untersuchungen zum traditionsgeschichtlichen Ort der Bilderreden des äthiopischen Henoch (SUNT 12)*, Göttingen 1975.

Thompson, G.H.P., "The Son of Man: The Evidence of the Dead Sea Scrolls", *ET* 72 (1960−1) 125.

−−, "The Son of Man − Some further Considerations", *JTS* NS 12 (1961) 203−9.

Thorion, Y., "אדם und בן אדם in den Qumrantexten", *RevQ* 10 (1980) 305−8.

Tillman, F., *Der Menschensohn*, Freiburg in Br., 1907.

Tödt, H.E., *Der Menschensohn in der Synoptischen Ueberlieferung*, Gütersloh 1959.

−−, *The Son of Man in the Synoptic Tradition*, London 1965.

Torrey, C.C., "The Messiah Son of Ephraim", *JBL* 66 (1947) 253−77.

−−, *Documents of the Primitive Church*, New York 1941.

Τουλουμάκος, I., (Cooperation of) "Τὰ ἑλληνικὰ κράτη τῆς Ἀνατολῆς ὡς τὴν πρώτη ἐπέμβαση τῶν Ρωμαίων στὴν Ἑλλάδα" (280−201 π.Χ.), *IEE* IV, 368−437.

Tuckett, Chr., "Recent Work on the Son of Man", *ScrB* 12 (1981) 14ff.

−−, "The Present Son of Man", *JSNT* 14 (1982) 58−81.

Turner, H.E.W., *Historicity and the Gospels*, London 1963.

−−, *Jesus Master and Lord*. A Study in the Historical Truth of the Gospels, London 1953.

Uloth, C.B.E., *Godgeleerde Bijdragen*, 1862.

Usteri, J.M., "Die Selbstbezeichnung Jesu als der Menschensohn", *TZ* a.d. Schweitz, 3 (1886) 1−23.

van Andel, C.P., *De Struktuur van de Henochtraditie en het Nieuwe Testament*, Utrecht 1955.

van Iersel, B.M.F., "Fils de David et fils de Dieu", in *La Venue du Messie*, Bruges 1962.

van Manen, W.C., "De 'Zoon des Menschen' bij Henoch", *Theol. Tijdschr.* 29 (1895) 263−7.

−−, "Naschrift", *Theol. Tijdschr.* 28 (1894) 177−87.

−−, "Het Evangeliet van Petrus", *Theol. Tijdschr.* 27 (1893) 517−72.

Vansina, J., *Oral Tradition*. A Study in Historical Methodology, London 1965.

Vassiliadis, P., "The Nature and Extent of the Q-Document", *NovT* 20 (1978) 49−73.

−−, "The Original Order of Q. Some Residual Cases", in *Logia* ed. J. Delobel, Leuven 1982.

Vermes, G., "Jewish Literature and New Testament Exegesis: Reflections on Methodology", *JJS* 33 (1982) 361−76.

−−, *Scripture and Tradition in Judaism: Aggadic Studies*, (Studia post-Biblica 4), Leiden 1961.

−−, *Jesus the Jew. A Historian's Reading of the Gospels*, London 1973.

−−, "The Use of בר נש / בר נשא in Jewish Aramaic", pp. 310−30 in M. Black, *An Aramaic Approach to the Gospels and Acts*.

−−, "The Present State of the Son of Man Debate", *JJS* 29 (1978) 123−35.

−−, "The 'Son of Man' Debate", *JSNT* 1 (1978) 19−32.

Vielhauer, Ph., *Aufsätze zum NT*, München 1965.

−−, "Gottesreich und Menschensohn in der Verkündigung Jesu", pp. 51−79 in *Festschrift G. Dehn*, Hrsg. W. Schneemelcher (1957) (= *Aufsätze zum NT*, pp. 55−91).

−−, "Jesus und der Menschensohn: zur Diskussion mit Heinz Eduard Tödt und Eduard Schweizer", *ZTK* 60 (1963) 133−77, (= *Aufsätze zum NT* pp. 92−140).

Vögtle, A., "Die Adam−Christus−Typologie und 'der Menschensohn' ", *TTZ* 60 (1951) 309−28.

−−, "Bezeugt die Logienquelle die authentische Redeweise Jesu vom 'Menschensohn'?" in *Logia*, 77−99, ed. J. Delobel.

——, " 'Der Menschensohn' und die paulinische Christologie" pp. 199—218 in *Studiorum Paulinorum Congressus Internationalis Catholicus* 1961 I (AnBib 17/18), Rome 1963.

Volkmar, G., *Die Evangelien. Oder Markus und die Synopsis der kanonischen und ausserkanonischen Evangelien nach dem ältesten Text mit historisch-exegetischem Kommentar*, Leipzig 1870.

Völter, D., "Der Menschensohn in Dan 7, 13", *ZNW* 3 (1902) 173—74.

——, *Die Menschensohnfrage neu untersucht*, Leiden 1916.

von Gall, A., *Basileia tou Theou*, Heidelberg 1926.

von Rad, G., *Old Testament Theology*, 2 Vols., Edinburgh 1962, rp. 1968.

——, *The Message of the Prophets*, London 1968.

Walker, W.O., "The Son of Man: Some Recent Developments", *CBQ* 45 (1983) 584—607.

——, "The Son of Man Question and the Synoptic Problem", *NTS* 28 (1981—2) 374—88.

——, "The Origin of the Son of Man Concept as Applied to Jesus", *JBL* 91 (1972) 482—90.

——, "The Kingdom of the Son of Man and the Kingdom of the Father in Matthew", *CBQ* 30 (1968) 573—79.

Wedderburn, A.J.M., *Adam and Christ. An Investigation into the Background of 1 Corinthians XV and Romans V 12—21.* (Dissertation, Cambridge University, Unpublished 1970).

——, "Philo's 'Heavenly Man' ", *NovT* 15 (1973) 301—26.

Weimar, P., "Daniel 7. Eine Textanalyse" pp. 11—36 in *Jesus und der Menschensohn*, Hrsg. R. Pesch, R. Schnackenburg.

Weiser, A., *Introduction to the OT*, London 1961, rp. 1969.

Weiss, B., *Lehrbuch der biblischen Theologie des Neuen Testaments*, Berlin 1868.

Weiss, J., *Die Predigt Jesu vom Reiche Gottes*, Göttingen 1892.

Weisse, Ch. H., *Die Evangelische Geschichte kritisch und philosophisch bearbeitet*, 2 Bd, Leipzig 1838.

Weizsäcker, C., *Untersuchungen über die evangelische Geschichte. Ihre Quellen und der Gang ihrer Entwicklung*, Tübingen ²1901.

Welch, A.C., *Visions of the End*: A Study of Daniel and Revelation, London 1922, rp. 1958.

Wellhausen, J., *Das Evangelium Marci*. Übersetzt und erklärt, Berlin 1903.

——, *Israelitische und jüdische Geschichte*, Berlin 1894.

Westcott, B.F., *The Gospel of John*, Cambridge 1881.

Westermann, C., "Sinn und Grenze religionsgeschichtlicher Parallelen", *TLZ* 90 (1965) 490—96.

Whitehead, J.D., "Some distinctive Features of the Language of the Aramaic Arsames Correspondence", *JNES* 37 (1978) 119—40.

Wifall, W., "Son of Man — A Pre-Davidic Social Class?", *CBQ* 37 (1975) 331—40.

Wilcke, H.A., *Das Problem des messianischen Zwischenreichs bei Paulus* (*ATANT*, 51), Zürich—Stuttgart 1930.

Wilckens, U., "Christus, der 'letzte Adam', und der Menschensohn", pp. 387—403 in *Jesus und der Menschensohn*, Hrsg. R. Pesch — R. Schnackenburg, Freiburg etc. 1975.

Wilcox, M., See Ellis, E.E. — Wilcox, M.

Willaert, B., "Jezus, de Mensenzoon", *ColBG* 5 (1959) 515—36.

Winter, P., "Das aramäische Genesis-Apokryphon", *TLZ* 82 (1957) 257—62.

Wiseman, D.J. (Ed.), *Ancient Records and the Structure of Genesis* (= P.J. Wiseman: New Discoveries in Babylonia about Genesis).

——, *Clues to Creation in Genesis* (= P.J. Wiseman: *New Discoveries* etc. and *Creation Revealed* etc.) 1977.

Wiseman, P.J., *Creation revealed in six days*, 1946.

——, *New Discoveries in Babylonia about Genesis*, London 1936.

Wittichen, C., *Die Idee des Menschen*, 1886.

Yadin, Y.—Avigad, N., See Avigad, N. — Yadin, Y.

Young, E.J., *The Messianic Prophecies of Daniel*, Delft 1954.

——, *Daniel's Vision of the Son of Man* (Tyn Mon), London 1958.

——, *The Prophecy of Daniel*, Grand Rapids 1949.

Zevit, Z. "The Structure and Individual Elements of Daniel 7", *ZAW* 80/3 (1968), 385—96.

Zöckler, O., *Der Prophet Daniel* (THBW 17), Bielefeld — Leipzig 1870.

Zorn, R.O., "The Significance of Jesus' Self-Designation 'Son of Man' ", *Vox Ref* 34 (1980) 1—21.

Index of Passages

1. Biblical Passages

A. Old Testament

Genesis
1-3	169
1:24	78
1:26	78
4:14	20, 24
5:3	59
6:1ff.	54
6:1-7	58
6:2	59
6:3	59
6:4	59
6:5-9	59
9:5-6	20
10	59
11	58
11:1-9	58
11:5	51, 52, 53, 54, 58
11:6	64
14:18ff.	76
41:55	63
50:25	54

Exodus
1:1	54
4:4f.	185
4:31	63
7:16	64
16:10	74
19:9	74

Leviticus
5:17	198

Numbers
11:1	64
11:8	64
23:19	52, 53, 55, 132

Deuteronomy
7:6	65
13:14	54
18:15	216
19:15	92
26:19	76
28:1	76
32:8	51
38:8f.	70

33:2	45
33:2-4	42
33:3	45
33:21	132

Joshua
24:24	66

Judges
15:4	178
16:12	54
19:22	54
20:13	54
21:25	236

1 Samuel
1:16	54
2:8	171
2:12	54
8:4f.	236
8:6-8	236
8:9ff.	236
9:13	63
10:27	54
12:14	66
15:10	236
16:1	236
25:17	54
25:25	54
26:19	51, 52, 53, 56
30:22	54

2 Samuel
7:14	51, 53, 56
7:15f.	236
7:16	216
15:23	64
16:7	54
18:5	64
20:1	54
23:3	107

1 Kings
8:39	51, 53, 57
11:11-14	236
18:21	64
21:10	54
21:13	54

2 Kings

2:3	54
8:17	54
14:14	54
15:2	54
18:2	54
19:32-35	90

3 Kingdoms (LXX)

21:10	178

1 Chronicles

3:24	135
29:23	171

2 Chronicles

6:30	51, 53, 57
13:7	54

Ezra

6:10	73
6:16	54
8:35	54
10:7	54

Nehemiah

3:35	178
5:13	64
8:1	64

Job

5:1	45
5:11	201
15:10	45
15:11	45
15:15	45
25:6	52, 53, 56
35:8	52, 55
36:11	66

Psalms

2	140
2:7	140
2:9	132
8	56, 76, 77, 169
8:4	52, 53, 56, 85, 164, 168, 169
8:5	13, 56, 164, 191
11:5f.	18
11:14	51
12:1	51
12:1f.	56
12:8	51, 56
14:1ff.	56
14:2	51, 53
16:3	45
18:8	130
18:10ff.	74
18:13	130
21:5	132
21:8	76
21:11	51
21:17	230

22	230
22:7f.	197, 230
22:16	230
31:19f.	56
31:20	51, 53
33:13	51, 57
34:10	45
36:8	51
45:2	55, 169
45:3	51
46:5	76
46:6	129
48:3	56
49:2	56
49:3	51, 53
53:1f.	56
53:2	51
57:5	51
58:2	51
62:9	56
62:10	51, 53
66:5	51
68:2	129
72:11	132
72:17	132
80	60, 76
80:17	54, 57, 168, 169, 223
80:18	52, 53
81:12	64
89:3	109
89:3f.	236
89:6	45
89:8	45
89:20ff.	216
89:23	54
89:27	76
89:36	138
89:47	56
89:48	51, 53
90:3	51, 56
97:2	74
97:5	129
103:12	176
104:3	74
104:12	176
107:8	51
107:15	51
107:21	51
107:31	51
110	225
110:1	80, 140, 141, 142, 172, 203, 204, 217, 218, 222, 223, 224, 225
110:4	138
115:16	51
118:22	177, 214
132:11f.	236
144:3	53, 56
145:10	56
145:12	51, 53
145:13	66
146:3	52, 53, 57

Proverbs
    8:4   51, 53
    8:4f.   56
    8:31   51, 55
    9:10   45
    15:11   51, 57
    15:33   201, 226
    18:12   201, 226
    22:4   201
    24:14   198
    30:3   45

Ecclesiastes
    1:13   51, 57
    2:3   51, 57
    2:8   51
    3:10   51, 57
    3:18   51
    3:18ff.   57
    3:19   51
    3:21   51
    8:11   51, 57
    9:3   51, 57
    9:12   51, 57

Canticles
    2:15   178

Isaiah
    6   87
    6:10   64
    8:18   207
    9:2-7   216
    9:6f.   138
    11:1-9   216
    11:4   130
    19:1   74
    20:2ff.   207
    22:23   171
    25:8   91
    29:13   64
    30:25   88
    32:1   107
    32:18   64
    34:3   129
    40:4   88
    41:15-18   88
    42:1   109, 227
    42:6   227
    43:3f.   191, 193, 230
    43:21   64
    44:3   88
    49:3   227
    49:7   227
    49:10   91
    49:18   52
    49:33   52
    50:4-5   227
    50:40   52
    51:7   64
    51:12   52, 53, 57
    51:43   52

    52:13   227
    52:13-53:12   226
    52:14   51, 53, 169
    52:15   227
    53   190, 191, 194, 197, 199,
                  230
    53:3   197
    53:4   132
    53:4-8   230
    53:10ff.   196, 230
    53:10-12   193
    53:11   107, 108, 227
    53:12   197, 199, 201, 230
    56:2   52, 53, 55, 168
    58:1   64
    61:1f.   232, 241

Jeremiah
    2:13   64
    5:23   64
    14:21   171
    16:13   132
    17:12   171
    23:5f.   216
    23:32   64
    27:7f.   69
    32:19   51
    33:14ff.   216
    43:3f.   191
    49:18   53, 57
    49:33   53, 57
    50:40   53, 57
    51:43   53, 57

Lamentations
    5:18   178

Ezekiel
    1   75, 77, 81, 87, 110
    1:26   39, 72
    2:3   60
    3:17   60
    3:18   60
    3:25   60
    4:1-17   60
    13:4   178
    17:23   176
    23:9   54
    23:15   54
    25:4   54
    27:11   54
    27:15   54
    31:6   176
    31:14   51
    34   230
    34:16   230
    34:23f.   216
    37:24   216
    37:25   138
    38:39   90

Daniel

2	176, 177, 178, 179, 198, 214
2:21	213
2:28	170, 198, 210
2:29	198
2:34	214
2:35	132, 177, 178
2:38	35, 69, 176, 177, 178
2:39f.	213
2:44	177, 213
2:45	177, 198, 210, 214
3:12	66
3:14	66
3:17	66
3:18	66
3:26	67
3:28	66
3:32	67
3:33	66
3:54	171
4	32, 177, 178, 179
4:3	213
4:9	176, 177
4:10ff.	177
4:11ff.	178
4:12	176, 177
4:14	67
4:17	103, 213
4:18	176, 177
4:20f.	177
4:20ff.	178
4:21	67, 176, 178
4:22	67
4:25	103, 213
4:29	67
4:30	103
4:31	67
4:32	213
4:34ff.	213
5:18	67
5:18-21	213
5:21	35, 67, 103
5:30	213
6:6	181
6:17	66
6:21	66
6:26	213
7	4, 5, 6, 7, 18, 27, 32, 40, 42, 44, 46, 47, 48, 62, 66, 67, 68, 70, 74, 75, 76, 77, 79, 80, 84, 95, 101, 102, 103, 104, 109, 110, 112, 118, 122, 123, 124, 125, 126, 127, 128, 129, 143, 144, 167, 169, 170, 175, 177, 179, 188, 189, 191, 192, 198, 199, 200, 201, 204, 206, 209, 211, 213, 214, 225, 227, 228, 229, 230, 231, 232, 236, 240, 248, 249, 250
7:1-8	42
7:7	103
7:7f.	227

7:9	80, 102, 104, 133, 142, 246
7:9f.	133, 163, 171, 204
7:9-10	42
7:9-14	40, 133, 191, 192, 193, 203, 230
7:10	191
7:10ff.	203
7:11	42
7:12	42, 68, 69, 213
7:13	13, 15, 17, 18, 19, 21, 27, 28, 29, 35, 39, 41, 42, 44, 47, 61, 62, 63, 72, 76, 79, 83, 84, 102, 104, 115, 128, 131, 132, 134, 135, 136, 137, 140, 141, 142, 163, 170, 173, 191, 203, 204, 205, 206, 210, 211, 218, 224, 225, 229, 240, 246, 248
7:13f.	4, 6, 14, 40, 41, 42, 47, 83, 115, 131, 132, 136, 138, 140, 164, 203, 204, 210, 212, 213, 223, 224, 225, 234, 240
7:13-14	213
7:14	42, 47, 61, 62, 66, 68, 69, 72, 118, 132, 188, 189, 232, 240
7:16	42, 74
7:17	42, 73
7:18	42, 61, 62, 63, 64, 66, 72, 73, 75, 213
7:18-22	47
7:19	129, 237
7:19-21	76
7:21	199, 227
7:22	61, 62, 63, 64, 66, 72, 73, 75, 76, 118, 210, 213
7:23	98
7:25	46, 63, 64, 66, 67, 75, 76, 98, 199, 200, 227, 230, 240
7:25ff.	118
7:26	68
7:26f.	213
7:27	43, 46, 47, 61, 62, 63, 64, 66, 72, 75, 118, 119, 132, 163, 203, 211, 240
7:27a	65, 68, 69, 72
7:27b	64, 65, 66, 68, 69, 70, 72, 74, 200, 240
8	213
8:10	98, 103
8:11	98
8:13	210
8:17	35, 42, 52
8:20	21
8:21-25	213
9:2	122
9:22	52
9:24ff.	122
9:25	79
9:26	219
9:27	210
10:11	52, 122
10:12	52
10:13	70, 213

10:16	35, 51, 52, 61, 102	5:8	208
10:20	70, 213	5:11	166
10:21	70	5:12	194
11:31	210	5:21-48	202
11:32.	64	5:22	221
11:34	42	5:28	221
11:36	199, 213	5:33	221
11:41	210	5:34	221
12:1	54, 64, 170, 210	5:39	221
12:4	52	5:44	221
12:7	65, 210, 213	6:10	233, 238
12:9	52	6:33	238
12:11	210	7:13f.	91
12:12	210	7:17f.	246
		7:24-29	202
Hosea		7:29	68
3:5	216	8:9	68
6:2	196, 199	8:20	19, 29, 30, 145, 146, 172,
12:1	45		175, 176, 178, 179
		8:20ff.	178, 179
Joel		8:25	231
1:12	51	9:2-6	221
		9:2-8	164
Amos		9:6	11, 29, 32, 146, 172, 179,
5:18	132		183, 202
9:11	134, 135, 216	9:8	19, 190
		9:21f.	231
Micah		9:27	216
1:4	129	9:34	70
5:6	51, 53	10:5ff.	241
5:7	55	10:7	215
		10:17-21	211
Nahum		10:22	231
1:3	74	10:23	146, 204, 205, 215, 235
		10:23f.	166
Haggai		10:28	231
1:2	64	10:32	196
		10:32f.	29, 32, 166, 202
Zechariah		10:37ff.	175
9:9	131	10:37-38	196
12:10	204	11:2-10	202
12:10f.	218	11:9	157, 169
14:2	64	11:10	202
14:5	45	11:16-19	29, 31
		11:19	11, 13, 19, 145, 146, 172
Malachi		12:1ff.	187
4:5f.	219	12:6	31
		12:6ff.	221
		12:8	15, 146, 172
		12:9ff.	187
B. New Testament		12:14	194
		12:22f.	216
Matthew		12:22-29	241
1:16	220	12:24	70
1:16f.	220	12:28	238, 241
1:18-25	220	12:28f.	239
1:20	220	12:28-32	233
1:21	231	12:32	15, 19, 29, 146
2:1	220	12:39	209
2:6	220	12:39f.	209
3:3-15	202	12:40	146, 207
4:17-24	240	12:41f.	31

13:4	146	23:37-39	194
13:11	238	24	169, 201, 204, 211, 212
13:19ff.	246	24:3	170, 208, 209
13:26	204, 210	24:4-29	208
13:31f.	177	24:6	170, 198, 210
13:32	177	24:6f.	121, 169
13:37	146	24:6ff.	121
13:37-43	215	24:10	210
13:40	172	24:13	231
13:40ff.	226	24:15	210
13:41	146, 226, 233, 239, 240	24:21	170, 210
13:57	194	24:27	146, 170, 204, 205, 206, 207,
14:30	231		208
15:1-14	194	24:30	121, 146, 205, 206, 207, 208,
15:22	216		209, 210, 211, 212, 226, 240
16:3	208	24:30a	205, 206, 207, 208, 209
16:4	209	24:30b	206, 207, 209, 210
16:4-12	194	24:30f.	146, 209
16:13	13, 15, 25, 26, 146, 152, 165	24:31	170, 234
16:21	192, 194, 195, 197, 198	24:36	209
16:24ff.	175	24:37	146, 204, 205, 206
16:24-26	196	24:37ff.	170
16:25	231	24:37-39	235
16:27	146, 196, 203, 226, 234, 239,	24:39	146, 204, 205, 226
	240	24:42-44	209
16:27f.	146, 215	24:44	29, 146, 148
16:28	146, 226, 233, 238, 240	24:45	230
16:29ff.	201	25:31	92, 146, 171, 204, 205, 206,
17:9	146		212, 226, 234, 235
17:10	198	25:31ff.	226, 239, 240
17:10-13	219	25:31-40	233
17:12	146, 197, 226	25:31-46	235
17:22	146, 198, 226, 230	25:34	235
17:22f.	146, 192, 195	25:34ff.	212
18:4	201	25:40	235
18:11	145, 231	25:41	172
18:16	92	26:2	146, 199, 226
18:18	189	26:16	169
19:9	226	26:21ff.	192
19:21	175	26:21-24	234
19:25	231	26:23f.	26
19:27ff.	175	26:24	146, 197, 198, 225
19:28	26, 93, 146, 171, 204, 226,	26:45	146, 200, 226
	234, 240	26:53	216
20:18	146, 195, 226, 230	26:54	198
20:18f.	146, 192	26:61	196
20:21	233	26:62ff.	139
20:26ff.	201	26:63ff.	205
20:28	146, 172, 190, 191, 193, 197,	26:64	80, 146, 164, 201, 203, 206,
	226, 230, 231		224, 225, 226, 234, 240
20:30f.	216	26:66	171
21:9	216	28:18	189, 240
21:42	214		
21:43	214	**Mark**	
21:44	177, 214	1:2-11	180, 202
21:45	214, 246	1:21ff.	187
22:14	121	2:1-12	180
22:41ff.	224, 225	2:3-5a	183
22:41-46	217, 218	2:3-11	164
22:45	80, 219	2:5	180, 184, 187
23:12	201	2:5b	183, 184, 186
23:29-35	194	2:5-9	180

2:5-10	187, 221
2:5b-10	180, 183, 186
2:5-11	184
2:5-12	186
2:6-9	180
2:6-10	180, 183
2:8-9	184, 186
2:9	184, 187
2:10	19, 145, 146, 152, 172, 179, 180, 181, 182, 183, 184, 185, 186, 188, 189
2:10a	184, 186
2:10b	183, 184
2:10f.	29, 32
2:11	180, 183
2:11-12	180, 183
2:12	180
2:23ff.	187
2:27f.	19, 221, 223
2:28	145, 146, 172
3:1ff.	187
3:3ff.	187
3:6	194
3:27	239
3:28	17
4:12	182
4:30ff.	177
4:31	178
5:12	182
5:23	181, 182
6:4	194
6:25	181, 182
6:56	231
7:5-13	194
8:11-15	194
8:12	209
8:27	25, 165
8:27-30	166
8:28	196
8:31	29, 146, 192, 194, 195, 197, 198, 202, 226, 230
8:31-38	174
8:34ff.	175, 201
8:34-37	196
8:34-38	234
8:35	231
8:38	26, 146, 148, 203, 226, 234, 239
8:38-9:1	234
9:1	226, 234, 238
9:1a	234
9:9	146, 226
9:11-13	219
9:12	146, 181, 197, 226, 230
9:31	25, 29, 146, 192, 194, 195, 198, 226, 230
9:35	201
10:21-25	175
10:28ff.	175
10:33	146
10:33f.	146, 192, 195, 226, 230
10:33-34	29, 194
10:35	182
10:43ff.	201
10:45	146, 172, 190, 191, 192, 193, 197, 226, 230, 231
10:47f.	216
10:51	181, 182
11:9f.	216
11:10	216
12:12	246
12:15	181
12:19	181
12:35	216, 218
12:35ff.	224
12:35-37	217
12:37	218
13	201, 204
13:4f.	208
13:5b-8	210
13:7	170, 198, 210
13:7f.	169
13:12	121
13:12-16	210
13:13	121, 210, 230, 231
13:14	210
13:19	170, 210
13:19-22	210
13:24-27	210
13:26	121, 146, 148, 205, 206, 210, 212, 226
13:26f.	146
13:27	170, 204, 234
13:28ff.	235
13:32	209
13:35-36	209
14:18ff.	192
14:18-21	234
14:20f.	26
14:21	146, 197, 198
14:26	225
14:35	200
14:38	181
14:41	146, 200, 226, 230
14:49	181
14:58	196
14:60ff.	139
14:61	225
14:62	26, 62, 146, 164, 171, 201, 203, 205, 206, 224, 225, 226, 234
14:62ff.	62
Luke	
1:19	91
1:27	220
1:32	220
1:32ff.	140
1:35	220
1:36	220
1:69	220
1:76	220
2:4	220
2:4ff.	220

2:11	220	13:23	231
2:15	220	13:32	178
2:19	221	13:33-35	194
2:33	229	14:1ff.	187
2:49	198, 220	14:11	201
2:51	221	14:26f.	175
3:3-17	202	17:19	231
3:22f.	220	17:20f.	238
3:23	220	17:20-30	233
4:18	232	17:21f.	215
4:24	194	17:22	146, 204, 205
4:31ff.	187	17:22-25	198
5:17-26	186	17:22-30	152, 174, 204
5:18-25	164	17:23-25	226
5:20-24	221	17:24	29, 146, 170, 204, 205
5:24	29, 32, 146, 179, 183	17:26	29, 146, 204, 205
5:38	224	17:26f.	170
6:1ff.	187	17:30	29, 146, 204, 205, 226
6:5	146, 172	18:8	146, 205
6:6ff.	187	18:8b	205
6:6-11	194	18:14	201
6:11	194	18:22-25	175
6:22	145, 146, 164	18:28ff.	175
7:18-27	202	18:31	146, 226, 230
7:24	202	18:31f.	226
7:31-35	29, 31	18:31ff.	146, 192, 230
7:34	13, 145, 146, 157, 169, 172	18:31-34	195
7:47	186	18:38f.	216
7:50	231	19:10	146, 172, 226, 230, 231
8:48	231	19:38	216
9:18	165	20:17f.	177
9:21	146	20:18	177, 214
9:21f.	226, 230	20:19	214, 246
9:22	146, 192, 195, 197, 198, 226	20:20	68
9:23ff.	175, 201	20:41ff.	224
9:24	231	20:41-44	217
9:24-25	196	21	201, 204
9:26	26, 146, 196, 226, 234, 239	21:8	208, 210
9:27	226, 238	21:9	170, 198, 210
9:35	109	21:9f.	169
9:44	146, 192, 195, 198, 226, 230	21:22	210
9:56	145, 231	21:24	210
9:58	29, 30, 145, 146, 172, 175	21:27	146, 206, 210, 212, 226
9:58ff.	178, 179	21:27-31	215
10:9	238	21:29ff.	235
10:17	241	21:31	233
10:18	241	21:36	146, 204, 205, 206
11:19	209	22:15-22	234
11:20	238	22:16ff.	233
11:20ff.	239	22:21f.	27, 192
11:30	29, 31, 146, 207	22:22	146, 197, 198
11:31f.	31	22:27	201
11:47-51	194	22:29f.	233
12:8	26, 146, 148, 196	22:30	204, 233
12:8f.	29, 32, 146, 166, 201, 202, 203	22:48	146
		22:53	200
12:10	29, 146	22:67	141, 225
12:31	238	22:67f.	141
12:40	29, 146	22:67ff.	139
12:51ff.	175	22:68	141
13:10ff.	187	22:69	140, 141, 142, 146, 164, 171, 201, 203, 204, 205, 206, 224, 226, 234
13:19	177, 178		

22:69f.	142, 172		13:31ff.	26
22:70	141, 225		13:34b	182
23:35	109		16:11	70
23:35ff.	231		17:1	200
23:42	233		17:24	31, 182
24:7 ·	146, 198, 226, 230		18:32f.	216
24:26	198		19:37	208
24:44	198		20:9	198
			20:23	189
John				
1:14	176		Acts	
1:19-34	202		1:7	209
1:39	208		2:29-34	218
1:50	208		2:34f.	218
1:51	147, 204, 205		3:14	108
1:52	11		7:52	108
3:12f.	172		7:56	25, 142, 164, 191
3:13	139, 147, 172		12:19-23	40
3:14	147, 198		17:28	213
5:9	187		22:14	108
5:16ff.	187		26:16	208
5:25	164			
5:26f.	27		Romans	
5:27	68, 92, 147, 239		3:20ff.	121
6:14f.	216		5:15	164
6:26f.	26, 32		5:15ff.	164
6:27	147		8:17	201, 226
6:37	31		8:28	70
6:39	31		12:3	122
6:53	147		16:1f.	182
6:62	147, 172			
6:62ff.	26		1 Corinthians	
7:1	194		1:17	31
7:23	187		2:6	70
7:30	194, 200		2:6ff.	200, 237
7:32	194		2:8	68, 70
7:40ff.	216		3:13f.	91
7:41f.	216		4:10ff.	226
8:11	186		6:2f.	204
8:20	194, 200		6:3	72
8:28	26, 138, 139, 147		7:2-5	182
8:37	194		7:9	182
8:40	222		7:12-13	182
8:59	194		7:27-28	182
9:14	187		7:29	182
9:16	187		7:29ff.	121
9:35	137, 138, 147		7:31	182
10:31	194		14:1	182
10:31-39	164		15:4	196
11:1	24		15:21	164
12:13	216		15:24	68
12:13f.	216		15:27	164, 169
12:23	138, 147, 200, 228		15:52	91, 121
12:23f.	228		15:53	121
12:24-33	138		16:15f.	182
12:27	200			
12:31	70		2 Corinthians	
12:32	27, 228		5:16	247
12:34	138, 139, 147, 165, 198, 247		8:7	181, 182
13:1	200		12:2f.	20
13:21	192			
13:31	147, 192			

Galatians
  2:9   181
  2:9f.   182
  2:10   182
  4:3-9   237
  4:4   222

Ephesians
  1:21   68, 69, 237
  1:22   164, 169
  2:2   69, 70, 237
  3:10   68, 70, 237
  5:33   181, 182
  6:12   68, 70, 237

Philippians
  2:5-11   229, 247
  2:6-11   201, 226
  2:7   222
  2:9ff.   164
  3:21   164

Colossians
  1:16   68, 69, 70, 237
  2:8-10   237
  2:10   68, 69, 70
  2:15   68, 70, 211, 237
  4:16   182
  4:16f.   182

1 Thessalonians
  4:13   182
  4:16   121

2 Thessalonians
  2:3ff.   199

1 Timothy
  2:5f.   190

2 Timothy
  2:12   201, 226
  4:8   108

Titus
  3:13f.   182

Hebrews
  2:5   246
  2:6   169, 191
  2:6f.   169
  2:9f.   201
  5:8f.   201
  12:4   208
  13:17   182

James
  4:10   201
  5:6   108

1 Peter
  3:18-22   201
  4:13f.   201
  5:6   201

1 John
  2:1   108

Jude
  6   68

Revelation
  1:7   163, 246
  1:13   15, 191, 246
  1:13ff.   163
  1:14   62
  2:26   68
  5:9-13   201
  6:9-11   121
  7:15-17   91
  10:9f.   60
  11:5   121
  14:14   191
  19:6-8   91
  21:3-4   91
  22:4   208

2. Apocrypha

1 Esdras
  4:37   84
  7:12   54
  7:13   54

Judith
  8:12   84
  8:16   84
  16:15   129

Tobit
  7:7   84
  8:12   181

1 Maccabees
  1:10   199
  1:34   199
  2:48   199

2 Maccabees
  1:9   181

Sapientia
  9:6   84
  9:10   171

Sirach

17:17   70

17:30   84
47:11   171

3. Pseudepigrapha

Apocalypse of Sophonias   69

Ascension of Isaiah
1:4   69

2 Baruch
25-27   170
29   84
30   84
30:1   125
39   84
40   84
40:1f.   88
53   170
72:2ff.   88

1 Enoch
1:6   129
6-36   39
6:1ff.   58
9:4   171
9:10   170
14   75
14:8   71
14:18-20   171
20:7   70
27:3   92
37-70   85, 129
37-71   39, 84, 106, 123, 124, 125, 126, 127, 128, 137, 141, 142, 188
37:4   122
38:1   125
38:2   94, 95, 105, 107, 108
38:2f.   107
39:4   108
39:6   94, 105, 109
39:6a   94, 105, 107, 108
39:6f.   95
40:2   96
40:5   94, 105, 108
40:5-45:3   103
40:6   95, 109, 170
40:7   170
40:8   96
41:2   125
43:1   98
43:4   98
45:2   125
45:3   94, 95, 105, 108, 109, 171, 203
45:4   94, 95, 105, 108, 109
45:5f.   125

46   7, 93, 95, 96, 98, 101, 102, 103, 104, 113, 117, 167, 173
46f.   77
46:1   85, 95, 102, 105, 106, 107, 112, 113, 127, 128
46:1f.   142
46:1:4   106
46:2   95, 105, 106, 110, 112
46:3   94, 95, 104, 105, 106, 107, 108, 113, 115, 116, 227
46:4   95, 105, 106, 108, 227
46:4ff.   113
46:4-6   116
46:5   108
46:6   108
46:13   110
46:14   110
16:14-17   110
47:1-2   98
47:2   170
47:3   104
48   95
48:1-7   223
48:2   93, 95, 104, 105, 106, 114, 142
48:2f.   108, 113
48:2-10   95
48:3   114
48:4   108, 117, 227
48:5   108, 119, 142
48:5f.   113
48:6   93, 107, 114
48:6f.   125
48:7   114
48:8ff.   118, 125
48:9f.   92
48:10   94, 105, 107
49:2   94, 105, 107, 108, 203, 223
49:4   94, 95, 105, 108
50:2ff.   125
51:1   92
51:2   170
51:3   92, 113, 171
51:5a   94, 95, 105, 108
52:3   94, 96, 105, 108
52:4   93, 105, 107
52:4-6   95
52:5   96
52:6   94, 105, 108, 129
52:9   105, 115
53-56   117
53:3   170

53:3ff.	125		62:9b	116, 119
53:3-7	170		62:9c	116, 119
53:4	96		62:9d	116, 119
53:6	94, 95, 105, 107, 108		62:9f.	189
53:7	87		62:10	92, 117
54:4	96		62:11	116
54:5	170		62:11ff.	125
55:3	170		62:12b	118
55:4	94, 105, 108, 117, 171, 203		62:12f.	117
			62:13	125
55:4-61:5	103		62:13a	118
56:1-8	170		62:13b	118
56:2	96		62:14	95, 105, 106, 108
56:5ff.	170		62:14b	118
56:5-7	87, 88, 90		62:14c	118
59	170		62:15c	118
60:69	170		62:15f.	125
60:1	98		62:16b	118
60:1-3	129		62:16c	118
60:5ff.	125		63	95
60:6	92		63:1-11	189
60:7-9	92		63:4a	118
60:22	98		63:4b	118
61:1	87, 92		63:7a	118
61:2	96		63:7b	118
61:3	96		63:7c	118
61:5	94, 105		63:7d	118
61:8	94, 105, 108, 113, 170, 171		63:11	95, 105, 106, 108, 170
61:10	69		63:11a	118
61:11	94, 95, 105, 108		63:11b	118
61:11f.	109		63:11c	118
62	95, 107, 116		63:1-69:26	103
62:1	94, 105, 116		64:2	96
62:1c	116		67:8-9	89, 91
62:1ff.	170		68:28f.	121
62:1-5	95		69	95, 112
62:2	107, 108, 113, 116, 129, 130, 171, 203		69:26	95, 105, 106, 107, 125
			69:26c	117
62:2a	116		69:26ff.	93, 117, 170, 189
62:2f.	108		69:27	95, 105, 106, 108, 109, 113, 116, 142, 171, 203
62:3	116			
62:3a	116		69:27a	117
62:3c	116		69:27b	117
62:3d	116		69:27f.	125
62:3e	116		69:27ff.	113
62:3f.	116		69:28	109
62:3ff.	116		69:28a	117
62:5	95, 105, 106, 107, 113, 116, 129, 171, 203		69:28c	117
			69:29	95, 105, 106, 109, 115, 116, 118, 125, 171, 203
62:5a	116			
62:5b	116		69:29a	117
62:5e	116		69:29b	117
62:5f.	116		69:29c	117
62:5ff.	113, 142, 170		69:29d	117
62:6	108, 113, 119		70	95, 112
62:6f.	93, 118, 125		70:1	95, 105, 106
62:6ff.	113		70-71	93
62:7	95, 98, 105, 106, 108, 113, 114, 115		71	88, 91, 95, 106, 112, 115
			71:13	110, 111
62:8	108		71:14	95, 105, 106, 107, 110, 111, 112
62:9	105, 106, 108, 116, 119			
62:9a	116, 119		71:14ff.	112

71:14-17	111		12:32ff.	126,130
71:15	107,109,111		12:32-33	126
71:15c	118		12:32-34	125,126
71:15d	118		12:33	126
71:16	111		12:34	125,126,130
71:16a	118		12:36	122
71:17	95,105,106,107,111,118		12:42	122
71:17a	118		12:44f.	124
71:17b	118		13	7,39,93,120,121,122,128,
89:76	70			130,141,142
104:1	170		13:1	128
			13:2	128
2 Enoch			13:3	128
3:1	71		13:3a	127,130
20:1	69		13:4	129
			13:10	121
3 Enoch			13:10-11	130
2:2	135		13:12	130
3:2	135		13:14	122
4:1	135		13:19	169
			13:26	123,129,130
IV Ezra			13:27-32	169
3-14	120		13:30	121
3:1	120		13:31	121
4:26	121		13:32	121,128,130,143,170
4:35	121		13:37	130,143,163
5:9	121		13:37f.	131
6:23	121		13:38	130
6:25	121		13:39ff.	130
6:49-52	92		13:48f.	131
7:16	129		13:52	123,129
7:28	124,129,130		13:53f.	122
7:28f.	121,130		14:9	112,129
7:28ff.	126,130			
7:29	125,126		**Jubilees**	
7:29ff.	125		4:15	58
7:29-33	125		5:1f.	58
7:31	121		15:31f.	70
7:31f.	121			
7:32f.	92		**Late Hebrew Testament of Naphtali**	
7:33	126		9:4f.	70
7:36	92			
7:37	92		**Psalms of Solomon**	
7:125	92		17	84
8:3	121		17:35	107
8:31f.	121		18	84
8:47ff.	122			
9:3	121		**Sibylline Oracles**	
11-12	120,122,125,126		III	43
11:11	122		III, 388-400	199
11:39	123		III, 785ff.	84
11:40-45	124		V, 414ff.	84
11:42	123		V, 414-33	39
12-13	88			
12:1	124		**Testament of Abraham**	
12:7	122		Rec A	92
12:9	122		A IV	91
12:10ff.	122		A VII	91
12:11	122,124		A XI	91
12:12-31	123		A XIII	91,92
12:32	124,125,126		A XX	91
12:32f.	125,131		Rec B	88,92
			Rec B XI	91

Testaments of XII Patriarchs

Test of Dan
  6:2ff.   70

Test of Levi
  3:8   69
  5:1   171
  5:7   70

Test of Ruben
  5:6f.   58

Testament of Solomon
  8:2   69, 237
  18:2   237
  20:15   69, 70

4. Qumran

1 QS
  XI, 7f.   45
  XI, 20   84

1 Q Sa
  II, 11f.   140

CD
  XX, 8   45

1 QH
  III, 21f.   45, 46
  IV, 24f.   45
  X, 35   45
  XI, 11f.   45

1 QM
  I, 16   45
  III, 4f.   45
  VI, 6   45
  VI, 14   54
  VII, 1ff. 54
  X, 10   45
  X, 11f.   45
  XII, 1   45
  XII, 4   45
  XII, 7   45
  XII, 8f.   45
  XV, 14   45
  XVI, 1   45
  XVIII, 2 45

1 Q Genesis Apocryphon
  II, 1   45

1 QpHab
  V, 3-6   84

1 Q 22
  IV, 1   45

1 Q 28b
  I, 5   45
  III, 25f.   45
  IV, 23   45

1 Q 36
  I, 3   45

4QS1
  I, 1, 23-25 45

4QFlor
  I, 4   45, 140

4QDan^c 86

4QpsDan A^a 140

4QpJsA
  19   171

11QMelch   112

4QOrNab   32

5. Rabbinica

Babylonian Talmud

Hagigah
  2:1 (14a) 133

Sanhedrin
  38b   80
  96bf.   134
  98a   131

Jerusalem Talmud

Berakoth
  3b   22
  5b   22
  5c   22

Kethuboth
  35c   22

Shebi'ith
  38d   22

Ta'anîth
  2:1   132

Midrashim

Genesis Rabba
  vii,2   22
  xxxiii,13   22
  lvii,1   237

Numbers Rabba
  13:14   132

Shir Rabba
  3:4   237

Midrash Tehillim (Psalms)
  2:7   140

Midrash Hag-gadol
  Gen 49:10   66, 132

Aggadath Bereshith
  14:3   132
  23:1   132

Pᵉsiḳta Rabbati
  34 (159a)   107
  37 (163a)   107

Tanḥuma Toledoth
  20 (70b)   134, 135, 136

Targumim

Cairo Targum B
  Gen 4:14   20, 24
  Gen 9:5-6   20

Fragment Targum
  Gen 4:14   22

Neofiti I
  Gen 4:14   24

Palestinian Pentateuch Targum
  Gen 4:14   20
  Gen 9:5-6   20

Pseudo-Jonathan Targum
  Gen 4:14   20
  Gen 11:7   70

6. Inscriptions etc.

Inscriptions

Sefire (ANET p.661; NERT p.265)
  III,16-17   28

Ugaritic Texts

CTA
  16f.   59
  32   59

UG
  2   59

7. Ancient Authors

Apollodorus

Bibliotheca
  I,i.1-ii.1 58

Arrian

Anabasis
  III,3   221
  IV,9f.   221
  IV,11   221
  IV,12   221

Curtius
  X, 1-2   221

Dio Cassius
  68:25, §6   87

Diogenes Laertius

Vitae Philosophorum 247

Herodotus
  I, 79   209

Hesiod

Theogonia
  71 ff.   58
  176 ff.   58

Homer

Odyssey
  XI, 307-317 58

Josephus

Antiquitates Judaicae
  I, 73   58
  XII, 146   178
  XIII, 330-69 90
  XIII, 419-21 90
  XIV, 119f.   90
  XIV, 337   90
  XIV, 398   90
  XVII, 171-3 89
  XX, 97   216
  XX, 167f.   216
  XX, 169-70 216

Bellum Judaicum
  I, 116   90
  I, 180-2   90
  I, 248-73 90
  I, 250   90
  I, 256   90
  I, 268f.   90
  I, 657-8   89
  II, 261f.   216
  II, 261-2 223
  V, 567   24

Lucian

Dialogi Mortuorum
  395   221

Philo

Gigantibus
  6   58

Sacrificiis
  5,4.5.6.   111

Philostratus

Vita Apollonii 247
  VI, 10   185

Plato

Leges
  4,713 Cf. 70
  5,738 D   70

Symposium
  202 E   70

Plutarch

Vitae Parallelae 247

Alexander
  28f.   221
  50   221
  51   221

Solon
  30,2   178

Sulla
  28,3   178

Strabo
  XVII 1.43 221

Suetonius

Vitae Caesarum 217

Thucydides
  I, 22   161

Virgil

Eclogae
  IV, 21f. 84

8. Christian Authors

Chrysostom

Homiliae
  1:1   91

Clemens Alexandrinus

Stromata
  V,11   69

Didymus Maximus

Trinitate
  2:7   91

Irenaeus

Adversus Haereses
  III,22,4   106
  IV,33.11   106
  V,19.1   106

Justin

Apologia
  52:3   92

Dialogus
  14:8   92
  31:1   92
  32:2   92
  40:4   92
  49:2   92
  51:2   92
  53:1   92
  54:1   92
  110:2   92
  111:1   92
  121:3   92
  124   106

Proclus
  CP   91

Index of Authors

Aalders 43
Abbott 4, 83
Albertz 190
Albright 44, 78
Alexander 135
Alford 14
Allegro 171
Allen 209
Appel 22, 110
Archer 86
Arndt (also BAG) 91, 137, 181, 197
Ashby 233
Atsalos 161
Avigad 46, 86

Badham 10
Baeck 10
BAG see Bauer, Arndt, Gingrich
Baker 59
Baldensperger 13, 123
Bammel 235
Bardtke 46
Barr 43, 68
Barrett 3, 137, 138, 142, 147, 149, 227
Barthélemy 64
Bartlet 223
Bauer, H. 67
Bauer, W. (BAG) 91, 181, 197
Bauernfeind 137
Baumgartner (also Koehler-Baumgartner) 42, 43, 67
Baur 12
Beasley-Murray 42, 71, 212, 214
Beekman 96
Beer 96, 97, 98
Behrmann 43, 78
Bentzen 39
Berger 143
Bernard 137, 138, 139, 164
BDB see Brown, Driver, Briggs
BDR see Blass, Debrunner, Rehkopf
Betz, O. 174
Bevan 67
Beyer 203
Beyerlin 28
Beyschlag 12, 13
Bietenhard 10
Billerbeck 107, 132, 136, 216, 237
Birdsall 149
Black, M. 1, 2, 3, 5, 9, 20, 21, 22, 23, 24, 26, 30, 31, 32, 33, 75, 85, 86, 89, 93, 94, 110, 140, 164, 175, 225, 229

Black, Max 214
Blass (BDR) 182, 183, 219
Bleek 43, 78
Blinzler 137, 139, 140, 142, 197
Bloch 121, 124, 125
Böhl 39
Bonsirven 223
Bornkamm 148, 201, 202
Borsch 2, 9, 23, 25, 36, 60, 85, 93, 94, 106, 121, 137, 140, 145, 149, 150, 165, 171, 175, 187, 192, 193, 194, 196, 203, 209, 210, 212, 224, 234
Bousset 150, 217
Bowker 9, 23, 59, 201
Bowman 9, 20, 43, 60, 75, 84, 106, 114, 135, 136, 212, 229
Box 92, 93, 120, 125, 127, 129
Brandenburger 41, 120, 164
Braun 147
Breech 120, 124, 129, 131
Brekelmans 42, 44, 45
Briggs (BDB) 56, 199
Bright 236
Brown, F. (BDB) 56, 199
Brown, J. B. 10
Brown, R. E. 137, 138, 222
Brown, T. S. 221
Bruce 10, 62, 65, 84, 90, 140, 144, 149, 203, 217
Brückner 12
Buber 132
Buchanan 42
Bultmann 10, 137, 145, 148, 151, 153, 160, 176, 180, 183, 186, 187, 201, 202, 217, 219, 236, 238, 239
Burger 217
Burkill 10
Busch 210, 212

Cacrides 161
Cadoux 182
Callow 96
Calvert 155, 157, 158
Campbell 9, 19, 20
Caquot 42, 55
Caragounis 68, 106, 200, 237
Carlston 159
Casey 2, 9, 11, 22, 23, 28, 29, 32, 33, 39, 42, 44, 47, 62, 94, 106, 109, 110, 127, 131, 133, 134, 135, 136, 137, 158, 164, 165, 166, 175, 187, 188, 190, 202, 209, 212, 241, 248

Catchpole 139, 140, 141, 154, 159, 160, 203, 204, 224, 225
Cavallin 111
Ceroke 180, 183, 184
Chamberlain 215
Charles 10, 47, 64, 67, 84, 85, 88, 93, 94, 96, 97, 98, 105, 106, 120, 129, 139, 170, 171, 211, 213, 223
Charlesworth 84, 89, 170, 237
Christensen 10
Ciholas 25
Collins 4, 43, 44, 46, 47, 48, 67, 68, 112
Colpe 2, 6, 9, 23, 36, 39, 40, 41, 43, 62, 106, 112, 120, 140, 145, 149, 150, 165, 175, 187, 188, 204, 205, 206, 208, 225, 232, 234
Conybeare 185
Conzelmann 3, 148, 232
Coppens 4, 10, 42, 43, 44, 68, 94, 147, 229, 248
Craibl 55
Cranfield 149, 220, 222
Creed 10
Croskery 10
Cross 64, 86
Cruvellier 43, 229
Cullmann 140, 141, 148, 149, 201, 202, 204, 220, 222
Culpepper 161
Cumont 61

Dalman 9, 16, 17, 18, 19, 20, 21, 50, 133, 136
Dascalakis 221
Daube 216, 218
Davies, Ph. R. 48
Davies, W.D. 44, 76, 110, 223, 227
Debrunner (BDR) 182, 183, 219
Dechent 108
Dehn 148, 232
Deissler 62
Delcor 41, 42, 43
Delling 10
Dequeker 42, 43, 44, 45, 66, 68, 213
Derrett 203
De Villiers 105
Dexinger 4, 42, 43, 59
Dhanis 43, 79
Δημητράκος 180, 181, 182, 183, 197
Dibelius 175, 180, 183, 184
Dieckmann 10
Diez-Macho 20
Di Lella 4, 42, 44, 45, 47, 48, 72, 86
Dillmann 106, 171
Dodd 20, 30, 76, 138, 147, 177, 179, 216, 223, 227
Doeve 234
Driver (BDB) 42, 56, 66, 67, 73, 136, 198, 199
Droysen 163
Drummond 10
Duling 237
Dumbrell 46, 61

Duncan, G.S. 84
Duncan, J. 10
Dunn 2, 4, 212, 225, 230
Duplacy 180, 181, 182, 185
Dupont, G. 10
Dupont, J. 9, 23

Eaton 18
Eckert 109
Edersheim 14, 43
Eerdmans 15, 16, 25, 136, 190
Eichrodt 43, 236
Eissfeldt 50, 53, 120, 213
Ellis 139, 140, 142, 177, 209, 210, 220
Emerton 6, 35, 39, 40, 44, 71, 75, 78, 95
Engnell 42, 47, 55, 227, 234
Epstein 132
Ewald 43, 78, 125, 127, 130

Fabry 77
Farrar 14
Farrer 184, 185, 186, 187, 194, 201, 203, 209, 225
Ferch 38, 130
Feuillet 39, 43, 71, 75, 221
Fiebig 9, 18, 19, 21, 106
Fitzmyer 2, 9, 23, 24, 25, 28, 86, 140
Flender 225
Foakes-Jackson 85, 145
Ford 140, 203, 247
Formesyn 9, 11, 22
France 43, 76, 79, 80, 157, 209, 217, 227, 229, 234
Freed 147
Freedman 132, 134
Frey, J.B. 85
Frey, L. 162
Friedrichsen 10, 223
Frietzsche 11
Fuller 3, 140, 202
Furger 147

Gadamer 161
Garnet 10
Gaster 42
Geden 231
Geissen 62
Gelin 10
George 65
Gerhardsson 162
Gero 121
Gese 44
Gesenius (G-K) 45, 54, 63, 65, 67
Gibson 28
Gildemeister 125, 127, 130
Gingrich (BAG) 91, 181, 197
G-K see Gesenius, Kautzsch
Glasson 39, 40, 41, 209
Goettsberger 43, 136
Goldschmidt 132, 133, 135
Goldstein 199
Goppelt 149, 175, 187, 194, 203

Gordon (UT, UM) 59
Goudge 20
Grant 151
Grässer 169
Grayston 212
Greenfield 28, 87, 89, 90, 93
Grelot 125
Griesbach 154
Grimm 191
Grotius 43
Grundmann 197, 198
Gry 10, 120
Guilding 43, 62, 80, 140, 203
Guillet 10
Gundry 209
Gunkel 42
Guthrie 147, 149, 150, 169
Gwyn 64

Haag 28, 54, 56, 59
Haase 10
Haenchen 138, 143
Hahn 3, 43, 140, 148, 183, 201, 202, 217, 218, 225, 226
Hammershaimb 85, 94, 96, 97, 98
Hammerton-Kelly 27, 31, 147, 175, 187, 189, 223, 233
Hanhart 42, 44, 45, 47
Harnisch 126, 131
Harrington 159
Harrison 4, 13, 50, 53, 84
Hartman, L. 109, 110, 162, 206, 210, 212
Hartman, L. F. 4, 42, 44, 72, 86
Hasel 44, 45, 46, 47
Hatch 49
Haufe 1
Hävernick 43, 78
Hay 221
Heaton 42
Hedinger 161
Helfmeyer 207
Hengel 56, 133, 134, 135, 140, 193, 194, 199
Hengstenberg 78
Herdner (CTA) 59
Herford 133
Hickling 159
Higgins 1, 2, 3, 145, 148, 149, 151, 158, 159, 166, 188, 201, 202, 203, 207, 208, 209, 222
Hilgenfeld 13, 43, 78
Hill 55, 187
Hindley 3, 87, 88
Hirsch 161
Hodgson 146, 148, 150, 151, 158
Hoffmann 10
Hofius 247
Holm-Nielsen 84
Holsten 13
Holtzmann 12, 17
Hommel 39
Hooker 1, 5, 42, 141, 149, 150, 151, 152, 154, 157, 158, 159, 160, 162, 165, 174, 180, 187, 209, 212

Horst 43
Horton 112
Hoskyns 138
Houk 60
Hunter 149
Huntress 10

Isaac 87, 171
Jacob 41
Jacobson 159
James, J. C. 10
James, M. R. 92, 120
Jannaris 181, 183, 185, 207
Jansen 35, 38
Janssen 92
Jeffery 36
Jellicoe 64
Jensen 39
Jeremias, A. 39
Jeremias, J. 2, 9, 23, 25, 85, 148, 163, 164, 190, 193, 201, 202, 204, 205, 206, 207, 220, 222, 223, 247
Jocz 80
Jones (LSJ) 180, 181, 182
Jüngel 3, 215, 233

Kabisch 120
Kahle 19
Kaminka 120
Κανελόπουλος 221
Käsemann 148, 153, 162, 232
Kautzsch (G-K) 45, 54, 63, 65, 67
K-B see Koehler, Baumgartner
Kearns 43
Keil 43, 78
Kertelge 221
Keulers 120, 122, 123, 126, 127, 129, 144
Kieffer 145
Kim 192
Kingsbury 10
Kinniburgh 147
Klausner 126
Klijn 84, 170
Knibb 85, 87, 88, 93, 96, 97, 98, 111
Knox 145, 146, 148, 150, 151, 192
Koch 65
Koehler (also Koehler-Baumgartner) 56, 67
Kraeling 36
Kranichfeld 43, 78
Kristensen 10
Kruijf 10
Kruse 43, 68
Kuhn 45
Kümmel 1, 22, 140, 149, 153, 154, 155, 159, 160, 162, 163, 187, 194, 205, 209, 210, 212, 238
Kurichianil 222
Kutscher 86

Ladd 145, 149, 150, 154, 157, 233, 238
Lagarde 12
Lagrange 94, 125

Lake 85, 145
Lambrecht 159
Lampe 91
Lane 139, 140, 177, 180, 181, 182, 183, 210,
    212, 216, 217, 218, 220, 225
Leander 67
Lebram 10
Leivestad 2, 9, 26, 138, 140, 149, 151, 152,
    187, 194, 202, 203
Lenglet 213
Leupold 43
Levy 136
Liddell (LSJ) 180, 181, 182
Lietzmann 9, 14, 15, 16, 17, 18, 19, 22, 25,
    33, 148, 151
Lindars 2, 3, 9, 10, 28, 29, 30, 31, 32, 33, 41,
    43, 137, 145, 147, 149, 152, 158, 164, 165,
    166, 172, 175, 180, 187, 188, 190, 194,
    196, 197, 202, 203, 209, 224, 241, 245,
    248
Lindeskog 148, 149, 203
Linton 203
Lisowski 48
Lohmeyer 219, 229
Lohse 46, 62, 121, 140, 216, 218, 220
Longenecker 43, 79, 165
Lövestam 140, 142, 216, 218
LSJ see Liddell, Scott, Jones
Lundström 238
Lust 62, 63

Maas 53
Maddox 41, 147, 149, 150, 152, 154, 157, 162,
    202, 203
Maier 42, 43
Manek 212
Manson, T.W. 4, 31, 42, 110, 114, 115, 175,
    176, 202, 207, 223
Manson, W. 44, 227
Marlow 1, 149
Marshall 1, 41, 43, 79, 137, 139, 140, 141,
    145, 149, 151, 163, 171, 175, 177, 180,
    184, 186, 187, 188, 193, 194, 197, 202,
    203, 204, 209, 210, 212, 214, 216, 217,
    218, 220, 222, 223, 225, 234
Martyn 27
McArthur 155, 156, 159, 161, 163
McCown 1, 149
McNeil 214
McNeile 188
Mearns 87, 88, 89, 91, 93
Meecham 182
Meloni 10
Mertens 45, 70
Messel 94, 106
Metzger 92, 120
Meyer 9, 14, 15, 16, 19, 133
Michel 149, 178, 226, 234
Μικρογιαννάκης (IEE) 90
Milik 3, 40, 75, 85, 86, 87, 88, 89
Milligan 182

Moloney 27, 56, 62, 147, 169
Montgomery 4, 42, 45, 62, 64, 73, 214
Moore, A. L. 137
Moore, G. F. 223
Morgenstern 6, 35, 37, 40, 41, 44, 59, 75, 78
Morris 137, 222
Mosley 161
Moule 27, 28, 76, 85, 127, 140, 149, 169,
    173, 203, 223, 227
Moulton, J. H. 181, 182, 207
Moulton, W. F. 231
Mowinckel 6, 35, 36, 38, 39, 44, 94, 112, 149
Muilenburg 39, 79, 117, 119
Muirehead 25
Müller, K. 43, 170, 214
Müller, M. 1, 9, 26, 43
Müller, U. B. 43
Müller, H. P. 190
Munck 137
Murphy O'Connor 180, 181
Mussner 142, 214
Myers 92, 93, 120, 126, 129, 130

Neander 11, 12
Neirynck 158
Nestle, Eb. 169
Neugebauer 215
Newman 10
Nineham 3
Nösgen 13
Noth 4, 42, 44, 45, 46, 47, 67, 68, 248

Oesterley 43, 53, 74, 78, 85, 120, 124
Olmstead 91
Oort 15, 18
Otto 10

Palmer 160
Pamment 27
Parker 84
Paul 10
Paulus 11
Peake 10
Pernot 180, 181, 182
Perrin 4, 8, 48, 110, 148, 150, 152, 153, 154,
    155, 156, 157, 160, 162, 163, 218, 224,
    236, 238
Pesch 137, 140, 142, 143, 166, 190, 225, 234
Pfammatter 147
Plöger 43
Plummer 177
Porteous 4, 42, 227
Porter, F. C. 43
Porter, P. 214
Poythress 42, 44, 46
Procksch 4, 38, 39, 42, 44, 67, 68, 72, 248
Pusey 43, 78

Quasten 106

Raatschen 222

Rahlfs 49
Rehkopf (BDR) 182, 183, 219
Redpath 49
Rengstorf 208, 221
Rhodes 43
Riedl 147
Riehm 43, 78
Riesenfeld 145, 226, 229
Riesner 54, 154, 157, 158, 161, 162, 163, 193, 194, 203, 215, 221, 222, 224
Robert 180
Roberts 64
Robertson 31, 181, 183, 207, 208, 219
Robinson, C. A. 221
Robinson, J. M. 147
Robinson, Th. H. 53
Rolland 159
Roscher 39
Rose 10
Rosenmüller 43, 78
Rosenthal 67
Ross 229
Rössler 126
Rost 10
Rowdon 10
Rowe 214
Rowlex 20, 40, 43, 45, 59, 85, 120, 199, 213
Ruckstuhl 147
Ruppert 108
Russell 4, 36, 40, 42, 85, 120

Sabourin 10, 165, 216, 224
Sahlin 42
Salmon 64
Sanders 89, 92, 126
Sandmel 166
Sarna 37
Scharbert 59
Schechter 132
Schenk 219
Schlatter 221
Schmidt, F. 92
Schmidt, H. 42
Schmidt, N. 18, 39, 43, 106, 127
Schmiedel 25
Schmithals 41
Schmitt, A. 64
Schnackenburg 137, 138, 147, 221, 228, 238
Schnedermann 14
Schneider, G. 107, 139, 140, 143
Schniewind 209
Schreiner 120, 125, 130
Schrenk 109
Schubert 42
Schulz, H. 43, 78
Schulz, S. 147
Schulze 13
Schürer 79, 80, 85, 90, 114, 120, 125
Schürmann 194
Schweitzer 10, 148
Schweizer 145, 146, 148, 152, 175, 187, 194, 197, 201, 202, 215, 226, 229, 234

Scott, R. (LSJ) 180, 181, 182
Scott, R. B. Y. 10
Segal 65, 75, 133, 134
Seitz 223
Sellin 42
Sharman 19, 215, 232, 233, 234, 238, 239
Sharp 180
Shea 39
Sherwin-White 139, 140, 160, 161
Sidebottom 147
Sierig 149
Simon 132
Σιμώτας 63
Sjöberg 9, 14, 21, 50, 51, 52, 53, 85, 89, 94, 106, 110, 111, 114, 115
Smaley 138, 147
Smith, D. 285
Smith, M. S. 55
Smith, W. 64
Snaith 49
Somervell 10
Sophocles 182
Staerk 106
Stauffer 149, 202, 224, 225
Stein 163
Stewart 220
St John Thackeray 64
Stone 83, 85, 87, 89, 90, 91, 93, 120, 122, 124, 125, 126, 129, 131, 144
Strack 107, 132, 136, 216, 237
Strauss 11
Stuhlmacher 85, 161, 163, 190, 191, 192, 200, 230
Sturch 27, 138

Tarn 221
Taylor 139, 140, 149, 177, 183, 187, 194, 196, 203, 217, 219, 225, 227
Teeple 3, 148, 159
Theison 88, 93, 171
Thompson 21, 85, 93, 139, 187, 189, 221, 228
Thorion 55
Tillman 123
Tödt 3, 8, 25, 148, 158, 174, 175, 176, 180, 193, 201, 247
Torrey 10, 209
Τουλουμάκος (IEE) 90
Tuckett 149, 154
Turner, H. E. W. 149, 161
Turner, N. 161, 183, 219

Uloth 12, 13, 15
Usteri 13

Vamvas 183
van Andel 94
van Iersel 219
van Manen 15, 16
Vansina 161
Vassiliades 159
Vermes 2, 3, 5, 6, 9, 11, 20, 21, 22, 23, 24, 26,

28, 29, 32, 33, 46, 86, 135, 136, 142, 166,
171, 190, 225, 241, 248
Vielhauer 3, 148, 201, 215, 232, 234, 235
Violet 84, 120, 121, 127, 130, 170
Vögtle 164, 202
Volkmar 15
Völter 10
von Gall 10
von Lengercke 78
von Rad 42, 236

Walker 1, 10, 154, 158, 233, 234
Wedderburn 43, 112
Weimar 39, 42
Weiser 50, 53, 120
Weiss, B. 13
Weiss, J. 13
Weisse 12
Weizsäcker 13
Welch 43, 44, 70, 78
Wellhausen 17, 18, 19, 25, 188
Westcott 14
Westermann 38, 190

Whitehead 28
Wifall 10
Wilcke 125
Wilckens 164
Willaert 43
Winter 86
Wiseman, D.J. 53
Wiseman, P.J. 53
Wittichen 12
Wolff 190
Wrede 14

Yadin 86
Young, E.J. 43, 79
Young, R. 49

Zevit 42, 43, 68
Ziegler 62, 64
Zimmerli 190
Zöckler 78
Zorn 165, 224

Index of Names and Subjects

Abel 92
Abbahu, R. 132, 133
Abraham 91, 92, 111
Adam 164
Adam-Christ typology 164
Adapa 39
Aeon, the new 211
Aeon, the old 211
Aesop 178
Aged One 62, 63, 71, 75, 78, 163, 228
Akiba, R. 80, 133, 134
Alexander the Great 70, 120, 221
Alexander Jannaeus 90
Ammon 221
Ammonites 175
Analysis 95, 96
– logical 7
– philological 7, 248
– semantic 7, 96, 127, 167
Anani 135, 136, 144
Ancient of Days 39, 40, 73, 78, 81, 101, 133
Ancient One 41, 71, 73, 74, 75, 77, 79, 80, 113, 211
Angel(s)
– fallen 58
– guardian 70
– holy 112
– interpreting 96, 99, 100, 102, 111
– of punishment 170
Animal symbolism 61, 76, 77
Anointed One 95, 104, 106, 107, 110, 112, 124, 131, 173
Anthropology 86
Anthromorphism, -phic 77, 103
Antigonus 90
Antioch 87, 90
Antioch earthquake 87
Antiochus III 42, 90
Antiochus IV 90
Antiochus VII 90
Antiochus X 90
Antiochus Epiphanes 37, 40, 46, 75, 199
Aphrahat 136
Apocalyptic 2, 81, 107, 124, 143, 170, 204, 223, 239
Apocalypticism 111
Apocrypha 84
Apollonius of Tyana 185, 186
Apotheosis of Israel 75
Arabic Version of IV Ezra 121, 125, 127, 130
Aramaic
– Biblical 19

– Christian Palestinian 19, 21
– Early Standard 28
– Galilean 16, 21
– Imperial 27, 86
– Jewish Galilean 21
– Literature 22, 24, 26
– Official 28
– Old 27, 30
– Palestinian 19
– Samaritan 21
– Syriac 21
Aramäisch, jüdisch-palästinische 17
Arameans 28
Armenia 87, 90, 121
Armenian Version of IV Ezra 121, 125, 127, 130
Armenians 87, 90
Asia Minor 90
Authenticity, -ic 147, 152, 153, 154, 157, 158, 160, 162, 163, 164, 165, 166, 175, 196, 201, 202, 205, 207, 210, 225, 226, 235, 250

Baal 39, 40, 41
Baal-Haddad 40
Baal-Shamem 40
Babel 59
Babylon 58, 69
Babylonian 32, 35, 38, 39, 77
– Invasion 236
Bactra 221
Bar Cochba revolt 134
Bar (e)nash(a) 15, 17, 22, 23, 24, 28, 30, 33, 134, 166, 245, 249
Bar Nafle 134, 136
Beasts
– concept of 61, 68, 69, 70, 72, 211, 237, 239, 250
– invisible potentates 69, 70, 71
– judgment on 228
– = kings 69, 71
– outrageous conduct of 228
– = state 70
– symbol for kingdoms 61
Belial 54
Belshazzar 35
Ben Adam 49, 50, 51, 52, 53, 56
– poetic expression 50
Bene Arwad 54
Bene Asshur 54
Bene Babel 54
Bene Dedan 54

Bene Kedem 54
Bethlehem 220
Birds, symbol for peoples 177
Blasphemy 140, 141, 142, 164
Book of Noah 86
Burden of proof 153, 162, 164
 — upon authenticity 153
 — upon inauthenticity 154, 162

Caesar 25
Caesarea 40
Caesarea Philippi 14, 194
Caiaphas 200
Cairo Geniza 22
Cairo Targum 24
Callirhoe 89, 91
Canaanite
 — background 38
 — hypothesis 41
 — myth and ritual 39
 — religion 77
Carrhae 90
Cassius 90
Celsius 217
Chaldean
 — background 36, 38
 — god of wisdom 39
Charybdis 220
Cherubim 87
Christian
 — art 77
 — writers, early 161
Christianity 94
 — Greek-speaking 25
Christology 86, 149, 154, 172, 220, 230
 — Incarnation 4, 230
Chrysostom 91
Church
 — hellenistic 25
 — Palestinian 191
Clouds, bearers of divine presence 71, 72, 74
Cosmas Indicopleustes 136
Cosmic struggle 211
Crassus 90
Criteria 147, 149, 152, 154, 155, 160, 163,
   165, 206, 237, 242, 249
 — of attestation by multiple forms 155, 159
 — of coherence 153, 154, 158
 — of discounting tendencies of developing
   traditions 155, 159
 — of dissimilarity 152, 153, 154, 155, 156,
   157, 158, 163, 191, 193
 — of elimination of Jewish or Christian material
   155
 — of formal consistency 150
 — of multiple attestation 153, 154, 155, 158,
   159, 163, 193
Criticism 165
 — Form 7
 — Literary 7
 — Redaction 7
 — Source 7

 — Textual 158
 — Tradition 7
Croesus 209
Cronos 58
Curtius 221
Cyprian 62
Cyrus 70, 209

Damascus 90
Daniel 35, 41, 42, 52, 74, 77, 80, 111, 132,
   173, 192, 210, 223, 246
Daughters of men 58, 59
David 56, 110, 111, 124, 125, 133, 134, 217,
   218, 219, 220, 222, 225, 226, 236, 237, 239
David *redivivus* 134
David's Kingdom conflated with God's King-
   dom 236
Dead Sea Scrolls 155
Deliverance 223, 232
Demetrius II 90
Demigods 58
Dio Cassius 87
Diogenes Laertius 247
Discipleship 175, 221
Dominions, the 63

Ea-Oannes 39
Early Church 4, 152, 154, 155, 156, 157, 164,
   166, 186, 187, 191, 194, 202, 210, 217,
   218, 224, 225, 226, 230, 247
 — Easter faith of 29
Ebed-Yahweh 20
Egypt 87
Eighteen Benedictions 209
El 39
El Elyon 39, 41
El\u1d49azar 24
Elect One 94, 95, 104, 105, 106, 107, 109,
   110, 112, 115, 116, 117, 129, 170, 173
Elephantine Papyri 21
Eliakim 171
Elijah 198, 219, 220
Elisabeth 220
'Elyonin (עליונין) 63, 64, 66, 67, 75, 81, 163,
   200, 204, 227, 228, 229, 230, 232, 240,
   247, 248
Emancipation 58
Enoch 71, 85, 88, 90, 94, 96, 106, 110, 111,
   112, 114, 115, 135,
Enthronement 39, 133
Ephialtes (giant) 58
Ephraem 136
Erniedrigung 229, 230
Erniedrigung und Erhöhung 226, 229
Eschatology (ical) 88
 — discourse 169, 171, 201, 205, 207, 210, 212
 — events before the End 198, 211
Esther 89
Eternal One 102, 113
Ethiopic
 — translator of I Enoch 85, 106
 — Version of IV Ezra 121, 125, 127, 130

Eve 106
Exaltation 145, 198, 201, 203, 225, 228, 230, 231
Exalted One 76, 248
Exodus 130
Exile 80
Exorcist, Jewish 32
Ezekiel 60, 76
Ezra 112, 122, 123, 124, 125
IV Ezra
— Christian influence on 119, 121
— no Christian influence on 119, 121, 123
— Christian interpolations in 120, 121, 123, 130
— Christological interpolations in 121
— Date of 120, 124
— Jewish Character of 123
— Self-complacency of 122

Forgiveness 32, 180, 184, 186, 187, 188, 202, 221
— the SM's right 215
Form-Criticism 160
Formgeschichte 160
Four Document Theory 53
Four Kingdoms (empires) 72, 73, 211

Gabriel 35, 42, 43, 47, 91
Galatians 92
Gallic War 25
Genesis Apocryphon 96
Georgian Version of IV Ezra 121
Germany 14
Gnosticism 37
God
— self-projection of 80
— triumph of 73
— Kingdom of (see Kingdom of God)
God-Anthropos 38
Gog 90
Greco-Aramaic 136
Greco-Roman Historians 160
Greece 43, 70, 237
Greek
— Byzantine 180, 186
— Colloquial Modern 183
— Hellenistic 180, 181
— Literary Modern 183
— Modern 180, 181, 182, 183, 186
— myths 58
— post-Classical 181
— sources for idea of guardian spirits 70
— translators 15
— views of underworld 40
Greeks 138
Griesbach hypothesis 154

Haggada-question 217, 218, 222
Hanina ben Dosa 32
Ha-nofeleth 134, 135
Hayyim ben Galipapa R. 137
Head of Days 75, 99, 100, 101, 103, 104, 110, 111, 112, 113, 129

Hellenistic
— background of SM 36
— Judaism 43
— motifs 38
— times 42
— theology 17, 25
Hellenists 138
Heracles 40
Hero, -es 58, 59
Herod Antipas 178
Herod the Great 85, 89, 91
Herodes 40
Herodotus 160, 161, 166, 209
High priest 140, 141, 142, 203, 225
Hilkiah 171
Hippolytus 43
Hiram 40
Historians
— ancient 161
— Greco-Roman 160
— Roman 160
Historiographers, modern 161
Historiography, modern 247
History
— ancient 247
— Partho-Jewish 90
— of Religions approach 41, 248
— -writing 247
Holland 14, 15
Holy ones 44, 45, 46, 47
Homeric times 250
Honi 32
Humiliation 76, 197, 198, 229
Humiliation-Exaltation schema 139, 198, 226
Humility 139

Iconography, Christian 87
Inauthenticity 150, 152, 154, 155, 162, 163, 166, 175, 205
Inscriptions from
— Nabatea 17, 21
— Palestine 17
— Palmyra 17, 21
— Sefire 27, 28, 50
— Tema 17, 21
Interpolations 95
— Christian, in IV Ezra 120, 121, 123
— Christological, in IV Ezra 121
Interpretation
— Jewish messianic (see under Messiah)
— principles of 242
Interpretative tradition 6, 83, 127, 131, 164, 214, 223, 227, 228, 250
Invasion
— Babylonian 236
— Parthian 89, 90
— Partho-Median 90
Iran 37, 74
Iranian
— background of SM 35
— origin of God-Anthropos 38
— son of man 41

— sources for SM 36
Irenaeus
Isaac, R. 134
Isaiah 207
Ishmael, R. 135
Ishodad of Merw 136
Israel 14, 36, 38, 39, 40, 41, 42, 43, 44, 47, 48,
   54, 60, 61, 66, 70, 71, 72, 76, 79, 90, 92,
   126, 131, 132, 135, 140, 143, 176, 207,
   236, 239
Jebusite beliefs about enthronement 39
Jeremiah 122
Jerusalem 80, 87, 89, 90, 120, 123, 126, 143,
   178, 194, 199, 216, 246
— fall of 123, 143
Jesus *passim*
— authority of 221, 222
—, character of 1
— condemned for SM claim 140, 141, 142
— Danielic influence on 212, 213
— David's son 218
— life of 1
— private teaching on SM 236, 245
— public teaching 236
— non-repudiation of OT 219, 220
— self-consciousness of 4, 11, 149, 151, 167,
   214, 222
— self-designation of 57, 150, 157, 165, 191,
   214
— teaching of 1, 155, 177, 194, 196, 212
— teaching of,: two *foci* 238, 241
Jew(s) 3, 4, 14, 21, 31, 32, 38, 44, 48, 64, 70,
   78, 79, 83, 85, 90, 91, 137, 139, 166, 199,
   232, 248, 249
— Babylonian 21
— pious 64, 232
Jewish
— Authorities 62, 141, 142, 193, 195, 200,
   204
— exorcists 32
— interpretations 83, 94
— interpreters 59
— literature 83, 84, 106
— people 65, 66
— remant 125, 126
— revolt 40
John 60, 62
John the Baptist 220
Jonah 31, 32, 207
— preaching of 207
— sign of 31, 207
Jonathan, the reviser 64
Jonathan ben Uzziel 64
Jonathan-Theodotion 64
Jose the Galilean, R. 134
Joseph 201
Joseph (of Mary) 220, 225
Josephus 40
Judah 60, 132
Judaism 86
— apocalyptic 3
— cabbalistic 94

— competing messianologies in 5, 144
— Hellenistic 43
— pre-Christian 3, 223
Judas Maccabaeus 40, 42
Judea 90
Judge, eschatological 196, 250
Judgment 73, 89, 92, 97, 100, 101, 103, 104,
   107, 115, 117, 125, 126, 131, 204, 206,
   211, 228, 234
— final 92, 100, 103
— first 92
— second 92
— third 92
Justin 43, 62, 92, 106

KAIGE recension 65
Kingdom of God 5, 7, 177, 179, 198, 213, 215,
   223, 231, 232, 233, 235, 236, 237, 238,
   239, 240, 241, 242, 250
— agent of 214, 225, 231
— and SM 179, 215, 233
— conceived dynamically 238, 239
— matrix for SM 179, 213, 215

Labienus 90
Last Supper tradition 193
Latin Version of IV Ezra 121, 125, 127, 128,
   130
Lazar(os) 24
Leben-Jesu-Forschung 11
Leopard symbolism 61
Lightning on Cloud 170
Lion symbolism 61
Little horn 103, 199, 200, 227, 232
Lord of Spirits 95, 97, 100, 101, 103, 107, 113,
   117, 122, 170
Luke 213, 220

Maccabaean
— date for Daniel 86
— interpretation of SM 42
— revolt 40, 144
Maccabees 115
Macrocosm (= Primordial Man) 38
Magical papyri 27
Man from the Sea 121, 122, 123, 127
Mandean motifs on SM 38
Mary 106, 220, 221
Matthew 220
Medes 87, 90
Media 87, 90
Melchisedek 112
Melqart, Melcarth 40
Mesopotamia 53, 90
Messiah 14, 20, 47, 66, 75, 79, 80, 81, 94, 95,
   109, 111, 124, 125, 130, 131, 132, 138,
   139, 215, 216, 218, 219, 223, 224, 226,
   228, 249
— David's son 217, 218, 219, 222, 225, 250
— David's lord 218, 219, 222, 225, 250
— Davidic 78, 79, 111, 125, 126, 129, 143,
   223, 232, 237, 238

– Davidic descent of 115, 125, 215, 216,
  218, 219, 220, 225
– death of 125, 126, 139
– earthly 78, 125, 126, 134
– Heavenly 126, 129, 134, 249
– hiddeness of, in IV Ezra 124
– political 78, 216, 220, 222, 231
– Son of God 140, 142
– suffering 76
– supernatural 80, 143, 173
– traditional 80, 125, 248, 249
– transcendental 124, 125
– two different models of, in IV Ezra 127
Messiahship, scribal view of 216, 217
Messianic
– expectations 107, 124, 143, 216, 249
– hope, early 79, 143, 239
– hope, latter 79, 143
– hope, new 80
– pretenders 125
– *testimonium* 225
'Messianic Secret' 217
Messianism 75, 78, 79, 84, 126, 216, 223, 238,
  249
Messianology 84, 143, 215, 223, 224, 225, 226,
  232, 249, 250
– various types of 84
Meṣir 106
Metatron 133
Methodological principles 37, 38, 136, 144
Michael 42, 43, 47, 48, 67, 70, 91
Microcosm (= First Man) 38
Middle East 178
Midrash 210
Miracle stories 179, 183, 186, 187
Mishnah 53
Mithridates II 90
Monotheism 133
Morphology 24
Moses 41, 42, 92, 185, 221
– law of 221
Moses *redivivus* 42
Most High 75, 98, 101, 103, 113, 114, 124,
  129, 130, 227
'Most High' (= *'Elyonin*) 63, 64, 66, 67, 69, 71,
  72, 73, 75, 76, 103, 126, 132, 173, 229

Na'ar (= Enoch) 135
Nabatea 17, 21
Nabonidus 32
Nafle 135
Nahman, R. 134, 135
Name, divine 141
Near East (-ern), ancient 41, 67
Nebuchadnezzar 69
– dream of 198
– haughty 35, 103
– humiliation of 35
– power of 35, 176
– symbolized by tree 177
Necessity, idea of divine 170, 196, 197, 198
Neofiti, see Targum

Nephilim 59
Ninevites 31, 207
Noah 59, 103, 170, 205
Nofeleth 134, 135

'Old Man' (= Ancient of Days) 78
Olympias 221
Onkelos, see Targum
Origen 217
Orodes 90
Otus (giant) 58
Ouranos 58
Oxford 21, 24, 86

Pacorus 90
Palestine 17, 87, 90, 126
Palmyra 17, 21
Palmyreans 87
Panthera 217
Papyri
– Elephantine 21
– Magical 27
Parables of Jesus 177, 235
Parables passim
– no Christian influence 89, 94
– date of 3, 86, 87, 88, 89
– Jewish character of 87, 89
– Jewish-Christian 88, 89
– pre-Christian date of 87, 89, 93
– post-Christian 3
– absent in Qumran 3
– structural elements 104
Parousia 92
– second 92
– SM sayings 92, 208
Paris seminar on Pseudepigrapha 87, 89
Parthia 87, 88, 90
Parthian invasion 89, 90
Parthians 87, 89, 90
Partho-Jewish history 90
Partho-Median invasion 90
Paul 15, 88, 92, 122, 164, 167, 190, 218, 222,
  237, 242, 246, 247
Pentateuchal origins 53
Persia 43, 70
Persian Gulf 87
Peter 194
Pharisees 233
Philip (of Macedon) 221
Philo 111, 112, 133
Philosophers, Egyptian Nudist 185
Philosotratus 186
Phoenicia 37
Pilate 200
Platea 166
Plato 156
Poetry, poetic 50, 51, 52, 53, 55, 60
– style 51, 52
Polemics
– Jewish 91, 92
– rabbinic 131, 133
Polychronius 136
Pompey 90

Porphyry 136
Powers, the 67, 68, 200, 241
— demonic 231, 232
— evil 232, 241
— invisible 72, 211, 237
— rebellious 240, 250
Primal Man 36, 41, 168
Primordial Man 38
Primordial silence (IV Ezra) 125
Principalities, the 67
Principles of interpretation 242
Principles, Two divine 75, 80
Pronouncement stories 183, 187
Prophets, violent death of 194
Proto-Theodotion 64
Pseudepigrapha 84, 121
Pseudo-Jonathan 24, 70
Pseudo-Saadia 66

Q (Document) 158, 159
Q-hypothesis 159
Qumran 3, 24, 40, 45, 46, 84, 85, 86, 88, 89,
    93, 140, 144, 151, 152
— absence of *Parables* in 151, 152
— negative evidence of, on SM 85, 93
— silence of, on SM 86, 88, 89, 93

Rabbinism, rabbinic 43, 84, 131, 144
— orthodox 133, 134
— polemic 131, 133
— writings 131
Rabbis 75, 143, 174, 221, 249
Religion
— Babylonian 77
— Canaanite 77
— Egyptian 77
— Greek 237
— Hebrew 77
— Tyrian 40
— Yahwistic 237
Religionsgeschichte 7
Remnant 125, 126
Research, Son of Man 6
Resurrection 121, 126, 145, 189, 196, 197,
    218, 225
Return, the 88
Revolt
— of Bar Cochba 134
— Jewish 40
— Maccabaean 40, 144
Righteous Branch 110
Righteous One, the 94, 95, 104, 105, 106, 107,
    110, 112, 116, 117, 173, 196
Roman
— army 87
— deserter 90
— domination 216
— Empire 43, 123, 124
— Historians 160
— times 92
Romans 232, 247
Rome 4, 132

Sabbath 187
Saints of the 'Most High' 63, 64, 66, 67, 71,
    72, 73, 74, 75, 76, 199, 227, 241
— angelic view 44, 46, 47, 48
— identifed with 'SM' 227
— Israelite view 227
— sufferings of 200, 201, 211, 227, 229
Salamis 166
Salome Alexandra 90
Salvation History 130
Samson 178
Samuel 236
Samuel ben Nissim 66
Sanhedrin 141, 142, 197, 204, 217
Sapor I 87
Sardeis 209
Saul 56
Scribes 184, 187, 188, 218, 222, 224, 226
— teaching of 216, 218, 219
Scylla 220
Sefire inscription 27, 28, 50
Seleucus II 90
Semantics, semantic 7, 96, 99
— analysis 96, 127, 167
Sennacherib 90
Seraphim 87
Servant Song 197
Servant of Yahweh 196, 197, 222
Shekinah 114
Sign of Jonah 31, 207
Signs of the times 208
Socrates 156
Sodom 205, 206
Solomon 31, 32, 40, 84, 171, 236
— wisdom of 31
"son of ..." 6, 54, 58, 106
Son of God 130, 141, 142, 163, 215
son of man (OT) 50, 53, 55, 61, 77, 84, 229
— creatureliness of 57, 76, 229
— deceitful 56
— determinate form of 51
— fickleness of 55
— indeterminate form of 51
— liar 56
— negative use of 55, 56
— neutral use of 55, 57
— parallelism to 'man' 55, 56
— positive use of 55, 57, 163
— transience of 56, 57
— ungodly 56
— vanity of 57
— weakness of 56, 76, 168, 229
— wickedness of 57, 76
Son of Man, SM, 'SM', *passim*
— absent in Paul 15, 167, 246
— Agent for God's Kingdom 81, 177, 198,
    213, 231, 232, 233, 235, 238, 239, 248
— apocalyptic 2, 3, 150, 151, 218
— background of 10, 35, 36, 37
    — Babylonian 35, 38, 39
    — Canaanite 35, 38, 41
    — Chaldean 36

- Gnostic 36, 41
- Hellenistic 36
- Iranian 35, 36, 38, 41
- Old Testament (see biblical identifications)
- Ugaritic 38
- bearer of human values 12
- biblical indentifications of 'SM' with 6
  - angels 42, 44, 48
  - angel prince 43, 47
  - Daniel 42
  - divine glory 43
  - the elect people 42
  - eschatological people of Israel 42
  - Gabriel 42, 43, 47
  - *hasidim* 42
  - 'holy ones' 44, 45, 46, 47, 61
  - pious Jews 173, 232
  - Judas Maccabaeus 42
  - Kingdom of God 43
  - men of insight 42
  - Messiah 43
  - Michael 42, 47, 48, 67
  - Moses 42
  - people of Israel 42, 44, 48, 61, 223
  - the persecuted of Israel 42
  - saints of the Kingdom 42
  - saints of the 'Most High' 62, 72, 84
  - suffering saints 227
- chosen 117, 227
- circumlocution for 'I' 2, 21, 24, 26, 167, 188, 190
- Circumlocution Theory 2, 6, 21, 25, 27, 33
  - bunkruptcy of 25
- coming 145, 204
- concept, many-sided 215
- confession of 203
- connected with Kingdom of God 215, 232, 233, 234, 236, 250
- not connected with Kingdom of God 215, 232, 233, 234, 236
- differentiated from Jesus 205
- not differentiated from Jesus 204
- distinct from King 235
- divine (being, status) 129, 132, 164
- Earthly 212, 150
- Enochic 5, 111, 234
- ensign (standard) of 209
- eschatological 3
- eschatological reign of 211
- exaltation 72, 199, 203, 212
- exalted (being) 139, 164, 169, 201, 204, 226, 250
- extra-biblical backgrounds 35, 36, 41
  - (see Background of)
- forgives sins 186
- not a fixed title 213
- heavenly (being) 79, 110, 132, 139, 189, 190, 200, 205, 214, 223, 224, 226, 227, 238
- hiddeness of 92, 114, 117, 123, 128, 227
- non-human 128
- humility of 12, 139

- Ideal Man 11, 12, 13, 168
- identification of 10, 41, 42, 44, 45, 48, 61, 72
- identified with
  - Anointed one (*Parables*) 95, 104, 106, 110
  - Elect One (*Parables*) 95, 104, 107, 109, 110
  - Enoch (of *Parables*) 91, 94, 106, 115
  - Jesus 133
  - Messiah 131, 132, 133, 138, 139
  - Righteous One (*Parables*) 95, 104, 106, 110
- interchangeable with 'I' 22, 23, 25, 166
- interpretations of
  - angelic 4, 43, 44, 46, 47, 48, 80, 223, 248
  - combined 44
  - corporate 136, 250
  - Israelite 4, 43, 44, 46, 47, 48, 72, 75, 80, 227
  - messianic 43, 47, 78, 140
  - mythological 44
- interpretative tradition of 83, 214
- Jewish 41
- Johannine 146, 147
- Judge 4, 79, 91, 92, 109, 117, 118, 119, 131, 170, 191, 200, 205, 215, 226, 227, 240, 250
- judicial functions of 88, 146, 207
- judicial functions denied 2
- King 4, 146, 207, 215, 226, 234, 250
- and Kingdom of God 179, 215, 233
- Kingly functions denied 2
- known to Paul 164, 247
- leader (of saints) 81, 189, 200, 229
- Lord of sabbath 215
- Messiah 14, 47, 133, 215
- messianic
  - significance of 228
  - title, a 13, 15, 80, 110, 132, 141
  - understanding of 193
- non-messianic 13, 16, 17, 18
- messianology 110, 112, 143, 144, 215, 222, 226
- a metaphor 213
- myth 2
- now at work 145
- a nickname 225
- object of worship 119, 191
- an oprobrius epithet 225
- origin of 115
- origin of Enochic 114
- 'Parable' of 245, 246
- Parousia of 92, 208
- Parousia sayings of 14
- philological debate on 5, 11, 15, 16, 18, 19, 20, 21
- pre-Christian 4, 136
- pre-existence of 4, 114, 115, 116, 129, 163, 189, 223, 232
- pre-mundane existence of 114, 123

- problem 2, 159
- in Qumran, implicitly 84
- revealed (*Parables*) 114, 117
- revealer (of secrets) 104, 116, 119
- research 6
  - two waves of 9
- right to forgive 189, 215
- saviourhood aspect of 117, 231
- sayings
  - authentic(ity of) 29, 30, 147, 149, 150, 151, 152, 155, 175, 180, 187, 190, 191, 193, 204, 205, 206, 210, 212, 217
  - inauthentic 29
- sayings, groups of 145, 174
  - apocalyptic 148, 150
  - earthly life 146, 148, 159, 174, 175, 193, 201, 250
  - eschatological 151, 152, 154
  - exaltation 146, 147, 148, 150, 151, 154, 159, 174, 175, 193, 201, 202, 205
  - humiliation 14
  - parousia 14
  - sufferings 146, 147, 150, 154, 159, 174, 192, 193, 197, 199, 200, 201, 230
- self-designation 5, 19
- two shifts in investigation 14
- sign (for coming) of 170, 207, 208, 209, 211
- sitting on God's throne 113
- sitting on throne of glory 93, 117, 171, 234
- Son of God 130, 141, 142, 163, 215
- studies on 1, 9, 10
- substitute for 'the Name' 141, 247
- suffering 76, 145, 174, 190, 193, 198, 200, 201, 212, 215, 226, 227, 228, 229, 250
- supernatural (character of) 41, 128, 129, 130, 163, 225
- not a surrogate for 'I' 26
- symbol for Israel (Jews) 4, 41, 48, 61, 65, 72, 79, 248
- symbolism 214
- synoptic 145
- *ein theologisches Phantom* 2
- titular 86
- transcendental 2, 81, 164, 223, 224, 225, 226, 227, 232, 238, 250
- transported by Clouds 71, 74, 76, 104, 128, 132, 141, 172, 198, 211
- universal Ruler 79, 118, 119, 191
- unknown to Paul 15
- vicarious sufferings of 191, 192, 229
- vindicator 81, 109, 117, 119, 211
- warrior (IV Ezra) 131
son of man (= Ezekiel) 60, 77
sons of God 58, 59
sons of man/men 6
Source-criticism 158
Status constructus 65
Stephen 142
Stone 132, 198, 214
- agent for God's Kingdom 214
- messianically interpreted 132, 214

Streitgespräche 180
Suetonius 247
Supra-history 67
Supreme Power 58, 78
Suffering-Exaltation 198, 201
Suffering Servant 117, 215, 227, 229
Symbolism, symbolic 47, 58, 60, 61, 76, 78, 123, 128, 129, 133, 229
- animal 61, 76, 77
- bear 61
- Danielic 124
- Ezekielic 77, 78
- leopard 61
- two level 67
- lion 61
Synoptic(s) 141, 160, 228
- interrelationships 141
Syria 28, 87, 90
Syriac (language) 18
Syriac Version of IV Ezra 121, 125, 127, 128, 130

Talmud
- Babylonian 132, 133, 135
- Jerusalem 16, 18
  - *Demai* 16
  - *Kelaim* 16
  - *Pea* 16
  - *Taanith* 16
  - *Yoma* 16
- Palestinian 132
Tammuz-Adon 40
- birth of 40
Targum 19
- Cairo B 24
- Fragment 19
- Geniza 19, 20
- Jonathan 16, 19
- Neofiti I 20, 24
- Onkelos 16, 17, 18, 19, 20, 21
- Palestinian Pentateuch 17, 21
- Prophet 21
- Pseudo-Jonathan 24
- Samaritan Pentateuch 17
Tema 17, 21
Temple 221
Tertullian 62
Text-linguistics 7, 96, 248
Texual-criticism 158
Theodore bar Koni 136
Theodotion 63, 64, 65
Theodotionic problem 64
Theophany 39, 72, 75, 77, 78, 113, 128, 129
Thermophylae 166
Throne-vision (Ezekiel) 60, 75, 77
Thucydides 160, 161
Tigranes 90
Tobias 84
Tobit 84
Torah 221
Tradition, pre-Markan 193
Trial of Jesus 142, 196, 203

Trinity, doctrine of 37, 40, 75
Two-Powers in Heaven 133
— doctrine of 75, 80
Two-source Hypothesis 154, 158
Tübingen seminar on Pseudepigrapha 89
Typology, Adam — Christ 164

Ugaritic 38, 39, 46, 55, 59, 131
— pantheon 39
— parallels 131
Unechtheit 162
Ur-Theodotion 65
Vatican Library 20
Ventidius Bassus 90

Waw-explicativum 59, 98, 101
Yahweh 39, 56, 60, 66, 72, 74, 77, 78, 222,
    236
— depicted in human form 77
— depicted as Old Man 78
— (Ugaritic) dragon-slayer 39
Yahwism 60, 238

Zacharias 91
Zenobia 87
Zeus (Olympios) 40, 58
Zion 124
Zir-amilûti 39